Royal Government in Colonial Brazil

Sebastião José de Carvalho e Melo, Marquis of Pombal

Royal Government in Colonial Brazil

With Special Reference to the Administration of the
Marquis of Lavradio, Viceroy, 1769–1779

by Dauril Alden

University of California Press
BERKELEY AND LOS ANGELES
1968

University of California Press
Berkeley and Los Angeles, California
Cambridge University Press
→ London, England
Copyright © 1968, by
The Regents of the University of California
Library of Congress Catalog Card Number: 68-26064
Printed in the United States of America

TO ENGEL SLUITER
Remarkable Historian-Detective,
Challenging Teacher, and Esteemed Friend

Preface

"No NATION has ever accomplished such great things, in proportion to its means, as the Portuguese . . . and whatever changes may take place, Brazil will always be the inheritance of a Portuguese people." So wrote the poet laureate Robert Southey at the conclusion of his celebrated *History of Brazil*. In the century and a half that has elapsed since Southey completed his massive three-volume work, Brazilian historians have examined many facets of their colonial past; but few foreigners, certainly few North Americans, have followed in his footsteps. Although a recently published directory lists eighty-three historians in the United States who claim to specialize in Brazilian history, only a handful are actually engaged in research and publication on topics that relate to the colonial period. That Brazil's colonial experience is worthy of serious scholarly investigation both for its own sake and for the opportunity that offers to make enlightening comparisons with contemporary developments in other former European colonies is the major premise upon which this study rests.

Scholarly projects commonly undergo many modifications in design between their original conception and ultimate completion. This one is no exception. It began—more years ago than I like to remember—as an analysis of the impact of the Marquis of Pombal, Portugal's celebrated minister of state between 1750 and 1777, upon Brazil, then Portugal's most important colony. After several weeks of intensive bibliographical searching, I reached the conclusion that, considering the number of archival and printed sources that would have to be utilized for such a study, the subject was too ambitious for the purposes of a doctoral dissertation. In the course of my search, however, I discovered that there was a good deal of source material in print and in manuscript concerning the administration of the Marquis of Lavradio, who held the post of viceroy of Brazil longer than anyone else during the Pombaline era. It seemed to me that by concentrating on his administration I could gain considerable insight into the aims and achievements of Pombal in Brazil. That assumption, in fact, proved correct, though the conclusions I have reached regarding Pombal's abilities as a statesman will appear less flattering to that so-called enlightened despot than those offered by many previous writers.

But to return to Lavradio, the more I looked into his administration, the more I became convinced that in order to understand his role as viceroy it was essential to have an adequate knowledge of the development of Portugal's administrative apparatus in Brazil, the relationships that existed among its various offices, the kind of persons who filled such positions, and their powers and limitations. Since an examination of existing studies of Brazil's colonial government failed to yield the answers to many questions, I found it necessary to turn to the sources. As a result of such investigations my project, instead of being merely another traditional study of a colonial viceroy's years in office, became a case study of how the Portuguese regime functioned in eighteenth-century Brazil with particular reference to the administration of the Marquis of Lavradio. As my research deepened, the scope of the study continued to enlarge. For example, I discovered that many of the problems and administrative guide lines of Lavradio's day had their origins decades or even centuries before his time and that some of the solutions he tried did not really bear fruit until long after he had left office. Consequently, although primarily focused upon the 1760s and 1770s, the book necessarily ranges from the sixteenth to the early nineteenth centuries. It also extends beyond the limits of the Portuguese empire, for in order to gain perspective on certain Portuguese administrative achievements and shortcomings, I found it fruitful to compare Portuguese practices with those prevailing in other parts of the Atlantic world. In a sense, therefore, this is an essay in comparative colonial history, although I have not pursued that particular approach systematically. Nor can I claim to have as full a knowledge of the relevant literature pertaining to the other empires as I have acquired with respect to Portuguese Brazil. My citations concerning institutional practices in the English, French, and Spanish empires are intended merely to suggest the sources that I found most useful for my illustrative purposes.

The text is divided into four parts, each of which consists of several topically or chronologically arranged chapters. Part I introduces the Marquis of Lavradio and some of his leading contemporaries, defines the nature of the office he filled, and describes the ambiance in which he worked. The second part emphasizes the most critical problem that confronted the viceroy throughout his administration, that of defending Portuguese positions within an area that I have called "the Debatable Lands," a long stretch of borderlands extending from the present state of São Paulo to the estuary of the Río de la Plata. Though Spain and Portugal had been sparring for a dominant position in that territory since the seventeenth century, their rivalry reached its climax during Lavradio's stay in Brazil. I have endeavored to indicate the relevant background to the complex military, naval,

and diplomatic maneuvering of each side during the critical decades
of the 1760s and 1770s and have examined both European and
colonial phases of the conflict during those decades with the aid of as
much of the available bilateral documentation as possible in order to
avoid the biased treatment that this subject usually receives at the
hands of partisan national historians. The struggle over the Debatable Lands was a constant preoccupation of the viceroy and provides
the best narrative thread for an understanding of his years in office. It
also directly or indirectly influenced many of Lavradio's other problems. Those of an economic nature are considered in Part III, which
analyzes a major attempt by the Pombaline regime to modernize the
management of imperial finances, assesses the impact of the borderlands' war upon the viceregal exchequer, demonstrates the role of the
viceroy in promoting new sources of nonmineral wealth in Brazil, and
describes his efforts and those of other royal agents to combat the activities of contrabandists. The last part examines the viceroy's relations with administrative officers on various levels in different parts of
Brazil and concludes with an evaluation of the Marquis of Lavradio
as viceroy and an appraisal of the regime in which he served.

Some names appear in this study in forms different from those in
which they are often spelled. Thus I have referred to the viceroy as
the Marquês *do* Lavradio instead of *de* Lavradio as have some
Brazilian and Portuguese historians, since I see no need to alter the
way by which he signed his name and the style by which most contemporaries addressed him. It is worth remembering that the street in
Rio de Janeiro which honors his name is called the Rua *do* Lavradio.
I have preserved the umlaut in João Henrique de Böhm, as Lavradio's Austrian-born general was known to the Portuguese, instead
of employing the circumflex as some Brazilian writers have incorrectly
done. In the primary and secondary literature there are many variant
spellings of the family name of the viceroy's Irish squadron commander, Robert MacDouall, but according to documents bearing his
signature in the Manuscripts Section of the National Library in Rio
de Janeiro, it is properly written as given here. A glossary following
the table of contents explains certain special terms used in the text.

Research in Brazil for this study was made possible by a traveling
grant from the Henry and Grace Doherty Charitable Foundation, for
which I remain very grateful. For additional financial assistance
which made it possible to continue this study during subsequent
years, I wish to thank the Social Science Research Council, the
American Philosophical Society, and the Graduate School of the University of Washington. A visiting appointment at the Berkeley campus of the University of California for the year 1962–63 enabled me
to continue to exploit the excellent collection of printed materials

conerning colonial Brazil housed in its library and to examine microfilm copies of documents in British and Portuguese archives available in the Bancroft Library.

The nature of this project made it necessary to impose upon the good will of many persons for whom a few words of thanks are wholly inadequate repayment. Among my Brazilian friends and acquaintances I particularly want to express my appreciation to Dr. José Honório Rodrigues, former chief of the Manuscripts and Rare Book Section of the National Library for his exceptional courtesies, wise counsel, and constant encouragement; to Sr. Marcos Carneiro de Mendonça of Cosme Velho, Rio de Janeiro, for generously according me unlimited access to his invaluable collection of Lavradio and Pombal papers in one of the finest private libraries in Brazil; to Sr. Cláudio Ganns of the Instituto Histórico e Geográfico Brasileiro, for helping me with books and manuscripts in the institute; and to Dr. E. Vilhena de Moraes, former Director of the Brazilian National Archives, for granting me special permission to use important manuscript collections in that facility. I should also like to record my deep appreciation to Professor Benjamin Woodbridge, Jr., of the Department of Spanish and Portuguese at the Berkeley campus of the University of California for his careful reading and criticism of an earlier version of the first half of this study. My interest in Brazilian history was first aroused by Professor Engel Sluiter of the Department of History of the same institution, and for many years I have benefitted from his exacting training, constant encouragement, unstinted assistance, infectious enthusiasm for the raw materials of history, and warm friendship.

The supervisors and staffs of every library and manuscript depository that I have been privileged to use have been most generous in their assistance, and I wish especially to thank Mrs. Margaret Urige and Mrs. Ruth M. Kirk, respectively interlibrary loan librarians at the University of California, Berkeley, and the University of Washington, for having successfully located for me many of the rare works used in this study. Miss Sheena Pugh typed the final draft of the manuscript with remarkable fidelity. My wife, Alice Alden, prepared the charts, figures, and maps, and I am grateful for her drafting and other skills and for her forbearance and that of my sons, Bryson and Grant, during my frequent and extended absences from home to finish the manuscript. Mrs. Sylvia Wells-Henderson gracefully bore the onerous chore of assisting with the proofreading and in spite of my protests saved me from many a gaucherie. I am likewise deeply indebted to Mrs. Wells-Henderson for her extraordinary generosity in allowing me to use her unique wilderness cabin, where I completed the manuscript during the past year. Finally, to those numerous well-meaning former students, colleagues, and other friends who for too many years have raised the perennial question, "Is the book done?" I wish to express my thanks for their persistent prodding and, with more than a slight sigh of relief, can at last reply in the affirmative.

E. J. Hobsbawm once wrote that "big broad subjects . . . are rarely tackled with full success before a man's fortieth year." The subject to which the following pages are addressed is patently a vast one, and I admit to having crossed the threshold of forty some time ago. Whether this contribution to an understanding of Brazilian history is a successful one is for others to say. Since, like the Portuguese sea captains of old, I have sailed upon imperfectly charted waters, I am, like John Colbatch, the chronicler of court life in seventeenth-century Portugal, "far from the Folly of thinking [my]self exempt from Mistakes; it is very likely that [I] may have been guilty of many, in that great variety of Matters which [I have] had occasion to mention."

DAURIL ALDEN

"STONEBANK"
WHIDBEY ISLAND
MARCH 1967

Contents

List of Figures and Maps   xviii

List of Tables   xix

List of Illustrations   xx

Glossary   xxii

Abbreviations   xxvi

PART ONE: THE SETTING OF THE SCENE

I. Lavradio's Apprenticeship as Captain-General of Bahia   3

Lavradio's Background   3
The Marquis of Pombal: Architect of Enlightened
Despotism   7
Lavradio as Captain-General of Bahia   13
Promotion to Rio de Janeiro   27

II. The Viceroyalty of Rio de Janeiro   29

The Delimitation of the Authority of the Governors-
General   30
The Captaincy-General of Rio de Janeiro   44
The City of Rio de Janeiro in the Time of the Marquis of
Lavradio   46
The New Viceroy Surveys His Government   51

PART TWO: THE DEBATABLE LANDS

III. The Beginnings of European Settlement   59

The Setting   59
The Coming of the Jesuits   63
The Founding of Colônia do Sacramento and the
Beginnings of Formal Luso-Spanish Platine Rivalry   66
Closing the Gap: The Occupation of Santa Catarina   71
Closing the Gap: The Occupation of Rio Grande   74

IV. Diplomacy and War, 1494–1769   83
   Early Luso-Spanish Negotiations   83
   The Treaty of Madrid—a Compromise That Failed   86
   The First Cevallos Campaign and the Emergence of a
      New Spanish Policy   96
   The First Portuguese Attempt to Recover Rio Grande   104
   Borderlands Diplomacy and the Projected Second
      Diplomatic Revolution (1766–1768)   106

V. The Years of Stalemate, 1769–1774   116
   Colônia do Sacramento, Beleaguered Outpost of Empire   117
   Borderland Tensions in Rio Grande   119
   The Vértiz Expedition to Rio Grande   125
   The First Portuguese Responses to the New Spanish
      Challenge   132
   Portuguese Reassessment of the Spanish Challenge   135

VI. Continued Stalemate: The Frustrations of a Viceroy,
1774–1776   143
   The First Portuguese Moves   144
   Bad News from Rio Grande   148
   The First Tests of Strength in Rio Grande   150
   The Beginning of the Algiers Crisis   154
   Francisco José da Rocha Renews the Debate Concerning
      Colônia   157
   High Strategy and the Purposeful Sacrifice of Colônia   160
   The Algiers Debacle and Its Influence on Luso-Spanish
      Policy   164
   Painful Progress Toward a Portuguese Offensive   168
   The Background to the Portuguese Order Suspending
      Hostilities   171

VII. The Portuguese Victory in Rio Grande and Its
Consequences   176
   Preliminaries to the Naval Attack of February 19, 1776   176
   The Fracasso   178
   The Postmortems   181
   The Portuguese Victories of March 26–April 1, 1776   182
   Reaction in Rio de Janeiro to the Portuguese Victories   187
   Diplomatic Reaction to the Portuguese Victories   189

VIII.   Action and Reaction: The Outfitting of the Cevallos
Expedition and Portuguese Efforts to Thwart It   195
  Origins of the Second Cevallos Expedition   195
  Lisbon's Reaction to the Spanish Threat   202
  *Lavradio's Efforts to Prepare Brazil for the
    Impending Attack*   206
  Lisbon Divines Cevallos' Operational Plan   213
  Lavradio's Final Preparations   215

IX.   The Second Cevallos Campaign   224
  The Outward Voyage   224
  The Fall of Santa Catarina Island   230
  The Capitulation of the Santa Catarina Garrison   235
  Cevallos Captures Colônia but Fails to Take Rio Grande 238

X.   The Trials of Viceroy Lavradio During the
Crisis of 1777   247
  *The Viceroy's Reactions to the Loss of Santa Catarina and
    Its Garrison*   247
  First Steps Toward a Portuguese Counteroffensive   252
  Bad News from the Court   256
  The Naval "Action" of June 12, 1777   258
  Arrival of the Colônia Officers   260
  The New Rapprochement Between Portugal and Spain   263
  The Question of Responsibility   267

PART THREE: THE VICEROY'S ECONOMIC
              PROBLEMS

XI.   The Reorganization of the Royal Fisc   279
  Structural Reorganization   279
  Departments of the Exchequer in Rio de Janeiro   282
  The Double-Entry System   287
  The Need for Accounting Reforms in the Colony   288
  The Nature of the Accounting Reforms   291
  The Filling of Public Offices   294
  Chief Expenditures of the Viceroyalty   298
  Sources of Royal Income   301
  Problems of Revenue Collection   307

XII.   Problems of Getting and Spending   312

   First Impressions   312
   The State of Viceregal Finances Before 1775   317
   The Shipment of Capital to the Kingdom   323
   Fiscal Consequences of the War with Spain, 1774–1777   332
   Desperate Measures   343
   The Persisting Debt Problem   347

XIII.   Problems of Economic Development   353

   Expressions of the Viceroy's Concern for Economic
     Development   354
   The Viceroy's Efforts to Promote Tobacco Cultivation   359
   The Fostering of Cereals: A Story of Success   362
   The Promotion of Fibers: A Story of Frustration   366
   Indigo, Cochineal, and the Scientific Society of
     Rio de Janeiro   372
   Factors that Impeded the Colony's Economic Development   381

XIV.   The Contrabandist Versus the Crown   388

   The Tightening of Controls over Imperial Trade   392
   Smuggling Rings in Lavradio's Brazil   396
   The Question of Responsibility for the Apprehension of
     Smugglers   399
   The Treatment of Unlicensed Foreign Ships in Colonial
     Ports: The Evolution of Procedure   403
   The Treatment of Unlicensed Foreign Ships: Some Case
     Histories   408
   Conclusion   416

PART FOUR: THE VICEROY AS ADMINISTRATOR

XV.   Relations with Municipal, Judicial, Ecclesiastical, and
Provincial Officials   421

   The Viceroy's Relations with the Câmaras   422
   The Viceroy and the Magistracy   430
   Lavradio as a Dispenser of Justice   434
   The Viceroy and the Church   437
   The Role of the Mestres de Campo   443
   Conclusion   446

XVI.   Relations with Governors and Captains-General   447

   The Viceroy and the Subordinate Governors   448

The Viceroy and the Captains-General 452
Lavradio Versus Luís Antônio de Sousa 459
Conclusion 471

XVII. Portrait of a Viceroy and Critique of a Regime 473

REFERENCE MATTER

Appendices

   I. *Distribution of the Population of Brazil, 1772–1782* 497
  II. *The Quest for Culpability for the Capitulations of 1777* 498
 III. *Money Struck at the Mint in Rio de Janeiro, 1768–1779* 506
 IV. *Account of What Is Owed to the Royal Treasury in the Different Captaincies of Brazil from the Yield of Contracts Rented and Administered [ca. 1781]* 507
  V. *Commodity Prices in Southern Brazil, 1740–1777* 509

Bibliography 513

Index 535

List of Figures and Maps

FIGURES

1. THE PLACE OF THE VICEROY IN THE ADMINISTRATIVE STRUCTURE OF BRAZIL IN THE 1770S.   41
2. ORGANIZATION OF THE ROYAL FISC IN RIO DE JANEIRO IN THE 1770S.   283
3. MILITARY AND NONMILITARY PAYMENTS OF THE VICE-REGAL EXCHEQUER, 1774 to 1777.   334
4. YEARLY INDEBTEDNESS OF THE RIO DE JANEIRO EXCHEQUER, PRE-1761 to 1780.   348

MAPS

1. DISTRIBUTION OF POPULATON OF BRAZIL, *ca.* 1772 to *ca.* 1782.   16–17
2. PLAN OF RIO DE JANEIRO, 1775.   47
3. THE FORTIFICATIONS OF GUANABARA BAY IN 1768.   55
4. THE DEBATABLE LANDS.   62
5. THE JESUIT MISSION ESTÂNCIAS, 1750.   65
6. THE FIRST CEVALLOS CAMPAIGN, 1762–1763.   98
7. THE VÉRTIZ EXPEDITION TO RIO GRANDE, 1773–1774.   128
8. ENTRANCE TO LAGOA DOS PATOS.   152
9. COLÔNIA DO SACRAMENTO, 1762–1777.   159
10. THE SPANISH INVASION OF SANTA CATARINA (FEBRUARY 1777).   232
11. THE TREATIES OF 1750 AND 1777.   266

List of Tables

1. EXCISES ESTABLISHED BY THE CÂMARA OF RIO DE JANEIRO.   305
2. ESTIMATED AVERAGE YEARLY INCOME OF RIO DE JANEIRO AND ITS DEPENDENCIES, 1768–1778.   318
3. ESTIMATED AVERAGE ANNUAL EXPENDITURES OF RIO DE JANEIRO AND ITS DEPENDENCIES, 1768–1778.   320–321
4. SHIPMENTS OF CAPITAL FROM RIO DE JANEIRO TO PORTUGAL IN WARSHIPS AND IN COMMERCIAL VESSELS.   328
5. CAPITAL REMITTANCES FROM BRAZIL TO PORTUGAL, 1714–1749.   331
6. MILITARY PAYMENTS OF THE VICEREGAL TREASURY, 1774–1777.   335
7. EXTRAORDINARY FUNDS RECEIVED BY THE JUNTA DA FAZENDA OF RIO DE JANEIRO, 1774–1777.   339
8. TOTAL INCOME AND TOTAL PAYMENTS OF THE VICEREGAL TREASURY, 1775–1777.   341

List of Illustrations

frontispiece

SEBASTIÃO JOSÉ DE CARVALHO E MELO, MARQUIS OF POMBAL

Reproduced from Luis Innocêncio de Pontes Athaide e Azevedo, *A Administração de . . . Marquez de Pombal*, II, Lisbon, 1841

following page 258

1. EXECUTION OF JOSÉ MARIA DE TAVORA, LISBON, JANUARY, 1759

Reproduced from Luis Innocêncio de Pontes Athaide e Azevedo, *A Administração de . . . Marquez de Pombal*, II, Lisbon, 1841

2. PLAN AND PROSPECT OF FORT SANTO ANTONIO DA BARRA, BAHIA DE TODOS OS SANTOS

Reproduced from Luiz dos Santos Vilhena, *Recopilação de noticias soteropolitanas e brasilicas*, I, Bahia, 1921

3. PALACE SQUARE, RIO DE JANEIRO, 1808

Reproduced from Gilberto Ferrez, *Aquarelas de Richard Bate: o Rio de Janeiro de 1808–1848*, Rio de Janeiro, 1965

4. PROCESSION OF THE HOST PASSING THE CARMELITE CHURCH, FROM THE PALACE SQUARE TOWARD RUA DIREITA

Reproduced from Gilberto Ferrez, *Aquarelas de Richard Bate: o Rio de Janeiro de 1808–1848*, Rio de Janeiro, 1965

5. DOWNTOWN RIO DE JANEIRO IN THE TIME OF THE VICEROYS

Reproduced from Gilberto Ferrez, *Aquarelas de Richard Bate: o Rio de Janeiro de 1808–1848*, Rio de Janeiro, 1965

6. MEDIA OF TRANSPORT IN RIO DE JANEIRO DURING THE ERA OF THE VICEROYS

Reproduced from Gilberto Ferrez, *Aquarelas de Richard Bate: o Rio de Janeiro de 1808–1848*, Rio de Janeiro, 1965

7. PROSPECT OF A PORTION OF THE CITY OF SALVADOR, CA. 1802

Reproduced from Luiz dos Santos Vilhena, *Recopilação de noticias soteropolitanas e brasilicas*, I, Bahia, 1921

8. COPY OF AN ORDER FROM THE QUEEN TO VICEROY LAVRADIO, 1778

    Bancroft Library Microfilm Collection

9. PATENT SIGNED BY THE MARQUIS OF LAVRADIO, 1773

    Bancroft Library Microfilm Collection

10. UNIFORMS OF AN ENLISTED MAN (LEFT) AND AN OFFICER (RIGHT) IN FIRST LINE REGIMENT, BAHIA, CA. 1802

    Reproduced from color plate in Luiz dos Santos Vilhena, *Recopilação de noticias soteropolitanas e brasilicas,* I, Bahia, 1921.

11. UNIFORMS OF AN ENLISTED MAN (LEFT) AND AN OFFICER (RIGHT) IN THE HENRIQUE DIAS MILITIA REGIMENT, BAHIA, CA. 1802

    Reproduced from color plate in Luiz dos Santos Vilhena, *Recopilação de noticias soteropolitanas e brasilicas,* I, Bahia, 1921.

Glossary

ALFÂNDEGA.—Custom house.

ALMOXARIFE.—Receiver of customs.

ALMOXARIFE DOS ARMAZENS.—Warehouse superintendent.

ALQUEIRE.—A grain measure during the colonial period; e.g., an alqueire of rice weighed 72 pounds. In modern Brazil an alqueire is usually a unit of agricultural land varying in size according to region.

ALVARÁ.—Royal decree beginning "Eu, el rei" and ending with "Rei" as signature. Unless specified to the contrary, an alvará remained in force for only one year, but an indefinite extension was usually provided.

ARRAIÁL.—An unincorporated settlement; also an encampment.

ARRIBADA.—A ship entering port allegedly under stress of weather.

ARROBA.—Unit of weight varying from 25 to 32 pounds.

AUTO DE POSSE.—Record of the act of taking public office.

AUXILÁRIOS.—First-line colonial militia.

BANDEIRANTES.—Prospectors and slave-raiders.

BANDO.—Proclamation.

CÂMARA (SENADO DA CÂMARA).—Municipal council.

CAPITÃO MOR.—In the sixteenth and seventeenth centuries a royal governor of a subordinate captaincy, but in Lavradio's time the governor of an unincorporated settlement and/or commandant of a company of second-line militia (that is, the ordenanças, s.v.).

CARIOCA.—Of or pertaining to the city of Rio de Janeiro, particularly a person born in that city.

CARTA FAMILIAR.—Dispatch written in an intimate style, often intended to flatter the addressee.

CARTA RÉGIA.—A royal provision intended to be permanent which began with the name of the person or authority to whom it was addressed, followed by "Eu el Rei vos envio muito saudar . . ." and signed "Rei."

CASAIS.—Married couples (pl. of casál). In eighteenth-century Brazil a term specifically referring to subsidized emigrants from Portugal's Atlantic Islands who colonized Santa Catarina, Rio Grande de São Pedro, and the lower Amazon. Also often used as the equivalent of households or families (*famílias*).

CIDADE.—A city whose citizens theoretically enjoyed special privileges and exemptions to which other town dwellers were not entitled.

CONSULTA.—A recommendation by a Peninsular council, especially the Conselho Ultramarino, to the king; also a decree-in-council with the force of law.

CONTO.—Monetary unit containing 1,000,000 *réis* (*s.v.*).

COPIADOR.—A copybook, often of selected documents.

CORTES.—The parliament of Portugal.

CRUZADO.—Monetary unit worth 400 réis (*s.v.*).

DEGREDADO.—A banished convict.

DESEMBARGADOR.—Senior royal magistrate.

DEVASSA.—A judicial inquiry sometimes the equivalent of *residência* (*s.v.*). A devassa might be either general or special. The former was intended to verify the existence of a suspected crime; the latter assumed a crime had been committed and was concerned with the determination of the persons guilty.

DÍZIMO.—Church tithe.

DONATIVO REAL.—So-called voluntary contribution of funds to defray the Crown's extraordinary expenses.

ENGENHO.—Sugar mill; by extension, a sugar plantation (*fazenda*), though some plantations possessed more than one mill.

ENTRADA.—In the singular, usually an official exploring party; when pluralized, generally customs duties levied on merchandise, livestock, and slaves shipped from coastal captaincies to Minas Gerais.

ESTÂNCIA.—A cattle or horse ranch.

FARINHA.—Flour; when unqualified, as *farinha de trigo* (wheat flour), usually manioc flour, which was processed in several different forms.

FROTA.—A fleet of ships, generally escorted.

JUIZ DE FÓRA.—A Peninsular-born, university-trained judge charged with administrative and judicial tasks within the limits of a municipality, and therefore inferior to a circuit judge (*ouvidor, s.v.*).

JUNTA DA FAZENDA.—Treasury board consisting of several high royal officials headed by senior administrative officer, charged with management of royal finances within a captaincy-general.

MAÇO.—A loose bundle of documents.

MAPA.—A map, chart, list, or table.

MESA DA INSPEÇÃO.—A board established in major colonial ports charged with overseeing production and export of sugar, tobacco, and other commodities of particular interest to the Crown.

MESTRE DE CAMPO.—In Lavradio's time the commander of a regiment of *auxilários* (*s.v.*) and a field administrator.

NORDESTE.—The northeastern part of Brazil.

ORDENANÇAS.—The second-line colonial militia composed of men fifteen to sixty who were considered physically unfit to be enrolled in the first-line militia, the *auxilários* (*s.v.*).

OUVIDOR.—A circuit magistrate who performed administrative and judicial duties within a *comarca*, a district significantly larger than a municipality; in the eighteenth century ouvidores in the larger captaincies-general were assigned either to civil or to criminal matters and were respectively called *ouvidor do civil* and *ouvidor do crime*.

OUVIDORIA.—The tribunal of an ouvidor.

PARDOS.—Mixed-bloods, probably most often meaning mulattoes.

PASTA.—A folder of documents.

PRAÇA.—Town or municipal square; also a fortified place.

PRESÍDIO.—In the colonial period a garrison or fortified place; in modern Brazil a prison.

PROVEDOR.—A term applied to the custodians of many kinds of government facilities during the colonial period such as the heads of the royal mint (*provedor da moeda*), but in the sense most often used in this study a royal treasurer or superintendent of royal treasurers and their staffs (*provedor mór da fazenda*).

QUINTO.—A Crown tax on bullion or hides, the latter called the *quinto do couro*.

RASCUNHO.—A sketch or rough draft, as of a letter.

REGIMENTO.—Used in two senses during the colonial period: (1) standing instructions specifying the duties, powers, and restrictions of a particular office; (2) *ad hoc* instructions to a particular official issued before he assumed a new post. In the second sense, equivalent to *instrução*.

REGISTRO.—Check point, an interior custom post.

REINÓL (pl., *ões*).—Person or persons born in the kingdom of Portugal.

RÉIS.—A Portuguese monetary unit (sing., *real*) which existed only as money of account.

RELATÓRIO.—A report, particularly a terminal account by a retiring official concerning problems encountered during his administration.

RESIDÊNCIA.—An official terminal inquiry into the conduct of a public official made by taking testimony from a group of witnesses concerning the former officeholder's behavior. Often used interchangeably with *devassa* (*s.v.*). The Portuguese residência was supposed to be limited to thirty days, whereas its Spanish equivalent often lasted several months.

SAUDADES.—Nostalgia, particularly homesickness.

SENTENÇA.—Judgment or sentence issued by a court or senior administrative officer.

SERTÃO.—The back country (pl., *-ões*).

VIA.—During the colonial period when the hazards of loss at sea were substantial, the Peninsular governments sent several copies of important dispatches to their overseas agents by different ships. The first original was titled *primeira via* (*1.a via*), or sometimes *única via* if only one copy was sent. The second original (also signed) was the *2.da via,* and the triplicate the *3.ra via.*

Abbreviations

ABNRJ—*Anais da Biblioteca Nacional,* Rio de Janeiro.

AHU/CU/LR—Arquivo Histórico Colonial, Lisbon. Conselho Ultra-marino. *Livros do registro.* Bancroft Library Microfilm Collection.

AHU/PA-RGS—Arquivo Histórico Colonial, Lisbon. *Papeis avulsos.* Rio Grande do Sul. Bancroft Library Microfilm Collection.

AHU/PA-SC—Arquivo Histórico Colonial, Lisbon. *Papeis avulsos.* Santa Catarina. Bancroft Library Microfilm Collection.

ANRJ—Arquivo Nacional, Rio de Janeiro.

BCRG—"Correspondencia passiva do Tte.-Gal. João Henrique de Böhm," *Boletim do centro rio-grandense de estudos históricos,* Ano I (1939), No. 1, 10–160.

BNRJ—Biblioteca Nacional, Rio de Janeiro.

Castro e Almeida, *Inventário*—Eduardo de Castro e Almeida, *Inventário dos documentos relativos ao Brasil existentes no Arquivo de Marinha e Ultramar de Lisboa.*

CB—Archivo General de la Nación, Buenos Aires. *Documentos referentes a la guerra de la independencia . . . Campaña del Brasil. Antecedentes coloniales.*

CCLE—*Collecção da legislação antiga e moderna do reino de Portugal.* Pte. II *Da legislação moderna. Collecção chronológica de leis extravagantes, posteriores a' nova compilação das ordenações do reino publicadas em 1603.*

CCLP—José Justino de Andrade e Silva, ed., *Collecção chronológica da legislação portuguesa.*

CLDA—*Collecção das leys, decretos e alvarás q. comprehende o . . . reinado del rey . . . D. Jozé o I . . . .*

CLP—António Delgado da Silva, ed., *Collecção da legislação portuguesa de 1750 a* [*1820*].

CMCM—Private manuscript collection of Sr. Marcos Carneiro de Mendonça, Rio de Janeiro.

Coelho e Sousa, *Systema*—José Roberto Monteiro de Campos Coelho e Sousa, ed., *Systema ou collecção dos regimentos reaes . . . .*

CTLA—Carlos Calvo, ed., *Colleción completa de los tratados de la América latina.*

DH—Biblioteca Nacional, Rio de Janeiro. *Documentos históricos.*

DI—Arquivo do Estado de São Paulo. *Publicação official de documentos interessantes para a história e costumes de São Paulo.*

HAHR—*Hispanic American Historical Review.*

IHGB—Instituto Histórico e Geográfico Brasileiro, Rio de Janeiro.

IHGB/AUC—The Arquivo Ultramarino collection of transcripts in the Instituto Histórico e Geográfico Brasileiro.

Lavradio, *Relatório*—"Relatório do Marquez de Lavradio . . . entregado a Luiz de Vasconcelos e Sousa . . . ," June 19, 1779, *RIHGB,* IV (1843), 409–486.

PAN—*Publicações do Arquivo Nacional,* Rio de Janeiro.

QE—Manoel de Barros Sousa [Visconde de Santarém] and L. A. Rebello da Silva, eds., *Quadro elementar das relações políticas e diplomáticas de Portugal com as diversas potências do mundo.*

RADF—Rio de Janeiro, Arquivo Municipal. *Archivo do districto federal: revista de documentos para a história da cidade do Rio de Janeiro.*

RAPM—*Revista do Arquivo Público Mineiro.*

RIHGB—*Revista do Instituto Histórico e Geográfico Brasileiro.*

RIHGB/TE—"Catálogo de documentos sôbre a história de S. Paulo, existentes no Arquivo Histórico Ultramarino de Lisboa," *RIHGB, Tomos Especiais.* 15 vols. (Rio de Janeiro, 1956–1959).

RIHGRGN—*Revista do Instituto Histórico e Geográfico do Rio Grande do Norte.*

RIHGRGS—*Revista do Instituto Histórico e Geográfico do Rio Grande do Sul.*

R/SPHAN—*Revista do Serviço do Patrimônio Histórico e Artístico Nacional.*

Teixeira Coelho, "Instrução"—José João Teixeira Coelho, "Instrução para o governo da capitania de Minas Geraes" (1780), *RIHGB,* XV (1852), 257–476.

VRL—José d'Almeida [Correa de Sá, 6th Marquis of Lavradio], *Vicereinado de D. Luiz d'Almeida Portugal, 2º marquez de Lavradio, 3º vice-rei do Brasil.*

2RGG—"Regimento que trouxe Roque da Costa Barreto, . . ." Jan. 23, 1677, *DH,* VI (1928), 312–466; VII (1929), 3–46.

PART ONE

The Setting of the Scene

I

Lavradio's Apprenticeship
as Capitan-General of Bahia

ON SEPTEMBER 25, 1767, in the throne room of the royal palace in Lisbon, Nossa Senhora da Ajuda, occurred a ceremony which had been repeated countless times over several centuries in Portugal and in the far corners of her empire. Sitting on his dais was the "Very High and Very Powerful King," Dom José I, and kneeling before him, his hands placed in those of his liege lord, Dom Luís de Almeida, fifth Count of Avintes and second Marquis of Lavradio. Observing the ritual were the Count of São Vicente, a member of the Council of State and colonel of the royal armada, and another councillor, the Count of São Paio, gentleman of the bedchamber of the infante, Dom Pedro. According to the "usages and customs of these Kingdoms," the vassal repeated his oath of fealty to the king, swearing by the evangelical saints to uphold the laws of Portugal and to obey blindly the commands of his lord. Rising, he signed the Book of Homages, and beneath his bold, neat signature the witnesses added theirs.[1] With this simple yet essential ceremony, the Marquis of Lavradio became the forty-fifth governor and captain-general of Bahia de Todos os Santos, and embarked upon an eventful and trying eleven-year career in Brazil as an instrument of Portugal's celebrated dictator, the Marquis of Pombal.

Lavradio's Background

What qualities should an ideal colonial governor possess? Pondering this question in 1711, a few months after the city of Rio de Janeiro had been successfully besieged and held for ransom by the French privateer Duguay Trouin, the attorney-general of Portugal stated that the candidate should be valorous, prudent, responsible, and experienced in

[1] Patent letter of Lavradio, Aug. 26, 1767, with appendix dated Sept. 25, 1767, signed by Francisco Xavier de Mendonça Furtado, *VRL*, pp. 147–148. Lavradio was appointed at a salary of 1,917,500 réis a year for three years "and more" until the king saw fit to replace him. He was to consider himself "subordinate only to the Viceroy . . . of the State of Brazil, as have the other governors. . . ."

war. Coursing through his veins should be the blood of an aristocrat, since "the Brazilians have much respect for those with illustrious blood." But good blood alone is not enough, he cautioned, for without other qualities a governor can become dangerous, even tyrannical, arousing the inhabitants to indignation and hatred of their king and his government. The governor should not be young, for those with few years do not have the requisite prudence or experience to rule, and their unsteadiness can be irritating to their subjects and jeopardize the empire. In addition the ideal governor should abstain from all commercial intercourse, for one cannot be a good governor, or soldier, or judge, as well as a good merchant, the attorney-general stressed, since one's pecuniary interests will inevitably affect one's impartial judgment.[2]

Whether these criteria were generally observed when the Crown made its colonial appointments, or whether family connections and friends at Court were more influential in determining nominations is a moot question.[3] Certainly it is one that cannot be answered with confidence until we know more about the careers of individual Portuguese governors than we do at present. The Marquis of Lavradio, for example, seems to have possessed most of the attorney-general's requisite qualities, but he was unquestionably favored in his professional advancement by his family status and palace connections.

Lavradio was born June 27, 1729, in the borough of Ribaldeira outside Lisbon, on the estate of Conceição, which had been in his family since 1475. He was the eldest son of Dom Antônio de Almeida, first Count and later first Marquis of Lavradio, an army officer and an experienced civil servant. His mother was Dona Franciscana das Chagas de Mascarenhas, sister of the last Duke of Aveiro. His grand-uncle was Cardinal Dom Tomás de Almeida, first patriarch of Lisbon.

It is not recorded whether Dom Luís' father and mother had difficulty in selecting his name. It is doubtful, however, that they omitted

---

[2] *Parecer* of the procurador da coroa (*ca.* 1715) quoted in Alberto Lamego, "As invasões francesas no Rio de Janeiro, Duclerc e Duguay Trouin," *Anais do IV congresso de história nacional,* VI (Rio de Janeiro, 1949), 154–157. The Portuguese appear to have seldom theorized about the qualities their colonial officers should possess. Another tantalizing example of such reflections is Francisco de Almeida Silva, "Dessertação [*sic*] instructiva sobre a escolha dos governadores das conquistas; a sua existência nos governos; e o seu regresso para a Côrte," listed in the "Catálogo da exposição de história do Brasil," *ABNRJ,* IX, No. 19625, as one of the manuscripts possessed by the Instituto Histórico e Geográfico Brasileiro. An extensive search in the institute unfortunately failed to turn up the document.

[3] Surely the generalization of João Francisco Lisboa (*Obras,* III [Maranhão, 1865], 82 *et passim*) that the majority of Portugal's colonial governors were "ignorantes, duros, rudes e incultos . . ." is overdrawn.

any significant branch of the family when they had their first son baptized Luís de Almeida Portugal Soares Alarcão Eça Melo Pereira Aguilar Fiel de Lugo Mascarenhas Silva Mendonça e Lencastre. In his later life Dom Luís always signed his name simply "Marquês do Lavradio"; in Brazil he was usually addressed by that title, though subordinates referred to him as "O Senhor Marquês" or "O Marquês Vice Rei."

Dom Luís' education followed the usual pattern for one of his station in society. When he was ten, he joined his father at Elvas, where the latter commanded an infantry regiment. In later years he told his own son that the first marquis always treated him more like a common soldier than a son.[4] Actually he saw very little of the elder Lavradio after 1740, for in that year the father was appointed governor of Angola, a post he held for thirteen years.[5] Evidently the father left his family behind when he journeyed to Africa. Probably he, like many colonial governors, decided the advantages of having his family near were outweighed by the hazards of travel, the discomforts of living abroad, and the inevitable *saudades* or nostalgia for relatives, friends, and familiar places. Later, when the son went to Brazil, he too went without his wife and children.

During his father's absence Dom Luís remained in Portugal under the tutelage of a French abbé selected by his uncle, Cardinal Almeida. When the youth reached his twentieth year, he was sent on a grand tour to complete his education by travel. He first visited close relatives in Madrid and then went to Paris, where he spent some time studying the arts of war and fraternizing with young French army officers.

After he returned to Portugal Dom Luís began an army career, following in his father's footsteps. He must have been both proud and grieved when his ill and aging father left Portugal, late in 1759, to become viceroy of Brazil. Within less than a year news came that the elder Lavradio, last of the Bahian viceroys, had died scarcely six months after reaching his post.

The young marquis' personal fortunes brightened two years later when he came to the attention of the Count of Lippe, the celebrated restorer of the Portuguese army. The English-born German Count William of Schaumburg-Lippe-Bükelburg had come to the Peninsula to head a group of foreign officers in British service loaned to Portugal in response to her plea for military assistance to defend her frontiers against massing Spanish forces. It was largely through Lippe's efforts that the invaders were repelled, so that Portugal

4 Lavradio to his son, Nov. 26, 1776, cited in *VRL*, p. 4, n. 1.
5 Elias Alexandre da Silva Corrêa, *História de Angola* (1792) II (Lisbon, 1937), 7-9.

emerged from the Seven Years' War without the loss of any European territory.[6]

During the war and the years immediately following, Lippe gathered around him a group of eager young Portuguese officers, including the Marquis of Lavradio, and instilled in them his ideas concerning army organization, discipline,[7] tactics, and the importance of artillery in warfare.[8] Among this group may have been some of Lavradio's fellow regimental commanders, such as colonels Antônio Carlos Furtado de Mendonça, Martim Lopes Lobo de Saldanha, and Dom Luís Antônio de Sousa Botelho, each of whom was to play an important part in Brazil during Lavradio's tenure there.[9]

Lavradio enthusiastically applied his master's teachings in commanding the Cascaes regiment, welding it into a model unit and winning for its colors the coveted motto "exemplo." While he allegedly served with distinction during the war of 1762, available evidence does not reveal whether he participated actively in the fighting.[10] In any case, on recommendation of Count Lippe, he was promoted from colonel to brigadier before the conflict was over.[11]

The next significant event in Dom Luís de Almeida's career was his appointment to Bahia. It came about when Dom José I was searching for a capable tutor for his grandson a few years after the war. Evidently his eyes settled on Dom Luís for the post. However, the powerful Marquis of Pombal dissuaded the king from giving Lavradio the appointment by arguing that the thirty-eight-year-old marquis was precisely the person needed to administer Bahia, where a series of weak, short-lived governors had followed the elder Lavradio.[12] La-

6 For the "guerra fantástica" of 1762 and Count Lippe's role in it, see José Maria Latino Coelho, *História militar e política de Portugal desde os fins do xviii século até 1814,* III (Lisbon, 1885–1891) , 60–75; João Lúcio d'Azevedo, *O Marquês de Pombal e a sua época,* pp. 235–242; and John Smith, *Memoirs of the Marquis of Pombal,* I, 325–335; and *Grande enciclopédia portuguesa e brasileira,* XXVII, 855–860. William Dalrymple, a British major stationed at Gibraltar, thought the effectiveness of the Lippian reforms had been overrated. *Travels through Spain and Portugal,* p. 147. Colonial aspects of this war are examined in Chap. IV.

7 Lippe was the author of the exceedingly harsh *Regulamento para o exercicio, e disciplina dos regimentos de infantaria dos exercitos de Sua Magestade Fidelissima . . .* (Lisboa, 1794) . A copy of this very rare work is in CMCM.

8 *VRL,* p. 5.

9 "Relação que Sua Magestade mandou baixar ao Conselho de Guerra com o seu real decreto de dez de maio deste presente anno de mil setecentos sessenta e tres sobre a redução das tropas do seu exercito e marinha," Ajuda, May 10, 1763, in CMCM, miscellaneous laws.

10 *VRL,* p. 5.

11 *Loc. cit.*

12 The first Lavradio was followed by a caretaker government (composed, as usual, of a senior churchman, an army officer, and a magistrate) , which gave way in 1766 to the distinguished but old and infirm Dom Antônio Rolim de Moura Tavares, Count of Azambuja, who went on to Rio de Janeiro as viceroy before the following year was out. When the second Lavradio arrived, he relieved still another interim regime.

vradio's biographer has suggested that Pombal had an ulterior motive for his recommendation, that he saw in Dom Luís a potential rival for the king's ear; but there is no convincing evidence that this contention is more than the wishful surmise of an admiring descendant.[13] Dom Luís had held no office at Court, and there is nothing in his later correspondence to suggest that he had designs on Pombal's job. On the contrary, the numerous exchanges between the two make it quite certain that Dom Luís was a protégé of Pombal, who evidently regarded the younger man as a conscientious, intelligent, able, and pliant person who could faithfully carry out his instructions regarding the administrative reorganization and economic development of Brazil.[14]

The Marquis of Pombal: Architect of Enlightened Despotism

During the years that the younger Lavradio was maturing and throughout most of his service in Brazil, the uncrowned ruler of Portugal was Sebastião José de Carvalho e Melo, Count of Oeiras and Marquis of Pombal.[15] Besides holding two of the three portfolios in the Portuguese cabinet, he was inspector-general of the Royal Treasury, lieutenant-general of the University of Coimbra, and secretary of the ruling house of Bragança.[16]

Born near Lisbon in 1699, Carvalho was the eldest of three sons of a country nobleman. He received his higher education from the Jesuits at Coimbra but reputedly quit the university in disgust. In 1733, after drifting in and out of the army, he obtained a position in the newly founded Academia Real de História, where he was assigned to do research on the history of the royal family. Evidently this experience made a profound impression upon him, for in later life he constantly appealed to history to justify his policies. He seems to have

13 *VRL*, pp. 5–6. According to William Beckford, popular rumor in Lisbon held that Lavradio had been "banished" to Brazil because of his talent for Court intrigue. *The Journal of William Beckford in Portugal and Spain 1787–1788*, Boyd Alexander, ed. (London, 1954) , p. 121.

14 Lavradio later wrote that he had had no wish to go to America and that he reluctantly accepted his appointment as a personal sacrifice to the king. To Patriarch Almeida, Dec. 23, 1770, *VRL*, p. 6. n. 1. Many another colonial officer could have echoed those words.

15 He became Count of Oeiras in 1759 and Marquis of Pombal in 1770.

16 For an introduction to the abundance of controversial literature on Pombal see Alfredo Duarte Rodrigues, *O Marquês de Pombal e os seus biógrafos* (Lisbon, 1947) . The best and most dispassionate study remains Azevedo, *O Marquês de Pombal e a sua época*, which is based on select use of manuscript and printed sources [hereafter cited as Azevedo, *Época*]. See also Jacome Ratton, *Recordacoens*. Ratton was a French-born, Portuguese-naturalized cloth merchant with important Court connections. He was an admirer of Pombal, as was John Smith [Marquis of Carnota], *Memoirs of the Marquis of Pombal*.

attempted to cut a smart figure in Lisbon society in the 1730s but was snubbed because of his inferior lineage, a mortification for which he was later to repay the *grandees*. Eventually he managed to force his acceptance in the ranks of the court nobility by a spectacular run-away marriage to a rich blue-blooded widow. The property he acquired from her and from some providential inheritances made him a wealthy landowner.

Carvalho's career took a decisive turn in 1740, when he became minister plenipotentiary to London, a post he held until 1744. Though he failed to score any major diplomatic triumph or even to learn the language of the host country, he developed a strong sense of antipathy mixed with admiration for the British after studying the sources of their prosperity, particularly the British East India Company and England's lucrative trade with Portugal.[17] He resolved some day to apply at home the lessons he had learned. He also examined the mode of the British government, but apparently concluded that parliamentary government was inapplicable to Portugal, where the *Cortes* had not met since 1698. In addition, he read of the accomplishments of the great triumvirate of seventeenth-century French ministers, Sully, Richelieu, and Colbert, choosing Henry IV's minister as his model in economics and the crafty cardinal in politics.[18]

After an uneventful four-year embassy in Vienna,[19] Pombal returned to Lisbon early in 1750, and languished among the unemployed until the death of fun-loving Dom João V.[20] Then in August the new king, thirty-six-year-old Dom José I, astonished palace habitués by naming Carvalho Secretary of State for Foreign Affairs and War.[21] The nomination prompted one of his court rivals to declare,

[17] While in London Pombal urged his government to create a Portuguese East India Company patterned on the famous British trading firm but was disappointed when the Crown turned a deaf ear to his detailed recommendations.

[18] Azevedo, *Época,* p. 89.

[19] It was uneventful from a diplomatic standpoint, but Pombal did acquire a second wife in Vienna, his first having died in a convent while he was in England. His second bride was Countess Leonor Ernestina Daun, daughter of an Austrian military hero and descendant of an ancient but impoverished family. The marriage had the approval of both Empress Maria Theresa and her daughter, the queen of Portugal.

[20] In recent years the Portuguese historian João Ameal has led efforts to rehabilitate the much-maligned João V (1706–1750), whom he compares favorably with Louis XIV. E.g., João Ameal and Rodrigues Cavalheiro, *Erratas à história de Portugal de D. João V a D. Miguel* (Porto, 1939), and *D. João V. Conferências e estudos comemorativos do segundo centenario da sua morte (1750–1950)* (Lisbon, 1952). Unfortunately Ameal has produced no new archival evidence to sustain his reappraisal but has contented himself with the testimony of contemporary foreign ambassadors as to the king's piety and pacific nature.

[21] There are at least three theories to account for the king's selection of Pombal:

"The Pasha has obtained his objective, such are the ways of the world! It is the people who will have to suffer for it, and the tidings will go down to future generations who will admire the effects of his expansive (largas) ideas in everything that pertains to his own department, if he does not interfere in the others." [22]

These words by Alexandre de Gusmão, the leading diplomat of the preceding reign, proved prophetic; for once in power Pombal ran roughshod over all opposition while implementing his program of reform for Portugal and her empire. He believed that only through the restoration of strong monarchical authority could Portugal, then a third- or fourth-rate power, regain her former greatness and influence. In carrying out his plans he tolerated no opposition or criticism—to him they were synonymous—whether from commoners, ministerial colleagues, the traditional ruling families, or the Jesuits, who for centuries had been the councillors and confessors of the royal family, the educators of the nation's privileged youth, and its most celebrated overseas missionaries. During the 1750s his vigorous action in dealing with a series of domestic crises—the great Lisbon earthquake and fire (1755), the Oporto revolt against his newly established royal wine monopoly company (1757), the attempted regicide (1758), and the expulsion of the Society of Jesus (1759)—and his ruthless treatment of nonconformists by medieval-type punishments, property confiscations, long imprisonments, and/or banishment from Court or homeland consolidated his position and left him with no formidable opposition.

Yet Pombal, the contemporary of Frederick the Great, Catherine of Russia, Maria Theresa, Louis XV, and Charles III, was no mere despot. Like those enlightened monarchs, he introduced many far-reaching measures designed to improve the administration, economy, and cultural life of Portugal and her empire. Brazil played a prominent role in his plans.

The fact that Pombal was never colonial secretary [23] mattered little, for his was the dominant voice in colonial affairs just as it was in domestic affairs. It was he who drafted the new legislation pertaining to the colony, and it was he who issued orders to colonial officials

---

(1) that he was influenced by the Austrian-born queen mother who was friendly with Pombal's second wife; (2) that the royal confessor, a Jesuit, recommended Pombal for the post; and (3) that Dom Luís da Cunha, a leading statesman of the preceding reign, had spoken highly of Pombal in his famous Testamento Político (ca. 1750).

[22] Alexandre de Gusmão to Martinho Velho Oldemberg, n. d., quoted in Azevedo, Época, pp. 96–97.

[23] An office created by the alvará of July 28, 1736, CCLE, II, 458–463, which expanded the number of secretaries of state from two to three. Like Spain, Portugal

either directly or through the office of the colonial minister, a post held by his brother Francisco Xavier de Mendoça Furtado, from 1762 until his death in 1770, and subsequently by Martinho de Melo e Castro. The major policy-making agency for colonial affairs in preceding reigns, the venerable Overseas Council (*Conselho Ultramarino*) [24] was reduced to handling purely routine matters after an early test of strength with Pombal.[25]

By Pombal's time Brazil's population was approaching 1,500,000,[26] scattered from the Amazon to the Río de la Plata, from the Atlantic coast to the foothills of the Andes. Though it was then Portugal's most important colonial possession, it had not always been regarded so highly. Discovered in 1500, Brazil was considered a second-rate colony so long as Portugal held on to glittering India. Rather than colonize it directly, the Crown entrusted its settlement to private entrepeneurs or donataries who were given territorial enclaves (captaincies) to defend, populate, and develop. As the fame of Brazil's red dyewood and fabulous sugar plantations spread, so many foreigners came to share in the riches that the Crown felt compelled to protect its interests by taking a more energetic role in the administration of its American possession. After the loss of the Portuguese far eastern empire in the first half of the seventeenth century, Brazil became Portugal's milch cow, to use the famous expression of King João IV, and her sugar, tobacco, and other products sustained the Portuguese monarchy during the difficult days after the restoration of Portugal's independence (1640). The discovery of gold (1694) and diamonds (1729) in the interior of Brazil enabled Portugal to indulge in a superficial sort of prosperity during the first half of the eighteenth

---

moved from a counciliar to a ministerial form of government during the eighteenth century.

24 It was founded in 1642 and, like its short-lived predecessor the Conselho da India (1604–1614), was patterned after the Consejo de las Indias of Spain. We badly need a study comparable to Schafer's standard work on the Spanish council. Marcelo Caetano's brief essay, *Do conselho ultramarino ao conselho do império*, is thin and disappointing, coming as it does from the pen of an able historian.

25 The incident involved mining legislation for Brazil. It is described in Azevedo, *Época*, pp. 102–103, and in Caetano, pp. 34–35, who emphasizes the significance of the affair in these terms: "O antigo órgão de govêrno, que francamente aconselhava o Rei, e de cujas consultas eram os Secretários de Estado meros intermediários junto do Soberano, ia assim transformar-se, por efeito da exaltação da função ministerial, em mero colaborador subalterno da orientação governativa deles" (p. 35). Another indication of the decline of the council was an order sent to the viceroy of Brazil and to various other colonial officers that henceforth no copies of any communications between them and the colonial minister should be sent to the council. Francisco Xavier de Mendonça Furtado to Count da Cunha, Nov. 22, 1765, ANRJ, Col. 67, Liv. 1-A, fol. 191ʳ (*1.a via*); *idem* to Marquis of Lavradio, Feb. 10, 1768, CMCM, cod. 23, fol. 75ʳ (orig.).

26 D. Alden, "The Population of Brazil in the Late Eighteenth Century: a Preliminary Survey," *HAHR XLIII* (May 1963), 173–205. See Appendix I, below.

century, the so-called golden age of absolutism, which was reflected in the lavish late baroque architecture of the kingdom.[27]

The Pombaline epoch was a period of important administrative, economic, and social innovations in Brazil.[28] Some of the administrative measures—such as the establishment of Brazil's second appellate court (Relação) in Rio de Janeiro (1751),[29] the extinction of all but one of the private captaincies,[30] and the shift of the nominal capital from Bahia (Salvador) to Rio de Janeiro (1763)—represented the continuance of long-standing trends. But many of the reforms need to be understood against the background of a severe and prolonged depression which beset the colony beginning in the 1750s; it was caused by declining production of gold, diamonds, and sugar and was reflected in the Crown's falling revenues.[31] The curtailment of Portugal's income from Brazil came precisely at a time when her military expenditures were vastly increasing because of the intensification of military rivalry with Spain in America.[32]

The remedies Pombal provided to meet this situation were more

[27] The best general history of Colonial Brazil in Portuguese remains Francisco Adolfo de Varnhagen, História geral do Brasil. The most illuminating works in English are those of Professor Charles R. Boxer. See Bibliography.

[28] Two studies of Pombal's impact upon Brazil are João Lúcio de Azevedo, "Política de Pombal relativa ao Brasil," Novas epanáforas: estudos de história e literatura (Lisbon, 1932), pp. 7–62, and António de Sousa Pedroso Carnaxide (Visconde de Carnaxide), O Brasil na administração pombalina (economia e política externa) (São Paulo, 1940). Azevedo's work, based largely on printed materials, rectifies some of the lacunae in his larger work on Pombal, but is sketchy. Carnaxide's is not as sound as its citations would imply, and his conclusions are not always reliable. Both are weak on institutional changes, and neither author consulted relevant Spanish materials for evaluating Luso-Spanish military and diplomatic relations during the Pombaline period.

[29] The first was created in Salvador in 1609, but was suspended in 1624 and reestablished in 1652. The Relação was a tribunal of second instance which confirmed, modified, or revoked the sentences of inferior tribunals where legal remedy was provided. It reviewed the conduct of all Crown officials upon the completion of their terms, and made special investigations upon orders from the Crown or governor-general. The limits of its authority in civil cases were 2,000 cruzados in reality and 3,000 in chattels; beyond these amounts, appeals could be taken to the Casa de Suplicação in Lisbon. Except for those favored by military or ecclesiastical privileges (foros), there was no appeal from the Relações' decisions in criminal proceedings. In some ways similar to the Spanish audiencias, the Relações never attained the importance or stature of their Spanish counterparts. Regimentos of Mar. 7, 1609, Sept. 12, 1652, and Oct. 13, 1751, Coelho e Sousa, Systema, VI, 290–315, IV, 484–502. See also the illuminating comments of César Trípoli, Historia do direito brasileiro, I, 228 ff.

[30] By means of settlements in the form of pensions, titles, or by confiscation. The only proprietorship to survive the Pombal era was that of Itanhaém (coastal São Paulo), which lasted until 1791.

[31] See Jorge de Macedo, A situação econômica no tempo de Pombal: alguns aspectos (Pôrto, 1951), pp. 159–190; idem, "Portugal e a economia 'pombalina' Temas e hipóteses," Revista de historia, No. 19 (São Paulo, Julho–Setembro, 1954), 81–100, and Carnaxide, pp. 76–82.

[32] See Chap. IV.

effective administrative controls, efforts to revive old and promote new colonial raw-material industries, and measures designed to increase the volume of trade with the mother country. In 1751 boards of inspection (mesas de inspeção) were established in Brazil's four leading ports, São Luís do Maranhão, Recife, Bahia, and Rio de Janeiro, to provide quantitative and qualitative controls for the export of sugar and tobacco and to promote either commodity where it was lagging.[33] The agricultural development of the backward northern part of Brazil became the province of the Companhia do Grão Pará e Maranhão, a government-sponsored monopoly trading company (1755); and four years later a similar organization was created to revive the sugar industry of the nordeste. In 1765 the system of organized fleets (frotas) between colony and mother country, which had existed since 1649, was scrapped to expedite ship movements across the Atlantic.[34]

The maritime captaincies were not the only parts of Brazil to feel the impact of the new regime. Indeed, the most vital part of Brazil from the Crown's point of view was the interior captaincy of Minas Gerais, the main source of both gold and diamonds. During the first half of the eighteenth century Lisbon experimented with various means of collecting the king's share of the mineral harvest; and in 1750 Pombal abolished the hated head tax on the miners' slaves (the capitação) in favor of direct collection of the quinto, or royal fifth, at the government smelteries (casas da fundição).[35] These were administered by intendants who were charged with the collection of the quinto, its remission to Rio de Janeiro, and the policing of the mining zone to prevent smuggling.[36] In this last capacity they also cooperated with the intendentes gerais do ouro in Rio de Janeiro and in Bahia.[37]

Another mining reform which represented the work of Pombal was

[33] Later the boards were given responsibility for promoting cereals, fibers, dyestuffs, and other commodities with attractive revenue-producing features. For the original regulations setting up the boards see the regimento of April 1, 1751, Coelho e Sousa, Systema, IV, 92–97. In 1755 the boards were placed under the supervision of the Junta do Commércio (not to be confused with an earlier junta bearing the same title, 1663–1720) in Lisbon, which had broad powers concerning industry, trade, and the suppression of smuggling. See Ratton, Recordacoens, pp. 258–282, and Chaps. XIII and XIV below.

[34] Alvará de lei of Sept. 10, 1765, CLP, II, 221–222. See Chap. XIII, n. 104.

[35] For the various methods the Crown devised to collect its share of Brazil's bullion, see Teixeira Coelho, "Instrução," p. 364–367, and Charles R. Boxer, The Golden Age of Brazil, p. 437, s.v. "Fifths, Royal."

[36] Regimento of Mar. 4, 1751, CCLE, III, 35–37; also in Coelho e Sousa, Systema, IV, 503–516.

[37] As their title suggests, these officers had charge of the shipments of gold to the Peninsula both for the Crown and for private individuals. They were ex-officio members of the Relações, and were also presidents of the boards of inspection. For further discussion of their duties, see Chap. XIV.

the creation of a special administration, the Royal Extraction, for the diamond district within Minas Gerais.[38] For a number of years the Crown had forbidden individual gem prospecting and had auctioned off the entire production of the district to a group of private contractors. This system failed to bring expected benefits to either the Crown or the contractors, largely because of the persistence of clandestine mining. In 1771, therefore, Pombal placed the area under rect royal control. The new governing body consisted of an inten-general, a locally appointed fiscal, and three treasurers nomi- by a directory of three in Lisbon. The directory was, in turn, ;ible to the inspector-general of the royal treasury, that is, to oal. The new administration had complete authority over all luction and persons within the district and was exempt from any erior authority in Brazil. Aside from the marked severity of the ministrators' judicial powers, the Royal Extraction represented a unique example in the Portuguese empire of highly centralized authority without the customary overlapping administrative checks.[39]

One of the most ambitious of Pombal's reforms was the creation of a new fiscal system for Portugal and her empire during the 1760s and 1770s. That reform, which involved extensive changes in administrative organization and procedure, will be examined in Chapter XI. Suffice it here to say that establishment of the new fiscal system in the captaincy-general of Bahia became one of the principal duties of the Marquis of Lavradio after he took up his new post.

Lavradio as Captain-General of Bahia

On April 18, 1768, the frigate *Madre de Deus* rounded Fort Santo Antônio da Barra and sailed into the broad bay of All Saints with Dom Luís de Almeida and his entourage, after a relatively quick voyage of fifty-seven days.[40] The new captain-general elected to re-

---

38 The original district was an elliptical area twelve leagues north to south, seven leagues east to west. As new discoveries were made outside the original boundaries, the limits of the intendancy were extended. J. Felicio dos Santos, *Memória do Distrito Diamantino da comarca do Serro Frio* . . . (Rio de Janeiro [?], 1868), p. 34. According to José Vieira Couto, "Memoria sobre a capitania de Minas Gerais . . ." (1799), *RIHGB*, XI (2d ed., 1872), 292–293, the *arraial* of Tijuco, the administrative center, was situated nearly in the middle of the district, which comprised an area about forty-two leagues in circumference. Besides these two classic accounts of the Diamond District, see W. L. von Eschwege, *Pluto Brasiliensis*, tr. and ed. by Domício de Figueiredo Murta, II (São Paulo, n.d.), 115–158, and Boxer, *The Golden Age*, Chap. VIII.

39 *Regimento* of July 12, 1771, *ibid.*, 123–148.

40 Corrêa de Sá erroneously states that the voyage lasted fifty-three days. *VRL*, p. 6. In his dispatches, however, Lavradio declared that he had enjoyed "57 dias de felis navegação." To the king and to Francisco Xavier de Mendonça Furtado, Bahia, Apr. 28, 1768, CMCM, cod. 16, fols. 95 and 97 (*rascunhos* in hand of author).

main on board until the morrow to prepare himself for the arduous day ahead when he would sorrowfully visit his father's sepulcher, and then participate in his triple installation at the cathedral, the council hall, and the governor's palace.[41]

The captaincy-general of Bahia was one of Brazil's key agricultural areas. Its economy rested upon sugar and tobacco, the one the mainstay of its European trade, the other of its African commerce.[42] Both depended upon a large and constant supply of Negro slaves, and Salvador, the capital of Bahia, was probably the largest Brazilian entrepôt for human merchandise.[43] In addition to sugar and tobacco, the latter a highly specialized industry concentrated around the *vila* of Cachoeira, Bahia was a major whaling port.[44] It also produced manioc, raw and tanned hides, construction woods, brandy, and molasses. As many as forty 8oo-ton ships a year carried its exports to Lisbon and Porto.[45] In return, Bahia bought cloth, wheat, wine, codfish, salt, butter, iron, copper, and lead from the Peninsula.[46] The port boasted at least three shipyards, which built mainly small craft,

[41] Lavradio to Mendonça Furtado, Apr. 28, 1768, *ibid.* fol. 95; *idem* to Cardinal Almeida, May 5, 1768, *VRL,* p. 6 n. 2. The solemn installation of the colonial governors is described in Edmundo Zenha, *O município no Brasil,* p. 107.

[42] As the famed army engineer and historian, José Antônio Caldas, wrote in 1759, "He sem duvida q' o asucar e tabaco são os generos mais principães desta capitania, os quaes carregando as Frotas, q' deste porto saem para o da Corte, e Cidade de Lisboa, serve do Estado de opulencia, e não pouco interesse aos Commerciantes." *Noticia geral de toda esta capitania da Bahia* (Fasc. ed., Salvador, 1951), p. 425 (hereafter cited as Caldas, *Noticia da Bahia*). During the latter part of the eighteenth century Bahian sugar was three times as valuable an export as its tobacco, and six times as important as its leather goods. Anon., "Discurso preliminar, histórico, introductivo, com natureza de descripção econômica da comarca e cidade da Bahia" (*ca.* 1790), *ABNRJ,* XXVII, 290–291.

[43] An informed contemporary estimated that 15,000 slaves annually entered Bahia and 10,000 came to Rio de Janeiro. He stated that fifty corvettes and sloops left Salvador each year for the Guinea and Angola coasts, four-fifths going to the former. José da Silva Lisboa (later Visconde de Cairú) to Dr. Domingos Vandelli, Oct. 18, 1781, *ABNRJ,* XXXII, 504–505; but for a lower estimate see Manoel da Cunha Menezes (captain-general of Bahia) to Martinho de Melo e Castro, Mar. 3, 1775, *ibid.,* 288. Many of the chattels entering Bahia passed illegally through the *sertões* to Minas Gerais, the premium slave market in Brazil. Mafalda P. Zemella, *O Abastecimento da capitania das Minas Gerais no século xviii* (São Paulo, 1951), pp. 77–78.

[44] According to an anonymous report of *ca.* 1771, a whaling station on the island of Itaparica at the entrance to All Saints Bay processed between fifty and two hundred carcasses a year. *ABNRJ,* XXXII, 253–254. But Portuguese whaling at Bahia and elsewhere along the Brazilian littoral was then on the verge of a serious decline as a consequence of Yankee and British competition. D. Alden, "Yankee Sperm Whalers in Brazilian Waters, and the Decline of the Portuguese Whale Fishery (1773–1801)," *The Americas,* XX (Jan. 1964), 267–288.

[45] Lisboa to Vandelli, Oct. 18, 1781 (see n. 43), 494–506; for the cargo of the frota of 1757 (thirty-three ships) see "Mapa geral da carga que levárão os navios de que se compos a Frota da Bahia . . . de 1757," in Caldas, facing p. 442.

[46] Thomas Lindley, *Narrative of a Voyage to Brazil,* pp. 258–259.

but which usually had one or more ocean-going craft on the stocks.[47]

The hub of the Bahian universe was its capital, Salvador, the home of nearly one-fifth of the captaincy-general's inhabitants.[48] Long the seat of royal government in Brazil, the city lost some of its luster when that honor passed in 1763 to its economic rival, Rio de Janeiro. Bahians, however, continued to hope that the king would restore their metropolis to its former preeminence "so merited by the dignity and primacy of the city, by the opulence of its captaincy, and by its natural position as the center of Portuguese America. . . ." [49]

Salvador must have reminded eighteenth-century travelers like the Marquis of Lavradio very much of Lisbon.[50] Both cities were built according to the medieval plan of the fortified hillside with narrow, winding streets, and buildings crowded upon one another.[51] Each was divided into two separate cities, joined by steep, meandering, ill-paved paths called ladeiras. In the commercial lower town (cidade baixa) were the royal arsenals, warehouses, waterfront shops, and vegetable marts, as well as the dwellings of prominent merchants and the humble classes. The upper city (cidade alta) sprawled along the montanha, a ridge of hills paralleling and overlooking the bay. Here the visitor found the more commodious homes and remarkably sumptuous churches, whose ornate, gilded interiors gave vivid testimony to the wealth and piety of their parishioners. A focal point of attention here was the praça do palácio, the nerve center of Salvador; for facing this square were the old, unpretentious governor's palace,[52] the royal mint, the chambers of the Relação and the municipal corporation (câmara), and the city jail.[53]

47 Petition of "capitão e commerciante" Theodosio Gonçalves da Silva (ca. Oct. 1775), ABNRJ, XXXII, 309.

48 Including its suburbs, Salvador's population numbered 57,000 out of a total of 288,848 persons reported for the captaincy-general. "População da capitania da Bahia, em janeiro de 1775," annex to Manuel da Cunha Menezes to Martinho de Melo e Castro, Mar. 3, 1775, ABNRJ, XXXII, 288–289.

49 "Representação do senado da câmara . . . da Bahia . . . ," July 4, 1785, ABNRJ, XXXII, 575–576.

50 See the excellent discussion and comparison in Robert C. Smith, "Some Views of Colonial Bahia," Belas artes, 2d ser., no. 1 (Lisbon, 1948), pp. 31 ff.

51 "The Portuguese discoverers were men of the Renaissance, but as town planners they belonged to the Middle Ages. . . . [T]hey clung to the medieval plan of the fortified hill-side . . . [claiming] that such a situation was essential for defense, but in reality they were preserving a tradition." Idem, "The Arts in Brazil: [I] Baroque Architecture," in Harold V. Livermore, ed., Portugal and Brazil (London, 1953), p. 349.

52 Lindley sarcastically noted "A small alley, descending from the palace to the city below [which] is noticed by every stranger from its excessive accumulation of nauseous rubbish; in the immediate sight and scent of the governor's window! to the great credit of the police and the cleanliness of his excellency." Narrative, p. 244 n.

53 Ibid., pp. 244–245.

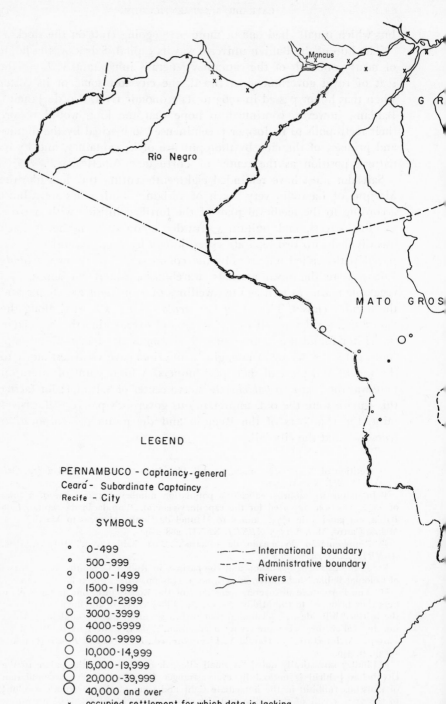

Manaus

G R

Rio Negro

MATO GROS

O °

LEGEND

PERNAMBUCO - Captaincy-general
Ceará - Subordinate Captaincy
Recife - City

SYMBOLS

°	0-499	.——.—	International boundary
°	500-999	-----	Administrative boundary
°	1000-1499	⟩—	Rivers
°	1500-1999		
O	2000-2999		
O	3000-3999		
O	4000-5999		
O	6000-9999		
O	10,000-14,999		
O	15,000-19,999		
O	20,000-39,999		
O	40,000 and over		
x	occupied settlement for which data is lacking		
*	21,972 persons in unspecified parts of interior Bahia		

Colônia

Map 1 Distribution of population of Brazil, *ca.* 1772 to *ca.* 1782.

Seen from the bay, the skyline of Salvador presented an impressive panorama with its white houses gleaming in the tropical sun, its confusing jumble of forts, churches, hospitals, and other public buildings.[54] Yet some of these pleasant impressions were dispelled once the visitor stepped ashore and inhaled the unpleasant aromas of decaying fish and vegetable matter scattered about the streets. He would experience further disillusionment when he noticed that the exteriors of the old seventeenth-century homes were dirty and unpainted.[55]

What the new captain-general thought of the appearance of Salvador is unrecorded. He seems to have been a bit uneasy as he prepared to assume his duties, for when the royal barge called for him and was five minutes late in reaching the frigate, he sharply reprimanded the crew for their tardiness. Somewhat testily he declared, "I begin to see the negligence with which orders given in the name of His Majesty are executed," and promised that he would enforce their strict observance. He also censored the boat company for the defacement of a picture on the barge, criticizing them for failing to take proper care of royal property.[56]

Three days after taking office (April 19, 1768), the captain-general crossed the palace square, doubtless accompanied by the usual retinue of uniformed soldiers, and entered the quarters of the Relação to become its *regedor,* or president. Although the captains-general and viceroys did not vote in the court's proceedings unless they were trained in law, as was also true of their counterparts in Spanish America, they were expected to see that justice was dispensed equally to all "without fear, favor, or prejudice." [57] They were required to make periodic visits to the prison of the court to see that no one was detained longer than thirty days without charges being brought against him. With the advice of the chancellor of the court they made

54 See the excellent colored panoramic map of the Salvadorian skyline, dated 1801, in Luiz dos Santos Vilhena, *Cartas de Vilhena: notícias soteropolitanas e brasílicas,* annotated by Braz do Amaral, I (Bahia, 1921–1922), xvi, which is based on the earlier map in Caldas, *Notícia da Bahia,* facing p. 226, but is more carefully rendered.

55 Lindley, *Narrative,* p. 247; for a jaundiced view of Salvador and its officialdom by an English Protestant lady see Mrs. [Nathaniel Edward] Kindersley, *Letters from the island of Teneriffe, Brazil, the Cape of Good Hope, and the East Indies* (London, 1777), pp. 22–48, recording her impressions of August–September 1764.

56 These anecdotes were recorded by Gaspar José de Matos, adjutant to Lavradio. *VRL,* p. 7.

57 As Secretary of State Melo e Castro put it in his instruction to the Marquis of Valenca (a later captain-general of Bahia), "devendo ser o seu principal cuidado a boa administracao da justica. . . ." Instruction of Sept. 10, 1779, *ABNRJ,* XXXII, 440, ¶ 25. The Relação normally met every Tuesday, Thursday, and Saturday from 7 A.M. to 2 P.M., but it is unlikely that the regedor remained there during those long hours. Caldas, *Notícia da Bahia,* pp. 46–47.

provisional appointments to the bench when vacancies occurred and assigned judges to take *residências* [58] and to perform other special tasks. The *regedor* also reported to the Crown on the court's proceedings and on the conduct of its magistrates. [59]

Lavradio had in mind the drafting of one of these papers when he first presided over the court. He was obliged to respond to an urgent inquiry from Colonial Secretary Francisco Xavier de Mendonça Furtado regarding the court's handling of a particular case. The existence of such an order suggests that the colonial courts were not immune from censorship during the days of Pombal. The case concerned one Francisco Gil Garcia de Araujo who had been accused of certain "atrocious crimes," a term often used for suspected acts of smuggling. The Relação originally sentenced Araujo to ten years' exile in Angola. Subsequently, for reasons unclear, it reviewed the case, and several of the magistrates voted to reduce the sentence to several years' exile in nearby Pôrto Seguro. Only by the margin of the tie-breaking vote of the president, Lavradio's predecessor, was the original sentence sustained. The colonial minister demanded to know the names of the judges who comprised the minority and their reasons for having voted for the lesser penalty. He also ordered the prisoner kept under close guard in Salvador until the king should determine otherwise. [60]

Within a week after his arrival, Lavradio sent the required information, but he confessed that he had not yet formed any definite impression of the particular merits of the judges. [61] Soon after, however, he complained that the court was so split into factions that it was difficult for him to know which of the magistrates to trust. Because of their bickering, the dispatch of the court's business was greatly delayed. He recommended that nine of the twelve judges be replaced as soon as their terms expired. [62] Later, he protested against the inconveniences resulting from the king's appointment of magistrates with-

[58] The *residência* was a means of checking on the performance of public officials upon completion of their service in office by means of a judicial inquiry which seems to have been considerably shorter in Portuguese America than it was in Spanish America.

[59] E.g., Lavradio endorsed the residência of retiring chancellor Joseph Carvalho de Andr[ad?]e, by stating that the chancellor had conducted himself well, had accepted no bribes, or committed any excess such as "tracto illícito com mulher," nor engaged in any unlawful business. Lavradio to the king, June 20, 1768 (rascunho in his hand) , CMCM, cod. 16, fol. 78.

[60] Mendonça Furtado to Lavradio, Oct. 21, 1767 (*única via*) , CMCM, cod. 23, fol. 174.

[61] Lavradio to Mendonça Furtado, Apr. 26, 1768 (rascunho) , CMCM, cod. 16, fol. 94ʳ [*sic for* 103ʳ].

[62] Lavradio to Count of Oeiras, May 5, 1768, *VRL*, pp. 149–151.

out previously consulting the governor as to those best qualified for the posts.[63] To have done so, however, would have encouraged colonial patronage machines, a practice the Crown always looked upon with disfavor.

The colonial minister acknowledged Lavradio's complaints, and promised that Dom Luís would find the court more harmonious when the new promotion list appeared.[64] Such was evidently the case, for after there had been some turnover in the personnel,[65] the captain-general pronounced himself satisfied with the Relação's conduct.[66]

One of the first duties of a new captain-general or governor was to inspect the garrison and military installations of his post and to report his findings to the Court. Captain-General Lavradio's observations concerning the inadequacy of his defenses typified the remarks of many colonial administrators. He stated that the fortifications of Salvador were crumbling through long neglect and that he could do little to remedy their defects since he lacked competent engineers and funds to rebuild them. The garrison lacked adequate quarters, weapons, uniforms, and discipline. He thought incompetent leadership primarily responsible for this situation, and characterized the commanding officers in Bahia as overage,[67] ill, and too inflexible to practice the new Lippian army reforms.[68] His complaints against old soldiers were echoes of similar criticisms expressed nearly a century before by that great Jesuit pundit, Antônio Vieira, and repeated by many others since then.[69]

The composition of the military forces of Bahia was similar to that of most of the captaincies-general, and reflected the three racial in-

---

[63] Lavradio to Count of Oeiras, Sept. 12, 1768, cited in *VRL*, p. 12.

[64] Mendonça Furtado to Lavradio, Aug. 19, 1768 (*única via*), CMCM, cod. 23, fol. 103.

[65] One of the new magistrates was Manoel José Soares, promoted from ouvidor of Mato Grosso to the Relação. The desembargadores were customarily invested with their office by the Casa de Suplicação in Lisbon, but a carta régia of Oct. 13, 1768 made a specific exception in Soares' case, stating that he could be given his *beca*, the garb of the office of desembargador, in Bahia, instead of having to come to Portugal. CMCM, cod. 23, fol. 119ʳ (*1.a via*).

[66] Lavradio to Oeiras, May 8, 1769, quoted in *VRL*, pp. 8–9; *idem* to Mendonça Furtado, June 29, 1769, *ABNRJ*, XXXII, 220.

[67] One of these was eighty-two-year-old Lt. Col. José Mirales, author of the first of many dull military histories of Brazil, "História militar do Brazil: desde [1549] . . . até 1762," *ABNRJ*, XXII (1900), 1–238.

[68] Lavradio to Oeiras, May 5, 1768, *VRL*, pp. 149–151; *idem* to Mendonça Furtado, May 5, 1768, *ABNRJ*, XXXII, 196–197.

[69] Vieira to Diogo Marchão Temudo, July 1, 1686, J[oão] Lúcio de Azevedo, ed., *Cartas do Padre Antônio Vieira*, III (Coimbra, 1928), 530. Vieira's remarks show that conditions had not essentially changed in ninety years: "Os soldados velhos da guerra do Brasil estao acabados; os dois Mestres de campo decrépitos; o presídio nao chega a ter a metade da lotacao . . . a cidade [Salvador] sem fortificacoes, sem armas, sem municoes. . . ." For examples of later complaints by various administrators see Azevedo, "Política de Pombal," p. 21.

gredients that had achieved victory over the Dutch invaders of
northern Brazil in the seventeenth century.[70] There were two white
infantry regiments, a military regiment of free mulattoes named after
the Negro hero of the Dutch war, Henrique Dias,[71] and several companies of Indian troops. Although Bahia was reputed to have had
25,000 men under arms in 1757, its garrison and reserves were far
below this strength in Lavradio's time.[72]

Dom Luís did what he could to obtain additional recruits, but he
was no more successful in finding them than his immediate predecessors or successors. Military service was far from popular in Brazil. The
period of active duty was long, the pay bad and usually far in arrears,
and the discipline exceptionally harsh. Anyone who could find a pretext for claiming exemption did so; [73] many, for example, allegedly
took religious vows merely to avoid entering the militia. Both
Lavradio and Count da Cunha, first viceroy of Rio de Janeiro, complained about the Church's competition for eligible young men,[74]
and Lisbon reacted by forbidding the Church to admit any more
novices without royal consent in each instance.[75]

After Lavradio had been in Bahia a year, he was able to report
some improvement in the infantry regiments. New quarters had been
built, and new uniforms and weapons passed out. His aides, members
of his old Cascaes regiment, had reorganized the regiments along
brigade lines, and were instructing the troops according to the doc-
trines of the Count of Lippe. Although the captain-general admitted
that he could not claim the regiments were in a "state of perfection,"
he insisted that he would have "no shame in presenting them to the
Professors of our art." He acknowledged his failure to make any improvements in the artillery regiment, and requested that trained
specialists be sent from Portugal.[76] In spite of his efforts, however, it
is clear from the dispatches of his successors in Bahia that Lavradio

[70] I.e., the Dutch occupation of Salvador, 1624–1625, and of the seven northern
captaincies, 1630–1654. For an introduction to the voluminous literature on this
epic theme see Charles R. Boxer, *The Dutch in Brazil 1624–1654* (Oxford, 1957) .

[71] There were also Henrique Dias units in Recife and in Rio de Janeiro.

[72] Caldas, *Notícia da Bahia*, p. 464; Lavradio to Oeiras, May 5, 1768, *VRL*, pp.
149–151.

[73] Modern draft-dodgers have invented few techniques unknown to these eighteenth-century Portuguese. See, e.g., petition of Manuel José Esteves to the interim
government of Bahia [1766], *ABNRJ*, XXXII 194, and Manoel da Cunha Menezes
to Martinho de Melo e Castro, Oct. 16, 1775, *ibid.*, 301–303.

[74] Lavradio to Oeiras, May 5, 1768, *VRL*, p. 149; Count da Cunha to Francisco
Xavier de Mendonça Furtado, Mar. 24, 1767, abstracted in J. C. Fernandes Pinheiro,
"Os últimos vice reis do Brasil," *RIHGB*, XXVIII:2 (1865) , 230–231.

[75] Mendonça Furtado to Lavradio, Aug. 19, 1768 (orig.) with an order to the
Archbishop elect of Bahia [D. Fr. Manuel de Santa Inês], Aug. 19, 1768, CMCM,
cod. 23, fols. 99–100.

[76] Lavradio to Mendonça Furtado, May 29, 1769, *ABNRJ*, XXXII, 217–218.

was unable to bring about any lasting improvement in the captaincy's defenses during his short tenure.[77]

Another branch of administration which caused the captain-general concern was the exchequer. He discovered that government warehouses were badly managed and that supplies were rotting because they were improperly stored. More serious was the state of the captaincy's finances. Although Bahia enjoyed an annual surplus of more than 82,500,000 réis in 1756,[78] the coffers were practically empty twelve years later, while the accounts were in confusion and payments long in arrears. Little wonder that Lavradio warned the Crown that public confidence was at a low ebb, and that businessmen were hesitant to bid for government contracts.[79]

Doubtless the several stopgap administrations of the captaincy-general since 1760 and the extraordinary military expenditures of 1762–1764 had contributed to this situation, but it is likely that the main factor was a series of large-scale embezzlements which had been discovered two years before Dom Luís' arrival. Those directly implicated included the head of the treasury (the *provedor mór da fazenda*), the comptroller-general, and the master (*provedor*) of the mint,[80] but there were probably others involved also. The report of the royal investigator, Desembargador Rodrigo Coelho Machado Torres, indicates that extensive thefts had occurred in the purchasing and disbursement sections of the *provedoria* over a number of years. Goods ordered for the treasury could not be found, many of them allegedly having been sold by fiscal officers for personal gain. After the closing of a nitrate plant in interior Bahia, the king's slaves assigned to it were sold at less than cost to the friends and family of the treasury superintendent without any record of the transactions appearing in the treasury files. The investigator estimated that the frauds ran to at least 30,000 cruzados, but warned that they might be considerably higher.

The activities of the ring made his work as difficult as possible. Ac-

77 E.g., Count of Povolide to Mendonça Furtado, Oct. 20, 1769, *ibid.*, p. 225; interim government to Martinho de Melo e Castro, June 20, 1774, *ibid.*, pp. 279–280; and Manoel da Cunha Menezes to *idem*, Nov. 2, 1774, *ibid.*, p. 282.

78 "Mapa do orsamento de todo o rendim.to e despeza anual . . . em toda esta capitania da Bahia . . . 15 de Julho de 1756," Caldas, *Notícia da Bahia*, p. 476. Caldas estimated the annual income at 302,634,802 réis and expenses at 220,089,651 réis.

79 Lavradio to Oeiras, May 5, 1768, *VRL*, pp. 150–151; *idem* to *idem*, July 21, [1768], cited in *VRL*, p. 11. With an income of 162,956,021 réis and expenses of 191,843,313, the 1768 deficit was 28,867,292 réis.

80 Manoel da Silva Ferreira, provedor of the mint, and Manoel de Matos Pegado Serpa, provedor mór da fazenda, had held office since at least the 1750s. Both were proprietors. Caldas, *Notícia da Bahia*, pp. 82, 104–105, 115. For others implicated, see Rodrigo Coelho Machado Torres to Mendonça Furtado, Dec. 23, 1769, *ABNRJ*, XXXII, 228.

counts were effectively juggled to conceal shady transactions, making it almost impossible to determine the real perpetrators of the thefts. Reliable witnesses were dismissed from their posts, and others were intimidated to prevent them from testifying. The comptroller-general reported that the wife of the provedor mór had offered him 100,000 cruzados to keep silent about her husband's conduct, a charge which, if true, gives a fair indication of the size of the illicit gains. The provedor himself escaped from jail and boasted openly that his great influence would prevent any injury to himself or his friends. Torres further charged that treasury officers concealed books and papers from him and declined to testify before him. Because of these obstacles an earlier investigator had given up trying to determine the guilt, and Torres declared that the only way he could accomplish his task was to be granted full authority to subpoena witnesses and accounts.[81]

Always sensitive where its purse was concerned, the Crown reacted decisively as soon as it learned of the Bahian scandals. It suspended the mint superintendent from his office and ordered him sent under close guard to the jail in Cachoeira across the bay. Investigator Torres was made acting provedor, and was given the authority for which he had asked. Later, both the treasury and mint supervisors were ordered sent to Lisbon on the first available ship for imprisonment in the famed Limoeiro dungeons.[82] Even though the comptroller-general had cooperated fully with the investigating officer and had twice received favorable reports on his conduct from the captains-general of Angola and Bahia, he too was removed from office.[83]

[81] This summary has been pieced together from Francisco Xaxier de Mendonça Furtado to Lavradio, Nov. 21, 1767, CMCM, cod. 23, fol. 162 (orig.) ; Rodrigo Coelho Machado Torres to Count de Azambuja, Bahia, July 17, 1767, ibid., fols. 151ʳ-154ʳ; Mendonça Furtado to Lavradio, Oct. 20, 1767, ibid., fols. 148-149 (orig.). Other aspects of the case are examined in S[everino] Sombra, História monetária do Brasil colonial . . . (Rio de Janeiro, 1938), pp. 241-242.

[82] Cartas régias to Torres, Oct. 20 and 21, 1767, ibid., fols. 150ʳ and 164ʳ; Lavradio to Mendonça Furtado, Sept. 25, 1768, ibid., fol. 163; Mendonça Furtado to Lavradio, April 21, 1769 (1.a via), ibid., fol. 36; idem to idem (única via), Nov. 22, 1767, ibid., fol. 186. Failing in her attempted bribe, the wife of the provedor mór petitioned Lavradio for permission to return to Portugal with her husband. The captain-general saw no reason why her petition should not be granted. Lavradio to Mendonça Furtado, May 2, 1768, CMCM, cod. 16 (rascunho in his hand), fol. 92ʳ [sic for 101ʳ].

As so often happened in such matters, the case dragged on for years. As late as 1782 the Crown was still asking the documents on ex-provedor Manoel de Silva Ferreira. ABNRJ, XXXII, nos. 10867-71.

[83] The case of Antônio Ferreira Cardoso, the comptroller-general, provides an example of how the Crown continued to keep fiscal officers under scrutiny even after they had apparently been cleared of charges of misappropriation of funds. Cardoso had formerly been an accountant in Angola. Before he left for his new post in Salvador, there were reports that he "looked after his own interests better than those of the king." An auditing of his accounts failed to reveal evidence of peculation and he departed from Africa with a high recommendation from the captain-

After familiarizing himself with the details of these frauds, La-vradio made several recommendations which he thought would pre-vent a repetition of the problem. He proposed to the Court that the sale of judicial and fiscal offices be abolished or that at least certain standards be met before proprietors or their deputies (*serventuários*) should be permitted to exercise their functions.[84] He also urged that the duties of the treasury superintendent be reorganized, pointing out that he had many unrelated responsibilities that were beyond the competence of a single administrator. He observed that it was illogi-cal for the provedor to be also a member of the treasury council [85] and thus be in a position to sit in judgment on his own conduct. Lavradio regarded the excessive jurisdiction of the provedores as "the principal cause of the ruin of the treasury," declaring that many peo-ple died or rotted in jail, their businesses and homes ruined because of long delays in appeals from the provedor mór's sentences. He therefore recommended that the authority of the treasury chief be curtailed by the creation of a new office, that of warehouse superin-tendent (*provedor dos armazéns*) to manage government stores, and by the transfer of all fiscal cases from the authority of the provedor mór to that of the treasury council.[86]

The treasury scandals in Bahia and elsewhere in Brazil [87] and the reports of Desembargador Torres and Captain-General Lavradio con-

---

general of Angola. In 1765, however, Mendonça Furtado ordered the Count of Azambuja, then captain-general of Bahia, to watch Cardoso closely. Dispatch of Oct. 29, 1765, CMCM, cod. 21, fol. 262ʳ. (*1.a via*). But Azambuja found nothing incriminating in Cardoso's performance and endorsed his request for a salary in-crease. Azambuja to Mendonça Furtado, Mar. 16, 1767 (rascunho) and memorial of Cardoso, May 27, 1767, *ibid.*, fols. 263ʳ–264ʳ, 56ʳ–62ʳ. Even so, Cardoso was later suspended without explanation. Mendonça Furtado to Lavradio, Mar. 4, 1769 (*1.a via*), *ibid.*, cod. 23, fol. 4ʳ. In reply, Lavradio praised the "zeal, activity, and com-petence" of the comptroller-general, but was apparently unable to lift the shadow of suspicion from him. Lavradio to Mendonça Furtado, May 1, 1769, *ABNRJ*, XXXII, 215.

84 Lavradio to Mendonça Furtado, July 21, 1768, cited in *VRL*, p. 10. The Count de Azambuja was another Bahian captain-general who protested against venality. See his dispatches of Aug. 28 and Sept. 20, 1767 to *idem, ABNRJ*, XXXII, 179–180.

85 The treasury councils, the forerunners of the juntas da fazenda, were estab-lished during the 1760s to exercise over-all supervision of royal finances in each captaincy-general. In Bahia the council consisted of the viceroy (later the captain-general), the chancellor of the Relação, the provedor, and two government at-torneys, the *procurador da coroa* and the *procurador da fazenda*.

86 To Mendonça Furtado, Sept. 12, 1768, *ABNRJ*, XXXII, 202–203.

87 Contemporary with the Bahian affair, the provedor da fazenda of Rio de Janeiro was sent home to answer charges of peculation, while the provedor of São Paulo died (1766) leaving his accounts in such disarray that his property was seized to liquidate his obligations. Extensive extortions were also reported in the exchequer of Goiás. Oeiras to Lavradio, Apr. 24, 1769, *ibid., DI*, XXIII (1896), 252–253; Martinho de Melo e Castro, Instruction to José de Almeida e Vasconcelos (capain-general of Goiás), Oct. 1, 1771, *RIHGB*, XXVII:2 (1864), 234–259.

vinced the Marquis of Pombal that it was time to extend his new fiscal reforms to America, and that Bahia was an appropriate place to begin. Accordingly, he ordered the replacement of the ineffective treasury council by a new board, called *junta da fazenda*, consisting of persons more directly familiar with fiscal problems. Two of the junta's key posts, those of the treasurer-general and the secretary, were appointive rather than proprietary offices as their equivalents had been in the past; and their duties were patterned after similar positions in the new Royal Treasury. At the same time the Crown abolished the office of provedor mór da fazenda in Bahia, and divided its duties between the junta da fazenda and the newly created office of marine intendant who was responsible for the management of royal warehouses, customs collection, shipyards, and ship inspection.[88]

As first secretary of the new Bahian junta, the Royal Treasury dispatched Sebastião Francisco Bettâmio with instructions concerning the new accounting procedures he was to introduce.[89] Bettâmio, accompanied by two assistants, was directed to recruit competent local bookkeepers to replace the old exchequer staff members, who were to be pensioned off. Since he and his assistants arrived at midyear, an awkward time to convert the books to the new system, they were instructed to employ the "new method" with entries beginning January 1, 1769. Meanwhile they were to confer with retiring functionaries to bring old accounts up to date, starting with those originating before 1762 (called *rendimentos pretéritos*) and then continuing with the intervening years 1762–1768 for which they were directed to compile annual balances of expenses and receipts. In the future the junta was required to submit such annual balances to the Royal Treasury in Lisbon.[90]

Captain-General Lavradio lent his full support to the implementation of the new system in his capacity as the presiding officer of the junta, which met regularly two afternoons a week and on other occasions when required. A good deal of effort was necessary to work out the details of the new accounting procedures each department was to

88 The Bahian junta da fazenda was established and its duties defined by several dispatches between 1767 and 1770, particularly Oeiras to Lavradio, Mar. 31, 1769, CMCM, cod. 23, fols. 22ʳ–24ʳ (orig.) and the alvará of Mar. 3, 1770, *CLP*, II, 451–456. A carta régia of Oct. 19, 1767, provided that every person handling government funds must take his receipts to the junta at the end of each month instead of clearing his accounts once every three years, as in the past. CMCM, cod. 23, fol. 144ʳ (*1.a via*). The functions of the juntas da fazenda are analyzed in detail in Chap. XI.

89 Bettâmio was to receive an annual salary of 1,200,000 réis, his assistants 600,000 réis each. Carta régia of Oct. 19, 1767, *ibid.*, f. 142ʳ (orig.). For Bettâmio's later career, see pp. 314–315, below.

90 Oeiras to Lavradio, Nov. 18, 1768, CMCM, cod. 23, fols. 123ʳ–126ʳ (orig.), published in *VRL*, pp. 151–157.

follow, and as moot points were appealed to Dom Luís, he undoubtedly consulted Secretary Bettâmio before rendering an opinion.
Before the end of 1768 the balance for 1762 was completed and sent
to Lisbon, where it met with the approval of the exacting inspector-
general of the Treasury, the future Marquis of Pombal.[91] During the
following year the balances for 1766–1768 were drawn up and forwarded to Lisbon.[92]

Dom Luís was particularly concerned about the need to reduce the
outstanding indebtedness of the king in Bahia, for he believed that
this was the best way to restore the community's confidence in the
exchequer. This meant, in part, collecting from the Treasury's own
debtors, but Lavradio preferred to give businessmen as much time as
possible to settle their obligations with the Crown, rather than to
induce their ruin for a trifling sum after which they could be of no
further use to the king.[93]

Another means of alleviating the exchequer's burdens was by increasing its revenues through the promotion of new economic activities. To this end Lavradio encouraged the exploitation of neglected
local resources, such as tree cotton and wild cinnamon, which local
exporters had been unwilling to purchase.[94] Dom Luís also became
interested in the commercial possibilities of a fiber plant said to be
similar to flax and offered a group of businessmen the former Jesuit
novitiate in Salvador for a sailcloth factory.[95] These interests foreshadowed one of the Marquis of Lavradio's major preoccupations in
Rio de Janeiro.[96]

Although he did not remain long as captain-general of Bahia, the
marquis succeeded in compiling an impressive record in fiscal man-

[91] *Provisão* of Manoel Pereira de Faria, contador geral da África occidental,
territórios da Relação da Bahia, Gram Pará e Maranhão (countersigned by Oeiras),
Mar. 31, 1769, CMCM, cod. 23, f. 9^{r-v} (orig.).

[92] In spite of its title, the "Livro de cartas correntes dos rendimentos reaes da
capitania da Bahia . . . principiado no anno de 1769," which constitutes codice 1
of the Mendonça Collection, is a folio volume containing fifty-seven double-entry
accounts for the years 1766–1769.

[93] See note 90, above. In one instance Lavradio intervened to save a local tithe
contractor who had difficulty in settling his accounts with his creditor in Lisbon.
The captain-general persuaded referees to give the Bahian merchant an additional
six months to complete his accounts, pointing out the extreme difficulties that he
faced in reaching settlers in the backlands to make his collections. [Lavradio] to
Mendonça Furtado, July 18, 1768, CMCM, cod. 23, fol 86^r (rascunho).

[94] The existence of tree cotton in Bahia had been known since the sixteenth
century. For an explanation as to why local entrepreneurs were unenthusiastic
about trying to market it abroad, see Manoel da Cunha Menezes (Captain-General,
Bahia) to Martinho de Melo e Castro (Colonial Secretary), Mar. 10, 1779, *ABNRJ*,
XXXII, 423.

[95] Lavradio to Oeiras, Sept. 12, 1768, *ibid.*, p. 202; Lavradio to Mendonça Furtado,
Dec. 28, 1768, cited in *VRL*, p. 14.

[96] See Chap. XIII below.

agement. According to a summary prepared by Secretary Bettâmio in 1770, the total income of Bahia's treasury during Lavradio's term amounted to 388,713,155.5 réis, of which 157,453,677.5 were from earnings prior to his arrival. During his stay a total of 107,124,977 réis were paid out on old claims, and 159,302,823 réis on current accounts.[97] When Dom Luís left office there remained a surplus of 122,285,353.5 réis, compared with only 11,845,728.5 réis which were in the coffers when he came to Salvador.[98]

Promotion to Rio de Janeiro

Lavradio's performance did not go unnoticed in Lisbon. No less a person than the Count of Oeiras himself wrote that Dom Luís' measures in Bahia were "not only wise and useful, but also necessary." [99] With obvious pleasure the Patriarch of Lisbon assured his nephew that "the ministers do not cease saying wonderful things about you and your government." The king had been impressed by Dom Luís's conduct, and the uncle was "certain that all your praiseworthy deliberations will be approved. . . ." [100] Confirmation of that prediction came from the colonial secretary, who expressed the king's pleasure at the "great zeal, activity, and judicious prudence" Dom Luís had displayed in his post.[101] Paulo de Carvalho, Oeiras' other brother and the inquisitor-general of Portugal, was another Court official who congratulated Lavradio for his achievements.[102]

But there was more in store for the Marquis of Lavradio than laudatory words. By a royal decree of April 8, 1769, he was promoted from Bahia to Rio de Janeiro to replace the ailing and aging Conde de Azambuja as viceroy of Brazil.[103] For Dom Luís this was a singular honor. Only twice before in the history of the colony had the son

[97] Bettâmio to Lavradio, Bahia, May 25, 1770, CMCM, cod. 21, fols. 5ʳ and 8ʳ (orig.).

[98] Loc. cit. One source of increased revenues was the tithe contract for Bahia, for which 133,000 cruzados were offered in 1769 compared with 125,000 in 1768. José Ferreira Cardoso da Costa (provedor da fazenda) to Mendonça Furtado, July 19, 1768, ABNRJ, XXXII, 200; Lavradio to idem, May 1 and 29, 1769, ibid., pp. 215 and 217; Oeiras to Lavradio, Aug. 25, 1769, CMCM, cod. 3, f. 50ʳ (orig.) (approving the 1769 agreement). However, it should be noted that the bids for both years were substantially less than the successful bid for the 1756 contract (Caldas, Noticia da Bahia, p. 473), one of the many indications of the contraction of Brazil's economy since ca. 1760.

[99] Oeiras to Lavradio, Nov. 18, 1768, VRL, pp. 151–157; idem to idem, July 12, 1769, CMCM, cod. 3, f. 42ʳ (orig.).

[100] The Patriarch's letters to Dom Luís are paraphrased in VRL, p. 14, n. 1.

[101] Mendonça Furtado to Lavradio, Apr. 21, 1769, CMCM, cod. 23, f. 34ʳ (orig.).

[102] Quoted without source or date in VRL, p. 14, n. 1.

[103] The patent is published in PAN, II, 31–32, and in VRL, p. 157.

of a governor-general or viceroy succeeded to Brazil's most exalted administrative post.[104] The precise circumstances behind the Crown's decision to elevate Dom Luís have not been revealed, but it seems safe to say that among other considerations were the experience he had gained with the new fiscal reforms in Bahia and the diligence he had shown there as an administrator.

[104] The two earlier examples were D. Luís de Sousa, 11th governor-general (1617–1621), whose father, D. Francisco de Sousa, was Brazil's 7th governor-general (1591–1602), and Vasco Fernandez Cézar de Menezes, the 4th viceroy (1720–1735), whose uncle, D. João de Lencastro (1694–1702), and father, Luís Cézar de Menezes (1705–1710), had been governors-general. One of Lavradio's immediate predecessors, D. Marcos de Noronha, Brazil's 7th viceroy (1755–1760), was the grandfather of Brazil's last viceroy, D. Marcos de Noronha e Brito, Conde dos Arcos (1806–1808).

II

The Viceroyalty of Rio de Janeiro

On Tuesday the second day of this month His Majesty's frigate Our Lady
of Nazareth sailed from our port . . . to conduct Luís de Vasconcelos,
. . . whom His Majesty has appointed as Viceroy of Rio de Janeiro, to
his destination.

Gazeta de Lisboa, February 5, 1779, supplement

Rio de Janeiro . . . certainly the most brilliant theater that the monarchy
of Portugal has today. . . .

Pombal to Lavradio, April 14, 1769

ALTHOUGH DOM LUÍS DE ALMEIDA learned of his promotion in
June 1769, it was mid-October before he was able to leave Salvador
for Rio de Janeiro.[1] He arrived there October 31 and relieved the
Conde de Azambuja four days later, "notwithstanding the fact that
my health was then hardly up to a post so laborious, so important,
and so hazardous." [2]

The nature of the office that Dom Luís had just occupied has occasioned wide differences of opinion among historians. Speaking of the
administrators of Rio de Janeiro after 1763, a popular local historian
recently reminded his readers that "it is unnecessary to recall that the
powers and the authority (*ação*) of the viceroys were not limited to
Rio de Janeiro, but extended to all the captaincies and frontiers that
constituted the State of Brazil." [3] Had he been so inclined, Vivaldo
Coaracy could have cited such well-known historians as Pizarro e Araujo, Carvalho Mourão, Rocha Pombo, Max Fleiuss, and Tavares de
Lyra to substantiate his statement. While they differ somewhat on the

[1] The royal frigate that was supposed to take Dom Luís to Rio de Janeiro was
scheduled to stop first at Recife to pick up his successor, the Conde de Povolide,
but sailed directly to Salvador instead because of leaky seams. After being repaired
and fetching Povolide, she transported the new viceroy to his post. Conde de
Azambuja to Francisco Xavier de Mendonça Furtado, Aug. 30, 1769, ANRJ, Col.
69, Liv. I, fol. 51 ʳ⁻ᵛ; Conde de Povolide to the Court, Oct. 15, 1769, *ABNRJ*,
XXXII, 225.

[2] *Auto de posse*, Nov. 4, 1769, *PAN*, II, 33–34; Lavradio to Pombal, Feb. 20, 1770,
IHGB/AUC, 1-1-29, fols. 213ʳ–227ʳ, at fol. 213ʳ.

[3] Vivaldo Coaracy, *Memórias da cidade do Rio de Janeiro* (Rio de Janeiro, 1955),
p. 569.

territorial extent of the viceroy's authority, they agree that he was a "true sovereign" with virtually limitless powers.[4] Yet had Coaracy consulted another group of writers, including Pereira da Silva, Marcelo Caetano, and Caio Prado, Júnior, he would have come to the conclusion that the authority of the viceroys was far more limited than he imagined.[5] And if he closely examined the initial royal instructions to Viceroy Lavradio [6] or his famous memorial to his successor,[7] the Carioca historian would have found supporting evidence for the latter group's conception of the realities of viceregal authority in colonial Brazil.

It is true that the eighteenth-century viceroys bore the imposing title of "Viceroy of [the] Sea and Land of the State of Brazil," and that their patents conveyed the impression that they possessed sweeping powers over a wide area. In practice, however, their authority was largely confined to the captaincy-general in which they resided, as the official state gazette quoted at the head of this chapter perhaps unintentionally confirmed. The title was, in fact, the vestige of an office whose powers had been gradually curtailed during the course of two centuries of administrative reorganization. In order to understand how the office of viceroy fitted into the administrative structure of Pombaline Brazil, it is necessary to review the development of royal government in the colony before the Marquis of Lavradio assumed his new post.

The Delimitation of the Authority of the Governors-General

Royal government was formally established in Brazil in 1549 when the colony was in peril of passing to a foreign power. The discovery

---

4 José de Souza Azevedo Pizarro e Araujo, *Memórias históricas do Rio de Janeiro*, V (Rio de Janeiro, 1948), 156; see also the prologue to Vol. VIII in which the author, whose work was first published in Rio de Janeiro 1820–1822, indicates that the last two parts of his chronicle would deal with the "Provincias anexas à jurisdição do vicerei do Estado do Brasil." See also João M. Carvalho Mourão, "Órgãos administrativos e judiciários da colônia no período . . . 1500 a 1763," IV Congresso de história nacional, *Anais*, IX (Rio de Janeiro, 1951), 411–412; José Francisco da Rocha Pombo, *História do Brazil*, V (Rio de Janeiro [1905]), 383–384; Max Fleiuss, *História administrativa do Brasil*, pp. 52–53; and A. Tavares de Lyra, *Organização política e administrativa do Brasil* (São Paulo, 1941), p. 31.

5 J. M. Pereira da Silva, *História da fundação do império brazileiro*, I, 134–136; Caio Prado, Júnior, *Formação do Brasil contemporâneo*, 4th ed., pp. 303–308; and Marcelo Caetano, "As reformas pombalinas e post-pombalinas respeitantes ao Ultramar . . . ," in António Baião, et al., eds., *História da expansão portuguesa no mundo*, III:1 (Lisbon, 1940), 254–355.

6 Pombal to Lavradio, April 14, 1769, *RIHGB*, XXX:1 (1868), 291–299, especially paragraph 23. This was one of four briefing instructions from Pombal to the future viceroy, all bearing the same date. See Chap. V, n. 1.

7 Lavradio, *Relatório*, June 19, 1779.

of Brazil (1500) had not caused large-scale Portuguese emigration to the new land, for Portugal's population was small and the attractions of fabled India were far more alluring than those of tropical America. Consequently, in the 1530s the Crown parceled out segments of Brazil to Court favorites called donataries, and bestowed vast powers and privileges upon them in exchange for their promise to colonize and defend their lands, or captaincies, at their own expense and to appoint a corps of officials to maintain respect for the king's laws and rights.[8]

Notwithstanding the generous inducements of their charters, many donataries failed to exploit their concessions; some who did exhausted their financial resources or paid with their lives in the effort; others simply became discouraged and gave up. As a result, many strategic areas, such as the coast between the Amazon and Cape São Roque and the bays of All Saints and Guanabara, remained unoccupied. As the midpoint of the sixteenth century approached, Brazil appeared ripe for conquest by Portugal's European rivals.

To prevent this possibility and to save the remaining settlements from collapse, the king sent Brazil's first governor-general, Tomé de Sousa, with a large expedition of soldier-colonizers and a staff of military, fiscal, and judicial officials to establish royal government in the abandoned captaincy of Bahia in 1549.[9] The responsibility of Sousa and his immediate successors extended to all of Brazil. Their tasks were to protect existing settlements, to conquer and fortify the unoccupied captaincies and defend them against Indian insurrection and foreign attack, to keep the donataries within the bounds of their charters, and to establish royal governments headed by *capitães mores* in each of the private and the recovered captaincies.[10]

Within their respective jurisdictions, the governors-general and the capitães mores exercised similar powers. Their authority was defined

[8] See the classic João Capistrano de Abreu, *Capítulos de história colonial (1500–1800)* (4th ed., Rio de Janeiro, 1954), Chap. V; also Pedro de Azevedo, "Os primeiros donatários," in Carlos Malheiro Dias, ed., *História da colonização portuguesa no Brasil*, III (Oporto, 1923), 189–216, and the essays on individual donataries in the same volume. Alexander Marchant, "Feudal and Capitalistic Elements in the Portuguese Settlement of Brazil," *HAHR*, XXII (Aug. 1942), 493–512, considers the extent to which the regime reflected modern or medieval thinking. Apart from studies on the founding fathers and an occasional article on the later captaincies granted in the seventeenth century, there are no comprehensive studies of the donatarial regime.

[9] Among the many studies of Brazil's first governor-general see Pedro de Azevedo, "A instituição do governo geral," in Dias, ed., *Hist. da col. port.*, III, 325–384; Ruth Lapham Butler, "Thomé de Sousa, First Governor General of Brazil, 1549–1553," *Mid-America*, N.S., XIII (Oct. 1942), 299–251; and the present writer's "The Early History of Bahia, 1501–1553," MS, M.A., University of California, Berkeley, 1952, Chaps. V–VI.

[10] In addition to the studies cited in ns. 4 and 5 on the general responsibilities of the governors-general, see Rodolfo Garcia, *Ensaio sôbre a história política e administrativa do Brasil*, Chap. III.

by their standing orders, or *regimentos*,[11] and by various types of legislation and special directives issued by agencies of the Crown.[12] Each executive was the nominal supervisor of the courts, the treasury, and the government of the secular church. He was expected to look after the welfare of the Indians and to cooperate with the missionaries in their endeavors to convert the aborigines; but he could also sanction military expeditions against recalcitrant tribes and camps of runaway Negro slaves. He was responsible for raising and training the militia and for the proper maintenance of all fortifications, arsenals, and warehouses within his jurisdiction. Until the late seventeenth century, the governors-general, but not the capitães mores, could fill vacant civil and military posts, subject to nominal royal approval. Another prerogative exclusively enjoyed by the governors-general was the right to bestow or reassign land grants in each captaincy. Every executive was responsible for preventing the theft of brazilwood and other articles belonging to the king, and for the enforcement of the laws against illicit trade with foreigners.[13]

These broad powers were hedged by numerous restrictions imposed by a suspicious, paternalistic Crown which insisted on spelling out the most petty details. In part these restraints undoubtedly reflected colonial protests against the abuses to which some royal officials were inclined when residing in remote places. Their frequent repetition suggests, however, that they were more honored in the breach than in the observance. Thus, for example, the prohibitions against any ranking official engaging in commerce, manufacturing, or agriculture, either directly or through third parties, was repeatedly renewed in response to colonial complaints against engrossing officials.[14] The governors were admonished to write by every homeward-bound ship

11 I.e., the permanent instructions concerning the duties of the office *per se*. The term *regimento* was also used for the specific instructions given to each new office holder.

12 Including official letters (*cartas régias, cartas de ofício*), laws (*alvarás, alvarás de lei*), resolutions (*resoluções, assentos, consultas*), and decrees (*provisões, ordens*).

13 The first regimento for the governor-general was that issued to Tomé de Sousa, Dec. 17, 1548, published in full in *RIHGB*, LXI:1, 39–57 and in Dias, ed., *Hist. da col. port.*, III, 345–350, and is summarized in Butler, "Thomé de Sousa," pp. 236–242. The earliest known regimento given to the capitães mores is one prepared for the capitão mor of Paraíba, May 9, 1609, *CCLP*, I, 267–269.

14 Carta régia, Mar. 29, 1671 and provisão of Feb. 27, 1673, *ABNRJ*, XXVIII, 133–134; alvará de lei, Jan. 10, 1678, *CCLE*, II, 86–88. The rule was temporarily set aside in 1709 when permission was granted for colonial governors to engage in commerce, but the privilege was withdrawn by the alvará de lei of Aug. 29 and the consulta of Dec. 16, 1720, and by the alvará of Mar. 27, 1721, *ABNRJ*, XXVIII, 134–136. Yet in 1757 all royal officials were permitted, if not encouraged, to invest in the government Companhia do Grão Pará e Maranhão. Alvará of Jan. 5, 1757, *CCLE*, IV, 1–3. One of the earliest governors-general to be accused of engaging in illicit commerce was Don Luís de Sousa (1617–1621) who survived three residências which exonerated him of the charge. See *Livro primeiro do govêrno do Brasil (1607–1633)* (Rio de Janeiro [1958]), pp. 333–416.

"even though it means repeating what has already been said," and to correspond frequently with the governor-general "since it is fitting that [he] be perfectly acquainted with all the news." [15]

Even the movements of the governors-general and the capitães mores were closely regulated. They were instructed to proceed directly to their stations and to remain there until ordered elsewhere or relieved of command. After 1614 the governors-general were forbidden to reside outside the captaincy of Bahia without specific royal authorization.[16] When their successors arrived, they were to embark on the ship that brought their replacements, on pain of having their estates seized for disobedience.[17] Like all royal officials, the senior and subordinate governors worked with the knowledge that their conduct was liable to examination by an ad hoc inquiry (devassa) during their term of office and by a terminal review (residência) upon its completion.[18]

As with all royal officials overseas excepting high court judges,[19] the governors-general and capitães mores were named to three-year terms, but they often served much longer. The governors-general remained at their post for an average of six and a half years in the sixteenth century, three and a half in the seventeenth, and a shade under six during the eighteenth century.[20] A surprising number of governors and captains-general spent twenty or even thirty years at one or more stations within Brazil.[21]

[15] Lei of Oct. 26, 1722, DI, XVIII 1896), 72.
[16] Carta régia, Mar. 13, 1614 and alvará of Feb. 21, 1620, CCLP, II, 98, III, 5.
[17] Carta régias of Nov. 10, 1638, and Mar. 4, 1639, CCLP, V, 175, 189.
[18] The devassa was the equivalent of the Spanish visita and, like the latter, could be general or special, i.e., it was used to verify the existence of a suspected crime and also to determine the guilty when a crime was known to have been committed. Devassa was often synonymous with residência, and the procedure for the latter was the same as that employed by the Spanish, except that the Portuguese ordinarily limited their investigations to thirty days, much less time than the Castilians allowed. Cândido Mendes de Almeida, ed., Código filipino ou ordenações e leis do reino de Portugal, Liv. I, tit. 60 and 65, paragraph 31–72 and notes there; see also José Caetano Pereira e Sousa, Esbôço de um dicionário jurídico, teorético e prático, remissivo às leis compiladas e extravagantes, under "devassa" and "residência." For the Spanish residencia see Clarence H. Haring, The Spanish Empire in America (New York, 1947), pp. 148–153.
[19] The members of the Relações were appointed for six years. A resolution of the Mesa do Desembargo do Paço, the supreme court of Portugal, of Nov. 1, 1668, declared that the terms of the desembargadores in Brazil should henceforth be eight years, but I am doubtful that it was ever put into effect. Virgínia Rau and M. F. Gomes da Silva, comps., Os Manuscritos do arquivo da casa de Cadaval respeitantes ao Brasil, I, 197
[20] Calculations based on Vicente S. P. de Lemos, "Catálogo dos governadores geraes do Brasil," RIHGRGN, VII, 183–196; Ignácio Accioli Cerqueira e Silva, Memórias históricas e políticas da . . . Bahia, Braz do Amaral ed., I and II (Bahia, 1919), passim; and Francisco Adolfo de Varnhagen, História geral do Brasil, V, annexes.
[21] See Varnhagen, loc. cit.

While long tenure in one post was a measure of the king's confidence (or of the governor's ability to avoid making too many enemies), it by no means followed that the governors were anxious to stay in Brazil. Far from it. Like their counterparts in other empires, they complained about the climate, the food, inadequate housing, insufficient salaries, personal infirmities, the disobedience of subordinates, the unruly character of the colonists, the lack of support from the home government, and numerous other irritants. Except for the relatively few who were sent home in disgrace, nearly all looked forward to the day when their terminal orders arrived so that they could turn their backs on the "Land of the Holy Cross" and sail for home to resume their careers at Court or to enjoy pensioned retirement.[22]

With few exceptions Brazil's colonial governors were drawn from the ranks of professional soldiers; they were seldom jurists and never prelates.[23] During the seventeenth and eighteenth centuries, commoners, some of them colonial-born, served in less important executive posts, but senior administrators (captains-general, governors-general, and viceroys) were generally members of the high nobility, counts, or marquises. Like the Bourbons of Spain, the Braganças, the ruling family of Portugal after 1640, seem to have looked more for previous administrative experience in selecting their governors-general than had the preceding dynasty. More than half of the last eighteen governors-general (eight of them styled viceroys) had served one or more terms as governor or captain-general in Brazil, Angola, or India before being appointed to Brazil's senior administrative post.[24]

As the conquest of Brazil progressed, the Crown experimented with several administrative reorganizations, each of which involved a curtailment of the effective authority of the Bahian governors-general. These innovations were made in response to several considerations: (1) the desire to provide more adequate defense for the thousands of miles of Brazilian littoral; (2) the hope of reducing the time lag between the issuance of orders in Lisbon and their execution in the far-flung captaincies; and (3) the need to blanket presumed mineral zones with a special apparatus to control exploitation and protect the Crown's interests, while preventing foreign participation.

22 *A terra de Sancta Cruz* was an early sixteenth-century name for Brazil. The generalizations above are based upon an extensive reading of the correspondence of the governors, both in MS and in the printed collections.

23 Two notable exceptions, both of them desembargadores and members of the Casa de Suplicação, one of Portugal's hightest courts, were Mem de Sá (1558–1572) and D. Luís de Vasconcelos e Sousa (1779–1790). Bishops often served as members of interim governments upon the death or removal of a governor, but were never appointed to regular terms, as was sometimes the case in the early Spanish empire.

24 See sources in n. 20. For Spanish Bourbon practice, see Haring, p. 128.

Between 1572 and 1621 Lisbon made three subdivisions of Brazil, only one of which endured. The southern captaincies were twice detached from Bahia (1572–1578, 1608–1612) and were placed under a separate governor-general at Rio de Janeiro.[25] Although both experiments were suppressed after brief trials, each tended to weaken the authority of Bahia over the southern region, as did the establishment of a circuit court (*ouvidoria*) at Rio de Janeiro in 1619 with cognizance over the captaincies from Espírito Santo southward.[26] In 1621 the recently conquered northern captaincies of Ceará, Maranhão, and Pará were joined together as the *Estado do Maranhão* and thereafter were administered separately from the rest of Brazil, which henceforth was called the *Estado do Brasil.*[27]

The authority of the Bahian governors-general was further weakened by the long Dutch war, an aspect of that epic struggle which has escaped the attention of its numerous chroniclers.[28] During that conflict the governors-general were primarily concerned with the defense of their own captaincy and with the encouragement of loyalist revolts in occupied Brazil. Consequently they were unable to act decisively in such important crises as the great Paulista raids on the Spanish missions of Guairá (1628–1632) and the explusion of the Jesuits from São Paulo in 1640.[29] Both problems were left to the governors of Rio de Janeiro and to the Crown.

After the war the governors-general tried to reassert their authority over the State of Brazil but met with indifferent success. Their failures were partly due to the unwillingness of the governors of Rio de Janeiro and Pernambuco to admit their subserviency to Bahia,

[25] The first division included Pôrto Seguro, Espírito Santo, Rio de Janeiro, and São Vicente; the second, all except Pôrto Seguro, which remained under Bahia.

[26] Regimento of the ouvidor geral of Rio de Janeiro, June 5, 1619, *CCLP*, II, 382–384. The ouvidores of Rio de Janeiro acquired greater prestige after the suppression of the first Relação of Bahia (1609–1626), though they were still to some extent subordinate to the ouvidor geral of Bahia. Regimentos of Mar. 31, 1626 and Mar. 21, 1630, *ibid*, III, 157, V, 166–167.

[27] On the separation of the two Estados see Garcia, *Ensaio sobre a história*, Chap. XI. The capital of the northern state fluctuated during the seventeenth and eighteenth centuries between São Luís do Maranhão and Belem do Pará. Antônio L. M. Baena, *Compêndio das eras da província do Pará* (Pará, 1838), pp. 638–641, and *idem, Ensaio corográfico* (Pará, 1839), pp. 134–136; see also Cézar Augusto Marques, *Diccionário histórico-geográphico do Maranhão* (Maranhão, 1870), pp. 274–280. Ceará was made partially dependent on Pernambuco in 1656.

[28] Between 1630 and 1641 the Dutch conquered the seven northern captaincies between Sergipe and Maranhão and made repeated efforts to recapture Salvador, which they had taken in 1624 but lost the following year. For guides to the literature see José Honório Rodrigues, *Historiografia e bibliografia do domínio holandês no Brasil* (Rio de Janeiro, 1949) and Charles R. Boxer, *The Dutch in Brazil*.

[29] On the Paulista raids see Chap. III, pp. 63–64; for the Jesuit expulsion see Affonso de E. Taunay, *A Grande vida de Fernão Dias Pais* (Rio de Janeiro, 1955), Chaps. V, VIII.

and to the lack of support from the Court, which was virtually paralyzed during the reign of Affonso VI (1656–1667) by a power struggle among the nobility.[30] The governors-general were also handicapped by the previously noted regulations which prevented them from traveling outside Bahia to impress recalcitrant governors with their authority.

The first to experience this frustration was Governor-General Francisco Barreto de Menezes (1657–1663), whose disputes with the governors of Pernambuco and Rio de Janeiro typified the jurisdictional battles waged by the senior governors during the rest of the century. Barreto had served as commander-in-chief (*mestre-de-campo general*) in Pernambuco during the Dutch war, and possessed temporary authority over all of the occupied territory during the years 1647–1656. When he was promoted to Bahia, he turned over his powers as governor of Pernambuco to André Vidal de Negreiros, another war hero. After coming to Salvador the new governor-general found that Negreiros claimed that he had succeeded to Barreto's former military authority and was therefore entitled to rule independently not only in Pernambuco but also in the island captaincy of Itamaracá.[31] Barreto denied Negreiros' contention and insisted that the latter was merely governor of Pernambuco and was subject to orders from Bahia. When Negreiros repeatedly flouted Barreto's directives, the governor-general appealed to Lisbon for a decision regarding Negreiros' claim of independent authority.[32] After vainly waiting eighteen months for a reply, the exasperated governor-general sent a desembargador and a military force to Pernambuco with instructions to convince the governor of the error of his ways or to bring him back to Salvador as a prisoner.[33] When the Crown learned of his action, it sternly rebuked Barreto but made no attempt to settle the question of the limits of Negreiros' authority.[34] However, when the next governor of Pernambuco not only followed Negreiros' policy of dominating Itamaracá but also intervened in Paraíba and Rio Grande do Norte, Lisbon directed him to stay out of the latter two captaincies.[35]

Meanwhile Barreto found his authority threatened on another flank. In 1658 the influential Salvador Corrêa de Sá, the liberator of

[30] See Charles R. Boxer, *Salvador de Sá and the Struggle for Brazil and Angola*, pp. 341–373.

[31] Both Pernambuco and Itamaracá had been sequestered by the Crown from their donataries in 1656.

[32] Barreto to the king, Feb. 21, 1658, *DH*, IV (1928), 326–332.

[33] Barreto to the king, Aug. 22, 1659, *DH*, IV, 369–371.

[34] Carta régia of April 5, 1659, *DH*, LXVI (1944), 161–162.

[35] Barreto to the king, June 9, 1661, *DH*, IV, 405–408; carta régia, Jan. 26, 1662, *DH*, LXVI, 178–180.

Angola and an old hand in Brazil,[36] obtained a patent naming him governor and captain-general of the southern captaincies in order to further the search for mines there. Because the Court failed to spell out the limits of Salvador's authority, he and Barreto became enmeshed in a dispute over the extent of his jurisdiction. Salvador contended that it extended as far north as Espírito Santo, whereas the governor-general believed that it was limited to Rio de Janeiro and the captaincies south thereof. Reluctantly Barreto recognized Sá's claim, and in a fit of bad humor wrote the Court that he would have given him control of the entire State of Brazil rather than risk a second rebuff.[37] A few months later when the Cariocas rose to expel the hated Sá dynasty from their city, Barreto found no reason to intervene in the dispute. In 1661, when Salvador retired, the southern captaincies were again made subject to Bahia.[38]

In 1663 Francisco Barreto was replaced by Dom Vasco de Mascarenhas, Conde de Óbidos (1663–1667) a nephew of the king and Brazil's second viceroy.[39] Óbidos, who had apparently been instructed to reestablish the authority of his office, found his jurisdiction "torn to shreds." He informed the governors that "with my coming to this State things are different," and he let it be known that he intended to be viceroy of Brazil in fact as well as in theory. Soon after taking office he directed that no royal order should be observed in any captaincy unless it had been cleared through Bahia. Then he issued a special regimento to the capitães mores,[40] redefining their duties and insisting that they were subordinate to Bahia and to no other colonial authority.[41]

Óbidos also wrote dispatches to the governors of Rio de Janeiro and Pernambuco, reminding them of the limits of their authority and of their subordination to him.[42] While the governor of Rio de Janeiro

36 Salvador had previously held the military post of "Superintendente em todas as matérias de guerra na Repartição do Sul" between 1637 and 1641. Boxer, *Salvador de Sá*, p. 144, n. 59. Boxer's is the fullest account of Salvador's colorful career.

37 Carta régia, Dec. 3, 1658, *DH*, LXVI, 160–161; Barreto to the king, Aug. 22, 1659, *DH*, IV, 367–369.

38 On the Carioca revolt (Nov. 1660–April 1661) see Boxer, *Salvador de Sá*, pp. 311–329.

39 The first viceroy was the unlucky Dom Jorge Mascarenhas, Marquis of Montalvão (1640–1641), who for obscure reasons was sent home in chains. Boxer, *The Dutch in Brazil*, p. 104.

40 I.e., applying to all governors except those of Rio de Janeiro and Pernambuco, who were the only ones styled *governadores*.

41 Alvará of July 21, 1663, and "Regimento que se mandou aos capitães-mores das capitanias deste Estado," Oct. 1, 1663, *DH*, IV, 115–125.

42 Óbidos to Pedro de Melo (governor of Rio de Janeiro), Oct. 16 and 23, 1663, *DH*, V (1928), 465, 467–469; Óbidos of Francisco de Brito Freire (governor of Pernambuco), Sept. 6 and Dec. 5, 1663, *DH*, IX (1929), 123–124, 133–137.

acknowledged (on paper) his inferior station, the governors of Pernambuco continued to manifest their independence by persisting in intervening in Itamaracá, prompting the angry Óbidos to order local authorities there to ignore any orders from Recife.[43] None the less in 1672 the Crown awarded the island captaincy to Pernambuco. The decision was a clear victory for the staunch Vidal de Negreiros and his successors and a blow to the pretentions of the governors-general, who thereafter found it more difficult than ever to dominate the northern governors.[44]

During the 1670s the Crown stepped into this long-standing controversy and drafted new regimentos concerning the responsibilities of the governors-general and the governors of Rio de Janeiro and Pernambuco.[45] The Bahian instruction was only the second (and last) prepared for that post.[46] Besides summarizing the voluminous

---

[43] Pedro de Melo to Óbidos, June 10, 1664, *DH*, VI, 43–44; Óbidos to Jerônimo de Mendonça Furtado, April 26 and Sept. 9, 1664, *DH*, IX, 162–167, 191–192. For later efforts of the governors-general to control the governors of Pernambuco see, e.g., Affonso Furtado de Castro do Rio de Sousa Coutinho, Sept. 3 and Nov. 6, 1671, *DH*, IX, 430–433, X, 8–19, "Memória" of Nov. 10, 1671, *ibid.*, 25–30, and Mathias da Cunha to Bishop Governor of Pernambuco, Sept. 27, 1688, *DH*, X (1929), 302–303. Each officeholder followed the policy of his predecessor in this protracted controversy, both in Bahia and in Pernambuco.

[44] Carta régia of Dec. 22, 1672, *DH*, LXVII (1945), 195–196

[45] "Regimento de que ha de uzar Fernam de Souza Coutinho [Governor of Pernambuco]," Aug. 19, 1670, with an endorsement stating that it was reregistered in 1740, *ABNRJ*, XXVIII (1908), 121–127; "Regimento fornecido ao Governador do Rio de Janeiro . . . [Dom Manoel Lobo]," Jan. 7, 1679, *RIHGB*, LXIX:1 (1908), 101–111; "Regimento que trouxe Roque da Costa Barreto, Mestre do Campo Geral do Estado do Brasil . . . ," Jan. 23, 1677, *DH*, VI (1928), 312–466, VII (1929), 3–46 (hereafter cited 2RGG). A hitherto unknown draft of this last document was the regimento apparently given to Affonso Furtado de Castro do Rio de Mendonça [Mar. 4, 1671], summarized in Rau and Gomes, *Cadaval MS*, I, 211–229. which agrees article by article with the well-known one issued to Barreto. These regimentos are all generically very similar. E.g., the first seven articles of the Rio, Pernambuco, and Bahia regimentos are almost identical, and the first thirteen articles of the Rio and Pernambuco instructions are the same except for minor word changes. The full story of the circumstances behind their preparation has never been told, nor can it be found in published document collections. It has been asserted that these regimentos were modeled after one granted to André Vidal de Negreiros as governor-general of the Estado do Maranhão, April 14, 1655, but a close reading makes it evident that the later instructions had nothing intrinsically in common with the 1655 document. There are copies of it in IHGB/AUC, 1, 3, 1 and in BNRJ, I-6, 2, 49, n. 10, and it is published in *Anais da Biblioteca e Arquivo Público do Pará*, I (Pará, 1902), 25–45. The Rio de Janeiro regimento served as standing orders for the governors of Minas Gerais, a fact deplored by desembargador José João Teixeira Coelho, who wrote in 1780 that "é incompleto e impraticavel, segundo o estado presente dos negócios e costomes d'aquelle continente." "Instrução," pp. 287–288.

[46] Both Fleiuss (p. 46) and Tavares de Lyra (p. 28) have asserted that a "novo regimento" was prepared for the first Rio viceroy, that Conde da Cunha, in 1763, but they fail to cite its source—since it never existed. Both misread Pizarro e Araujo, who stated that the Conde "executando o número 3° do Regimento dos Governadores . . . que ordenou aos governadores das capitanias . . . visitasse pes-

legislation issued since 1548 regarding the duties of the governors-general, it contained an explicit statement of the subordination of the governors of Recife and Rio to the governor-general.[47] Curiously, however, such a reminder was omitted from the junior governors' instructions.[48] Moreover, for the first time both were given the right to make temporary military and civil appointments, a prerogative hitherto reserved exclusively to the governors-general. This delegation of authority proved to be an omen for the future.

Throughout the remainder of the seventeenth and during the first half of the eighteenth centuries, the Crown continued to reorganize the administration of Brazil along regional lines. Beginning with Itamaracá in 1672, it transferred some of the older captaincies [49] from the jurisdiction of the governors-general to that of the governors of Rio de Janeiro and Pernambuco. In some cases the smaller captaincies were absorbed by the larger; [50] in others their entity was preserved, but their capitães mores were placed under the governors of the principal captaincies.[51] Beginning in 1697 the governors of Rio de Janeiro were given the title "governor and captain-general." The term captain-general had hitherto been reserved for the governors-general and referred to the military aspect of their offices, but by 1715 the governors of Pernambuco were also styled as "governor and captain-general." The lands administered by both officials were thereafter termed captaincies-general.[52]

---

soalmente todas as fortalezas . . ." (Memórias, V, 158). But Pizarro e Araujo was referring to paragraph 3 of the Barreto regimento, not to a new instruction. See the explicit comments of Viceroy D. Fernando José de Portugal e Castro (2RGG) upon the preamble and paragraph 3 of the Barreto instruction. Viceroy Portugal, the penultimate viceroy of Brazil, was ordered to analyze the 1677 instruction and make recommendations for a new regimento for his office. His annotations and the "Instrução" of Teixeira Coelho [see abbreviations] stand as sui generis in the very impoverished coeval literature on Portuguese administrative practice in Brazil. Rodolfo Garcia rightly called the annotated 1677 regimento "o melhor código administrativo comentado que tivemos no Brasil Colonial." Ensaio, p. 260.

47 2RGG, par. 39.

48 However, the relevant paragraph seems to have been sent to the governor and câmara of Rio de Janeiro to be registered. Roque da Costa Barreto to Matias da Cunha, idem to the provedor-mór of Rio de Janeiro, Mar. 22, 1678, DH, X, 95–98. In all likelihood, it was also sent to Recife.

49 Including those which reverted to the Crown from time to time by the grant of pensions or titles to the donatarial families or by confiscations. The process was virtually complete by 1761, when only the small captaincy of Itanhaen (littoral of São Paulo, immediately south of Santos) remained.

50 E.g., Ilhéus and Pôrto Seguro by Bahia; Alagoas and Itamaracá by Pernambuco; Cabo Frio and Paraíba do Sul by Rio de Janeiro.

51 E.g., the capitães mores of Ceará and Paraiba were under the governors of Pernambuco.

52 According to the "Catálogo dos capitães mores, governadores, capitães gerais, e vice-reis que têm governado a capitania do Rio de Janeiro de 1565 . . . até 1811," Artur de Sá e Menezes (1697–1700) "foi o primeiro a quem S. M. fez a mercê do governo desta capitania com patente de capitão general, sendo que seus antecessores

As royal regimes were organized in São Paulo, Minas Gerais, Goiás, and Mato Grosso during the first half of the eighteenth century, they too became captaincies-general.[53] By 1772, the year the *Estado do Maranhão* was dissolved, Brazil possessed nine captaincies-general and an equal number of subordinate captaincies (*capitanias subalternas*) : [54]

Captaincies-General	Subordinate Captaincies
Grão Pará	São José do Rio Negro
Maranhão	Piauí
	Ceará
Pernambuco	Rio Grande do Norte
	Paraíba
Bahia	Sergipe
	Espírito Santo
Rio de Janeiro	Santa Catarina
	Rio Grande de São Pedro [55]
São Paulo	
Mato Grosso	
Minas Gerais	
Goiás	

The reorganization of the colony into captaincies-general meant a further diminution of the effective authority of the governors-general, whose position was upgraded to the rank of viceroy in 1720 with commensurate increases in salaries. By the early decades of the eighteenth century the viceroys lost the right to intervene in the internal affairs of administrative entities headed by captains-general, and they no longer made appointments or removals or issued titles to land grants or instructions to local authorities outside of their own captaincy-general. Nor were official directives from Lisbon ordinarily channeled through Bahia as in the past.

On the contrary, they were sent to the captains-general themselves, and they in turn corresponded directly with the Crown.[56] How far

eram chamados de capitães mores governadores . . ." *RIHGB*, II, 75. Official correspondence between the Court and the governors of Pernambuco in *ABNRJ*, XXVIII indicates that the latter were regularly styled captains-general by 1715.

[53] São Paulo and Minas Gerais were a joint captaincy-general from 1709 to 1720, and after the latter date became separate captaincies-general. Goiás and Mato Grosso were separated from São Paulo in 1748.

[54] The following list is based on documentation too extensive to cite here. The process by which each captaincy-general was organized remains to be worked out by scholars.

[55] Until 1777 the captaincy-general of Rio de Janeiro also included the entrepôt of Colônia do Sacramento.

[56] The best source on the curtailment of the viceroys' authority is the commentary of Viceroy Portugal, 2RGG, *passim*.

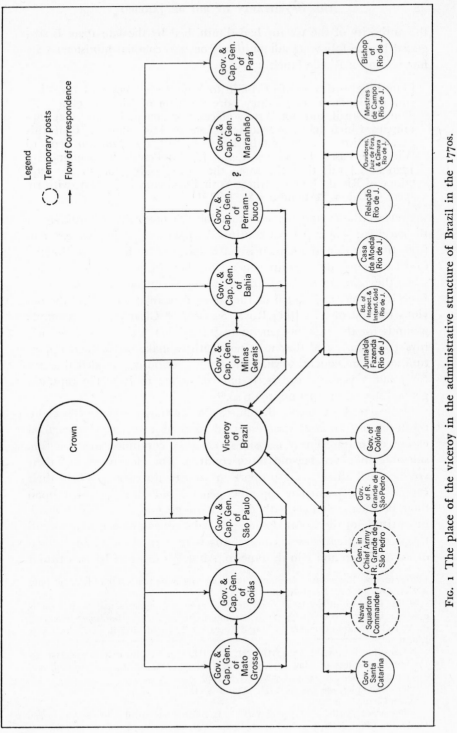

FIG. 1 The place of the viceroy in the administrative structure of Brazil in the 1770s.

Legend

◯ Temporary posts

→ Flow of Correspondence

Crown

Viceroy of Brazil

Gov. & Cap. Gen. of Pará

Gov. & Cap. Gen. of Maranhão

Gov. & Cap. Gen. of Pernam-buco

Gov. & Cap. Gen. of Bahia

Gov. & Cap. Gen. of Minas Gerais

Gov. & Cap. Gen. of São Paulo

Gov. & Cap. Gen. of Goiás

Gov. & Cap. Gen. of Mato Grosso

Junta da Fazenda Rio de J

Bd. of Inspect. & Intend. Gold Rio de J

Casa de Moeda Rio de J.

Relação Rio de J.

Ouvidores, Juiz de Fora & Câmara Rio de J.

Mestres de Campo Rio de J.

Bishop of Rio de J.

Gov. of Santa Catarina

Naval Squadron Commander

Gen. in Chief Army R. Grande de São Pedro

Gov. of R. Grande de São Pedro

Gov. of Colónia

the authority of the viceroy had diminished by the late 1720s is suggested by the following admonition from the colonial minister to the first viceroy of Rio de Janeiro:

> [The king] orders me to explain to Your Excellency that the Viceroys of Bahia, although they bore the title of Viceroys of all the State of Brazil, did not bestow offices, nor govern in the other captaincies which had governors subject to His Majesty. That this . . . practice . . . was established . . . [in] the *provisão* sent to [Viceroy] Vasco Fernandes Cezar [de Menezes] on January 29, 1729 . . . [and] that the same therefore holds good in the captaincy of Rio de Janeiro, where Your Excellency is Viceroy, with respect to Bahia, Pernambuco &c. [sic] [57]

Even so, the captains-general remained theoretically subordinate to the viceroys. Their patents continued to state that they were,[58] and from time to time the Crown issued reminders to that effect. But the Court enjoined the captains-general to obey the viceroys' orders only when they did not conflict with their own regimentos, with directives from the Overseas Council or the colonial secretary, or with "the obvious interest of . . . [the] Royal Service." [59] Clearly this left ample grounds for the captains-general to justify their defiance of the viceroys' commands, and they were not loath to make use of their opportunities.[60] Consequently, when the Crown seriously intended them to carry out a viceroy's orders, it felt compelled to issue the captains-general special instructions to do so.[61]

For pactical purposes, therefore, the authority of Brazil's eighteenth-century viceroys was restricted to their own captaincy-general except on extraordinary occasions. Yet they continued to exert considerable influence beyond those confines. The effectiveness of their voice varied directly in proportion to the distance between their capital and a particular captaincy-general but also depended upon their personal relations with the captains-general [62] and the prevailing attitude of the Court. As long as Bahia remained the residence of the viceroys, their closest connections were with the captains-general of Pernambuco and Rio de Janeiro. After Rio became Brazil's titular

[57] Francisco Xaxier de Mendonça Furtado to Conde da Cunha, Feb. 4, 1765, ANRJ, Col. 67, Liv. I-A, fols. 76^{r-v} (orig.).

[58] The usual formula was "e gosará de todas as honras, poderes, mando, jurisdição, e alçada, que tem, e de que gosou o seu antecessor, . . . com subordinação sòmente do V. Rei e Capitão General do Mar e Terra do Estado do Brasil. . . ." See Chap. I, n. 1.

[59] Consulta of Nov. 14, 1724, *ABNRJ*, XXVIII, 127; see also carta régia, Oct. 29, 1714 and consultas of May 27, 1716 and Oct. 26, 1722, *ibid.*, pp. 127–129, and carta régia of Nov. 9, 1709, *DI*, XLVII, 65–68.

[60] For examples, see Chaps. VIII, X, and XVI.

[61] See Chap. V, p. 39.

[62] For a noteworthy example of Viceroy Lavradio's successful intervention in São Paulo, see Chap. XIII, p. 362; but cf. Chap. XVI, pp. 457–458.

capital, the viceroys communicated most frequently with the captains-general of São Paulo, Minas Gerais, and Bahia.[63]

Concomitant with these reorganizations, important changes occurred also in the major responsibilities of Brazil's governors. By the second half of the seventeenth century the remaining donataries had become so impotent that they no longer posed serious disciplinary problems for the governors-general. By the following century the complex problem of Luso-Indian relations, a major concern of the early governors-general, had become a minor preoccupation of the viceroys,[64] though Indian raids still constituted a source of considerable annoyance to governors of the interior captaincies and the administration of Indian labor remained a primary task of the governors of the northern captaincies. As a consequence of the intensification of Iberian rivalry for hegemony over southern South America during the late seventeenth and eighteenth centuries, the military duties of the viceroys and the captains-general became increasingly burdensome.[65] However, the viceroys were displaced as field commanders by more professionally trained soldiers; and instead of directing campaigns personally, as their predecessors had, they were chiefly concerned with logistics and with finding the means to defray the costs of defense. As a consequence of mounting military expenditures, the viceroys and captains-general became far more directly involved with problems of fiscal management and economic development than had Brazil's early royal governors.[66]

Far from being a "sovereign," the eighteenth-century Portuguese viceroy was much closer to being, like his Spanish counterpart, "a mere royal commissioner" charged with the execution of the king's commands, or rather those of his dominant ministers.[67] The so-called "Estado" over which the viceroy nominally ruled was in fact an "intimate association and [theoretically a] close defensive alliance" of separately administered captaincies-general, united only through the Crown.[68] When the Crown designated Rio de Janeiro as the new viceregal capital in 1763, it actually shifted only a title.[69] Nothing else needed to be transferred—neither administrative agencies, nor

---

[63] See the accompanying chart (fig. 1) and particularly Chap. XVI.

[64] For example, Indians are virtually unmentioned in the Lavradio Relatório.

[65] See Chaps. III–X.

[66] See Chaps. XI–XIV.

[67] Cf. Haring, Spanish Empire, p. 121.

[68] Pombal to Luís Pinto de Sousa (Portuguese ambassador to Madrid), Nov. 25, 1775, in Simão José de Luz Soriano, História do reinado de el-rei d. José e da administração do Marquez de Pombal, II (Lisbon, 1867), 637; Pombal to José Cézar de Menezes (Governor of Pernambuco), July 23, 1774, IHGB, lata, 439, doc. 1.

[69] In a carta régia of June 27, 1763, the Crown notified the interim governors of Rio de Janeiro that the Conde da Cunha was coming to act as viceroy, but gave no explanation of why it decided to transfer the title; nor did it indicate that any governmental agencies would be moved from Salvador to the Carioca capital. None were. BNRJ, I-2, 4, 4, n. 70.

courts, nor personnel, nor files, nor furniture, for all were already duplicated in Rio de Janeiro.

The Captaincy-General of Rio de Janeiro

The political and economic leadership that Bahia and Pernambuco enjoyed during the sixteenth and seventeenth centuries passed in the eighteenth century to Rio de Janeiro and its economic vassal, Minas Gerais. Second only to Pernambuco as a source of dyewood and long one of Brazil's three most important sugar-producing captaincies,[70] Rio's rise during the second half of the colonial period was due to its importance as a military base and as a commerical emporium. It was the staging area for the Portuguese reconquest of Angola from the Dutch in 1647, and for the expedition that founded Colônia do Sacramento in 1680.[71] During the later seventeenth and eighteenth centuries Rio ranked next to Salvador as a market for African slaves, retaining some to work in her numerous plantations while sending others to fetch fat profits in the gold and diamond fields of the interior or to Colônia, whence they were smuggled into Spanish America. The opening of the "new" road to the interior in 1707 enabled Rio to supplant São Paulo, the mother of Minas Gerais, as the chief supplier of slaves, locally produced foodstuffs, and imported European merchandise to the mining captaincies. It was also through Rio de Janeiro that the heavily laden chests of gold and diamonds passed on their way to Portugal.[72] The Carioca capital also became the principal supply base for the newly opened southern captaincies of Santa Catarina and Rio Grande de São Pedro, and reexported their hides and other products to the Peninsula.[73]

[70] On the relative positions of Pernambuco, Bahia, and Rio de Janeiro as sugar producers at the beginning of the eighteenth century, see André João Antonil [pseud. João Antônio Andreoni, S. J.], Cultura e opulência do Brazil por suas drogas e minas (3rd ed., São Paulo, [1922]), pp. 170–172.

[71] For Rio's contribution to the liberation of Angola see Boxer, Salvador de Sá, Chap. VI; on the establishment of Colônia see Chap. III, below.

[72] For the opening of the new road see Antonil, pp. 243–245. Concerning the economic relationship between Rio and Minas Gerais, see Mafalda P. Zemella, O Abastecimento da capitania das Minas Gerais no século xviii, University of São Paulo, Faculdade de Filosofia, Ciências e Letras. Bull. 118 (São Paulo, 1951), especially pp. 124–132. Commenting on the rise of Rio at the beginning of the eighteenth century, an anonymous writer noted, "He esta pouoação do Rio de Jan.ro poucos annos atras nada; hoje [é] a segunda praça daquelle Estado. . . ." "Informação sobre as minas do Brasil" [ca. 1711], ABNRJ, LVII (1935), 163.

[73] According to Antonil (writing ca. 1711) "a parte do Brazil que tem menos gado, he o Rio de Janeiro, porque tem curraes sòmente nos campos de Santa Cruz . . . nos campos novos do Rio de S. João . . . e nos Goitacazes . . . ; e em todos estes campos não passão de sessenta mil as cabeças de gado. . . ." in cf. with Bahia,

During the middle decades of the eighteenth century, Rio became a major administrative center. From its founding, Colônia was Rio's responsibility; and between 1738 and 1742 the Crown awarded Santa Catarina and Rio Grande to her over the claims of her rival, São Paulo.[74] Throughout much of his long term, Gomes Freire de Andrada (1733–1763) was separately captain-general of Rio and of Minas Gerais, as well as the chief administrator of São Paulo.[75] In 1751 Brazil's second Relação (High Court) was established in Rio,[76] as was an intendancy-general of gold [77] and a board of commercial inspection.[78] These agencies joined Rio's mint, which was founded in 1703 and was one of two permanently operated in Brazil.[79] When in 1763 the Crown decided to raise Rio de Janeiro's captains-general to the status of viceroys, it was only making a logical, if belated, recognition of her political and economic ascendancy.

Notwithstanding her importance, Rio de Janeiro was one of Brazil's smallest captaincies, as it is one of her smallest states today.

---

then producing more than half a million head, and Pernambuco with more than 800,000. *Cultura e opulência*, p. 246. Since Rio became a major exporter of cattle products in the later eighteenth century, it is a fair inference that they came primarily from her southern dependencies. See Chap. III.

[74] See Chap. III, n. 41.

[75] Andrada, later the Conde de Bobadela, was captain-general of Rio de Janeiro from 1733 and of Minas from 1735 to his death. He was interim governor of São Paulo, 1737–1739, and governed São Paulo as a comarca of Rio de Janeiro from 1748 to 1763. Varnhagen, *História*, IV, 283, 285. Strangely enough, no adequate biography of this powerful colonial officer has ever been published.

[76] Colonials had petitioned for a second Relação since 1734. When established, it was given jurisdiction over the thirteen southern comarcas, from Espírito Santo to Santa Catarina and west to Mato Grosso. Regimento of Oct. 13, 1751, Coelho e Sousa, *Systema*, IV, 484–502. At one point the Crown seemed to be considering the abolition of the Bahian Relação. See Martinho de Melo e Castro to Marquês de Valença, Sept. 10, 1779, *ABNRJ*, XXXII, 441.

[77] The gold superintendents registered all private shipments of bullion to Portugal and were responsible for the detection and seizure of suspected contrabandists. In the latter task they worked closely at times with the interior intendants of Minas Gerais, and with the gold superintendents of Salvador. Alvará of Apr. 7, 1770, *CLDA*, III, 463–465. Both maritime intendants were also presidents of the commercial board of inspection (*mesa de inspeção*).

[78] Boards of inspection were established simultaneously at Salvador, Recife, and São Luis do Maranhão. Their initial purpose was to provide quantitative and qualitative controls over the export of sugar and tobacco, and to promote either commodity where it was lagging. Regimento of April 1, 1751, Coelho e Sousa, *Systema*, IV, 92–97. Later they were given responsibility for the promotion of indigo, cotton, and other crops which the Crown was interested in developing. The Rio board was theoretically independent of the viceroy but in practice worked closely with him. The Brazilian boards were made subordinate to the junta do commércio established in Lisbon in 1755. For the role of the latter, see Jacome Ratton, *Recordacoens*, pp. 258–282.

[79] "Carta monetária do Brasil colonial," in S[everino] Sombra, *História monetária do Brasil colonial*, following p. 293.

Tropical in climate and vegetation,[80] it is squeezed between the Atlantic Ocean and the Great Escarpment on the south and the Paraíba River and the Serra da Mantiqueira on the north and west. According to eighteenth-century reckoning, the captaincy extended fifty-five leagues in its longest (east-west) direction, and varied in width from twenty leagues at Cabo Frio to only six near the vila of Paratí in the mountainous southwest.[81] Within these confines were two cities (Rio de Janeiro and Cabo Frio), five vilas, and seven lesser settlements. A census of about 1780 gives the captaincy's population as 167,760, nearly half of whom were Negro slaves. More than a quarter of the captaincy's inhabitants, 51,000, lived in the capital and its environs. There, also, the proportion of blacks to whites was very high.[82]

The City of Rio de Janeiro in the Time of the Marquis of Lavradio [83]

Though few Caricocas would concede it, the beauty of their *"cidade maravilhosa"* derives more from its matchless site than from what man has done to it. Rio de Janeiro is situated on the bay of Guanabara, one of the world's most spectacular harbors. The appeal of its deep blue waters and white sandy beaches which grace its margins is enhanced by the rugged granitic mountains that guard its entrance, and the serrated pinnacles of the Serra dos Órgãos that form an impos-

[80] The city of Rio de Janeiro lies just north of the Tropic of Capricorn.

[81] Lavradio, *Relatório*, 410–411. He noted, however, that if all the coastal sinuosities were included, the length of the captaincy was seventy-five leagues.

[82] "Mappa geral das cidades, villas e freguezias que formão o corpo interior da capitania do Rio de Janeiro" (1780), *RIHGB*, XLVII:1 (1884), 27–29. Between Lavradio's time and the end of the colonial period the captaincy's population doubled (to 333,056), and the ratio of Negroes to whites reached 52 percent. "Mappa dos fogos, pessoas livres, e escravos comprehendidos nas freguezias da cidade e provincia do Rio de Janeiro" (1821), *ibid.*, XXXIII (1870), 137–[142].

[83] The following description is based primarily on contemporary travel accounts including: [John Byron], *A Voyage Round the World in His Majesty's Ship the "Delphin,"* pp. 15–24; Louis de Bougainville, *Voyage Round the World in the Years 1766 . . . [to] 1769 . . .* (London, 1772), pp. 73–85; J. C. Beaglehole, ed., *The Journals of Captain James Cook on His Voyages of Discovery*, I, *The Voyage of the Endeavour 1768–1771*, especially pp. 32–34; Evariste Désiré de Forges [Vicomte de Parny] to his brother, Sept. 1773, *Oeuvres d'Evariste Parny*, I, 205–216; John White, *Journal of a Voyage to New South Wales*, pp. 48–72; Sir George Staunton, *An Authentic Account of an Embassy from the King of Great Britain to the Emperor of China*, especially 174–181.

Two contemporaneous sources unequaled for their sketches of life in Rio within a generation of Lavradio's time are the very rare *Views and Customs of the City and Neighbourhood of Rio de Janeiro . . . from Drawings taken by Lt. Chamberlain . . . 1819 and 1820 . . .* (London, 1822) and *O Velho Rio de Janeiro através das gravuras de Thomas Ender* (São Paulo [1957]), the impressions of an Austrian artist who was in Rio 1817–1818. Ender gives the better details of structures and persons, but Chamberlain's panoramas of the bay and city are superior.

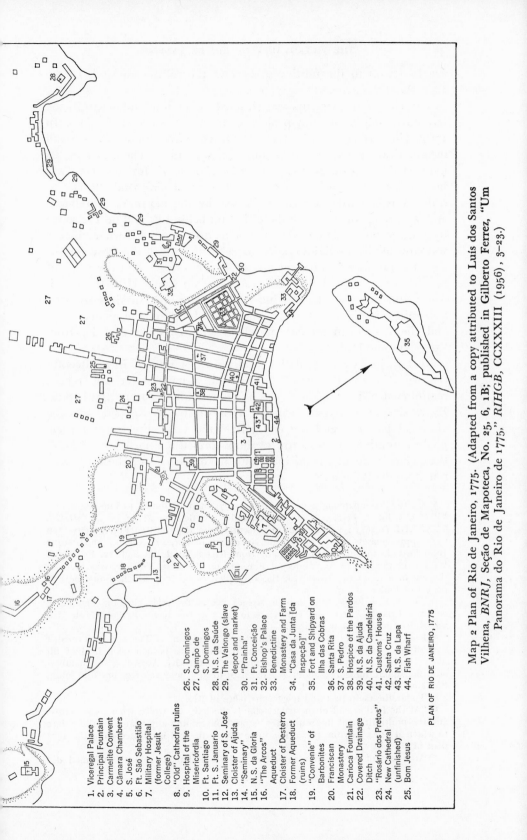

PLAN OF RIO DE JANEIRO, 1775

1. Viceregal Palace
2. Principal Fountain
3. Carmelite Convent
4. Câmara Chambers
5. S. José
6. Ft. São Sebastião
7. Military Hospital (former Jesuit College)
8. "Old" Cathedral ruins
9. Hospital of the Misericórdia
10. Ft. Santiago
11. Ft. S. Januario
12. Seminary of S. José
13. Cloister of Ajuda
14. "Seminary"
15. N.S. da Gloria
16. "The Arcos" Aqueduct
17. Cloister of Desterro
18. Former Aqueduct (ruins)
19. "Convenie" of Barbonites
20. Franciscan Monastery
21. Carioca Fountain
22. Covered Drainage Ditch
23. "Rosário dos Pretos"
24. New Cathedral (unfinished)
25. Bom Jesus
26. S. Domingos
27. Campo de S. Domingos
28. N.S. da Saúde
29. The Valongo (slave depot and market)
30. "Prainha"
31. Ft. Conceição
32. Bishop's Palace
33. Benedictine Monastery and Farm
34. "Casa da Junta [da Inspeçaõ]"
35. Fort and Shipyard on Ilha das Cobras
36. Santa Rita
37. S. Pedro
38. Hospice of the Pardos
39. N.S. da Ajuda
40. N.S. da Candelária
41. Customs' House
42. Santa Cruz
43. N.S. da Lapa
44. Fish Wharf

Map 2 Plan of Rio de Janeiro, 1775. (Adapted from a copy attributed to Luís dos Santos Vilhena, *BNRJ*, Seção de Mapoteca, No. 25, 6, 1B; published in Gilberto Ferrez, "Um Panorama do Rio de Janeiro de 1775," *RIHGB*, CCXXXIII (1956), 3–23.)

ing backdrop to the northwest, beyond the rolling lowlands of the Baixada Fluminense.

The city of the viceroys was situated about four miles within the bay on a tongue of land projecting from the Serra da Carioca. In 1767 Rio was estimated to extend three miles "in compass," and measured about twelve blocks long and six wide.[84] Then, as now, its most striking features were its hills (morros), for the city was bounded on the southeast by the outeiro da Glória and the clover-leafed Castle Hill;[85] on the northeast by the morro de São Bento and by a range of smaller hills rolling up behind it; and on the south by the morros of Santa Teresa and Santo Antônio. Each eminence was crowned by a religious edifice or a fort, of which the most notable were the military hospital (a former Jesuit college) and the ruins of fort St. Sebastian and the "old" cathedral on Castle Hill; the formidable and peaceful Benedictine monastery, which survives as tranquil refuge in the midst of the hustle and bustle of the modern city; and the Franciscan monastery, which still overlooks the city from Santo Antônio Hill.

Next to its hills, one of the focal points of interest in eighteenth-century Rio was the Praça do Palácio, a large waterfront square reminiscent of the marine plazas at Luanda and Goa and the famous Piazza di San Marco of Venice.[86] Fronting on its east side was the viceregal palace[87] and the city jail;[88] the Carmelite convent occupied the south side, and a row of shops formed the north side. Behind the palace were the municipal council chambers and those the city rented to the Relação.[89]

[84] See the accompanying map, based on a 1775 map attributed to Luís dos Santos Vilhena. Gilberto Ferrez, "Um Panorama do Rio de Janeiro de 1775," RIHGB, CCXXXIII (1956), 1–23. In terms of present landmarks, the limits of the city then were approximately from Praça 15 de Novembro to Largo da Carioca and Parque Júlio Furtado in depth and in length from Rua Santa Luzia and Av. Presidente Wilson on the east to Av. Marechal Floriano on the west. The city was then on the eve of a rapid expansion. Cf. the 1812 plan of the city which forms the end papers of Ender, O Velho Rio.

[85] The Morro do Castello was the second site of the early city, the first being on Urca, beneath Sugar Loaf Hill, close to the entrance to the harbor. Castle Hill was sluiced into the bay in 1921.

[86] Robert C. Smith, "Baroque Architecture," p. 367, n. 1. The square formed a part of the present Praça 15 de Novembro. There has been a good deal of fill (aterro) here, as everywhere about the margins of the city. According to Chamberlain, the square measured about 450 feet east-to-west, and 280 feet north-to-south. Views and Customs, text to Pl. 2.

[87] Today the main post and telegraphy office of Rio.

[88] "At the farther end of the palace stands the jail . . . which from its structure, and the multiplicity of its iron grates, is far from adding any beauty to the palace to which it joins." Byron, p. 20. For some reason the jail is omitted from the 1775 plan of the city.

[89] At a cost of 200,000 réis annually. At least as late as 1781 the tribunal did

The viceregal palace was a large two-story structure that had formerly housed the bureau of accounts (*casa dos contos*). Rectangular in design, it was an unimpressive structure save for its glass windows, the only ones the city possessed. The French poet Parny who saw it in 1773 wrote that neither the exterior nor the interior of the palace corresponded with his notions of the "richness of the colony." [90] The English surgeon John White, who visited it fifteen years later, agreed that the building was far from princely. The only furnishings he observed in the anteroom were six card tables, a few chairs, and two portraits, one of King Sebastian, the other of Maria I, the reigning monarch. But, he added, "the passage we walked through was adorned on each side with odoriferous flowers and aromatic shrubs, which while they charmed the eye, spread a delightful fragrance around." The reception room, remodeled since Lavradio's time, was "furnished and painted in a neat and elegant style; the roof displayed well-executed representations of all the tropical fruits, and the most beautiful birds of the country. The walls were hung . . . with prints, chiefly on religious subjects." [91]

The principal thoroughfare, Rua Direita (today 1º de Março), began at the square and extended to the foot of the Morro de São Bento. Fronting on the main street were many of the better shops, the customs house, and other government buildings. The back streets extended at right angle to Rua Direita, and were described as "so narrow that two persons can not walk with convenience together" along them.[92] Each of their intersections was marked by a ten-foot pole supporting a glass-encased crucifix or saint's image, before which pedestrians instinctively genuflected, just as religious Cariocas pause today to cross themselves when passing a church.

Most of the city's better dwellings were two- and three-story brownstones. The families lived on the upper floors to escape some of the

---

not have its own quarters. Luís de Vasconcelos e Sousa to Martinho de Melo e Castro, July 15, 1781, *RIHGB*, LI:2 (1888), 189.

90 Parny to his brother, Sept. 1773, *Oeuvres*, I, 212.

91 *Voyage to New South Wales*, pp. 48, 56–57. The viceroys were not indifferent to the defects of their residence. The Conde da Cunha wished to move to the former Jesuit college on Castle Hill, and though his request was approved, his successor refused to occupy the college, claiming that it was too far from the government office, and that the *ladeira* was so steep that he would have to bind himself into his carriage to prevent his tumbling out. Apparently Viceroy Lavradio was content to remain in the old residence, but his successor complained that it was far less luxurious than the palace of the former viceroys of Bahia, and undertook its renovation. Carta régia, July 23, 1766, *RADF*, II (1895), 565–566; Azambuja to Mendonça Furtado, May 9, 1768, quoted in J. C. Fernandes Pinheiro, "Os últimos vicereis do Brasil," *RIHGB*, XXVIII, 234–235; Vasconcelos to Melo e Castro, April 23, 1779, IHGB/AUC, 1-2-1, fol. 11ʳ.

92 White, p. 59.

heat, and left the ground floor to shops and servants' quarters. As in Salvador, the interiors seemed underfurnished to visitors and featured numerous religious pictures of indifferent quality. Lattice-covered balconies extended over the streets, permitting the occupants of the home to cool off during hot summer days while gazing at passersby below and gossiping for hours on end, just as their descendants do today. The objects of their attention included brightly uniformed soldiers, slaves carrying burdens on their heads, richly dressed planters or businessmen equipped with swords and riding in sedan chairs, beribboned young girls with flowers in their hair, mounted militiamen whose elaborate uniforms revealed their particular unit, and Carmelite, Franciscan, and Benedictine priests garbed in the distinctive robes of their Orders.

In the early evening before curfew the Cariocas indulged in their traditional promenade, often going to the palace square to hear the latest news. In the center of the square was the city's principal water fountain, the terminus of the famed Carioca aqueduct. Completed in 1740, the aqueduct was a double-arched stone structure designed to carry water from Corcovado peak at the head of Laranjeiras Valley to the city, and extended from the Morro de Santa Teresa to Santo Antônio Hill, from where the waters were piped to the central square.[93] A member of the viceregal constabulary regularly stood guard at the fountain to prevent disorders among the queues of boisterous slaves, lower-class men, and sailors waiting their turn, bucket in hand.

Even in the eighteenth century Rio was a noisy town. Church bells seemed to peal at all hours of the day and night. Large-wheeled mule carts loaded with merchandise or military stores creaked over the paved streets, provoking one irate visitor to exclaim that "the fertile powers of the imagination could scarcely have devised a more effectual method of producing a horrid din." [94] A more sinister source of noise was the frequent brawls among soldiers and civilians that often occurred in front of the palace. It was there that Bougainville's surgeon was set upon and murdered. Even in the days of the viceroys, Rio was noted for its homicides.[95]

In Viceroy Lavradio's time the city offered few social diversions.

[93] See Chamberlain, Pl. 17, and Ender, p. 64. The "arcos" are used today as a roadbed for tram lines from the Largo da Carioca to Santa Teresa.

[94] Staunton, I, 179–180.

[95] Bougainville, p. 75. About 1740 warrant gunner John Bulkeley, a survivor of the Anson expedition who spent some weeks in Rio, declared that the city was a very dangerous place in which to live, "for here ruffians are to be hired at a small Expense; and there is no Place in the World where People will commit Murder at so cheap a rate." Bulkeley and John Cummins, *A Voyage to the South Seas in His Majesty's Ship the Wagner*, p. 137. A century before, Father Ruiz Montoya, S.J., no friend of the Portuguese, declared that the Cariocas were so unruly that they killed

There were as yet no inns or coffee houses; indeed there was hardly any coffee. But there were numerous taverns where one could quench his thirst with that vile stuff called *cachaça* (sugar brandy), and where contacts could be made with contrabandists and other members of the underworld.[96] On important occasions, such as a military victory or the birth or death of a member of the royal family, the capital's forts alerted the city with their salvos and the heavens were pierced by sky-rockets. Almost any evening had its share of taper-lit, friar-led processions, which wound their way through the streets, seeking alms or demonstrating their veneration for a particular saintly protector.

For the upper classes there were also masquerades, palace receptions, and performances at the opera. The "tolerable handsome hall" near the *Largo* de São Domingos, where Bougainville saw "the best works of Metastasio represented by a band of mulattoes, and heard the divine composition of the great Italian masters, executed by an orchestra . . . under the direction of a hump-backed priest" was destroyed by fire in 1769. But it was soon replaced by another, built near the Praça do Carmo, close to the palace.[97] For some unexplained reason Parny was denied permission to visit the new hall in 1773; but he did attend a "joli concert" followed by a ball where he danced the minuet and made unfavorable comparisons between the local damsels and the mesdemoiselles he had left behind in Paris.[98] Such, in brief, was the city where the Marquis of Lavradio was to spend the most trying years of his career.

The New Viceroy Surveys His Government

As he familiarized himself with each department, the new viceroy reported its condition to the Crown. He was pleased to discover the Relação unhindered by the dissensions that had characterized its sister tribunal in Salvador. Nonetheless, Dom Luís declared that the court

---

each other "as if they were bed-bugs." Boxer, *Salvador de Sá*, p. 113. That life is still cheap in Rio may be confirmed by reading its daily newspapers.

[96] In 1771 the taverners petitioned Viceroy Lavradio to set aside a decree of the câmara of Rio closing the taverns from 10:00 P.M. to daybreak. Lavradio refused to do so on the ground that to have the bars open all night would constitute "hum grande prejuízo ao povo e a perturbação do socego público," and asserted that they were dens of iniquity "donde se refugião os ladroens a venderem os furtos. . . ." Lavradio to Antônio Pinheiro Amado (Ouvidor da Comarca), Feb. 11 and 25, 1771, ANRJ, Col. 70, Liv. V, fols. 159ᵛ–160ʳ, 164ᵛ–165ʳ.

[97] *Voyage*, p. 76; cf. Varnhagen, *História*, IV, 186, n. 24, and Rodolfo Garcia, Introduction to "Almanaques da cidade do Rio de Janeiro . . . 1792 e 1794," *ABNRJ*, LIX, 220. For Viceroy Lavradio's humorous description of the behavior of an opera audience in his time see *VRL*, p. 22.

[98] Parny to his brother, Sept. 1773, *Oeuvres*, I, 215.

was behind in its work, partly because of the existence of two vacancies on the bench but also because of the extra burdens the court had assumed when the Crown assigned it reponsibility for administering the estates of the Jesuits who had been expelled from Brazil in 1759. Lavradio, who never had reason to complain about the Rio court, recommended that its vacancies be filled and that two additional judges be assigned to it to help clear up the backlog of cases.[99]

When he examined his military establishment, the viceroy had serious misgivings, especially about the generals in charge. They included Lieutenant-General J. H. Böhm, an Austrian who was in charge of the troops, and a Swedish fortification expert, Jacques Funk. Both were mercenaries who had been in British service before entering that of Portugal. In 1767 Pombal had sent them with high recommendations to Rio de Janeiro to supervise a military buildup there.[100]

Though he had never met Böhm before,[101] Lavradio soon formed a lasting dislike for him. It is difficult to say whether his aversion stemmed from Böhm's foreign nationality, his high rank, his Protestant faith, or his past associations with the English.[102] The viceroy contended that, although he was an able inspector of troops, Böhm was excessively arrogant, supercilious, and harsh. He resolved to "put the general in his place" by making him serve as his aide-de-camp at parades and other public functions and by setting aside some of the general's unpopular orders. Lavradio found the troops well disciplined and trained, but believed that their morale was very low because Böhm insisted on conducting the traditional maneuvers during the same months as in Europe, even though they constituted the hot, wet season in America, and because the general refused to approve marriages beyond the regimental quotas prescribed in the official regulations. He countermanded Böhm's directives on both counts, and alleged that the spirits of the troops immediately improved and that the rate of desertions showed a corresponding decline.[103]

99 *VRL*, p. 33.

100 Pombal to Conde da Cunha, June 20, 1767, *RIHGB*, XXXV:1, 227–236. For biographical details and the circumstances behind the generals' dispatch to the colony, see Chap. IV, pp. 106 to 112.

101 An inference based on Lavradio's personal, get-acquainted letter to J. H. "Bôme [sic]," Salvador, June 20, 1769, and Böhm's reply, Rio de Janeiro, Aug. 11, 1769, BNRJ, 13-4-1, nos. 42 (orig.) and 43.

102 Writing at a time when there was a good deal of friction between Britain and Portugal (see below Chap. IV, pp. 109 to 115), Lavradio professed doubts about the loyalty of Böhm and Funk in the event of hostilities between the two powers, owing to the generals' prior British service and to Böhm's reputed contact with a British warship (undoubtedly Cook's) in Rio de Janeiro. Lavradio to Pombal, June 26, 1770, IHGB/AUC, Arq. 1-1-29, fols. 234ʳ–239ʳ (carta familiar, marked confidential).

103 Lavradio, *Relatório*, pp. 413–414. Nevertheless desertions were to plague the

The garrison of the captaincy-general consisted of three grades of troops. The so-called "first line" included three European and two colonial infantry regiments [104] and a locally formed artillery regiment. These were backed up by militia companies called auxiliaries and by a reserve militia known as the *ordenanças*.[105] The regulars were supposed to number more than 6,000 men when Dom Luís took office, but he found that there were actually only 4,175 effectives.[106] The viceroy proposed three means of compensating for his manpower shortage: (1) that he be authorized to go ahead with the projected organization of a colonial regiment on Santa Catarina Island; (2) that he be permitted to draft youths in church seminaries who had failed to make satisfactory progress in their studies; [107] and (3) that the Crown send him an additional 400 to 500 recruits.

The viceroy also proposed the creation of a regular cavalry regiment in Rio de Janeiro. He contended that there was need for a mobile force to discourage enemy landings along the extensive beaches near Guanabara Bay, as well as to prevent desertions and to protect communications between Rio and São Paulo. While Rio already had an auxiliary cavalry, it was inadequate for these purposes since it was composed of farm folk who had little inclination for military service. Dom Luís wanted to use his personal guard as the nucleus for the new outfit, but he complained that although two companies of select mounted troops had been authorized for the vice-

---

viceroy throughout his term, and he repeatedly issued *bandos* asking soldiers (and sailors) to return to their posts within a grace period of twenty to thirty days. The first of these was published in November 1769. Circular letter to all mestres de campo of Rio de Janeiro, Nov. 27, 1769, ANRJ, Col. 70, Liv. V, fol. 4ᵛ, ordering the proclamations posted in a public place. Lavradio also wrote to the ouvidor geral of Espírito Santo and to the captains-general of Minas Gerais and São Paulo asking their cooperation in rounding up AWOLs. To José Ribeiro Guimarães e Athayde, May 28, 1770, *ibid.*, fol. 50ᵛ–51ᵛ; *idem* to Conde de Valadares (captain-general of Minas), Dec. 1, 1769, CMCM, cod. 15, fol. 3ᵛ, with notation that a similar *ofício* was sent to São Paulo.

104 Respectively called the "old" and the "new" Rio regiments, owing to the time when each was organized.

105 The *ordenanças*, the sixteenth-century militia, were composed in the eighteenth century of men unfit for service in the two front lines, and were intended to replace the fighting units when they were sent to a battle area. In modern parlance, they were the Home Guard.

106 Lavradio to Pombal, Feb. 20, 1770, IHGB/AUC, 1-1-29, fols. 213ʳ–227ʳ; *idem* to Martinho de Melo e Castro, June 23, 1770, *ibid.*, fols. 229ᵛ–231ᵛ. Except when otherwise noted, the following paragraphs are based upon these two dispatches.

107 As he had in Salvador, Lavradio complained that the Church was competing unfairly for the able youth of the captaincy. He stated that the bishop of Rio got around a royal decree forbidding the ordination of additional priests without specific authorization from the Crown by sending seminary students to Buenos Aires, via Colônia, for investiture there, after which they returned to Rio. Lavradio to Pombal, June 23, 1770, *ibid.*, fols. 227ʳ–229ᵛ; see also Conde da Cunha to Francisco Xavier de Mendonça Furtado, Mar. 24, 1767, *RIHGB*, XXVIII:2 (1865), 230–231 for similar complaints.

roys of Rio in 1763, they still lacked sufficient officers, uniforms, and discipline.

After inspecting the artillery regiment and conferring with General Funk, Viceroy Lavradio reported that the gunners were poorly trained and were too few to man the numerous marine fortifications of Guanabara Bay. These included three forts at the entrance—Santa Cruz, the principal bastion; the island of Lage in the center and São João on the left flank—and four forts within the bay—Boa Viagem, Gravatá or Caraguatá, and the islands of Villegaignon and Cobras.[108] The fortifications had been allowed to decay during the long years of peace coinciding with most of Gomes Freire's term; and Lavradio stated that the repairs instituted by Viceroy da Cunha had been poorly made, while the Conde de Azambuja had been in office too short a time to execute any major renovation. Relying on information supplied by Generals Funk and Böhm and upon his own observations, the new viceroy stated that the list of urgent requirements included quarters for the garrisons of the forts, water cisterns, and magazines, as well as large quantities of supplies to replace those damaged over the years by spoilage and neglect, and new cannon to enable the bar forts to cross fire and prevent an enemy fleet from entering the bay.

The viceroy also stressed the need for adequate land defenses in the immediate vicinity of the capital. Generals Funk and Böhm had worked on various projects to strengthen the city's defenses since their arrival but had failed to agree on what should be done.[109] The Swedish officer informed Lavradio that Rio would be compelled to surrender if an invasion fleet penetrated the outer marine defenses, as the French had on two occasions (1710, 1711),[110] for the existing installations about the city were incapable of offering resistance against a determined siege. Lavradio ordered the brigadier to put his ideas on paper and within a short time had three plans, one from Funk, another from Funk's adjutant, Captain Francisco João Roscîo, and a third from Colonel José Custódio de Sá e Faria. The viceroy submitted the proposals to General Böhm for his opinion, and then

[108] See the accompanying map, prepared by Jacques Funk and contained in his "Relacion génerále de toutes les forteresses à Rio de Janeiro, 1768," BNRJ, I-28, 23, 10. Note that Fort Gravatá (Caraguata) is garbled, and that the mountain here labeled Gávea is now known as Corcovado.

[109] Copies of a number of Böhm's early reports to the crown (1767–1768) are in IHGB and some of Funk's are in *BNRJ*. Several of the former's are quoted in extenso (but not with a clear indication as to their author) in J. B. Magalhães, "A defesa do Rio de Janeiro no século xviii . . . ," *RIHGB*, CC (1948), 1–32; see also [Miguel Angelo Blasco], "Reparos e annotações sobre a barra do Rio de Janeiro, suas fortalezas e defesas" (*ca.* 1766) and Böhm's devastating critique of it dated Feb. 25, 1768, *ibid.*, XXXIII:1, 281–292.

[110] For an introduction to the voluminous literature, see Augusto Tasso Fragoso, *Os Franceses no Rio de Janeiro* (Rio de Janeiro, 1950) , and Charles R. Boxer, *The Golden Age of Brazil, 1695–1750*, Chap. IV.

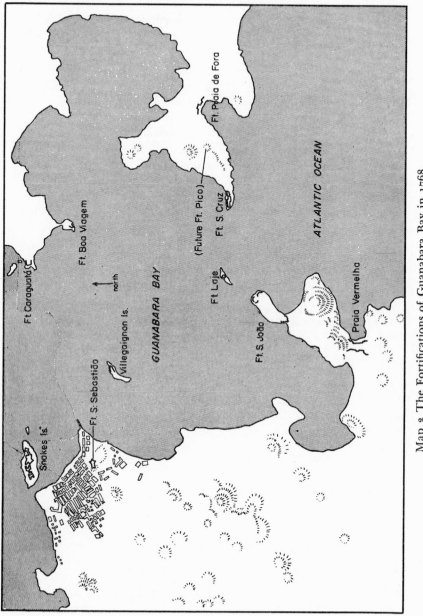

Map 3 The Fortifications of Guanabara Bay in 1768.

ordered the engineers to incorporate Böhm's recommendations. Both he and Böhm favored Roscîo's plan since it entailed the least expense, but Lavradio sent all three to Lisbon for the Court's approval.[111] However, he warned the Crown that its sanction of any of these plans and its approval of his other recommendations would require the allocation of additional revenues, for the viceregal branch of the royal exchequer was in much worse financial shape than the Bahian branch.

The viceroy's report on the status of the Rio exchequer in 1769 will be considered later when the fiscal reorganization of Brazil at this time will be analyzed.[112] As will become apparent then, Dom Luís' fiscal record in Rio de Janeiro was not one of spectacular success. Indeed, the Crown's indebtedness in Rio de Janeiro and its dependencies increased by 60 percent during Lavradio's administration. That increase was not a consequence of bad management by the viceroy or his staff but of the protracted borderlands conflict between Spain and Portugal which occupied most of his term. Before discussing the marquis' role in that conflict, it is necessary to examine its background.

111 The plans of Roscîo, Sá e Faria, and Funk were first published in *RIHGB*, LXV:1 (1902), 183–204; see also Lavradio to Böhm, Jan. 26, 1770, and Böhm to Lavradio, Feb. 2, 1770, *ibid.*, CC (1948), 9, 20–23. Lavradio's dispatch of Feb. 20, 1770 to Pombal (see n. 106) was the covering letter for these reports.
112 See Chaps. XI and XII.

❀ ❀ ❀

PART TWO

The Debatable Lands

III

The Beginnings of European Settlement

Together these border struggles constituted a drama covering two centuries. All the acts had features in common. But each had its own peculiar incidents and characters, and each made its particular contribution to the larger story of American history.

Herbert E. Bolton, *The Debatable Land: A Sketch of the Anglo-Spanish Contest for the Georgia Country* (Berkeley, 1925), p. v.

THROUGHOUT THE SIXTEENTH and most of the seventeenth centuries there existed a vast "no-man's-land" of fertile soils and temperate climate in eastern South America beyond the limits of Portuguese or Spanish settlement. These unoccupied lands were bounded on the east by the Atlantic Ocean, on the north by the Portuguese captaincy of São Paulo, on the south by the estuary of the Río de la Plata, and on the west by the Uruguay and Paraná rivers. In the nineteenth century this area became the Brazilian states of Paraná, Santa Catarina, and Rio Grande do Sul, and the Republic of Uruguay. During the second half of the colonial era, however, when Spain and Portugal vied for control of this territory,[1] it comprised the *comarca* of Paranaguá,[2] the captaincies of Santa Catarina and Rio Grande de São Pedro, and the geographical entity called the Banda Oriental. After a century and a half of neglect, these became the "Debatable Lands" of southern South America.

The Setting[3]

Throughout their history, geography has played an important role in shaping the destiny of the Debatable Lands. South of the port of Paranaguá, near the present-day Paraná–Santa Catarina border, the

[1] For diplomatic and military aspects of Luso-Spanish rivalry over the Debatable Lands to 1769, see Chap. IV.

[2] The *comarca* (county) of Paranaguá, the future state of Paraná, was administratively part of São Paulo.

[3] For extended treatments of the geography of the area see Pierre Denis, "Ameríque du Sud" in P. Vidal de la Blache and L. Gallois, eds., *Géographie universelle* (Paris, 1927), I, 171–184, and II, 453–455, and Preston James, *Latin Amer-*

crystalline escarpment, the predominant surface feature of the Brazilian coast as far north as Bahia, is broken into a broad zone of
faulted blocks, forming a rugged terrain of block mountains separated by rift valleys. Midway along the coast of Santa Catarina a segment of the escarpment became separated from the continent by a
narrow strait, the result of a sinking of the coast. This segment consists of the twenty-nine-mile-long island of Santa Catarina and a few
smaller fragments.[4] South of latitude 28° S. the escarpment narrows
and rejoins the coast, terminating not far below the port of Laguna.

In Paraná and Santa Catarina the escarpment forms the eastern
limits of the broad Paraná lava plateau, whose southern edge is
defined by the east-west Serra Geral, north of Pôrto Alegre. The passage from the plateau to the southern plains (*campanha, campos*)
consists of a series of ridge and terrace steps called the *subida da serra*.
Here, red sandstones have weathered into a series of low hills (*coxi-
lhas* in Rio Grande; *cuchillas* in Uruguay) with at first sharply etched
slopes. Farther south these hills gradually decline in altitude and
soften their contours, so that they give the appearance of being a
"solidified sea in which the waves succeed one another until lost from
sight."[5] This surface feature continues into Uruguay, where a low
range of hills, the Cuchilla Grande, cuts diagonally across the country, intersecting the coast behind Montevideo.

The littoral of the Debatable Lands possessed few protected ports.[6]
Wherever found, harbors were generally the first sites appropriated
and fortified by Europeans. The earliest of the Platine ports of the
Banda Oriental, controversial Colônia do Sacramento, situated behind San Gabriel Island, was never more than a roadstead. Less
highly regarded by contemporaries was Montevideo, which has become a major port in modern times only after the addition of break-

---

ica (3rd ed.; New York, 1959), Chap. 15. See also Carl O. Sauer, "Geography of
South America," *Handbook of South American Indians,* Julian H. Steward, ed., VI
(Bureau of American Ethnology, Smithsonian Institution, Bull. No. 143, Washing-
ton, D.C., 1950), 322, and maps 8 and 9 following this page, and map 10 after 338;
and Hilgard O'Reilly Sternberg, "The Physical Basis of Brazilian Society," *Brazil
Portrait of Half a Continent,* T. Lynn Smith and Alexander Marchant, eds. (New
York, 1951), pp. 82–83.

4 Similar structural weaknesses have been responsible for two other island remnants of the escarpment—Ilha Grande, off the state of Rio de Janeiro, and Ilha de
São Sebastião, off the coast of São Paulo. Both of these islands exceed Santa Catarina
in elevation.

5 F[rancisco] de Paula Cidade, *Lutas, ao sul do Brasil, com os espanhóis e seus
descendentes* (Rio de Janeiro, 1948), p. 8. Pages 7–13 contain an excellent appreciation of the military geography of Rio Grande. Known in colonial days as Rio
Grande de São Pedro and in modern times as Rio Grande do Sul, the southernmost
part of Brazil is usually referred to as Rio Grande in this study.

6 For useful description of the littoral and the modern port development see
Sailing Directions for South America, I, *East Coast* (U.S. Hydrographic Office, H.O.
172, 5th ed.; Washington, D.C., 1952), 226–270.

waters and extensive dredging.[7] Like Montevideo, Maldonado, the easternmost port of the Platine estuary, is exposed to southwesterly winds, particularly the *pamperos*.[8]

Between Maldonado and Laguna (28° 30' S. latitude), the shoreline consists of low, monotonous white sand dunes, visible at sea for only a few miles even when the weather is clear, a fact which accounts for this being one of the graveyards for shipping on the eastern coast of South America. Seldom is the coast sufficiently indented to permit the formation of good harbors. Castillos Bay (34° 21' S. latitude) formerly served as a refuge for ships seeking a haven from southerly or southeasterly winds, but shipmasters alertly put to sea if the guage shifted to the northeast, for they knew that northeasterlies here raise a heavy sea. Between the Arroio Chuí at the Brazil-Uruguay frontier and the Rio Mambituba, the dividing line between the States of Santa Catarina and Rio Grande do Sul, centuries of buffeting by Atlantic waves have created a series of sand bars, some of which have solidified to form elongated lagoons behind them. The two largest, Lagoa Mirim and Lagoa dos Patos, extend almost the entire length of Rio Grande. The narrow entrance to the Lagoa dos Patos, which gives access to the only ports on this long stretch, has always been a sailing hazard because of its constantly shifting sand banks.

The coast of Santa Catarina, by contrast, offers numerous small harbors such as Laguna, Desterro (on the western shore of the island), Tijucas, Garoupas [Pôrto Belo?], São Francisco do Sul, and Paranaguá. But in colonial times, as today, these harbors too posed special navigational hazards because of shifting banks and alluvial fill from tributary watercourses.

The rivers that drain the area of its abundant, year-round rainfall have played a vital role in the history of the Debatable Lands. Some, like the westward-flowing Tietê, Paranápanema, Iguaçú, and Ibicuí and the eastward-moving Jacuí-Guaíba,[9] have served as inviting avenues for penetration of the interior.[10] On the other hand, the two major waterways of the region, the Paraná and the Uruguay, have acted as barriers to east-west movement because of their deep canyons and spectacular waterfalls.

Favored by some of the best soils on the continent, the lands of

[7] E.g., a half century after its occupation the experienced Don Pedro de Cevallos referred to "Montevideo, a donde V.E. quiere dirigirse no merece el nombre de Puerto. . . ." Cevallos to Marquis of Casa Tilly, Feb. 7, 1777, *CB*, III, 455.

[8] See the vivid, succinct description of these southwesterlies in *Sailing Directions*, I, 243.

[9] As far as the Rio Pardo tributary, this river is known as Guaíba; thereafter it changes its name to Jacuí.

[10] Within Rio Grande, wherever the Ibicuí, Jacuí-Guaíba, and Camaquam and their tributaries make sharp bends or are joined by other affluents, they form peninsulas (*rincões*) which have been attractive to cattlemen as places to confine

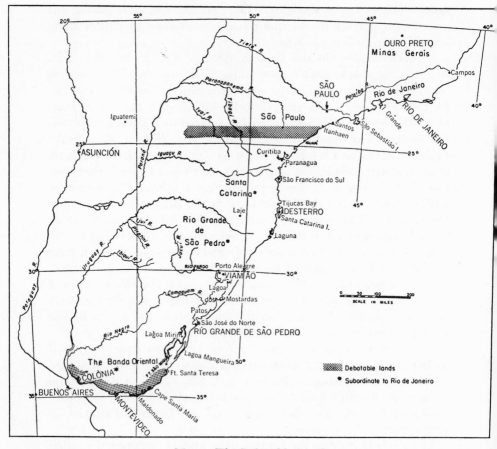

Map 4 The Debatable Lands.

southern Brazil and Uruguay comprise an important agricultural, lumbering, and ranching area. In parts of Paraná, Santa Catarina, and Rio Grande, beds of relatively recent basalt and red sandstone overlay the older rocks of the Paraná plateau and have weathered into deep, wine-red, productive *terra roxa* soils, creating some of the finest farmland in Brazil. Along the littoral, the dense tropical rain forest extending from southern Bahia gradually gives way to a lighter, semideciduous forest north of Pôrto Alegre, forming a band of frost-resistant Araucária pine forests along the broad arc of the Uruguay. Important stands of *Ilex paraguayensis,* the source of mate tea, exist in western Paraná and in parts of western Rio Grande, while the lower alluvial basin of the Jacuí-Guaíba is southern Brazil's rice bowl. On the plateau the vegetation gradually changes from tropical, semideciduous forest to pure grass prairie. The prairies, which occur in

their herds and to military strategists as staging areas for troop movements. Paula Cidade, p. 11.

patches throughout Paraná and Santa Catarina, attain greater prominence than the forests in Rio Grande (except along tree-covered stream margins) and Uruguay, making these last two excellent cattle- and horse-raising country.

The Coming of the Jesuits

Notwithstanding their great economic potential, the Debatable Lands were neglected for nearly two centuries after their discovery. While the Portuguese were preoccupied with the tropical captaincies of Brazil, which yielded sugar and other high-unit value commodities, the Spanish were concerned with the exploitation of the silver-rich Andes and the development of tributary agricultural colonies in northwestern Platine provinces and in interior Paraguay. Except for the Spanish Jesuits, European settlement of the Debatable Lands was primarily limited to the fringes of the area during the colonial centuries.

The Spanish Jesuits made two efforts to establish themselves in the heart of the Debatable Lands. Three years after the new Jesuit province of Paraguay, Chile, and Tucumán was created, the Black Robes began opening up four mission fields: Itatín, along the tributaries of the upper Paraguay; Guairá, between the Paranápanema and Iguaçú, both eastern affluents of the Paraná; Paraná, in the delta between the middle Paraguay and the Uruguay; and the derivative Uruguay-Tape group east of the Uruguay. Two of these fields, the Guairá and the Uruguay-Tape reductions, constituted the first attempts by Europeans to occupy the Debatable Lands permanently.

Between 1610 and 1628 the Fathers founded fifteen missions in Guairá, thirteen of them in present-day western and central São Paulo and Paraná. Before the Jesuits had had opportunity to establish their new field on a stable basis, the missions were repeatedly attacked by slave-hunting Paulistas, the famous (or infamous) *bandeirantes,* who carried away undetermined thousands of neophytes (1628–1632). As a consequence, the Black Robes abandoned Guairá, and transferred their remaining charges to the Uruguay-Tape field farther south.[11]

[11] By 1632 the Spanish were also forced to evacuate three recently established towns in Guairá—Villa Rica, Ciudad Real, and Santiago de Jérez—because of the menace of the Paulistas. Not without reason the Viceroy of Perú, the Conde de Chinchón, suggested to the king that Spain either purchase São Paulo from its donataries or destroy all Portuguese settlements there. Basílio de Magalhães, *Expansão geográfica do Brasil colonial* (Rio de Janeiro, 1944), p. 164.

A fully adequate study of the Guairá missions remains to be written. Magnus Mörner, *The Political and Economic Activities of the Jesuits in the La Plata Region* . . . (Stockholm, 1953), pp. 72–74, 89–91, is sketchy. *Ramón I. Cardozo, La antigua provincia de Guayrá y la Villa Rica del Espíritu* (Buenos Aires, 1938), utilizes printed and manuscript Spanish materials, but not Portuguese, and is concerned with a broader theme than the missions themselves. Herbert Raffeld, "The Jesuit

After the marauding bandeirantes finished hunting for Indians and gold in Guairá, the area remained virtually untouched by Europeans for more than a century.[12]

From 1626 to 1634 the Jesuits established fifteen reductions between the Ibicuí and Jacuí-Guaíba rivers, in the heart of Rio Grande do Sul. The Fathers seem to have intended to continue founding missions as far east as the Lagoa dos Patos, where they would have obtained an outlet to the sea. Had they achieved this goal, the story of Luso-Spanish rivalry in the Debatable Lands might have been a very different one, for the Portuguese would have been cut off not only from Rio Grande but also from the Plata. Once again, however, the bandeirantes attacked. By 1640 all of the Uruguay-Tape reductions had been either destroyed or abandoned. Their survivors fled to the Paraná missions, across the Uruguay. After the decisive Jesuit-Indian victory over the bandeirantes at Mbororé (March 1641), those missions served as a barrier to further Paulista depredations.[13] The Jesuits did not return to the Debatable Lands for nearly half a century.

Left behind when the Fathers withdrew were an unknown number of cattle that had been intended for the support of the missions. Fattening and multiplying upon the lush prairie grasses of western Rio Grande, these animals were augmented from time to time by additional cattle and horses that the Jesuits drove across the Uruguay from their Paraná missions as a hedge against their future needs. These were the probable ancestors of the vast wild herds that roamed throughout the Debatable Lands during the late seventeenth and the eighteenth centuries from the pampas of the Banda Oriental (the Vaquería del Mar) to the upland pastures of Santa Catarina (the Vaquería dos Pinhais). These bovine riches stimulated the Spanish Jesuits' resolve to return to Rio Grande and kindled the interest of others in the area as well.[14]

Missions of Guayrá, 1588–1633," University of California, M.S., M.A. (Berkeley, 1947), relies on printed sources in Spanish and Portuguese.

[12] During the 1760s and 1770s the Paulistas rediscovered Guairá and sent numerous gold-hunting expeditions into the interfluvial area between the Ivaí (a tributary of the Paraná) and Tibagí (an affluent of the Paranápanema). See Chap. XVI, pp. 462–463.

[13] The first Jesuit missions in Rio Grande have been closely studied by [Afonso] Aurélio Porto, *História das missões do Uruguai*, I (Pôrto Alegre, 1954), 76–228; for an excellent brief treatment see José C. Canales, "Rio Grande do Sul in Luso-Spanish Platine Rivalry, 1626–1737," M.S., Ph.D. (Berkeley, 1959), Chap. II. See also Jónatas da Costa Rego Monteiro, "As primeiras reduções jesuíticas no Rio Grande do Sul, 1626–1638," *RIHGRGS*, XIX:1 (1939), 15–45, for an exacting study of the location of each mission.

[14] The origins of the cattle and horses of the Debatable Lands has been the subject of a long controversy. For a summary of the evidence with respect to Rio Grande see Porto, I, 265–269. He concludes, "lícito é afirmar que a origem de toda a

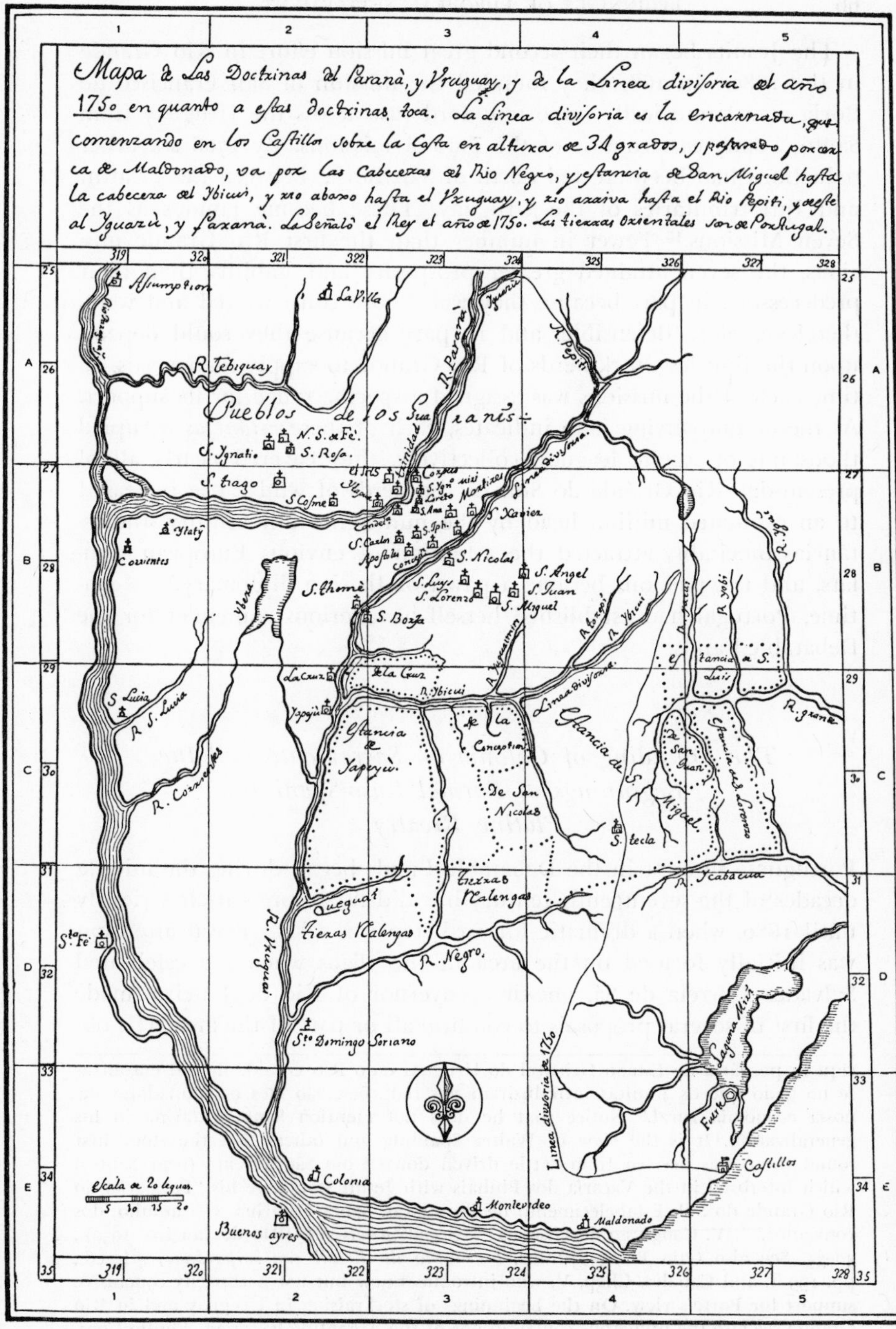

Mapa de Las Doctrinas del Paranà, y Vruguay, y de la Linea divisoria del año 1750 en quanto a estas doctrinas toca. La Linea divisoria es la encarnada, que comenzando en los Castillos sobre la Costa en altura de 34 grados, y pasando por cerca de Maldonado, va por las Cabeceras del Rio Negro, y estancia de San Miguel hasta la cabecera del Ybicui, y rio abaxo hasta el Vruguay, y rio arriva hasta el Rio Pepiri, y de este al Yguazù, y Paranà. La Señalò el Rey el año de 1750. Las tierras Orientales son de Portugal.
Assumption
La Villa
R. tebiquay
Pueblos de los Guaranis
N. S. de Fè.
S. Ygnatio
S. Rosa.
S. tiago
S. Cosme
Corpus
Candel.
S. Carlos
Apostolo
S. Xavier
S. Nicolas
S. Angel
S. Juan
S. Miguel
S. Luys
S. Lorenzo
S. Thomè
S. Borja
Corrientes
La Cruz
Yapeyù
R. S. Lucia
R. Corrientes
R. Ybicui
Linea divisoria
Concepcion
De San Nicolas
S. tecla
R. Ycabacua
R. grane
Tierras Realengas
Queguay
R. Negro.
R. Vruguay
Sto Domingo Soriano
Sto Fè
Laguna Mini
Fuerte
Castillos
Colonia
Montevideo
Maldonado
Buenos ayres
Escala de 20 leguas.
5 10 15 20
Linea divisoria de 1750

Map 5 The Jesuit Mission estâncias in 1750. (Guillermo Furlong Cardiff, S.J., *Cartografía Jesuítica del Río de la Plata* (Buenos Aires, 1936), No. XXXIII.)

The Jesuits began their second great mission effort in Rio Grande in the 1680s. In 1682 they founded the mission of San Francisco de Borja at a strategically important ford just across the Uruguay from Santo Tomé, easternmost of the Paraná missions. By 1706 six other reductions had been erected north of San Borja, between the Piratiní and Ijuí tributaries of the Uruguay. These became famous as the Seven Missions.[15] Fewer in number than the first Rio Grande missions, the seven attained greater prosperity and stability than their predecessors, in part because they were more concentrated and were, therefore, more defensible, and in part because they could depend upon the limitless stock herds of Rio Grande to supply their needs. In time each of the missions was assigned a specific range for its support. As the accompanying map indicates, each of these *estâncias* occupied thousands of square leagues; collectively, they covered nearly all of present-day Rio Grande do Sul. As the herds of wild cattle increased to an estimated million head by the mid-eighteenth century, the estâncias inevitably attracted the attention of envious European seculars, and the missions became a pawn of Iberian diplomacy.[16] Meantime, Portugal had established herself as a serious contender for the Debatable Lands.

The Founding of Colônia do Sacramento and the Beginnings of Formal Luso-Spanish Platine Rivalry

Portuguese interest in the Debatable Lands began during the middle decades of the seventeenth century but did not express itself seriously until 1680, when a dramatic forward step was taken. Royal attention was initially focused on the area in the 1640s when the celebrated Salvador Correia de Sá, one-time governor of Rio de Janeiro, made the first of several proposals to colonize all or part of the area. His ob-

riqueza pecuária do Estado Oriental do Uruguai e do Rio Grande do Sul encontra-se no gado que os Jesuítas introduziram nas reduções. São eles os fundadores da nossa economia rural." Notice that he does not mention Santa Catarina in his generalization. It is the view of Walter Spalding and others that the stock first found there was derived from cattle driven down from São Vicente (near Santos) which interbred in the Vacaría dos Pinhais with Jesuit stock. See his "Formação do Rio Grande do Sul. Estabelecimento de Fronteiras. Santa Catarina. O caminho 'dos conventos,'" IV. Congresso de Historia Nacional, *Anais*, VI (Rio de Janeiro, 1950), 30–34. See also Caio Prado, Júnior, *Formação do Brasil contemporâneo*, 4th ed., pp. 199 ff, and Canales, Chap. V, who introduces new but not necessarily conclusive support for Porto's view. On the beginnings of stockraising in Uruguay and in Rio Grande see also the numerous contributions of the Argentine historian, Emílio Coní.

[15] Porto, II, 31–85, 162–197, gives a detailed account of the missions; see also Canales, Chap. V.

[16] See below, Chap. IV, pp. 88 f.

jectives were to exploit anticipated mineral, timber, and other resources and to forestall occupation of the vacant lands by Spain.[17] In the wake of the discovery of small gold deposits in 1653, the first Portuguese settlements in the Debatable Lands were made at their northern margins. These included Curitiba on the Paraná plateau, and Paranaguá and São Francisco do Sul on the coast. Though permanently maintained, none of these towns lived up to their early promise as major mineral producers.

While continuing to hope for a large mining strike around Paranaguá, royal interest shifted to the opposite extremity of the Debatable Lands. In 1676 Salvador de Sá finally obtained a grant to territory extending from Cape Santa María, then regarded as marking the north entrance to the Plata, to the approximate latitude of Pôrto Alegre.[18] In the same year Pope Innocent XI made a significant contribution, innocently or intentionally, to Portugal's previously unsupported claim to the north bank of the Plata. In a bull reorganizing the ecclesiastical administration of Brazil, the Pope referred to the "province of Rio de Janeiro" as extending from "the captaincy of Espírito Santo . . . to the Rio de la Plata, along the shore and inland." [19] While this was grist for the mill of Prince Pedro, ruler of Portugal, he realized that Spain would not be easily disposed to subscribe to the papal interpretation of Brazil's southern boundary. What better way existed to buttress Portugal's claim than to establish a settlement in the Plata?

The desire to plant the Portuguese flag firmly in the soil of the Banda Oriental was one of several reasons that inspired the Prince to order in 1679 the erection of a fortified outpost, subsequently called Colônia do Sacramento, on the Platine estuary.[20] Possibly a more compelling motive was the hope that, by offering African slaves and European merchandise at the entrepôt, the flow of Spanish silver, cut off since the cessation of the once profitable contraband trade between Rio de Janeiro and Peru via Buenos Aires,[21] would be re-

[17] Charles R. Boxer, *Salvador de Sá*, pp. 295, 302.

[18] Boxer, p. 378.

[19] *Romani Pontificis*, Dec. 16, 1676, quoted in Canales, Chap. IV, n. 17.

[20] A half century ago the eminent Brazilian historian Capistrano de Abreu asked "Por que fundá-la [Colônia] tão afastada dos outras possessões portuguezas? porque este era o meio de evitar as costas aridas do Rio Grande do Sul? ou porque julgou el-rei que o melhor meio de sustentar e affirmar seus direitos era leva-los ao extremo?" And replied, "A última hypothese parece a mais justa." "Sobre a Colonia do Sacramento," *Ensaios e estudos (crítica e história)* 3.a série ([Rio de Janeiro], 1938), p. 73. This essay (pp. 57–105) is a reprint of the introduction Capistrano wrote to Simão Pereira de Sá, *História topográphica e béllica da Nova Colônia do Sacramento do Rio da Prata* (Rio de Janeiro, 1900), the first account of Colônia, written *ca.* 1737.

[21] The trade was cut off in 1640 when Portugal began her twenty-eight-year war for independence from Spain. See Alice P. Canabrava, *O comércio português no Rio*

sumed to the benefit of Pedro's nearly exhausted exchequer.[22] A Platine base would also make possible exploitation of reputedly large cattle herds in the Vaquería del Mar and search for the fabled mines the Jesuits were believed to possess in the interior.[23]

These ambitions were only partially realized after Colônia's founding early in 1680.[24] Instead of locating the base on San Gabriel Island, as the Crown intended,[25] Dom Manoel Lobo, Rio de Janeiro's new governor and commander of the expedition, picked a

---

da Prata, 1580–1640 (São Paulo, 1944). For some indication that Portugal was still trying to establish a direct trade between Rio de Janeiro and Buenos Aires in Lavradio's time, see Francisco Xavier de Mendonça Furtado (colonial secretary) to Count da Cunha (viceroy of Rio de Janeiro), July 23, 1766, *RIHGB*, XXXIII:1 (1870), 243–244.

[22] Portugal's treasury was drained by the long Dutch war for control of northern Brazil (1624–1654), the large indemnity Portugal agreed to pay the Dutch in 1661, the war of independence from Spain (1640–1668), and the expenses of the marriage of Catherine of Bragança to Charles II of England. Owing in part to competition from the newer producing areas of the Carribbean, the sugar industry of Brazil was in decline during this period, bringing about a consequent fall of royal income at a time when Brazil had become Portugal's most important colony. These factors were behind the extensive economic and administrative reforms undertaken during the reign of Prince, and later King, Pedro II (1667–1706). See Mario Rodríguez, "Dom Pedro of Braganza and Colônia do Sacramento, 1680–1705," *HAHR*, XXXVIII (May 1958), 179–208. It should be added that Professor Rodríguez' thesis that these reforms were the personal work of Dom Pedro is not conclusively proved. It is more likely that they reflected the views of the Conde de Ericeira, his chief adviser.

[23] For a more detailed discussion of the motivation for Colônia, see Rodríguez, *passim*.

[24] Though growing in volume, the literature on Colônia continues to emphasize the early years, stressing military and diplomatic aspects, and is uniformly thin on the last years. See Luis Enrique Azarola Gil, *Contribución a la historia de Colonia del Sacramento: La epopeya de Manuel Lobo . . . 1680 hasta 1828* (Madrid–Buenos Aires, [1931]), which is more valuable for its documentary appendices than for its slender text; Jônatas da Costa Rego Monteiro, *A Colônia do Sacramento, 1680–1777* (2 vols., Pôrto Alegre, 1937) devotes Vol. II to a rather disorderly array of key documents. Antonio Bermejo de la Rica, *La Colonia del Sacramento* (Toledo, 1940) publishes useful diplomatic sources, to which Luís Ferrand de Almeida, *A Diplomacia portuguesa e os limites meridionais do Brasil*, I (1493–1700) (Coimbra, 1957), has contributed some important additions. The economic background is ably presented in Mario Rodríguez, "Colônia do Sacramento: Focus of Spanish-Portuguese Rivalry in the Plata, 1640–1683," M.S., Ph.D. (Berkeley, 1952); Canales restudies the years to 1737 in Chaps. IV, VII, and VIII. See also the essay of Capistrano de Abreu, cited in n. 20. A promising source apparently still in private hands is Sebastião da Veiga Cabral (third governor of Colônia), "Reprezentação estudiosa & vtil para as magestades, grandeza & vassalos de Portugal," n.d., of which the table of contents is published in Virgínia Rau and Maria Fernanda Gomes da Silva, eds., *Os manuscritos do arquivo da casa de Cadaval respeitantes ao Brasil*, II, 411–418, one of two known extended contemporary accounts, the other being that of Pereira de Sá, cited in n. 20, above.

[25] Portugal wanted to tap the trade flowing down the nearby Uruguay and Paraná rivers and the commerce of Buenos Aires. "Regimento que o governador do Rio de Janeiro, Dom Manuel Lobo, levou para a fortaleza do Sacramento no Rio da Prata," Nov. 18, 1668 [sic for 1678], Rego Monteiro, *Colônia*, II, 5–16, and in *DH*, LXXIX, 324–345.

sandy peninsula behind the island. Whatever the reasons for its selection,[26] the site proved to be a poor one defensively; the roadstead did not make an especially good port, and the *praça* could be dominated from higher ground to the east and north.[27] Though the Portuguese succeeded at times in conducting a lucrative illicit trade with Spanish merchants and hide hunters,[28] their commercial connections with the Spanish and with their own bases were made hazardous by enemy *guardacostas* and shore patrols. The latter drove the livestock herds away from Colônia toward Montevideo Bay, so that the Portuguese were forced to rely primarily on Spanish intermediaries to procure the hides they had hoped to gather directly.[29] Nor were the expected mines ever found. Nevertheless, as long as it remained a Portuguese possession, Colônia served to support the Portuguese dream of control of the eastern coast of South America from the Amazon to the Plata, a vision that was not finally dispelled until the last quarter of the nineteenth century.

Although Colônia was almost immediately erased by a Spanish punitive force (August 7, 1680), the base was rebuilt three years later and remained an irritating thorn in the flank of the Spanish empire for nearly a century. During that time it was often besieged by hostile Spanish troops aided by Jesuit Indian neophytes, and was overrun four times. However, Spain's successes in the Plata were counterbalanced by her weakness in Europe, and Colônia was thrice restored to Portugal at the peace table.

Colônia's vulnerability to enemy attack stemmed from its exposed location. While it was only fifteen miles from Buenos Aires and sixty miles from Montevideo Bay, the entrepôt was hundreds of miles from its headquarters, Rio de Janeiro, and from other Brazilian settlements. In terms of sailing time, Colônia was less than a day from Buenos Aires, two days from Montevideo, seven from Santa Catarina,

26 See Lobo to Prince Pedro (March 12, 1680?), Rego Monteiro, *Colônia*, II, 28, for his comments on the site.

27 Though the Portuguese occasionally posted batteries on the heights, they never really fortified them.

28 The true economic significance of Colônia remains to be assessed. The occasional data that have come to light—the number of hide ships leaving for Portuguese ports in a given year, the number of hides on a specific vessel, reports of foreign ambassadors on the amount of silver arriving in Lisbon—is insufficient to make possible a reliable appraisal of Colônia's commercial importance. Disappointing are the eight codices of ANRJ, Col. 157, entitled "Termos de fiança q. dão os capitães de navios que sahem deste porto [Colônia]," since while they indicate names of vessels leaving port, their captains, and their destinations, they do not indicate the quantity nor value of their cargoes. Judging from scattered treasury reports, Colônia was very likely always a fiscal liability to the Crown, whose expenses there greatly exceeded revenues received from the praça. For a report which supports this assumption, see Chap. IV, n. 20.

29 Porto, II, 111.

and fourteen from Rio de Janeiro. These facts were apparent to Portuguese authorities from the time of Colônia's founding. They realized that its security depended on the attraction of substantial numbers of settlers—especially farmers who could double as militiamen—the establishment of other Portuguese bases in the Plata, and the closing of the gap between settled Brazil and the Banda Oriental.[30]

Though Colônia's founder urged the Crown to send Portuguese families to the praça, his suggestion was apparently not adopted until 1718; nor was it consistently followed thereafter.[31] Instead, the Crown supplemented the base's complement of troops, government workers, and merchants' factors with degredados,[32] exiles who included political and criminal offenders, army misfits, prostitutes, and the like. Such people could be expected to be among the first to desert to the enemy in time of trouble[33] and to discourage useful

[30] Thus, an anonymous royal inspector who had toured Brazil from Pará to Colônia recommended: "Para se conservar a povoação do Sacramento houvera Sua Magestade ter mandado fazer outra no Monte Video, e outra no cabo Negro, assim para a estabilidade, e communicação de umas para as outras povoações, como para nos irmos senhoreando das terras que ficam da nossa parte, com os gados, lenhas e madeiras." "Informação do estado do Brasil e de suas necessidades" (ca. 1690), RIHGB, XXV, 473. In 1715 Councillor Antônio Rodrigues da Costa, a member of the council for colonial affairs (Conselho Ultramarino), observed "E como esta Colônia fica mui separada das mais povoações do Brazil e da última que temos para a parte do Sul . . . . Laguna . . . será muito conveniente procurar que se fundem mais algumas naquelle districto para atar esta Colônia com os mais dominios da America Portugueza . . ." and recommended (though not for the first time) occupation of Montevideo and Maldonado. Rego Monteiro, Colônia, II, 62. See also Lobo to Prince Pedro (Mar. 12, 1680?), cited in n. 26, above.

[31] Governor Lobo differed from the anonymous royal inspector who recommended that Paulistas be sent to Colônia by urging that sturdy farmers be dispatched from Entre Douro e Minho and Alentejo, since there were "too few" Brazilians and since they would be unwilling to put up with the hard winters of the Plata. See n. 26, above. On the 246 members of Portuguese families (casais) transported from Tras os Montes to Colônia between 1716 and 1718, see Rego Monteiro, Colônia, II, 63–70.

[32] A royal decree of Oct. 29, 1689, provided that men and women who had been sent to Brazil as degredados could have their sentences commuted to Colônia. CCLP, X, 205. The first degredados sent to the praça arrived in 1690. See the list of Jan. 25, 1690, in Rego Monteiro, Colônia, II, 54. The typical attitude of the Portuguese government toward the employment of exiles in defending important remote outposts was expressed by the influential Duke of Cadaval in a parecer of Feb. 11, 1722. He recommended that 200 "degredados e vadios" be transported to Colônia "porque era uma forma de limpar o reino daquella gente." Rau and Gomes, II, 262–263. A royal decree of 1722 prohibited the sending of additional degredados to Brazil. It by no means follows, as Borges Fortes concluded, that the practice of shipping exiles to Colônia ceased, however; for the captains-general and viceroys of Rio de Janeiro continued to sentence soldiers and civilians to Colônia from the capital down to the 1770s. Cf. João Borges Fortes, Casais (Porto Alegre [?], 1932), p. 12. Examples of sentences of convicts to Colônia in the 1770s are in Viceroy Lavradio's correspondence with the governors of Colônia during the 1770s in CMCM, cods. 4 and 15, passim.

[33] E.g., three years after Colônia's second restoration, Governor D. Manuel Gomes Barbosa reported that 95 soldiers of his garrison of 289 had defected to

colonists from coming to Colônia. As a result of the unattractive reputation that the outpost acquired—because of its precarious military situation and the type of people who were forced to live there— voluntary immigrants were never numerous. Indeed, Colônia's total population of troops and civilians probably never exceeded 3,000 and was usually considerably smaller.[34]

Notwithstanding the repeated plans and the several attempts the Portuguese made to establish additional bases in the Plata to buttress Colônia, no other Portuguese settlement was ever made in the estuary. The story of Portuguese efforts to occupy the key harbors of Montevideo and Maldonado is told elsewhere and is one of repeated lost opportunities.[35] After the Spanish belatedly fortified both bays, Montevideo in 1724 and Maldonado by 1740, a Portuguese effort to expel them miscarried.[36] Thereafter, Colônia was doomed to ultimate extinction unless the Portuguese-settled frontier succeeded in reaching the beleagured outpost from the north.

Closing the Gap: The Occupation of Santa Catarina [37]

If Colônia represented the first major step in the Portuguese *Drang nach Süden*, the occupation of Santa Catarina was the second. Unlike Colônia, however, the development of Santa Catarina was initially

the enemy since February 1718. Barbosa to the king, Dec. 26, 1719, Rau and Gomes da Silva, eds., *Os manuscritos de Cadaval*, II, 259–260. Desertion was a common problem of colonial governors in Brazil, but it was a particularly serious one in Colônia, where a sizable proportion of the garrison was often immobilized by illness, and where it was difficult to find replacements.

34 This is a general impression based upon a reading of many scattered sources. At the time of its fall in 1762, Colônia probably had the largest garrison that the Portuguese ever maintained within the citadel—2,355 men. "Lizta das praças da goarnica'o melittar da Nova Colonia do Sacramento, durante o sittio" [*ca.* 1762], *CB*, III, 16–19. The number of civilians living there at the time is not given. When the outpost capitulated for the fourth time in 1777, its garrison was down to less than 1,000 men. In addition, there were 533 civilians and seven priests in the praça. "Families que ficaram na praça da Colonia, quando esta se rendeu ao Espanhoes na guerra de 1777 . . . ," ANRJ, Col. 67, liv. IV, fols. 24^r–27^r.

35 See Rodríguez, "Colônia do Sacramento: Focus" pp. 184–191, and Canales, Chap. VIII.

36 Canales, Chap. IX.

37 Compared with the historiography of colonial Rio Grande do Sul, that of Santa Catarina is quantitatively and qualitatively inferior. Santa Catarina-born Alfonso de E. Taunay's "Santa Catarina nos annos primevos," and "Em Santa Catarina colonial—capítulos da história do povoamento," *AMP*, IV, 201–320, and VII:2, consist of anecdotes based upon travelers' accounts. More comprehensive is Lucas A. Boiteux, *Notas para a história catharinense* (Florianópolis, 1912) a work evidently based on local archival sources but lacking notes or bibliography and factually careless. Admiral Boiteux, the dean of Santa Catarinense historians, has published numerous books and articles on his state, but all must be used with care. Useful in spite of its age and sketchiness is José Feliciano Fernandes Pinheiro (Visconde de São Leopoldo), "Resumo histórico da província de S. Catarina,"

left to private rather than royal enterprise. Its founders were restless Paulistas, lured to the southern lands by the possibilities of mineral wealth, free lands for farms and ranches, and escape from royal tax gatherers, justices, and recruiters. The foundations of the captaincy's three principal settlements were laid at widely separated bays between 1653 and 1684: Nossa Senhora da Graça do Rio São Francisco (1653) in the north; N. S. dos Anjos da Laguna (1684) in the south; and in the center, N. S. do Desterro (1678) situated on the western shore of Santa Catarina Island.[38] For the next few decades, however, Santa Catarina's progress was unspectacular.[39] As before formal occupation, its numerous small harbors continued to serve as havens for ships in distress and for contrabandists, pirates, and other outlaws.

With the coming of the eighteenth century, Santa Catarina assumed new economic and military importance. Laguna became the center of a clandestine cattle trade with renegade Spaniards who drove stock up from the Vaquería del Mar. The opening of a road across the plateau to São Paulo via Curitiba and Sorocaba (1727–1732) enabled the captaincy to furnish cattle, horses, and mules to the burgeoning mining communities of Minas Gerais.[40] At the same time Santa Catarina Island became an important way station for vessels plying between Colônia, Rio Grande de São Pedro, and points farther north.

Concomitant with the founding of Rio Grande (1737), Santa Catarina was brought under more direct royal control. As part of a general administrative reorganization of Brazil, both Santa Catarina and Rio Grande were detached from São Paulo and made subcaptaincies of Rio de Janeiro.[41] Desterro became the new capital [42] and

in *Anais da província de S. Pedro* (3rd ed., Rio de Janeiro, 1946), pp. 307–354. On the founding period, see also Canales, Chap. VI.

38 Considerable differences of opinion exist as to the founding dates of these communities. I have followed Canales, *loc. cit.*

39 See "Relação da diligencia que fez Manuel Gonçalves de Aguiar . . . por todos os portos do sul," April 20, 1711, and "Relação da diligencia que . . . Manuel Gonçalves de Aguiar [fez] a todos os portos do sul, desde de Santos até a Laguna . . . ," July, 1714 [sic for 1715], *ABNRJ*, XXXIX, 403–407; the "Informação dos moradores da Ilha de Santa Catharina," Jan. 25, 1715, indicates there were only 22 settlers on the island at that time. *Ibid.*, 408.

40 On the significance of this "caminho dos conventos" see Spalding, "Formação do Rio Grande do Sul (cited in n. 14 above), pp. 71–85, and João Borges Fortes, *Cristóvão Pereira—A familia Fortes* (Pôrto Alegre, 1931), *passim.*

41 In 1737 Gomes Freire de Andrada (captain-general of Rio de Janeiro, Minas Gerais, and São Paulo, 1733–1763) recommended the "utility" of having all the littoral of southern Brazil as far as Colônia administered from Rio de Janeiro. Andrada to the king, Nov. 14, 1737, cited without source in Boiteux, *Notas*, p. 206. Two clear precedents existed for this proposal: (1) Colônia had belonged to Rio de Janeiro since its founding, and (2) the port of Santos was under Rio de Janeiro from 1711 to 1720. Cartas régias, May 18 and June 6, 1711, alvará, Dec. 2, 1720, *DI*, XLVII (1929), 75–78, 94–96.

Andrada's recommendations were implemented by (1) the provisão of Aug. 11, the headquarters of a governor, an *ouvidor*,[43] and a fiscal subdivision of the parent captaincy. During the 1740s the strait and prominent points on the island were fortified and manned by a regular garrison.[44]

Still the settlement of Santa Catarina lagged. In 1749 its population was estimated at, 4,197.[45] In the same decade the Crown began to offer generous inducements to attract homesteaders from its Atlantic islands and even from foreign lands; [46] and between 1747 and 1753 some 4,000 *casais* (couples) settled in the subcaptaincy, whose population grew to between 6,000 and 7,000 by the late 1760s.[47]

1738, *ibid.*, 109–110, transferring Santa Catarina Island and Rio Grande from São Paulo to Rio de Janeiro; (2) the provisão of Jan. 4, 1742, *RIHGB*, XXIV (1861), 585–586, which placed the vila of Laguna and its *termo* (i.e., environs extending from Garoupas Bay indefinitely south) under Rio de Janeiro; while (3) the provisão of Sept. 11, 1748, *DI*, XLVII (1929), 120, declared that the governors and commandants of Colônia, Santos, Santa Catarina Island, and Rio Grande were subordinates of the captain-general of Rio de Janeiro. In 1750 Gomes Freire ordered (with or without royal authorization) the vila and termo of São Francisco du Sul detached from São Paulo and made a part of Santa Catarina. Andrada to Manuel Escudeiro Ferreira de Sousa, June 18, 1750, *ibid.*, 140. Finally, between 1748 and 1765 São Paulo was itself reduced to a *comarca* (district of Rio de Janeiro.

42 Upon recommendation of Santa Catarina's first governor, José da Silva Pais (1739–1749), Desterro was made the new capital instead of Laguna. However, his successor, Manuel Escudeiro Ferreira de Sousa (1749–1753), regarded Desterro as unsuitable, suspended work on government buildings, and laid plans to move to the mainland pending royal approval. The Court rejected his proposal, aided by the advice of Silva Pais, then in Lisbon. Later, the third governor, D. José de Melo Manuel (1753–1762), found the plans for the new capital, but not the order turning them down. His request for clarification brought a stiff note instructing him to continue the building of Desterro and adding that the Court wished to hear no more about any proposed shift of the capital. And there it remains today as headquarters for the state of Santa Catarina, but with its name changed to Florianópolis. Boiteux, pp. 207, 228–229, 231.

43 An *ouvidor* was a circuit judge whose jurisdiction and court were called an *ouvidoria*. In 1723 the ouvidoria of Paranaguá (compromising the area between Iguape and the Plata) was detached from that of São Paulo. In 1748 the headquarters of the ouvidoria was moved to Desterro, and for the balance of the period of this study, it embraced the subcaptaincies of Santa Catarina and Rio Grande.

44 Fortification of the island was recommended as early as 1711 by Manoel Gonçalves de Aguiar. See n. 39, above. The fortress of Santa Cruz (on the island of Anhatomirim), forts Santo Antônio (Raton Island) and Ponta Grossa (on a promontory of the main island facing the channel) in the straits, and fort N. S. da Conceição at the south end of the main island were built between 1740 and 1744. Boiteux, pp. 208, 212. By the late 1760s the subcaptaincy's garrison had grown from 150 to 679 men. See n. 47, below.

45 Boiteux, *Notas*, p. 216. The estimate, based upon an uncited report of Governor Silva Pais made at the end of his term, undoubtedly included persons living in Rio Grande de São Pedro, then a part of Santa Catarina.

46 For the privileges the Crown offered Roman Catholics regardless of nationality, see provisão of Aug. 9, 1749, *RIHGB*, XL:1 (1877), 215–222; Boiteux, *Notas*, pp. 224–228; and *idem*, "Açorianos e Madeirenses em Santa Catarina," *RIHGB*, CCXIX (1953), 122–169.

47 An inference based on "Informação sobre a Ilha de Santa Catarina," a report

In spite of the arrival of the newcomers, Santa Catarina continued to be one of the most sparsely occupied parts of Brazil. Its inhabitants engaged in subsistence agriculture, ranching, and fishing, and exported manioc flour (*farinha*), salted fish, fibers (for cables), and whale oil. Except for the town of Lajes (founded by Paulistas in 1766),[48] the occupied frontier did not extend inland more than a few leagues at any point.[49] By the 1770s there were only three *vilas* and a few scattered villages between Santa Catarina's northern and southern limits (Rio São Francisco do Sul to Rio Tramandaí), a distance of eighty leagues.[50] But it is fair to add that Santa Catarina might have developed more rapidly during its first century of colonization had it not been for the superior attractions offered by its sister to the south, Rio Grande de São Pedro.

Closing the Gap: The Occupation of Rio Grande [51]

Portuguese forces took formal possession of Rio Grande in 1737, after more than twenty years of investigations, proposals, and discussions. Though none of the several private offers to colonize Rio Grande materialized, they, along with recommendations by various colonial officers, constantly focused the Crown's attention upon the area.[52] But the government failed to order its occupation until it became convinced that it was both necessary and justifiable to do so. Lisbon's caution was based upon two considerations: (1) the likelihood that

---

prepared by Governor Francisco de Sousa de Menezes for Count de Azumbuja (Viceroy), Dec. 8, 1767, BNRJ, 7, 3, 47 (orig.).

48 See Chap. XVI, p. 462.

49 Sousa de Menezes to Azambuja, Dec. 8, 1767 (cited in n. 47 above); Francisco João Roscîo Xavier da Veiga Cabral da Câmara (Governor of Rio Grande), Aug. 18, 1797, *RIHGRGS*, XXVII (1947), 83.

50 Each of the three original towns had been raised to the rank of vila—Laguna in 1714, Desterro *ca.* 1726, and São Francisco do Sul at an unknown date.

51 The historiography of colonial Rio Grande de São Pedro is comparatively rich, especially for the early years. For a good, brief introduction, particularly to *ca.* 1750, see José Honório Rodrigues, *O continente do Rio Grande*. The names of three nonprofessional historians, all of them active during the 1930s but now deceased, dominate *Riograndense* historiography: Jônatas da Costa Rego Monteiro, Alfonso Aurélio Porto, and João Borges Fortes. All were prolific, and all worked with both local and national archives; unfortunately, however, they did not always clearly identify their sources, a criticism particularly applicable to Borges Fortes. Nevertheless every historian of colonial Rio Grande de São Pedro is indebted to the contributions of these three who helped to make the *RIHGRGS* the best historical journal in Brazil. Because of the number of high-quality articles and documents it continues to publish, the *RIHGRGS* has attained the stature formerly enjoyed by the *RIHGB*.

52 Except as otherwise noted, the following paragraphs are based on the excellent, though incomplete, account in Porto, *História das missões*, II, 86–100.

Spanish authorities in the Plata and in Paraguay would make reprisals, particularly against isolated Colônia do Sacramento, as soon as the Portuguese attempted to plant a colony in Rio Grande,[53] and (2) the realization that so long as eastern Rio Grande remained unoccupied, it would serve as a buffer between Spanish- and Portuguese-held territory, whereas colonization by either side would inevitably intensify Luso-Spanish rivalry for control of the Debatable Lands.

Portuguese interest in Rio Grande was at first local, then regional, and finally imperial. By 1715 the *Lagunenses* were already well acquainted with the unoccupied lands south of them. In that year the governor (capitão mor) of the port of Laguna received instructions from the captain-general of Rio de Janeiro to undertake a survey of an overland route connecting Laguna with Colônia, then about to be returned to the Portuguese for the second time. While he was making that survey,[54] the câmara of Laguna strongly urged that Rio Grande be occupied. Among the reasons that it gave for its recommendation were (1) the fertility of the area's soil and the salubrity of its climate, (2) the capaciousness of its port (the Lagoa dos Patos), (3) the (presumed) existence of gold and silver mines in the lands occupied by the Seven Missions of the Spanish Jesuits, and (4) the abundance of wild cattle roaming between the Lagoa dos Patos and the bays of Maldonado and Montevideo.[55]

Evidently, the Overseas Council bore the câmara's remarks in mind when it first recommended the occupation of Rio Grande five years later. While deliberating on the need to establish bases at Montevideo or Maldonado to buttress Colônia, the council declared that the ports of Garoupas [56] and Rio Grande (the Lagoa dos Patos) should be occupied "because those ports are so good that they are looked upon as the best of our America, and [since] their lands [contain] such an abundance of cattle and [such] palpable expectations of great riches of gold and silver mines, it is certain that if we do not occupy . . . that coast, the other nations of Europe will. . . ." [57] Nevertheless, the royal instructions ordering the expulsion of the Spaniards from Montevideo and the establishment of a Portuguese

[53] This was the specific reason for the Overseas Council's rejection of the offer of Manuel Jordão da Silva to colonize Rio Grande in 1695. *ABNRJ*, XXXIX, 227, and Porto, II, 87. Silva claimed familiarity with Rio Grande and proposed "novamente" to colonize it with Christianized Indians in return for a loan of 6,000 cruzados guaranteed by the revenues from two engenhos (sugar mills) that he owned.

[54] Francisco de Brito Peixoto to the king, Aug. 20, 1732, *DI*, XIII (1895), 203–205.

[55] Câmara of Laguna to questions posed by Manuel Gonçalves de Aguiar (sergeant major of the praça of Santos), Jan. 6, 1715, *ABNRJ*, XXXIX, 407–409.

[56] A port in Santa Catarina highly regarded by contemporaries, possibly modern Pôrto Belo.

[57] Consulta of Sept. 25, 1720, quoted in Porto, II, 88.

fort there failed to say anything about the need to occupy the Lagoa dos Patos.[58]

While the Crown procrastinated, the captains-general of São Paulo and Rio de Janeiro ordered their own investigations on the feasibility of founding a colony in the lagoon.[59] When the Conselho Ultramarino reviewed the resulting reports, it advised the king that further delay in reaching a decision on this matter might not only prejudice his claim to the unoccupied lands south of Laguna but also endanger the mines of Minas Gerais in the event that the area was occupied by a hostile power.[60] Still no action was taken.

Two years later, in 1730, the council drew up a comprehensive plan for the occupation of Rio Grande. It emphasized that the south shore of the Lagoa dos Patos ought to be fortified "since by this part we will become masters of the great plains [extending from there to] . . . the Serra do Maldonado, . . . which will not happen if we establish the colony on the north part." After detailing the composition of the proposed expedition and suggesting the name of a qualified person to lead it, the council urged the king to subsidize persons willing to settle in Rio Grande, as the Crown was preparing to do in order to populate Colônia and Santa Catarina. After examining the rival claims of São Paulo and Rio de Janeiro to jurisdiction over the proposed new colony, the councillors recommended that it should be made dependent upon Rio de Janeiro "like the praça of Nova Colônia," since Rio possessed greater resources than did São Paulo to support the new venture.[61] Although the council's recommendations were temporarily shelved, they are noteworthy in that they contain the essentials of the plan finally executed seven years later.

In 1736 two new proposals for the colonization of Rio Grande came

58 Carta régia of June 29, 1723, RIHGB, XXXII:1 (1869), 22–25.

59 Among these investigations was the controversial expedition of João de Magalhães, son-in-law of the capitão mor of Laguna, to the Lagoa dos Patos in 1725. Although some historians have contended that he founded a settlement there, others (including the present writer) believe that his work was merely exploratory. In 1721 the captain-general of Rio de Janeiro sent a significant questionnaire to Gonçalves de Aguiar, the well-informed sergeant major of Santos. To question 21, "Em que parte se pode fazer uma povoação conveniente assim para se aproveitar de toda a utilidade, como para o augmento da nova Colônia, e promptidão para os seus soccorros, assim, dentro deste Porto do Rio Grande como fóra da Costa do Mar, ou perto da Ilha da Santa Catarina," Aguiar replied that both the Lagoa dos Patos and Santa Catarina Island should be effectively occupied. Aguiar to Antônio de Brito e Menezes, Santos, Aug. 26, 1721, RIHGRGS, IX, 359. The captain-general of Rio de Janeiro reported in 1728 that thirty Portuguese and sixty Spaniards, "gente criminosa em Buenos Aires e bandoleiros," were living around the Lagoa dos Patos; this remark hardly supports Canales' statement that Rio Grande was "already heavily populated" at this time. Luís Vahia Monteiro to the king, Aug. 3, 1728, quoted in Porto, II, 93; cf. Canales, Chap. IX.

60 Consulta of Nov. 26, 1728, quoted in Porto, II, 89–90.

61 Consulta of Apr. 19, 1730, quoted ibid., II, 90–92.

before the Overseas Council. The first concerned the offer of a syndicate in Rio de Janeiro to establish colonies in the unoccupied borderlands. The council observed that there appeared to be two alternatives for the occupation of the area: it could be carried out either by the proposed company or by expenditures from the royal treasury, "which would make the execution of this project more prompt." In either case the colonists would need protection, since it was likely that the Spanish would dispute control of Rio Grande. The council again suggested that homesteaders be sent from the Atlantic islands to populate Rio Grande and other points along the coast, "because the continuation of these settlements will be the best means of deciding the question of limits . . . between the two crowns." [62]

The second offer came from an individual entrepreneur who wanted to colonize Rio Grande in return for the right to make land grants and collect certain fees there. His scheme was approved by José da Silva Pais, interim governor of Rio de Janeiro, but its execution was blocked by Gomes Freire de Andrada, his superior.[63] The matter was referred to the Overseas Council, which managed to save the face of both officers in rendering its opinion: Gomes Freire had acted correctly in staying the project since he believed that the proposed colony lay within territory disputed by Spain and Portugal. There was no evidence that Spain had laid claim to lands more than a few leagues north of Cape Santa María,[64] but since she could not be trusted, the council recommended that Colônia's garrison be augmented so that in the event that the Castilians marched against the new settlement, Montevideo could be captured by way of retaliation. Once again the council urged that the south shore of the Lagoa dos Patos be occupied to facilitate exploitation of the "quantity of cattle and horses" grazing in its vicinity.[65]

The final decision to plant the Portuguese flag in Rio Grande came as a direct consequence of the outbreak of an undeclared war between Spanish and Portuguese forces in the Rio de la Plata.[66] After

[62] Consulta of Jan. 26, 1736, quoted *ibid.*, II, 94.

[63] Andrada was then on an inspection tour of Minas Gerais.

[64] The council's reasoning is both interesting and revealing: "Como, porém este sítio não está comprehendido no território que os Castelhanos nos contestão, pois no parecer que seus cosmógraphos dérão, em virtude do tractado provisional de 7 de maio de 1681, não estendião a sua pretensão mais que até a distância de 38 léguas ao norte do cabo de Santa Mariá e o Rio de São Pedro fica em distância de 60 léguas do mesmo Cabo, para a nossa parte não pode esta consideração embaraçar o estabelecimento desta colônia. . . ."

[65] Consulta of Jan. 28, 1736, *ABNRJ*, XLVI, 233–235; also quoted in Porto, II, 96–99, where the date is omitted.

[66] For the precipitating diplomatic incidents, see Canales, Chap. IX, n. 45. In April 1735 Spanish Prime Minister Don José Patiño notified the Governor of Buenos Aires that war was imminent and ordered him to anticipate its outbreak by capturing all Portuguese vessels in the Plata and by seizing Colônia. Patiño to Miguel

learning that the governor of Buenos Aires was seizing Portuguese ships and was preparing to besiege Colônia, Lisbon responded by ordering the expulsion of the Castilians from Montevideo and the fortification of the entrance to the Lagoa dos Patos.[67]

Though the Montevideo project badly misfired,[68] the mission of Brigadier José da Silva Pais to Rio Grande was crowned with success.[69] His orders were to assure Portuguese possession of the Lagoa dos Patos by fortifying key positions around it. Upon his arrival on February 19, 1737, the brigadier found that a substantial number of settlers from Laguna had already taken up lands on the peninsula separating the lagoon from the Atlantic Ocean and around the river mouths at the north end of the lagoon.[70] To protect these settlers Silva Pais planted the fort of Jesus-Maria-José on a landspit extending from the south shore of the entrance channel some two leagues above the bar (precisely as the Conselho Ultramarino had recommended seven years earlier). Besides building several small earthworks to guard approaches to the presídio, Silva Pais selected sites for two royal stock farms (estâncias) to be supplied with wild cattle and horses selected from the mission ranches to the west.[71] Such animals were intended for the use of Rio Grande's garrison, which was soon

---

Salcedo, April 17, 1735, quoted in Rego Monteiro, Colônia, II, 217–218. For subsequent operations in the Plata see ibid., II, 217–331, and Canales, Chap. IX. Formal hostilities were averted by the mediation of France, England, and the Netherlands; and an armistice was signed at Paris on March 15, 1737. For the Spanish and Portuguese texts see CTLA, II, 210–224.

[67] Carta régia, Mar. 24, 1736, RIHGRGS, XXVIII (1948), 4–6, and Carta régia, Apr. 17, 1736, RIHGB, XXXII:1 (1869), 42–45. The second is an amplifying instruction that cautions that in the event that the Portuguese ships had already been restored and the Spanish had not actually menaced Colônia, no attempt should be made to take Montevideo. It stressed, however, that the occupation of Rio Grande should proceed in any case, though it could be delayed until essential preparations for the expedition had been completed.

[68] See Canales, Chap. IX.

[69] The most comprehensive discussion of Silva Pais' accomplishments in Rio Grande is João Borges Fortes, "O Brigadeiro José da Silva Paes e a fundação do Rio Grande," RIHGRGS, XIII (1933), 3–119, which is based upon archival investigations. See also José Carlos Canales, "Rio Grande do Sul, Keystone of Platine Trade and Communications," V Colóquio Internacional de Estudos Luso-Brasileiros, Actas, II (Coimbra, 1965), 5–25.

[70] Some were squatters, but others had already procured formal land deeds from Gomes Freire de Andrada, captain-general of Rio de Janeiro. Squatters evidently began to occupy the margins of the Lagoa dos Patos in the late twenties. The first sesmarias (formal land grants) were issued in 1733. João Borges Fortes, Rio Grande de São Pedro (Povoamento e conquista) (Rio de Janeiro, 1941), pp. 24–44.

[71] One, the estância of Torotama, was situated on the west side of the Lagoa dos Patos about three leagues from the presidio. The other, the estância of Bojurú, was located twelve leagues up the peninsula. In June, 1738, Silva Pais reported that the estâncias already contained 1,500 mares and more than 2,500 head of cattle, and that he hoped eventually to have 45,000 head of livestock in them. To Gomes Freire de Andrada, June 18, 1738, quoted in Borges Fortes, "O Brigadeiro," p. 74. By the 1770s these stock farms had so deteriorated through neglect and thefts that royal officials in Rio Grande urged that they be sold.

to include a company of dragoons, the nucleus of the *Riograndense* mounted constabulary.[72] To shield the new colony from attacks launched from Spanish positions in the Plata, Silva Pais marched forty leagues down the narrow strip of land separating Lagoas Mangueira and Mirim,[73] and erected fort São Miguel on a low hill immediately south of the larger of these two lagoons. After making provision for the distribution of lands to future colonists [74] and for the administration of the new colony by a military regime (*commandância militar*),[75] the brigadier returned to Rio de Janeiro, confident that the colony he had organized would have an important future.[76]

Silva Pais' optimism was justified. As the fame of Rio Grande's fertile lands, flourishing flora, and limitless herds of unclaimed livestock spread, Brazilians flocked to the promised land from Santa Catarina, Minas Gerais, São Paulo, Rio de Janeiro, Bahia,[77] and even Colônia.[78] The Azores, too, contributed their sons and daugh-

[72] In 1742, three years after the dragoons were formed, they rose in revolt because of ill-treatment by their officers and lack of pay. After their commander pardoned them, Gomes Freire ratified his action on the ground that he did not have troops available to send to punish them! Porto, II, 148–150.

[73] Borges Fortes plausibly contends that it was while on this trip that Silva Pais made the initial discovery of Lagoa Mirim. "O Brigadeiro," pp. 88–91; see also the "carta de todo o terreno comprehendido desde a barra do Rio Grande de S. Pedro a the Castilhos Pequeno . . . 1737," *ibid.*, between pp. 56 and 57. An examination of other early maps of the area shows that all omitted the Lagoa Mirim until *ca.* 1750. See, e.g., Guillermo Furlong Cardiff, S.J., comp., "Cartografía jesuítica del Río de la Plata," *Publicaciones del Instituto de Investigaciones Históricas*, LXXI, *passim.*

[74] Gomes Freire cautioned Silva Pais not to make land grants "situadas da parte do Norte [i.e., on the peninsula] . . . pois são até agora pertencentes ao governo de S. Paulo que, posto para esta parte estivesse ainda incerto, sem dúvida pertence áquele govêrno até o Rio menos a nova fortaleza que como fica sendo parte da fortificação que S.M. põe debaixo da ordem êste govêrno se há de conservar por êle até real resolução a qual nos determinará também a decisão de êsse território." Mar. 12 [1737?], quoted in Borges Fortes, "O Brigadeiro," p. 82.

[75] From 1739 to 1760 Rio Grande was ruled by a military commander subordinate to the governor of Santa Catarina, who, in turn, was responsible to the captain-general of Rio de Janeiro. By the carta régia of Sept. 9, 1760, Rio Grande was detached from Santa Catarina and was given a governor equal in status to his colleagues at Desterro. *RIHGB*, XL:1 (1877), 228–229. Father G. J. Pauwels, S.J., has argued, wrongly I think, that the governors of Rio Grande enjoyed more independence from Rio de Janeiro than did their brother officers at Desterro. There is nothing in the correspondence between the governors and the viceroys of Rio de Janeiro from 1763 to 1789 to support such an assertion.

[76] E.g., Silva Pais to Gomes Freire, June 21, 1737, quoted in Borges Fortes, "O Brigadeiro," pp. 38–39.

[77] Controversies continue to exist as to the relative contributions of each area to the early settlement of Rio Grande. José Honório Rodrigues, for instance, proud Carioca that he is, insists that Rio de Janeiro's share was particularly large, but his evidence is not especially impressive. *O continente*, pp. 35–36.

[78] While a few families emigrated da Colônia after the rigorous siege of 1735–1737, a much larger number came after the fall of the praça in 1777. According to Bettâmio (see n. 87, below) a majority of the inhabitants of the vila of Rio Grande de São Pedro in 1780 were refugees from the Platine outpost.

ters to the new colony, though in smaller proportions than they did to Santa Catarina.[79] By 1780 there were more than 18,000 persons, 5,102 of them Negro slaves, living in the new captaincy.[80] Within less than two generations Rio Grande had become more than twice as populous as Santa Catarina.

By this time the gaúcho landscape was dotted with numerous small settlements. Some, like Rio Grande de São Pedro, the captaincy's first vila and original capital,[81] and Rio Pardo, the guardian of the frontier, grew under the protection of presídios. Others, such as Viamão and São Luís de Mostardas, developed around parish chapels; while still others, including Santo Antônio da Patrulha, sprang up at prominent river crossings where interior customs posts (registros) were situated. Geography also influenced the locations of the small port of São José do Norte on the peninsula opposite Rio Grande and the interfluvial town of Pôrto Alegre, the captaincy's third and permanent capital.[82]

But town dwellers were distinctly in the minority in eighteenth-century Rio Grande, most of whose inhabitants lived on isolated plots (datas) or on large ranches (estâncias).[83] Their homes consisted of sparsely furnished, windowless cabins (cabanas) with only a rawhide curtain at the doorway to keep out inclement weather and inquisitive animals and human beings. Their culture was typified by the three c's, o churrasco, o chimarrão, and o cavalo—barbecued beef, bitter mate tea, and the horse. The last was indispensable for rounding up untamed cattle for food and hides for export. Stockraising, or more properly a colheita dos campos, to coin a phrase,[84] was regarded with

[79] João Borges Fortes, Casais, passim.

[80] "Mapa das freguesias e moradores de ambos os sexos com declaração das diferentes condições e idades com que se achão em 7 de outubro de 1780," BNRJ, I-5, 4, 9, where it is appended to a "Mappa geográfica do Rio Grande . . . ," following f. 106ʳ. The covering letter, Sebastião Xavier de Veiga Cabral da Câmara (Governor of Rio Grande) to Luís de Vasconcelos e Sousa (Viceroy of Rio de Janeiro), Oct. 11, 1780, fols. 81ᵛ–82ʳ, gives no hint as to how the census was compiled, but it was evidently taken from parish registers since it omits children under age seven (i.e., the so-called age of reason). Nor are Indians, even Christian Indians, included. The census lists the rolls of fourteen parishes with a total of 17,923 [sic for 17,903] inhabitants. It is published in Jônatas da Costa Rego Monteiro, Dominação espanhola no Rio Grande do Sul, 1763–1777 (Rio de Janeiro, 1937), Appendix 23, but without full information as to source.

[81] I.e., from 1760 to 1763, when the vila was captured by the Spanish and the capital was transferred to Viamão.

[82] For a useful, if unimaginative, discussion, see Paranhos Antunes, "Origens dos primeiros núcleos urbanos no Rio-Grande-do-Sul (municipalismo)," Anais do segundo congresso de historia e geografia sul rio-grandense, II (Pôrto Alegre, 1937), 359–374.

[83] The estâncias derived from sesmaria grants. For the distinction between the size of datas and sesmarias see Borges Fortes, Casais, pp. 131–132.

[84] One suggested by Caio Prado's well-known term a colheita da floresta, that is, the harvesting of the forest, the gathering of forest products without undertaking any deliberate effort to encourage or regulate their growth. In the sense used

more favor than crop growing, a fact reflected in Rio Grande's dependence on Santa Catarina and Rio de Janeiro for manioc flour.[85]

Forty years after Portuguese colonization began, the rude pastoral society of Rio Grande revealed some of the characteristics common to the inhabitants of the Spanish pampa and to those of the more familiar cattle frontier of the United States. Land grabbing and swindling were frequent occurrances. Disputes were often settled by brawling, knife-play, and the use of firearms. Army deserters, felons, and other miscreants found asylum in homes of sympathetic citizens in spite of severe penalties for such hospitality. It was a society where the evidence of the infidelity of the captaincy's leading citizen could be casually recorded in the parish register,[86] and one where offers to participate in rustling cattle from the Spanish mission estâncias—the famous *corridas*—and in smuggling ventures were considered sporting propositions, as they are to this day. No wonder a veteran governor stated that one of his most urgent needs was a stout, escape-proof jail.[87]

Six months after arriving in Rio Grande, José da Silva Pais made some extremely interesting remarks concerning the new colony's potential value to Portugal. They were based on his observations there and on his earlier experience in the Plata during the abortive attack on Montevideo. His conclusion: "I am convinced that it is much better to keep Rio Grande than Montevideo [or] even Colônia because it is contiguous with our territory [*continente*]. . . . If it becomes a question of abandoning this or that presídio [i. e., Colônia], I would

---

here, a *colheita dos campos* refers to the practice of contemporary Riograndenses, Orientales, and Argentines of permitting stock to breed indiscriminately and slaughtering animals whenever the need or desire arose.

[85] Because of its cool climate and not infrequent frosts, Rio Grande lies beyond the limits tolerated by manioc. Beginning with administration of the Marquis of Lavradio, it became a significant producer of wheat. See Chap. XIII, pp. 363–364.

[86] The entry reads "Eufrazia, filha natural do Mestre-de-Campo André Ribeiro Coutinho e de Ana Maria da Conceição, chamada a Mineira, casada com Manuel de Almeida. O dito Mestre-de-Campo é casado em Lisboa. Padrinhos licenciado Sebastião José de Carvalho [future Marquis of Pombal] e a sua mulher D. Maria de Oliveira." Porto, II, 153, n. 20. As Porto writes, Ribeiro Coutinho left "more than a memory" in Rio Grande!

[87] Two valuable contemporary sources which contain incidental references to society in Rio Grande are Sebastião Francisco Bettâmio, "Notícia particular do continente do Rio Grande do Sul" (1780), *RIHGB*, XXI (1858), 239–299, and Francisco João Roscîo, "Compêndio noticioso do continente do Rio Grande de São Pedro" (1781), *RIHGRGS*, XXVII:1 (1947), 47–84. The most remarkable social document on the period is "Reflexões sobre o estado actual do continente do Rio Grande de S. Pedro," *RIHGB*, XLI:1, 251–261, written in 1783 by Governor Veiga Cabral da Câmara. To the present writer's knowledge, this source has never been utilized by any Brazilian historian, perhaps because of the adverse picture it paints of gaúcho life at the time.

be in favor of giving up the latter in order to retain and improve [Rio Grande] . . . , since the same advantages can be reaped from here as from [there] . . . and at considerably less expense. . . ." [88] Whether or not these reflections were transmitted to Lisbon, they expressed a conviction soon to be shared by prominent Portuguese leaders on both sides of the Atlantic. The retention and expansion of Rio Grande became the cardinal aims of Portugal's Platine policy, objectives which Spain bitterly contested both in Europe and in America.

[88] Silva Pais to Gomes Freire, Aug. 20, 1737, quoted in Borges Fortes, "O Brigadeiro," p. 39.

IV

Diplomacy and War, 1494-1769

Two THEMES that dominated the history of the Debatable Lands from the beginning were diplomacy and war. Even before their discovery, the borderlands were included in the first agreement between Spain and Portugal concerning the division of the New World, the Treaty of Tordesillas (1494). Although the two Iberian powers subsequently disagreed upon interpretations of the terms of that document, their differences remained inconsequential until the founding of Colônia (1680), which initiated the military phase of the region's history. Throughout the eighteenth century the Debatable Lands figured prominently in every war fought between Spain and Portugal and in all major diplomatic negotiations to which both were parties.

Early Luso-Spanish Negotiations

As already intimated, Luso-Spanish Platine rivalry was an unintended by-product of the famous treaty signed at Tordesillas in 1494. That venerable agreement was an attempt by the two Iberian powers to compromise their claims to the new lands then being discovered in the Atlantic. It provided that all territories west of a meridian drawn 370 leagues west of the Cape Verde Islands would be Spain's, those to the east, Portugal's.[1] However, the two nations failed to stipulate the precise length of a league intended for the purposes of such a calculation and the particular island within the Cape Verde group that would serve as a bench mark for scribing the polar line. These ambiguities, as well as ignorance of the contours of American geography and the absence of reliable instruments for determining longitude prior to the late seventeenth century, enabled writers of both nations

---

[1] For an introduction to the literature see Charles E. Nowell, "The Treaty of Tordesillas and the Diplomatic Background of American History," in *Greater America: Essays in Honor of Herbert Eugene Bolton* (Berkeley-Los Angeles, 1945), pp. 1–18.

to reach widely divergent conclusions as to where the demarcation line intersected the South American continent. This was especially the case with the southern intercept, for Spanish writers believed that it occurred near the Portuguese port of São Vicente, next to the present port of Santos, while Lusitanian authors contended that it was somewhere in the Platine estuary, if not further south.[2]

Such differences of opinion remained academic until Portugal staked her claim to the north bank of the Plata by establishing Colônia do Sacramento.[3] In the diplomatic discussions that followed the first expulsion of Portuguese forces from that outpost, each nation insisted that Colônia lay within its sector in conformity with the Tordesillas agreement. Ultimately, Spain restored the base to Portugal pending a determination of the question of sovereignty by a joint conference of specialists. Commissioners for each power then drew up briefs studded with authorities sustaining the claims of their respective monarchs; but, not surprisingly, the conference failed to produce a settlement. The problem was then submitted to Rome for arbitration, but no papal decision was ever reached.[4]

While the Portuguese continued to hold Colônia, they found themselves confined by blockading Spanish forces to an area measured by the trajectory of a twenty-four-pound shot from the entrepôt's main square. Though apparently contrived by local Spanish authorities to justify their armed vigilance over the praça, the formula of the *tiro de cañón* became the official Spanish definition of Colônia's limits by 1716.[5]

In the meantime a series of treaties signed in 1701, 1703, and 1715 transformed Portugal's temporary claim to Colônia into a permanent title. In 1701 the French pretender to the vacant Spanish throne offered Portugal a clear title to the Platine outpost in exchange for

---

[2] E.g., according to a sixteenth-century Portuguese chronicler, Dr. Pedro Nunes, royal cosmographer of King Sebastião, believed that Portuguese territory ran as far south as the gulf of San Matías. Gabriel Soares de Sousa, *Tratado descriptivo do Brasil em 1587* (2nd ed., Rio de Janeiro, 1879), p. 100. Various interpretations of Spanish and Portuguese authorities were summarized in the briefs presented at the conference of Elvas and Badajoz (1681). See n. 4, below.

[3] A fundamental diplomatic study of the Colônia question which includes many essential documents from Spanish archives is Antonio Bermejo de la Rica, *La Colonia del Sacramento: su origen, desenvolvimiento y vicisitudes de su historia* (Toledo, 1920), to which Luís Ferrand de Alemeida, *A diplomacia portuguesa e os limitis meridionais do Brasil*, I (*1493–1700*) (Coimbra, 1957), is an important supplement.

[4] Preliminary treaty of May 5, 1681, Bermejo de la Rica, pp. 83–90; for a detailed discussion of the treaty and the subsequent conference of Elvas and Badajoz see Mario Rodríguez, "Colônia do Sacramento," pp. 277–285.

[5] On the origins of this concept see *idem*, "Dom Pedro of Braganza and Colônia do Sacramento, 1680–1705," *HAHR*, XXXVIII, 199. The doctrine was confirmed by royal cédulas in 1716, 1724, 1734, and 1736. *CTLA*, II, 164–165, n. 1.

her neutrality during the impending struggle over the Spanish succession.[6] Portugal's acceptance was nullified two years later when she joined the Grand Alliance, which also guaranteed her Platine title.[7] Spain responded by declaring war against Portugal, and in 1705 Colônia fell for the second time to Spanish troops.[8]

In the general European settlement at Utrecht (1713–1715) concluding the War of the Spanish Succession, Spain was obliged to hand Colônia back to Portugal and to recognize her right of sovereignty over the outpost. That recognition was hedged by two stipulations: (1) Portugal promised not to use the base to engage in commerce with Spanish subjects or to permit foreigners to do so; and (2) she agreed to cede Colônia to Spain if offered a satisfactory equivalent for it.[9] While official Portuguese circles had long debated the merits of retaining Colônia,[10] it is doubtful whether the government of João V was seriously inclined to give up the praça, for that would have been tantamount to abandoning Portugal's claim to the north bank of the Plata. As it turned out, Lisbon declared unacceptable the alternatives Madrid proposed,[11] and Portuguese forces took possession of Colônia again in 1716. Less than half a century later, when the idea of a quid pro quo was revived, the Portuguese Court found it more attractive.

[6] Treaty of Alfonza, June 18, 1701, summarized in Bermejo de la Rica, pp. 133–135.

[7] I.e., by the Methuen treaties of 1703. See Sir Richard Lodge, "The Treaties of 1703," Edgar Prestage, ed., *Chapters in Anglo-Portuguese Relations* (Watford, England), pp. 152–169.

[8] The siege and capture of Colônia are described in the monographs cited above in Chap. III, n. 24.

[9] Treaty of Utrecht, Feb. 6, 1715, arts. 6 and 7, *CTLA*, II, 167–177.

[10] For early Portuguese debate on the value of retaining Colônia, see Rodríguez, "Dom Pedro of Braganza," pp. 202–204.

[11] The equivalents suggested to Lisbon by the Spanish minister included: (1) the cession to Portugal of a Galician estuary for Portuguese ships needing a refuge from bad weather; (2) the right of two Portuguese ships to trade annually with Buenos Aires, exchanging Brazilian products for Platine commodities, and including the right to take out silver; (3) the annual payment of three hundred horses or mules to the king of Portugal. Marquês of Capecelatro to João V, Lisbon, Sept. 22, 1716, Bermejo de la Rica, pp. 153–155; see also pp. 32–34. The influential Duke of Cadaval advised João V against acceptance of the second proposal, contending that there would be no advantage to Portugal in being able to send Brazilian tobacco and sugar to Buenos Aires for dried meats and hides when Colônia could furnish far more of the latter two. *Parecer* of Aug. 21, 1716, Virgínia Rau and Maria Fernanda Gomes da Silva, eds., *Os manuscritos de Cadaval*, II, 183–184.

The Treaty of Madrid—a Compromise
That Failed [12]

In 1737, when the Iberian powers called off their undeclared war in the Plata,[13] they agreed to make a new attempt to settle their differences in America.[14] That pledge was redeemed thirteen years later when the Treaty of Limits was signed, climaxing three years of remarkable negotiations between the two Courts.[15] Those discussions began shortly after the accession to the Spanish throne of peace-loving Ferdinand VI (1746–1759) and his Portuguese wife Maria Bárbara, who favored permanent reconciliation with Portugal. To that end D. José de Carvajal y Lencastre, President of the Council of the Indies and chief minister of Spain, renewed his government's offer to exchange Colônia for a suitable equivalent.

There were several very important motives behind Carvajal's overture. He was convinced that the entrepôt was responsible for the loss of large quantities of badly needed Peruvian silver, notwithstanding all the surveillance measures that Spain could devise to prevent illicit commerce between her colonials and the praça.[16] He also felt that, if Spain were to develop the full economic resources of her Platine colonies, Portuguese competition for those resources must be eliminated. The Spanish minister was likewise anxious to remove a major cause of continual strife between the Iberian kingdoms, since war with Portugal always meant the likelihood of a costly conflict with Great Britain, the principal foe of Spain and the ally of Portugal.[17]

---

[12] The latest contribution to a growing shelf of literature on the ill-fated Treaty of 1750 is Father Wilhelm Kratz, S.J., *El tratado hispano-portugués de límites de 1750 y sus consequencias* . . . (Institutem Historicum SI, Biblioteca Instituti Historici S.I.; Rome, 1954), V, which provides a good introduction to the extensive published and archival sources and to the abundant secondary material. Though purporting to be an objective study, the work is primarily devoted to proving (1) that the treaty was essentially bad and (2) that the Society of Jesus was not responsible for its failure. The work is vitiated by (1) its anti-Portuguese bias, (2) its superficial explanation of the background to the treaty, and (3) its painful style.

[13] See above, Chap. III, n. 66.

[14] Convention of Paris, Mar. 15, 1737, *CTLA*, II, 210–224, giving Spanish and Portuguese texts.

[15] The fundamental published source for these negotiations is Jaime Cortesão, ed., *Alexandre de Gusmão e o Tratado de Madrid (1750)*, IV:1–2 *Negociações* (Rio de Janeiro, 1953), which makes available for the first time the largest part of the relevant Luso-Spanish correspondence between 1746 and 1750.

[16] See Alexandre de Gusmão, [Discourse on the Treaty of 1750], *ibid.*, p. 529.

[17] Carvajal to D. Ricardo Wall (Spanish ambassador to Britain), May 20, 1751; *idem*, secret instruction to Marquis of Valdelirios, 1751; and *idem* to Conde de Perelada (new Spanish ambassador to Lisbon), May 30, 1753, Bermejo de la Rica,

Carvajal's proposal elicited a favorable response from Lisbon, where Alexandre de Gusmão, a long-time royal adviser and an experienced diplomat, became the chief Portuguese architect of the resulting treaty.[18] An astute student of Brazilian history and geography, Santos-born Gusmão [19] sensed the far-reaching advantages his nation stood to gain from an accommodation with Spain. But Gusmão wanted to go beyond the mere settlement of the Colônia problem. Candidly admitting that the Portuguese had repeatedly trespassed on the Spanish side of the Tordesillas line, he believed that it was time to abandon that unworkable agreement and to devise a new treaty of limits in accord with each nation's de facto possessions on the South American continent. He was quite willing to give up Colônia, for he contended that Spain would never allow Portugal to expand her beachhead to link it with the rest of Brazil, and that the base had not justified the king's heavy expenses necessary to sustain it.[20] He conceded that by surrendering the entrepôt Portugal would be renouncing her claims to the Plata, but he was convinced that Brazil's real future lay not in the Plata but in the development of the Amazon. Moreover, he agreed with José da Silva Pais [21] that the new colony of Rio Grande promised all of Colônia's advantages without its inherent disadvantages. Yet the councillor considered Portugal's title to Rio Grande doubtful,[22] and feared that her hold on the cattle-rich

---

Colonia del Sacramento, pp. 163–164, 174–179, and 188–198. For further analyses of Carvajal's objectives, see *ibid.*, pp. 41–48, and J. O. Lindsay, "The Western Mediterranean and Italy," in *The New Cambridge Modern History*, VII (Cambridge, 1957), pp. 285–286.

[18] For the behind-the-scenes role of Gusmão in the negotiations, see Cortesão, IV:1, 7–8.

[19] Gusmão (1695–1753) was educated at the Jesuit college of Cachoeira (Bahia) and at the University of Coimbra. He served as a diplomatic agent to Rome from 1720 to 1728, and two years later became private secretary to the king. He was subsequently named to the Overseas Council and to the Royal Academy. Besides being the author of important legislation pertaining to Brazil and of important instructions to the diplomatic corps of Portugal, he wrote Classical Latin epigrams and at least three opera librettos. Jaime Cortesão, "Alexandre de Gusmão e o Tratado de Madrí," *Revista de história*, I (São Paulo, 1950), 437–452.

[20] Shortly after the treaty was signed, the Spanish ambassador to Lisbon reported a most interesting conversation with "un Ministro de los más confidenciales de esta Corte" who had been closely connected with the treaty negotiations. His source told him that it was calculated that 600,000 cruzados' worth of merchandise (primarily of foreign origin) was sent to Colônia annually; and that while the king received only 150,000 cruzados in revenues from the entrepôt each year, his expenses there ran to 470,000. Duke of Sotomayor to Carvajal, Lisbon, 1752, Bermejo de la Rica, pp. 184–188, and reprinted in *CB*, II, 105–107. It seems almost certain that the ambassador's informant was Gusmão, for the views expressed were consistent with his remarks in the papers cited in n. 35, below.

[21] See above, Chap. III, pp. 81–82. Significantly, Silva Pais returned to Lisbon from Santa Catarina on the eve of the signing of the agreement.

[22] Gusmão believed that the line of demarcation extended only to the entrance to the Lagoa dos Patos.

temperate land, which he regarded as the logical complement to the mining zone of central Brazil, would remain precarious so long as it was limited to the littoral. What Rio Grande needed, Gusmão concluded, was *Lebensraum*. Therefore, in a counterproposal, he indicated Portugal's willingness to exchange Colônia for territory north of the Rio Negro in the Amazon and east of the Uruguay in Rio Grande.[23]

That was a higher price for Colônia than Carvajal had been prepared to pay.[24] Moreover, since the territory Gusmão coveted in Rio Grande included the flourishing Seven Missions, the Spanish minister realized that the Society of Jesus and its allies would vigorously oppose their cession to Portugal. But so great was Madrid's desire to end the vexing Colônia problem that the Spanish government finally conceded most of Lisbon's demands after the latter made certain concessions, particularly in the Amazon Valley.[25]

The Treaty of Madrid, the first comprehensive agreement between Spain and Portugal concerning their overseas possessions since the Tordesillas settlement, was signed on January 13, 1750. By specifically abrogating all earlier agreements, the two nations abandoned the unworkable Tordesillas formula and adopted instead the principle of *uti possidetis;* effective possession rather than prior discovery or earlier treaty rights thus became the primary basis for determining their common colonial boundaries. However, four key articles, the heart of the new treaty, constituted exceptions to this criterion. By Articles XIII and XV Portugal renounced all claims to Colônia and other Platine lands, while in articles XIV and XVI Spain relinquished the triangle formed by the Ibicuí and Uruguay rivers and promised to evacuate the Jesuits and Indian neophytes from the ceded territory.[26] The accepted limits between Portuguese and Spanish territory in South America were outlined on the famous "Map of the Courts." [27] Beginning at Mount Castillos Grande in the Banda Oriental, the recognized boundary extended along various stream banks and ridge summits north to the middle of the Amazon Valley. To survey the new line, two joint commissions were created, one to begin its work at

23 Cortesão, "Alexandre de Gusmão," pp. 447–449, and Gusmão's defenses cited n. 35, below.

24 He originally offered 150,000 pesos for the outpost. "Tréplica" of Carvajal to Visconde da Vila Nova de Cerveira, Nov. 1748, Cortesão, *Negociações,* IV:1, 218.

25 Portugal also renounced all claims to the Philippine Islands. Treaty of Limits, Jan. 13, 1750, Art. 2. Among other places, the treaty is published in *CTLA,* II, 244–260.

26 By contrast, the Colônia settlers and the Indians of territories to be exchanged in the Amazon had the option of remaining in their homes or moving to other lands belonging to their sovereign. Arts. 15–16.

27 A facsimile of the original of this 1749 map is reproduced in *ABNRJ,* LII, facing p. 16.

the confluence of the Rio Negro and the Amazon, the other to start at Castillos.[28] In a unique reversal of the seventeenth-century doctrine of "no peace beyond the line," often articulated by Spain's European rivals, the two powers declared that their American colonies would always remain at peace toward one another regardless of the status of their mother countries in Europe.[29]

The Treaty of Limits, one of the most celebrated documents of its time, was also one of the most bitterly criticized.[30] As soon as its secretly drafted terms became known, Spanish and Portuguese leaders at home and abroad condemned the agreement as prejudicial to the best interests of their respective nations. The powerful Jesuit Order, which stood most to lose by the treaty, was understandably reluctant to give up the fruits of many years of labor. Though officially submissive to the will of Ferdinand VI, the Society nonetheless carried its opposition to the pact in appeals to the highest colonial and Peninsular civil and ecclesiastical authorities, many of whom subscribed to its point of view.[31] The Black Robes contended that the accord was contrary to the spiritual and temporal interests of the Crown, that it was unchristian to expect the loyal Guaraní to give up their homes, that the aborigines would fight before doing so voluntarily, and that the acquisition of the missions would put the Portuguese in dangerous proximity to the silver of Potosí.[32]

Portuguese opponents of the treaty also focused their attention upon the exchange provisions. The Lisbon business community, doubtless reflecting the views of British commercial interests who en-

[28] Concerning the northern commissioners, see n. 37, below.

[29] Art. 21. Article 23 provided that the exchange of Colônia for the missions would be made within one year. When it proved impossible to organize and dispatch the commissions within that time, the period was extended by one of several supplemental agreements signed at Madrid, Jan. 13, 1751, including one of detailed instructions to the commissioners. They are published in *CTLA*, II, 261–290, and in *CB*, II, 51–64.

[30] The controversy has persisted to the present. Brazilian writers from Capistrano de Abreu to José Honório Rodrigues have viewed the treaty as an honorable and essentially just compromise. On the other hand, Argentine, Uruguayan, and Colombian historians such as Barba, Ravignani, Lobo, Zeballos, and Bauzá have ridiculed the agreement as a shameful Spanish "sellout" to Portugal. They have been effectively answered by Spanish defenders of Carvajal y Lencastre, notably Cánovas del Castillo and Bermejo de la Rica. See Cortesão, "Alexandre de Gusmão," p. 439, for a division of historical opinion on the treaty into four schools of thought.

[31] E.g., the representation of the province of Paraguay to Viceroy of Peru, Córdoba, Mar. 12, 1751, and cabildo of Tucumán to Marquis of Valdelirios, Apr. 6, 1752, *CB*, II, 37–51. Contemporary Luso-Spanish reaction to the treaty is discussed in detail in Kratz, pp. 30–45 and 59, n. 44.

[32] The Jesuit position is summarized *ibid.*, pp. 45–72; for a contemporary appraisal of Luso-Spanish opposition to the treaty see [Francisco Auzmendi] (director general of the secretariat of dispatch) to Ricardo Wall (Carvajal's successor), Madrid, Apr. (?), 1754, *ABNRJ*, LII, 31–40.

joyed a dominant position in the trade of Portugal and her empire, complained that they would suffer serious losses if their Platine outlet were closed. Their position was strongly supported by António Pedro de Vasconcelos, long-time governor of Colônia (1721–1749), whose memorial against the treaty[33] included some of the same arguments raised against it by Spanish remonstrants[34] and prompted Alexandre de Gusmão to draft two notable defenses of his handiwork.[35] The ex-governor's opposition to the settlement was also shared by the newly appointed Secretary of State, Sebastião José de Carvalho e Melo, who not only regretted the proposed cession of Colônia, but was skeptical of Madrid's willingness to deliver the missions, especially over Jesuit opposition. Consequently he secretly directed Gomes Freire de Andrada, chief Portuguese commissioner in the south, to retain control of the praça until the missions had been evacuated and were in his possession.[36]

With so much ill will, even the treaty's most ardent supporters must have realized that it had little prospect of being successfully carried out. Nevertheless, for seven years agents of the two nations did attempt to implement its provisions in the Debatable Lands.[37] Early in 1752 the Marquis of Valdelirios,[38] chief Spanish commissioner, arrived at Montevideo with his staff, which included Father

[33] Vasconcelos to the king, Lisbon, 1750, *CB*, II, 16–18; also published in Jônatas da Costa Rego Monteiro, *A Colônia do Sacramento*, II, 140–142, and in Cortesão, *Negociações*, IV:1, 510–515. The memorial was supposedly written just after the former governor's return to Lisbon; it is not unlikely that Secretary of State Carvalho e Melo had a hand in its drafting.

[34] Notably his argument that the abandonment of Colônia would give Spain or a foreign power (clearly meaning Great Britain) the "master key to our American treasures," the mines of central Brazil; cf. Kratz, pp. 35–36.

[35] The longer of the two is Gusmão to Vasconcelos, Sept. 8, 1751, which is published in full [?] in *CB*, II, 18–37, and as an undated excerpt in *RIHGB*, I (2nd ed., 1856), 334–344; the second is the so-called "Discurso," which seems to have been intended for public consumption. See Cortesão, *Negociações*, IV:1, 529–534.

[36] Carvalho e Melo to Gomes Freire de Andrada, Sept. 21, 1751 (two dispatches), Francisco Adolfo de Varnhagen, *História geral do Brasil*, IV, 146–155. Carvalho's opposition to the treaty was well known to the Spanish government from reports sent by its ambassador to Lisbon, who possibly obtained inside information from Carvalho's enemy, Alexandre de Gusmão. E.g., Carvajal y Lencastre to Ricardo Wall, May 20, 1751, Bermejo de la Rica, pp. 163–164.

[37] In the Amazon Valley the Portuguese commissioner, Francisco Xavier de Mendonça Furtado, Captain-General of Pará and brother of Carvalho e Melo, vainly waited for two years (1754–1756) on the Rio Negro for the arrival of his counterpart, D. José de Iturriaga. Reputedly Iturriaga was unable to locate canoes to take his staff through the llanos of Venezuela to the rendezvous.

[38] Gaspar de Munibe Garavito de León y Tellos, Marqués de Valdelirios, was born in Peru in 1711. He was regarded as an able diplomat and a skilled politician, but his reputation was greatly damaged by his lethargic conduct during the attempt to carry out the treaty. After being recalled in 1760, he became a member of the Council of State, and devoted much of his remaining years to writing. He died in 1793. *CB*, II, xx.

Lope Luis Altamirano, special delegate of the general of the Society of Jesus, charged with facilitating the transfer of the missions. The Marquis was approached by the provincial of Paraguay and by the superior of the missions, who asked for a three-year delay of the commission's activities in order to evacuate the missions and to select new sites for their 30,000 neophytes and pastures for a million head of cattle. The two Jesuit leaders emphasized the need for time and tact to convince the Guaraní of the wisdom of their sovereign's decision, warning that hasty action might precipitate a major uprising. While sympathetic to the Fathers' pleas, Valdelirios could do no more than forward them to his Court. Then he made preparations to join his counterpart, Gomes Freire, who was waiting impatiently in Rio Grande, to officiate at the marking of the southern terminus of the new frontier.[39]

In August 1752 the Spanish and Portuguese commissioners and their staffs met at Castillos Grandes, where they remained until the following December.[40] While the engineers made soundings in the harbor both nations were to share and the geographers examined the terrain in its vicinity, the commissioners discovered certain discrepancies between the actual land features and those described in their instructions. After prolonged discussion, they agreed upon certain minor modifications of the boundary, subject to confirmation by their respective Courts. Then they presided over the installation of three huge marble markers, carved with the arms of His Most Catholic and His Most Faithful Majesties. After these formalities Valdelirios returned to Montevideo and Gomes Freire proceeded to Colônia, leaving the survey party to establish the boundary as far as the Rio Ibicuí

The survey team, consisting of astronomers, cosmographers, engineers, chaplains, and physicians, slowly made its way into the interior, accompanied by dragoons. They made satisfactory progress until early 1753, when they reached Santa Tecla, an outlying cattle station belonging to the mission San Miguel. There a party of Indians barred their advance. The Guaraní stated that while the Spaniards might proceed, they would never permit their traditional enemies, the Portuguese, to do so. The survey party, under instructions to avoid hostilities, withdrew and advised their superiors that they were unable to advance further inland.

After a year and a half of procrastination, the chief commissioners agreed upon pacification of the rebels by force. The world was then

39 Kratz, pp. 66–72.

40 On the following paragraph, see "Actos celebrados no campo de Castilhos Grandes, entre os Comissários Principais de S.M. e Fidelíssima e de S.M. Católica, para regular o modo e forma de dar inteiro cumprimento ao Tratado de limites . . ." (Sept. 1 to Dec. 5, 1752), Varnhagen, IV, 162–166.

treated to the strange spectacle of 4,000 Spanish and Portuguese troops fighting together against the vassals of the king of Spain. During the initial campaign (1754) a Spanish army under Don José Andonaegui, Governor of Buenos Aires, advanced up the Uruguay toward mission San Borja, intending to cut off the Indians' supplies and reinforcements from the Paraná missions. At the same time a Portuguese force, led by Gomes Freire, proceeded up the Jacuí valley from its new base at Rio Pardo (founded in 1752) toward the northernmost missions. Bad weather, desertions, and shortages of provisions caused Andonaegui to retire, having accomplished nothing. Gomes Freire was then obliged to arrange a truce with the insurgents and to retire to Rio Pardo. The withdrawal of the Europeans encouraged the spread of the revolt, and the Guaraní made defensive preparations to repel a new invasion, including an alliance with the bellicose Charruas of the Banda Oriental.

The Guaraní War created an embarrassing situation for the Spanish government, which became convinced from field reports by Valdelirios and others that the uprising was the work of the Jesuits.[41] Aware of Carvalho e Melo's hostility toward the treaty, fearful that he might use the insurrection as a pretext to denounce the agreement, and anxious to gain possession of Colônia, Madrid named Don Pedro de Cevallos to replace the ineffective Andonaegui.[42] Cevallos was provided with an expeditionary force of 1,000 men and instructions to quell the rebellion, determine those guilty for it, and complete the exchange.[43]

By the time the new governor arrived, the Indians had finally been pacified. Late in 1755 the Spanish and Portuguese armies joined forces near the headwaters of the Rio Negro, and advanced in two columns

[41] Even Father Altamirano wrote the king's confessor that he regarded the missionaries themselves as "os causadores da rebellião e da má fama que d'ella possa resultar á Companhia." Quoted and tr. in João Lúcio de Azevedo, *O Marqués de Pombal*, p. 135. In the royal instructions to Don Pedro de Cevallos (see n. 43) the king of Spain declared, "Tengo algunas noticias de q. los PP.es Jesuitas daquella Provincia han sido y son los únicos que mueven la disobediencia de los Indios . . ." (par. 12). However, after making his own investigation, Don Pedro concluded that none of the Jesuits had inspired the rebellion, and that all had done their best to quell it. Cevallos to Ricardo Wall, San Borja, Nov. 30, 1759, Bermejo de la Rica, pp. 214–217. The charges and countercharges regarding the role of the Jesuits in the Guaraní War have been debated inconclusively by their defenders and detractors ever since. There is no question, however, but that Kratz is correct in stating that their involvement in the controversy over the Treaty of 1750 hastened the movement for their expulsion from America and the subsequent suppression of the Order.

[42] For a valuable, though incomplete biography, see Enrique M. Barba, *Don Pedro de Cevallos: governador de Buenos Aires y virrey del Río de la Plata*. See also Chap. IX, n. 1.

[43] Instrucción reservada, Jan. 31, 1756, *CB*, II, 157–163; also in Bermejo de la Rica, pp. 204–212.

north and northwest across the rolling hills of central Rio Grande toward the cluster of mission villages. At the decisive battle of Caibaté on February 10, 1756, the principal Indian commander was slain, and by June the remaining Guaraní resistance had been broken.[44]

So ended the tragic Guaraní War.[45] Its futility became apparent in the ensuing disagreements between the conquerors over the implementation of the exchange provisions. Valdelirios and Cevallos were willing to hand over the missions at once, but Gomes Freire declined to accept them until the Guaraní had been evacuated. Even after Cevallos managed to transfer the Indians across the Uruguay in August 1758, the Portuguese commander contended that their proximity to their former villages made them a menace to future Portuguese settlers. Spanish authorities insisted that there was nothing in the pacts signed by their governments stipulating the whereabouts of the neophytes after their relocation, and that the costly and lengthy proceedings in Rio Grande should be brought to a conclusion.[46] At the same time they demanded that Freire return several hundred mission Indians whom he had taken back to his headquarters at Rio Pardo. He refused, claiming that they were all volunteers and had come of their own free will.[47] Another source of dissension arose over which of two branches of the Ibicuí was the "principal origin and headwaters" designated in the treaty as part of the southern boundary between Portuguese and Spanish territories. Tired of the fruitless disputes and having pressing business back at the capital, Gomes Freire left Rio Grande late in 1758 and returned to Rio de Janeiro, where he arrived in February 1759.[48]

44 The "Manifiesto de las operaciones del Then.te Gen.l . . . Dn. Joseph de Andonaegui . . . ," July 9, 1757, CB, II, 164–214, is one of the amplest of many contemporary accounts of the war. Among the secondary accounts see F[rancisco] de Paula Cidade, Lutas, ao sul do Brasil, com os espanhóis e seus descendentes (Rio de Janeiro, 1948) , pp. 47–62.

45 The war inspired the famous epic poem "O Uraguay" (1769) by José Basílio da Gama, one of the so-called Mineiro school, who, however, did his writing in Portugal. The poem, generally accounted to be of great merit, drew this famous censure from Capistrano de Abreu: "Um poeta de mais talento que brio commetteu a indignidade de architectar um poema épico sobre esta campanha deplorável." "Sobre a Colônia do Sacramento," Ensaios e estudos (3rd ser. [Rio de Janeiro], 1938) , p. 84.

46 See the exchanges of Gomes Freire with Valdelirios and Cevallos, Apr. 4, 1757 to July 29, 1758, CB, II, 215–253.

47 Valdelirios to Gomes Freire, July 28, 1758, ibid., pp. 252–253; Freire to Cevallos, Rio de Janeiro, Jan. 29, 1762, and Cevallos to Freire, July 15, 1762, ibid., pp. 462–473.

48 Contemporary and later Spaniards contend that there was no justification for Freire's departure, but as Kratz notes he returned to Rio de Janeiro to supervise the expulsion of the Jesuits from there. On the breakdown of the treaty in the Debatable Lands, 1757–1761, see idem, pp. 217–223; also CB, II, xxvi–xxix, and José F. Fernandes Pinheiro, Anais da província de São Pedro, pp. 75–76.

The same month Don Pedro de Cevallos warned Madrid that since the end of the war Gomes Freire's conduct was part of a calculated Portuguese plan of endless procrastination. Don Pedro was convinced that the Portuguese hoped to consolidate their gains in Rio Grande, but had no intention of giving up Colônia.[49] He reported that since the treaty had been announced the entrepôt had enjoyed a flourishing contraband trade, and that far from showing any sign of preparing to hand it over, the governor had been stockpiling munitions and strengthening his fortifications.[50] Subsequently, the general complained that Portuguese soldiers were illicitly taking large numbers of cattle from the mission ranges without his consent, and that the Portuguese were engaged in warlike preparations in Rio de Janeiro, Rio Pardo, and Colônia.[51] By no means of a pacific disposition himself, Cevallos forwarded a war plan calling for the expulsion of the Lusitanians from Colônia, Rio Grande, and Santa Catarina,[52] and sent a personal representative to Madrid to acquaint his Court with the rapidly deteriorating situation in the borderlands.[53]

The news from America strengthened sentiment in Spain for the abandonment of the treaty. The deaths of Carvajal (1754), Queen Maria Bárbara (1758), and Ferdinand VI (1759) had removed the treaty's chief supporters in Spain; and the new monarch, Charles III (1759–1788), never had looked upon it with favor. Soon after ascend-

[49] Spanish authorities contributed unwittingly to the substantial contraband trade at Colônia during the mid-1750s. One of the supplemental agreements signed at Madrid in January 1751 provided that, since the Colônia inhabitants would be moving to the mission lands and had many heavy possessions that would be too difficult to transport there, they could sell them to the Spaniards if the chief Spanish commissioner approved. *CB*, II, 53–54. By an edict dated April 6, 1754, the Marquis of Valdelirios permitted inhabitants of Buenos Aires to buy "bienes muebles y raizes" in Colônia "por los precios á que se ajustassem con sus vecinos . . . exceptuando en esta venta los géneros de comercio, por que solo hán de tratar de ella con una Persona que se embiará á su tiempo por parte de SM para tomarlos de su cuenta. . . ." *CB*, II, 126–128. Cevallos reported that the Portuguese were bringing in large quantities of merchandise to Colônia from Rio de Janeiro and were disposing of them under license from the Portuguese governor declaring that they were personal effects of Colônia's inhabitants. To D. Julián de Arriaga, Oct. 3, 1758, *CB*, II, 342–343; see also Joseph Martínez Fontes (Spanish officer at the blockade camp) to Cevallos, Oct. 3, 1758, *ibid.*, pp. 412–413, and Cevallos to D. Francisco Graell (Spanish commander at the blockade camp), Sept. 8, 1759, *ibid.*, pp. 344–345.

[50] Cevallos to Wall, Feb. 20, 1759, *CB*, II, 257–260.

[51] Cevallos to D. Thomas Luís Osório (Portuguese commandant of Rio Pardo), Dec. 2, 1759, and *idem* to Arriaga, Dec. 9, 1759, *ibid.*, pp. 429–432.

[52] Cevallos to Arriaga, Sept. 15, 1759, *ibid.*, pp. 422–427. Cevallos also urged an attack on Rio de Janeiro but stated that, since it would require 7,000 to 8,000 men, it should be left to an ally of Spain (i.e., France) while Spanish forces concentrated their efforts farther south.

[53] Cevallos to Arriaga, Feb. 29, 1760, *ibid.*, pp. 336–339; see also Informe of Capitán Joseph de Molina (Cevallos' representative) to Arriaga, Jan. 14, 1761, concerning available troops and their payroll in the Plata. *Ibid.*, pp. 433–437.

ing the throne, he called for a review of the status of the agreement, then decided to abandon it.[54] In September 1760 the Spanish ambassador to Lisbon was instructed to advise the Portuguese government that his master was obliged to rescind the treaty because of the Portuguese refusal to give up Colônia.[55] Without objection, Lisbon agreed, and at Pardo (February 12, 1761) the two nations signed a brief treaty abrogating the Treaty of 1750 and restoring the *status quo ante*.[56]

The Treaty of Pardo was a tacit admission by the Iberian powers of their failure to achieve a peaceful adjustment of their dispute in the Debatable Lands. It was also a prelude to war. While it revived all the pre-1750 boundary pacts, it failed to recognize explicitly Portugal's title to Santa Catarina or coastal Rio Grande at a time when Spanish authorities for the first time were questioning Portugal's right to either captaincy.[57] Furthermore, although the 1761 agreement pledged both sides to resume their pre-1750 limits, Portuguese colonial officers showed no disposition to honor that pledge, either claiming ignorance of the new treaty [58] or asserting that the territory they held had always been Portuguese.[59] Thus Governor Cevallos informed his government that the governor of Colônia refused to evacuate cattle lands around the entrepôt and certain islands near it, and that the Portuguese commandant in Rio Grande had spurned his request to withdraw from lands south and west of the Lagoa dos Patos, even though such districts were indisputably Spanish prop-

[54] Cevallos and Valdelirios were advised of the king's decision to abrogate the treaty by the *real orden* of June 24, 1760, three months before Charles III officially denounced the agreement. *CB*, II, 359–360.

[55] One cédula of Sept. 19, 1760, ordered the Indians returned to their ancient possessions and declared that the Portuguese should retire from the missions and withdraw to their former limits at Colônia. Another of the same date advised Valdelirios that the treaty was being annulled, and that he could come home at his convenience, being assured that the king had approved his conduct. *Ibid.*, pp. 360–361, 363.

[56] *CTLA*, II, 348–354 and *CB*, II, 373–375. The best discussion of the circumstances leading to the abrogation of the Treaty of 1750 is Kratz, pp. 234–240.

[57] See Valdelirios to Cevallos, May 12, 1761, *CB*, II, 377–378; Cevallos to Arriaga, May 28, 1761, and *idem* to Gomes Freire de Andrada, July 15, 1762, *ibid.*, pp. 445–447, 467–473.

[58] It is not unlikely that the Portuguese governors were still unaware of the abrogation of the Treaty of 1750. Spanish colonial authorities in the Plata generally enjoyed more rapid communication with the Peninsula than did Portuguese authorities in Brazil during the second half of the eighteenth century.

[59] Cevallos to Vicente da Silva Fonseca (governor of Colônia) Jan. 30, 1761 *CB*, II, 368, 440; Fonseca to Cevallos, Feb. 22, 1761, *ibid.*, pp. 442–445; Ignácio Eloy de Madureira (governor of Rio Grande) to Cevallos, Apr. 8, 1761, *ibid.*, pp. 438–439; Cevallos to Madureira, May 4, 1761, *ibid.*, p. 439. Cf. Alonso Berdugo (governor of Santa Cruz de la Sierra) to Dom Antônio Rolim de Moura (captain-general of Mato Grosso), Aug. 4 and 10, 1761, and Moura's reply, Oct. 22, 1761, *ibid.*, pp. 397–401, concerning the Portuguese refusal to evacuate the town of Santa Rosa (western Mato Grosso).

erty.[60] He advised that he was tightening the blockade of Colônia and had established a camp at San Carlos, a league from the praça, in order to keep it under close surveillance.[61] A few months later the general warned that there was no way, short of war, to compel the Portuguese to respect Spain's sovereign rights.[62]

Madrid not only approved Cevallos' conduct, but gave him carte blanche to take whatever action he deemed necessary to defend the rights of Charles III.[63] The general responded by implementing his two-year-old plan to expel the Portuguese from the Debatable Lands, thereby initiating a new phase of their turbulent history.

The First Cevallos Campaign and the Emergence of a New Spanish Policy

The first step in Cevallos' plan called for the taking of Colônia to terminate its flourishing contraband trade.[64] In August 1762 the general landed a large force from Buenos Aires close to the walls of the citadel and began formal siege preparations. Two months later he learned that Spain and Portugal were at war and immediately presented the governor of the entrepôt with a surrender ultimatum. Upon its rejection, he began bombardment of the citadel; after twenty-five days the defenders signified that they had had enough. On October 31, 1762, Colônia saw victorious Spanish troops march through its gates for the third time since its founding.[65]

Two months later, on January 6, 1763, Cevallos repulsed a joint Anglo-Portuguese expedition consisting of nine ships and 500 troops

60 Cevallos to Arriaga, May 28, 1761, *ibid.*, pp. 445–447.

61 Cevallos to Arriaga, June 16, 1761, *ibid.*, pp. 450–453, and *idem* to *idem*, Aug. 3, 1761, *ibid.*, pp. 455–457.

62 Cevallos to Arriaga, Mar. 27, 1762, *ibid.*, pp. 460–462.

63 *Real orden* to Cevallos, Dec. 8, 1761, and [Arriaga?] to Cevallos, Feb. 16, 1762, *ibid.*, pp. 458–460.

64 Contraband trade prospered until the eve of Cevallos' siege. According to British Minister Hay, the frota of 1761 from Rio de Janeiro brought "4,000,000 crusados in silver, the produce of the trade at Nova Colônia. . . . This silver the government has ordered to be conveyed with the greatest secrecy not to give umbrage . . . to Spain." Hay to Halifax, May 24, 1764, quoted in Allan Christelow, "Great Britain and the Trades from Cadiz and Lisbon to Spanish America and Brazil, 1759–1783," *HAHR*, XXVII (Feb., 1947), 5. A few years before, Secretary of State Carvalho e Melo (by then Conde de Oeiras) took cognizance of the Spanish ambassador's indignation at the arrival of some 3 million cruzados of silver from Brazil; and since "é notorio a todos q. Sahirao da America hespanhola, p[o]r q. este metal se nao lavra nas minas do Brasil," he ordered that in the future silver bullion should not be sent to Portugal in warships, as was done with gold and diamonds, but should be shipped aboard merchant vessels in specially identified sugar chests. Oeiras to Bobadela, Nov. 21, 1759, *RADF*, I, 101–103.

65 For contemporary documents bearing upon the siege and fall of Colônia, see *CB*, III, 8–47; Varnhagen, IV, 206–224; and D. Miguel Lobo, *Historia general de las antiguas colonias hispano-americanas*, III, 75–124. According to Barba, *Don Pedro de Cevallos*, p. 118, the Spaniards found more than a million pesos' worth of merchandise in the entrepôt.

sent from Rio de Janeiro to retake the outpost and to assault Buenos Aires and Montevideo. After the Spanish succeeded in blowing up the English flagship, killing the expedition's commander, the survivors weighed anchor and departed from the Plata.[66]

Winter was approaching, and Cevallos was convinced that it was unlikely that the enemy would send another expedition to the Plata until the following summer. However, there was still time for him to conduct a limited offensive against the Portuguese positions in Rio Grande. Accordingly, he assembled about 1,000 men in April 1763 and led them along the littoral of the Banda toward the Portuguese fortresses of Santa Teresa and São Miguel, south of Lagoa Mirim. Don Pedro claimed that both were potential springboards for an attack on Maldonado, but it is more likely that his primary reason for assaulting them was that they blocked his advance into Rio Grande.[67]

Not for long, however. After a week's march the Spanish army arrived in the vicinity of Santa Teresa, a newly constructed bastion containing a 700-man garrison. Like São Miguel seven leagues away, Santa Teresa was advantageously situated on high ground surrounded by swamps.[68] While Cevallos carefully deployed his troops so that the defenders could not determine the size of his forces, the Portuguese sent a scouting party to evaluate the enemy's strength. The patrol returned with an alarming report, and immediately a large part of the garrison deserted en masse, leaving their commander little choice but to sue for terms.[69] The victors then moved north to São Miguel, one of the oldest and strongest Portuguese forts in Rio Grande. Regardless of this fact, the morale of its garrison had already been undermined by the tales of refugees fleeing from Santa Teresa; when the attackers threatened to put them to the knife if they offered resistance, they readily agreed to surrender.

The swift-moving Spanish army then had a clear road to the vila of Rio Grande, clear except for throngs of frightened Portuguese ranchers and army deserters who raced into the vila ahead of the invaders. The result was that when three Spanish detachments entered the Portuguese capital on April 24, they found that it had been freshly evacuated. The troops from its garrison were already on the penin-

---

[66] Cevallos to Fray Julián de Arriaga, Feb. 20, 1763, *CB*, III, 36–39.

[67] Cevallos to Fray Julián de Arriaga, Feb. 26, 1763, *ibid.*, pp. 48–49.

[68] "Mappa da fortificação levantada na fronteira de Castilhos com a invocação de S. Teresa," [*ca.* Jan. 1763], *RIHGB*, XXI (1858), facing p. 332.

[69] As happened so often, it was the commander, Tomás Luís Osório, a veteran of the Guaraní War, who bore responsibility for the loss of his post and paid for it by spending the rest of his days in prison. Riograndense historians have argued for and against his guilt ever since. See, e.g., Paula Cidade, *Lutas*, pp. 74–75, n. 40; also Fernando Luís Osório, "A Trincheira de Castilhos (Forte de Santa Teresa)," *Anais do 2ᵈᵒ congresso de história e geográfia Sul Rio-Grandense*, II (Pôrto Alegre, 1937), 287–335, a defense of the author's ancestor, and cf. the cool evaluation of the critics which follows, pp. 335–337.

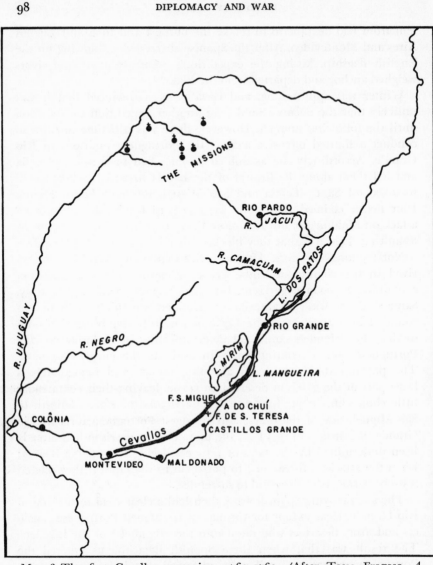

Map 6 The first Cevallos campaign, 1762–1763. (After Tasso Fragoso, *A Batalha do Passo do Rosário,* facing p. 66.)

sula, headed for Viamão at the opposite end of the Lagoa.[70] Before the Spanish were able to catch up with them, word reached Rio Grande that Spain and Portugal had suspended hostilities.[71]

[70] Less fortunate were the civilians, many of whom fell into the invaders' hands and were afterward transported as involuntary colonists of one of Cevallos' pet projects, the new town of San Carlos, a league from Maldonado. Fernandes Pinheiro reported that he found many of their descendants still living in the Banda Oriental when he campaigned there in 1812. *Anais,* p. 92, n. 1.

[71] On the Spanish campaign in Rio Grande see Cevallos to Arriaga, Aug. 24, 1763, *CB,* III, 49–53, and the documents which follow, pp. 53–59. See also *RIHGB,* XXI, 325–342, and XXXII:1 (1869), 299–327.

The Seven Years' War was concluded by two peace agreements. The first, the Treaty of Fontainebleau (November 7, 1762), was a preliminary settlement, while the second, the Treaty of Paris (February 10, 1763), was the definitive agreement. Both treaties were negotiated without knowledge of the progress of the Luso-Spanish war in America, but both documents included provisions intended to terminate the conflict and to provide for mutual territorial restitutions. There was a significant difference between the two texts of the article governing the latter point. Article XX of the preliminary treaty stipulated that, if any Portuguese overseas lands had been occupied during the war, "they will be returned to the same footing on which they were before the present war," [72] while the equivalent clause in Article XXI of the final treaty declared that such lands "will be returned to the same footing on which they were, *and in conformity with existing treaties* . . . between the Courts of Spain, France, and Portugal before the present war." [73] In its original form the clause obviously meant that all Spanish conquests in South America must be given back to Portugal. The revised article,[74] however, enabled Madrid to claim that she was obliged to return only Colônia to Portugal since Spain had not ceded her rights to Rio Grande by any *existing* treaty with Lisbon.[75] This, in fact, became the official Spanish interpretation of Article XXI of the Treaty of Paris for the next fourteen years, whereas the official Portuguese view—that Rio Grande properly belonged to Portugal—was grounded on the same article in the preliminary treaty.

Yet it would be incorrect to assume that Spain's decision to retain Rio Grande was merely an act of diplomatic sophistry or territorial cupidity. On the contrary, it was an expression of the determination of the government of Charles III to exclude Portugal from the Plata and of its conviction that possession of Rio Grande was vital to the

[72] Art. XX, par. 2. The treaty of Fontainebleau is published in Frances Gardiner Davenport and Charles Oscar Paullin, comps., *European Treaties Bearing on the History of the United States and Its Dependencies,* IV (Washington, 1937), 86–90.

[73] Italics added. For the Treaty of Paris see *CTLA,* II, 363–377.

[74] The question of who was responsible for the alteration of the wording remains a matter of debate. Somewhere in his writings, Pombal attributed it to British diplomats who wished to appease Spain. Ismael Buchich Escobar, editor of *CB,* II and III, contends that the clause was "introducida sin lugar a duda por el negociador portugués ante la convención de la paz, e inspirada en la reconocida perspicacia de los diplomáticos lusitanos, que en este caso presentián la posibilidad de un mal suceso militar en América del Sur, la Colonia del Sacramento tenía que ser devuelta a quien las poseía antes de la guerra, es decir: a Portugal." *CB,* III, xviii. He seems to overlook the fact that the clause weakened Lisbon's position and strengthened Madrid's elsewhere in the contested area.

[75] Perhaps the earliest official statement of the new Spanish position, one Spain consistently maintained in all of her diplomatic notes on the subject to 1777, was Marquis of Grimaldi (Spanish Foreign Minister) to Ayres de Sá e Melo (Portuguese ambassador to Madrid), Feb. 6, 1765, *CB,* III, 133–137.

military and economic defense of the lands bordering on the Plata system. In reaching this conclusion Madrid was strongly influenced by the advice of two of its old hands in the Debatable Lands, the Marquis of Valdelirios and Don Pedro de Cevallos.

The conqueror of Rio Grande was strongly adverse to seeing all of the territory won by his campaign sacrificed at the peace table and did his best to convince Madrid that it should retain Rio Grande and certain Platine islands. Upon receiving a copy of the Treaty of Fontainebleau, he directed his commander in Rio Grande to sign an armistice with a delegate of the Portuguese governor. The latter's agent was either in ignorance of the preliminary treaty or failed to understand the meaning of the paper he signed, for it recognized Spain's exclusive right to the possession of the vila of Rio Grande and to the control of navigation and trade passing through the Lagoa dos Patos.[76]

In a significant series of dispatches written between August and November 1763, Don Pedro showed his superiors how Spain could justify retention of the bulk of his conquests in spite of the peace treaties. He declared that it pained him to think of having to hand back "Spanish" territory to the Portuguese who had usurped it "in time of Peace and which we have recovered in Just War." [77] Moreover, he expressed doubt whether the Fontainebleau provision should apply to the lands between the Arroio Chuí and Rio Grande since, he contended, they belonged to Spain under the only existing agreement affecting them—the Tordesillas treaty.[78] While preparing to restore Colônia in conformity with a royal cédula,[79] Don Pedro indicated that he did not feel obliged to hand back two offshore Platine islands [80] because they had never been Portuguese territory, and reaffirmed his intention to retain Rio Grande unless specifically directed to evacuate it.

Cevallos realized that his attitude was certain to produce a Portuguese protest in Europe and justified his stand by calling attention to the fact that Article XXI spoke only of territory *belonging* to

76 The terms of the armistice of Aug. 6, 1763, are published in Fernandes Pinheiro, pp. 89–91, whence they were reprinted in *CTLA*, II, 382–383. Cevallos ordered that the agreement be strictly enforced, that no Portuguese ships be permitted to enter or leave the Lagoa dos Patos, and that all civilians be removed from the "recovered" territory and be sent to San Carlos. Cevallos to Captain D. Joseph de Molina, Rio Grande, Aug. 31, 1763, *CB*, III, 76–77.

77 Cevallos to Arriaga, Aug. 24, 1763, *CB*, III, 52.

78 Cevallos to Arriaga, Aug. [between 24 and 31], 1763, *ibid.*, pp. 74–75.

79 Cédula of June 9, 1763, *CB*, III, 93. Colônia was formally transferred to its new Portuguese governor, Pedro Soares de Figueiredo Sarmento, on Dec. 27, 1763. "Acta de la entrega . . . ," *ibid.*, p. 99.

80 Martin García and Dos Hermanos, located about eight leagues from Colônia.

Portugal, not that which had been usurped by her. Further, he contended that Rio Grande and the Platine islands had been occupied since the Convention of Paris (1737), and that Spain had not recognized them as legitimate Portuguese possessions by any treaty. Referring to the field armistice concerning Rio Grande, he emphasized that it was of the "highest importance to the service of the King" that the port remain in Spanish hands. He also stated that he had resumed the blockade of Colônia [81] because he believed that it was in accord with the king's wishes that he do so.[82]

As it turned out, Madrid was already favorably disposed toward Cevallos' recommendations because of a memorandum prepared by his former colleague, the Marquis of Valdelirios. The Peruvian wrote his observations in June 1763 in response to a request from Fray Julián de Arriaga, the Minister of War, for an analysis of the significance of the Portuguese occupation of Rio Grande. In his reply the marquis stated that Portuguese interest in the area began with the opening of the Conventos road between southern Santa Catarina and São Paulo.[83] He contended (correctly) that the road was opened to facilitate an illegal trade in domestic animals belonging to Spain. The cattle and mules, Valdelirios added, were driven up from estâncias around Montevideo, Santa Fé, and Corrientes by "robbers" who exchanged them for clothing and brandy supplied by the Portuguese.

Subsequently, continued the Peruvian adviser, the Portuguese moved into Rio Grande and established estâncias and protected them with forts so as to be in a better position to exploit the livestock reserves of Spain. Noting the distances between the various Portuguese fortifications and the closest Spanish settlements, he stated that several of the key forts, notably São Miguel and Jesus-Maria-José (Rio Pardo), were actually gateways for animals supplied by renegades from the ranges in the Banda Oriental and the Jesuit missions. Valdelirios concluded by declaring that in his estimation all Portuguese settlements in Rio Grande were contrary to the treaties of 1494 and 1761, and warned that unless the Lusitanians were expelled

---

[81] Two days after Colônia was handed back, Cevallos caused a proclamation to be published forbidding any trade or communication with the Portuguese. This was answered by a bando signed by Governor Sarmento, who declared that notwithstanding the Spanish order Colônia would always welcome its Spanish friends, though Portuguese inhabitants had been forbidden to introduce any articles of trade in the dominions of Spain. The last was strictly *pro forma*. Bandos of Don Joseph Nieto, Dec. 29, 1763, and of Pedro José Soares de Figueiredo [Sarmento], Apr. 6, 1764, BNRJ, I-2, 4, 6, nos. 69–70.

[82] Cevallos to Arriaga, Colônia, Nov. 30, 1763 (two dispatches), *CB*, III, 96–98, 103–105.

[83] On the Conventos road see above Chap. III., n. 40.

Spain would continue to experience serious losses of her stock animals.[84]

Late in 1763, Madrid was agreeably surprised to receive Cevallos' dispatches announcing his conquests in Rio Grande. After deliberating some months on his recommendations,[85] the government advised the general that the king fully endorsed his views, agreed that the Platine islands and Rio Grande should remain in Spanish possession, and cautioned that Rio Grande should be adequately defended against the Portuguese. In addition the king commended Don Pedro for resuming the blockade of Colônia, and instructed him to utilize all possible means to "shut off the contraband which has been carried on with such great wantonness and prejudice to the royal interests (*haveres*) in the past." [86]

When Sebastião José de Carvalho e Melo, Portugal's dominant minister, learned of Spain's refusal to restore all of her wartime conquests to Portugal, he was furious and declared that Cevallos was a tool of the Jesuits and had acted on orders from the unscrupulous Marquis of Grimaldi, Spain's foreign minister.[87] The indignant Portuguese statesman drafted one remonstrance to Madrid and sent another for the viceroy of Brazil to write himself to Cevallos. In them he demanded the return of all Portuguese lands in accordance with the "exact and literal execution" of the Treaty of Paris.[88]

Spanish authorities in Spain and America, however, summarily rejected these protests. In fact, Don Pedro de Cevallos countered by demanding Portuguese evacuation of "Spanish" territory in the Jacuí valley, the campos de Viamão, and in the Llanos de Moxos (between Brazil and Perú), as well as the return of Tape Indians held by the Portuguese since the Missions War.[89]

---

84 Valdelirios to Arriaga, Madrid, June 6, 1763, *CB*, III, 89–92.

85 In April 1764 Cevallos thanked Arriaga for the Minister's private letter of congratulations for the capture of Colônia and repulse of the Anglo-Portuguese expedition. He added that he hoped his conquests in Rio Grande would cause similar pleasure at Court "por que en la realidad há sido mui ventajoso para nosotros este suceso, y será de gran consequencia en adelante si nos quedamos con el, como lo espero de las razones que en mis antecedentes . . . expuse á V. Ex." Cevallos to Arriaga, Apr. 6, 1764 (*carta particular*) *CB*, III, 106–107.

86 Arriaga to Cevallos, July 5, 1764, *ibid.*, pp. 107–108.

87 Oeiras to Conde da Cunha, Jan. 26, 1765, ANRJ, Col. 67, Liv. II, fols. 74ʳ–77ʳ (orig.).

88 The *minuta* that Viceroy da Cunha was to write to Cevallos was enclosed in *loc. cit.* For the viceroy's protests see Cunha to Cevallos, Feb. 27 and July 16, 1765, *CB*, III, 108–109, 111–113. On Jan. 6, 1765 the Portuguese ambassador to Madrid delivered Pombal's protest to the Spanish government. Ayres de Sá e Melo to Grimaldi, Jan. 6, 1765, *ibid.*, pp. 131–133.

89 See n. 75, above; Cevallos to Viceroy da Cunha, June 15 and Dec. 3, 1764, *CB*, III, 109–111.

While colonial officers on both sides continued a war of ink over each nation's alleged violations of the peace,[90] Portugal appealed to her ally to intervene in the dispute.[91] When London firmly declined to do so,[92] the threat of an immediate renewal of war between the Iberian powers subsided.

With the war scare over, an informal truce settled upon the borderlands, reflecting the uneasy peace that existed in Europe during the years immediately after the Seven Years' War. While each of the participants in that conflict was striving to recover from the effects of the war and to deal with pressing domestic problems, none wanted to be responsible for igniting a new conflict. Yet, given the record of Luso-Spanish rivalry over the Debatable Lands, especially their antithetical ambitions there, a resumption of strife was as inevitable as was the renewal of the contest for world domination between their allies, Britain and France.

The borderlands had, in fact, become an area of major concern to Spain. Her strategists saw Rio Grande as a buffer beyond which Portugal must not be allowed to pass.[93] There still remained Colônia, but Spanish authorities were hopeful that enforcement of the blockade and the constant harassment of Portuguese ship movements in and out of the entrepôt would again convince Lisbon that it was not worth keeping.[94] But with extensive imperial commitments elsewhere and the prospect of a new war with Great Britain never far removed, Spain was content for the time being to remain on the defensive in the borderlands. Having thrown down the gauntlet by holding on to Rio Grande, she dared Portugal to take it from her so

[90] See the exchanges between D. Carlos Morphi (Spanish commandant in Rio Grande) and José Custódio de Sá e Faria (Portuguese governor of Rio Grande), Dec. 14–30, 1765, *ibid.*, pp. 117–121. In September 1765 Cevallos reported that the Portuguese were moving troops and warships to northern Rio Grande, leaving Rio de Janeiro almost undefended. He believed that he had sufficient forces in case war broke out, but asked for orders to attack Colônia again as well as Rio de Janeiro. To Arriaga, Sept. 12, 1765, *ibid.*, pp. 116–117.

[91] Pombal wrote Viceroy da Cunha (Nov. 18, 1765) that the future of the boundary question did not lie with the pertinacious Cevallos, but depended on the cooperation of Great Britain, "our necessary ally and [the] guarantor of the dominions of His Majesty by many treaties." ANRJ, Col. 67, Liv. II, fols. 94^r–96^v.

[92] See below, pp. 109–110.

[93] See especially the "Plan de operaciones en que . . . se expone lo que parece mas combeniente al R.l servicio para estas provincias del Rio de la Plata," Montevideo, Feb. 21, 1771, *CB*, III, 203–210.

[94] Governor Sarmento reported that Cevallos had declared that, if "El Rei de Portugal quer conservar este [Colônia], não ha de ser á custa de os Viveres de Hespanha," and stated that the Spanish guards were spreading the rumor that they would take the praça again when it was convenient to do so and that this time they would demolish its installations. Psychological warfare was not unknown to the eighteenth century. Sarmento to Conde da Cunha, Apr. 28, 1764, Rego Monteiro, *Colônia*, II, 194–195.

that she could represent Portuguese aggression to France and Britain as an unwarranted breach of the peace.

For Portugal the Spanish challenge in the Debatable Lands posed a major problem, one that Lisbon could not ignore unless she were willing to sacrifice Rio Grande and her Platine ambitions. The loss of Rio Grande meant not only a setback to the Portuguese drive to the Plata, but also deprived the mining regions of Brazil of an important source of livestock and the king of badly needed revenues. Moreover, Spanish occupation raised the prospect that the Castilians would use their new acquisition to flood Brazil, especially the gold camps of Minas Gerais, with contraband goods or that they would use it as a base for further territorial aggrandizement.[95] Unwilling to wage an all-out war over the borderlands unless or until assured of British support, the Conde de Oeiras adopted an opportunistic course, seeking occasions to improve the Portuguese situation there by means short of provoking a major conflict. The first test of this policy came after the Portuguese attack on the vila of Rio Grande in 1767.

The First Portuguese Attempt to Recover Rio Grande

The initial Portuguese effort to expel the Spaniards from Rio Grande came without official sanction and was the responsibility of Colonel José Custódio de Sá e Faria. José Custódio was an army engineer who had served with the joint boundary commission in Rio Grande from 1752 until it was dissolved in 1760; during its last two years he was chief Portuguese representative on that commission.[96] In 1764 he became Rio Grande's first postwar governor.[97] It was his task to reunite the widely scattered Portuguese settlers, many of whom had fled as far away as Laguna and Desterro during the Spanish invasion, and to organize his defenses to prevent the Spaniards from successfully launching a new offensive. The Portuguese position in Rio Grande was then restricted to the north end of the peninsula separat-

---

95 "Memórias políticas sobre os nossos dominios da parte do Rio da Prata," an undated memorial (ca. 1764–1765) of Oeiras to Martinho de Melo e Castro (Portuguese ambassador to Great Britain), BNRJ, I-2, 25, 6. Similar views were expressed by the same minister to Viceroy Lavradio during the 1770s.

96 A number of José Custódio's dispatches relating to his activities on the commission are in ABNRJ, LII and LIII.

97 He received an interim appointment from Viceroy da Cunha on Feb. 24, 1764, that was confirmed by the king three years later. Jônatas da Costa Rego Monteiro, Dominação espanhola no Rio Grande do Sul, 1763–1777 (Rio de Janeiro, 1937), p. 123; Francisco Xavier de Mendonça Furtado to Conde da Cunha, Mar. 18, 1767, ANRJ, Col. 67, Liv. II-A, fol. 13ʳ (orig.). Since he was also commander of one of Rio de Janeiro's two colonial infantry regiments, he was technically on detached service in the borderland captaincy.

ing the Lagoa dos Patos from the Atlantic, the upper end of that lagoon, and along the Jacuí or Guaíba River valley from its mouth as far as the fort at Rio Pardo. For three years the governor endeavored to rebuild the captaincy's fortifications, to restore the morale of his troops, and to reopen supply lines to Santa Catarina and further north.[98] He also engaged in several vitriolic exchanges with his Spanish counterpart, whose headquarters was in the vila of Rio Grande at the south end of the lagoon. Their disputes concerned such typical frontier issues as thefts of cattle and slaves and demands for the return of army deserters.[99]

In May 1767 José Custódio felt that he had had enough of the Spanish governor's threats to attack his positions. Without obtaining approval from higher authority (so far as is known), he decided to drive the Spaniards out of Rio Grande. His plan called for Colonel José Casimiro Roncali to lead one contingent of 200 dragoons south from Rio Pardo to a point behind the vila to cut off the enemy's retreat. Concurrently, 500 men were to float down the lagoon in canoes and fishing boats to make a frontal attack on the town, while a third group, consisting of mounted troops, was to prevent a Spanish counterattack up the peninsula by raiding the enemy's stock and ambushing his cavalry near the town of São José do Norte, part way up the peninsula.

Whatever chance José Custódio's plan may have had of success was wrecked by bad weather and by the loss of the element of surprise. Heavy rains turned the Riograndense rivers into raging torrents, slowing down Roncali's progress, while the amphibious troops, who embarked at midnight May 28, soon became separated and lost in a heavy fog. The next morning when part of the boats emerged from the mist near the vila, they were spotted by Spanish lookouts who immediately gave the alarm. Subsequently, the landing party of about 100 men was deposited on what was supposed to be a safe beach near the vila; the troops had to wade in water up to their shoulders, while holding their arms and powder above their heads. Once ashore, they found themselves in marshy ground and under fire from two nearby batteries. After making a sortie against the vila and being repulsed, the attackers retired. Fortunately the elements now turned in their

---

[98] In 1765 the câmara of Viamão, then the Portuguese capital of Rio Grande, wrote the Overseas Council that because the Spaniards had closed the entrance to the Lagoa dos Patos they were completely dependent for supplies on the port of Laguna, and complained that the Lagunenses were taking advantage of their plight by levying excessive duties on goods sent to Rio Grande. The Council ordered the Laguna câmara to desist from that practice. In a second appeal the Viamão corporation declared that local merchants had lost heavily during the Spanish invasion, and pleaded for a moratorium on debts they owed merchants in Rio de Janeiro. Consultas of Apr. 2 and 13, 1766, DH, XVC, 65–69.

[99] See n. 90, above.

favor, for a protecting mantle of fog enabled them to return to their headquarters.

Three days later the Portuguese made a second attempt against the Spanish positions. This time they concentrated on São José do Norte on the peninsula opposite the vila. But upon entering the town, they found that the Spaniards had anticipated them, and, after spiking their guns, had crossed over to the vila. Separated by the waters of the entrance canal of Lagoa dos Patos, the two opposing forces thereafter contented themselves with looking menacingly at each other, and awaited the reaction of their respective Courts.[100]

Borderlands Diplomacy and the Projected Second Diplomatic Revolution (1766–1768)

The first reports of the action in Rio Grande reached Lisbon early in September 1767; [101] but far from arousing the Court's pleasure, José Custódio's activities were officially disavowed. The Portuguese ambassador to Madrid expressed Dom José I's regrets for the "ridiculous war of the subordinates," and promised that his government would make full restitution.[102] Orders were quickly dispatched to Viceroy da Cunha to send a representative to Buenos Aires with the same message to the Spanish governor there. Subsequently the viceroy himself was removed in a manner which suggested rebuke for having permitted the attack; and the officer responsible for it—José Custódio —was ordered sent to Lisbon under guard.[103]

The explanation for Lisbon's strange behavior lies in the negotiations then in progress between the two Iberian courts, and indirectly with France as well, toward what might have become the second *renversement des alliances* within little more than a decade. Though formal discussions did not begin until the spring of 1767, the ground was prepared the previous year when Portugal manifested uncommon solicitude for a domestic crisis afflicting her neighbor. In March 1766 a series of popular uprisings known as the Squillace revolts broke out in major Spanish cities in protest against the unpopular

100 On these operations see Sá e Faria to Dom Luís Antônio de Sousa Botelho Mourão, June 1, 1767, and José Marcelino de Figueiredo to *idem*, June 8 [?], 1767, *DI*, XXIII (1897), 215–218, which is followed by an inventory of the articles that the Spanish left behind on the peninsula (pp. 218–219). Among the secondary accounts see Rego Monteiro, *Dominação*, pp. 132–138, and Fernandes Pinheiro, pp. 95–99.

101 Oeiras to Ayres de Sá e Melo, Sept. 10, 1767, *RIHGB*, XXXIII:1 (1870), 264.

102 Ayres de Sá e Melo to Grimaldi, Sept. 18, 1767, *CTLA*, III, 95.

103 Oerias to Conde de Azambuju (Viceroy of Brazil), Sept. 11, 1767, *RIHGB*, XXXIII:1, 264–267.

Italian ministers of Charles III.[104] Upon learning of the riots, the Conde de Oeiras closed Portugal's borders to the participants, and his master offered Charles III the use of Portuguese troops to quell the disturbances.[105] But at the same time Oeiras wrote Viceroy da Cunha to alert his subordinates to take every possible advantage of Spain's predicament.[106]

Portugal's apparently friendly gestures appreciably thawed Madrid's attitude toward her neighbor. While Ayres de Sá, Portuguese ambassador to Spain, became overnight the most popular foreign diplomat in Madrid, the Spanish ambassador to Lisbon was seen entertaining the entire Portuguese ministry. [107] In America the bellicose Don Pedro de Cevallos was replaced by the more tractable Don Francisco de Bucareli y Ursúa as Governor of Buenos Aires.[108] In July 1766 both courts sent orders to their colonies to suspend hostilities,[109] and six months later the Spanish minister of war prepared a memorandum for the foreign minister suggesting the basis for a compromise settlement with Portugal concerning the borderlands in America.[110]

The official cordiality between the two Iberian courts continued throughout 1767. On March 1, Madrid followed Portugal's lead and

[104] The revolts began in Madrid on Mar. 23 and spread throughout the principal cities of Spain. Antonio Ballesteros y Beretta, *Historia de España e su influencia en el mundo*, V (Barcelona, 1929), 167–174. There is also a very good account of the uprisings in Ludwig, Freiherr von Pastor, *The History of the Popes . . .* , XXVII, E. F. Peeler tr, (St. Louis, Mo., 1950), 49–71, based upon both manuscript and secondary sources.

[105] Oeiras to D. Vicente de Souza Coutinho (Portuguese ambassador to Paris), Jan. 24, 1766, *QE*, VIII, 129, referring to a carta régia of Apr. 9, 1766 to Ayres de Sá e Melo; see also Saint-Priest (French minister to Lisbon) to Choiseul, Apr. 16, 1766, *QE*, VII, 202.

[106] Oeiras to Conde da Cunha, June 22, 1766, referred to in *idem* to *idem,* June 20, 1767, *RIHGB*, XXXIII:1, 254–260.

[107] João Lúcio de Azevedo, *O Marquês de Pombal e a sua época*, p. 261; Saint-Priest to Choiseul, Apr. 18, 1766, *QE*, VII, 202.

[108] But not before Cevallos had again proposed to settle outstanding differences with Portugal by an attack on Rio de Janeiro. Cevallos to Arriaga, May 30, 1766, quoted in Octavio Gil Munilla, *El Río de la Plata en la política internacional: génesis del virreinato*, pp. 112–113, n. 64. The timing of Cevallos' replacement made it appear that he was being recalled as a gesture calculated to please Portugal, but in 1763 he had asked to be relieved for reasons of health. Cevallos to Arriaga, Nov. 30, 1763, *CB*, III, 104–105.

[109] *Real orden* to President of Audiencia of Charcas, July 4, 1766, cited in Gil Munilla, p. 114, n. 66; Oeiras to Azambuja, Sept. 11, 1767, cited in n. 103 above, referring to an order of July 22, 1766. Following the expulsion of the Jesuits from Spanish America, instructions were sent from Lisbon to the viceroy and to the captain-general of São Paulo calling a halt to Paulista penetration of northeastern Paraguay because it was not "conveniente que rompamos pela nossa parte uma guerra, que se incendiará em toda a parte." Francisco Xavier de Mendonça Furtado to Conde da Cunha, Mar. 22, 1767, *RIHGB*, XXXIII:1, 246–252.

[110] Arriaga to Grimaldi, Dec. 28, 1766, summarized in Gil Munilla, p. 114.

expelled the Jesuits on the pretext that the Order was responsible for the Squillace revolts.[111] That decision was warmly praised by the sponsor of the Jesuit expulsion movement, the Conde de Oeiras, who regarded it as the next logical step in the total suppression of the Society, and also as a sign that the Spanish government would no longer be Jesuit-dominated, and would therefore be more reasonable in its dealings with Portugal.[112] To test this possibility both he and King José I made proposals to the Spanish ambassador suggesting that both governments unite in their efforts to bring about Papal suppression of the Black Robes and also settle their differences in America.[113]

The Marquis of Grimaldi, Spanish Foreign Minister, was quick to see the advantages that Spain could derive from these proposals. In framing his favorable reply the following month, Grimaldi made the bold offer of a political alliance with Portugal, but noted that France would also have to be included since Spain could not enter into a new arrangement unless it also embraced her ally.[114]

Oeiras did not immediately respond directly to Grimaldi's proposal. Instead he asserted that it was first necessary for the two powers to settle the "very important business of the suppression of the Jesuits" before going on to other matters of common concern. Persevering, Grimaldi renewed his offer, this time sweetening it by stating that the question of boundaries in America could be settled in a manner favorable to Portugal.[115] There the matter rested for some time.

Before considering the ultimate fate of these negotiations, it is pertinent to examine the motives behind the proposed alliance. The common adversary that brought the three Latin powers closer together was Great Britain, the colossus which emerged from the Seven Years' War as the first power in Europe, thanks to a series of spectacu-

---

111 Pastor, XXXVII, 91–202.

112 [Oeiras] to Conde da Cunha, June 20, 1767, *RADF*, IV (1897), 420–422. The belief that Madrid was Jesuit-influenced was one of Pombal's favorite theses; and when the negotiations with Spain broke down, he accused the Spanish government of still being Jesuit-controlled, even though the only Black Robes then in Spain were in prison!

113 For conflicting accounts of the negotiations of 1767–1768 by the two principals most intimately familiar with them, see Grimaldi to Almodóvar (Spanish ambassador to Lisbon), May 20, 1768, Gil Munilla, Appendix II, and Oeiras, "Compéndio analytico das negociações entre as cortes de Lisboa e de Madrid desde 1759 até ao fim . . . de 1775," in Pombal to Luís Pinto de Sousa, Apr. 12, 1776, *QE*, XVIII, 393–399; see also Oeiras to D. Vicente de Sousa Coutinho, Mar. 20, 1768, *QE*, VII, 274–280, and *idem* to *idem*, Jan. 24, 1776, *QE*, VIII, 129–131.

114 Grimaldi to Almodóvar, May 20, 1768, Gil Munilla, p. 397.

115 *Loc. cit.;* see also Gil Munilla's remarks on the significance of the Grimaldi proposals (p. 125).

lar global victories over Spain and France. Though badly beaten, both members of the Family Compact longed for an opportunity to strike a major blow at their tormentor.[116] An alliance with Portugal would contribute to that objective since it would deprive Britain of Portugal's strategic harbors in wartime and would facilitate France's efforts to secure a commercial treaty with Portugal that would give her concessions equal to those long enjoyed by Britain.[117] In addition, an accord with Portugal would put an end to the explosive frontier disputes between the two Iberian powers in America and allow France and Spain to concentrate their military energies against Britain.

As an old Spanish proverb laments, "I can take care of my enemies, but God protect me from my friends." This complaint must often have come to the minds of British and Portuguese statesmen during the era of the Marquis of Pombal. Since the Peninsular war of 1762, when Britain had saved Portugal from being overwhelmed by Spanish troops, relations between the two powers had seriously deteriorated. One of the several sources of friction between Lisbon and London concerned the Debatable Lands directly. During the post-1763 crisis over Spain's refusal to evacuate Rio Grande, the Portuguese minister to London, Martinho de Melo e Castro, sought support from prominent persons in and out of the government for Portugal's position in her dispute with Spain. The answers he received were completely unsympathetic. The British contended that the situation in Brazil was not serious and refused to send a fleet to the Portuguese colony because of the likelihood that such action would provoke a general war. The British government also declined to give Portugal new subsidies on the ground that it was too deeply in debt to do so. Worse still, Portugal's pride was hurt and her suspicions aroused by Lord Halifax' advice that Portugal should look after her ruined fortifications in Rio de Janeiro, which, he boasted, were not strong enough to resist a British battalion for more than twenty-four hours. Ruefully, the Portuguese minister wrote his government that "Only when Great Brit-

[116] Commenting on the Luso-Spanish discussions, the Duc de Choiseul wrote the French ambassador in Madrid that "Pombal loses his head whenever there is talk of Jesuits. But with skill and discretion some profit may be derived from the negotiations if we draw Portugal into our alliance." Choiseul to Ossun, Nov. 24, 1767, quoted in Pastor, XXXVII, 324.

[117] In his instruction, the new French minister to Lisbon, Chevalier de Clermont D'Amboise, was told that consummation of a commercial treaty with Portugal was one of his most important tasks. Instruction of Aug. 7, 1768, *Recueil des instructions données aux ambassadeurs et ministres de France . . .*, III (Paris, 1886), 361. France had hoped to conclude such a treaty during the late 1740s, but realized that such a possibility would follow only if Spain and Portugal settled their differences over Colônia. See Marquis d'Argenson to Chavigny (French minister to Lisbon), Aug. 2, 1746 and Puissieux to *idem*, Apr. 11, 1747, *QE*, V, 341-344, 362-363.

ain sees us powerful and resolute . . . will she have to treat us as allies and not as dependents." [118]

Another source of irritation between Britain and her ally concerned their divergent economic aspirations. Long Britain's most lucrative European market, Portugal under Pombal was attempting to reduce British preeminence by developing domestic industries, by promoting the economic growth of various regions of Brazil through government-sponsored monopoly companies, and by enforcing existing laws against the export of bullion from Portugal. These measures naturally aroused bitter protests from British businessmen, who charged that Portugal was infringing upon Britain's ancient treaty rights. During the mid-1760s a plethora of British pamphlets and articles attacked the new economic policies of Portugal. One of the most notable was a pamphlet entitled "Occasional Thoughts on the Portuguese Trade" (1767), which anticipated Adam Smith in questioning the real value of the trade to England, but went beyond Smith in urging a renunciation of Britain's traditional alliance in favor of one with Spain.[119] Given his own great antipathy for the Jesuits and his jealousy of British opulence, it was easy for Oeiras (soon to be Marquis of Pombal) to see the sinister hand of the Black Robes behind these attacks on his policies.[120]

A third reason for Portuguese hostility toward England was the belief that Britain had illegitimate commercial, and possibly territorial, designs on Brazil. Though Britain supplied over fifty percent of the manufactures sent to Brazil via Portugal, the English were thought to be actively engaged in smuggling in Brazilian waters with the help of Jesuit sympathizers.[121] Moreover, Portuguese authorities were gravely concerned about the detailed remarks concerning Brazilian ports and resources that had appeared in recent published accounts of British naval expeditions which had stopped at such ports. To men as suspicious as the future Marquis of Pombal, those remarks confirmed Lis-

---

[118] To Oeiras, April 7, 1766, quoted in Azevedo, *Época*, pp. 252–253; see also pp. 246–253. Excerpts of Melo e Castro's dispatches are quoted in Alberto Lamego, "As invasões franceses no Rio de Janeiro . . . ," IV Congreso de história nacional, *Anais*, VI (Rio de Janeiro, 1949), 129–131, where the suggested date is 1763, though internal evidence makes it almost certain that they were written in 1767. E.g., Melo e Castro noted with alarm the book by John Byron, *Voyage Round the World in HMS "Delphin,"* (1st ed., London, 1767), in which "Foul-weather Jack" Byron described in considerable detail the harbor and fortifications of Rio de Janeiro.

[119] See A. B. Wallis Chapman and V. M. Shillington, *The Commercial Relations of England and Portugal* (London, n.d.), p. 278. There is a copy of "Occasional Thoughts" in the Newberry Library, Chicago. For Adam Smith's famous remarks regarding the questionable value of the Methuen Treaty to the British economy, see *An Inquiry into the Nature and Causes of the Wealth of Nations*, II (Edinburgh, 1811), 370–376.

[120] Oeiras to Conde da Cunha, June 6, 1767, *RADF*, IV, 421–422.

[121] *Loc. cit.*; also Oeiras to Lavradio, Apr. 14, 1769 IHGB, *Lata* 9, MS 192.

bon's suspicion that the British were planning an invasion of Brazil in cooperation with the Jesuits.[122]

Under these circumstances it was easy enough for Portugal's chief minister to give credence to a warning from the Duc de Choiseul that the British were about to invade the Plata with the help of the Jesuits.[123] Once before, in 1741, Pombal was convinced that a British force, the Vernon expedition, was destined for the Plata. At that time he had regarded the prospect with misgivings, for he felt that a British base in that estuary would pose a strategic threat to Brazil.[124] Choiseul's warning therefore struck a responsive chord, and Pombal wrote Viceroy da Cunha that any British attack in southern South America against Spanish possessions would be regarded by his government as menacing to Brazil and would automatically make Britain an enemy of Portugal.[125]

To check the alleged British-Jesuit conspiracy,[126] Pombal decided to strengthen the defenses of Brazil, particularly those of Rio de Janeiro. In 1766 he reactivated the colonial militia [127] and the follow-

122 Byron said scornfully, for example, that a British naval squadron could capture Rio in twenty-four hours. *Voyage*, pp. 15–16. James Cook, who had a copy of Byron's account with him when he visited Rio in 1768, reached the same conclusion and even paraphrased Byron to say so. "A De[s]cripcion of the Bay or River of Rio de Janeira," [sic] J. C. Beaglehole, ed., *The Journals of Captain James Cook*, I, 29–34.

123 Oeiras to D. Vicente de Sousa Coutinho, Mar. 20, 1768, *QE*, VII, 277. Perhaps Choiseul had got wind of the secret British instructions to their ministers in Madrid and Lisbon to obtain the best possible information, including maps and charts, on the strengths and weaknesses of Spain and Portugal in South America, the "strength and amount of discontent which are supposed to prevail there . . . , the state of the military fortifications, [and] the points which may be supposed to be open to attack. . . ." Possibly London had already learned of the negotiations between the Iberian powers and was merely taking prudent precautions. See Christelow, "Great Britain and the Trades," p. 24.

124 Carvalho e Melo to Marco Antônio de Azevedo Coutinho, July 8, 1741, *PAN*, IV (1903), 15–20. (Later Pombal claimed credit for having diverted the expedition to northern South America.) It is possible that Pombal also knew about the earlier bizarre proposals of a renegade Portuguese slaver, Antônio da Costa, to found either a British or a Russian base in the entrance to the Lagoa dos Patos to engage in trade with the Portuguese and Spanish colonies. See A[ntônio] Béthancourt, "Proyecto de un establecimiento ruso en el Brasil (1732–33)," Consejo Superior de Investigaciones Científicas. Instituto "Gonzalo Fernandez de Oviedo," *Miscelanea Americanista*, I (Madrid, 1951), 189–206.

125 Oeiras to Conde da Cunha, June 20, 1767, *RIHGB*, XXXV:1, 227–236.

126 In the eighteenth century many persons feared Jesuits as much as contemporaries do Communists. Black Robes then, like alleged Communists today, were often accused of conspiratorial acts on the basis of little or no persuasive evidence. Thus they were charged with attempted regicides in France, Portugal, and Spain; and Spaniards accused them of being responsible for the long-delayed British return of Manila to Spain after 1763. In 1767 Lisbon warned the viceroy of Brazil to be on guard against attempts by ex-Jesuits to land in Brazilian ports in the garb of other religious Orders or by posing as laymen. Mendonça Furtado to Conde da Cunha, Apr. 25, 1767, *RIHGB*, XXXIII:1, 252–254.

127 Carta régia, June 30, 1766, *ABNRJ*, XXXII, 280–281.

ing year sent three of Portugal's best regiments, the Bragança, the Moura, and the Estremoz, to Rio de Janeiro. J. H. Böhm, an Austrian-born general who had passed from British into Portuguese service, was assigned to take charge of Rio de Janeiro's newly augmented garrison.[128] Pombal then warned the viceroy that the British had greatly improved their siege techniques since their defeat at Cartagena (1741), and therefore ordered improvements in the capital's fortresses. To supervise such alterations and to establish an artillery and engineering school in Rio de Janeiro, he named a well-traveled Swedish fortification expert, Jacques Funk, as Böhm's assistant.[129] Provided that Rio's defenses were properly improved, Pombal predicted that if the British tried to seize the Carioca capital, Böhm and Funk would teach them a lesson they would not soon forget.[130]

Meanwhile, Portugal's real and imagined difficulties with England and Spain's expulsion of the Jesuits seemed to draw the two Iberian powers ever closer toward alliance. As Pombal wrote Viceroy da Cunha, "the expulsion of the Jesuits from Spain has converted our enemies into friends, and according to all appearances, those who were our friends and allies into enemies." [131] In a dispatch to Cunha's successor, the Portuguese secretary spoke glowingly of the "close friendship and intimate union" of Portugal and Spain. In fact, he declared, both powers "have determined to adjust amicably [their] differences" in America.[132] Even the news of José Custódio's ill-timed attack did not seriously disturb the honeymoon, and Madrid seemed convinced of the sincerity of Lisbon's explanations.[133] Brazilian authorities, moreover, were ordered to refrain from giving any

128 Böhm, former adjutant to the Conde de Lippe, was given the title of inspector general of the troops of Brazil, but in practice his authority was limited to troops within the captaincy-general of Rio de Janeiro

129 After spending his early years in the Swedish army, Funk joined French forces in the 1740s and participated in the seige of Maestrich (1745). Subsequently he went to India in the service of the British East India Company, returning to Europe in time to distinguish himself in the British attack on Havana (1762). Two years later he was recruited in England for Portuguese service by ambassador Martinho de Melo e Castro. Francisco Marquês de Sousa Viterbo, *Diccionário histórico e documental dos architectos, engenheiros e constructores portuguezes* I (Lisbon, 1899), 400–401; Clado Ribeiro de Lessa, "Breve notícia sôbre Jacques Funk e seus trabalhos de engenaria civil e militar no Brasil (1768–1781)," IV Congreso de historia nacional, *Anais*, X (Rio de Janeiro, 1949), 383–402, is mainly a listing of archival sources concerning various projects Funk drafted during the 1770s.

130 Oeiras to Conde da Cunha, June 20, 1767, *RIHGB*, XXXIII:1, 227–236. Since the regiments were not complete, 600 "volunteers" were to be sent from the Azores to fill the ranks. Mendonça Furtado to *idem*, Mar. 23, 1767, ANRJ, Col. 67, Liv. II-A, fol. 18ʳ (*1.a via*).

131 Oeiras to *idem*, June 20, 1767 (cited in n. 130 above).

132 Oeiras to Azambuja, Oct. 2, 1767, ANRJ, Col. 67, Liv. I, fol. 90ʳ (*orig.*).

133 Arriaga to Bucareli, Sept. 20, 1767, ordering the governor to accept the Portuguese apology and the restoration of the peninsula in the Lagoa dos Patos to Spanish control. Cited in Rego Monteiro, *Dominação*, p. 139.

offense to Spain lest such action imperil the discussions in progress.[134]

Notwithstanding this admonition, Pombal did not intend to neglect the opportunity afforded by the new cordiality with Spain to strengthen the Portuguese position in the Debatable Lands. Craftily, he ordered that, in case the Spanish should be forced to withdraw their forces from the Lagoa dos Patos to conquer the missions from the Jesuits or to go to Buenos Aires to defend that city against an Anglo-Jesuit attack, Portuguese troops might occupy the places from which the Spanish had withdrawn "under the pretext of defending them against the invasions and machinations of the Jesuits." [135] He also directed the viceroy to write a personal letter to Governor Bucareli protesting the continuance of the Colônia blockade as constituting an act of war and as entirely contrary to the new Luso-Spanish friendship.[136]

However, that friendship did not endure beyond the spring of 1768. The Marquis of Grimaldi made it clear that his government would consider modifying its stand on the frontier question only if Portugal adhered to the Family Compact.[137] After delaying his answer for seven months, Pombal declared that the price of the package was too high and that Portugal could not think of abandoning her traditional ally.[138] His answer was doubtless based on several considerations, among them (1) José Custódio's advance in Rio Grande, a step in the right direction and certainly one that Pombal could have

134 Mendonça Furtado to Conde da Cunha, Mar. 22, 1767, *RIHGB*, XXXIII:1, 246–252.

135 Oeiras to Conde da Cunha, June 20, 1767, *ibid.*, pp. 254–260.

136 *Loc. cit.* Pombal's order was prompted by the viceroy's report that the blockade seemed to have been somewhat relaxed. Wryly, the minister observed that judging from the flow of silver patacas into Lisbon, Cunha must be right; but he ordered that henceforth all silver should be exchanged at the Rio de Janeiro mint for gold so that only the latter arrived in Portugal, thereby preventing the Spanish ambassador and his agents from obtaining an indication of the volume of the illegal trade.

137 "De suerte que mi proposición fue absolutamente indivisible, dependiendo en todo y por todo la primera parte de la segunda; sin que en defecto de la una, pueda subsistir ni alegarse la otra." Grimaldi to Almodóvar, May 20, 1768, Gil Munilla, p. 400. The foreign minister went on to deny that he had ever intimated Spain would consider abandoning any territory legitimately belonging to her.

138 Grimaldi wrote Almodóvar that Pombal's negative reply was dated May 8, but Pombal himself stated that he gave his answer on Apr. 14. *QE*, XVIII, 398. Almost certainly he had decided much earlier on the course he would follow. On Jan. 28, 1768, he wrote Viceroy d'Azambuja that Portugal was still holding out for complete control of the north bank of Plata on the basis of the treaties of Utrecht and Paris, but that Spain would not give up the Banda Oriental. He pointed out that switching allies would expose Portugal to war with England, and that Spain was in no position to aid her in such a situation. While the negotiations were continuing, he said, he was pessimistic about their outcome because of the continued "bad faith" of Madrid. *RIHGB*, XXXIII:1, 278–280.

had no serious intention of forsaking; (2) the failure of the expected British invasion of Brazil to materialize; and (3) Pombal's chagrin over the unwillingness of France and Spain to accept his leadership in the formation of a Catholic league against Pope Clement XIII.[139] For their part, both members of the compact had come to suspect that Pombal had merely initiated the negotiations in order to strengthen his hand in dealing with Great Britain, and that he had sent the Peninsular regiments to Brazil not to forestall an English attack, but to employ them against Spain.[140] Considering the devious way Pombal's mind often worked, his critics may not have been far wrong.

The end of the Luso-Spanish rapprochement was signaled by a resumption of the familiar pattern of incidents and mutual recriminations in America. In spite of Portuguese promises, Colonel José Custódio did not come home to face punishment for his bold acts,[141] nor was the recently won strip of territory in Rio Grande given back to the Spaniards.[142] Far from relaxing the blockade of Colônia, the

[139] The league was organized to defend the duchy of Parma in its dispute with the Holy See and to bring pressure on the Pope to abolish the Jesuit Order. Pastor, XXXVII, 281–282, 321–325. In his dispatch to Azambuja of Sept. 11, 1767, Pombal boasted that at present "se acha SM unido com França e Hespanha, para em causa commum obrigarem a côrte de Roma á extincção dos jesuitas," adding "porque sem isso, nem póde subsistir a igreja de Deus, nem podem se conservar as monarchias da terra." *RIHGB*, XXXIII:1, 264.

[140] Arriaga to Bucareli, May 6, 1768, *CB*, III, 178–179; Choiseul grumbled to Grimaldi: "M. d'Oeyras est tout feu quand il est question de Rome et des Jésuites, pour lesquels nous n'avons pas besoin de lui et où il n'est qu'incommode; mais lorsque nous traitons l'alliance contre l'Angleterre il me persifile, comme on dit dans ce pays-ci; et je crois qu' il fait pire, car il négocie un nouveau traité de commerce avec l'Angleterre." May 3, 1768, quoted in Pastor, XXXVII, 281, n. 4. In his instruction to minister Clermont (Aug. 1768), Choiseul declared: "On se feroit illusion si l'on se flattoit que cette union entre les cours de Londres et de Portugal cessera d'exister." *Recueil*, III, 361.

[141] The Crown obviously did not regard Custódio as being guilty of a serious crime. In his second order for the colonel's return to the Peninsula, the colonial secretary stressed that he need not be sent under guard. Mendonça Furtado to Azambuja, Mar. 30, 1768, ANRJ, Col. 67, Liv. I, fol. 115 (orig.). Later, in a summary of one of Viceroy Lavradio's instructions, appears the following note: "Carta de 30 de Março de 1768 ratificando a ordem de vir prego o Coronel Jozé Custódio, que depoiz se soube obrou, o que devia fazer; e.q. em lugar de castigo merece ser premiado." *Ibid.*, Liv. III, fol. 27ᵛ. He was—by being promoted to brigadier general. Carta régia of Oct. 2, 1771, BNRJ, 10, 4, 8 (unnumbered).

[142] On Jan. 30, 1768, Bucareli wrote Viceroy d'Azambuja demanding the restoration of the territory the Portuguese had occupied in May 1767 in view of the negotiations then going on between their respective courts. At the same time he complained of the protection given by the Portuguese commandant of Rio Pardo to "mas de trecientos Desertores y Guaderios que se emplean no solo en robar las Familias establecidas en estas Campañas sino tambien los ganados que del mismo modo sacan." Referring to a previous dispatch of Dec. 23, 1767, he also complained that Colônia's governor was still giving protection and arms to Spanish contraband runners. *CB*, III, 177–178. On Mar. 3, 1769, Azambuja wrote Bucareli claiming that the officer who was supposed to execute the restitutions to Spain had been delayed in Rio because of illness and the lack of a ship to take him to Rio Grande. *Ibid.*, p. 187. In fact the viceroy's agent never left Rio.

Castilians actually tightened their grip [143] and continued to deny Portuguese shipping the right to enter the Lagoa dos Patos.[144] At the same time the Spanish intensified their efforts to seal off the wild cattle preserves of the missions from the Portuguese.[145]

The failure of the negotiations in Europe and the renewal of tension along the southern frontier of Brazil did not immediately lead to war, for neither power was yet willing to go that far. Spain soon had her hands full with England concerning ownership of the Falkland Islands. For his part, Pombal was unwilling to press colonial issues until the Jesuit question was definitely settled with Rome, and for that he needed Spain's help. Moreover, relations with Portugal's only ally, Great Britain, continued strained for several years.[146] Significantly, however, both the settlement of the Jesuit question [147] and the healing of the breech in Luso-British relations occurred in 1773.[148] Thereafter Portugal's policy in the Debatable Lands became increasingly aggressive, prompting countermeasures by Spain and bringing the threat of war ever nearer. The new stalemate that began in 1768 coincided with the first years of the administration of the Marquis of Lavradio as viceroy in Rio de Janeiro.

143 Bucareli to Arriaga, Oct. 15, 1768, *ibid.*, pp. 182–183.

144 Arriaga to Bucareli, June 28, 1769, *ibid.*, pp. 188–189, ordering Rio Grande defended as the "actual y el eterno Dominio Del Rey sin permitir su navegaz.n á los Portugueses teniendo aq.as embarcaz.s q. se colocaron para su resguardo defendiendo con toda su fuerza qualquer nueba imbasion. . . ."

145 In late 1768 Spanish soldiers in the missions seized a Portuguese patrol including a Paulista, a mulatto, and several Indians who were poaching. Significantly, the missions' commander dispatched the mulatto and the Paulista to Buenos Aires, but sent the Indians to the other side of the Rio Paraná with the warning not to help the Portuguese to steal livestock again. Both sides were actually playing for the support of the Guaraní. Francisco Bruno de Zaballa to Bucareli, San Miguel, Dec.`18, 1768, *CB*, III, 183–185.

146 Owing primarily to Portuguese seizures of British ships in African and Brazilian ports of Portugal on the grounds that they were contrabandists, and because in retaliation an English frigate threatened to bombard Lisbon (1770). *QE*, XVIII, 384–385. See also Chap. XIV, below.

147 The Holy See finally gave in to pressure from most of the Catholic powers and suppressed the Society of Jesus by the brief *Dominus ac Redemptor*, July 23, 1773. Pastor, XXXVIII, Chaps. 1, 3, and 4.

148 As João Lúcio de Azevedo so well put it, "D'este modo a questão dos jesuítas effeituara quasi separar-nos da Inglaterra. A mesma questão nos reconduzia aos braços d'ella." *Época*, p. 266.

V

The Years of Stalemate, 1769-1774

For every given action there is an equal and opposite reaction.

Isaac Newton, Third Law

THE EVENTS DISCUSSED in the two preceding chapters were summarized in three of the four lengthy instructions the Marquis of Pombal drafted for the new viceroy's guidance.[1] He emphasized that it was necessary for Dom Luís de Almeida to guard against not only the machinations of Spain and the Society of Jesus, but also against the activities of Great Britain and France. For while Spain posed the immediate military threat to Brazil by her hostile acts in the borderlands, Britain and France were attempting to undermine Portugal's economic ties with Brazil by their flagrant contraband operations conducted off the lightly defended southern coast and within colonial ports. Contending that the Jesuits had excited British cupidity for Brazil's gold and diamonds, the chief minister stated that English smugglers found ready collaborators among the reputedly pro-Jesuit merchant community of Rio de Janeiro, and warned the viceroy to be extremely circumspect about permitting foreign ships to gain admission to his ports.[2]

Although Pombal provided detailed instructions concerning the economic defense of Brazil, he was conspicuously silent about the precise measures the viceroy should take to alleviate the military threat in the south. Since he did not authorize Dom Luís to employ force to recover the part of Rio Grande that Spanish forces still held or to relieve encircled Colônia, the viceroy was left with no choice but to mark time and try to contain the Spanish until the Court determined otherwise.

[1] The four instructions, each on a different topic, were dated April 14, 1769, and were termed *carta primeira, carta segunda,* and so forth. Each was accompanied by copies of pertinent legislation and correspondence addressed to Lavradio's predecessors. The first originals (*1.a vias*) of all four are in CMCM, cod. 18 together with their appendices. ANRJ, Col. 67, Liv. III contains second originals (*2.as vias*) and most of the appendices, while a third original of the "first letter" is in IHGB, *Lata* 9, MS 192. The 2nd, 3rd, and 4th letters are published without their annexes in *RIHGB,* XXXI:1, 291-303.

[2] For Lavradio's literal compliance with that injunction, see Chap. XIV below.

Caution, therefore, became the watchword of Viceroy Lavradio in his correspondence with the governors of Colônia and Rio Grande during the early seventies. He enjoined them to write "prudent" protests when the Spanish violated Portuguese rights, but to refrain from the use of force unless overtly attacked.[3] As the years went by, however, events in the borderlands made it increasingly difficult for the viceroy and his subordinates to continue a policy of inaction.

Colônia do Sacramento, Beleaguered Outpost of Empire

One officer who did not need to be told to observe caution in his relations with the Spanish was the governor of Colônia, whose base lay within the tight embrace of Spanish land and maritime forces. In 1770 the new governor of Buenos Aires, Don Juan José de Vértiz y Salcedo,[4] published a *bando* condemning the persistence of Spanish trade with the *praça*.[5] Vértiz ordered his *guardacostas* to patrol the harbor and offshore islands of the entrepôt, inspect all outgoing Portuguese ships, and seize those carrying Spanish goods.[6]

During the early seventies the Spaniards intercepted a few Portuguese small craft leaving Colônia, but most of the vessels that cleared the *praça* seem to have slipped through the blockade to destinations in Santa Catarina, Rio Grande, and Rio de Janeiro.[7] The number of such clearances was quite small, varying from twenty-five in 1733 to a

---

[3] E.g., Lavradio to Pedro José Soares de Figueiredo Sarmento (governor of Colônia), Feb. 14, 1771 and June 2, 1772, CMCM, cod. 15, fols. 76–77, 119ᵛ; *idem* to José Marcelino de Figueiredo (governor of Rio Grande), Apr. 7, 1771, *ibid.*, 58ᵛ–60ᵛ; *idem* to Antônio de Veiga de Andrade, Oct. 26, 1771, *ibid.*, fols. 89ᵛ–90ᵛ. If the Spanish broke the "peace," José Marcelino was authorized to attack "sem entrar em considerações da Fronteira." *Idem* to *idem*, Oct. 25, 1769, quoted in Jônatas da Costa Rego Monteiro, *Dominação espanhola no Rio Grande do Sul*, p. 144.

[4] Mexican-born Vértiz y Salcedo (sometimes written Vertíz, sometimes without accent) was an old Platine hand, having come to Montevideo in 1747 as inspector-general of troops. He was governor of Buenos Aires 1770–1776 and viceroy of the Plata 1777–1784. He left an able record as an administrator, but as a military commander he was distinctly inferior to Don Pedro de Cevallos, his predecessor, whom he admired and envied. So far as I am aware, no adequate biography of Vértiz exists, but see José Torre Revello, "Juan José de Vertíz y Salcedo, governador y virrey de Buenos Aires. . . ." Faculdade de Filosofia e Letras. *Publicaciones del Instituto de Investigaciones Históricas*, LX (Buenos Aires, 1932), and Vértiz's *memoria* in Sigfrido A. Radaelli, ed., *Memorias de los virreyes del Río de la Plata* (Buenos Aires, 1945), pp. 25–197 (hereafter cited Vértiz, *Memoria*).

[5] *Bando* of Nov. 5, 1770, CB, III, 197–200, issued because of the "Maior evidencia de la continuacion del ilicito commercio" with Colônia.

[6] When he learned of the *bando*, Viceroy Lavradio wrote Governor Sarmento that he should never consent to these inspections, but should protest against them. In a postscript, however, he added "Tudo o que acabo de dizer se deve praticar com a mayor prudência." June 2, 1772, CMCM, cod. 15, fol. 119ᵛ.

[7] Lavradio to the Court, Sept. 19, 1772, *RIHGB*, XXVII:1, 233.

low of seven two years later.[8] According to the sureties of their captains, all carried unspecified quantities of hides, showing that that sort of trade with Spaniards still existed. Significantly, however, none of the declarations mentions silver, an omission that suggests why there was a shortage of that metal at the mint in Rio de Janeiro during these years.[9]

The Spanish blockade also restricted the volume of shipping entering Colônia. Although their number is not known, Governor Sarmento frequently complained about shortages of provisions and firewood because of the failure of ships to bring such supplies from Santa Catarina or Rio de Janeiro. On one occasion he bitterly criticized supply officers in Rio de Janeiro for sending him a load of codfish so ill-smelling that it had to be thrown overboard.[10]

Viceroy Lavradio was sensitive to the governor's problems, but could not solve them. Until 1775 he seldom had warships available to take supplies to the outpost, and the hazards of the voyage and the irregularity of government payments discouraged private shippers from contracting to carry government cargoes to the praça.[11] Nevertheless Lavradio managed to send smacks at irregular intervals to Colônia

[8] The "Termos de fiança que dão os capitães de navios que sahem deste Porto [Colônia]," ANRJ, Col. 157, Liv. VIII, indicates the following vessels obtained clearances between May 3, 1771 and Jan. 16, 1777:

1771	7 corvettes	2 yachts	9 smacks	1 navio	1 galley
1772	3 "	1 "	9 "	[none]	[none]
1773	8 "	3 "	11 "	1 navio	2 galleys
1774	4 "	1 "	7 "	[none]	1 galley
1775	4 "	[none]	2 "	[none]	1 galley
1776	10 "	[none]	3 "	[none]	1 "
1777	1 "	[none]	2 "	[none]	[none]

[9] Lavradio to Conde de Valladares (captain-general of Minas Gerais), Aug. 7 and 26, 1771, and Feb. 1, 1772, CMCM, cod. 15 fols. 71^r, 73^v, and 101^r. In these dispatches the viceroy advised that the mint was unable to supply silver coin "pela falta que hâ de prata nesta cidade."

The mint normally manufactured silver coins in 600, 300, and 150 réis units. Between 1768 and 1780, however, it was only able to emit the 600 réis coin in 1770, 1771, and in 1774, while only in 1771 did it produce the 300 and 150 réis denominations. The total silver minted in these years was 8,031,600 réis (1770), 15,668,400 réis (1771), and 11,662,800 réis (1774). See Appendix 3. For the efforts of Spanish authorities to prevent the leakage of silver through Colônia during these years, see Guilhermo Céspedes del Castillo, "Lima y Buenos Aires. Reprocusiones económicas y políticas de la creación del virreinato del Plata," *Anuario de estudos Americanos*, III (Sevilla, 1946), 773.

[10] Lavradio to Sarmento, Mar. 4, 1773, CMCM, cod, 4, fol. 26^r.

[11] The case of Nicolãs Antônio Bonarrote is an example. Bonarrote, a Rio merchant, signed a supply contract in 1768, agreeing to send a shipload of farinha to Colônia. Later the government refused to honor the agreement because of certain irregularities in its terms, for which it admitted the shipper was not responsible. More than two years later, the contractor was still petitioning for his money. Conselho Ultramarino to Viceroy Azambuja, April 23, 1769, and Lavradio to the king, Nov. 4, 1770, BNRJ, 10, 4, 8, nos. 114–115.

with farinha, munitions, and especially money to pay the garrison to retain its loyalty.[12]

The effectiveness of the blockade was also reflected in other ways. Desertions, always a serious problem at Colônia, continued to plague its commander, sometimes involving the flight of individual soldiers and even of entire families to the enemy.[13] The viceroy was concerned about the loss of manpower; to offset it he occasionally sent military prisoners to Colônia to serve out their sentences,[14] but at the same time he directed that "prejudicial persons and useless families" be returned to Rio de Janeiro to eliminate sources of dissension within the praça.[15] Because of the danger of capture by the Spaniards, he ordered Portuguese traders not to venture outside the gates to rendezvous with their correspondents, insisting that the latter should run the risk of detection by coming to the entrepôt themselves.[16] Under these conditions it was impossible for the Spanish to carry away anything that could not be readily concealed, and late in 1770 Lavradio prohibited the dispatch of slaves, long one of the main staples of Colônia's trade, to the Plata.[17]

Even though Colônia could no longer effectively fulfill its primary commercial function, it continued to serve as a useful listening post. Since any American-based Spanish offensive against Brazil would most likely be mounted in the Plata, the viceroy urged the governor to keep him informed of all suspicious movements by the Castilians by interrogating enemy prisoners and by paying informers in Buenos Aires, Montevideo, and the blockade camp of San Carlos.[18] The governors of Rio Grande de São Pedro were under similar instructions.

Borderland Tensions in Rio Grande

During the early seventies each side in divided Rio Grande persisted in harassing the other with the means at its disposal. The Portuguese continued their raids on the old mission estâncias for cattle and

12 This statement is supported by numerous dispatches between Lavradio and Sarmento in CMCM, cods. 4 and 15. See also Chap. XII below.

13 Lavradio to Sarmento, Dec. 24, 1771 and Mar. 4, 1773, CMCM, cod. 15 fol. 88ᵛ, and cod. 4, 26ʳ–29ᵛ.

14 "Carta circular para todos os commandantes dos regimentos de infantaria assim desta praça como dos da Europa," Mar. 20, 1771, ANRJ, Col. 70, Liv. V, fol. 174ᵛ, Lavradio to Sarmento, Mar. 20, 1771, CMCM, cod. 15, fol. 55.

15 Lavradio to Sarmento, Dec. 24, 1771, ibid., fol. 88ᵛ.

16 Lavradio to Sarmento, Mar. 4, 1773, ibid., cod. 4, fols. 26ʳ–29ᵛ.

17 Lavradio to Pedro Correa dos Santos (Ouvidor Geral do Crime), Oct. 10, 1770, ANRJ, Col. 70, Liv. V, fol. 101ᵛ.

18 Lavradio to Sarmento, Apr. 21, 1770, Feb. 14, 1771, May 13, 1772, and Mar. 17, 1773, CMCM, cod. 15, fols. 17ᵛ, 76ʳ–77ʳ, 107ʳ, 157ʳ.

horses in spite of Spanish protests that the stock belonged exclusively to Spain. The Lusitanians also established new estâncias south of the Jacuí-Guaíba as far as the Rio Camaquam, and erected guard posts to protect them from Spanish attack.

While the Portuguese could move freely in the interior, the Spanish made certain that they could not do so within the entrance to the Lagoa dos Patos. They erected several fortifications along its southern shore, and reinforced them by anchoring a number of armed ships in the channel. Every time the Portuguese tried to run a supply ship through this gauntlet it was met by a rain of fire, and upon at least two occasions the vessels became Spanish prizes.

Each incident produced protests and counterblasts from local Spanish and Portuguese authorities who tirelessly repeated the arguments dictated by their superiors in Buenos Aires, Rio de Janeiro, Madrid, and Lisbon. Spanish officials complained that the Lusitanians were violating the existing "peace and harmony" between their Courts by stealing Spanish property (livestock) and by attempting to navigate in Spanish waters. They contended that the Portuguese themselves had recognized Spain's right to control navigation in the Lagoa dos Patos by the "Treaty of the Frontier," the field armistice of August 6, 1763.[19] Portuguese officers rejoined that the so-called treaty had no force since it had never been approved by their government, whose representative had acted without authorization. Moreover, they pointed out that the armistice had been superseded by the Treaty of Paris which, according to Lisbon's interpretation, restored all of Rio Grande to Portugal. Hence Portuguese ships had a perfect right to sail freely in the lagoon, and Spain had no justifiable grounds for keeping warships there.[20] The net result of this spate of paper and ink was the addition of more fuel to an already smoldering fire.

Disturbed about the unstable situation in Rio Grande, the viceroy decided to send one of his aides to the frontier to act as an observer. His choice fell on Francisco José da Rocha, one of his personal retainers (criados),[21] who was appointed sergeant major of the dra-

[19] See above, Chap. IV, p. 100.

[20] The foregoing is based on correspondence between Spanish and Portuguese authorities in DI, XXXV (1901), 241–255, 259–265, and CB, III, 241–245, 258–259; see also Rego Monteiro, Dominação, pp. 144–147.

[21] Francisco José da Rocha Campos Frontoura e Távora had served under the viceroy in the Cascaes regiment, and by his own statements had been a member of the Marquis' household in Portugal. His letters to Lavradio bear the mark of a respectful intimate rather than that of the usual reserved subordinate. Sixteen of his dispatches to Lavradio, written in his own bold hand, and replete with archaic spellings, cover his service in Rio Grande, 1771–1773. They comprise cod. 28 of CMCM. A later series, cod. 29, covers the first year (1775) of his ill-fated governorship of Colônia, and is discussed in other chapters.

goons, but whose primary function was to report to Lavradio every-thing he saw and heard.[22] After a leisurely journey by land and sea,[23] Rocha arrived at Viamão, the temporary capital of Rio Grande, in August 1771.[24] Following conferences with the governor, José Marcelino de Figueiredo, a fellow countryman,[25] the sergeant major traveled up the Guaíba to his post at Rio Pardo.

Rocha was not favorably impressed with his new station, and doubted whether there were sufficient men available to defend the open frontier against enemy attack. After reviewing the dragoons, he reported that many of them were old and infirm, and that their horses were unfit for cavalry duty. He was shocked at the neglect in the arsenals, for strewn about the floor were stacks of arms, some so old that "the *bichos* (insects) have eaten their stocks," and others broken and useless.[26]

Because of the viceroy's concern about Portuguese treatment of the Indians,[27] the sergeant major paid special attention to the Indian vil-lages near his post. He found their inhabitants [28] bereft of clothing and dependent for food upon "the miserable ration of beef" the king

[22] Lavradio indicated Rocha's unique role by referring to him as "Sargento Mayor Francisco Jozé da Rocha, a quem tenho nesse continente para tambem me informar de tudo o que nelle succede e me avizar de quanto se deixão de executar as minhas ordens." To Antônio da Veiga e Andrade, May 19, 1772, *ibid.*, cod. 4, fol. 13.

[23] En route Rocha stopped at Santos, the city of São Paulo, Desterro, and Laguna. At each place he was feted by public officials who clearly recognized that he was an influential person and tried to make a favorable impression upon him. In his first letters to Lavradio he described the geography, inhabitants, economy, and de-fenses of each locality through which he passed. From Santa Catarina he sent the viceroy as gifts "hum barris [*sic*] de agoa ardente da melhor, da mais clara e de menos cheyro, q. aqui achey . . . tao bem hum galo muzico de casta com quatro galinhas . . . [e] huas moscas, ou bezouros . . . os coaes julgo serem de huns q. a V.Ex. ouvidizer tinha a Rainha." Rocha to Lavradio, July 5 and 8 (Santa Catarina) and 27 (Laguna), 1771, *ibid.*, cod. 28, fols. 34ʳ–39ʳ, 47ʳ, 51ʳ–52ʳ. Quota-tions are from the second letter.

[24] Rocha to Lavradio, Viamão, Aug. 11, 1771, *ibid.*, fol. 18ʳ.

[25] I.e., they were apparently both from the same part of Portugal, a district never mentioned in the correspondence of either. For a sketch of the governor, see below, Chap. XVI, pp. 449–450.

[26] Rocha to Lavradio, Rio Pardo, Aug. 30, 1771, *ibid.*, fol. 60ʳ–61ᵛ.

[27] Before Rocha's arrival, Lavradio had written two significant statements to Governor José Marcelino regarding the proper treatment of the Indians in Rio Grande. He believed that the Indians should be assisted and protected to (1) pro-mote the development of agriculture, (2) populate vacant lands, and (3) attract other Indians away from Spain. Dispatches of Mar. 9 and 14, 1771, CMCM, cod 15, fols. 51ʳ–52ʳ, 52ᵛ–54ᵛ.

[28] The Indians are nowhere identified as to family, but they seem to have been the Guaraní "volunteers" who returned from the missions with Gomes Freire in 1759, when the Spanish vigorously pressed for their return. See above, Chap. IV, p. 93. In 1767 José Custódio de Sá e Faria reported that there were more than 3,000 Indians living in *aldeias*, but this estimate probably did not include many living on Portuguese estâncias. To Conde de Azambuja, Jan. 10, 1768, *RIHGB*, XXX:1 (1868), 280–284; cf. Vértiz, *Memoria*, p. 80.

provided. Observing that the whites were accustomed to treat them with contempt, Rocha reproved his fellow countrymen in front of the Indians and invited one of their chiefs to his table. He also encouraged his men to marry Indian girls, acting as godfather at three mixed marriages attended by his entire regiment. He urged the viceroy to provide such couples with dowries in the form of seed and agricultural implements, stating that soldier-farmers were the best means of holding the frontier.[29] The sergeant major also arranged with a priest to provide education for the Indian children, and selected promising boys to become apprentices as carpenters, tailors, and blacksmiths. He suggested that some of the girls ought to be entered in the "college of orphans," presumably in Rio de Janeiro.[30]

Before Rocha had been in Rio Grande many months, he became caught up in the intense factionalism that divided that frontier captaincy's leading figures. His involvement began late in 1771, when the viceroy suddenly recalled Governor José Marcelino[31] and instructed Rocha to assist his temporary successor, Antônio da Veiga e Andrade. Although Rocha pledged that he would, he soon found it impossible to work with Veiga e Andrade because of the shady dealings of the new governor and his friends.[32]

Rocha charged that "the two principal objects of this government are the round ups (corridas) of the cattle of Spain (that is to say, thefts [sic]), and the administration of the Indians."[33] With respect to the former, he accused Veiga e Andrade of permitting his former associate, Rafael Pinto Bandeira, to conduct the corridas for his own rather than the king's benefit: Bandeira allegedly signed contracts to supply stock for the king's service, used the king's horses and Indian vassals to obtain the spoils, and then controlled the bidding for them in such a way that he secured for himself the choicest animals at a minimum of cost.[34] Rocha also contended that the new governor permitted Bandeira and a few cohorts to monopolize the annual

29 Viceroy Lavradio expressed the same views in the dispatches cited in n. 27 above and on many other occasions.

30 Rocha to Lavradio, Aug. 30 and Oct. 22, 1771, CMCM, cod. 28, fols. 60ʳ–61ᵛ, 6ʳ–9ᵛ, both from Rio Pardo.

31 The circumstances are discussed in Chap. XVI, pp. 450–451.

32 Rocha stated that it was common knowledge that when Veiga e Andrade had served as commander of the Rio Pardo post some years before, he had collected 400,000 réis as his share of the profits from a large corrida. Rocha to Lavradio, Viamão, Jan. 27, 1772, CMCM, cod. 28, fol. 53ʳ.

33 Ibid., fol. 54ʳ.

34 Ibid., fols. 54ʳ–55ʳ and Rocha to Lavradio, Feb. 1 and 28, 1772, fols. 68ʳ–69ʳ, and 75ʳ⁻ᵛ. In the same file is a signed copy of one of Bandeira's proposals: "Eu me ofereço a V.Sa p.a hir correr as egoas por conta del Rey . . . e polas nesta Capella [Viamão] donde podem render a C[o]roa 6 ou 7 mil cruzados a p.a esta dilig.a preciso de coatro sentos cavallos e outenta peças sendo coarenta indios e a despeza

roundup of new mares from public ranges and that Bandeira illegally substituted calves and colts for fully grown animals belonging to the royal stock farms. But Bandeira was not the only one whom Rocha accused of fraud. He reported that an "infinity [of] traders who negotiate [here] in horses, mares, mules, and cattle . . . are not [local] estancieiros, [for] the majority [are] Paulistas from Minas," who evaded the taxes on animals exported from the captaincy by sending their herds over back trails where customs posts did not exist. Rio Grande, said Rocha, is "a nest of thieves." [35]

Another official whom the dragoon commander singled out for taking advantage of his position was the long-time local Indian commissioner, Pinto Carneiro. He accused him of exploiting the tribesmen by assigning them to work on his own properties and those of his friends or sending them on the corridas and diverting their earnings into his own pockets. No one knew, the Sergeant Major said, how much the commissioner had stolen because he had never been required to render an accounting.[36]

The assignment of lands in Rio Grande was another object of Rocha's criticism. He reported that most of his own officers had taken up lands south of the Jacuí near Rio Pardo, and recommended that plots be awarded to enlisted men to give them an economic stake in the captaincy and to discourage desertions. He indignantly complained that Governor Veiga e Andrade had asked his advice concerning which persons ought to get lands in a district about to be opened up, then ignored his recommendations and parceled out the lands among his favorites.[37]

Sergeant Major Rocha strongly recommended that the viceroy order a judicial inquiry to verify these charges, since a devassa would show that Governor Veiga e Andrade, Rafael Pinto Bandeira, Pinto Carneiro, and even former governor José Custódio were responsible

---

q. hé preciza para esta dilig.a hé ordem p.a pagar a estes trabalhadores em egoas e potros da mesma corrida q. poderão chegar ao . . . 300 animais e eu levarei coarenta cavallos c/pioins suficientes meus sem mais emterece q. servir al El Rey." To Viega e Andrade, Dec. 21, 1772, fol. 57ᵛ (orig.). According to Rocha, Bandeira and 150 Indians captured 1,500 horses in one raid, but lost nearly half of them. In a later expedition Bandeira was more successful and netted 1,016 stallions, mares, and colts. To Lavradio, Feb. 1, and 28, 1772, and Mar. 15, 1773, *ibid.*, fols. 68ʳ–69ʳ, 75ʳ and 20ʳ.

35 Rocha to Lavradio, Oct. 22, 1771 and Feb. 28, 1772, cited in the notes above.

36 Rocha to Lavradio, Jan. 27, 1772, *ibid.*, fols. 55ʳ–57ʳ.

37 Rocha to Lavradio, Nov. 29 and Dec. 8, 1771, Jan. 21 and Feb. 11, 1772, *ibid.*, fols. 12ʳ–15ʳ, 73ʳ–74ᵛ, 45ʳ–51ʳ, 59ʳ. Curiously enough, in the second of these dispatches Rocha coyly suggested that if Lavradio felt his criado should be rewarded for his services, he would be glad to have a small ranch either for himself ("to sustain my family with decency") or as a dowry for his daughter, who was, he reminded the viceroy, the latter's godchild!

for "the ruin of this continent," that is, Rio Grande.[38] However, he asked that Lavradio not make public his bill of particulars because these men had already promised to take vengeance upon him as soon as the viceroy retired. Whether or not Rocha had really been threatened, one is not surprised to find him begging "for the love of God" to be transferred to another post.[39]

It is difficult to gauge how many of Rocha's charges were based on fact, and to what extent they reflected the recriminations of persons excluded from the spoils.[40] He admitted, for example, having listened to a number of aggrieved public officials as well as to several of his own relatives who were on military duty in Rio Grande.[41] No doubt influential persons did obtain preferential treatment in land distributions, and the Indians of Rio Grande probably were exploited for their labor as they were elsewhere in Brazil. As for cattle rustling, it had long been an important activity in the captaincy, but most Portuguese officials shared Viceroy Lavradio's view that the corridas were quite legitimate since the stock belonged to the Indian vassals of Portugal, not to the Spanish successors of the Jesuits.[42]

Nevertheless, Rocha's unsavory charges undoubtedly stimulated Viceroy Lavradio's desire to visit Rio Grande himself. For several years he had been disturbed about the persistence of the military stalemate, and had repeatedly warned the Court that he had neither the troops nor the armament necessary to repel a possible Spanish attack along the broad front extending from Colônia to São Paulo.

---

38 Rocha to Lavradio, Feb. 1, 1772, *ibid.*, fol. 69ᵛ. The precise meaning of the word *continente* has occasioned considerable debate among Brazilian historians. E.g., Francisco Adolfo de Varnhagen, *História geral do Brasil*, IV, 20 and n. 40. The documents used in this study make it clear that it was intended merely as a synonym for *terra* (land, or mainland).

39 Rocha to Lavradio, Feb. 27, 1772, fol. 57ᵛ.

40 In one reply to Rocha, Lavradio thanked him for his reports and urged him to continue them, but warned him to stay out of the intrigues and plots which "have always been the ruin of the officers who have been stationed there." In another, he cautioned his aide against believing everything that he heard, stating wisely "hê certo, que quem se acha em empregos semelhantes, sempre tem infinitos inimigos, e que estes empregào toda a arte para fazerem parecer verdade o que nem sombra tem della. O interesse dos máos homens em toda a parte hê dezunirem as pessoas mais principaes, que junto podem concorrer para se lhe castigar as suas maladades, e lhes embaraçarem os seos excessos." June 11 and July 21, 1772, CMCM, cod. 15, fols. 117ʳ–118ᵛ.

41 Five of the latter are identified in Rocha's dispatches, and the sergeant major specifically recommened three of his relatives in the Bragança regiment for promotions.

42 Thus Lavradio praised the efforts of José Marcelino to aid the Indians and relieve the treasury of the expense of sustaining them by encouraging the tribesmen to gather "gado bravo, sem dono nem marca dos Dominios de Espanha," adding "nem para a corrida de gado era precizo o parecer dos Moralistas, quando sabemos que este era dos mesmos Indios, que o deixarão por eses Campos, na ocazião em que vierão com o Sr. Conde de Bobadela." Oct. 9, 1770, CMCM, cod. 15, fols. 32ʳ–34ʳ.

He was particularly concerned lest a renewed surge of Paulista expansionism south and southwest of São Paulo provoke a Spanish attack on Rio Grande or on the lightly defended captaincy-general of São Paulo.[43] Several times during 1773 the viceroy requested permission to lead a contingent of reinforcements to Rio Grande in order to organize its defenses.[44]

In spite of Lavradio's warnings, Lisbon appeared to be unconcerned about the military situation in Brazil. Indeed, his complaints about the bellicose activities of the captain-general of São Paulo drew a rather irritated reminder that the Court expected its viceroys and captains-general to cooperate in the defense of southern Brazil and to refrain from quarreling about so serious a matter.[45] In a further slap the Crown instructed the viceroy to send Luís Antônio de Sousa, captain-general of São Paulo, whatever men and money he needed to carry out his projects within "Portuguese territory." [46] Not until 1775 did the Court acknowledge Lavradio's request to travel to Rio Grande, and then the colonial secretary informed him that it would be inexpedient for him to do so.[47]

Time would show that Lavradio's apprehensions concerning the borderlands were justified, and that the Court was indulging in wishful thinking when it assumed that Spain would permit the stalemate to continue indefinitely. Only after the unsuccessful Spanish expedition of 1773–1774 was Lisbon sufficiently aroused to adopt a policy of decisive action in Rio Grande.

The Vértiz Expedition to Rio Grande [48]

Juan José Vértiz y Salcedo had long been anxious to attack the Portuguese. Shortly after becoming governor of Buenos Aires, he sent Madrid a summary of recent Portuguese acts in violation of his na-

43 For the revival of Paulista expansionist activities in the 1760s and 1770s, see Chap. XVI, pp. 462–463.

44 See the extracts from Lavradio's letters to the Court, Mar. 1772 to Dec. 1773 in *RIHGB*, XXVII:1 (1864) , 231–243, and those of Mar. 16, July 9 and 16, 1773 cited in *VRL*, pp. 44–46. I have not been able to find complete texts of these dispatches.

45 Martinho de Melo e Castro to Lavradio, Oct. 10, 1771, CMCM, cod. 3, fol. 144ʳ (orig.) ; *idem to idem*, Nov. 20, 1772, *ibid.*, fols. 188ʳ–195ʳ (*1.a via*) , published in *VRL*, pp. 171–181.

46 Two cartas régias, Aug. 13, 1771, CMCM, cod. 3, fols. 134ʳ and 136ʳ (*únicas vias*) , published in *VRL*, pp. 166–167.

47 See below, Chap. VI, n. 1.

48 The most complete accounts of the expedition, Octavio Gil Munilla, *El Río de la Plata en la política internacional*, pp. 189–197, 229–230, and Rego Monteiro, *Dominação*, pp. 179–201, pay scant attention to the motives behind it or to its impact on subsequent Portuguese borderlands policy, lacunae which justify the space given to these themes in this chapter.

tion's legitimate rights. He reported that the Portuguese governor in Rio Grande openly sanctioned plundering raids against Spanish live-stock, and that "robbers" were supported by armed troops. The governor of Colônia "consents to, foments, and maintains" illicit trade with Spanish colonials by sending smacks to the Río de Solís, close to Maldonado, to exchange merchandise for hides. He stated that he was complaining about these matters to Viceroy Lavradio, but that if the latter refused to stop them, he considered the only alternative was to undertake reprisals himself.[49]

Vértiz was not the only Spanish official to view Portuguese activities with concern. In Peru Viceroy Manuel Amat had received reports of a new Paulista fort on the Rio Iguatemí, only thirty leagues away from the Spanish *villa* of San Isidro Labrador de Curuguatí in north-eastern Paraguay. Since Amat was convinced that the Paulistas' purpose was to establish clandestine trade with the Paraguayans, he ordered Vértiz to expel them. The governor declined to organize such an expedition, however; for he considered it would be "dangerous, costly, and of dubious results." He pointed out that because of the Falkland Island dispute with Great Britain he did not dare to leave the Plata, and suggested an alternative venture that would be less risky and more productive.[50]

That alternative was an attack on Colônia. Early in 1771 he convoked a military junta in Montevideo to formulate future Platine strategy. One of several plans the junta drew up called for the bombardment and capture of Colônia and the destruction of its installations by mining. The committee also proposed that concomitant with this attack a diversionary expedition be sent to assault Portuguese positions in the vicinity of Rio Pardo to prevent relief from being sent to the entrepôt.[51] This dual proposal contained the seeds of both Vértiz' expedition of 1773–1774 and the Cevallos' conquest and efface-ment of Colônia in 1777.

Early in 1772 Vértiz sought the Court's authorization to proceed with an attack on Colônia. The request was referred to the Council of the Indies, which viewed it with misgivings, for the Council feared the British would intervene if the outpost were taken again. Conse-quently Vértiz' request was shelved, and he was told to guard the points most seriously menaced by Portuguese aggression and to re-cover any territory the enemy invaded.[52]

[49] Vértiz to Julián de Arriaga, Nov. 8, 1770, *CB*, III, 200–201.

[50] See the exchange of letters between Carlos Morphi (governor of Paraguay), Viceroy Amat, and Vértiz, 1768–1771, *CB*, III, 214–235.

[51] Plan II of the "Plan de operaciones y acta de la junta militar celebrada por orden del Governador de Buenos Aires en . . . Montevideo para tratar en particu-lar la defensa de esa Plaza," Montevideo, Feb. 21, 1771, *CB*, III, 202–203.

[52] Vértiz to Arriaga, Jan. 5, 1772, and *parecer* of the Consejo, Dec. 22, 1771, cited in Gil Munilla, p. 193. At this time Spanish forces in the Plata numbered

As the months passed, it became plain to Vértiz that while the Portuguese in Colônia were not in a position to do the Spanish serious harm, their compatriots in Rio Grande definitely were. In August 1772 he wrote the Crown that the corridas were committing "great thefts" of Spanish livestock, and that the Portuguese had established seventy new estâncias south of the Rio Jacuí. The governor sought permission to expel the invaders, and this time his request was granted.[53]

Vértiz was anxious to carry out his mission successfully, but only after a year of careful planning and several unexpected delays was he able to set out for Rio Grande.[54] In April 1773 he dispatched reinforcements to the Vila of Rio Grande with instructions to its commander to keep the Portuguese on the peninsula busy while he struck in the back country.[55] The governor also directed local authorities in Corrientes and Sante Fé to provide men and horses to join him on the march, and ordered Captain Don Antonio Gómez, in charge of the Rio Grande missions, to proceed southeast toward Rio Pardo with 300 Indians and 100 militiamen.[56] By September the governor began withdrawing troops from Buenos Aires, Montevideo, and San Carlos ostensibly to conduct training exercises. Satisfied with his preparations, Vértiz wrote his Court on the eve of his departure that he was certain of success.[57]

3,202 men and 210 officers. Vértiz to Arriaga, Nov. 8, 1770, *ibid.*, 190–191, n. 37. Most of them were stationed in island or mainland positions around Colônia, at Montevideo, Maldonado, Santa Teresa, San Miguel, and in Rio Grande. *Memoria* of Governor Bucareli, quoted in Emilio Ravignani, "El Virreinato del Rio de la Plata (1776–1810)," Ricardo Levene, ed., *Historia de la nación Argentina*, IV:1 (2d ed., Buenos Aires, 1940), 66.

53 Vértiz to Arriaga, Aug. 25, 1772, summarized in royal order of Dec. 14, 1772, *CB*, III, 213–214; cf. Emilio Coni, *El Gaucho: Argentina-Brasil-Uruguay* (Buenos Aires [1945]), pp. 173 ff., for a revealing account of Luso-Spanish conflict over the cattle of Rio Grande and the Banda Oriental.

54 One of the reasons for Vértiz' delay was a serious drought which swept through the Plata early in 1773. Vértiz to Arriaga, Apr. 20, 1773, cited in Gil Munilla, p. 197. On the advice of Captain Molina (Spanish commander in Rio Grande), he decided to wait until November when the rains had ceased and the interior waters had receded, for Molina assured him that his proposed route would be impassable for heavily laden troops in winter. Molina to Vértiz, Mar. 30, 1773, *CB*, III, 261. Vértiz seems to have had some reservations about his mission, for he again wrote Arriaga for approval of his project on April 25, 1773, *ibid.*, 257–258.

55 Vértiz to Molina, April 25, 1773, *ibid.*, pp. 256–257.

56 "Extracto del diario de las operaciones del destacam.to que el 7 de Nov.e de 1772, salió de Montevideo al mando del S.r D.n Jph de Vértiz," n.d., *ibid.*, pp. 267–284 (hereafter cited as "Diario").

57 Vértiz to Arriaga, Montevideo, Nov. 2, 1773, *ibid.*, pp. 265–266. Two letters written by a soldier in Vértiz' army to an intimate in Buenos Aires were intercepted by the Portuguese at Colônia and were later forwarded to the viceroy. They provide some interesting details on the preparations for the march, and reveal that the Spanish were confident that the Portuguese would be easily defeated since they were expected to be besotted with *agua ardente*. Christovão Gutierres de Aguirre to Estevão Solha, [Montevideo?], Oct. 12 and off Martín García Island, Oct. 22, 1773, CMCM, cod. 29, fols. 48r–49v.

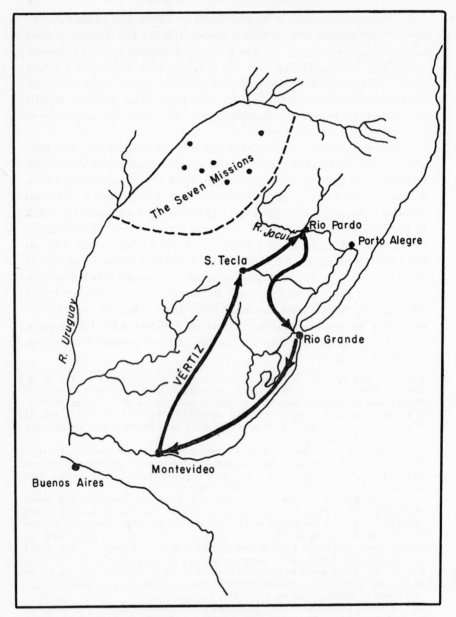

Map 7 The Vértiz expedition to Rio Grande, 1773–1774. (After F. de Paula
Cidade, *Lutas, ao sul do Brasil . . .* , fig. 2.)

The Spanish army—1,014 men,[58] 114 wagons, and 1,400 horses —left Montevideo on November 7, 1773,[59] and proceeded in a generally northeasterly direction through the Cuchilla Grande toward the former Jesuit estâncias.[60] When it had reached the headwaters of the Rio Camaquam in the Serra de Bagé, Vértiz paused to erect the fort of Santa Tecla on a commanding height near the site of the first Guaraní resistance twenty years before. The fort, a formidable one, was situated at the crossroads of several trails connecting Paraguay, Rio Grande, and the Plata, and was intended to prevent Portuguese depredations to the south and to cut off the illicit movement of Spanish stock to the north.[61]

After leaving a well-supplied garrison at Santa Tecla, the governor renewed his march on December 21. He was somewhat perturbed by Captain Gómez' failure to report on his progress, for Vértiz wanted to effect a pincers movement on the Portuguese fortified settlement of Rio Pardo. Consequently he sent the captain a message to hurry his advance. From Santa Tecla the Spanish army moved across the Serra dos Tapes, fording several small streams, detouring around falls, and passing through box canyons and thick woods until, on January 5, 1774, it reached the Rio Piquirí, a southern tributary of the Jacuí. There a Portuguese post of twenty-one men was quickly overrun.[62] Encouraged by his "victory" at fifty-to-one odds, Vértiz sent an ultimatum to the Portuguese commandant of Rio Pardo, informing him that if all his people did not immediately retire from "Spanish" territory between Rios Camaquam and Jacuí, they would be treated as "robbers and disturbers of the public peace." [63]

[58] Contemporary Portuguese accounts, like the Spanish, generally grossly exaggerate enemy strength. In the case of the Vértiz force, Portuguese estimates range from 5,000 to 8,000 men, figures still accepted by some Brazilian historians (excepting Rego Monteiro). The estimates given in the text are the ones in the "Diario" and in the "Estado de la tropa que D. Juan Joseph de Vértiz llevó para su propria defensa, quando salió á reconocer en el año de 1773 los dominios de S.M. en las provincias de su mando," [Marquis of Grimaldi], *Respuesta a la memoria que presentó en 16 de Enero de 1776 el Exmo Señor Don Francisco Inocencio de Souza Coutiño* (Madrid, 1776) p. lxxviii (reprinted in *CTLA,* III, 98), and are consistent with the sources cited in n. 52 above.

[59] "Diario," 267–268.

[60] This was the same route taken by Spanish forces during the second phase of the Guaraní War, and followed a natural but seldom used land route to the missions. F[rancisco] da Paula Cidade, *Lutas, ao sul do Brasil* (Rio de Janeiro, 1948), p. 88.

[61] There is a good description of Santa Tecla in Alcides Cruz, *A Vida de Rafael Pinto Bandeira* (Pôrto Alegre, 1906), p. 45. See also Teodoro Becu and José Torre Revello, "La colección de documentos de Pedro de Angelis . . . ," Facultad de Filosofía y Letras. *Publicaciones del Instituto de Investigaciones Históricas,* LXXV (Buenos Aires, 1941), Plate VII.

[62] Vértiz boasted in his *memoria* of 1784 "me avanzé al rio Piquirí donde ya tenía noticia se hallaban atrincherados los Portugueses, que cedieron el terreno sin gran resistencia no obstante su ventajosa situación." p. 81.

[63] Vértiz to commandant of Rio Pardo, Bank of the Piquirí, Jan. 5, 1774, Rego Monteiro, *Dominação,* pp. 189–192.

The Vértiz expedition represented a very real threat to the Portuguese hold on Rio Grande. To resist the Spaniards, Governor José Marcelino had only 714 men, most of them stationed near São José do Norte on the peninsula. There was but a single company of Santa Catarina militia in the new capital of Pôrto Alegre,[64] and 263 effectives on the Rio Pardo front, where they faced an adversary more than five times as numerous.[65] As soon as he learned of Vértiz' departure from Montevideo,[66] José Marcelino ordered one of his subordinates to round up all available men near Rio Pardo and concentrate them within the fort. Then the governor went to São José do Norte to prepare for a possible cross-channel attack. Since he did not know what Captain Molina, the Spanish commander of the vila, might do, José Marcelino did not dare weaken the peninsular garrison in order to strengthen his defenses in the interior. Returning to Pôrto Alegre, he mobilized all militia units and sent instructions for two scouting parties, one under Rafael Pinto Bandeira and the other under Miguel Pedroso Leite, to keep under surveillance the movements of the converging Spanish forces.[67]

In the ensuing operations, Captain Rafael Pinto Bandeira proved that he was not only a successful leader of corridas but also a resourceful guerrilla fighter.[68] Assigned to patrol the westernmost sector and to intercept Spanish forces expected from the missions, Bandeira left his post at Encruzilhada late in December 1773, and with about forty men marched west to the Rio Irapúa. There he was

[64] The capital of Portuguese Rio Grande was moved from Viamão to Pôrto Alegre, a few leagues away, in 1773, and has remained there ever since.

[65] "Mappa das tropas que guarnecem a Cap.nia do Rio Grande de S. Pedro," Pôrto Alegre, July 9, 1773, DI, XXXV, 163. The Spanish believed that the Portuguese had four times as many troops in Rio Grande. Relying on "informes contextes de varios desertores y otras personas," they estimated the Portuguese garrison at 2,942 men. Vértiz to Arriaga, Sept. 28, 1773, CB, III, 261–263.

[66] Late in November, 1773, the Riograndense governor received a warning from the governor of Colônia that Vértiz was about to march northward. José Marcelino de Figueiredo to Lavradio, Nov. 28, 1773, DI, XXXV, 257–259.

[67] The best account of José Marcelino's movements is Cruz, pp. 46–47.

[68] On Bandeira's colorful career (1740–1795) the only biography is the old, thin, romanticized one by Alcides Cruz cited above in n. 61. A less favorable account of his activities is Florêncio Abreu, "Govêrno de José Marcelino de Figueiredo no govêrno de São Pedro—1769 a 1780," Anais do segundo congresso de história e geografia sul Rio-Grandense, III (Pôrto Alegre, 1937), 177–207. A controversial figure even in his own time, as has already been mentioned, Bandeira was the subject of a lengthy devassa because of charges brought against him by one of his most prominent enemies, José Marcelino. In spite of strong evidence that he had greatly profited from his wartime activities, Bandeira was fully exonerated, and later made a triumphant visit to Lisbon, where he was introduced at Court. Subsequently he returned to Rio Grande, and for a time filled the post of interim governor. The devassa of 1779–1780 is published from materials in ANRJ in the very rare No. 23 of the Revisita do Archivo Público do Rio Grande do Sul (1931), of which there is a copy in CMCM.

joined by the Paulista Cypriano Cardoso de Barros Leme who headed a detachment of fifty-five militiamen and ten dragoons. His forces now numbering slightly more than 100 men, Bandeira went in search of Don Antonio Gómez.

Gómez, accompanied by 310 Indians and two companies of Corrientes militia, had instructions to proceed to within three leagues of a Portuguese post on the Rio Tabatingaí where he was to receive further orders. But somehow he became lost, and on January 2, 1774 he was encamped on the bank of the Santa Bárbara, another tributary of the Jacuí, but considerably to the west of the Tabatingaí. As dawn broke that day, Pinto Bandeira suddenly emerged from the mist-covered woods and attacked the Spanish camp. The issue was quickly decided, for Gómez' Indian troops, who were armed with lances and arrows, panicked before the musket-firing Portuguese and fled the field. The captain, two of his officers, and eighty men quickly became Bandeira's prisoners. Besides a large quantity of horses, cattle, and mules, the victors also captured a copy of Vértiz' orders to Captain Gómez.[69]

Meanwhile, ignorant of the fate of Gómez, General Vértiz continued to advance on Rio Pardo. After reaching the Rio Piquirí he divided his forces, and while leading one column himself, sent the other under Don Francisco Bruno de Zabala down the Rio Tabatingaí to establish connections with Gómez. When Vértiz had arrived within two leagues of Rio Pardo, he made a new camp and confidently sent a second ultimatum to the Portuguese.

Vértiz' confidence was misplaced, for Zabala was about to become Bandeira's second victim. Commanding a force of 400 Corrientes and Santafecino militia, Don Francisco crossed the Tabatingaí and advanced toward a Portuguese post he intended to capture, situated on a hill between the river and some swamps. Suddenly he found himself in the midst of an ambush prepared by the returning Pinto Bandeira. Throughout the entire day (January 14) Bandeira, whose knowledge of the terrain was unrivaled, proved himself a master of Fabian tactics as he taunted the Spanish by firing upon them and then withdrawing into the trackless swamps, only to emerge again and take pot shots at his bewildered adversaries. After vainly trying to pin down the Portuguese and suffering untold casualties for his pains, the thoroughly demoralized Zabala finally retired and headed for Vértiz' camp.[70]

---

[69] There is a good account of the action in Cruz, p. 47; see also José Marcelino de Figueiredo to Lavradio, Jan. 4/5, 1774, *VRL*, pp. 54-55, and Francisco Bruno de Zavala to [Vértiz], Jan. 10, 1774, *CB*, III, 281-282.

[70] See Rego Monteiro, *Dominação*, pp. 192-195 and sources cited there; also Cruz, pp. 49-55. It is amusing to see how the "Diario" (p. 280) glosses over these actions.

Zabala's unexpected return and the news of two Spanish defeats within a fortnight greatly discouraged Vértiz. He abruptly notified Governor José Marcelino, who had just reached Rio Pardo, that he had completed his "inspection" of the frontier, and was proceeding to examine other parts of his government.[71] The General then wheeled about and marched south toward the vila of Rio Grande. Until he crossed the Rio Camaquam his movements were carefully watched by Portuguese guerrillas.

When he had reached the vila Vértiz addressed several irate letters to José Marcelino, complaining that Pinto Bandeira's attack on Captain Gómez' forces was an "express insult . . . contrary to the rights of man" and to "the perfect peace and good correspondence" which existed between their respective sovereigns. He warned the Portuguese governor that any attempt to restore his former guard posts would be regarded as a "clear and evident infraction of the peace."[72] Unimpressed, José Marcelino replied with equally pompous language and reposted his guards. Then he reported the Spaniards' repulse to the viceroy.[73]

The First Portuguese Responses to the New Spanish Challenge

It was not until the last day of November 1773 that the viceroy had definite information concerning Vértiz' departure from Montevideo.[74] Correctly surmising that the general was headed for Rio Grande, Lavradio immediately made arrangements to reinforce that captaincy. He assembled two companies of his personal guard and 400 "volunteers" selected from the capital's regiments, and dispatched them to the Lagoa dos Patos [75] under Colonel Sebastião Xavier da

71 Vértiz to José Marcelino de Figueiredo, Jan. 16, 1774, cited in Rego Monteiro, *Dominação*, p. 193. Vértiz' own account of why he withdrew is incredible, for he states that he had received word of the departure of General Böhm with two complete regiments from Rio de Janeiro for Rio Grande and of the dispatch of a battalion for Colônia. In fact, Böhm did not leave Rio de Janeiro until Dec. 5, 1774, and the reinforcements were not sent to Colônia until late 1775. See below, Chap. VI; cf. Vértiz, *Memoria*, pp. 81–82 and "Diario," 277–281.

72 Vértiz' three dispatches of Feb. 17 and 18, 1774 are published together with José Marcelino's reply of Mar. 6, 1774, in *DI*, XXXV, 261–280. In Vértiz' protests, he reiterated Spain's position that her rights to Rio Grande rested on the "Treaty of the Frontier."

73 The governor's dispatches of Jan. 15 and 19, 1774, are mentioned in Lavradio to José Marcelino de Figueiredo, Feb. 28, 1774, *VRL*, pp. 187–192.

74 Lavradio to the Court, n. d. [probably Dec. 12, 1773], *RIHGB*, XXVII:1, 240–241.

75 The guard companies were led by their commander, Gaspar José de Matos Ferreira e Lucena, who was elevated from captain to sergeant major for this mission. For his later career, see Chap. XVI, n. 17.

Veiga Cabral da Câmara; he named the latter as military commander of Rio Grande, a post which made him superior to its governor.[76] To organize land and sea transport for the relief force, he designated Captain Francisco João Roscîo and sent him to Santa Catarina.[77] Dom Luís also called upon the administrators neighboring captaincies-general for support. He asked the captain-general of Minas Gerais to send him as many recruits as possible,[78] and directed the captain-general of São Paulo to forward to Rio Grande three companies of the "old" Rio de Janeiro regiment, then on loan to São Paulo, an artillery company, and several "picked" Paulista militia companies.[79]

While engaged in these preparations the marquis found time to unburden himself in a long dispatch addressed to the colonial secretary. The present crisis, the viceroy intimated, was the direct result of the Court's failure to heed his repeated supplications for men, munitions, weapons, and a naval squadron to defend Brazil. He complained that his fellow governors depended upon him to furnish them military aid to defend their captaincies, but that he was unable to

76 Veiga Cabral was promoted from lieutenant colonel to colonel for this assignment. With the rank of brigadier general, he served as governor of Rio Grande de São Pedro from 1780 to 1801.

77 Subsequently Lavradio ordered Roscîo to proceed to Rio Grande "para n'elle fazer dirigir as obras, e o mais, que for necessario para a defeza do mesmo Continente . . . fazendo . . . ao mesmo tempo todas as observações que lhe forem possiveis para se haver de forma um mappa do mesmo continente mais certo, e com menos defeito que até agora se tem feito." To Roscîo, Feb. 15, 1774, *RIHGRGS*, XIX:1 (1939), 15–17. The result of Roscîo's extensive travels and note-taking was his "Compêndio noticioso do continente do Rio Grande de São Pedro" (1781), *ibid.*, XXII:2 (1942), 29–56 and republished *ibid.*, XXVII (1947), 49–75, where Aurelio Porto calls it "the oldest known document concerning Riograndense geography." Unpublished are Roscîo's "Mappas particulares extrahidos da carta da Capit.nia do Rio Grande de S. Pedro e suas circunuinhanças [sic] ate o R.o da Prata," BNRJ, 5-4-35. The text is dated "Lisboa, June 21, 1781," and the maps "Rio de Jan.ro em Jan.ro 1783."

78 Lavradio to Antônio Carlos Furtado de Mendonça (temporary captain-general of Minas), Dec. 14, 1773, CMCM, cod. 4, fol. 23ʳ. Later Lavradio thanked Antônio Carlos for the "admirable recruits" he sent. *Idem* to *idem*, Jan. 25, 1774, *ibid.*, fols. 33ʳ–34ʳ, but the same codex shows that many of these "admirable" Mineiros deserted as soon as they reached Rio de Janeiro.

79 Lavradio to Dom Luís Antônio de Sousa, Dec. 14, 1773, CMCM, maço 15 (rascunho). This was a very bitter dispatch, in which the viceroy blamed Sousa's headstrong expansionist activities as partially responsible for the "great risk" in which Rio Grande and São Paulo had been placed. At the bottom of the draft appear the following figures:

583
300
859
400
―――
1,842 [sic for 2,142]

These were apparently Lavradio's calculations of the total number of troops he hoped to have in Rio Grande when the various reinforcements had arrived.

accede to their appeals because his regiments were undermanned, his warehouses were virtually empty,[80] and his exchequer was close to exhaustion. "I leave to the consideration of Your Excellency," he added bitterly, "the affliction in which I find myself." With obvious heat he declared that the captain-general of São Paulo had his own ideas on how Rio Grande should be defended, and "with the most obstinate caprice" had withheld aid that the viceroy intended for the stricken captaincy. In short, Lavradio concluded, everything appeared to be conspiring to bring stain upon his honor and an unhappy destiny to Brazil.[81]

Coming from one who normally exercised great restraint in his dispatches to the Court, this was rather strong language. Probably Dom Luís realized that his intemperate remarks were likely to draw a severe rebuke, but he doubtless regarded his situation as so critical as to warrant such a hazard.

Far from reprimanding him, however, both the colonial secretary and the Marquis of Pombal replied that the viceroy had their full support. They approved all the measures he had taken to meet the crisis, as well as his recommendation that General Böhm be sent to Rio Grande. The colonial minister stated that the general ought to be named supreme commander in the south with instructions to defend all Portuguese rights there, particularly that of free access to the Lagoa dos Patos, and to take the offensive if the Spaniards showed a disposition to resume their attack on Portuguese positions and ignored all appeals to desist.[82]

The viceroy was also promised that armaments and additional troops would soon be sent secretly to him,[83] to include 600 barrels of powder, an artillery train consisting of eleven cannon and four bronze six-inch howitzers, and 100 Madeiran "volunteers." Lavradio

---

[80] His assertion was not strictly true. In 1772 the Court had sent large amounts of clothing of every size and description for the dragoons in Rio Grande and other soldiers at Colônia, Santa Catarina, and Rio de Janeiro. In a covering letter the colonial secretary explained that because of the limited productive capacity of the royal cloth factories, a schedule had been devised to equip the military units stationed in various parts of Brazil during different times of the year. The allowance for troops in Grão Pará was to be available on January 1; those in Pernambuco and Bahia, on April 1; and those in Rio de Janeiro and its dependencies on July 6. Melo e Castro to Lavradio, Nov. 20, 1772, CMCM, cod. 3, fol. 206^r (orig.). Bills of lading (*conhecimentos*) for clothing shipments to Rio de Janeiro follow, fols. 207^r–225^r.

[81] Lavradio to Melo e Castro, Dec. 13, 1773. There is an undated copy in CMCM, *maço* 15, and a dated draft in *maço* 31 which contains a PS omitted in the first copy. An excerpt, misdated Dec. 16, 1773, is in *VRL*, pp. 50–51.

[82] Melo e Castro to Lavradio, April 22, 1774, CMCM, cod. 13 (45/20), fols. 32^r–37^r (orig.). There are copies (dated April 21) in BNRJ, 6, 3, 24, fols. 244^r–248^v, and in ANRJ, Col. 67, Liv. III, fols. 40^v–41^r, and an excerpt in *VRL*, pp. 51–52.

[83] Melo e Castro to Lavradio, Apr. 21, 1774, CMCM, cod. 13 (45/15), a draft possibly in Melo e Castro's hand; there is a copy in BNRJ, I-2, 4, 6, n. 49.

was also authorized to select recruits from two convict ships scheduled to stop at Rio de Janeiro while en route to the Indian Ocean.[84]

Besides these pledges of material aid, the Court took pains to reassure the viceroy that he also had its moral support. One way this was achieved was by the drafting of a severe reprimand to Captain-general Sousa of São Paulo for his alleged lack of cooperation with the viceroy. The dispatch was sent via Lavradio and left open for him to read and seal before forwarding it to Sousa.[85] In addition, the Marquis of Pombal took pen in hand and wrote the viceroy a warm personal letter (carta familiar) which began: "My sterile pen is an inadequate witness of my unalterable affection and most constant veneration and friendship [for Your Excellency]. . . ." These sentiments, he assured Dom Luís, motivated his interest in the "reputation of your government" and his desire to do whatever he could to lighten the viceroy's burdens. He added that he was confident that the measures then being taken to thwart the Spaniards would achieve that goal if the Portuguese remained united.[86]

Portuguese Reassessment of the Spanish Challenge

Three months after his reassuring letter to the viceroy, the Marquis of Pombal decided that he had underestimated the seriousness of the Spanish threat, and revamped his strategy accordingly. His decision to do so was based in part on Lavradio's reports concerning Vértiz' misadventure,[87] and in part on a warning from Robert Walpole, British

---

[84] The two ships were bound for Mozambique and India with degredados and munitions. Their captains were given sealed orders to stop at Rio de Janeiro and receive new instructions from the viceroy. These countermanded their original orders, directing that the munitions be unloaded at Rio de Janeiro and that the viceroy would select their sturdiest prisoners as recruits. Melo e Castro to Lavradio, Apr. 21, 1774, CMCM, cod. 13 (45/26) (orig.). Earlier the Colonial Minister advised the viceroy that in view of the "deploravel situação em q. se acham os seus Dominios na Azia," the Crown was dispatching a new governor to India to undertake reforms. He added that the official would be aboard one of these two vessels and would spend three weeks in Rio de Janeiro, where Dom Luís was to render him every possible assistance. Implicitly, this was a reminder that the Crown had more on its mind than his problems in Brazil. Melo e Castro to Lavradio, Feb. 18, 1774, ibid., (45/23) (orig.).

[85] Melo e Castro to Lavradio, Apr. 22, 1774, ibid., fol. 20ʳ (orig.). For the background to this reprimand, see Chap. XVI, pp. 463–468.

[86] Pombal to Lavradio, April 22, 1774, CMCM, cod. 14 (49/2) (orig.); copies in BNRJ, I-2, 4, 6, n. 55, and in ANRJ, Col. 67, Liv. III, fols. 52ᵛ–53ʳ.

[87] Lavradio's dispatches of Feb. 22 and 28, 1774 were received in Lisbon June 3. "Compêndio dos insultos commettidos pelos castelhanos ao sul do Brasil e ùltimamente continuados pelos factos . . . nas duas cartas de 22 e 28 de fevereiro deste . . . anno de 1774 . . . do marquez de Lavradio," Pombal to Walpole, June 10, 1774, in Simão José de Luz Soriano, História do reinado de el-rei d. José e da administração do Marquez de Pombal, II, 546 ff. I have not discovered copies of the

ambassador to Lisbon, that the Spanish were massing four warships and 2,700 men in El Ferrol, northwestern Spain, for an unknown destination.[88] Pombal concluded that the fleet's destination was the Río de la Plata, and that it was intended to reinforce Vértiz so that he could resume his offensive against Rio Grande and possibly assail Colônia as well. To forestall the Spanish, the Portuguese minister decided to take appropriate diplomatic and military measures.

When in distress Portugal, as usual, turned to her one ally, Great Britain, for assistance. Through diplomatic channels Pombal asked for a British fleet to concentrate around El Ferrol so as to force the Spaniards to disarm or, if they refused, to blockade the port. In phrasing his appeal, the secretary raised three strong arguments to justify British action: (1) that the Spanish armada posed a threat to British command of the seas, a palpable exaggeration, to be sure, but one calculated to prick British pride; (2) that the British could easily force the Spanish to back down, just as they had the French when the latter recently attempted to revive their navy at Toulon; and (3) (playing an old Portuguese gambit) that if Spain achieved military dominance in southern South America, she would close the Plata to British as well as to Portuguese trade.[89]

In commenting to the viceroy on his overtures to Britain, Pombal emphasized that Portugal stood to gain substantially if Britain cooperated. If Spain elected to defy England, El Ferrol would be blockaded, and a redeployment of Portuguese forces in southern Brazil would give Portugal clear preponderance in the Debatable Lands. If Spain were foolhardy enough to challenge the British fleet, she would be thoroughly defeated. Then Portugal could easily become master of the Banda Oriental, and unite Colônia, Montevideo, and Maldonado with the rest of Brazil, a prospect which must have brightened the countenance of the crafty old Carvalho.[90]

---

viceroy's dispatches, but they cannot have contained his final remarks on the Vértiz expedition, since on Feb. 28 he wrote Governor Marcelino that he still had not received "uma completa notícia de quais são verdadeiramente as forças dos nossos inimigos, quais teem sido as acções que temos tido, as vantagens delas, o numero que ha de prisoneiros, e que tambem ha de desertores; e finalmente aquelas noticias particulares que eu devo saber, para o meu governo e para informar a nossa corte como sou obrigado." *VRL*, p. 192.

[88] "Plano militar da guerra defensiva," BNRJ, I-2, 4, 6, n. 67; published in part in *BCRG*, pp. 13-17. The Plan comprises Appendix I of Pombal to Lavradio, July 9, 1774, BNRJ, I-2, 4, 6, n. 60; published in full in Visconde de Carnaxide, *O Brasil na administração pombalina*, pp. 255-273, and in excerpt in *CB*, III, 294-313. This dispatch, hereafter cited as General Instruction, amplified *idem* to *idem*, July 15, 1774, BNRJ, I-2, 4, 6, n. 81; also published in *RIHGB*, XXXI:1, 303-307. Despite their chronological differences, the second dispatch was prepared *before* the first and went on its way to Rio de Janeiro before the General Instruction was completed. When not otherwise noted, statements in the following paragraphs rest upon one or both of these dispatches.

[89] General Instruction, pars. 4-11.

[90] *Ibid.*, pars. 12-14.

Much as he hoped for British intervention, the Portuguese minister was not so much of a visionary that he ignored the possibility that Britain would reject his plea, and he cautioned Lavradio that Portugal must be prepared to tackle Spain alone. The borderlands must, therefore, be further reinforced to protect them against a potentially vastly superior Spanish army in the Plata.[91] During the first part of July 1774, Pombal and Colonial Secretary Melo e Castro prepared voluminous instructions for the viceroy indicating how this buildup was to be carried out.

It was first necessary to strengthen the Portuguese position in Rio Grande so that the Spaniards would be forced to relinquish their remaining hold on that captaincy. To this end, Pombal ordered the three Peninsular regiments in Rio de Janeiro transferred to Rio Grande and placed under command of General Böhm, who would continue to be under Lavradio's direction.[92] When added to existing forces in Rio Grande, the regiments would give the general 7,395 men, an army considerably larger than the 6,000 Vértiz was erroneously assumed to possess. After Böhm had deployed his troops to block all mountain passes and river crossings to prevent the Castilians from attacking from the south, or from reinforcing their garrison in the Lagoa dos Patos, he was to send the Spanish commander in the vila of Rio Grande an ultimatum to evacuate all Portuguese territory or risk the consequences. If the Spaniard accepted, his troops could retire to Buenos Aires, but his ships must sail to Rio de Janeiro to compensate José I for the expense he had undergone to recover his legitimate patrimony. Alternatively, if the Spanish chose to fight, they should be bombarded into submission, and upon their capitulation they should be held as prisoners of war.[93] However, their Indian allies were to be well treated so as to attract them to the Portuguese flag. After having liberated the vila, the Austrian was to advance south as far as the Río Chuí and anchor his defenses on Mount Castillos and the former Portuguese fort of São Miguel.[94]

[91] There was no question in the mind of Pombal or of any of his top subordinates, including the viceroy, that man for man, the Portuguese were far superior as fighters to the Spaniards and their Indian levies; yet prudence dictated that the enemy must not be underestimated. As Pombal wrote, "nenhuns inimigos, por pequenos que sejam, se devem desprezar [sic]." *Ibid.*, par. 26.

[92] In his patent as commander of the army, Pombal urged Böhm to work in common accord with Lavradio "ao fim de que entre ambos se divida a m.ta glória, que as Armas de El Rey . . . promettem às direções de dous tão distinctos Generaes." July 22, 1774, *BCRG*, p. 17.

[93] General Instructions, pars. 28, 31, 35–40, and 48.

[94] The General Instructions called for Böhm to suspend hostilities after taking the vila since (1) Portugal would have the diplomatic advantage of appearing to regain only what clearly belonged to her; (2) it would be relatively easy to anchor the defense of Rio Grande by control of both sides of the Lagoa dos Patos; and (3) Pombal wished to avoid the possibility of the army outrunning its supply lines. *Ibid.*, pars. 41–47. Later, however, Pombal happened upon a report, "Reparos sobre

Pombal recognized that a Portuguese assault on Spanish positions in Rio Grande would place Colônia in jeopardy of a retaliatory attack, and insisted that the entrepôt should be defended "to the last extremity." He was noticeably vague as to how the isolated garrison could hope to hold out, and significantly made no provision for its strengthening. Since the viceroy had indicated a lack of confidence in Governor Sarmento, Lavradio was authorized to replace him with a person in whom he placed more reliance.[95]

By contrast, Pombal was more specific about what needed to be done to defend Santa Catarina Island, which he considered one of the keys to control of southern Brazil. Its fall could not only sever sea communications between Rio de Janeiro and her dependencies, but also give the Spaniards an opportunity to establish a smuggling base on Brazil's southern flank. To guard against its capture, he ordered all Santa Catarina militia units mobilized and a colonial regiment sent to the island from Rio de Janeiro.[96] The defense of Santa Catarina Island was made the responsibility of Brigadier General Antônio Carlos Furtado de Mendonça, an experienced officer then serving as interim captain-general of Minas Gerais, who, like General Böhm in Rio Grande, became superior to the subcaptaincy's civil governor.[97]

A measure intended to strengthen the defenses of Santa Catarina as well as the rest of the Debatable Lands was the assignment of a naval squadron to Viceroy Lavradio. It was to consist of the *naus Santo Antônio* (64 guns), *Ajuda* (64), and *Belém* (50), and the frigates *Graça* (40), *Nazareth* (40), and *Assumpção* (30), plus several small converted merchant vessels. To mask the fact that these ships were to be organized in Brazil as a single force, they were scheduled to sail separately from Lisbon to escort new governors to their stations, to

---

a defeza do Rio Grande de São Pedro e seus territórios," prepared seven years earlier by the Milanese engineer Miguel Ángelo Blasco who had served in Rio Grande during and after the Missions War. Blasco, who wrote a similar analysis of the defenses of Rio de Janeiro (see Chap. II, n. 109), stated that the best defensive positions in Rio Grande were Monte Castillos and Fort São Miguel. Accordingly Pombal, who sent this report to Lavradio, modified his original instructions. Pombal to Lavradio, Aug. 8, 1774, BNRJ, I-2, 4, 6, nos. 88–90 [sic]; other copies in ANRJ, Col. 67, Liv. III, fols. 116ʳ–123ᵛ and IHGB, *Lata* 109, MS, 1844. I am indebted to D. Adelaide Morosini Alba of the IHGB for a typescript of this dispatch and its enclosure. It has since been published in *RIHGB*, CCXXXIV (1957), 324–335.

95 General Instruction, pars. 57–64. Par. 62 recommends the purchase of Spanish spies to keep the viceroy and Lisbon informed concerning Spanish military movements in the Plata.

96 There is a discrepancy between par. 51 of the General Instructions, which orders one of the Rio de Janeiro regiments sent to Santa Catarina, and par. 9 of Pombal to Lavradio, July 15, 1774, which specifies that the Pernambuco regiment should proceed to the island. In practice, the latter order was followed.

97 General Instruction, pars. 49–56; Melo e Castro to Lavradio, Sept. 19, 1774, CMCM, cod. 13 (45/4) (orig.), repeating the order for Furtado de Mendonça to be sent to the island.

pursue troublesome Algerian pirates off the Azores, and to engage in routine patrol work off the Portuguese coast.[98] Once at sea, each captain was to open secret instructions telling him to sail to Rio de Janeiro, and terminating his commission there. After assembly, the squadron was to be placed under command of an Irish captain, Robert MacDouall.[99]

As mentioned, one mission of the outgoing squadron was to escort new governors to their posts. The Crown utilized the emergency of 1774 for a wholesale reassignment of governors in various parts of Brazil and in the Azores.[100] Each new appointee was given secret orders—to be opened when he reached his destination—informing him of his particular duties during the crisis. Thus Diniz Gregório de Melo e Castro was directed to dispatch the Pôrto regiment from the Azores to Rio de Janeiro as soon as he reached the islands. Similarly, Manoel da Cunha de Menezes was relieved as captain-general of Pernambuco by José Cézar de Menezes (no relation), and was transferred to Salvador, where he was specifically placed under command of the Marquis of Lavradio. The already-noted Antônio Carlos Furtado de Mendonça was scheduled to be succeeded as captain-general of Minas Gerais by Dom Luís Antônio de Sousa who, in turn, was to be replaced in São Paulo by Martim Lopes Lobo de Saldanha. Saldanha was directed to hold conferences with the viceroy before taking up his post, and was also put under the command of Lavradio and enjoined to cooperate with General Böhm in Rio Grande.[101] Later, in 1775,

98 Details on the squadron's size and mission are in the General Instruction, par. 34, and Pombal to Lavradio, July 15, 1774; also in an untitled appendix of *idem* to *idem*, Aug. 8, 1774, CMCM, cod. 14 (49/6a), and in two *cartas régias* of July 9, 1774, one to Guilherme MackDuval [sic for Robert MacDouall] and the other to Lavradio, BNRJ, I-2, 4, 6, nos. 74 and 59.

99 Portuguese contemporaries had a difficult time with the spelling of MacDouall's name, and subsequent historians have contributed their own novel variations. The one given in the text is based upon an examination of his signature on more than twenty letters in BNRJ, 13, 4, 5. He was one of five British subjects who skippered Portuguese warships in Brazilian waters at this time. The others were George Hardcastle, Arthur Phillip, Thomas Stevens (or Stivens), and John Nicolas Schmerkel, who died in Bahia in 1776. MacDouall had served in the British Navy during the Seven Years' War and appears to have been a protégé of Colonial Secretary Martinho de Melo e Castro.

100 Multiple shifts of governors were not an unusual practice for the Portuguese government. Frequently the Crown made several appointments at one time, and dispatched new governors on the same frigate to save shipping. What is significant here is the number of changes, and the fact that each new governor carried special orders making him militarily dependent on the viceroy. See Pombal to Lavradio, July 15, 1774 (cited above in n. 88).

101 [Martinho de Melo e Castro], "Instrução militar para Martim Lopes Lobo de Saldanha," Jan. 14, 1775, *RIHGB*, IV (2nd ed., 1863), 350-362, reprinted in *DI*, XLIII (1903), 29-52. Saldanha was originally scheduled to go to Pernambuco. Carta régia, May 31, 1774, *ibid.*, pp. 8-9. His departure for Rio was delayed several months because of a tumor.

the roll of new governors was completed when the viceroy exercised his options and replaced Governor Sarmento of Colônia by his former observer in Rio Grande, Francisco José da Rocha, and Governor Francisco de Sousa de Menezes of Santa Catarina by another of his aides, Pedro Antônio da Gama e Freitas.

Also scheduled for shipment to Rio de Janeiro in the squadron were large quantities of munitions, clothing, and tents [102] as well as additional troops. Among the last was the five-hundred-man Lagos artillery regiment, which was to board the warships secretly and replace the normal contingent of soldiers on the ships, 800 recruits from the Azores, and another 200 from Madeira.[103] The Pôrto regiment, also reassigned from the Azores to Rio de Janeiro, was to be joined there by the first and second Bahian regiments, these being the three replacements for the units transferred to Rio Grande.

In authorizing these reinforcements, the Crown made it clear that Portugal lacked the manpower to provide sufficient regular troops to defend Brazil, and that it was up to the Brazilians themselves to share that burden. This was a reasonable demand, said Pombal, since the Brazilians were only protecting their own homes, and their familiarity with the local terrain made them superior to Peninsular troops for that purpose. He added that this was particularly true of the Paulistas, those "scourges of the Jesuits and the Castilians," for whom both he and the colonial minister had great esteem.[104]

Besides supplying more manpower, the Court acceded to the viceroy's repeated requests for promotions for officers in the European regiments and on his personal staff. More than thirty were advanced one or two ranks to become sergeant majors, lieutenants, and full colonels.[105] At the same time Brigadier Funk, who was to join Böhm in Rio Grande, was raised to field marshal and Martim Lopes Lobo de Saldanha, the incoming captain-general of São Paulo, was made a

---

[102] Some idea of the size of the military stores involved is given in a covering letter of Melo e Castro to Lavradio (Aug. 8, 1774) detailing weapons, tents, powder, and clothing for seven infantry regiments and one artillery, a regiment of Rio-grandense dragoons, five companies of Paulistas, and two companies of Lavradio's guard. All these stores were aboard the nau *Ajuda*. CMCM, cod. 13 (45/12) (orig.).

[103] Melo e Castro to Lavradio, July 22, 1774, *ibid.*, (45/13) (orig.); *idem* to *idem*, Aug. 8, 1774, *ibid.*, (45/11) (orig.). The Madeirans oversubscribed their quota as "muitos Moças de Famílias distintas" volunteered to go to Brazil. While at sea these recruits were to be trained in naval tactics as well as in land-fighting. *Idem* to *idem*, Sept. 18, 1774, *ibid.* (45/30) (orig.).

[104] General Instructions, Appendix I. Another who had high regard for the prowess of the Paulistas was the Milanese Blasco in his "Reparos" cited in n. 94 above.

[105] Martinho de Melo e Castro to Lavradio, July 15, 1774, CMCM, cod. 3 (45/29) (orig.), which includes the promotion lists of June 14 and Nov. 11, 1774. In his introduction, the secretary stated that the promotions were intended to fill vacancies of which the viceroy had complained on five occasions between 1770 and 1773.

brigadier.[106] As the senior military officer in Brazil, the Marquis of Lavradio was elevated from field marshal to lieutenant general, though not until after an embarrassed Pombal had discovered that through an oversight the king had promoted the viceroy to field marshal, a title he already held! [107]

In addition to a more exalted military title, the viceroy was given full war powers and authority equal to that of the former viceroys of India.[108] He had discretionary authority to determine how and when the new borderland policy was to be implemented, and was empowered to draft General Böhm's formal instructions. To meet the expenses of the campaign, he was authorized to utilize all extraordinary revenues from his own captaincy-general, and to draw upon those of São Paulo, Minas Gerais, Bahia, Pernambuco, and Angola.[109] Finally, Pombal sent Lavradio his congratulations for the "limitless confidence" the king had shown in Dom Luís' ability to carry out his difficult assignment, and sent the viceroy a personal gift as a token of his own affection.[110]

By mid-September Lisbon learned that the Spanish had called off the El Ferrol expedition.[111] This welcome news was offset by reports that the 1,400-man Galicia regiment and 500 deserters had already left Cádiz for the Plata.[112] In spite of their departure, Lisbon was

106 Pombal to Lavradio, June 21, 1774, *ibid.*, cod. 14 (49/3) (orig.). For some reason the promotions of Saldanha and Funk were declared secret.

107 Pombal wrote a personal letter of apology to Lavradio for the mistake. Dispatch of Sept. 12, 1774, containing the corrected patent of July 22, 1774, CMCM, cod. 14 (49/4 and 49/4a), both originals, the latter rubricated by the king.

108 Pombal to Lavradio, July 9, 1774, BNRJ, I-2, 4, 6, n. 80; carta régia, same date, *ibid.*, n. 58. The latter is no more specific as to precisely what Lavradio gained by these added powers than this: "Me parece authorizarvos, como por esta vos authorizo, com todo o Pleno Poder, e com todas as amplas faculdades necessarias, . . . á mesma intensão do que se tem praticado com os Vice Reis da India. . . ."

109 General Instructions, pars. 21-23. Essentially this meant that all important revenues from these jurisdictions save the quinto were to go to Rio de Janeiro. The fifths had still to be sent to Portugal. See Chap. XII below.

110 Carta familiar of July 23, 1774, BNRJ, I-2, 4, 6, n. 86.

111 [Pombal], "Orçamento das forças terrestres e navaes, que verosìmilmente se póde julgar que os castelhanos tenham no Rio da Prata e sul do Brasil . . . ," *RIHGB*, XXXI:1, 311-316. The Estimate is an appendix to Pombal to Lavradio, Sept. 18, 1774, BNRJ, I-2, 4, 6, n. 93, where it is mentioned by title but is omited from the codex.

112 The Galicia regiment was sent early in August 1774 aboard five warships and three small merchant vessels. The purpose of this force was to defend the Plata against the anticipated Portuguese attack, for Madrid had been receiving alarming reports of Portuguese warlike preparations from both Vértiz and the Spanish ambassador to Lisbon. The reinforcements reached Montevideo late in November, and were secretly debarked on the pretext that they were replacements for other troops stationed in the Plata. Vértiz was ordered to maneuver the Portuguese into firing the first shot before attacking their positions at Colônia and in Rio Grande. Arriaga to Vértiz, Aug. 5, 1774, *CB*, III, 316-319.

confident that General Böhm would soon have sufficient men to contain any offensive that Vértiz might throw against him.[113] Consequently the colonial minister ordered the viceroy to continue his war
preparations, and assured him that the troops and matériel would
soon arrive.[114]

[113] The Orçamento cited in n. 111 calculates that Vértiz would have 2,700 regular
foot and horse troops, and 5,200 militia and Indian levies, against 5,394 Portuguese
regulars and 2,000 auxiliaries. The Spanish numerical advantage, it was reasoned,
would be offset by the superior fighting ability of the Portuguese.

[114] Melo e Castro to Lavradio, Nov. 20, 1774, CMCM, cod. 13 (45/41) (orig.),
printed in RIHGB, XXXI:1, 319–324. This dispatch also contains a severe and unjust criticism of José Marcelino de Figueiredo for failing to crush Vértiz. Actually
the governor had neither the forces nor the authorization to achieve such a result.

VI

Continued Stalemate: The Frustrations of a Viceroy, 1774-1776

I am like a bell: I am here calling to all; I cry, I persuade, I give them [every] possible assistance; as my cries are from afar, sometimes they are heard; and most of the time they make little or no impression.

Lavradio to Pombal, December 30, 1775

IN ITS VOLUMINOUS INSTRUCTIONS of July, August, and September 1774 the Crown conceded every important military request but one that Viceroy Lavradio had made during the previous four years. While this represented a personal victory for Lavradio, the planned build up of Portuguese land and sea forces also meant a substantial increase in his burdens in terms of responsibility and sheer paper work. Furthermore, having agreed to provide the assistance he had called for, the Crown expected him to produce tangible results; failure to do so was likely to prove costly not only to the State but also to the career of Dom Luís de Almeida.

The privilege that the marquis had particularly sought, that of directing the military operations in Rio Grande himself, was refused. That was a keen disappointment to Dom Luís, but in denying his petition the colonial minister stated that it was "indispensably necessary" for him to remain in Rio de Janeiro to supervise the extensive preparations requisite for the recovery of occupied Rio Grande and the protection of the rest of southern Brazil.[1]

The viceroy thus remained an intermediary between the Court, his commanders afield and afloat, and the captains-general who were supposed to contribute to the success of the operations. It was his task to get the men, ships, guns, munitions, provisions, and money to the military theater where they were needed. The supplies and some of the men, the Court said, would soon be forthcoming from across the Atlantic. The captains-general would furnish additional troops, and all would be combat-ready. But as it turned out, the troops and the equipment reached Rio de Janeiro only after many months of delay,

---

[1] Martinho de Melo e Castro to Lavradio, Nov. 21, 1774, CMCM, cod. 13 (45/35) (orig.); published in *RIHGB*, XXXI:1, 324.

often arriving in such poor condition as to provoke sharp criticism from the disappointed viceroy.

In theory, the military campaign was to be coordinated with the fluid diplomatic situation which prevailed in Europe. In practice, however, coordination became impossible, partly because of the hesitations of the land and sea commanders, but particularly because of what more than one historian has termed the "time-distance" factor. In Lavradio's time it required seventy to one hundred days for dispatches from Lisbon to reach Rio de Janeiro; a week to forward their substance from there to São Paulo, Minas Gerais, and Santa Catarina; two weeks to Rio Grande; and three to four weeks to Colônia, Bahia, and Pernambuco.[2] Consequently, by the time the Court's directives arrived at their points of execution, the circumstances that had prompted them not infrequently had altered, necessitating the dispatch of new instructions, causing further delays and confusion. For these and other reasons, the years 1774 to 1776 were destined to be years of frustration for Viceroy Lavradio.

The First Portuguese Moves

The dispatch of a large expeditionary force like General Böhm's required extensive preparations not only in Rio de Janeiro, but also in the other captaincies-general that were expected to support the venture. As soon as he received his instructions,[3] the viceroy wrote to his fellow governors asking them to send the troops, money, and supplies the Court had assured him they would provide.[4] He spoke to his old adversary, Dom Luís Antônio de Sousa, of the role that the "intrepid, valorous, dependable, and ever distinguished Paulistas" were to play in the campaign, and ordered him to prepare an infantry regiment and an artillery company for immediate dispatch to Rio Grande, and to assemble a reserve force of 2,000 militia to be on call for duty there.[5]

Not until November 1774 did the first elements of the Pernambucan and Bahian regiments arrive in Rio de Janeiro, thereby reliev-

[2] These estimates are based upon the active and passive correspondence of Viceroy Lavradio with the places mentioned. The dates the dispatches were sent and received are usually indicated in the opening sentence.

[3] They began to arrive in Rio late in September or early in October 1774, but the major instruction, that of July 9, 1774, did not reach the viceroy until about January 1775, for it was brought by Captain MacDouall. See n. 17 below.

[4] E.g., Lavradio to Manoel da Cunha Menezes, Sept. 20, and Dec. 24, 1774, *ABNRJ*, XXXII, 288, 283.

[5] Lavradio to Sousa, Sept. 22, 1774, CMCM, cod. 26 fols. 85ʳ-86ᵛ.

ing the Peninsular regiments for duty in Rio Grande.[6] All three colonial regiments were incomplete, and contained many over aged, ill, and otherwise useless men whom the viceroy returned to their homes with strong rebukes to their captains-general for having sent such people, and for having neglected to bring their regiments up to full strength before sending them.[7]

On December 5, 1774, General Böhm left for Rio Grande with the first elements of the Bragança and Moura regiments.[8] The general carried with him lengthy instructions written by the viceroy[9] and copies of pertinent royal directives.[10] Lavradio's instructions formalized points that the viceroy had made during his conversations with the general concerning the latter's offensive and defensive mission in Rio Grande.[11] Dom Luís cautioned Böhm to maneuver the Spaniards into firing the first shot so that Portugal could play the role of the aggrieved party who was merely defending herself. How and when Böhm was to accomplish this trick was not specified. In the ensuing months the general proved reluctant to play his cards, while the anxious viceroy, hundreds of miles away from the realities that confronted Böhm, repeatedly insisted that the general held the winning hand and that all he had to do was call the enemy's bluff. The viceroy concluded Böhm's standing orders with a *pro forma* prophecy which hardly expressed his true feelings regarding the Austrian, with whom he was never especially congenial: "The talents, qualities, and virtues of Your Excellency are so well known to all that I have no

6 The first Pernambucan troops arrived Oct. 2, 1774, and included many men sixty to seventy years old; others were too ill to serve; and all were poorly equipped and clothed. Lavradio to Governor José Cézar de Menezes, Oct. 8, 1774, IHGB, *Lata* 439, n. 1 fols. 9ʳ–11ʳ. The two Bahian regiments seem to have arrived about mid-November to judge from the *portarias* of Nov. 19 and 20, 1774, ordering disbursement of their pay. CMCM, cod. 2, fols. 89ʳ–90ʳ.

7 There are numerous examples of such complaints in the viceroy's correspondence with captains-general Cézar de Menezes (see n. 6, above) and Cunha Menezes, CMCM, cod. 4, *passim*. Typical of their rejoinders was Cézar de Menezes' admission that there were deficiencies in the units he sent but that "the speed with which I was ordered to send this expedition prevented me from remedying the faults" and that after serving His Majesty for twenty-seven years, he thought he knew something about the organization of troops. To Lavradio, Nov. 12, 1774, IHGB, *Lata* 439, n. 1, fols. 13ʳ–17ʳ.

8 Lavradio to Dom Luís Antônio de Sousa, Dec. 12, 1774, CMCM cod. 26, fol. 87ʳ. The rest of these regiments and the Estremoz were expected to follow shortly, but actually did not reach Rio Grande until the spring of 1775.

9 Lavradio to Böhm, Dec. 3, 1774, BNRJ, 13, 4, 2, n. 1 (orig.) ; printed from another copy in *BCRG*, pp. 17–30.

10 Included was the "Minuta para a carta do manifesto" that Böhm was to present to the Castilians when ready to order them out of Rio Grande. *BCRG*, pp. 25–27.

11 Lavradio refers to these conversations in his dispatch of Mar. 12, 1775 to Böhm, BNRJ, 13, 4, 2, n. 13 (orig.) ; *BCRG*, pp. 42–45.

doubt that good success will attend all your actions, and that at the end of this expedition I shall have the good fortune of seeing Your Excellency return to this capital covered with the greatest glory."

If the viceroy felt some relief on the departure of the vanguard of the expeditionary force, he was certainly unable to relax. He fretted about the safety of the troops until he had received assurances that they had arrived in Santa Catarina.[12] Then Governor Sarmento warned him that the Spaniards had just landed a large contingent of troops from Spain at Montevideo. From Spanish inquiries regarding Santa Catarina and Santos, the governor concluded that they were preparing to attack one or both ports.[13] The viceroy discounted this supposition, and rightly concluded that the reinforcements were intended to strengthen Montevideo and the force blockading Colônia.[14] Nevertheless, he instructed the governor of Santa Catarina to be prepared for an attack, and promised that the Pernambuco regiment would be sent as soon as shipping became available.[15] He also wrote Böhm to hasten his preparations so as to relieve the pressure on Colônia, and to expel the Spanish from the Lagoa dos Patos before they should have time to bring up reinforcements.[16] Dom Luís could do little more than issue these instructions until he had a naval arm with which to harass the Spanish in the Plata. Elements of the squadron began to arrive in December 1774, but it was still not fully assembled when Captain MacDouall arrived to take charge.[17]

MacDouall's appearance made it possible for the viceroy to take more positive steps to meet the new Spanish threat. Even though the Pernambuco regiment was still incomplete, Lavradio put it aboard the nau *Ajuda* and sent her, along with the frigates *Graça* and *Nazareth*, to Santa Catarina Island. Also aboard were 200 infantrymen and an artillery company for Colônia, the new governor of the entrepôt, Francisco José da Rocha, and Field Marshal Antônio

12 The anxious viceroy waited two and a half weeks for word from Böhm, and then rebuked him for neglecting to keep him properly informed on his progress. Lavradio to Böhm, Dec. 22, 1774, BNRJ, 13, 4, 2, n. 6 (orig.) ; BCRG, pp. 31-32. Curiously, Böhm's first dispatch was written the following day. Böhm to Lavradio, Laguna, Dec. 23, 1774, CMCM, *maço* 6.

13 Pedro José Soares de Figueiredo Sarmento to Lavradio, Oct. 22 and 29, 1773, *CB*, III, 263-265. The troops in question were the deserters from the Galicia regiment sent out from Cádiz in August 1774. See above, Chap. V, n. 112.

14 *Loc. cit.*

15 Lavradio to Francisco de Souza de Menezes, Dec. 22, 1774, CMCM, cod. 4, fols 64^{r-v}.

16 Lavradio to Böhm, Dec. 22, 1774 and Jan. 26, 1775, BNRJ, 13, 4, 2, nos. 5 and 9 (origs.) ; BCRG, pp. 36-38.

17 MacDouall, who was overdue and feared lost, arrived sometime between Dec. 22, 1774 and Jan. 21, 1775. By Jan. 26, 1775 the squadron included the naus *Ajuda* and *Santo Antônio*, and the frigates *Graça*, *Nazareth*, *Assumpção*, and *Príncipe do Brasil*. Lavradio to Böhm, Jan. 26, 1775, cited in n. 16, above.

Carlos Furtado de Mendonça, commander of the defenses of Santa Catarina.[18] Before their departure, Lavradio conferred with each officer and promised to assist him to the extent of his means.[19]

At the same time, the viceroy gave MacDouall his general instructions.[20] His duty was to protect Santa Catarina Island, "the only port through which we can succor our Southern establishments," and to apprehend Spanish vessels en route to the Plata with troops and munitions.[21] But since the squadron was the only naval force available for the defense of the coast, Lavradio cautioned the captain to avoid any engagement that might expose his ships to possible destruction. As soon as he thought it safe to proceed from Santa Catarina, he was directed to escort Governor Rocha and his troops to Colônia. En route, he was to inquire at Rio Grande whether General Böhm had begun offensive operations and to cooperate with him in the event that he had.

Late in February 1775, MacDouall was ready to convoy the Colônia reinforcements to their destination. While at sea, he dispatched a ship to Rio Grande to learn whether Böhm was ready to attack.[22] Finding that the general was far from ready, MacDouall continued on to the vicinity of Montevideo. After assigning the *Graça* to escort the transports to the entrepôt, he lay off the Spanish port with four warships. Within the harbor he spied several attractive targets, warships prepared to winter at Montevideo before returning to Europe.[23] As he debated whether to fire upon them, the Spanish suddenly awakened from hibernation, unfurled their sails, and trained their guns on him. This display of energy was sufficient to dissuade MacDouall from testing the enemy, for he concluded that the Spaniards were too strong for him to attack without risking his own ships, an eventuality the

18 MacDouall seems to have left port first and to have been followed a few days later by the other ships. It is certain that General Furtado de Mendonça left Rio on Jan. 28, and arrived at Santa Catarina Feb. 5. Lavradio to Böhm, Jan. 26, 1775, cited in n. 16, and Furtado de Mendonça's apology cited in n. 19 below.

19 Precisely what commitments the viceroy made at these conferences is uncertain. For one version, see Antônio Carlos Furtado de Mendonça to the Queen (*ca.* 1779), BNRJ, I-31, 26, 1, n. 17; published in *RIHGB*, XXVII:1, 291–322; see especially pp. 293–294. For a discussion of this document, see the last section of Chap. X. So far as is known, Lavradio never disclosed what promises, if any, he offered the field marshal.

20 Lavradio to MacDouall, Jan. 20 and 28, 1775, *VRL*, pp. 197–200, 202–205.

21 The pretext for these seizures was to be that the dispatch of military supplies and troops was an unfriendly act while both nations were at peace. As will be seen later, Spain resorted to the same practice to intercept Portuguese ships going from the Peninsula to Brazil in 1776.

22 MacDouall to Böhm, Santa Catarina, Feb. 23, 1775, BNRJ, 13, 4, 5, n. 63 (orig.); *idem* to J.N. Schmerkel (captain of *Graça*), Feb. 27, 1775, *ABNRJ*, XXXII, 340–341.

23 Presumably these were the vessels that brought the Galicia regiment to Montevideo.

viceroy had ordered him to avoid; so he set course for Santa Catarina, having missed a great opportunity, as he later admitted.[24]

MacDouall's lost opportunity provoked the first of his many controversies with the viceroy. With justification the captain defended his conduct by pointing to Lavradio's ambiguous orders. He also insisted that it was not his responsibility but General Böhm's to initiate hostilities. For his part, the viceroy contended that the Irishman had greatly exaggerated the size of the enemy and should have destroyed him.[25]

Bad News from Rio Grande

If Lavradio was dissatisfied with MacDouall's performance, he was even more disappointed by General Böhm's first reports from Rio Grande. The general declared that the Portuguese forts on the peninsula were "no more than batteries, very poorly constructed, inadequately garrisoned, semi-ruined, [and] open to the rear or closed for appearance's sake by palisades."[26] Because of the ravages of the sea and the wind, the entrance fort of Santa Bárbara, "the key to the port," and Conceição, the next in line, would have to be completely rebuilt, while the rest required extensive restoration.[27] He was amazed to find no hospital in Rio Grande and no provision storehouses or carts on the peninsula. He warned that unless the viceroy continued to send flour regularly his men "would die of hunger or be reduced to the state of our brothers of creation, the tigers, vultures, and urubús."[28]

24 MacDouall to Furtado de Mendonça, off Montevideo, Mar. 31, 1775, VRL, p. 63, n. 2; idem to Böhm, Santa Catarina, Apr. 9, 1775 BNRJ, 13, 4, 5, n. 64 (orig.).

25 MacDouall to Böhm, loc. cit.; Lavradio to Pombal, May [?], 1775, VRL, pp. 62-65.

26 Böhm to Lavradio, Feb. 9, 1775, CMCM, maço 6 (orig.); BNRJ, I-28, 26, 2 n. 1 (rascunho). The following summary of Böhm's remarks is based on this long report and another of the same date, of which one original (in Portuguese) is in CMCM, maço 6, and another (in French) is in IHGB, Lata 9, MS 190; also pertinent is another Böhm dispatch of Mar. 6, 1775, of which there is a draft in BNRJ, I-28, 26, 2 n. 2.

27 For the locations of the Spanish and Portuguese forts in the channel see Map 8. A useful study of the origins and architecture of these fortifications is J. C. Rego Monteiro, "Fortificações do canal e cidade do Rio-Grande," Anais do 2do congresso . . . sul-rio-grandense, II (Pôrto Alegre, 1937), 243-264. Böhm found by experiment that cannon balls fired from the Portuguese side would not carry effectively to the Spanish, so these fortifications were primarily useful (if at all) for repelling invasion and for harassing shipping in the channel. To Lavradio, July 19, 1775, CMCM, maço 6 (orig.). For another contemporary criticism of Rio Grande's fortifications, see F. J. Roscîo, "Compêndio noticioso do continente do Rio Grande de São Pedro," RIHGRGS, XXVII (1947), 72.

28 The urubú is a Brazilian vulture.

The general also complained that his forces were insufficient in numbers or quality to undertake the proposed offensive. Besides lacking elements of the three European regiments, still in transit in February 1775, he discovered that some of the expected Riograndense militia units existed on paper only. Although expressing qualified approval of the famed dragoons whom he described as "handsome, strong, extraordinarily agile, as much at home on a horse as the Arabs," and admirable for keeping order, he doubted whether they could be counted on in battle.

On the other hand, the general was pleased with some of his officers and singled out for praise Camilo Maria Tonelet, commander of the viceregal guard companies,[29] and the *guerrilhéiro* chief and newly promoted major, Rafael Pinto Bandeira. In his dispatches Böhm frequently lauded Bandeira's abilities, but nowhere more eloquently than in the following characterization: "He is a man in the flower of youth, educated rather like a noble tartar, robust, bursting with health, frank but retiring. He is not boastful, but he answers with spirit and frankness. Perhaps he does not have the furor of a drunken grenadier or of a wounded wild boar, but I believe he's a man with a head on his shoulders." [30]

Böhm left Pinto Bandeira in charge of the Rio Pardo frontier patrols, under the nominal authority of Governor José Marcelino, who remained at Pôrto Alegre. The general decided to concentrate the bulk of his troops on the peninsula between the southern tip and São José do Norte, opposite the main Spanish force. He wrote the viceroy that in time he would capture Santa Tecla, Vertiz' new fort, but that to employ all of his forces in such a mission would be to fall into a trap and expose the vital peninsula to possible attack. Yet he warned Lavradio against the assumption that he would be ready to launch his campaign soon. The conquest of the Spanish forts in the Lagoa would be difficult, for they were formidable, and the currents in the channel were tricky to negotiate. If compelled to attack at once, he would do so, for his duty was to execute orders and close his eyes. The implications were plain.

The general's sobering words disturbed the viceroy. He expressed surprise that adequate preparations had not been made to receive Böhm and his men, and that sufficient supplies had not already been

<hr>

[29] Tonelet, another of the viceroy's aides, apparently assumed command of the guard from Sergeant-Major Gaspar de Matos, who returned to Rio de Janeiro. Like Matos, he remained in Brazil after his chief's return to Europe, and like Matos, he rose to high rank. He was promoted to brigadier in 1808, and in that year commanded the Moura regiment at the welcoming parade for the royal family when it reached Rio de Janeiro. He was then known as "olho de vidro" because of a glass eye. He died in 1831 at the age of eighty-two. *ABNRJ*, LIX (1937), 197–198.

[30] Böhm to Lavradio, Feb. 9, 1775 (no. 2) cited in n. 26 above.

stockpiled, but he contended that the fault was not his but Governor José Marcelino's. He promised that the supply problem would be solved shortly, when shipments he was dispatching reached Rio Grande, and assured the general that he would continue to furnish him with all the men and matériel at his disposal. Böhm's plan to improve his two principal forts on the peninsula met with Lavradio's approval, but he cautioned that the other fortification projects would need royal consent—and that meant further delay.

Actually the viceroy doubted that it would be necessary to rebuild the other peninsular forts, since they would immediately become obsolete as soon as Böhm crossed the channel. He tried to convince the general that he already had sufficient manpower to expel the Spanish from the Lagoa.[31] He minimized Böhm's complaint that he had fewer men than promised, and pointed out that he could always call up nearly 3,000 Paulista reserves, and that he would have 500 artillerymen as soon as they arrived from Portugal. Again he urged Böhm to force the enemy to a decision before the latter had time to bring up more troops from the Plata or to send them from Europe. Dom Luís also suggested that the general work out a plan with MacDouall whereby the squadron could make a diversionary strike in the Plata at the moment when Böhm presented his ultimatum to the Spanish in Rio Grande.[32]

The First Tests of Strength in Rio Grande

The viceroy's sanguine expectation of an early decision in Rio Grande was rudely shattered by two preliminary tests of strength in the Lagoa dos Patos in April, 1775, when each side tried to send naval reinforcements through a gauntlet of fire in the channel. The first to try were the Portuguese.

Early in February, Lavradio sent a supply convoy to Rio Grande under command of an English captain, George Hardcastle.[33] Hardcastle's force included four smacks and three escorts, the frigate-rigged

---

[31] Yet as late as May, 1775, Böhm was still awaiting the arrival of eight companies of the Moura and Bragança regiments. *Idem* to *idem*, May 5, 1775, CMCM, *maço* 6 (orig.) ; BNRJ, I-28, 26, 2, n. 5 *(rascunho)*.

[32] Lavradio to Böhm, Jan. 12 and 26, Mar. 21, April 12, and May 7, 1775, BNRJ, 13, 4, 2, nos. 7, 9, 13, 15, and 16; *BCRG*, pp. 34–38, 42–53. Similar advice concerning a combined offensive was apparently sent to MacDouall who, beginning in April 1775, made regular reports to Böhm on the number of warships he had available for duty in Rio Grande or in the Plata. MacDouall to Böhm, April 17 and May 9, 1775, BNRJ, 13, 4, 5, nos. 65–66 (origs.) , and later MacDouall dispatches cited below. MacDouall indicated a willingness to undertake a Platine attack whenever Böhm felt it would help, but the latter contended that the Plata was out of his jurisdiction and never showed any interest in such a project.

[33] Lavradio to MacDouall, Feb. 13, 1775, *VRL*, pp. 205–206; *idem* to Böhm, same date, BNRJ, 13, 4, 2, n. 10 (orig.) ; *BCRG*, pp. 31–48.

Invencivel, and the *Sacramento* and *São José,* both corvettes. The convoy reached the improvised port of Lagamar[34] on March 16, but immediately encountered a severe storm that dispersed all of the transports.

After waiting two weeks for the weather to improve, Hardcastle and Böhm agreed that the escorts should try to enter the channel even though the transports had not reappeared.[35] Hardcastle was to hold his fire unless the Spanish guns spoke first. At 8:00 A.M. on the morning of April 4 he began his run, and as he drew abreast Fort S. José de la Barra, the Spanish batteries opened up. The Portuguese ship and shore guns immediately replied with such vigor that three Spanish ships anchored in the channel cut their cables and scurried back under the protecting guns of Fort Mangueira.

Throughout the early part of the engagement, the Portuguese pilots tried to avoid the rain of shot from both sides and at the same time stay away from the shifting sand banks of the canal. Nevertheless both the *Invencivel* and the *Sacramento* soon ran aground in front of the Portuguese battery of Patrão-mor, and there they remained for a time—sitting ducks for what fortunately proved to be inaccurate Spanish gunners. Notwithstanding the Spanish bombardment, Hardcastle was able to liberate his stranded vessels with launches and towlines, and by 3:00 P.M. all three were safely anchored upstream.[36]

While this was the largest Portuguese naval force that had successfully entered the Lagoa for many years, that achievement was offset ten days later when four out of five Spanish warships also ran up the channel in spite of efforts of the Portuguese batteries to turn them back.[37] Far from condemning his own gunners for their failure to bar

---

[34] Lagamar was a lagoon formed by a sand bank. The roadstead, thought (erroneously) to be out of range of the Spanish guns of Fort S. José de la Barra, was used to debark supplies for the army on the peninsula. Since it was unprotected, shipping was not safe there in foul weather.

[35] One transport later beached herself on the Spanish-controlled coast, but the others were apparently never seen again. Böhm to Lavradio, Mar. 20, 1775, CMCM, *maço* 6 (orig.) ; BNRJ, I-28, 26, 2, n. 3 *(rascunho)* . A typical officer of his time, the general bemoaned the loss of the much-needed supplies, but expressed no concern for the lost crewmen.

[36] Details on the engagement are given without major discrepancies in Hardcastle to MacDouall, April 11, 1775, *VRL,* pp. 65–67; Böhm to [?], April 5, 1775 *CB,* III, 330–332; and *idem* to [?], Apr. 17, 1775 (begun Apr. 4) , in Simão José de Luz Soriano, *História do reinado de el-rei d. José,* II, 623–624. See also an excerpt of Lavradio to Pombal, May [?] 1775, *VRL,* pp. 62–65. According to Hardcastle's report, his ships expended 10.25 quintals of powder, 765 balls, and 325 "pirâmides de metralha" during the seven-and-a-half-hour engagement. The Portuguese suffered no casualties, and the only damage to their ships consisted of two holes near the waterline of one vessel and shredded rigging on all three. Spanish losses are not known.

[37] The most detailed account of this action is Francisco Betbezé de Ducós (commander of S. José de la Barra) to [Vértiz?], Apr. 23, 1775, *CB,* III, 332–333. These reinforcements gave the Spanish nine ships in the Lagoa. It is noteworthy that

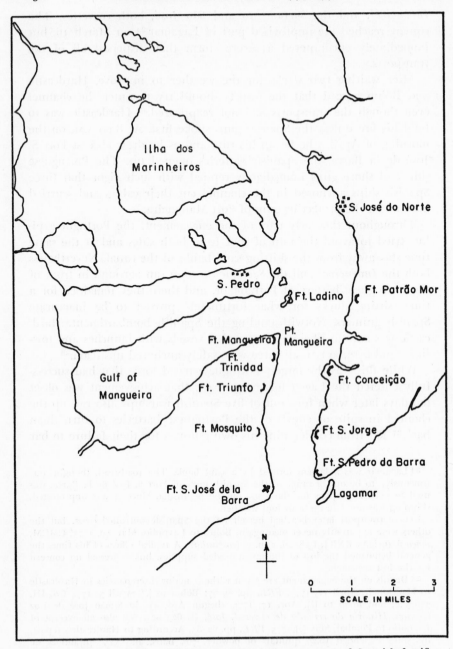

Ilha dos
Marinheiros

S. José do Norte

S. Pedro

Ft. Ladino

Ft. Patrão Mor

Pt.
Mangueira

Ft. Mangueira

Ft.
Trinidad

Gulf of
Mangueira

Ft. Triunfo

Ft. Conceição

Ft. Mosquito

Ft. S. Jorge

Ft. S. Pedro da Barra

Ft. S. José de la
Barra

Lagamar

N

0   1   2   3

SCALE IN MILES

Map 8 Entrance to Lagoa dos Patos showing Portuguese and Spanish fortifications, April 1, 1776. (After Tasso Fragoso, *A Batalha do Passo do Rosário*,
facing p. 70.)

the entry of the enemy vessels, General Böhm insisted that Captain MacDouall should have intercepted them at sea.[38]

This countervailing Spanish success was irritating to the viceroy, who realized that it would provide General Böhm with a new excuse for procrastination. Consequently he wrote the general a lengthy letter calculated to overcome his doubts and inspire him to proceed with his mission. Dom Luís admitted that the Spanish were now defensively stronger than before, and he conceded that Böhm did not have as many men as he believed that he needed; however, he contended that the Portuguese troops made up in quality for what they lacked in numbers. With more enthusiasm than accuracy he stated that they were carefully selected, well paid, adequately clothed, contented, faithful, valorous, and confident in the leadership of their general; also they possessed one characteristic essential to the success of any fighting troops—the desire to win. He emphasized that he was not speaking in his capacity as viceroy of the State of Brazil but as the Marquis of Lavradio, comrade in arms, friend, and admirer of his general. As such, he desired nothing more than to demonstrate his fidelity and interest in Böhm's accomplishments, and his conviction that the general had the ability to achieve a glorious victory.[39]

This is a typical example of Lavradio's resort to the paternalistic approach in delicate situations. But he had more than flattering words with which to inspire his reluctant field commander. He had just received an ominous dispatch from the Court, a copy of which he forwarded for Böhm's reflection.

Hardcastle's ships took no part in the engagement, owing to adverse winds which prevented them from descending the channel.

[38] Böhm to Lavradio, June 7, 1775, CMCM, maço 6 (orig.) ; BNRJ, I-28, 26, 2, n. 7 (rascunho). Only after the Spanish flotilla's arrival did MacDouall order two ships to patrol between the Lagoa and Cabo Santa Maria. MacDouall to Böhm, June 20, 1775, BNRJ, 13, 4, 5, n. 68 (orig.) , with enclosures of his orders to Antônio Januário do Valle (captain of Belém) José dos Santos Ferreira (captain of Ajuda) , and Antônio Jacinto da Costa (captain of Príncipe do Brasil). While each skipper was directed to contact Böhm for news and special instructions before beginning his patrol, none did so, as MacDouall learned long after.

MacDouall seldom had his entire squadron available for service. Often one or more of its units were detached for special missions or were laid up for repairs. E.g., on May 29, 1775, he advised Böhm that the Ajuda and Príncipe do Brasil were on patrol off Rio Grande, the Graça was taking the quintos to Portugal, and the Nazareth was in Rio for repairs, so that he had only the nau Belém and three other warships at Santa Catarina. Of these, he said, only the Belém was capable of going to the Plata in winter. This fragmentation of his squadron obviously irked him, and he added a postscript stating "Sir the face of this intrest Negocio I am every day at more dificulty to understand, but be asurd. sir I shall act with spirit in every part of his Majestys service." BNRJ, 13, 4, 5 n. 67 (orig.) .

[39] Lavradio to Böhm, June 22, 1775, BNRJ, 13, 4, 2, n. 18 (orig.) ; BCRG, pp. 56–61.

The Beginning of the Algiers Crisis

The Algiers crisis began in April 1775, and was over by early July. Although brief in duration, it had important, generally unappreciated, implications for Portuguese policy concerning the Debatable Lands. In his first dispatch on the subject, Secretary Melo e Castro informed Lavradio that in Cádiz and other Peninsular ports the Spaniards were massing "a formidable armament" consisting of warships, fireships, and a great number of transports, some equipped to carry a huge number of troops, others artillery, military stores, and provisions sufficient for several months. The "public" objective of this armada, said the secretary, was Algiers, for Madrid intended to punish the dey for encouraging the king of Morocco to rebel against Spain by besieging the presidio of Melilla. However, Lisbon considered the expedition too large to be limited to that objective, and suspected that after a brief campaign in Africa, the troops would be reboarded and taken to America for an attack on southern Brazil, the real but "hidden" goal.

It was therefore necessary to take steps to prevent Spain from succeeding with such a secret design. Melo e Castro directed the viceroy to order the captains-general of Minas Gerais and São Paulo to place their military forces at his disposal, and to call upon the captains-general of Bahia and Pernambuco for sufficient troops to complete the regiments assigned to him. Since the Court considered Santa Catarina Island to be in particular danger, Captain MacDouall's squadron was to be brought up to full strength as soon as possible to protect it. As for Rio Grande de São Pedro, the secretary emphasized that it was "indispensably necessary" for General Böhm to drive out the Spaniards before the arrival of the Spanish expeditionary force made it impossible for him to do so.[40]

The viceroy transmitted a copy of Melo e Castro's dispatch to the general with the tactful suggestion that he act accordingly,[41] but he warned the Court that he doubted that Böhm would ever take the offensive. He was an able and an experienced officer, but he was too cautious and exaggerated the risks. He feared possible failure and the effect it would have upon his reputation. Moreover, he insisted that

[40] Melo e Castro to Lavradio, April 5, 1775, *RIHGB*, XXXI:1, 329–333. This dispatch was supplemented by another, dated April 6, from Pombal to Lavradio, CMCM, cod. 14 (49/11) (orig.), in which Böhm was ordered to scorch the pastures of Rio Grande to force the Spanish to bring forage with them so as to burden them down. Pombal predicted that this hardship would discourage the enemy and force him to desist from his aggressive designs.

[41] See n. 39, above.

the viceroy must take the responsibility for ordering an attack; but, Dom Luís declared, the general at the front was in a far better position than he was in Rio de Janeiro to judge the proper moment to move forward.[42]

The marquis also advised his superiors that he had found Captain MacDouall both wanting in ability and insubordinate. The Irishman did not even know how to draft proper orders to his captains; one captain had blundered by capturing a Spanish ship headed for Callao de Lima when the viceroy's instructions had specified that only militarily laden ships bound for the Plata should be stopped. In addition, he criticized MacDouall for having ignored the advice of one of his Portuguese captains, a man reputedly familiar with Platine waters, whom he sent back to Rio de Janeiro as useless. Even more irritating to the viceroy was an order from MacDouall forbidding anyone under his command to present complaints to Dom Luís except when the captain himself was in attendance.[43]

In detailing the alleged inadequacies of both chiefs, the viceroy's purpose was clearly to demonstrate why it was essential for him to be in Rio Grande in order to supervise both officers. But the Court continued to refuse to grant him the license he so eagerly sought.

Meanwhile, in Rio Grande the general continued to postpone and complain. A particular source of grievance to him was the newly organized treasury board (junta da fazenda) of Pôrto Alegre. Headed by Governor José Marcelino, it was set up to handle Böhm's fiscal and logistic problems.[44] However, he asserted that it had rendered him practically no assistance beyond sending him some useless supply commissioners and a few "skeleton" oxen, mules, and horses. He was so disgusted that he resolved to speak with the board himself while on a general tour of inspection.[45]

---

[42] Lavradio to Pombal, June 26, 1775, *VRL*, p. 70 (excerpt); [*idem*] to [*idem?*], July 1, 1775, CMCM, cod. 14 (49/10a) (*rascunho*); *idem* to *idem*, n. d. (*ca.* July 1775), CMCM, *maço* 15 (draft in Lavradio's hand).

[43] Such a directive was, of course, contrary to the spirit of Portuguese administrative practice. One can, however, sympathize with MacDouall's position, for he realized that the viceroy was hostile toward him, and that he was therefore naturally receptive to Portuguese officers with complaints against him; consequently, in order to defend himself, he wanted to be present when the charges were made.

[44] The junta was established in 1775 and terminated after the war in 1779. It was an exception to the usual rule that no junta was subordinate to another, for it was directly under the junta of Rio de Janeiro and reported to it as well as to the junta of São Paulo, to the latter only on the balance of receipts from the latter. Sebastião Francisco Bettâmio, "Plano para a administrasão da Faz.a R.al no Ryo gran de [sic] do Sul," Rio de Janeiro, Nov. 14, 1774, BNRJ, 13, 4, 4, n. 1 (copy signed by Bettâmio).

[45] Böhm to Lavradio, June 7, 1775, CMCM, *maço* 6 (orig.); BNRJ, I-28, 26, 2, n. 7 (draft).

Böhm's tour of the Pôrto Alegre and Rio Pardo frontiers lasted nearly a month, from June 7 to July 5, 1775.[46] During that time he traveled by launch, brigantine, canoe, and horse to visit troops, fortifications, warehouses, arsenals, and a shipyard. Upon returning to his headquarters, the general summarized his findings in a lengthy and gloomy report to the viceroy.[47] He was especially critical of the supply system which was run by incompetents. Many of the supply commissioners were "imbeciles" totally unfamiliar with the nature of their duties.[48] He had repeatedly spoken to the junta about this situation but, he said, that body was incapable of making any improvement. The only board member whom the general found sympathetic with his problems was Sebastião Francisco Bettâmio, Lavradio's one-time fiscal expert in Bahia; Böhm took him back to the peninsula to organize his supply lines.

Böhm also reported deficiencies among the troops and their installations in the interior. He labeled customs stations (registros) that were also serving as guard posts as militarily "useless and superfluous." Commenting on the 200 mounted dragoons whom he had inspected near Rio Pardo, he snorted that "the ablest officer in the world will never make them into a regular regiment." Much as he admired Major Bandeira, that admiration did not extend to his corps of irregulars, which included a company of thirty-three Indians. The major's outfit would have to be thoroughly reorganized before it would be fit for service.

In short, Böhm concluded, he had seen nothing during the past month to change his mind with regard to the proposed offensive. Considering what he knew to be the facts, the Court was asking the impossible. The risks would be very grave, the issue in doubt. Another person might see the situation differently, but so far as he was concerned, he would proceed only upon explicit command. If allowed a choice, "I would not commence the war in the form prescribed. . . . Your Excellency . . . [will be] the judge."

46 During the general's absence a triumvirate, consisting of General Funk, Col. José Raimundo Chichorro da Gama, commander of the Estremoz regiment, and Col. Sebastião da Veiga Cabral e Câmara, carried on his duties. The use of three-man executive committees to replace royal officials unable for one reason or another to perform their duties was characteristic of both the Spanish and Portuguese colonial regimes.

47 Böhm to Lavradio, July 19, 1775, CMCM, maço 6 (orig.) ; Jônatas da Costa Rego Monteiro, Dominação espanhola no Rio Grande do Sul, 1763–1777, pp. 213–214, which is based on the "Diário" written in the course of Böhm's tour (BNRJ, II-35, 36, 26).

48 He gave as an example one Antônio Silveira d'Ávila e Matos of Rio Pardo, who served as paymaster, quartermaster of provisions, munitions of war, hospital and "certame" [?], yet "por sua própria declaração sabe apenas escrever seu nome, ignora as operações, e que se encontra já quasi arruinado, sendo antes um dos melhores trabalhadores."

It is not difficult to feel sympathy for the old general, who bears some resemblance to George B. McClellan, another reluctant warrior. Like McClellan, Böhm tended to exaggerate the size and strength of his enemy while belittling his own forces. Obviously he erred in judging the Brazilians by European standards. He forgot that in spite of their apparent lack of discipline and military bearing, they had won significant military victories in the past. Moreover, he failed to appreciate the fact that the Castilians faced the same problems that he did, and that they, too, possessed troops who displayed nonprofessional characteristics. But in one important respect Böhm differed from the "Little Napoleon": the Austrian was a mercenary soldier, fighting for the defense of a foreign land.

One can visualize this earnest, lonely soldier sitting in his quarters after a long day of cajoling his intractable subordinates, bending over his candle- or whale oil-lit letter book, now browned with age and badly riddled with worm holes,[49] taking up his quill and composing in French his complaint-filled dispatches to the viceroy. Böhm rewrote frequently, scratching out words, lines, whole paragraphs; he scribbled on the margins, at the top, the bottom, and the verso of the page, always trying to make his position clear to the insistent Lavradio. But the general had no heart for his assignment. Since 1773 he had petitioned unsuccessfully to be allowed to return to Europe, and now his wife lay dying in Rio de Janeiro while he was hundreds of miles away, unable even to console her in her last hours.[50]

Francisco José da Rocha Renews the Debate Concerning Colônia

Lisbon and Rio Grande were not the only sources of disconcerting news for the viceroy during 1775. Disturbing dispatches also came from Colônia, where Francisco José da Rocha had recently taken office as governor.[51] In his reports on the state of his post, Rocha told of the usual negligence in the warehouses; of soldiers and marines unfit for service because of their extreme youth or age or disabilities;

---

49 His letter book is conserved today in BNRJ as I-28, 26, 2.

50 After Böhm's wife died in August 1775, Lavradio wrote a personal letter conveying the sad news to Böhm as delicately as possible. Dispatch of Sept. 22, 1775, BNRJ, 13, 4, 2, n. 33. Thereafter Böhm apparently lost the desire to return to the continent. Nor did he. After being injured in a fall from a horse in 1781, he became a Catholic and died the following year. He lies buried in the monastery of Santo Antônio in Rio.

51 Rocha took possession on Mar. 25, 1775. "Acto de posse . . . Colônia bloqueada pelos Hespanhoés," Mar. 25, 1775, ANRJ, Col. 94, Liv. VII, fól. 2ʳ.

and of serious shortages of funds,[52] fuel, and food, the last undoubtedly contributing to the fact that one quarter of his garrison was on
the sick list.[53] Months went by, he noted wistfully, without a single
ship coming from Rio de Janeiro or Santa Catarina with supplies and
news from the outside.[54] As if this were not enough to depress the
morale of the inhabitants, there were constant rumors of an impending Spanish attack on the outpost.[55]

As many a governor had before him, Rocha began to reflect on
whether his post was really worth keeping. He expressed his doubts in
a very revealing dispatch to the viceroy [56] and thereby contributed
another negative voice to the ninety-odd-year Portuguese debate on
Colônia's utility. As will be recalled, the last time the question had
arisen was during the Portuguese controversy over the merits of the
Treaty of 1750.[57] When Rocha was in Rio Grande, he discovered a copy
of Alexandre de Gusmão's famous reply to Antônio Pedro de Vasconcelos.[58] After pondering Gusmão's arguments, he had forwarded the
paper to the viceroy with the remark that he believed Portugal ought
to reach a permanent agreement with Spain concerning the status of
Colônia. He returned to this idea after seeing the praça at first hand.[59]

"Colônia, Senhor," he wrote, "is not a praça, it is really a prison,
and the ruin of its inhabitants." [60] He added that it was surrounded
by land and sea by Spaniards camped a mere cannon's shot away. The
Portuguese garrison was grossly inadequate; the batteries poorly constructed; the bulwarks too thin to deflect the balls of siege guns; it

---

[52] One type of expenditure that put a strain upon existing funds was the amount
Rocha paid out of a secret account to confidants in Buenos Aires, Montevideo,
and the siege camp at San Carlos. Rocha to Lavradio, May 20, 1775, CMCM, cod.
29, fol. 45ʳ (orig., as are all of the governor's dispatches bound in this codex). One
of the Montevideo agent's reports, entitled "Novidades de Montevideo," is appended to idem to idem, Aug. 14, 1775, ibid., fols. 64ʳ–66ʳ.

[53] Idem to idem, Apr. 18, May 23 and 26, Aug 11 and 16, 1775, ibid., fols. 18ʳ, 44ʳ,
55ʳ, 62ʳ–64ʳ, and 76ʳ.

[54] Rocha complained that the Spanish continually received information from the
peninsula, even in winter, but that "nós havemos de estar aqui como no Seyo de
Abraão sem sabermos o que vai pelo mundo senão de Seis em Seis Mezes, e as
vezes mais, porem paciencia seja Deos louvado." Dispatch of Aug. 11, 1775, cited
n. 53 above.

[55] The Portuguese also indulged in psychological warfare at Colônia. About
the time Rocha was writing, his opposite number in the blockade camp reported
a rumor that the Portuguese were expecting fourteen warships (eight of them
English and 1,500 troops who would besiege Montevideo. Elorduy to Vértiz,
July 7, 1775, quoted in Octavio Gil Munilla, El Río de la Plata en la política
internacional, p. 242.

[56] Rocha to Lavradio, April 20, 1775, CMCM, cod. 29, fols. 37ʳ–44ᵛ (containing
both the draft and the signed original).

[57] See above, Chap. IV, pp. 89–90.

[58] Rocha did not indicate which of Gusmão's two replies he read.

[59] So Rocha wrote in his dispatch of April 20, cited in n. 56 above.

[60] "A Collonia Senhor não he Praça he verdadeiramente hum Prezidio, e Ruyna
dos seos [h]abitadores. . . ."

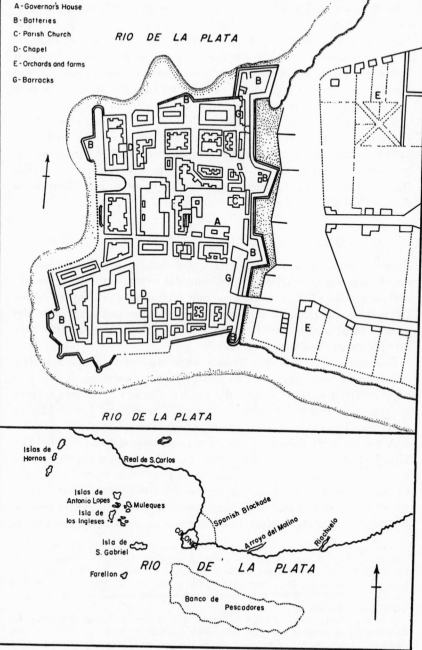

Map 9 Colônia do Sacramento, 1762–1777. (After Rego Monteiro, *Colônia*, II, facing p. 216.)

would be impossible for the outpost to withstand a concerted attack.

If, Rocha added, the king really intended to use Colônia as a base from which to conquer Montevideo, Maldonado, and the rest of the Banda Oriental and to unite this territory with Rio Grande, then all of his expenditures and the privations of his subjects would be justified. Otherwise a convention should be signed ceding Colônia to the Spanish, putting an end to the useless drain on the royal exchequer and to the suffering of the king's subjects living in the praça.[61]

Such was the grim but realistic testimony of Colônia's precarious condition in the 1770s by one of the viceroy's most trusted confidants. Whether Lavradio forwarded Rocha's dispatch to the Court, as the governor evidently hoped he would,[62] is uncertain. If he did, Rocha's counsel merely confirmed a decision that the Marquis of Pombal had already made.

High Strategy and the Purposeful Sacrifice of Colônia

Pombal's plan to sacrifice Colônia was a consequence of his growing conviction that the Algiers expedition was destined to attack Brazil, and of his inability to persuade "our ever tardy [British] allies" of the need to intervene in Portugal's behalf. Accordingly, he wrote the viceroy in May 1775 that it was necessary to revise the Crown's military policy on the Debatable Lands.[63]

Portuguese forces in Rio Grande were ordered to adopt a strictly defensive posture. They were to occupy strategic locations in order to fight guerrilla warfare against the enemy. Paulista irregulars were to cut up and destroy his convoys, burn his lands, and harass him in every possible way so as to discourage him from waging war.

A spectacularly different policy was to be observed in Colônia. The king had come to realize, the minister continued, that the defense of the entrepôt was "chimerical and impossible." Therefore he ordered Colônia's regiment back to Rio de Janeiro under the pretext that it required retraining and additional recruits, and that these could be best obtained in the capital. Governor Rocha was directed to inform

---

61 Presumably he meant a convention of cession. The pertinent wording is "he impossivel durar a conservação da Collonia, e por estes motivos digo a V.Ex. como fiel Vaçalo, que emporta muito a El Rey . . . fazer com esta praça algúa Comvenção, antes que fique sem húa couza e sem outra." He referred to this proposal again in the same vague manner in his second dispatch of Aug. 25, 1775, CMCM, cod. 29, fol. 84ʳ.

62 In a postscript to his April 20 dispatch (n. 56 above), Rocha stated that he had thought of sending his recommendation directly to the king's ministers, but decided it would be better to place the matter in the viceroy's hands so that he could decide whether the dispatch merited forwarding. I cannot determine whether Lavradio actually forwarded the letter, but it is likely that he did so.

63 Pombal to Lavradio, May 9, 1775, BNRJ, I-2, 4, 7, n. 6; RIHGB, XXXI:1, 333–343. Received by Lavradio before Aug. 20. Lavradio to Böhm, Aug. 20, 1775, BNRJ, 13, 4, 2, n. 25 (orig.); BCRG, pp. 63–66.

the Spanish that this measure was being taken because of the certainty that Lisbon and Madrid would soon reach a settlement of their differences in America. In case Colônia was subsequently attacked, "as it naturally will be as soon as the Castilians see that it is unprotected by regular troops," Rocha was to make a token defense, and to protest that the attack was contrary to the peace that prevailed between the Courts. When obliged to surrender, he was personally to burn all correspondence with Rio de Janeiro and all orders from Lisbon to prevent such papers from falling into enemy hands. This admonition included the viceroy's order for the recall of the regiment, which Rocha should preserve "in his memory only."

Before continuing with Pombal's new instructions for the defense of Santa Catarina, it is pertinent to speculate upon his motive for sacrificing Colônia. There is no reason to doubt that he spoke the truth when he stated that the Crown realized the praça was indefensible. The record of Colônia's fall on three out of four occasions when it had been besieged certainly supported such a conclusion. Moreover, since its most recent restoration, in 1764, little or nothing had been done to improve the entrepôt's defenses owing to the continuance of the Spanish blockade and to the penury of the royal exchequer. Furthermore, the possibility of sending relief from outside after the Spaniards had begun an assault on the outpost was remote, both because of the need to concentrate available warships around Santa Catarina Island and because the reported size of the Algiers armada made it unlikely that a Portuguese relief force could get through to the praça.

It does not necessarily follow that Pombal intended to abandon Colônia permanently. He undoubtedly believed that England would eventually come to Portugal's aid in the event of formal war between Portugal and Spain, and that Colônia would, as usual, be given back to Portugal at the peace table.

If the British defeated the Spaniards in time, he could look forward to the liberation of occupied Rio Grande and possibly the Portuguese conquest of the Banda Oriental. But it was first necessary to persuade Great Britain to enter the fight; Pombal elected to do that by offering Colônia as bait to goad the Spaniards into the position of aggressors so that England would become convinced that Portugal was in serious trouble.[64] This, it is reasonable to conjecture, was Pombal's real objective in denuding Colônia of its regiment whose recall, so incomprehensible to some historians,[65] was the crafty minister's supreme gambit.

[64] This was precisely what the astute Conde de Aranda, Spanish ambassador to France, suspected was Pombal's intention. Aranda to Grimaldi, Aug. 12, 1776, cited in Gil Munilla, p. 290.

[65] E.g., J. C. Rego Monteiro, who refers to the withdrawal as "êsse inexplicável e incompreensível transporte de tropa," as "o primeiro ato para a entrega da

The gambit could fail, of course, and it was essential to take steps to prevent loss of other territory in Brazil. Therefore, as soon as the Colônia regiment arrived in Rio de Janeiro, another of the capital's regiments was to be sent to Santa Catarina Island to strengthen its defenses. In addition, the captain-general of Pernambuco was ordered to send the six-hundred-man Henrique Dias battalion of free Negro troops and another battalion of *pardos* to the island.[66] Pombal predicted that these colored troops would throw the Spanish into a "grande terror pánico" just as the strikingly attired Zouaves of Bohemia had baffled the French during the Seven Years' War.[67] Finally, he repeated his earlier injunction that every able-bodied man on the island should be armed to defend his homeland.

While Portuguese officers concerned with the withdrawal of the Colônia regiment referred to the matter with considerable circumspection in their correspondence, no effort was made to conceal the operation from the Spanish.[68] It was not until September 22, 1775, more than a month after he had received Pombal's new orders, that Viceroy Lavradio penned two dispatches to Governor Rocha[69] concerning the Court's decision. In the first, which bears the earmarks of having been intended for delivery to the Spanish, as indeed it appar-

---

Colônia do Sacramento." *Colônia do Sacramento,* I, 432. What he did not know was that the regiment was soon returned with additional reinforcements. See also the unwarranted inferences drawn by Luis Enrique Azarola Gil, *La epopeya de Manuel Lobo,* p. 52.

[66] Martinho de Melo e Castro to José Cézar de Menezes, May 12, 1775, cited in Cézar de Menezes to Melo e Castro, July 30, 1775. See n. 67. There were Henrique Dias black regiments in Recife, Salvador, and Rio de Janeiro. This was not the first time in recent years that the Crown had called for the use of Negro troops against the Spaniards. See Pombal to Conde da Cunha, Jan. 26, 1765, ANRJ, Col. 67, Liv. II fols. 74ʳ–77ʳ (orig.) ; *idem* to Luís Antônio de Sousa, same date, *RIHGB, TE,* V (1957) , 355.

[67] João Lúcio de Azevedo for some strange reason ridicules this plan as an "infantil recurso, próprio das civilizações inferiores." *O Marquês de Pombal e a sua época,* p. 272. Both he and the Visconde de Carnaxide (*O Brasil na administração pambalina,* pp. 204–205) assume that the battalions actually were sent to the island; in fact, they were not. Cézar de Menezes experienced great difficulty in assembling the troops, and to prevent their desertion locked them up in the former Jesuit college in Recife until the transports were ready. In October 1775 he received a countermanding order from Secretary Melo e Castro, and the troops were immediately released. That night there were fireworks and vivas to the king in Recife for having spared Pernambuco's vaunted blacks and *pardos.* A shortage of provisions that had existed when the captain-general was attempting to find food to accompany the troops suddenly ceased, enabling the captain-general to send ample supplies to Rio de Janeiro. Cézar de Menezes to Melo e Castro, July 30 and Oct. 10, 1775, IHGB/AUC, 1-1-15, fols. 61ʳ–69ʳ.

[68] The evident reason for secrecy was to prevent the public in Brazil and Portugal from learning of what appeared to be the shameful abandonment of Portuguese territory. See also n. 72 below.

[69] The cause for the delay was apparently a shortage of shipping. The *Nazareth,* one of two ships sent to bring the troops back, was in Rio de Janeiro undergoing repairs from the end of May until the end of August. MacDouall to Böhm, May 29 and Sept. 6, 1775, BNRJ, 13, 4, 5, nos. 67 and 70 (origs.) .

ently was,[70] Dom Luís paraphrased Pombal's suggested pretext for the withdrawal of the troops.[71] In the second he gave Rocha secret instructions, those which he was to retain "in memory only" when he burned the official records.[72]

On September 28, 1775, the frigate *Nossa Senhora do Pilar* arrived at Desterro with orders for Captain MacDouall to dispatch her and the frigate *Nazareth* to bring back the troops.[73] Two and a half weeks later (October 14), Colônia's regiment was drummed to a formal parade, and without any warning or explanation the men were ordered aboard the ships.[74]

[70] Gil Munilla states (p. 290) that Vértiz received a copy of the viceroy's order on Oct. 14, the same day the regiment boarded the ships.

[71] Lavradio to Rocha, Sept. 22, 1775, interleaved with *idem* to Böhm, BNRJ, 13, 4, 2, n. 31 (orig.). In the latter dispatch the secret information about the impending retirement of the Colônia troops has been cut out of the middle of the folio, apparently by a knife, and has been replaced by paper of a lighter weight and color. The cut begins at the end of one paragraph and extends to an incomplete sentence which begins "sou tãobem obrigado a comunicar a V.Ex. este importante negocio debaixo do mesmo segredo, e de V. Ex. tãobem fazer queimar este officio de que El-Rey . . . q.er fique só memoria delle no R.o de Janeiro, em livro q. fique debaixo da minha chave." The printed version (*BCRG*, pp. 66–67) contains suspensive points where the deleted part occurs, but supplies no explanation for the hiatus. See also n. 73 below.

[72] The viceroy's instruction to Rocha (cited in n. 71) contains no reference to the burning of documents or to the token defense the governor was expected to make, yet in a dispatch to the Court, probably written in September, Lavradio advised that he had sent such orders. *VRL*, pp. 71–73. That Rocha actually received them is evident from his dispatches of Oct. 12 and 13, 1775, CMCM, cod. 29, fol. 91^{r-v} and 93^{r-v}. In the first he states that he had put the viceroy's instruction of Sept. 22 into execution, and that all of the garrison except the lame and apoplectic were departing, adding that he feared that the Spanish would attack and give him no quarter. In the second he reported that he had burned "mais cento e tantas hordeins q. achey na Secretaria, que fallavão em Comtrabandos e igualmente dos livros de Registo dellas."

Rocha later wrote that as soon as his troops left, the Spanish began making inquiries as to the reasons for the embarkation of the garrison and that he replied with the contrived official explanation. Some credence may have been given to his story, since, he says, four days later a packetboat arrived with Madrid's first suspension order (discussed below in the text). But then came news that in late October the Portuguese had captured a Spanish patrol in the missions (the seizure of S. Martinho by Pinto Bendeira, Oct. 28, 1775, also described below). This report convinced the Castilians that there was more than appeared on the surface to the Portuguese troop retirement, and the Spanish immediately increased the size of their force blockading Colônia. Rocha to Lavradio, Dec. 4 and 20, 1775, CMCM, cod. 29, fols. 102^{r}–103^{v}, 123^{r}–125^{v}.

[73] On Oct. 6 MacDouall wrote Böhm that the *Pilar* had arrived at Desterro with three companies of infantry and artillery. He added, "no dia 30, fis sahir as Fragatas Nazareth e Pilar, a hum serviço Particular, e por 2, athé 3 Mezes não espero que se ajuntem a esta Esquadra. . . ." On Oct. 22 he noted in a postscript to another report to Böhm that "The 2 frigats Nazareth & Pillar ar gone to Colonia to take in what the Governor is pleast to give them—and cary it to the riodejaneiro." BNRJ, 13, 4, 5, nos. 71 and 73 (origs.).

[74] Petition of Col. Domingos Correa de Mesquita (commander of the Colônia regiment) to Lavradio, *ca.* 1777 or 1778, in Rego Monteiro, *A Colônia do Sacramento*, II, 165–174; a manuscript copy [?] formerly existed in the National Library (BNRJ, I-31, 26, 1, n. 6) but is curiously missing from its *pasta*.

Those soldiers must have been happy when they saw Rio de Janeiro again.[75] At last they could fill their shrunken stomachs and drink fond farewells, minus the usual *saudades,* to their former station. There was even the possibility that they might receive part of the six years' back pay the king owed them.[76] But eight days after their arrival,[77] they were mustered once more and told to board the warships again. Consternation and disillusionment spread as the word was passed: they were returning to Colônia!

The explanation for this apparently heartless and arbitrary action mystified contemporaries,[78] and has escaped the searches of previous historians. But when the scattered evidence is properly assembled, the solution to the puzzle becomes apparent.

The Algiers Debacle and Its Influence on Luso-Spanish Policy [79]

The Portuguese government was correct in believing that there was more to the Algiers expedition than the punishment of the dey, but it was probably wrong in concluding that the "hidden" purpose of the armament was an attack on Brazil. What seems to have been in the

[75] From the portarias cited in n. 76, it appears that the regiment arrived in Rio during the second week of November.

[76] Mesquita to Lavradio, *ca.* 1777 or 1778. Actually the troops were paid only for October and November 1775. Portarias of Nov. 14 and 15, 1775, CMCM, cod. 26, fols. 11ᵛ-12ʳ, showing disbursements to the regiment amounting to 8,078,890 réis.

[77] Mesquita says six, but Lavradio wrote Saldanha (captain-general of São Paulo) "Devo partecipar a V.Ex. q. o Regimento da Colônia, veyo a esta Capital, a onde se demorou 8 dias por não permitirem os ventos q. elle tornasse a sahir mais depressa. . . ." He added, "Este movimento parecerá hum pouco extraordinário, porém em o praticar fis o q. devia." Dispatch of Nov. 26, 1775, CMCM, *maço* 15; *DI*, XVII (1895), 43-48.

[78] Mesquita clearly did not understand why his regiment was being sent back. Governor Saldanha, in reply to Lavradio's dispatch of Nov. 26 (previous note), stated with evident bewilderment, "Creyo que V.Ex.a com justos fundamentos, faria recolher a retroceder o regimento da Colônia, porque longa experiência me tem mostrado q. V. Ex.a nada obra sem altos fins e acertos felices." Dispatch of Dec. 16, 1775, *DI*, XLII (1902), 69.

[79] For a brief bibliography of sources on the Algiers expedition see Antonio Ballesteros y Beretta, *Historia de España*, V, 188, where the statement that "no modern account exists" still stands. Vicente Rodríguez Casado, *Política marroqui de Carlos III* (Madrid, 1946), pp. 235-244, is a disappointing, narrowly conceived account which, like all previous studies, fails to establish the relationship between the Algiers disaster, the Portuguese campaign of 1776 in Rio Grande, and the punitive Cevallos expedition of 1777. In spite of its age, William Coxe, *Memoirs of the Kings of Spain of the House of Bourbon . . . 1700 . . . to 1788*, V (2d ed., London, 1815), is still useful; see also *The Annual Register, or a View of the History, Politics, and Literature for the Year 1775* (5th ed., London, 1791), pp. 142-146.

mind of the ministers of Charles III was something quite different, namely recovery of the prestige that Spain had lost in the recent Falkland Islands dispute with Great Britain. A massive display of Spanish military strength and a spectacular victory in North Africa would serve as a reminder to the nations of Europe that Spain was still a major power.[80]

To this end nearly 40,000 men and approximately 400 ships were secretly assembled in four of Spain's principal ports,[81] where they were placed under the command of General Alejandro O'Reilly—the infamous "Bloody" O'Reilly of New Orleans fame. The armada sailed during the last days of June 1775, and on July 1 its six columns presented themselves before the mainland between Algiers and El Harrach. But the landing did not occur until a week later, giving the estimated 80,000 Moors ample time to prepare their defenses. When O'Reilly finally ordered his men ashore, he did so without laying down a preliminary bombardment, so confident was he of an easy victory. The Moors initially gave way, and when the Spaniards had advanced about a mile, they became entangled in obstacles left behind by their adversaries. Suddenly the Moors turned upon them and drove them back into the sea. Having lost part of his artillery and most of his provisions, and having suffered casualties in excess of 2,600, O'Reilly returned to Spain and to personal obscurity.[82]

The unexpected outcome of the Algiers venture produced an immediate shift in Spanish policy vis-à-vis Portugal and Brazil. Though Madrid tried to conceal the extent of the catastrophe, the news soon leaked out [83] and a ministerial crisis resulted.[84] The possibility of renewing the attack on Algiers was debated at an emergency meeting of the Council of State, which rejected the proposal and ordered the ex-

[80] See the revealing remarks of Aranda and Grimaldi in Gil Munilla, pp. 250–251.

[81] Estimates of the size of the expedition vary considerably. William Dalrymple, who was in Spain when the survivors returned, states that there were fifty-one warships and 344 transports which carried 24,447 men. *Travels through Spain and Portugal*, p. 178. Portuguese intelligence sources reported that the armament included fifty-four warships, 422 Spanish and foreign transports, and 23,840 men. See n. 90 below.

[82] Estimates on the number of Spanish casualties also differ. Official sources set the figure at 2,600, but Dalrymple, who interviewed survivors and had sources of information in Algiers, said that it was closer to 5,000.

[83] At midday on July 15 a courier rode up to the royal palace in Madrid with the first news of the disaster. He was immediately confined to the guardhouse. That evening the Portuguese ambassador heard rumors of the defeat, and the following day he went to Court, where Charles III's unperturbed countenance at first deceived him into believing that the reports were false. A look at the Duke of Lousada, however, told him that they were true. Sousa Coutinho returned to his residence to "work for the truth" by means of his spies. Sousa Coutinho to Ayres de Sá e Melo (Portuguese Foreign Minister), July 17, 1775, BNRJ, I-2, 4, 7, n. 11.

[84] Ballesteros y Beretta, V. 192–195.

pedition disbanded.[85] The same day Foreign Minister Grimaldi suggested to the Portuguese ambassador, Dom Francisco Innocêncio de Sousa Coutinho, that their governments resume negotiations toward a settlement of their dispute in America.[86] Thus began another round of Luso-Spanish diplomatic discussions concerning the borderlands.

Grimaldi's overture was conditioned partly by the Algiers debacle, and partly by the arrival of an alarming report from Governor Vértiz concerning Rio Grande. After making a careful investigation, the governor concluded that it would be impossible for him to expel the Portuguese from their positions on the peninsula where they were daily augmenting their forces and behaving as if they would soon attack his troops.[87] Grimaldi's proposal therefore appears to have been designed to forestall such a Portuguese attack,[88] as does his instruction to the Count of Aranda, Spanish ambassador to Versailles, to try to persuade Louis XVI to mediate the Iberian dispute.[89]

In Lisbon the Marquis of Pombal reflected on Grimaldi's proposal and examined fresh dispatches from ambassador Sousa Coutinho on the magnitude of the Spaniards' defeat.[90] Realizing that Grimaldi was negotiating from a position of weakness, Pombal determined to profit from his adversary's distress. He instructed Sousa Coutinho to discuss with Grimaldi the possibility of a peaceful solution to their differences in the borderlands, but his new orders to Viceroy Lavradio were conceived in an entirely different spirit.

Acting on Pombal's instructions, the Portuguese ambassador ad-

[85] Pombal to [Lavradio], Aug. 26, 1775, BNRJ, I-2, 4, 7, n. 15. According to this dispatch, presumably based on Sousa Coutinho's reports, Grimaldi and the Conde de Ricla, Minister of War, wanted to rebuild their forces, punish the Moors, and restore the reputation of Spanish arms. Their proposal was vetoed by the Minister of Finance, Don Miguel de Mosquiz, who said there was no money for a new undertaking, and by the Minister of Marine, D. Julián de Arriaga, who declared that the navy was unfit for another attempt. I cannot find a Spanish source to corroborate or refute this story.

[86] Gil Munilla, pp. 262–263, and the dispatches of Pombal to Lavradio of July 26 and 27 and Aug. 26, 1775 cited in this section.

[87] Vértiz to Arriaga, Mar. 14 and May 9, 1775, CB, III, 326–330.

[88] Possibly Grimaldi was also trying to maneuver Pombal into the position of the aggressor so that Spain could retaliate and appear to be repelling an unjust Portuguese attack. Such is the implication of Grimaldi's remarks to Aranda of Aug. 7, 1775. After rejecting Aranda's suggestion of an attack on Portugal, he went on "parecería más acertado esperar que los portugueses nos atacasen en alguna parte de las que no pueda haber pretexto de suponerlas contenciosas; y entonces enviar de una vez un armamento grande de tierra y de mar para que los hundiese; en fin gastar de una vez y con provecho, lo que se parta en años, sin él." Quoted in Gil Munilla, p. 254.

[89] Ibid., pp. 255–258.

[90] Pombal to Lavradio, July 27, 1775, CMCM, cod. 14 (49/10) (orig.); copies in BNRJ, I-2, 4, 7, n. 9, and in ANRJ. Included in this dispatch was a copy of ambassador Sousa Coutinho's first report on the Algiers disaster and an intelligence summary entitled "Relasion de las Tropas embarcadas de los quatro puertos de Espana . . . y los numbres de los Principales Gefes."

vised Grimaldi on August 12, 1775, that his government was willing to resume the long-interrupted negotiations concerning their respective colonial limits provided that those discussions were based upon the terms of the Treaty of Paris. Ignoring that stipulation, Grimaldi countered with the suggestion that both governments immediately order a suspension of hostilities in America pending the conclusion of their talks.[91] With only a vague oral agreement from Sousa Coutinho, the Spanish foreign minister at once arranged for the dispatch of such an order to General Vértiz.[92] Two days later he notified Aranda that French mediation was no longer necessary.[93]

While Grimaldi was congratulating himself on having prevented a further blow to Spanish prestige until Spain had recovered from her wounds at Algiers, the Marquis of Pombal was preparing new instructions for Viceroy Lavradio. In them he reviewed what was known concerning the Algiers debacle, concluding that it proved that the Spaniards were obviously a "less formidable" adversary than in the past. Therefore he countermanded his earlier pessimistic orders and directed Lavradio to resume efforts to achieve victory in Rio Grande. No longer was Colônia to be sacrificed, and its governor should be notified that the praça must be "defended, secured, and maintained against any and all Castilian attacks." [94]

When the Court's new instructions reached the viceroy, Colônia's regiment was already en route to Rio de Janeiro, having left the entrepôt ten days earlier.[95] Realizing that it was probably too late to intercept and turn back MacDouall's frigates, Lavradio immediately sent 100 picked soldiers from the first Bahian regiment and Pombal's revised instructions to Governor Rocha.[96] As soon as the Colônia reg-

---

91 Gil Munilla, pp. 255-258.

92 Arriaga to Vértiz, Aug. 12, 1775, *CB*, III, 337-338. The order reached Montevideo on Oct. 18. Vértiz, "Memoria" in Sigfrido A. Radaelli, ed., *Memorias de los virreyes del Río de la Plata*, p. 84.

93 Gil Munilla, pp. 264-265. Unaware that Grimaldi had initiated the discussions, Aranda was amazed that Portugal would be so ready to treat with all the aces in her hand. Aranda to Archbishop of Tebas, Oct. 11, 1776, *ibid.*, p. 264, n. 7. Always strongly suspicious of Pombal and hostile toward Portugal, Aranda proposed that Spain immediately send four to six battalions to Buenos Aires to anticipate Portuguese deception. Grimaldi, however, rejected the suggestion on the ground that the reinforcements would be insufficient to check the Portuguese, and that a larger force would tempt the British to aid Portugal. *Ibid.*, pp. 266-267.

94 Pombal to Lavradio, July 27, 1775, CMCM, cod. 14 (49/7) (orig.); copy BNRJ, I-2, 4, 7, n. 12.

95 Lavradio to Böhm, Oct. 31, 1775, BNRJ, 13, 4, 2, n. 35 (orig.); *BCRG*, pp. 71-73. The viceroy stated that the Court's new instructions (n. 94 above) arrived in Rio de Janeiro on October 24.

96 *Loc. cit.*, and *portaria* of Nov. 15, 1775, CMCM, cod. 26, fol. 12ʳ. The Bahians were sent on the pretext that they were model troops sent to retrain the Colônia regiment.

iment landed at Rio de Janeiro, the gaps in its ranks were filled with members of the Lagos artillery regiment and preparations were made for the troops' return to the Plata.[97] Thus what at first glance appears to have been a viceroy's caprice was actually a consequence of the humiliating defeat that Spain sustained at the hands of infidels in North Africa.

Painful Progress Toward a Portuguese Offensive

A week after the viceroy received Pombal's new orders, he forwarded a copy of them to General Böhm. Once more he emphasized that the time was ripe for a land-sea attack upon Spanish positions in Rio Grande and in the Plata, and once more he urged that the general and Captain MacDouall work out details for such a joint operation.[98] Böhm curiously replied that the viceroy's suggestion amounted to a "change of our plan," but agreed to cooperate to the limit of his abilities.[99]

Actually, forces under the general's command had already been active against the Spanish. On October 31, 1775, Major Rafael Pinto Bandeira climaxed one of his frontier patrols with a surprise attack on the important post of San Martín [São Martinho], which lay athwart the lines of communication between the old Jesuit missions and their estâncias about thirty leagues west of Rio Pardo. Upon its surrender Bandeira captured eighteen Spanish dragoons and twenty-one Indians, but another hundred Indians managed to elude him.[100] After slitting a few Indian throats, the major warned survivors that he would be back, and returned to Rio Pardo with considerable booty.[101]

[97] Governor Rocha acknowledged his new instructions, which he received two weeks before the troops returned (December 14), and begged for men, matériel, and munitions to carry out the Court's directive. He stated that morale within the praça was extremely low; he had only four men available for guard duty, and they were so old and crippled that he gave them permission to sit rather than stand at their posts. Rocha to Lavradio, Dec. 1, 1775, CMCM, cod. 29, fols. 94ʳ–96ʳ.

[98] Lavradio to Böhm, Nov. 18, 1775, BNRJ, 13, 4, 2, n. 36 (orig.); BCRG, pp. 73–76; also published in VRL, pp. 210–214 (where the year is omitted).

[99] Böhm to Lavradio, Dec. 9, 1775, BNRJ, I-2, 26, 2, n. 15 (rascunho).

[100] Böhm to Lavradio, Nov. 9, 1775, ibid., n. 11 (rascunho). The best account of the attack is D. Francisco Piera to Vértiz, Nov. 7, 1775, CB, III, 341–342. San Martín's fall produced a new flood of protests from Vértiz and denials from Böhm, who refused to entertain the former's complaints, on the ground that he was not the governor of Rio Grande and was therefore unqualified to discuss questions of limits or jurisdictional violations. This drew an angry retort from Vértiz, but Böhm remained impassive. Ibid., pp. 343–346. Lavradio fully approved of the way Böhm had handled the exchange. Lavradio to Böhm, Jan. 11, 1776, BNRJ, 13, 4, 3, n. 1 (orig.); BCRG, pp. 79–86.

[101] The spoils included more than 270 oxen, 168 mares, 980 stallions and colts, and an unspecified number of sheep and cattle valued at 7,518,980 réis. Rego Monteiro, Dominação, pp. 217–22.

The fall of San Martín was encouraging to the viceroy, but even more cheering was Böhm's announcement that he and MacDouall were at last actively planning their long-talked-about offensive.[102] Early in November the general wrote the captain that he would require the squadron's assistance to destroy the Spanish warships in front of the enemy forts in order to proceed against the latter. MacDouall sent a liaison officer who spent a week with Böhm and Hardcastle discussing the proposed operation. Subsequently Böhm suggested two plans to MacDouall: (1) that he enter the Lagoa with forces equal to those of the enemy and attack him immediately, or (2) that he sail past the Spanish forts and unite with Hardcastle's flotilla, return downstream, and attack. He added that he would need several small craft to transport a battalion of grenadiers from the peninsula to assault the Spanish forts.[103] MacDouall replied that he would forward the general's proposals and the recommendations of his own lieutenant to the viceroy for his approval. He added: "I have propos.d to the Vice King 8 [?] Vessels armed with 16 piecs of artil.a [artillery] and 125 men each, and two smaler Vessels for a reserve[. I]f the Vice King sends them, . . . I think—with gods permission we can have no other dificulty to give you a free passage in the river." [104]

MacDouall's proposals meant further delay, since it would take time to procure the small craft and the armament. Why it took months for the general and the squadron commander to decide what they needed to carry out their instructions was beyond the viceroy's comprehension. He was also annoyed by Böhm's constant carping about the deficiencies of civil officers in Rio Grande and by his disparaging remarks on certain Paulista reinforcements he was expecting. Noting that Captain-General Saldanha considered it necessary to send six companies of ragged "volunteers" by sea since he feared the men would desert if marched overland,[105] Böhm had sarcastically asked Lavradio: "Is it possible that people who [are thus] animated by the martial ardor of their ancestors will be able to defend and conquer provinces? I pray Your Excellency to reflect upon this." [106]

The viceroy sent the Court copies of his subordinates' dispatches in a letter containing a refutation of their complaints and a defense of his own conduct. He assured the Court that MacDouall already had ample ships for his special mission, that the morale of Böhm's army

102 Böhm made his proposal in a letter of Nov. 2, to which MacDouall promptly responded. MacDouall to Böhm, Nov. 11, 1775, BNRJ, 13, 4, 5, n. 74 (orig.) ; Böhm to Lavradio, Nov. 2 and 17, 1775, BNRJ, I-28, 26, 2, nos. 9–10 (rascunhos) . Lavradio approved Böhm's plans in his dispatch of Dec. 15, 1775, BNRJ, 13, 4, 2, n. 38 (orig.) ; BCRG, pp. 77–78.

103 Böhm to Lavradio, Nov. 29, 1775, CMCM, cod. 6 (orig.) ; BNRJ, I-28, 26, 2, n. 14 (rascunho) .

104 MacDouall to Böhm, Dec. 13, 1775 (postscript) , ibid., 13, 4, 5, n. 75 (orig.) .

105 Saldanha to Böhm, Oct. 21, 1775, DI, XLII (1903) , 38–40.

106 See n. 103 above.

was high, and that the general possessed sufficient forces to expel the
enemy. Caustically he observed that if he had been worthy of the
king's confidence to direct the troops in person, the men would already have had an opportunity to prove their mettle in battle.[107] Instead, he was forced to remain in Rio de Janeiro, where "I am like a
bell: I am here calling to all; I cry, I persuade, I give them [every]
possible assistance; as my cries are from afar, sometimes they are not
heard, and most of the time they make little or no impression." [108]

There was more than self-pity behind Lavradio's remarks, for he
was burning under two stinging rebukes from Colonial Secretary
Melo e Castro. In the first the minister severely reproved him for writing dispatches

> full of complaints about the dearth of things you consider necessary
> and with criticisms of everything that has been sent to Your Excel-
> lency from Lisbon, [the] Islands, Pernambuco, and Bahia, when
> [the king] . . . is certain that it is public knowledge in Brazil that
> never before have so many soldiers, munitions, provisions, or pecu-
> niary resources gone to the State which Your Excellency gov-
> erns . . . ; [and that] with only the troops and resources of Rio de
> Janeiro the Count of Bobadela fought the Glorious Uruguayan
> War, triumphing simultaneously over the forces of the Indians and
> the Jesuit Engineers and the treacheries of the Spanish Generals
> . . . [and every one knows] that the Castilians of those times and
> now are the same Castilians.[109]

In the second reprimand, dated October 29, 1775, the secretary gave
the viceroy and his military subordinates an even stronger dressing
down. Without suggesting where the fault lay, he declared that it was
incomprehensible after "so many repeated and decisive letters" that
the king's orders concerning Rio Grande were still being flouted. The
present grave situation is due entirely to the "sinister and contrary"
conduct of those charged with the defense of southern Brazil. Because
of their "frivolous, affected, and invalid pretexts" for inaction, "the
only thing left to do is to put the interests of this Crown relative to
its dominions of Brazil and [particularly the] southern parts of it in
the Hands of Divine Providence. . . ." [110]

---

[107] To Field Marshal Antônio Carlos Furtado de Mendonça Lavradio wrote,
"Your Excellency can be certain that if the choice of commandants was mine,
[you] would be . . . second in the dangers, discomforts and in the most important
actions . . . [for] I would reserve the first place for myself; however God does not
wish it, and the King does not permit it. The Remedy is to cross our arms, obey
the command, and suffer with drops of blood the pain which the heart feels with
these troubles." Jan. 31, 1776, CMCM, cod. 26, fol. 97ʳ⁻ᵛ; see also *idem* to the Court,
Dec. 1775, *VRL*, pp. 73–75 (excerpt).

[108] To Pombal, Dec. 30, 1775, *VRL*, p. 216.

[109] To Lavradio, Aug. 4, 1775, CMCM, cod. 13 (44/17) (orig.); copy in BNRJ,
I-2, 4, 7, n. 14.

[110] [Melo e Castro] to Lavradio, Oct. 29, 1775, CMCM, cod. "C," fol. 158ᵛ.

The Background to the Portuguese Order
Suspending Hostilities

The tone of exasperation and despair in Melo e Castro's reprimands was prompted by Lisbon's growing awareness that time was fast running out for the attainment of a favorable military decision in Rio Grande without serious diplomatic consequences. Madrid could not be expected to wait much longer for definite assurances that Lisbon had followed her lead in suspending hostilities in America. By the end of October 1775 it was becoming apparent that either the Portuguese government would have to issue such an order or risk war with Spain, and possibly with France as well, without any guarantee of British assistance.

As soon as Grimaldi's original proposal had reached him, the Marquis of Pombal appealed for military support to the British government through ambassador Walpole and through the Portuguese plenipotentiary to London, Luís Pinto de Sousa.[111] As he had during the El Ferrol and Algiers crises, Pombal drew up lengthy memorials, buttressed by copies of pertinent dispatches from Viceroy Lavradio and General Böhm, demonstrating that Spain was the continual aggressor and Portugal the needy ally.[112] He asserted that the two members of the Family Compact were actively planning to attack Portugal and Brazil, intending to divide the colony between them and to impose Spanish rule upon Portugal. To meet such a threat he asked for six British (or German) regiments, four ships of the line, and a few frigates. Belittling Spain's offer to assist Great Britain in the suppression of the disturbances within her colonies,[113] he contended that the situation in the British colonies was not serious and that England could easily spare the few ships and soldiers that Portugal needed to defend herself.[114]

Meanwhile Grimaldi was becoming restive. Two months had

---

[111] Luís Pinto de Sousa, later visconde de Balsemão, was captain-general of Mato Grosso from 1769 to 1772, and then succeeded Melo e Castro as minister plenipotentiary to England, a post he retained until 1788. For a characterization of his abilities see Jacome Ratton, *Recordaçoens*, pp. 334–336.

[112] E.g., he construed the action of April 5, 1774, when Hardcastle forced the canal of Rio Grande, as evidence of Grimaldi's "jesuitical plan" for the conquest of São Paulo and Minas Gerais. Pombal to Pinto de Sousa, Sept. 8, 1775, Luz Soriano, *História do reinado de d. José*, II, 619–623.

[113] The Spanish ambassador to London had declared that his government viewed the contagion of revolt as dangerous to all colonial empires, and was willing to assist Britain in stamping it out. Pombal regarded the offer as a deliberate attempt to wean Britain away from Portugal.

[114] Pombal to Pinto de Sousa, Nov. 25, 1775, Luz Soriano, II, 627–639.

passed since Madrid had sent General Vértiz orders suspending hostilities against the Portuguese, yet there was still no assurance that Lisbon had followed suit.[115] If the Portuguese government had not, the Spanish Foreign Minister realized, he was out on a limb. Therefore, in mid-October Grimaldi sent a worried message to Aranda to inquire whether France would come to Spain's aid in the event of war with Portugal. If Paris replied negatively, the ambassador was to determine whether France would join with Great Britain in mediating the Iberian dispute.[116] Late in November 1775 Grimaldi called in ambassador Sousa Coutinho and flatly told him that Madrid must have positive information whether Lisbon had also issued a suspension order to its agents in Brazil.[117]

Grimaldi's insistence and the absence of any indication from Viceroy Lavradio that a campaign was under way in the borderlands forced Pombal to alter his strategy. While residing temporarily at Pancas, not far from Lisbon, he communicated his views to Melo e Castro who was staying by the king at the Ajuda palace.[118] Admitting that he had opposed the issuance of a suspension order in July, Pombal stated that he now believed that it was necessary to take such a step and to equip Sousa Coutinho with full powers to negotiate an agreement with Spain. He had been led to these conclusions by several considerations: (1) his belief that Portugal's procrastination was giving Spain the opportunity to present her in a bad light to Britain and France; [119] (2) the failure of Lavradio and Böhm to act in Rio Grande; (3) the existence of new pressure from France to treat with Spain; [120] (4) the lack of a positive response from Great

[115] Arriaga warned Vértiz on October 31 that Madrid had no guarantee that Lisbon had sent the order, and urged him to be on guard against Lusitanian treachery. *CB*, III, 341.

[116] Gil Munilla, p. 271.

[117] *Ibid.*, pp. 277-278.

[118] A nineteenth-century copy of this exchange of Dec. 2-6, 1775, including Melo e Castro's replies, is in BNRJ, I-3, 9, 135.

[119] British Foreign Secretary Weymouth wrote Lord Stormont (British ambassador to France) on December 15, 1775, that he had given Walpole instructions "that he express in the strongest terms to Mo^r. Pombal the necessity there is to give the Court of Spain Satisfaction with respect to their question whether orders are given to the forces of His Most Faithful Majesty in South America not to act on the offensive . . . their unwillingness to answer . . . gives ground for suspicion that they may take advantage of their superior strength in that part of the world. . . ." L. G. Wickham Legg, ed., *British Diplomatic Instructions, 1689-1789*, VII, *France*, Pt. IV, Royal Historical Society, Camden 3rd ser., XLIX (London, 1934), 149.

[120] Early in November the French chargé in Lisbon tried to learn from Ayres de Sá e Melo, newly appointed Secretary of Foreign Affairs, why Portugal had delayed giving Spain positive assurances. The secretary replied that all Portugal wanted was respect for the provisions of the Treaty of Paris, and that until Spain complied, Portugal had an "incontestable right" to prepare for any eventuality in Brazil. Count d'Hennisdal to Vergennes (French Foreign Minister), Nov. 7, 1775,

Britain to his pleas for aid; and (5) his hope that Britain might still come around if he had more time to persuade her. The king acceded to Pombal's recommendations, and full powers were sent to Sousa Coutinho, as well as a bizarre instruction to the Portuguese representative in England that was calculated to persuade the British government to grant home rule to its rebellious colonies so that it would be in a position to help Portugal.[121]

On December 10, 1775, Sousa Coutinho presented Pombal's reply to Grimaldi concerning the suspension order. The note read: "His Most Faithful Majesty *has ordered the dispatch* of a ship for Rio de Janeiro with the most positive and inflexible orders to his Generals and Commandants . . . of the said government and the others situated in the South not only to suspend all proceedings against their Spanish neighbors along the said frontiers, but also (in case there be any change) to restore everything to the state in which it was on July 17 of this year, the day on which the [current] negotiations began. . . ."[122]

It is not surprising that Grimaldi rejected the note as unacceptable. He denied its insinuation that he had been the instigator of the talks, and he was dissatisfied with its vague statement on the transmission of the Portuguese suspension directive. Had José I actually *sent* the instruction, or had he merely *ordered* it sent? There could be a vast difference, and the Spanish foreign minister insisted that the note's language be clarified. Also he demanded that the territorial restitutions go back to 1767, the year when the Portuguese occupied the peninsula of the Lagoa dos Patos.[123]

Eleven days later the Portuguese ambassador handed Grimaldi a new note replacing the rejected one but bearing the same date.[124] The revised pledge omitted any reference to the restoration of occupied territories, but declared positively that the king *"has dispatched"* the suspension order. On Pombal's insistence, the ambassador asked for written assurance that similar orders had been sent to

---

QE, VIII, 109–110. Soon after, the Marquis of Blosset, newly posted French ambassador to Lisbon, raised the same question, to which Sá e Melo replied that his hands were tied and that it was necessary to speak with Pombal. When the ambassador did so, Pombal declined to accept France's good offices. Blosset to *idem*, Nov. 14 and 17, 1775, *QE*, VIII, 111–115. Nevertheless, the French government still offered to mediate the Iberian dispute. Vergennes to Blosset, Dec. 5, 1775, *ibid.*, p. 115.

121 D. Alden, "The Marquis of Pombal and the American Revolution," *The Americas*, XVII (Apr. 1961), 369–382.

122 Quoted in Gil Munilla, p. 282, and paraphrased in *QE*, VIII, 116, and XVIII, 391–392, where the editor indicates that copies of the Portuguese statement were sent to the Portuguese ambassadors at London and Versailles.

123 Gil Munilla, pp. 282–283.

124 The text is given in Carnaxide, *O Brasil na administração pombalina*, p. 213.

Governor Vértiz, a request with which Grimaldi readily complied.[125]

But, contrary to the ambassador's positive assurances, the king had *not* suspended hostilities in Brazil. In fact, Pombal did not send such an order until January 15, 1776. One able historian has confessed perplexity as to the reason for Pombal's delay, [126] but the explanation seems quite obvious—he was still hoping to receive news from Brazil of the expulsion of the Spaniards from Rio Grande before ordering a stop to the fighting. By mid-January he realized that he could wait no longer, and in disgust finally sent the directive.[127] Less than a week before, however, he hopefully began preparations to brace Europe for a possible Portuguese victory in Rio Grande.[128]

In Rio de Janeiro the oppressively warm month of February was drawing to a close, and the viceroy was still unaware of his government's suspension order.[129] Yet he had reason to suspect that such an order might soon arrive, [130] and he was certain that the decisive moment in Rio Grande was fast approaching.[131] Though uninformed of Pombal's double dealing, he sensed that a Portuguese victory in the borderlands might come at an inopportune time for his superiors. With this disturbing possibility in mind, Dom Luís penned a dispatch to Lisbon that was as much a reflection of his character as it was of his powers of divination. He suggested that if Pombal felt it necessary to do so, he could assert that General Böhm had taken the initiative on the viceroy's authority and contrary to the Court's in-

---

125 *Ibid.*, p. 214. Vértiz (*Memória*, p. 84) refers to two additional suspension orders from his government, one dated January 6, the other February 6, 1776.

126 João Lúcio de Azevedo, *O Marqués de Pombal*, p. 274.

127 Pombal to Lavradio, Jan. 15, 1776, BNRJ, I-31, 26, 11, n. 1 (*1.a via*). The first paragraph indicates that this was his first dispatch to the viceroy since Aug. 26, 1775. In the order, Pombal contends that he was responding to the wishes of the kings of Britain and France to authorize the suspension. He urged the viceroy to observe extreme caution in order to be certain that Vértiz had a similar directive, and called for Böhm to withdraw his troops very gradually from Rio Grande.

128 On Jan. 9, 1776, Pombal visited the residence of the French ambassador. Responding to the latter's renewed offer to aid in settling the dispute with Spain, Pombal assured him that the question could easily be adjusted with Madrid, and that French mediation was unnecessary. "You know," he said, "it is not men who determine events (*negócios*), but circumstances. All that a minister can do is to profit from those which give him the privilege of affording proofs to the Nations of his personal good will." Blosset to Vergennes, Jan. 9, 1776, *QE*, VIII, 121–122.

129 The order did not reach Rio de Janeiro until April 1, 1776. Lavradio to Böhm, April 3, 1776, BNRJ, 13, 4, 3, n. 4 (orig.) ; *BCRG*, pp. 88–90.

130 On December 4, 1775, Governor Rocha wrote the viceroy that following the arrival of a mail boat from Spain, the local Spanish governor had sent him a letter expressing his desire to keep harmonious relations with the Portuguese, and that he had reciprocated in the same spirit. CMCM, cod. 29, fol. 102ʳ.

131 Since MacDouall had announced his departure from Santa Catarina for Rio Grande by a dispatch which arrived in Rio de Janeiro on Feb. 16. Lavradio to Melo e Castro, Feb. 21, 1776, IHGB/AUC 1-1-29, fols. 267ʳ–272ᵛ, and *VRL*, pp. 217–221.

structions. As a loyal vassal of the king, Lavradio said, he was prepared to sacrifice himself because of "my honor and the obligations
with which I was born." He would accept the guilt to save the State
embarrassment, but he was confident that the record of repeated
Spanish insults would justify his action before the world.[132] With
this display of *noblesse oblige,* Dom Luís rested his quill and eagerly
awaited news from Rio Grande.

[132] *Idem* to Pombal, Feb. 22, 1776, *VRL,* pp. 222–223.

VII
The Portuguese Victory in Rio Grande
and Its Consequences

... if the Spaniards resist me, I will avenge the insult, and if they permit
me to enter I will sail past them and confer with Your Excellency.

MacDouall to Böhm, February 3, 1776

I flatter myself that Your Excellency will receive with satisfaction the news
of the happy success that the arms of His Majesty won on the night of
March 31–April 1 . . . that I owe principally to our brave grenadiers
whom I caused to cross the River. . . .

Böhm to [Lavradio], April 3, 1776

HAD THE VICEROY known the outcome of the Portuguese attack
in the Lagoa dos Patos two days earlier, it is unlikely that he would
have been so willing to sacrifice himself upon the altar of expediency.
While the humiliation that the Portuguese experienced on that occasion was avenged less than a month and a half later, the tardy
Lusitanian victories in the borderlands proved difficult for Lisbon to
justify before the bar of international opinion, as Lavradio had
feared, and produced serious consequences.

Preliminaries to the Naval Attack of
February 19, 1776

After three months of preparations, Robert MacDouall announced
on February 3, 1776, that he was nearly ready to depart from Santa
Catarina Island for Rio Grande. He wrote General Böhm that his
forces included nine vessels—two small frigates, a sloop, two corvettes,
a brigantine and three smacks—armed with 110 guns, three to eight
caliber, and 770 men. He stated that he would sail as soon as two snows
arrived from Rio de Janeiro.[1]

The snows failed to appear, and four days later MacDouall left
without them. He was anxious to carry out his mission as soon as pos-

[1] MacDouall to Böhm, Feb. 3, 1776, BNRJ, 13, 4, 5, n. 77 (orig.) .

sible because of the lateness of the season, General Böhm's insistence that he have naval support, and the positive injunction from the viceroy that the operation be conducted during the new moon when the tides would be most favorable for crossing the bar. To tarry longer at Santa Catarina would mean postponing the operation for a month, said MacDouall, and he might have added, would surely have invited the wrath of the viceroy. Although the Irishman was far from pleased with the size or quality of his makeshift flotilla, he was confident that he would rout the enemy.[2]

After seven storm-tossed days the flotilla arrived off Lagamar on February 14. Originally MacDouall had intended to sail directly into the Lagoa, but adverse winds and the failure of three members of his squadron to meet him off Rio Grande prompted him to anchor in the roadstead.[3] The following day he went ashore to confer with the general and Captain Hardcastle. He informed them that he preferred to challenge the enemy as soon as he entered the channel rather than wait for Hardcastle's flotilla to join him, as Böhm had alternatively suggested. He was convinced that the five Spanish ships anchored in the canal would try to escape rather than oppose him. Böhm thought the Irishman too optimistic, but failed to shake his confidence. He informed MacDouall that he had three regiments poised to cross the channel as soon as the enemy vessels had been eliminated, but he made it clear that his men would not embark until the Spanish ships' guns had been silenced.[4]

After this exchange of views MacDouall returned to the *Santo Antônio,* his flagship, and assembled his captains to go over the particular assignment of each ship. According to his battle plan, the ships would enter the canal in a single column, led by MacDouall in the sloop *Expedição,* which would proceed to an anchorage opposite Fort Mosquito, and cover the rest of the flotilla as they passed to take up stations before the enemy vessels further upstream. After each captain had anchored opposite his target, he was to await a signal from the *Graça* before opening fire. Three vessels—the smacks *Monte* and *Belém* and a ship identified only as "the royal brigantine"—were to serve as a reserve to replace any ship damaged or unable to take her

2 *Idem* to *idem,* Feb. 14, 1776, *ibid.,* n. 79 (orig.). A note in Böhm's hand indicates that MacDouall delivered the letter personally.

3 On Jan. 27 MacDouall sent the frigate *Pilar* in search of the nau *Belém* and the frigate *Princesa do Brasil,* both on patrol, with orders for all three to join him at the entrance to Rio Grande. He intended to use their longboats and those of the *Santo Antônio,* his flagship, to transport Böhm's troops across the channel. For unexplained reasons, none of the three ships ever appeared while he was in Rio Grande.

4 Böhm to Lavradio, Feb. 23, 1776, BNRJ, I-28, 26, 2, n. 18; a polished version appears in *CB,* III, 357–360; cf. MacDouall to Lavradio, Feb. 29, 1776, *VRL,* pp. 223–228.

position. As each Spanish ship surrendered, the Portuguese warship assigned to her would shift to assist its sister in forcing the next enemy ship in line to make a similar decision.[5] The commander stressed that the success of the operation depended on the ability of each ship to find her station and to make her gunfire count. He added that the infantrymen in the yards ought to hold their musketfire until they could see the "beards of the enemy." [6]

For several more days the winds continued to be contrary, compelling MacDouall to delay his entrance. This gave the Spaniards time to appraise the size of the Portuguese flotilla and to plan their defense. The Castilian captains agreed in a meeting aboard their flagship that the rapidity of the current in the channel made it unsafe for them to leave the protection of their forts, and they decided to wait for MacDouall to approach them. They pledged that in the event of imminent capture they would run their ships aground and set them afire rather than allow them to fall into the Irishman's hands.[7]

The Fracasso [8]

On February 19 the winds abated and shifted from northeast to southwest, and MacDouall signaled his ships to cross the bar. It required all morning and the early afternoon to complete this operation, but it was accomplished with only one minor mishap, when the smack *Penha* crashed against the anchor flukes of the *Graça* and sustained slight damage. The frigate *Graça*, the largest member of the flotilla, was found to draw too much water to clear the bar, and it was necessary to unload her heavy guns first and then reinstall them after she was over. When the cannons were again in place, her Danish captain, Fredrick Kesselberg,[9] urged MacDouall to postpone the attack until the morrow because his men had not eaten all day and were exhausted from their exertions. The Irishman refused to consent to fur-

[5] The intended role of Hardcastle's ships is obscure. Apparently MacDouall wanted them to make a feint against the north end of the channel while he was advancing from the south. MacDouall to Böhm, Jan. 4, 1776, BNRJ, 13, 4, 5, n. 76 (orig.). However, adverse winds kept Hardcastle from participating at all, or so Böhm reported in his dispatch of Feb. 23, cited in n. 4 above.

[6] MacDouall to the flotilla, Feb. 14, 1776, BNRJ, 13, 4, 5, nos. 80 and 82 (by error the first and second folios are separated by an unrelated insert, so that the third folio is incorrectly numbered separately). A note by Böhm indicates that he obtained this copy from the reports of the various captains after the battle.

[7] Report of Francisco X.r de Morales, Brigantín *Santiago*, Rio Grande, Mar. 2, 1776, *CB*, III, 353–355.

[8] A fracasso is a complete "snafu," a "bust," or as the dictionary puts it, "a sudden or unexpected misfortune."

[9] This is one of several variant spellings of the Dane's name which appear in contemporary accounts.

ther delay, and after ordering a ration of brandy for the entire flotilla, set course for Fort Mosquito.

As the tiny *Expedição* boldly led the way up the channel the Spanish gunners held their fire, waiting until all the Portuguese ships were within range. Then the cannons of San José de la Barra opened up, and the rest of the Castilian batteries ashore and afloat followed suit. *Graça* immediately gave the signal to fire, but that was hardly necessary. The initial Spanish barrage threw the flotilla into complete disorder, and only four of MacDouall's ships were able to take their stations. The *Bom Jesus* sprung a leak from a near miss and ran aground. The smack *Victória* sailed beyond her anchorage, and took so long in coming about that she missed most of the brief action. The *frigatinha Glória* anchored in the wrong place, cut her cable, and drifted beyond the range of the enemy guns, while the *Penha* beached herself on the sand bank surrounding Lagamar.

Only the sloop *Expedição,* the frigate *Graça* and smacks *Belém* and *Monte* reached their proper positions, and they attacked the enemy ships forthrightly. The sloop and the smacks concentrated their fire on the first and second Spanish ships in line, forcing them to slip their cables and beach themselves. Meanwhile the *Graça* became engaged in a deadly duel with the *galeta Pastoriza,* and soon mortally wounded the latter's captain. As Captain Kesselberg was contemplating boarding his adversary, a volley of Spanish muskets felled him and seven Portuguese marines.

This was the turning point of the battle. Kesselberg expired almost immediately, and since no one aboard had been designated to succeed him in command, three junior officers fought for the privilege. Meanwhile the demoralized crew deserted their guns, and the *Graça* became a helpless target.

Now it was the Spaniards' turn to prepare a boarding party,[10] but as they were planning to do so MacDouall arrived upon the scene. After observing that most of his ships had failed to reach their stations, the Irishman had taken to his longboat and, rowed by "nine brave fellows," went from ship to ship urging their captains to get into position and their gunners to sharpen their fire. Noticing the erratic behavior of the silent *Graça,* MacDouall directed his longboat to her side to learn what was the matter. By the time he reached the

<hr />

10 So the Spanish naval commander at Rio Grande later told Lavradio when his ship entered Rio de Janeiro, and credited the skipper of the smack *Victória* with firing upon him so vigorously that he desisted from the attempt. Lavradio to Melo e Castro, Aug. 31, 1776, *VRL,* pp. 296–303. No mention of the *Victória's* accomplishment appears in any other contemporary account. MacDouall merely states "José Correia de Melo [captain of *Victória*] foi mais chegado á chalupa e . . . nunca chegou ao seu posto e passou muito distante e deu fondo acima de todos." MacDouall to Lavradio, Feb. 29, 1776, cited in n. 4 above.

frigate, the *Expedição* had received a twenty-four caliber ball at her waterline and was taking so much water that she had to pull out of the fight. That left two, possibly three, Portuguese ships against three Spanish warships and the forts behind them. Sizing up his situation, MacDouall decided to break off the engagement before he sustained further losses in what had become a very unequal contest. Consequently, he signaled the flotilla to cut their cables and to head for the protection of the Portuguese forts.[11]

Such was the two-and-a-half-hour naval engagement of February 19, 1776. In spite of heavy fire on both sides, casualties were negligible.[12] No Spanish ships had been severely damaged, although two had beached themselves. The Portuguese, however, had lost the *Expedição* and the *Bom Jesus,* the latter being set afire to prevent her from falling into Spanish hands.[13] MacDouall's flotilla also suffered substantial damage to rigging and masts, but the most serious loss was that of the anchors, for they could not be replaced in Rio Grande, and without them it was impossible for the ships to fire accurately in the canal.

After surveying the extent of the damage, the dispirited MacDouall

11 In addition to sources previously cited, the battle is reported in José Correa Lisboa (pilot of *Penha*), "Relação e mapas em que se mostra toda a ordem, disposição e successos, que houverão na tomada da terra do sul do Rio-grande . . . desde o . . . 6 de Fevereiro . . . 1776 até 1 de Abril do mesmo anno," Rio de Janeiro, 1776, *RIHGB*, XVL:1 (1882), 97–120. A similar account, probably by another pilot or a captain, is "Relação da esquadra por ordem de Roberto Mac-Dowal principio em 6 de fevereiro de 1776 . . . ," BNRJ, I-5, 1, 19, incorrectly attributed to MacDouall. Also in the same depository is Manoel [?] to "Mano de Coração," Rio de Janeiro, Apr. 18, 1776, written by someone in the viceregal palace to an intimate, probably in Lisbon. The first part concerns the Portuguese victory of April 1, 1776, and the second, the action of Feb. 19. It is chiefly valuable for revealing the attitude of the viceregal court, and has been published in J. C. Rego Monteiro, *Dominação*, pp. 324–326. The best secondary account is Rego Monteiro, *ibid.*, pp. 230–234; cf. F. A. Varnhagen, *História do Brasil*, IV, 196–197, and J. F. Fernandes Pinheiro, *Anais da província de S. Pedro*, pp. 113–115.

12 The most authentic account of Portuguese losses is the "Rellaçam dos mortos e feridos do combate do dia 19, de fev.ro de 1776 . . . ," an enclosure in Antônio Carlos Furtado de Mendonça to Lavradio, Mar. 3, 1776, CMCM, *maço* 31 (orig.), which lists twelve killed and thirty-eight wounded. The anonymous "Notícia circunstanciada do Rio Grande," Feb. 20, [1776] in Manoel Lobo, ed., *Historia general de las antiguas colonias hispano-americanas*, III, 72–73, gives Spanish losses as thirteen killed, twenty-five seriously wounded, and an unspecified number slightly wounded, but a considerably lower estimate appears in the "Relación de los oficiales, Marinería, y Tropa del Rey que han sido muertos y heridos en el combate . . . [de] 19 de Fevrero de 1776," *CB*, III, 356–357.

13 The *Expedição*, a sloop MacDouall had built at Desterro, sank in the canal. After grounding off the Spanish bar fort, the *Bom Jesus* was refloated only to run aground again off Fort Mosquito. The second time the Portuguese removed the crew, powder, and part of her guns during the night of the nineteenth. The next day the Spanish took the rest of the guns, and vainly tried to refloat the smack. That night Böhm ordered it destroyed.

decided against renewing the battle. Declaring that he had no authority to remain in Rio Grande, and that his primary responsibility was the defense of Santa Catarina Island, the Irishman turned command of the flotilla over to Captain Hardcastle, and set sail for the more tranquil waters of Santa Catarina.[14]

The Postmortems

Among contemporaries there was a considerable divergence of opinion on the causes and significance of the Portuguese reverse. Captain MacDouall attributed the outcome of his unsuccessful attack to several factors over which he had no control, among them (1) the inferior quality of his ships, (2) the defective seamanship exhibited by his captains and their pilots, (3) the failure of those officers to follow his orders, and (4) the lack of cooperation from General Böhm, who should have attacked the enemy forts while the battle was in progress to distract the Spaniards from concentrating their fire on his ships.[15] For his part, the general, who observed the action from the peninsula and later inspected the ships and talked with their crews, concluded that poor seamanship, indiscriminate naval fire, and the failure of the Portuguese ships to follow up their initial attack when victory was almost in sight were the major reasons for the debacle.[16]

As far as Viceroy Lavradio was concerned, there could be only one explanation for the disaster, and that was the incompetence of Robert MacDouall. He criticized the Irishman for (1) failing to heed Captain Kesselberg's advice and allowing his crews to fight while in a "stupor" occasioned by the brandy they had drunk just before the battle; (2) failing to issue proper instructions designating seconds in command on each vessel; (3) failing to select proper commanding officers and crews for the operation; [17] and (4) failing to assume command of the Graça himself when the day could still have been saved. In short, said Lavradio, "Were it not for the grave and unpardonable blunders of the chief . . . [the action] could have been very glorious for Portuguese arms." [18] But, he said caustically, and one suspects wistfully,

14 Böhm to Lavradio, Feb. 23, 1776, cited in n. 4 above.

15 MacDouall to Lavradio, Feb. 29, 1776, cited in n. 4 above.

16 Böhm to Lavradio, Feb. 23, 1776, cited in n. 4 above, and Mar. 11, 1776, IHGB/AUC, 1-1-29, fols. 288ᵛ–292ᵛ. The latter includes the relations of each captain "avec leurs obscurités et leurs erreurs," emphasizing how valiantly each had performed.

17 This was an unfair criticism, since Lavradio admitted great difficulty in finding suitable officer material for MacDouall, who was obliged to make his selections from among the motley group the viceroy sent him. Lavradio to MacDouall, Feb. 13, 1775, VRL, pp. 205–206.

18 Lavradio to [Melo e Castro], [Mar.], 1776, VRL, pp. 79–83.

"God still does not wish it, and perhaps reserves this good fortune for another time, and another Viceroy who is more deserving of this glory." [19]

Though the marquis clearly intended to discredit MacDouall and to persuade the Court to recall the troublesome naval officer,[20] Lisbon responded quite differently. In a dispatch glowing with praise for the Irishman and critical of the attitudes the viceroy and General Böhm had displayed toward him, the Marquis of Pombal asserted that MacDouall's brave and determined action had demoralized the enemy and thereby contributed substantially to the subsequent Portuguese victory of April 1. He emphasized that no other officer in the navy possessed as much experience or more fighting spirit than MacDouall.[21] Far from removing or rebuking the Irishman, the Court promoted him from captain to commodore (coronel do mar) ! [22] One wonders whether MacDouall would have fared so well had not the Court been able to evaluate his conduct in the light of General Böhm's success a month and a half later.

The Portuguese Victories of March 26–April 1, 1776

The military operations of March 31 to April 1, 1776, represented the third step in General Böhm's plan to expel the Spaniards from positions they occupied in Portuguese-claimed territory in Rio Grande. When he first arrived in the captaincy, Böhm found the Spaniards

[19] Lavradio to Melo e Castro, Mar. 13, 1776, *VRL*, pp. 344–347. Here Lavradio indicates his sources of information on the engagement consisted of MacDouall's report (which he clearly ignored) ; a letter from Böhm to Furtado de Mendonça in Santa Catarina; and the testimony of the captain and crew of a [merchant?] ship who claimed to have witnessed the action.

[20] So bitter was their relationship that the viceroy attempted to make MacDouall appear a coward in the action. He asserted that the Irishman "ordered his colors hoisted on the *Graça* [presumably to draw fire upon her], and took to the longboat disguised with a very old blue coat, and thus went speaking . . . [to] our ships, and as he appeared in the guise of an aide who was distributing the orders of the chief, the Castilians were prohibited from firing upon him, as we afterwards came to know, respecting also the courtesy with which he passed in sight of them, always bowing with hat in hand." See n. 18, above. No other source confirms the viceroy's allegation with respect to the Spanish order to withhold fire from MacDouall.

[21] Pombal to Lavradio, July 31, 1776, BNRJ, I-31, 26, 11, n. 3 (*2.a via*). There is not a shred of proof that MacDouall actually softened up the Spaniards, but this is typical of how Pombal leaped to conclusions without assessing the evidence. His thought processes mark him in many ways as a man of the Middle Ages rather than of his own times. On the medieval habit of overgeneralization and exaggeration, see J[ohan] Huizinga, *The Waning of the Middle Ages* (New York, 1954) , pp. 234–235.

[22] Pombal to Roberto MaKDouell [sic], July 31, 1776, BNRJ, I-31, 26, 11, n. 6. In the same *pasta* there is a letter of commendation to General Böhm for having repaired the damaged ships and for his subsequent victory over the Spaniards. Both letters were left open for the viceroy to read before sealing with the "sello volante" and forwarding to the two officers. *Idem* to Lavradio, July 31, 1776, *ibid.*, n. 5 (orig.).

dominating Rio Grande at three principal points: San Martín (or São Martinho), defending the missions west of the Rio Pardo; Santa Tecla, guarding the cattle ranges in the south and southwest; and the vila of Rio Grande and its protecting forts, blocking the entrance to the Lagoa dos Patos.[23] As has been noted in the preceding chapter, the first of these positions, San Martín, fell into Portuguese hands in October 1775.[24] Böhm originally intended that the attack on Santa Tecla would coincide with his own assault on the Spanish forts in the canal of the Lagoa dos Patos, the final step in his campaign.

The capture of Santa Tecla was entrusted to the victor at San Martín, Major Rafael Pinto Bandeira. In January 1776 Governor José Marcelino de Figueiredo asked the major whether he regarded seizure of the fort as feasible. The major had no doubt of his ability to overrun the fort if he had sufficient troops and supplies, emphasizing that its possession would make the Portuguese "masters of all the *campanha* and even the ranches of Montevideo." [25]

Late the next month Major Bandeira began his march. His expedition consisted of 619 men, 3,000 horses, 150 oxen, two falconets, and several thousand head of cattle. As was his custom, he planned to take the enemy by surprise, but this time he was deprived of the opportunity to do so when several members of a patrol intercepted by his men escaped to warn their comrades. Consequently, as the Portuguese came within sight of the fort they were greeted by cannon fire. Rather than risk heavy casualties by a direct assault, Bandeira settled down to an uncomfortable siege that lasted until March 26. Two days earlier the Spaniards offered to surrender, and after the usual bargaining the fort capitulated. Under terms of the armistice, its garrison—250 men, including sixty Indians—was allowed to retire to Montevideo.[26] Subsequently the major leveled the fort built by General Vértiz scarcely two years earlier,[27] and returned to Rio Pardo with a large quantity of booty.

23 Rego Monteiro seems to be the only historian who has seen the taking of San Martín, Santa Tecla, and Rio Grande as part of the same master plan. *Dominação*, pp. 217 ff.
24 See above, Chap. VI, p. 168.
25 Pinto Bandeira to José Marcelino, Feb. 1, 1776, Rego Monteiro, *Dominação*, pp. 323–324.
26 *Ibid.*, pp. 235–246; see also Bandeira's letters of Feb. 28, Mar. 1, 15, and 26 to Böhm, *VRL*, pp. 254–259; the terms of the capitulation are given on pp. 268–271. José Marcelino reported the victory to Governor Saldanha on Mar. 31, 1776, *DI*, XVII (1895), 164–166, but did not write the viceroy until April 3. *VRL*, pp. 260–261.
27 Böhm and José Marcelino both assumed credit for having given this order on the ground that Santa Tecla, fifty leagues south of Rio Pardo, was too remote to be supported. Nevertheless what Bandeira had said was true. Santa Tecla was such an obvious strategic locale that the Spanish rebuilt the fort in 1777, and thereby regained control of the southern campanha.

The third and most crucial step remained to be carried out. March 31, 1776, fell on a Sunday that happened to be the birthday of Maria Anna, Queen of Portugal. Like all anniversaries of the royal family, this one was cause for celebrations in all corners of the Portuguese empire, even in the remote Lagoa dos Patos. There the frigate *Graça* fired twenty-one guns in salute to the Queen, and they were answered by an equal number of salvos from the shore batteries. Across the channel the Spanish garrison watched the Portuguese merrymaking and relaxed, certain that their adversaries would be in no condition to attack them for some time to come.

However, unknown to the Spaniards, General Böhm selected that very evening to hold a secret conference with his principal officers. There he divulged his plan to assault the Spanish positions on the opposite shore during the early hours of the next day.[28] To transport the troops across the canal, an amphibious flotilla consisting of specially constructed *jangadas*[29] was to be inconspicuously distributed at various points along the peninsula before dawn. Surprise attacks were to be delivered against Fort Mosquito (also called Santa Barbara) and Fort Trinidad in the center of the Spanish defensive perimeter.[30] One party, composed of two grenadier companies, one from the Estremoz and the other from the first or "old" Rio de Janeiro regiment, was assigned to Major Manoel Soares Coimbra, who was ordered to rush Fort Mosquito. Another party, commanded by Major José Manuel Carneiro de Figueiredo and consisting of two grenadier companies, one from the Moura, the other from the Bragança regiment, was simultaneously assaulting Fort Trinidad. A second wave—four companies each from the Estremoz and Bragança regiments headed by their respective regimental commanders—was to follow the first after an interval of half an hour. Its mission was to help secure the two forts or, if they had already fallen, to push on to other objectives. Subsequent waves were assigned to attack the remaining forts.

Böhm's surprisingly well-conceived plan[31] was in the main carried

28 The plan is revealed in two of Böhm's reports to Lavradio, the first, an undated draft, BNRJ, I-28, 26, 2, n. 20, seems to have served as the basis for the second, dated April 3, 1776. *VRL,* pp. 246–252. The latter omits many details contained in the former.

29 Jangadas are the elementary fishing craft still used in northeastern Brazil as far south as Bahia. They consist of several logs lashed together, a simple mast and sail, and a tiller. Lavradio ordered hundreds of them sent from Recife to Rio de Janeiro and from there to Rio Grande to be assembled for the cross-channel attack.

30 See Map 1. Apart from the bar fort, these were the main forts in the Spanish defense system, and it was beneath their guns that the Spanish squadron was anchored.

31 Though Böhm stated that he was the author of the war plan, the viceroy rather ungraciously and inaccurately claimed credit for it himself: "Tudo o que se empregou nesta ação, foi segundo as providências que eu dei: o plano dela foi meu, ainda que um pouco desfigurado e praticado em diferente tempo. . . ." But he

out. The first waves left the peninsula about 3:00 A.M. the next day. Major Coimbra's group had an easy time of it. After overrunning a few sentry posts near the beach, the grenadiers, led by the sword-wielding major, attacked the astonished garrison of Fort Mosquito and set to flight those whom they could not kill or capture. By 4:15 A.M. observers on the peninsula descried three rockets from the fort, the signal that it was in Portuguese hands.

The second assault wave landed on a beach between Fort Trinidad and Fort Mangueira. This time the Spanish had been forewarned of the enemy's approach, since some of the landing craft ran aground on a shoal and were seen by lookouts on the brig *San Matilde,* which immediately opened fire. The gunfire apparently frightened the defenders of Fort Trinidad as much as it disturbed the Portuguese, and in the ensuing confusion the grenadiers of Moura and Bragança were upon their adversaries before the latter realized what had happened. A three-rocket burst soon told of the fall of the second Spanish fort.

The next objective was Fort Mangueira, situated on a point marking the entrance to the gulf of Mangueira. Although the attack was scheduled to be made at 4:00 A.M., it was delayed when the troop-laden launches ran aground in the predawn darkness and mist. Yet the delay worked to the advantage of the Portuguese. While they were trying to free themselves from the mud, refugees were arriving at the fort from Fort Trinidad, bearing tales that the Lusitanians were putting everyone to the sword. This rumor helped to demoralize the garrison of Fort Mangueira, and when a ball from a Portuguese-manned piece in Fort Trinidad hit their powder magazine, they decided that the better part of valor lay in flight to the vila. By 8:00 A.M. the third fort was flying the Portuguese flag.

With the light of day the Spanish ships anchored off the forts observed Captain Hardcastle's armada preparing to bear down upon them from the north end of the channel. Leaving their brothers ashore to their fate, the six Spanish captains cut their cables and headed to sea. Thanks to favorable winds, they outdistanced Hardcastle's ships, but as they approached the exit of the canal they came within range of the Portuguese shore batteries. In the ensuing fight three of the six ships ran aground on the sand bar at Lagamar, where they were abandoned.[32]

---

hastened to add that he was only "blindly" attempting to execute the "wise and very prudent" orders of Pombal. Lavradio to Pombal, Apr. 19, 1776, IHGB/AUC, 1-1-29, fols. 300ʳ–303ʳ; published in *VRL,* pp. 240–244. In fact, neither Pombal nor Lavradio detailed precisely how Böhm was to oust the Spaniards from Rio Grande, and so far as is known, the actual operational plan was his, not theirs.

[32] A corvette, a frigate, and a *saetía* were lost, but a brigantine, another saetía, and a schooner got away. Of this latter group, one vessel later returned and surrendered to the Portuguese. Böhm to Lavradio, Apr. 3, 1776, cited in n. 28 above, and *idem* to Saldanha, May 15, 1776, *DI,* XVII (1895), 181–183.

Hardcastle's flotilla was still to perform useful service during the battle. Unable to catch the Spanish ships downstream, the English captain trained his guns on the small fort of Ladino, situated on an island between Point Mangueira and the vila. The fort's outnumbered defenders soon had enough, spiked their guns, and crossed over to the Spanish town. But the soldiers within Fort Triunfo, newly built and named after the Spanish victory over MacDouall, showed more mettle than their compatriots on tiny Ladino, and put up such a heavy fire that Hardcastle's leading frigates were obliged to retire. Nevertheless, as the day wore on Triunfo's defenders observed their sister forts silent and themselves surrounded by Portuguese, and by 5:00 P.M. they struck their colors and retired. By this time the Spanish had also fired their warehouses in the gulf of Mangueira as well as two ships, one of which was a Portuguese prize, anchored in the mouth of the gulf.

Around 6:00 P.M. a small launch crossed from the vila to São José do Norte with a message from the Spanish general, Miguel de Tejada. Tejada asked for three days in which to evacuate the vila, but General Böhm replied with an ultimatum to get out in as many hours. When the Spanish general sent a second appeal, his messenger was told that Böhm had retired for the night.[33] Next morning (April 2) a Portuguese patrol found the vila deserted except for some wounded in the hospital, and hoards of cats and rats in the foul-smelling streets.

Of all the Spanish forts, the most active the preceding day had been San José de la Barra, which had continuously fired upon the Portuguese forts across the channel and on shipping in the Lagamar roadstead. San José was the principal Spanish fort in the canal, and until the Portuguese captured it they would be unable to send ships into the lagoon without grave risk. Moreover, since it was strongly fortified and was equipped with thirty-six-caliber guns, a Portuguese assault was likely to be a costly one. Fortunately it proved unnecessary to make such an attack. During the early hours of April 2 a number of loud explosions were heard from within the fort, and the next morning smoking ruins and a bannerless flag pole were mute testimony that the Castilians had evacuated their last fort in the Lagoa dos Patos.[34] A few days later, on Easter Sunday, the trium-

---

[33] D. Miguel de Texada to Böhm, 8:00 P.M., Apr. 1, 1776, Rego Monteiro, Dominação, p. 329.

[34] In addition to the sources previously cited, the Portuguese victory in the canal is discussed in Böhm to José Marcelino de Figueiredo, Apr. 1, 1776, ibid., p. 330, idem to Antônio Carlos Furtado de Mendonça, Apr. 1, 1776, VRL, pp. 244–246, and idem to Lavradio, Apr. 11, 1776, VRL, pp. 262–268; Lisboa, "Relação" (see n. 11, above) contains an excellent account of the sequence of events. The best secondary treatment of the action is Rego Monteiro, Dominação, pp. 247–251.

phant Austrian general ordered a Te Deum sung in the mother church of the vila to celebrate his long-awaited conquests.[35] Böhm had reason to celebrate. In spite of what had seemed to be endless procrastination, he successfully gave the coup de grâce to Spanish pretensions to eastern Rio Grande.[36] Never again would the Castilians be able to inhibit Portuguese movements within the Lagoa dos Patos, the key to control of Rio Grande de São Pedro.[37] Having now attained his major objectives,[38] the general awaited the reception of his victories in Rio de Janeiro and in Lisbon.

Reaction in Rio de Janeiro to the Portuguese Victories

By a curious coincidence, the Marquis of Pombal's tardy suspension order arrived in Rio de Janeiro the same day that General Böhm's grenadiers were overrunning the Spanish forts in Rio Grande. It was also on April 1 that the viceroy received General Böhm's second report on MacDouall's debacle the previous February.[39] Hence the viceroy was not in a very happy mood when he wrote the general to comply with the Court's directive. He ordered Böhm to retire his forces from Rio Grande "com muita lentidão," very sluggishly, using various pretexts to justify his dilatory action. Böhm was to notify General Vértiz that his withdrawal was occasioned by the armistice agreed upon by the two Courts, and that Vértiz would be expected to honor that agreement.[40] But the viceroy ordered Portuguese forces to remain

35 Böhm was then still a Protestant. He was converted to Catholicism shortly before his death in 1782. His conversion was reported in great detail by Viceroy Luís de Vasconcelos e Sousa to Martinho de Melo e Castro in his dispatch of Aug. 16, 1782, IHGB/AUC, 1-2-1, fols. 114ᵛ–120ʳ and was described in the "Sermão em ação de graças pregado na igreja de N. S. da Conceição de Hospício em 18 de Agosto de 1782 pela conversão que fez para a Fé Cathólica João Henrique de Böhm," IHGB, Lata 68, MS 1251 (orig.). It is symptomatic of the times that the same issue of the Gazeta de Lisboa (that of Oct. 3, 1782) that gave more than half a page to the Austrian's conversion devoted only two lines to the death of the Marquis of Pombal.

36 A good critique of Böhm's accomplishment is Vértiz to Arriaga, Montevideo, Mar. 14, 1775, CB, III, 326–330, in which the governor specifies various reasons why he regarded a cross-channel attack as impossible.

37 On the other hand, the Spanish continued to control the Southern campanha and the northwest missions until 1801.

38 Böhm, however, failed to capture the enemy troops or to recover Santa Teresa or São Miguel. The suspension order arrived before he could attack the latter two, and later he showed no interest in trying. Apparently he had intended to use Pinto Bandeira's mounted dragoons to sweep behind the retreating Spaniards, but they were still at Santa Tecla, and Böhm's own cavalry units reached the other side of the canal too late to catch the rapidly retreating enemy.

39 Lavradio to Böhm, Apr. 3, 1776, BNRJ, 13, 4, 3, n. 4 (orig.?); BCRG, pp. 88–90.

40 Böhm complied and naturally drew an angry retort from the Spanish governor. Vértiz to Bohn [sic], May 22, 1776, CB, III, 391–393, in reply to Böhm's letter of May 13.

alert for possible Spanish treachery. In the event that Böhm had occupied any territory previously held by the Spaniards, continued Lavradio hopefully, his forces should retain possession, and he should advise the governor of Buenos Aires that he could not hand back his conquests without orders from the viceroy, who could not sanction such action without Lisbon's approval.[41]

Two and a half weeks later, on April 17, 1776, the first news of the Portuguese triumphs reached the viceroy. As word quickly filtered throughout the capital, high government officials and the local aristocrats (nobreza) came to the palace to congratulate Lavradio and kiss his hand. Meanwhile the commoners crowded into the streets, dressed in their finest garments, and reacted by dancing, hugging one another, and shouting vivas to the king and to his wise minister, the Marquis of Pombal. As night fell, Guanabara Bay became the scene of brilliant illuminations. Even though a heavy rainfall soon extinguished the fires, it failed to quench the well-known exuberance of the Cariocas, who continued to celebrate far into the night.[42]

The viceroy vainly tried to restrain such merrymaking, not because he was opposed to it in principle, but because under the circumstances he found it more than slightly embarrassing, partly because the festivities were witnessed by the crew of a Spanish ship then in port. And the marquis knew, as the king's subjects did not, that the victory was a tarnished one and would require some dexterous explaining on the part of his superiors.

He had their problem in mind when he reported Böhm's achievement in the Lagoa dos Patos to Lisbon. Dom Luís expressed regret that the victory came so late in spite of his constant efforts to produce it at a more propitious time. As he had done earlier, the viceroy alluded to the probable complications that Portuguese aggression would make for Pombal's diplomacy, and he again suggested how that aggression could be justified. First, he pointed out that by the time the Court's suspension order reached him it was obviously impossible to prevent General Böhm from launching his attack.[43] Second, while admitting that Spanish authorities claimed to have received a similar order months before, Lavradio contended that they had repeatedly violated the spirit of the armistice by continuing to harass Colônia.[44]

41 See n. 39 above.

42 Rio de Janeiro's enthusiastic reaction is reported in Lavradio's dispatches cited in notes 43 to 45 below. Some additional details are given in Manoel [?] to "Mano de Coração," Apr. 18, 1776, cited in n. 11 above.

43 To give added force to this argument Lavradio obliged the crew of the Spanish ship in port to sign a statement that the action had occurred before the receipt of the suspension order. The viceroy forwarded their questionable testimony to Lisbon. Lavradio to Pombal, Apr. 19, 1776 (postscript), IHGB/AUC, 1-1-29, fols. 300ʳ–303ʳ; published in VRL, pp. 240–244.

44 Lavradio to Melo e Castro, Apr. 19, 1776, VRL, pp. 261–262.

Two weeks later the viceroy was able to tell the Court about the fall of Santa Tecla, the news of which arrived in Rio de Janeiro at the end of April. Once more he emphasized that the action had occurred before receipt of the suspension. order. Were it not for that directive, Lavradio boasted, Portuguese forces would push on to the Plata.[45]

Diplomatic Reaction to the Portuguese Victories

The news of the Portuguese offensive arrived in Europe while negotiations toward a settlement of the Iberian question were continuing in several European capitals. After having rejected a French offer of mediation early in January,[46] the Marquis of Pombal reversed himself two weeks later. He was prompted to do so by the discovery that a new memorandum from Sousa Coutinho to Grimaldi had been revised by the helpful English ambassador to Madrid, Lord Grantham, to make it more palatable to the Spanish foreign minister. In its revised form, the note offered immediate settlement of the boundary question in America on the basis of the Treaty of Utrecht (1715). This unauthorized proposal compromised Portugal's claim to Rio Grande since that treaty contained no clear provision recognizing the territory as Portuguese. Moreover, the offer was contrary to Pombal's consistent position that Portugal was entitled to the disputed territory by virtue of the Treaty of Paris, and that Spain had actually recognized her sovereignty to Rio Grande by a cédula of June 9, 1763.[47]

The tampered note of Sousa Coutinho forced Pombal to resort to a new strategy of delay. He wanted neither to concede Spain's title to the disputed area nor to go to war with her without British support; consequently he decided to accept the previously tendered offers of France and Britain to mediate the dispute. On January 23, 1776, he visited the French ambassador at his residence and told him of his de-

---

45 Lavradio to Melo e Castro, Apr. 30, 1776, *VRL*, pp. 252–254.

46 See Chap. VI, n. 120.

47 The Visconde de Carnaxide (*O Brasil na administração pombalina*, p. 216) completely misses the point why Pombal objected to this proposal, stating that the minister opposed it merely because it offered the possibility of a definite settlement to the question when he wanted to prolong the dispute. No doubt he did wish to keep the matter up in the air, but, much more important, he did not want to surrender the position he had consistently maintained since 1763: that Rio Grande was legally Portuguese. After he had fallen from power, Pombal wrote a bitter criticism of British interference in these negotiations, a pamphlet entitled "Compêndio histórico e analytico do juízo que tenho formado das dezeseis cartas estampadas em Londres" (1779), which purported to be a reply to another pamphlet, "Letters from Portugal on the late and present state of that kingdom" (1777), thought to have been written by Pombal, too. Excerpts from the "Compêndio histórico" are given in John Smith, *Memoirs of the Marquis of Pombal*, II, 311–336.

cision. He justified his new position on the ground that it was impossible to continue discussions with the intractable Grimaldi, who was a "Jesuit in a short robe . . . an instrument chosen by the rest of the Society . . . to exercise vengeance against Portugal and even against Spain." [48]

Pombal's new move was acceptable to Paris and London, for neither wished to be dragged by the Iberian powers into an unwanted war.[49] Spain went along less enthusiastically, even though Charles III had twice before urged the French to mediate. Preliminary discussions began in London, Paris, Madrid, and Lisbon among the various ambassadors and heads of state,[50] but difficulties arose almost immediately. Great Britain declined to propose a mediatory congress to Madrid on the ground that her close connection with Portugal would prejudice such a recommendation.[51] French Foreign Minister Vergennes also refused to author the plan, contending that it was up to José I to declare himself "in the usual form." [52]

A new issue suddenly arose when Grimaldi learned that two Spanish ships had been seized off Brazil and were being held in Rio de Janeiro. He promptly suspended the talks until Portugal had given a satisfactory explanation for the seizures.[53] Since both Paris and London supported the demand of the Spanish foreign minister, in April

[48] Blosset to Vergennes, Jan. 23, 1776, QE, VIII, 123–125.

[49] Characteristically, however, the French and the British took quite different views of the meaning of Pombal's new proposal. Blosset wrote pessimistically that its only result would be a deluge of memorials and countermemorials by Pombal who would manage to obscure thoroughly the substance of the dispute. Blosset to Vergennes, Feb. 20, 1776, QE, VIII, 163–164. On the other hand, Robert Walpole wrote Weymouth that "every day" he found Pombal "more desirous of having the affairs between the two Courts settled, and even the apprehensions of them . . . I am persuaded that he sincerely wishes . . . to finish with . . . Spain in a permanent and substantial manner." Walpole to Weymouth, n. d. [ca. Feb. 1776], Smith, Memoirs, II, 236. Weymouth agreed that "the proposals made by . . . Pombal are fresh proofs of the rectitude of his intentions." Weymouth to Walpole, Feb. 18, 1776, ibid., 235–236.

[50] Pombal advised D. Vicente de Sousa Coutinho to assure Vergennes first that his policy had always been one of "truth tempered with prudence," and then to review the Portuguese case beginning in 1763. Pombal to V. de Sousa Coutinho, Jan. 24, 1776, and instructions from idem to idem, same date, QE, VIII, 125–145. As Blosset had predicted, on Apr. 12, 1776, Pombal addressed another "Analytical compendium of the negotiations between . . . London and Madrid from 1759. . . ." for presentation by Pinto de Sousa to the British government. QE, XVIII, 393–399.

[51] Pinto de Sousa to V. de Sousa Coutinho, London, February 25, 1776, QE, VIII, 166.

[52] V. de Sousa Coutinho to Pinto de Sousa, Paris, Mar. 2, 1776, ibid., pp. 169–170. Pombal complied and the Portuguese ambassador to Madrid delivered such a proposal to Grimaldi on March 17. Pombal to Pinto de Sousa, Apr. 17, 1776, QE, XVIII, 404.

[53] Grimaldi to Francisco de Sousa Coutinho, Feb. 12, 1776, quoted in Carnaxide, O Brasil na administração pombalina, pp. 217–218. The two ships were the Príncipe de S. Lorenzo and La Aurora. Lavradio to Rocha, Oct. 30, 1776, VRL, pp. 331–336.

Pombal grudgingly expressed Portugal's willingness to furnish such a statement, and the tedious negotiations resumed.[54]

While these endless preliminaries were continuing, the news of the Portuguese offensive in Rio Grande reached Europe, arriving in Madrid during the last week in June 1776, and in Lisbon nearly two weeks later.[55] Thereafter hopes for a peaceful solution to the Iberian controversy rapidly dwindled. In vain did Pombal utilize Viceroy Lavradio's arguments that it was impossible for his suspension order to have reached the borderlands in time to prevent the military action, and fruitless were the efforts of worried Portuguese ambassadors to convince London, Paris, and Madrid that unseasonable weather had delayed the crossing of the messenger ship.[56]

In Spain the ministers of Charles III resolved to send a large punitive force to South America.[57] This was a calculated risk, for such a move might bring Great Britain to Portugal's aid; however, the Marquis of Grimaldi was convinced that England was too deeply involved in colonial problems of her own to assume those of Portugal too.[58]

[54] Vergennes to Blosset, Mar. 26, Apr. 12, and 23, 1776, *QE*, VIII, 177–179; Weymouth to Walpole, Apr. 16, 1776, *QE*, XVIII, 400–401, the latter expressing serious concern lest Pombal precipitate a new European war. Pombal to Pinto de Sousa, Apr. 17, 1776, and *idem*, "Minuta da memoria," same date, *QE*, XVIII, 402–405; *idem* to V. de Sousa Coutinho, same date, enclosing a long *pièce justicative*, *QE*, VIII, 182–196. It was not until Vergennes exerted additional pressure that Pombal finally sent a memória to F. de Sousa Coutinho to communicate first to the mediatory ambassadors and then to Grimaldi a statement admitting that Portuguese officers had exceeded their instructions in seizing the ships. Pombal to F. de Sousa Coutinho, June 12, 1776, *QE*, VIII, 242–244. Pombal stated that orders had been sent to Viceroy Lavradio to release the ships and to punish "de novo" the officers responsible for their confiscation. I have found no trace of such orders.

[55] Vértiz' reports to Arriaga concerning the Portuguese attack in the Lagoa dos Patos seem to have reached Madrid June 24 or 25. *CB*, III, 386–387. Lavradio's acknowledgment of the suspension orders and report on MacDouall's fiasco arrived in Lisbon about July 6. Pombal to V. de Sousa Coutinho, July 6, 1776, *QE*, VIII, 251–252; *idem* to F. de Sousa Coutinho, July 8, 1776, *QE*, XVIII, 406–407. The viceroy's dispatches of April 19 and 30, telling of Böhm's victory (cited in notes 43 to 45 above), arrived in Lisbon on July 12 and 13. Pombal to F. de Sousa Coutinho, July 22, 1776, BNRJ, I-31, 26, 11, n. 10.

[56] Pombal to F. de Sousa Coutinho, July 22 and 26, 1776, BNRJ, I-31, 26, 11, nos. 10 and 16; *idem* to Luís Pinto de Sousa, July 20, 1776, *QE*, XVIII, 407–409; see also *QE*, VIII, 255–279, for the reactions of the British and French governments and their diplomats abroad.

[57] See below, Chap. VIII.

[58] See the very important report of the Prince of Maserano (Spanish ambassador to London) to Grimaldi, July 19, 1776, transcribed in Octavio Gil Munilla, *El Río de la Plata en la política internacional*, pp. 416–418. Maserano stated that he had sounded out Lord Weymouth concerning his reaction to the possible dispatch of Spanish troops to Buenos Aires, and that the lord had replied that (1) his government would never defend another in an unjust cause, and (2) Britain would not object if Spain sent forces equal to those Portugal had in Brazil. The ambassador added: "Lord Weymouth dijo que era justisimo que el Rey mi amo enviase tropas para la defensa de sus estados de Buenos Ayres, y para igualar sus fuerzas a los que tienen en el Brasil los portugueses. . . ." While this report undoubtedly reassured

Moreover, he had assurances from Paris that France would stand by Spain as "a good relation and faithful ally."[59] Nevertheless, until the eve of the departure of the Spanish expedition Charles III kept the door open for a possible settlement of the crisis.[60]

Fully apprised of Spain's preparations for war, the Marquis of Pombal confidently addressed a long series of instructions to the viceroy and other authorities in Brazil designed to meet and defeat the Spaniards.[61] He still hoped that Great Britain would come to Portugal's assistance,[62] but whether or not she did, he was determined to keep the lands Portuguese forces had recovered in Rio Grande. Having at last achieved his minimum objective, Pombal was convinced that Spain could not (or would not be allowed to) take it from him.

In spite of the viceroy's apprehensions, Pombal had not the slightest hint of reproof for him or for General Böhm for their tardy performance in Rio Grande. On the contrary, he thanked Lavradio for his "wisdom and skill" in executing his long-standing orders, and asked him to convey the king's appreciation to all of the officers involved.[63] Each of the regimental commanders who participated in the victories won a one-step promotion, and both General Böhm and Captain MacDouall received special letters of commendation, the latter, as we have seen, being advanced to commodore.[64] Yet the most substantial rewards were reserved for the victor of Santa Tecla, Rafael Pinto Bandeira. Besides gaining a two-step promotion to colonel, he was privileged to raise and lead a special corps, the "Legion of

---

Madrid, Gil Manilla patently exaggerates when he says that "Las noticias de Maserano eran la *garantía internacional* que necesitaba la expedición. Por primera vez, Inglaterra dejeba una relativa liberdade de acción a España, enfrentada con Portugal; y Carlos III decidió aprovechar la ocasión." *Ibid.*, p. 307 (italics added). "International guarantee" is certainly too strong a phrase to attribute to a biased ambassador's report! Moreover, as Gil Munilla later states, Grimaldi continued to worry about the equivocal British attitude. E.g., on Nov. 27, 1776 (after the dispatch of the Spanish expedition), he wrote a colleague "Estamos *casi* [*sic*] ciertos de que nuestras operaciones militares en aquellas Regiones no seran causa de que los ingleses nos declaren la guerra." *Ibid.*, p. 345, n. 90; see also p. 327, n. 52.

[59] Vergennes to Ossun (French ambassador to Madrid), July 12, 1776, quoted *ibid.*, p. 303. At the same time, Vergennes urged Spain to strike quickly and suggested that measures be taken to prevent Lisbon from sending more forces to Brazil. Aranda to Grimaldi, July 12, 1776, *ibid.*, pp. 409–411.

[60] *Ibid.*, p. 315.

[61] See below, Chap. VIII.

[62] As late as August 20, 1776 he wrote Lavradio that the recent British mobilization implied that either the British fleet would soon call Spain's bluff or Britain would join Portugal in war against the Family Compact. So little did Pombal comprehend the seriousness of the American Revolution! BNRJ, I-31, 31, 1, n. 17.

[63] Pombal to Lavradio, July 31, 1776, *ibid.*, I-31, 26, 11, n. 2. (2.ª *via*), of which there is an excerpt in *RIHGB*, XXXI:1, 347–348. Received in Rio on Oct. 18. No praise or commendation was reserved for the enlisted men who contributed to the Portuguese victories, but then, foot soldiers seldom received their due before the twentieth century.

[64] Pombal to Böhm and to MacDouall, July 31, 1776, *ibid.*, nos. 6 and 7.

Adventurers," to be composed exclusively of Riograndenses. In addition he was promised a coveted knighthood in the military Order of Christ with a pension of 200,000 réis.[65]

During the second half of 1776 both France and England continued to try to smother the fires of war before they ignited a new global conflagration. British authorities in London and Lisbon persistently tried to persuade the Portuguese government to restore to Spain the territory its troops had occupied since July 17, 1775.[66] The French, though convinced that war could not be averted, wanted to localize hostilities to southern Brazil, preferring to fight a larger conflict for the recovery of French territory, not Spanish.[67] At the same time both major powers kept a careful watch on each other's movements, knowing that if either gave military aid to its Iberian ally, the other must assist its partner and that a general war would surely result.[68]

[65] Before the habit could be conferred, Bandeira was required to submit full names, birthplaces, and baptismal records of himself, his parents, and his four grandparents. Also "useful," said Pombal, would be written testimony of persons well acquainted with him. This information was to be forwarded to the "Official Mayor" in the office of the Secretary of State for Domestic Affairs (do Reino) for presentation to the Mesa da Consciência e Ordens. Pombal to Lavradio, July 31, 1776, cited in n. 63 above. As Bandeira's chief rival, Governor José Marcelino, bitterly pointed out, Pombal considerably exaggerated the difficulty of the major's achievement and said nothing about the governor's efforts to make it possible or to encourage Bandeira to continue the siege when he was about to give it up. To Martim Lopes Lobo de Saldanha, Nov. 22, 1776, DI, XVII, 170–171. The governor was not, however, the first or the last colonial official to feel neglected by an ungrateful Court. The promotions and rewards given to Bandeira were a typical expression of the Crown's policy of bestowing special favors upon outstanding colonials to encourage other Brazilians to strive to earn similar benefits.

[66] Blosset to Vergennes, Sept. 3, 10, and 24, 1776, QE, VIII, 279–283, reporting Walpole's lack of success in his conferences with Pombal. Weymouth to Stormout, Sept. 27, 1776, L. G. Wickham Legg, ed., British Diplomatic Instructions, 1689-1789, VII, France, Pt. IV, 1745–1789, Royal Historical Society. Camden 3rd ser., XLIX (London, 1934), 153; see also Richard W. Van Alstyne, Empire and Independence. The International History of the American Revolution (New York, 1965), pp. 93–94. The French ambassador to Lisbon reported that in Pombal's long-delayed reply to Weymouth's appeals the Portuguese minister expressed regret that his government could not accede to the desires of that of Great Britain to restore Rio Grande to Spain.

[67] Vergennes to Ossun, July 12, 1776, Gil Munilla, p. 303; idem to idem, Aug. 23, 1776, ibid., p. 330. Earlier, in the summer of 1775, Vergennes had already sent a secret agent to the English colonies to sound out the possibility of revolt. Samuel Flagg Bemis, The Diplomacy of the American Revolution: The Foundations of American Diplomacy, 1775–1823 (New York-London, 1935), p. 20.

[68] Vergennes to Blosset, July 19, and Nov. 14, 1776, QE, VIII, 257, 290; cf. Weymouth to Stormout, Oct. 25, and Dec. 20, 1776, Wickham ed., Br. Dip. Instr.: France, pp. 153–157, and especially idem to idem, Feb. [?], 1777, pp. 158–159, in which the British ambassador was instructed to make clear to the French government that "inexplicable as M.ᵒʳ de Pombal's conduct is," it did not proceed "from any encouragement given him from hence." For another expression of official British concern over the possible consequences of the Iberian dispute, see Lord George Germain to General William Howe, Oct. 18, 1776, Historical Manuscripts Commission. Report on the Manuscripts of Mrs. Stopford-Sackville of Drayton House, Northamptonshire, II (London, 1910), 42.

As 1776 gave way to 1777, diplomats in Lisbon still hoped that war could be prevented. It was apparent that Dom José I was failing rapidly, and it was generally felt that Pombal would not remain in office many days after his master's demise. The removal of Pombal, it was predicted, would lead to the formation of a more conciliatory Portuguese government, one disposed toward a compromise solution of the Iberian question.[69]

These assumptions proved correct, but their realization came too late. Dom José I expired on February 24, 1777, and his successor dismissed Pombal a few days later. But on February 22 the powerful Casa Tilly fleet appeared before Santa Catarina Island with thousands of Spanish troops. Having failed to find a solution in the chancelleries of Europe, the thorny dispute over the Debatable Lands seemed destined to be resolved on the battlefields of America.

[69] See the exchanges between Vergennes and Blosset, Dec. 13 to Feb. 24, *QE*, VIII, 292–296, 298–300, and 303.

VIII

Action and Reaction: The Outfitting of the Cevallos Expedition and Portuguese Efforts to Thwart It

The Monarch who has the greater sea power can always become Master of the Island of Santa Catarina.

MacDouall to Lavradio, November 21, 1776

ALTHOUGH THE DOUBLE-DEALING of the Marquis of Pombal had apparently paid off in the liberation of Rio Grande, it remained to be seen whether Portugal could prevent Spain from avenging her defeat. Madrid's reaction to the Portuguese triumph was swift and vigorous: the oufitting of the largest military expedition Spain had ever sent to America, commanded by one of her ablest officers, Don Pedro de Cevallos. Even though the Spanish government hoped to keep Lisbon guessing as to Cevallos' mission, the Portuguese Court obtained remarkably complete intelligence concerning the scope of his authority and the nature of his forces. This information was passed along to Viceroy Lavradio and his fellow governors, together with elaborate countermeasures by which the Crown expected to administer a new defeat to Spanish arms.

Origins of the Second Cevallos Expedition [1]

On July 12, 1776, three weeks after the arrival of news of the Portuguese victories in Madrid, José de Gálvez, newly appointed Minister

[1] We still await a complete account of the second Cevallos expedition. Useful but not definitive are Enrique Barba, *Don Pedro de Cevallos gobernador de Buenos Aires y Virrey del Río de la Plata* (Buenos Aires, 1937), a doctoral dissertation based on MSS in Spanish archives, but vitiated by the author's failure to consult even the relevant printed Portuguese literature; Enrique Arana, *Expedición de Don Pedro de Cevallos al Río Grande y Río de la Plata* (Porto Alegre, 1937) prints some new documentation, but his introduction is untrustworthy; Filemón Arribas, *La expedicion de D. Pedro de Cevallos y la fundación del virreinato del Río de la Plata, 1776–1778* (Valladolid, n.d.) is apparently a sound, brief study based on archival work, but I have not seen it. In many ways one of the best accounts of the signifi-

of the Indies, made an important announcement to the viceroy of Peru and to the governor of Buenos Aires. Because the government of Portugal had not fulfilled its repeated promises to keep the peace, Gálvez wrote, Charles III was determined to send a large military expedition to America to exact revenge for the "perfidy" of his neighbor.[2] This was the first official notice sent to Spanish colonial authorities of the impending departure of the huge force then assembling in Cádiz. Behind the king's decision to wage war across the Atlantic lay months of discussions among prominent Spanish officials concerning the best way to meet the Portuguese challenge in the Debatable Lands.

By 1774 it had become evident to Madrid that only a major military effort could dissuade Portugal from her attempt to recover Rio Grande and resume her expansion toward the Plata. The Vértiz expedition of 1773–1774 demonstrated that the governor of Buenos Aires lacked the talent necessary to direct a conclusive campaign against the Portuguese, while the subsequent buildup of Portuguese troops under General Böhm showed that additional Peninsular troops would be needed to throw back the Lusitanians.

Within official Spanish circles there was a division of opinion as to the most effective means of dealing with Portugal.[3] One view, expressed particularly by the Conde de Aranda and Don Pedro de Cevallos, was that Spain should attack Portugal directly and either reincorporate that kingdom within the Spanish empire or compel her to sign a definitive treaty that would remove the long-standing Portuguese threat to Spain's Platine possessions. The other view, championed by the Ministers of War and of Foreign Affairs, the Conde de Ricla and the Marqués de Grimaldi, regarded the Peninsular plan as visionary and likely to involve Spain in war with England. Instead, they favored dispatch of a large force to America to punish the Portuguese there.

The first concrete proposal regarding the American project was made by the Conde de Ricla in October 1775 after the Algiers debacle, when Madrid was anxiously waiting to see whether Lisbon would

cance and accomplishments of Cavallos is Emilio Ravignani's fine essay, "El virreinato del Río de la Plata (1776–1810)," in Ricardo Levene, ed., *Historia de la nacion argentina*, IV:1 (2nd ed., Buenos Aires, 1940), 33–234, which is unique in reflecting the best work in both Spanish and Portuguese and in its use of MSS in Buenos Aires and in Seville. Much more partisan and superficial is Juan M. Monferini, "La historia militar durante los siglos xvii y xviii," *ibid.*, IV:2, 221–312. Remaining to be exploited are substantial quantities of documentation in Spain, Argentina, and Great Britain.

2 Gálvez to Vértiz and to the viceroy of Peru, July 12, 1776, *CB*, III, 402–406.

3 Barba, p. 170; Octavio Gil Munilla, *El Río de la Plata en la politica internacional*, p. 272 and n. 22.

follow her lead in suspending hostilities in America.[4] In a memorandum to his senior military advisor, Lieutenant General Pedro de Cevallos, the minister of war suggested that 8,000 troops be sent to America under the command of Cevallos, "the most experienced [general] in this country," who should first capture Santa Catarina Island and then Rio de Janeiro. The success of both operations could be assured, Ricla wrote, if the governor of Buenos Aires made a diversionary threat against Colônia, since such a feint would cause the Portuguese to divide and therefore weaken their defenses.[5]

In his thoughtful reply, Cevallos analyzed the implications of Ricla's plan and pointed out its major defects. He regarded any attack on Rio de Janeiro as risky and expensive, and believed it would provoke England to declare war on Spain.[6] Moreover, he considered it unwise to undertake any expedition until the country had recovered from the losses it sustained at Algiers. At that time, said the General, a campaign against Portugal would be preferable to one in the colonies. It would be less costly and less hazardous, and it might be possible to secure French help for such a venture.[7] There can be little doubt that Don Pedro himself wanted the honor of directing that campaign.[8]

Cevallos' counterproposal impressed Charles III, who ordered the minister of war to examine it closely. Ricla in turn called upon Cevallos and three other generals to study its feasibility and report their findings to him. The following month (December 1775) Cevallos prepared a lengthy brief in which he discussed the climate, geography, economy, and military installations of Portugal and the number of troops Lisbon would be able to deploy against an invasion;[9] but that is as far as the Peninsular project ever got. It may have been shelved because of uncertainties concerning British and French reactions to a Spanish conquest of Portugal, or because the deceptive declarations of the Marquis of Pombal regarding the suspension of hostilities in America made such an attack appear unwarranted.[10]

4 See above, Chap. VI, pp. 171–172.

5 Barba, p. 171; Gil Munilla, pp. 272–273.

6 Cevallos consistently had a higher regard for the defenses of Rio de Janeiro than did the British. In his 1759 project for attacking Brazil he stated that "7 or 8,000 men" would be necessary to capture Rio, and recommended that it be left for the French to take. Cevallos to Arriaga, Sept. 15, 1759, Gil Munilla, pp. 393–394.

7 Informe of Oct. 22, 1775, Gil Munilla, pp. 407–409; see also pp. 272–274.

8 Barba, p. 171.

9 Ibid., p. 172.

10 Neither Barba nor Gil Munilla provides an adequate explanation of why the Peninsular project was dropped; neither seems to have been aware of the concurrent diplomatic negotiations between Madrid and Lisbon. Almost certainly the notes of Dec. 10 and 21 delivered by ambassador Sousa Coutinho to Grimaldi concerning Portugal's suspension of hostilities in America were instrumental in the scrapping of the project.

By the spring of 1776 new warnings from Vértiz gave Madrid reason to doubt the peaceful intentions of Portugal. In April José de Gálvez called upon Cevallos to evaluate the latest dispatches from the governor of Buenos Aires, and to render an opinion upon the most "opportune means" and the land and sea forces necessary not only for the defense of the Platine provinces, "but also for the conquest of the island of Santa Cathalina and Colonia del Sacramento with the object of demolishing [the latter]." [11]

Early in May, Cevallos forwarded his recommendations. He envisaged a moderate-sized force, 4,000 men, four ships of the line, two frigates, and six packetboats as sufficient for the purposes Gálvez mentioned. Cevallos suggested that the task force leave for America between August and November, and that Don Victorio de Navia be made its commander. Revealing his own coolness toward the American project, Don Pedro noted that in deference to His Majesty's command, he had refrained from expressing an opinion as to whether "it would be more convenient to take satisfaction here than in America." [12] Unenthusiastic as the general was about the American plan, he had actually sketched in outline the campaign he was soon to undertake.

Before anything was done about Cevallos' recommendations, news came of the Spanish defeats in Rio Grande. Once Pombal's deception was recognized, there was no longer any doubt as to the course Madrid would follow. On July 2 Don Alejandro O'Reilly, commandant of Andalucía, was ordered to begin preparations to assemble a large expedition bound for America.[13] Ten days later the governor of Buenos Aires and the viceroy of Peru were notified that the force would be sent during August or September, and that its objectives "should be" the conquest of Santa Catarina and the subsequent destruction of Colônia. Governor Vértiz was instructed to assemble cattle, horses, and transport, and to cooperate with the armada's commander in carrying out his mission.[14]

Although Gálvez implied that the armada's itinerary was already settled, it actually remained tentative until the task force was at sea. When a draft of the proposed instructions to the still-unnamed commander was referred to Cevallos, he took strong objection to the article calling for the fleet to proceed directly to Santa Catarina Island. The minister of war and other members of the cabinet considered the taking of the island to be of crucial military and diplomatic importance. They argued that its capture would sever Portuguese commu-

---

11 Quoted in Barba, p. 174 (see also p. 174, n. 1) and in Gil Munilla, p. 292.
12 Barba, p. 175.
13 Gil Munilla, p. 312, n. 6.
14 See n. 2 above.

nications with the south, and would facilitate the seizure of Colônia and the recovery of Rio Grande, and thereby force Portugal to abandon her conquests south of the point where the old Tordesillas Line intercepted the coastline. Moreover, they pointed out, Santa Catarina would be a useful port for Spanish ships plying between Spain and the Plata.[15]

Cevallos was not blind to these advantages—in 1759 he had advocated the capture of Santa Catarina.[16] But in 1775 he argued that no one could be certain how far south General Böhm had already proceeded, or would advance before the expedition arrived. If the Austrian had captured Forts Santa Teresa and San Miguel, the entire Banda Oriental would be menaced, and the armada's commander would have to divide his forces to attack the enemy on two fronts. The general therefore urged that the fleet proceed directly to Montevideo where its commanding officer could formulate his plans according to prevailing circumstances. When the cabinet persisted in favoring the taking of Santa Catarina first, Cevallos modified his objections, and agreed that the expedition could safely sail to the island if its commander had already received assurances from the governor of Buenos Aires that the Banda Oriental was still securely in Spanish possession.[17]

Cevallos' views strongly influenced the character of the instructions drafted for the commander of the expedition and the orders to the governor of Buenos Aires. The commander's instructions identified the several objectives of his expedition: (1) the recovery of all Portuguese-occupied posts "in my Dominions of Rio-Grande"; (2) the capture of Santa Catarina Island on the outward voyage "according to the news you have of the enemy's progress" in the Banda Oriental; (3) the destruction of Colônia; and (4) the taking of any other suitable Portuguese territory. Although the king stated his preference for the order in which these objectives should be attained, the commanding officer was given discretionary authority to determine priorities himself.[18]

The appointment of the task force commander was not made until July 25,[19] but the selection of Don Pedro de Cevallos for that post

[15] See Gil Munilla, pp. 318–319 and sources cited there; also Conde de Ricla to Cevallos, July 19, 1776, CB, III, 407. So anxious was the cabinet to be sure that Cevallos would capture Santa Catarina Island that Gálvez wrote him en route urging him to spare no effort "para conseguir el intento principalisimo de sua Expedición q. es de conquistar la Ysla de S.ta Catalina." Madrid, Dec. 5, 1776, CB, III, 452–453.
[16] See n. 6, above.
[17] Cevallos to Conde de Ricla, July 17 and 20, 1776, CB, III, 406–409.
[18] Instrucción reservada, Aug. 4, 1776, CB, III, 413–417; cf. Barba, pp. 176–177, who compares the minuta of July 17, to which Cevallos had taken exception, with the final draft, showing the incorporation of Cevallos' thoughts.
[19] Real orden of July 25, 1776, CB, III, 409–410.

was an obvious choice, both because of the part he had played in planning the forthcoming operation and because of his peerless military record. Born in Cádiz in 1715, he was a scion of the ancient Santander nobility. He began his public career at fifteen when he occupied the first of a succession of municipal administrative offices to which his privileged status entitled him. Entering the army at twenty-four, he rose rapidly to the rank of colonel. During the War of the Austrian Succession he distinguished himself in the Italian campaigns, and was promoted to brigadier and later to lieutenant general.

In 1756 Cevallos was named governor of Buenos Aires and was sent to the Plata with an expedition of 1,000 men. His assignment was to bring the embarrassing Guaraní War to a successful conclusion and to carry out the terms of the boundary treaty of 1750. Personally opposed to the concessions Spain had made to Portugal in that agreement, Don Pedro helped to defeat its execution. As has already been noted, after the denunciation of the Treaty of Madrid, Cevallos carried out a highly successful campaign against the Portuguese, sweeping them from Colônia, the northern Banda Oriental, and from southern Rio Grande.[20]

Relieved of his Platine responsibilities in 1767, Don Pedro returned to Spain where he was rewarded with various military promotions. In 1773 he was made a member of the Supreme Council of War, and two years later he was named governor and commandant general of Madrid. In 1775 Cevallos was the first to be offered command of the Algiers expedition; but when he demanded a force that the king and his ministers considered excessively large, he was passed over in favor of Don Alejandro O'Reilly, who agreed to conduct the operation with half as many men. O'Reilly's defeat further enhanced the prestige of Cevallos, who then got whatever he asked for in the composition of his second Platine expedition and the nature of his authority.[21]

Besides being appointed commander of the expeditionary force, Cevallos was also secretly appointed the first viceroy of the Plata.[22] Various colonial authorities had been advocating creation of a Platine viceroyalty for some time,[23] but it is probable that the decisive voice in favor of such a step belonged to Don Pedro himself.[24] The

20 See above, Chap. IV, pp. 96–98.
21 Biographical details are taken from Barba, *passim*.
22 Cédula of Aug. 1, 1776, *CB*, III, 412–413.
23 Ravignani, pp. 59–80; Barba, p. 169.
24 In his *informe* of July 20, Cevallos recommended that "el que fuese mandado [as chief of the expedition] ha de tener precisamente con el Gobierno y mando Militar, el Gobierno y Mando de la Provincia de Buenos Aires porque sin él no podrá mover aquellas Gentes. También conviene que su mando se estienda a las Provincias de Paraguay, Tucumán, Potosí, Santa Cruz de la Sierra y a todas las que

decision to establish the new viceroyalty was considered so important that only the king and his closest ministers were aware of Cevallos' dual mission. Neither the viceroy of Peru nor the governor of Buenos Aires was informed of Don Pedro's administrative capacity until his arrival in America.[25]

Soon after being invested with his new authority, Don Pedro took his leave of the Court and proceeded to Cádiz where the expedition was assembling. It was scheduled to sail toward the end of August or early in September, but was not ready to leave that soon. The general insisted on personally inspecting every weapon, powder barrel, and piece of equipment before it was stowed aboard the ships. He reviewed his troops, eliminating the unfit, particularly all foreigners, for he considered them most likely to desert. By the first of October Don Pedro was ready to leave, but he discovered that the escort commander, the Marquis of Casa Tilly, a naturalized Spaniard of Flemish extraction, was not. As the weeks went by Cevallos became increasingly anxious to get under way, for he wanted to complete his campaign before the approach of the devastating *pamperos* that begin in May. The ensuing conflict between Cevallos, Casa Tilly, and their staffs concerning the date of the expedition's departure foreshadowed their later clashes during the outward voyage.[26] Not until mid-November did the armada finally put to sea.[27]

Meanwhile, Madrid was undertaking additional steps to ensure the success of the operation. Spanish troops were massed on the Portuguese frontier to discourage Lisbon from sending more troops to Brazil.[28] On Cevallos' recommendation a powerful fleet of warships was sent to patrol the waters between the Canaries and the Peninsula to intercept Portuguese ships carrying war matériel across the Atlan-

---

comprehende la jurisdicción de la audiencia de Charcas, *porque con todas ellas confinan las Posesiones antigas y las usurpaciones modernas de los Portugueses.*" Quoted in Gil Munilla, p. 375; see also his comment at that point. (Italics added.)

[25] According to Gil Munilla, neither the Council of State nor the Council of the Indies was informed of Cevallos' appointment until the following year. He contends that the establishment of the viceroyalty was provisional, and that its permanency depended upon (1) the success of the expedition, and (2) Cevallos' reports on how the new reorganization was working in practice. *Op. cit.*, pp. 375–390.

Another explanation for the secrecy of the nomination is suggested by the *parecer* of Gálvez on the cédula to be sent to Vértiz on his role during the campaign. He recommended that neither the governor of Buenos Aires nor the viceroy of Peru be informed of Cevallos' status before his arrival since they were likely to be less cooperative in supporting him if they learned in advance of his nomination. *Parecer* of July 27, 1776, *CB*, III, 410–411. As will be seen later, the Portuguese were fully cognizant of Cevallos' status before he crossed the Atlantic.

[26] See Chap. IX, pp. 225–226.

[27] "Noticia individual de la expedición encargada al Excmo. Sr. D. Pedro de Cevallos . . . ," D. Miguel Lobo, ed., *Historia general de las antiguas colonias hispano-americanas*, III, 41–42, a contemporary source Barba apparently overlooked.

[28] Grimaldi to Aranda, July 22, 1776, cited in Gil Munila, p. 318.

tic.[29] In the Plata Governor Vértiz had orders to collect military information on both the enemy's and his own resources, and to forward the data by fast ship to the armada before it reached Santa Catarina.[30]

Lisbon's Reaction to the Spanish Threat

The several months required to mobilize the Spanish armada gave Lisbon ample time in which to inform Viceroy Lavradio as to the composition, probable destination, and tentative dates of departure of the enemy fleet. From fruitful sources within Spain [31] the Portuguese government furnished Lavradio with the names of the Spanish warships and transports, the number of officers, men, and guns aboard each vessel, and even a copy of Cevallos' signal book.[32] Of less value were the Court's inspired but often impractical directions for repelling the invasion, based as they were upon hearsay evidence, ignorance of Brazil's limited military resources, inexact geographical knowledge, and naïve assumptions.

Despite its impressive size, Lisbon was convinced that the Spanish expedition was less menacing than the one that had unsuccessfully assaulted the Algerian beaches the year before. Pointing out that Cevallos possessed fewer than half the number of men O'Reilly had when they "served as breakfast for the Moors," the Marquis of Pombal was persuaded that "God . . . will not make [the Spaniards] more successful against us who are Christians . . . than He did against . . . the inexperienced, barbarous Moors." [33] He contended that the enemy troops and sailors were of very poor quality, the former being raw recruits or dispirited survivors of Algiers, and the latter inexperienced country boys (saloyos).[34] His colleague, Martinho de Melo e Castro, predicted that the armada would have many

29 Cevallos recommended this measure in his *informe* of July 20. The Spanish squadron, commanded by D. Miguel Gastón, consisted of four ships of the line and two frigates, which were later to be reinforced by two ships of the line, three frigates, and a brigantine. Pombal to Lavradio, Sept. 9, 1776, BNRJ, I-31, 31, 1, n. 25 (appendix). In spite of its size, the Gastón squadron was largely ineffective. Of fifteen ships that left Lisbon for Rio de Janeiro between April 13 and Oct. 9, 1776 carrying war matériel and troops, only four were stopped, searched, and later released. "Navios que sahiram de Lisboa com Provizoens de Guerra para o Rio de Janeiro desde o Mez de Abril até Octubro de 1776 . . . ," [ca. Dec. 3, 1776], IHGB, *Lata* 21, MS, 443.

30 Gálvez to Vértiz, Aug. 10, 1776, *CB*, III, 421–422.

31 Notably the paid informers of ambassador Sousa Coutinho in Madrid and another spy (possibly a ring) in Cádiz.

32 The signal book was sent via Martinho de Melo e Castro to Lavradio, Oct. 9, 1776, BNRJ, I-31, 31, 1, n. 50. After the war it was ordered returned to Lisbon.

33 Pombal to Lavradio, July 31, 1776, BNRJ, I-31, 26, 11, n. 8 (orig.).

34 Pombal to Lavradio, Sept. 9, 1776, BNRJ, I-31, 31, 1, n. 21 (orig.).

stragglers since the Spanish had been forced to scour their harbors to find sufficient transports and had indiscriminately taken "large, small, good, bad, and very bad" ships.[35] The long crossing was expected to exact a fearful toll in shipwrecks, water and provision shortages, and to produce such fatigue among the ship-bound troops that they would be no match for the Portuguese defenders.[36] The Portuguese Court concluded from the repeated postponements of the armada's departure that Cevallos realized the great odds facing him and was consequently reluctant to leave port.[37]

This was the confident view that the Portuguese ministers expressed in their dispatches to the viceroy between the end of July and mid-October 1776. During those weeks they warned Lavradio where the enemy seemed likely to strike, and instructed him how to repel the Spaniards.

It was logical to assume that Cevallos would try to recover Rio Grande, and to prevent him from doing so, General Böhm was ordered to block all means of access to that captaincy.[38] He was to seal the Lagoa dos Patos by stationing two frigates and two floating batteries between the two bar forts. This would prevent the Spanish from entering the port[39] and force them to sail on to Maldonado, the closest alternative harbor. To stop an overland attack from the south, Böhm was directed to construct a series of rather extraordinary, semicircular redoubts between Monte Castilhos and Lagoa Mirim.[40] While these fortifications would interdict one approach to Rio Grande, there was always the possibility that Cevallos would follow Vértiz' inland route of 1773–1774; to take care of that eventuality guards were to be posted at all strategic passes along the Monte-

---

[35] Melo e Castro to Lavradio, Aug. 21, 1776, *ibid.*, n. 18. In a subsequent dispatch the secretary urged the viceroy to encourage Carioca merchants to emulate the Yankee corsairs, then harassing Anglo-Portuguese shipping. They were to be promised title to all prizes they captured, though the king reserved the right to select and purchase the ones his service required. *Idem* to *idem*, Oct. 9, *ibid.*, n. 48.

[36] Melo e Castro to Lavradio, Oct. 9, 1776, cited in n. 32 above.

[37] Pombal to Lavradio. Oct. 8, 1776, BNRJ, I-31, 31, 1 n. 37; published in *CB*, III, 444–447.

[38] Pombal to Lavradio, July 31, 1776, cited in n. 33 above.

[39] Actually most of the units in the Casa Tilly fleet drew too much water to cross the bar of the Lagoa dos Patos.

[40] See n. 33, above. The area mentioned is referred to as "Salto Grande," but the only place by that name on contemporary maps is far to the west on the Rio Paraná, so that this seems to be an error in geography. Some idea of Pombal's fuzzy-headed military thinking is suggested by his recommendation that the redoubts "consistam só nas frentas voltadas para a parte dos Castelhanos, ou do Sul; e que aliás fiquem abertos pelo lado do Norte, ou do Nosso Exército. Para q. não venha a seceder servirem contra Nós, no cazo de vir a ser precizo abandonallos." Obviously he failed to consider that such open-ended works could be flanked and taken from the rear! Implicit, of course, is the supposition that such construction would facilitate a hasty Portuguese retreat!

video-Santa Tecla and the Missions-Rio Pardo lines. Though the Court believed Böhm had sufficient troops to carry out these extensive preparations, it advised him to treat the Paulistas under his command with particular solicitude "so that they will not grow weary of service in Rio Grande." [41]

Shortly after drafting these intructions, the Marquis of Pombal became convinced that the Spanish did not intend to make Rio Grande their primary objective, and that they were planning an initial strike against a port of northern Brazil. He was led to this conclusion largely by a report from his ambassador in Madrid and by the implications he drew from it. "Today," wrote Sousa Coutinho, "I learned with positive assurance from [a] faithful and intelligent Person, that the great expedition which is arming . . . is certainly not [to be sent] against Rio Grande, or [to] . . . Buenos Aires; but rather will proceed elsewhere. It seems likely that it is [destined] for a hot country, because in Barcelona 4,000 light uniforms are being made with great haste. . . . [This news] and the great number of bombs and galiots to launch them that they are taking makes one presume that they expect to besiege a fortress." [42]

Pombal gave great credence to this report in spite of the likelihood that the ambassador's "faithful and intelligent Person" was a Spanish counterspy under orders to plant a false lead as to Cevallos's destination.[43] One reason the minister found the story so plausible was that it appeared consistent with earlier reports from Sousa Coutinho that leading Spanish statesmen had told him they regarded the Portuguese positions in Rio de Janeiro and Rio Grande as impregnable.[44] Another was his assumption that Spain knew that Bahia's garrison had been weakened by the transfer of Salvador's two prime regiments to Rio de Janeiro. To Pombal the "evidence" pointed to an attack upon Salvador or possibly Pernambuco.[45]

Of the two, the secretary was most concerned about the defenses of the former viceregal capital. He ordered the immediate return of the two regiments in small craft that could scurry into coastal harbors if challenged by Spanish warships.[46] At the same time Viceroy Lavradio

---

41 Melo e Castro to Lavradio, Aug. 2, 1776, BNRJ, I-31, 31, 1, n. 1.

42 Francisco de Sousa Coutinho to Pombal, July 24, 1776, quoted in Pombal to Lavradio, July 31, 1776 (postscript), BNRJ, I-31, 26, 11, n. 17. The postscript was evidently added to this second original after the first original (BNRJ, I-31, 26, 11, n. 16) had already been sent.

43 This seems a reasonable surmise, although no Spanish contemporary or later account refers to such a planned leak. Certainly Bahia was never an objective of the armada.

44 Several dispatches of Sousa Coutinho are quoted in Pombal to Lavradio, July 31, 1776, cited in n. 42 above.

45 See n. 42 above and the notes to the following two paragraphs.

46 Pombal to Lavradio, Aug. 3, 1776, BNRJ, I-31, 31, 1, n. 2 (orig.); published in Francisco Adolfo de Varnhagen, *História geral do Brasil*, IV, 226–227; Pombal to Manoel da Cunha Menezes, Aug. 3, 1776, BNRJ, I-31, 30, 17 (orig.).

was cautioned not to send "a single man" from Rio Grande or Santa Catarina to Salvador lest the Castilians find out and conclude that both were more vulnerable to attack, yet Pombal transferred Brigadier José Custódio de Sá e Faria and several other artillery experts from various parts of Brazil to Bahia to assist its captain-general in preparing his defenses.[47]

A flurry of instructions was sent to Captain-General Manoel da Cunha Menezes telling him how to protect his capital. Besides the return of his two regiments, he was promised a shipload of artillery, munitions, 4,000 muskets, and 1,000 swords from Portugal,[48] but he was warned against making "indiscriminate" (that is, costly) repairs to the capital's fortifications. The captain-general was directed to enroll and train as many sugar planters and farmers as possible as well as 8,000 to 10,000 Negro slaves who Pombal believed would be able to duplicate the Moors' recent success against the Spaniards. Small craft used by the planters were to be converted into fireboats. Manned by specially selected slaves who had been promised their freedom, these incendiary craft were to be sent into the enemy fleet "with a good wind" behind them, after which the Negroes were to escape in canoes. To minimize losses from the expected bombardment of the city, the *cidade baixa* was to be completely evacuated, and since Salvador might be cut off for a time from its trans-bay sources of supply, food reserves were to be accumulated. All pilots and fishermen were to be confined to port so that the Spaniards would be unable to find anyone to guide them into All Saints Bay, and would therefore run the risk of striking the false bar at its entrance "as we have seen happen so many times to our own navigators." [49]

Once Cevallos had been repulsed, as Pombal was confident he would be, the Portuguese could proceed to punish the Spanish for their treachery. Cunha Menezes was to inform the viceroy promptly of

---

47 Pombal to Lavradio, Aug. 3, 1776, BNRJ, I-31, 31, 1, n. 4 (orig.) .

48 Incredible as it may seem, the captain of the *Princeza do Brazil*, which carried these armaments to Bahia, reported on his arrival that ten twenty-four caliber cannon "were forgotten" in Lisbon, but he assured Pombal that he had brought the balls for them! J. N. Schmerkel to [Pombal], Oct. 31, 1776, *ABNRJ*, XXXII, 332–333.

49 Pombal to Cunha Menezes, Aug. 3 and 11, 1776; Melo e Castro to *idem*, Aug. 11, and 12, 1776, BNRJ, I-31, 30, 15, I-31, 30, 17, I-31, 30, 20. Similar instructions were sent to José Cézar de Menezes (captain-general of Pernambuco) , but they have not turned up. Cunha Menezes' energetic, if not frantic, efforts to prepare for the worst are beyond the scope of this study. They may be traced in detail in BNRJ, I-3, 2, 8, which contains many of his orders to local officials. See also *ABNRJ*, XXXII, 322 ff. Captain Schmerkel was apparently instructed to report on how well the captain-general was performing his tasks, for he wrote in detail about Cunha Menezes' accomplishments, concluding "Deus tem dado ao Sr. General hum dom muito especial para tudo, elle é engenheiro e artilheiro; elle he ferreiro, alfaiate, e á tudo acode com huma incansável vigilância. . . ." See n. 48 above.

his victory over the Spaniards so that Lavradio could order Mac-Douall's squadron and the troops of General Böhm and Governor Rocha to launch joint attacks upon Maldonado, Montevideo, or even Buenos Aires.[50] As a preliminary to such an offensive, Böhm was authorized to disregard the January order suspending hostilities and to proceed with the capture of forts Santa Teresa and San Miguel.[51]

No sooner had Pombal penned and dispatched this authorization than he canceled it. His reasons for doing so indicate that he still counted upon some form of British support, and that he did not want to be embarrassed by another unexpected Portuguese victory. After writing Lavradio to spur Böhm to resume his advance, the minister received a message from ambassador Luís Pinto de Sousa that George III had ordered full-scale mobilization of his land and sea forces. Forgetting about England's own burning colonial problem, Pombal concluded that her mobilization meant one of two things: either Britain was about to employ her fleet to force Spain to call off the Cevallos expedition and to resume peace talks with Portugal, or she was ready to make war with Portugal against the members of the Family Compact. If the first alternative came about, a new Portuguese offensive in the Debatable Lands would obviously prejudice the resumption of peace discussions. On the other hand, if England did join Portugal in war against their common enemies, Pombal wrote, there would be sufficient time to advise the viceroy and the general accordingly.[52]

Lavradio's Efforts to Prepare Brazil for the Impending Attack

The first dispatches from Lisbon reached Viceroy Lavradio between October 18 and the first weeks of November 1776. In advising his subordinates of the critical situation they all faced, Lavradio echoed the Court's assurances that Cevallos would be defeated provided every officer properly carried out his duties. Yet as he shifted men and matériel to the areas the Court believed most seriously threatened,

[50] Pombal to Lavradio, Aug. 3, 1776, BNRJ, I-31, 31, 1, n. 4 (orig.) ; *idem* to *idem*, Aug. 11, 1776, *ABNRJ*, XXXII, 362. The latter also published in *CB*, III, 435, but dated as a PS to the dispatch of Aug. 3, indicating that the Aug. 11 *ofício* was probably a 2.a *via*.

[51] Pombal to Lavradio, Aug. 13, 1776, BNRJ, I-31, 31, 1, n. 10; excerpted in *ABNRJ*, XXXII, 361, and published in garbled form by Balthasar Silva Lisboa, *Annaes do Rio de Janeiro*, III (Rio de Janeiro, 1835), 169–171. (Silva Lisboa telescoped part of one of Pombal's July 31 dispatches with this document and erroneously assigned Melo e Castro as author). It is published correctly in *CB*, III, 436–437.

[52] Pombal to Lavradio, Aug. 20, 1776, BNRJ, I-31, 31, 1, n. 17. Lavradio ignored this dispatch entirely, and repeatedly enjoined Böhm to attack in accordance with Pombal's earlier directive.

the viceroy found it necessary to plead with some correspondents, to cajole others, and to sympathize with all while asserting that his own tasks were more demanding than theirs and that his own resources were equally insufficient for the magnitude of the Spanish threat. Throughout the Cevallos crisis the viceroy served as the interpreter of the Court's commands, as the primary source of official news from the Peninsula, and as the coordinator of colonial defense from Bahia to Colônia.

One of Lavradio's major concerns was the procurement of sufficient soldiers for the defense of Guanabara Bay. Much as it pained him to do so, he immediately complied with the Court's directives and ordered the two Bahian regiments back to Salvador.[53] Their departure caused "consternation" in the capital,[54] but it is not clear whether the Cariocas were primarily concerned about their own safety or the resulting loss of business. Certainly the viceroy regretted the departure of two-thirds of his regular troops at so critical a juncture.

It is true that Lavradio was not entirely bereft of soldiers to man the capital's defenses. In addition to one remaining regiment of regulars, he could use the captaincy's militia companies, which were encamped near the city. But while Lavradio liked to show off his auxiliaries and home guardsmen (ordenanças) [55] to foreign visitors,[56] he did not place great reliance upon their fighting abilities. Nor was he

[53] The Bahians were ready to depart on October 22, four days after Lavradio received orders for their transfer. With pride he informed the Court that although they had come to him in a very unprofessional state, he was sending them home as "verdadeiro soldados," these being the same men for whom he had formerly been directly responsible as captain-general of Bahia. Lavradio to Pombal, Oct. 31, 1776, *VRL*, pp. 336–344. Although Dom Luís preferred to ship the regiments aboard two frigates bound for Salvador for repairs, he complied with the Court's directive and put the men in small smacks. That proved unfortunate since many of the Bahians later became stranded at various points along the coast of Rio de Janeiro and Espírito Santo as a consequence of bad weather and the exhaustion of provisions. By February 1, 1777, only six companies of one regiment had reached Salvador. Eventually the viceroy ordered those troops who had not proceeded beyond the limits of his captaincy to return to Rio de Janeiro. Manoel Cunha Menezes to Pombal, Feb. 1, 1777, BNRJ, I-3, 2, 9, n. 105; Lavradio to Capitão Mór Anast[ásio] Joaq[ui]m Moita Furtado, Feb. 8, 1777, CMCM, cod. 25, fol. 172ʳ.

[54] Lavradio to Pombal, Oct. 31, 1776, cited in n. 53 above.

[55] The auxiliaries were the first-line militia, composed of able-bodied men between fourteen and fifty, while the ordenanças consisted of men unfit for service in the regulars or the auxiliaries. The latter could be sent on military missions outside of the captaincy in which they were formed; the ordenanças could not. Except for their seconds in command, sergeants major drawn from the regulars, no militiamen were supposed to receive money for their service, though colonial administrators sometimes found it necessary to pay them to ensure their loyalty. Martim Lopes Lobo de Saldanha to Melo e Castro, Apr. 14, 1777, *DI*, XXVIII (1898), 333–337; *idem* to Lavradio, Mar. 29 and Apr. 6, 1777, *DI*, XLII (1903), 214, 226.

[56] For one such instance, see Lavradio to Melo e Castro, Aug. 31, 1776, *VRL*, pp. 296–303.

enthusiastic about the several hundred Azorian recruits the Court was sending him.[57] Experience had taught Dom Luís that raw recruits were no compensation for the loss of trained regulars.

As the Bahians were preparing to move out, he wrote to Dom Antônio de Noronha, captain-general of Minas Gerais, to obtain additional forces.[58] The viceroy recounted the latest news from Court and cautioned Noronha to keep it to himself, though he admitted that the public would learn of it soon enough through private correspondence.[59] "I must beg Your Excellency," he continued, "to send immediately to this capital the excellent and good Cavalry Regiment (these are the express words of the Court's dispatch) that you have created there." He added that it would be "very appropriate" if the captain-general could send him additional recruits without causing a public disturbance, and would also station several militia companies at a point from which they could be quickly summoned to the capital in the event of an emergency.

Noronha's response was one of many examples of how frustrating the position of a viceroy often became in dealing with nominal subordinates, and of the extent to which they could avoid or delay compliance with his orders even when they were clearly authorized by the Crown.[60] The captain-general agreed to send part of his cavalry regiment, but stated that the rest were on patrols and in guard posts in various parts of the captaincy. If Lavradio really wanted them, he would issue the appropriate orders, but it would take some time to replace the regulars with militiamen. He doubted whether he could raise any additional recruits without causing public unrest which, he reminded the viceroy, the latter cautioned should be avoided. For the same reason it would be impossible for him to station militia companies close to the boundary between their governments. He explained that Minas Gerais had relatively few whites proportionate to the

57 Of the 600 the Court promised, 400 were sent aboard the nau *N. S. da Prazeres,* the remainder on two merchant vessels. Melo e Castro to Lavradio, Aug. 5 and Sept. 15, 1776, BNRJ, I-31, 31, 1, nos. 6 and 32.

58 Lavradio to Noronha, Oct. 19, 1776, *VRL,* pp. 364-367. The viceroy was following almost verbatim the recommendations of Melo e Castro to Lavradio, Aug. 5 and Sept. 29, 1776, BNRJ, I-31, 31, 1, nos. 6 and 35.

59 "V. Ex.a guardará a respeito destas notícias aquele segredo q. lhe parecer conveniente, ainda q. eu julgo q. todas elas, bem depressa se divulgarão pelas cartas que forem desta capital em consequência das q. os particulares tem tido da Bahia." Lavradio to Noronha, Oct. 19, 1776 (postscript).

60 It should be noted that beyond the royal orders cited in n. 58 above, Noronha was obligated to aid the viceroy by art. 3 of his own instructions: "A capitania de Minas Gerais . . . como no centro de todas as outras, e servindo-lhe por consequência cada uma de barreira, particularmente do Rio de Janeiro, é de indispensável obrigação da primeira, de acudir com todas as suas forças ao socorro da última, logo que ellas lhe forem regueridas pelo vice-rei. . . ." Instruction of Jan. 24, 1775, most recently republished in *Anuário do Museu da Inconfidência,* Ano II (Ouro Prêto, 1953), 177-182.

number of its Negroes and mulattoes, and that all the whites "are useful to the Royal interests, and [if] they are removed [along] with the regular cavalry regiment, this captancy will remain exposed to some uprising of the Negroes." He added that he was having a great deal of trouble with fugitive slaves living in outlaw camps (*quilombos*), particularly those situated near public highways, and that the removal of the royal troops would encourage their depredations and alarm the rest of the inhabitants.[61]

Behind the captain-general's powder-keg thesis lay the real reason for his unwillingness to send men to Rio de Janeiro. Noronha, like most Mineiro governors who came after 1760, was concerned about the captancy's serious decline of gold production.[62] Ignoring the fact that the placers were simply becoming exhausted, Noronha was convinced that the decline was brought about by a *falta de braços,* a lack of sufficient workers, one of Brazil's most enduring myths and always a convenient excuse for any form of backwardness. The captain-general therefore opposed the departure of the miners and their slaves from the pits for unproductive military service outside Minas. Though at first sight his concern for the maintenance of public order seems legitimate, its absurdity is apparent when his opposition concerned the release of about 1,000 men out of a total population of close to 320,000, over 76,500 of them whites.[63]

The viceroy was understandably dissatisfied with Noronha's explanations. He repeated his demand for the entire cavalry regiment, and asked Noronha to accompany it to the capital.[64] In addition, he ordered him to recruit a corps of the least essential whites, blacks, and mulattoes including "useless" vagabonds. He also suggested that the whites should leave their slaves behind so that mining production would be unaffected.[65]

Noronha replied with truculence and injured feelings that he was only trying to keep Minas tranquil and promote the mining of gold, "which is the first object of this government." He pointed out that Lavradio's recommendation that the whites leave their slaves behind contravened privileges the king had granted militiamen in 1768 when auxiliaries were permitted to take their slaves with them to care for

[61] Noronha to Lavradio, Oct. 28, 1776, BNRJ, 2, 2, 24, n. 17.

[62] The best index to declining Mineiro gold yields from 1750 to 1777 is the precipitate fall in the quintos or fifths which ranged from a high of 118 arrobas (omitting fractions) in 1753–1754 to a low of 70 during 1777–1778. Teixeira Coelho, "Instrução," p. 372.

[63] "Mappa dos habitantes actuaes da capitania de Minas Geraes e dos nascidos e felecidos no anno de 1776," in José Joaquim da Rocha [?], "Geographia histórica da capitania de Minas Gerais" [ca. 1776], PAN, IX (1909), 73. Cf. n. 67 below.

[64] As suggested by Melo e Castro's dispatch of Aug. 5, cited in n. 58 above.

[65] Lavradio to Noronha, Oct. 30, 1776, paraphrased in Noronha to Lavradio, Nov. 17, 1776, BNRJ, 2, 2, 24, n. 18.

their horses while they were on active duty. With some heat he took exception to Lavradio's reference to "useless" vagabonds. Whatever their behavior might be elsewhere, retorted Noronha, the *vadios* of Minas Gerais were useful citizens. With few exceptions, he continued, "all are mulattoes, mestiços, *cabras,* and free Negroes" who populated remote areas, defended the frontier against Indian raids, opened new roads, and participated in the hunt for escaped slaves. He closed by observing that he would be glad "to learn part of the great deal that I do not know about the Art of War" from the viceroy, but insisted that the latter must appoint a temporary successor before he could leave Vila Rica.[66]

Eventually Noronha did send the viceroy a sizeable contingent of militia and part of his cavalry regiment.[67] He did not accompany them, however, for Lavradio never named his replacement, probably because he decided it was best to keep the opinionated Dom Antônio as far away as possible.

Another officer whose cooperation the viceroy continued to seek was General Böhm, Portuguese commander in Rio Grande.[68] After enclosing a copy of the Court's initial orders concerning the defense of that captaincy, Lavradio observed that since the enemy armada was still in Spain, this was a propitious time for Böhm to advance into the Banda Oriental and seize Fort Santa Teresa, which Dom Luís regarded as one of the keys to the defense of Rio Grande. He also suggested that Colonel Rafael Pinto Bandeira be sent south with his new legion of mounted troops to raid Oriental ranches to deprive Cevallos of their cattle and horses.

When the general produced his usual list of complaints, the viceroy did his best to assuage him. He reiterated his earlier statements that Böhm possessed supreme authority in Rio Grande and that the governor had no right to interfere with his orders. He was sorry that Böhm had been shipped some inferior equipment, but he could only forward the matériel Lisbon sent to him. Dom Luís agreed with Böhm's recommendation to dismantle all but the two bar forts in the canal in

---

66 *Loc. cit.,* and *idem* to *idem,* Nov. 19, 1776, *ibid.,* n. 31.

67 Noronha reported in January that he had dispatched to Rio de Janeiro 241 praças from the cavalry regiment and 928 militiamen and irregulars (*francas*) "todos escolhidos, muito bem armados, e fardados, e capazes de deffeza." Noronha to the Court, Jan. 7, 1777, *ibid.,* n. 37.

68 After the successful campaign in Rio Grande both Generals Böhm and Funk asked to be allowed to return to Rio de Janeiro. Lavradio, however, insisted that Böhm, the "Restorer" of Rio Grande, must remain until the emergency had definitely passed, but he agreed that Funk, who had pleaded ill health, might come back. Lavradio to Böhm, Aug. 8, 1776, BNRJ, 13-4-3, n. 7 (orig.) ; *VRL,* pp. 277–288, and *BCRG,* pp. 94–101. The viceroy had intended to replace Funk by José Custódio de Sá e Faria, but since the Court ordered the latter to Bahia, the Swedish officer had to remain at his post "athé nova ordem da corte." *Idem* to *idem,* Oct. 23, 1776, BNRJ, 13-4-3, n. 20 (orig.) .

order to conserve manpower. He conceded that it was "impractical" to guard the entire coastline, but contended that it was unnecessary in any case since Cevallos was most likely to land near the entrance to the Lagoa dos Patos.

Realizing that Böhm had not gained in self-confidence in spite of his victories, the viceroy employed various stratagems to inspire the general to acts of audacity. He noted that the Court was unimpressed by the quality of Cevallos' troops and compared them unfavorably with Böhm's "seasoned" veterans who, he hoped, would have an opportunity to gain new victories "not only for the glory of the Fatherland and of the State, but also for the honor and glory of the General who commands them." Once again he expressed his earnest wish that he could be at the general's side to observe the "wise and prudent measures" that "a General should take on occasions of such importance." [69] Yet flattery did not win Lavradio a convert, for the stolid Austrian refused to tempt Fortune a second time.[70]

Though he had as yet received no specific instructions regarding the defense of Colônia, the marquis recognized its peril. However, when he wrote to Governor Rocha the viceroy minimized the entrepôt's danger. He observed that if Cevallos landed at Bahia or Rio de Janeiro, he would have few uncommitted troops to use for a Platine venture. The further south Don Pedro launched his attack, Dom Luís admitted, the greater danger Colônia faced. He regretted that he could not spare additional troops or warships for Colônia, but he asked Rocha to reflect upon the perilous situation of Rio de Janeiro, "without troops and almost without officers." He emphasized that he expected his former military aide to put up a stout defense in the event of a Spanish attack so that the squadron and General Böhm's troops would have sufficient time to relieve him. Lavradio did not suggest how long that might be.[71]

While Lisbon indicated that it was satisfied that Santa Catarina Island was well defended and it was not on Cevallos' itinerary,[72] the viceroy did not share these convictions. In forwarding the pertinent paragraphs of the Court's dispatches to Field Marshal Antônio Carlos Furtado de Mendonça, Lavradio amended Pombal's remarks in two important respects. First, he ordered all provisions and equipment that might be of use to the Spaniards removed from the coast or de-

[69] To Governor Saldanha, however, the viceroy complained that "El Rey . . . não quer q. eu vá, nem tenho outro remedio que conservarme no pulpito. Deos queria q. os meus ouvintes queirão prestar algum fé as minhas palavras. . . ." Nov. 8, 1776, DI, XVII, 130–135.

[70] Lavradio to Böhm, Oct. 20, Nov. 3, Dec. 9, 1776, and Feb. 10, 1777, BNRJ, 13-4-3, nos. 13, 21, 24, and 27; BCRG, pp. 107–113, 115–127.

[71] Lavradio to Rocha, Oct. 30, 1776, VRL, pp. 331–336.

[72] Pombal to Lavradio, July 31, 1776, BNRJ, I-31, 26, 11, n. 8 (orig.).

stroyed. Second, he directed the field marshal to prepare a fortified supply base on the mainland where he could reassemble his garrison if forced to give up the island after having displayed "a very singular and exemplary resistance." Once again he expressed regret that he was unable to send additional troops.

In the same dispatch the viceroy referred to one burden which he shared with the field marshal, Commodore Robert MacDouall. With evident regret he informed Furtado de Mendonça that the Court had seen fit to continue the Irishman as squadron commander. They would have to try to get along with him, Lavradio said, and overlook his "very coarse and scandalous" language, trusting that he would soon learn to conduct himself "with the requisite moderation." [73]

Not long after expressing this advice, the viceroy found an opportunity to practice what he preached. The occasion was an interview with the Irishman, ostensibly called so that Lavradio could deliver MacDouall's promotion to him and discuss strategy, but planned with an ulterior motive. He was determined, Dom Luís wrote the Court, to treat the officer "with the greatest obsequiousness, as if he were the greatest of my friends . . . not the one who has so much affronted my person and position" in order to bring him to his senses. At first MacDouall displayed his usual "arrogance," reported the viceroy, but he soon manifested such "demonstrations of affection . . . not typical of his character or of his nation" that Lavradio became convinced that the Irishman was genuinely ashamed of his past behavior and wished to make amends. Dom Luís proceeded to lecture MacDouall on the niceties of the Portuguese language, and assured him that because he was a foreigner, he did not realize the "force of the terms" he frequently employed.[74] Then in a remarkable about-face, Lavradio proceeded to praise the commodore for the "valor" and "skill" he had exhibited during the previous February's naval action. Although MacDouall probably saw through the viceroy's transparent encomiums,[75] he decided to exploit Lavradio's rare good disposition—rare at least where he was concerned. According to European custom, he pointed out, squadron commanders were entitled to the honorary rank of brigadiers, and he asked to be accorded that status

---

[73] Lavradio to Furtado de Mendonça, Oct. 20, 1776, *VRL*, pp. 312–315.

[74] Lavradio made the same contention in the above dispatch to Furtado de Mendonça, but he later provided ample evidence that MacDouall was fully aware of what he was saying. Writing in 1777, the viceroy complained that Mac-Douall had scandalously displayed disrespect "contra mim, contra todos os generais de S.M., até ao ponto de dizer em publico diante de todos os oficiais, que os fidalgos portugueses e toda a nação não eram senão uns traidores, e ignorantes, e q. emquanto S.M. não mandasse tirar a cabeça aos generais q. tinha. nunca havia de ser bem servido"! To Visconde Vila Nova de Cerveira, June 20, 1777, *VRL*, p. 91.

[75] Cf. MacDouall's comments on Lavradio's written instructions given to him on Dec. 11, 1776, *ABNRJ*, XXXII, 363–366.

while in Brazil. Seeing how much he "had flattered himself . . . with this," the marquis agreed that he could fly a brigadier's pennant and promised that he would order all military and naval personnel to render him appropriate honors.[76]

The following day the corvette *Nossa Senhora da Boaviagem* entered port bearing important news.[77]

Lisbon Divines Cevallos' Operational Plan

According to the latest information from Spain, wrote Pombal, the Spaniards were no longer planning to assault Bahia but would strike farther south, specifically at Santa Catarina Island.[78] A "trustworthy confidant" in Cádiz had reported that informed persons in the port believed that the task force would try to capture the island first and then proceed on to the Plata.[79] This intelligence agreed with an earlier dispatch from ambassador Sousa Coutinho, advising Lisbon of Don Pedro de Cevallos' "secret" appointment as viceroy four days after his nomination.[80] Taken together, the two reports made it appear certain that the Spanish armada was headed for the Plata.

Before reaching that destination, Pombal predicted, the armada would stop at Santa Catarina Island. He was convinced that Cevallos

---

[76] Lavradio to Pombal, Nov. 20, 1776, IHGB/AUC, 1-1-29, fols. 311ᵛ–316ᵛ; printed in *VRL*, pp. 347–353.

[77] Just before the *Boaviagem's* arrival, two merchant vessels sailed in. One brought a rumor that France had forced Spain to cancel the Cevallos expedition, and that in consequence Lisbon had suspended departure of several warships for Brazil. Though inclined to give some credence to this report, Lavradio wisely ordered General Böhm to remain on guard until official news had come from Court. The second ship reported that while off the Canaries she had been stopped and searched by the Gastón squadron. The viceroy immediately warned all governors to be especially careful to take proper precautions when they sent their dispatches. Lavradio to Böhm, Nov. 11, 1776, BNRJ, 13-4-3, n. 22 (orig.); *BCRG*, pp. 113–115.

[78] Pombal to Lavradio, Sept. 9, 1776, BNRJ, I-31, 31, 1, n. 21 (orig.). By early September, Lisbon had concluded that the Spanish had intended to attack Bahia only if they were certain it was not in a state of preparedness, and that they had learned the contrary was true as a result of the implementation of the Court's earlier directives. Nevertheless, the captains-general of Bahia and Pernambuco were urged to continue training their militia and to maintain a vigilant watch of their coasts and harbor entrances. Melo e Castro to Manoel da Cunha Menezes and *idem* to José Cézar de Menezes, Oct. 9, 1776, *ibid.*, I-31, 30, 16 (orig.) and I-31, 31, 1, n. 59.

[79] "Cópia da última informação q. recebemos do confidante seguro de Cadiz, escripta naquella cidade em 19 de Agosto de 1776 . . . ," Pombal to Lavradio, Sept. 9, 1776, appendix IV, BNRJ, I-31, 31, 1, n. 26.

[80] Sousa Coutinho to Pombal, Aug. 5, 1776, *ibid.*, n. 11. Melo e Castro notified Lavradio of Cevallos' appointment on August 21 (*ibid.*, n. 18), and the viceroy passed along the news to his subordinates. Cevallos' status was thus known to more persons in Brazil than in Spain or her colonies!

wanted to take that island to compensate Spain for the loss of the "port" of Rio Grande, and also to permit his troops to recuperate from their long Atlantic crossing.[81] While the Portuguese chief minister erred in assuring that Don Pedro was the prime advocate of the capture of the island at this stage in his campaign,[82] he came close to anticipating the general's plans by surmising that he intended to couple the invasion of Santa Catarina with simultaneous attacks from Platine bases upon Colônia and Rio Grande.[83]

The Court's new instructions to the viceroy were based on these assumptions and contained measures which it felt certain would prevent the fall of Santa Catarina, whose loss might doom Rio Grande as well. Calling attention to the "good and clear" chart he was enclosing, Pombal pointed out that the key to the control of the island was its capital, N. S. do Desterro, which could only be approached by sailing south through the channel separating the island from the mainland. He believed that the shallow depth of that passage would force the Spanish fleet to pass close to the four "well-located and -armed" forts that guarded the channel and that would be able to rake the enemy with destructive incendiary shot. To reinforce these defenses, he ordered Commodore MacDouall to construct a chain of armed merchant vessels and floating batteries between Fort Ponta Grossa on the main island and Fort Santa Cruz on the islet of Anhatomirim. MacDouall should anchor his numerically inferior squadron behind this cordon in a protective cove until after the enemy had been repulsed, then he could safely attack the shattered remnants of the invasion fleet. Even if Cevallos succeeded in making a landing, said Pombal, the absence of sources of fresh water and the island's rugged terrain would force his quick withdrawal.[84]

Viceroy Lavradio was instructed to communicate this defense plan to Field Marshal Furtado de Mendonça and other "principal persons" on the island, who should be assured that "they have nothing to fear from the attacks of their fantastic and futile enemies." [85] The Court directed Lavradio to remit to Santa Catarina all the munitions and weapons he could spare and to transfer Brigadier José Custódio from

[81] Pombal also knew that only the lack of warships had prevented Cevallos from trying to capture the island in 1763, and he rightly concluded that none of the Platine ports was sufficiently commodious to accommodate all of the Casa Tilly fleet, so that securing additional harbors appeared essential. Pombal to Lavradio, Sept. 9, 1776, cited in n. 78 above.

[82] See the first section of this chapter.

[83] This surmise is particularly developed in Melo e Castro to Lavradio, Sept. 29, 1776, BNRJ, I-31, 31, 1, n. 35.

[84] "Última instrucção sobre a Ilha de S. Catherina [sic] que acompanha a carta de 9 de Setembro de 1776," Pombal to Lavradio, Sept. 9, 1776, Appendix II, ibid., n. 24. (Appendix I was the chart mentioned above.)

[85] Pombal to Lavradio, Sept. 9, 1776 (cited in n. 78 above).

Bahia to that island to contribute his knowledge as a fortification engineer and his experience in fighting the Spanish. Secretary Melo e Castro stressed that the island's survival depended upon the degree of cooperation achieved by the field marshal, the brigadier, the commodore, and the governor.[86] If they worked together harmoniously, and if the Court's instructions were carried out, Lisbon forecast that the Spaniards would experience a reverse comparable to that they had sustained at Algiers.

Lavradio's Final Preparations

After digesting the Court's new instructions, the viceroy sent urgent messages to the captain-general of Bahia and the field marshal. He directed the former to return Brigadier José Custódio at once so that he could take up his duties on Santa Catarina as soon as possible.[87] The viceroy sent Furtado de Mendonça copies of the Court's latest intelligence concerning the Spanish fleet,[88] its chart of the island, and its defensive plan. He instructed the field marshal to follow the plan scrupulously, departing from it only if "absolutely necessary to save the Island and our arms. . . ." Lavradio also repeated his injunction to denude the island and mainland coasts of anything that the Spaniards might find useful. Borrowing an idea from the Crown's earlier directions to the captain-general of Bahia, Lavradio suggested that the small craft from the nearby whaling factory be used as fireships to "disturb the night" of the enemy armada. As in Bahia, they should be manned by slaves who had been promised their liberty and further privileges for faithful service.[89]

Curiously, the viceroy said nothing in his covering letter to Furtado de Mendonça about the inherent defects of Lisbon's plan for the defense of the island. It seems impossible to believe that he failed to perceive them.[90] In any case he was soon enlightened by the commo-

---

[86] Melo e Castro to *Idem*, Sept. 11, 1776, BNRJ, I-31, 31, 1, n. 31.

[87] Lavradio to Cunha [Menezes], Nov. 19, 1776, *VRL*, pp. 353–355.

[88] Included was a copy of Pombal to Lavradio, Sept. 9, 1776, encl. 3, entitled "Títulos do General Dom Pedro de Cevalhos," detailing Cevallos' formal titles as viceroy and captain general of the Platine provinces, his warships, their armament, and the names of their commanders and of the regiments accompanying the expedition. BNRJ, I-31, 31, 1, n. 25.

[89] Lavradio to Furtado de Mendonça, Nov. 19, 1776, *VRL*, pp. 355–359

[90] As early as 1771 F. J. Rocha had warned Lavradio that Santa Catarina was poorly defended. Rocha to Lavradio, July 5, 1771, CMCM, cod. 28, fols. 34ʳ–39ʳ (orig.). Later both Generals Funk and Böhm examined the fortifications on their way to Rio Grande in accordance with the viceroy's orders, and recommended that "a defeza se devia reduzir ás partes mais próximas da mesma Ilha, e onde as forças estivessem mais juntas para em um posto vantajoso fazerem a sua defeza." Lavradio to Pombal, Nov. 20, 1776, IHGB/AUC, 1-1-29, fols. 311ᵛ–316ᵛ; *VRL*, pp. 347–353.

dore, who, as he listened to Lavradio reading the Court's defensive plan "put his hand to his head, telling me in a loud voice that . . . it could not be carried out." [91] Dom Luís questioned MacDouall at length, then asked him to take the plan, analyze it, and report back with a written critique. That critique he later forwarded to the Court.[92]

MacDouall's convincing critique serves to illustrate the differences between Lisbon's fantasies and the realities confronting its agents overseas. He pointed out that the chart upon which the Court's strategy was based bore only a remote resemblance to the actual geography, and that the forts were neither so advantageously placed nor as heavily gunned as it thought. He predicted that they would not be able to withstand a vigorous bombardment by a single, seventy-gun frigate, much less salvos from the nineteen warships Cevallos was expected to have. He regarded the construction of a cordon of ships and rafts to block the channel between the island and the mainland as totally impractical since (1) the distance involved exceeded one and a half leagues; (2) such small craft, assuming their availability in sufficient numbers, were not sturdy enough to support heavy guns; and (3) their gunners were certain to be mowed down by enemy sharpshooters. Moreover, the commodore saw no reason to assume that the enemy task force would actually sail into the so-called port of Santa Catarina. There were plenty of unguarded beaches around the island, such as that of São Francisco de Paula, between Ponta das Canavieiras and Ponta Grossa, where the Castilians could land with impunity and where they would discover an abundance of fresh water and an easy passage to the island's capital.

MacDouall was particularly critical of the idea of hiding his squadron in a protected bay until the enemy had been battered by the forts. This strategy violated the very purpose for which his ships had been sent to Brazil, the defense of the island. He insisted that he could perform that function better by remaining at sea so as to harass the task force and pick off stragglers. Whether the commodore really believed there was much chance of saving Santa Catarina is doubtful, for he concluded with the warning that "the Monarch who has the greater sea power can always become master of the island of Santa Catarina." [93]

In making this comment the commodore was doubtless thinking about the difference between the Court's estimates of the size of the

[91] Lavradio to [Visconde da Vila Nova da Cerveira?] [June, 1777?], *VRL*, p. 91.
[92] In his dispatch of Nov. 20, 1776, cited in n. 90 above.
[93] MacDouall to Lavradio, Nov. 21, 1776, *VRL*, pp. 315–319. As will be seen, the commodore's suggestion of where the Spanish might land was prophetic.

enemy task force and that of his own diminutive squadron. Of the four naus and seven frigates under his command, the nau *Ajuda* and three of the frigates required extensive refitting. Two other vessels were so unseaworthy that they had been decommissioned; another was on detached service at Colônia, and a fourth, a converted merchant vessel, had already been returned to her owners. His only combat-worthy vessels were the naus *Belém, Prazeres,* and *Santo Antônio.*[94]

It is a striking commentary on the sad state of the Portuguese navy at this time that the Crown was unable to provide the viceroy with a single additional warship to defend the entire coast of Brazil against the huge Spanish armada.[95] Consequently Lavradio was obliged to order his ailing frigates patched up, and to seek additional merchant vessels that might be adapted to stretch out his meager naval forces. After finding no commercial ships at Rio de Janeiro that could be converted to serve as armed auxiliaries,[96] he appealed to the captain-general of Bahia for one or more ships recently built there, and asked him to expedite repairs to two of the squadron's frigates.[97]

[94] The following was the status of the squadron *ca.* November 1776:

SHIP	WHERE LOCATED	REMARKS
Ajuda	Santa Catarina	Due to be sent to Rio Janeiro for repairs
Nazareth *Graça Divina*	En route to Salvador	For refitting
Princeza do Brazil	Rio de Janeiro	After "um imenso concerto," was returned to owners, the whaling monopoly company
Principe do Brazil	Rio de Janeiro	Being refitted "com toda a força, porém . . . a ruína foi muita. . . ."
Belém *Santo Antônio*	Rio de Janeiro	Seaworthy
Pilar	At sea	Left Lisbon Oct. 14; had not reached Rio de Janeiro by this time
Prazeres	Rio de Janeiro	Seaworthy

Lavradio to Pombal, Nov. 20, 1776, cited in n. 90 above; "Navios que sahiram de Lisboa . . . para o Rio de Janeiro," cited in n. 29 above.

[95] The Portuguese navy consisted of between fifteen and seventeen capital ships, ten of them naus and the rest frigates. "Marinha de guerra portugueza em 10 de Novembro, 1775," *QE*, VIII, 175–176, n. 268; "Relación de los navíos y fragatas de guerra de Portugal, útiles en 1777," appended to Conde de Almodóvar (Spanish ambassador to Lisbon) to Floridablanca, April 8, 1777, in Caetano Beirão, *D. Maria I (1777–1792)*, p. 22, n. 52. See also William Dalrymple, *Travels through Spain and Portugal*, p. 149.

[96] Lavradio to Pombal, Nov. 20, 1776, cited in n. 90 above. He wrote: "como todos os navios de q. agora se servem os commerciantes, não são que umas más corvetas, é impossível o eu servir-me delas e por consequência o é tambem que eu possa aumentar a força da Esquadra."

[97] *Idem* to Cunha Menezes, Nov. 19, 1776, cited in n. 87 above.

Faced with the viceroy's request, Manoel da Cunha Menezes proved even more adroit than Dom Antônio de Noronha in avoiding compliance. As he explained his behavior to the Court, he had previously sent Lavradio a frigate constructed in Salvador at a cost to the Crown of fifty-eight contos, only to be told that she would not make a good warship. Consequently, when the viceroy asked for other ships, "I resolved not to send any . . . [for I am convinced that] merchant ships, armed in war, besides making an extraordinary expense to the Royal Treasury, are always defective" for naval warfare. Therefore, instead of providing Lavradio with a ship, the captain-general dispatched a load of timber to Rio de Janeiro so that the viceroy could have one constructed there according to his own specifications.[98] But by the time the boards arrived, the enemy was already carrying out their assignments!

Meanwhile, on December 12, 1776, MacDouall left for Santa Catarina with his three naus.[99] Aboard were shipments of clothing and powder for the island and for Rio Grande,[100] as well as letters from the viceroy to the governor and the field marshal emphasizing the need for them to work closely with the naval commander in defending Santa Catarina.[101]

The commodore also carried with him formal instructions prepared and delivered to him by the viceroy on the eve of his departure.[102] There was nothing in them that he did not already know from reading the royal dispatches and from conversations with Lavradio, yet they provided a summary of what the Court expected of MacDouall and, even more important, a written record that could be later used in passing judgment upon his performance. Nor did this escape the Irishman. He subsequently claimed, not without considerable justification, that his orders were deliberately contrived to transfer the mantle of responsibility for carrying out the Court's mandates from

---

[98] Cunha Menezes to Pombal, Jan. 27 and April 4, 1777, BNRJ, I-4, 3, 16, nos. 103 and 112.

[99] *Prazeres, Belém,* and *Santo Antônio* were the three naus. Subsequently they were joined by the *Graça, Princeza do Brazil,* and *Pilar.* The latter two arrived at Desterro Jan. 7, 1777. Antônio Carlos Furtado de Mendonça to Böhm, Jan. 8, 1777, BNRJ, 13-4-9, n. 53 (orig.). MacDouall hoped to get additional ships, but from where he did not say. MacDouall to Böhm, Dec. 17, 1776, *ibid.,* 13-4-5, n. 88 (orig.).

[100] *Portaria* of Dec. 4, 1776, CMCM, cod. 19, fol. 134^{r-v}; covering letters from Lavradio to Furtado de Mendonça, Dec. 5 and 6, 1776, *ibid.,* cod. 4, fols. 101^v–102^r.

[101] Lavradio to Furtado de Mendonça and to Pedro Antônio da Gama e Freitas, Dec. 6, 1776, *ibid.,* cod. 4, fols. 102^{r-v}.

[102] Lavradio to MacDouall, Dec. 11, 1776, *ABNRJ,* XXXII, 363–366; also published in Silva Lisboa, *Annaes do Rio de Janeiro,* III, 171–178, and in *VRL,* pp. 367–372. The first source, however, is the best since it contains the annotated criticisms of MacDouall, written about May 1777. MacDouall described the circumstances under which the viceroy handed him his orders in MacDouall to Lavradio, Mar. 10, 1777, *ABNRJ, XXXII,* 360.

the viceroy's shoulders to those of the commodore and his colleagues at Santa Catarina.[103]

The viceroy informed MacDouall that his primary duty was to protect Santa Catarina and any other ports threatened by enemy attack. Though he admitted that the Spaniards would outnumber the Portuguese squadron, he contended that their numerical advantage would be offset by the "skill, honor, and valor of all those who have the distinction of serving" under the able Irish commander.[104] In view of MacDouall's objection to being confined within the channel, he was permitted to station himself at Garoupas Bay, north of the island,[105] in order to surprise the enemy's flank. After the expected enemy defeat, continued Lavradio, the squadron could slip down to the Plata and join the forces of General Böhm and Governor Rocha in attacks against suitable Spanish targets.[106]

Shortly after MacDouall left Rio de Janeiro the viceroy received new dispatches from Lisbon, the last the Court sent prior to the sailing of the Spanish expedition.[107] Included was a revised estimate of the size of the enemy armada, a copy of Cevallos' signal book,[108] and the prediction that the general would not leave Spain until mid-October. It was now virtually certain, wrote Melo e Castro, that Don Pedro intended to attack Santa Catarina, Rio Grande, and Colônia. After restating the Crown's previous orders for the defense of the first

103 E.g., he cited Art. 16 of his instructions in which the viceroy stated ". . . se este plano não for bem combinado, se V. S. o General do Sul e o Governador da Colônia não obrarem de commum accordo, . . . não só, não conseguiremos as felicidades *q. eu supponho quazi certas* se praticar e debaixo dos mais sinceros sentimentos, mas pelo contrário virá a ser a nossa total ruína." Italics added.

104 Art. 5, which prompted MacDouall to observe that these were only "compliments" and therefore meaningless.

105 Apparently either Bahia de Sepultura, North of Pt. Garoupas, or Enseada do Porto Belo. Contemporary maps show that the coastal geography of mainland Santa Catarina was very poorly known at this time. See José Torre Revello, "Mapas y planos referentes al virreinato del Plata," *Publicaciones del Instituto de Investigaciones Históricas*, LXXIII, nos. 26–28.

106 As soon as MacDouall arrived at Santa Catarina he wrote Böhm that he was willing to cooperate if the general had any plans for a Platine operation. Böhm replied as he had a year and a half before: that he had none and that the matter was the exclusive concern of the governor of Colônia. That was the end of the Marquis of Pombal's Platine schemes. MacDouall to Böhm, Dec. 17, 1776, cited in n. 99; Böhm to MacDonall [sic], Jan. 2, 1777, *ABNRJ*, XXXII, 361.

107 Included were the *ofícios* of Sept. 29 and Oct. 8 and 9, cited below. Presumably they arrived during the week of Dec. 20 aboard the dispatch boat (*hyate de avizo*) *S. Francisco Xavier*, which left Lisbon Oct. 9, 1776, bound for Rio de Janeiro after a stop at Bahia. "Navios que sahiram de Lisboa . . . para o Rio de Janeiro," cited in n. 29 above. The yacht reached Salvador *ca.* Dec. 8, 1776. Cunha Menezes to Melo e Castro, Dec. 8, 1776, *ABNRJ*, XXXII, 335.

108 Pombal to Lavradio, Oct. 8, 1776, BNRJ, I-31, 31, 1, n. 37; published in *CB*, III, 444–447. Melo e Castro to *idem*. Oct. 9, 1776, *BNRJ*, I-31, 31, 1, n. 50.

two points,[109] the secretary made two puzzling references to Colônia. In one dispatch he enlarged upon an earlier order from Pombal again authorizing the retirement of the citadel's garrison, stating that all civilians capable of bearing arms should also leave,[110] but in another carrying a later date he stipulated that the troops and civilians must remain to defend the praça.[111]

It was late in December when these directives reached the viceroy.[112] They came at a particularly hectic time for the marquis, who was engaged in frequent consultations with his aides concerning the dispatch of ships and supplies to the south, the selection of places to station newly received recruits from Minas and from the Azores, and the strengthening of the capital's defenses.[113] Besides supervising these activities, Lavradio corresponded frequently with the captains-general and his immediate subordinates, seeking additional supplies, particularly funds, from the former, and calming the fears of the latter.[114]

Early the following January Lavradio completed a lengthy report informing the Court of what he had done to prepare his defenses to meet the expected enemy attack.[115] He observed that since he had not received the Crown's second order for withdrawal of the Colônia regiment, the troops were still at the praça, where they would remain.[116] He protested that the Court's impression that the entrepôt

109 And denying MacDouall's request (made on May 5, 1776) to be relieved of his command. The colonial secretary insisted that he was needed in the colony because of its acute danger, and enjoined MacDouall and Lavradio to work together. Melo e Castro to Lavradio, Sept. 29, 1776, *ibid.*, n. 34; *idem* to MacDouall, Sept. 29, 1776, BNRJ, 6, 3, 24, fols. 268ʳ⁻ᵛ. The latter was left unsealed for the viceroy to read.

110 Melo e Castro to Lavradio, Sept. 29, 1776, cited in n. 109.

111 Melo e Castro to Lavradio, Oct. 9, 1776, cited in Lavradio's reply of Jan. 3, 1777. See n. 116 below.

112 See n. 107 above.

113 To one captain-general Lavradio wrote that the "grandíssimo trabalho em que me acho para expedir todas as ordens, que se fazem necessárias aos oficiais, generais, e commandantes destas differentes partes e dar ao mesmo tempo todas as providências que se fazem precizas." Lavradio to Saldanha, Dec. 10, 1776, *DI*, XVII (1895), 135–136. A common closure for the viceroy to use at this time was "A preça e o inexplicável trabalho, com que me acho sem ter quasi ninguém, que me ajude, não permitte, que eu seja mais extenço. . . ." Lavradio to Böhm, Nov. 3, 1776, BNRJ, 13-4-3, n. 21.

114 E.g., Saldanha to Lavradio, Dec. 19, 1776, *DI*, XLII (1903), 189–190; Lavradio's reply, Dec. 29, 1776, *DI*, XVII, 139–145; and Saldanha's acknowledgement, Jan. 29, 1777, *DI*, XLII, 191–193.

115 Lavradio to Melo e Castro, Jan. 8, 1777, IHGB/AUC, 1-2-1, fols. 317ʳ⁻335ᵛ; *VRL*, pp. 376–398. This was probably the longest ofício the viceroy wrote during his administration, its ninety-eight paragraphs being exceeded in length only by his *relatório* to his successor. Much of the information he supplied was unsolicited. This is a typical dispatch of colonial administrators, who always sought opportunities to boast, albeit indirectly, of their accomplishments.

116 On January 3, 1777, Lavradio wrote Melo e Castro: "Pelos últimos ofícios que recebi de V. Ex.a recebo um com data de 9 de Outubro do ano passado em q. V. Ex.a me manda suspender a ordem que se me tinha expedido para ser retirado o Regimento da Colônia e os Paisanos capazes de pegar em armas." *VRL*, pp. 373–374.

was adequately defended did not agree with the facts.[117] Echoing the words of Governor Rocha two years earlier, the viceroy declared that Colônia's fortifications urgently needed to be rebuilt, but that it had been impossible to do so because of the proximity of hostile Spanish patrols.[118] Because of the enemy's blockade, he continued, it had become extremely difficult to supply the outpost. Some ships were apprehended by the guardacostas; others managed to elude them but arrived with spoiled cargoes, particularly meat. Although the governor had requested naval support, Lavradio had been unable to spare any warships because of the need to protect Santa Catarina Island. The marquis concluded his remarks on Colônia by expressing the hope that its governor would have sufficient supplies to hold out in the event of a Spanish attack.[119]

Though the viceroy said little about Rio Grande, he spoke confidently about the situation at Santa Catarina where, he affirmed, everything possible was being done to complete the defenses. The governor and the field marshal were cooperating closely, and animated the defenders by personally assisting the construction of the fortifications. The commodore, Lavradio continued, had been given flexible instructions and all available warships.

The viceroy then described the various measures he had taken to improve his capital's defenses. As soon as he had learned of the outfit-

---

The dispatch Lavradio referred to has not been found in Brazilian archives, and is probably lost. By inferences too lengthy to detail here, it appears that the original of this order from Pombal again directing the withdrawal of the Colônia regiment was written between Aug. 13 and 20. As Lavradio suggested in his January 3 dispatch, the order was probably thrown over the side by the captain of one of four ships stopped and searched by the Gastón squadron off the Canaries. Yet since the Court customarily sent two, sometimes three, copies of its dispatches by separate ships, and since it frequently repeated important directives in subsequent dispatches, it seems strange that the order did not reach the viceroy in one way or another.

117 Not long before writing this report, Lavradio received a grim message from Arthur Phillip, captain of the frigate *Pilar*, which had been sent with supplies to Colônia. Phillip advised the viceroy that the praça badly needed provisions and armed corvettes, stating that his ship was the only war vessel at the entrepôt. He added ominously, "Eu não fallo a V. Ex. do perigo q. correm as embarcações q. vem para esta praça com os Guarda Costas Castelhanos, q. sempre andão girando: nem da força q. pode ser preciça nesta Rio, se a Guerra se principiar, V. Ex. o sabe melhor do q. eu o posso dizer." Phillip to [Lavradio], Colônia, Nov. 18, 1776, CMCM, *maço* 31 (orig.).

118 On Dec. 7, 1776, Vértiz wrote Gálvez that there was "mucha aplicación a reparar sus fortificaciones [those of Colônia], y aun á añadir algunas a las q. tenían anttes p.r la parte del Rio. . . ." *CB*, III, 449–450.

119 Besides the *Pilar* Lavradio sent at least five corvettes and smacks to Colônia between Oct. 3, 1776, and Feb. 24, 1777. Lavradio to Rocha, Oct. 11 and 24, 1776, CMCM, cod. 26, fols. 130^{r-v}; *portarias* of Oct. 3 and Dec. 9, 1776, *ibid.*, cod. 19, fols. 106^{r-v}, 134^{v}–135^{r}; Lavradio to Rocha, Feb. 24, 1777, *ibid.*, cod. 26, fol. 135^{r}. The terms he was obliged to make with shippers reflect the seriousness of the supply problem. They were promised immediate payment for goods they delivered to the praça as soon as their boats returned to Rio de Janeiro or "just value" for their vessels in the event of capture. It was most unusual for a Portuguese colonial officer to have to offer such terms.

ting of the Cevallos expedition, Dom Luís had assumed that Rio de Janeiro would be one of its objectives [120] and had intensified his program of strengthening existing fortifications around Guanabara Bay.[121] To direct that program he had appointed the able engineer Francisco João Roscîo, who bore the title of inspector of fortifications.[122] Under Roscîo's direction batteries were mounted on São Bento hill, where they could sweep Snakes' Island, the Valongo, and a nearby beach (called the Prainha), where the French had landed in 1711. Earthworks were erected in front of the palace square and along the eastern side of the city next to the harbor. An effort was made to rebuild the ruined seventeenth-century fort of São Sebastãio atop Castle Hill, near the military hospital, the former Jesuit college. Without obtaining the customary royal approval, the viceroy also went ahead with the construction of a major new fortification, called O Pico, overlooking Fort Santa Cruz, one of three forts protecting the entrance to Guanabara Bay. He also added several batteries to protect the Atlantic beaches immediately east and west of the entrance.

Besides proceeding with these costly improvements to his land defenses,[123] the viceroy called upon Captain Hardcastle to work out a method to prevent enemy ships from sailing into Guanabara Bay.[124]

[120] In December 1776 the viceroy still expected the Spaniards to test Rio de Janeiro's defenses, and boasted "Tenho procurado prepararme para receber estes hospedes, e pôr-me em estado de lhe agradecer este obzequio quanto o permittirem as pouquissimas forças com q. me acho. . . ." Lavradio to Saldanha, Dec. 29, 1776, *DI*, XVII (1895), 145.

[121] Soon after taking office, Lavradio called upon General Funk, Colonel José Custódio de Sá e Faria, and Captain Francisco J. Roscîo to submit detailed plans for improving Rio de Janeiro's defenses. After criticism by General Böhm and subsequent revision, the viceroy forwarded the three proposals to Lisbon for a decision. Back came the curt order "se não intente obra alguma nessa Cidade, sem que SM assim o determine." Lavradio to Oeiras, Feb. 20, 1770, IHGB/AUC, 1-1-29, fols. 213ʳ–227ʳ; Melo e Castro to Lavradio, Aug. 15, 1770, CMCM, cod. 3, fol. 87ʳ (orig.). During the crises of 1774–1775 the viceroy went ahead with a modest program of fortification improvements without obtaining royal sanction.

[122] The viceroy had an especially high regard for Roscîo, of whom he wrote "talvez seja o único em toda esta capitania de quem se possa acreditar as cartas e plantas que elle tem feito porque não põe em papel se não o que elle viu, mediu, e examinou, o que todos os outros fazem pelo contrário, riscando a maior parte das vezes por estimação ou informações." Lavradio to Melo e Castro, June 21, 1776, *RIHGRGS*, XIX:2 (1939), 20–22. He repeatedly sought promotions for the engineer, and wrote the just-cited letter in protest after the Overseas Council had failed to confirm his nomination of Roscîo as sergeant major. On the eve of his departure for the kingdom, the retiring viceroy addressed a "to whom it may concern" letter summarizing his knowledge of the engineer's abilities. *Ibid.*, pp. 17–19. Roscîo followed Lavradio to Portugal, returning to the colony three years later as a lieutenant colonel, a promotion that may have been the result of the marquis's intervention in his behalf.

[123] For the outlay made for fortification construction in Rio de Janeiro during the years 1774–1777, see Chap. XII below.

[124] Hardcastle returned to Rio de Janeiro about September 1776, when General Böhm indicated that he had no further use for naval craft in Rio Grande de São Pedro.

Under the captain's supervision an unseaworthy frigate was anchored off Fort Santa Cruz, while another was stationed close to Fort Laje on the other side of the main passage into the bay. A heavy iron chain was stretched between the two vessels,[125] and in the event that the enemy succeeded in breaking this barrier, a flotilla of fireships was concealed in the Saco de Santa Cruz, ready to strike panic among unwanted visitors.

Although these defense preparations were as yet unfinished, the viceroy expressed satisfaction with what had already been accomplished. He predicted that if the Spaniards tried to invade Guanabara Bay, they would pay a fearful price for their "imprudence."

Early in December Lavradio wrote Governor Vértiz that he had information the Spanish were about to violate the armistice by dispatching a powerful armada to "invade, oppress, and conquer the incontestable dominions of the King, my Lord." He warned that while Spanish merchant vessels would continue to receive the customary hospitality of Brazilian ports, all warships encountered would be seized as legitimate prizes.[126] Vértiz denied all knowledge of any armament at Cádiz, and replied that Lavradio had been misinformed. He countered by asserting that it was the Portuguese, not the Spaniards, who had repeatedly violated the truce by committing insults against the flag of his sovereign.[127] The rules of etiquette having now been observed, the game of war could resume.

[125] That chain has attracted some interest among Brazilian military historians. A portaria of July 10, 1777, authorized payment for 4,357 pounds of "ferro de suecia estreito" at 6000 rs/cwt. "o q.l f.ro a corrente q. se fez no mesmo [Casa do] Trem p.a feixar a barra desta cid.e." CMCM, cod. 19, fol. 195ʳ.

The idea of blocking the harbor by such a means goes back at least to the time of the Duguay-Trouin invasion of Rio. The Duke of Cadaval, a royal advisor, suggested the means by which such a catastrophe could be prevented in the future. He observed, "Também seria importante averiguar se a corrente das águas permitiria que se fechasse a barra com uma cadeia; esta podia ser de ferro, ou madeira, sendo preferível esta última por ser o Brasil muito abundante dela, principalmente a de 'mangue' que se não corrompia na água." *Parecer* of Mar. 15, 1712, Virgínia Rau and Maria Fernanda Gomes da Silva, eds., *Os manuscritos de Cadaval*, II, 87–88. A dissenting opinion was voiced by one Gaspar da Costa, who had apparently been charged with that project before the invasion. He wrote that it was impossible to construct the barrier "pela grande distância que ia de [L]age que estava no meio da barra até à fortaleza de Santa Cruz (umas 600 braças) . . . para a qual não havia em todo o Rio de Janeiro ferro que chegasse. Também sondara a barra, achando-lhe 27 a 30 braças de fundo e uma grande corrente pelo que não poderia meter a pique qualquer navio que defendesse a sua entrada. . . ." Costa to Cadaval, Limoeiro, Oct. 20, 1712, *ibid.*, pp. 104–108.

[126] Lavradio to Vértiz, Dec. 9, 1776, *DI*, XVII, 137–139. The viceroy's protest was sent via General Böhm (*idem* to Böhm, Dec. 9, 1776, BNRJ, 13-4-3, n. 24), and copies were sent to all captains-general with whom Dom Luís regularly corresponded, a fact which accounts for the many places where this particular document may be found today.

[127] Vértiz to Lavradio, Montevideo, Jan. 31, 1777, *CB*, III, 451–452.

IX

The Second Cevallos Campaign

> . . . any [Portuguese] mother annoyed by the excessive flood of tears from her children used to tell them: *here comes Cevallos,* and . . . they . . . immediately quieted down. Even today there are some people in Buenos Aires who have been in Brazil and have seen this method [used] . . . to calm the little ones.
>
> "Noticia individual de la expedición
> [de] . . . D. Pedro de Cevallos
> contra los Portugueses" (1777)

> My intention is to conquer the Island of Santa Catalina and the adjacent mainland during February and part of March; to clear out Rio Grande during the rest of March and April, and in May I expect to appear before Colônia. . . .
>
> Cevallos to the Marquis of Casa Tilly,
> aboard the ship *Poderoso,* at sea
> February 7, 1777

THE DIPLOMATS had had their say, and so had the royal ministers. Now it was up to their pawns to make the moves that the chessmasters had predicted would bring about defeat of their adversaries. Upon their success depended the fate of the Debatable Lands, possibly a new world conflagration, and certainly a number of promising careers.

The Outward Voyage [1]

Shrouded in secrecy as to its destination and the special authority possessed by its commander, the Spanish armada set sail from Cádiz on the morning of November 13, 1776. The task force consisted of 116 sail, twenty of them warships, and carried nearly 10,000 troops, 8,500

---

[1] Among the many primary sources on the crossing see: "Extracto del viaje y noticia de los acahecimentos del Ex.to destinado a la conquista de . . . Santa Cathalina y demás operaciones en la América meridional . . . en los años . . . 1776 y 1777," *CB,* III, 456–463, taken from the account Mariscal de Exército D. Victorio de Navia gave his nephew, the Marquis de Santa Cruz [hereafter cited Navia, Relation]; [Anon.] "Noticia individual de la expedición encargada al Excmo. Sr. D. Pedro de Ceballos, contra los portugueses . . . ," Buenos Aires, Dec. 18, 1777 in Miguel Lobo, *Historia general de las antiguas colonias hispano-americanas,* III, 40–59 [hereafter cited Noticia individual]; in the same volume, pp. 59–67, there is an anonymous letter dated "Bay of Santa Cathalina, Feb. 21, 1777," apparently

sailors, and 500 service personnel (*maestranza*), and supplies sufficient for a six-month's campaign.[2] These statistics added up to make this the largest expeditionary force Spain had ever sent to America.[3]

The first part of the armada's crossing was relatively swift and uneventful. The convoy followed the customary route from the Peninsula to the Canaries, passing between Tenerife and the Grand Canary on the seventh day. By the end of the second week the pilots calculated that they were off Cape Verde. Thus far the convoy commander, the Marquis of Casa Tilly, had been fortunate in keeping all his ships together, but on November 30 the first straggler dropped behind. Thereafter nearly every day saw one or more ships unable to keep up. On December 23, after two and a half dreary weeks in the equatorial calms, course was altered and the fleet headed for the uninhabited island of Trindade.[4]

The unscheduled call at Trindade was made to permit thirty-two laggards to rejoin the task force. During an anxious fortnight (January 17 to 30) off that island, a long-smoldering dispute between army and naval staffs broke to the surface when the latter learned that Cevallos intended to proceed to Santa Catarina Island rather than sail directly to the Plata. The navy pointed out that none of its pilots was familiar with the waters around the island, and that it lacked reliable information on the island's defenses.[5] In addition,

written by an army officer of high rank [hereafter cited SC, Anon. ltr.]; a source previously unused is the anonymous "Relación abreviada de los acontecimentos occoridos en la navegación e conquista de la isla de Santa Catelina," BNRJ, I-2, 4, 7, n. 78 [hereafter cited BNRJ Relación]. Among the secondary accounts, the most helpful is Enrique M. Barba, *Don Pedro de Cevallos*, pp. 185–190. Emilio Ravignani, "El virreinato del Río de la Plata (1776–1810)," in Ricardo Levene, ed., *Historia de la nación Argentina*, IV:1 (2d ed.; Buenos Aires, 1940), 33–234, notes 100, 101, 105, and 106, indicates manuscript sources concerning the expedition in Argentine archives, while Enrique Araña, *Expedición de Don Pedro de Cevallos*, pp. 16–17, identifies others in Spanish archives. The several catalogues of Portuguese documents in the British Museum reveal the existence of a large number of relevant materials there.

2 No two contemporary accounts agree precisely on the composition of the expedition. See the summary in Lobo, III, 1–14, and in Araña, pp. 14–15. Neither gives details on the number of cannon and men aboard each vessel. Such information exists, however, in the "Compêndio da armada naval q. se acha a partir de Cádiz . . . ," BNRJ, I-31, 31, 1, nos. 51 and 54 (duplicate copies), an appendix of Martinho de Melo e Castro to Lavradio, Oct. 9, 1776, *ibid.*, n. 50. See also Cevallos to Gálvez, Nov. 20, 1776, *CB*, III, 456, n. 1, where the total number of ships is given as 116.

3 The expedition was not the largest punitive force sent to the New World up to this time. For their 1740 expedition against Cartagena, for example, the British assembled 27,000 men, 3,000 pieces of artillery, and 190 warships.

4 Spanish accounts call the island "Trinidad o Ascención," but it is clear from the SC, Anon. ltr. that it was Trinidade (20° 30′ 32″ S. lat., 29° 50′ W. long.), not the British island of Ascension (7° 55′ S. lat., 14° 25′ W. long.).

5 Apparently the navy believed a story put out by Lisbon that the Portuguese had 15,000 men under able foreign officers guarding the Debatable Lands, and that MacDouall's squadron was numerically superior to the Spanish. SC, Anon. ltr.

their leader, the Marquis of Casa Tilly, argued that Cevallos' invasion would be handicapped by the absence of 2,000 troops and much essential equipment aboard their missing ships. But the general, although once opposed to an attack on Santa Catarina as the first step in his campaign, [6] now insisted that the royal instructions must be followed regardless of any difficulties involved in their execution. After thirteen stragglers rejoined the convoy, the commanders decided that no more time could be spared to wait for the rest. Leaving a *saetía* behind to direct them to Santa Catarina, the task force resumed its voyage, with the navy still protesting their intended destination.[7]

A week later the Spaniards were blessed by an incredible windfall that greatly strengthened the army's arguments in favor of an immediate invasion of Santa Catarina. On February 6 and 7 three Portuguese ships blundered into the convoy and were captured.[8] One was a corvette out of Rio de Janeiro bound for Lisbon with a cargo of whale oil and "a copious number of letters"; the others were smacks from Santa Catarina Island, destined for Bahia. Through intercepted correspondence and interrogation of their prisoners,[9] the Spaniards

---

[6] See above, pp. 198–199. Barba has argued (pp. 187–189) that Cevallos continued to vacillate as to whether to proceed directly to Montevideo or to attack Santa Catarina first, and that Don Pedro Cermeño, a field marshal and member of Cevallos' staff, finally convinced Don Pedro to go after Santa Catarina first. His interpretation rests upon a letter of Cermeño of Jan. 8 to Cevallos, but Barba apparently failed to realize that it was written in response to a letter from Cevallos, written Jan. 7, asking why Cermeño had expressed doubts about going on to the island. Both are printed in Araña, pp. 32–35. Read together, they make it obvious that Cermeño, in his reply, was backing water, not converting Cevallos.

Minister of the Indies José de Gálvez was evidently aware of the ill-feeling between the services with respect to their initial military objective. In view of this and the apparent desire of the queen regent of Portugal to sue for peace with her brother, Charles III, Gálvez wrote an urgent dispatch to Cevallos dated Dec. 5, 1776, in which he ordered him in the strongest possible terms to take Santa Catarina Island first "a fin de apoderarse de ella antes de emprender la conquista de la Colonia, ni las demás operaciones ulteriores . . . no perdonará V. Ex. trabajo, fatiga, ni esfuerzo alguna para conseguir *el intento principalísimo de su Expedición q. es de conquistar la Ysla de S.ta Catalina.*" CB, III, 452–453, where it is endorsed by Cevallos certifying that he handed it to Casa Tilly at 9:00 A.M. on Mar. 25, 1777 (italics added).

[7] The best account of interservice bitterness before and during the voyage is the SC, Anon. ltr., which represents the army's point of view. I am unaware of any document showing the navy's attitude.

[8] The Navia Relation makes it February 8 and 9, but all other accounts agree with the dates in the text.

[9] It will be recalled that intercepted letters also helped the Dutch estimate the resistance they would meet in taking Pernambuco in 1630. See Charles R. Boxer, *The Dutch in Brazil,* p. 32. According to the SC, Anon. ltr., the Portuguese "dijeron la verdad en sus declaraciones, y como nada sabían de declaración de guerra, descuidaron de la diligencia de echar las cartas al agua al tiempo de rendirse. . . ." They were nonetheless guilty of grave dereliction of duty. Since late 1774 all governors and ship captains had been ordered to take security measures to prevent correspondence from falling into enemy hands at sea. E.g., on Oct. 11,

learned the size of Santa Catarina's garrison and its distribution; the
location and condition of each of the captaincy's forts; the kind and
quantity of rations the Portuguese possessed there; the number of
MacDouall's ships, their station, and the instructions the commodore
had received from the viceroy; [10] and the fact that Cevallos' appearance before the island was anticipated. Don Pedro would not disap-
point his expectant hosts.

Armed with this invaluable intelligence, General Cevallos defended
his intention to proceed with the invasion of Santa Catarina. In a letter to the fleet commander, Don Pedro contended that it would be
impossible to winter with the entire fleet at Montevideo "which does
not deserve the name of port" because it lacked protected anchorages.
Drawing upon his previous Platine experience, he thought it very unlikely that Vértiz could have assembled supplies or funds sufficient to
sustain the entire expedition at one time. He then outlined his time-
table, as quoted at the head of this chapter, and assured Casa Tilly
that he had made proper provision for a retirement in the event that
the invasion of Santa Catarina miscarried.[11]

A week later Don Pedro called a staff meeting and reviewed his
plans. During the conference the army officers signed a statement
affirming their faith in his leadership in spite of the navy's lack of cooperation.[12] On February 14 the convoy learned for the first time
that Cevallos had been named the first viceroy of the Plata.

The next day came the welcome cry of "land." As the armada com-
menced the last leg of its three-month-old voyage, it wheeled south
and sailed along the littoral of mainland Santa Catarina. Two days
later contact was made with the Portuguese squadron.

A few days before the rival naval forces first made visual contact
MacDouall had decided to foresake Garoupas Bay for the island of
Arvoredo, which guards one of the northern approaches to Santa

---

1774, Melo e Castro wrote Lavradio "ordena SM q. V. Ex.a mande fazer primeiras
e segundas vias, q. venhão sempre por dous differentes navios; com ordem aos
capitaens delles de as ligarem a balas de artilharia do calibre de 24, para as
lançarem ao mar, no cazo de serem attacados, durante a sua viagem." ANRJ, Col.
67, Liv. III-A, fol. 12ʳ (orig.). Similar orders were sent to the captain-general of
Bahia and to other administrators. There can be no question but that this intelligence greatly helped the Spanish; yet so far as I know, no Portuguese captain
was ever punished for such negligence.

[10] As one Spaniard noted in commenting upon the information regarding Mac-
Douall's intentions to surprise the enemy fleet, "poco sabían los portuguese de esta
escuadra, las preparauciones q. se habíen tomado para evitar una sorpressa de esta
naturaleza. . . ." Noticia individual.

[11] Cevallos to Casa Tilly, Feb. 7, 1777, Araña, pp. 25–27.

[12] Quoted in Barba, p. 190. This was in retort to a statement signed by Casa
Tilly's officers two days earlier declaring "que si antes de entrar en el Puerto de
Sta. Cathalina, nó se encuentran las fuerzas de mar de los Portugueses, ò, que no
sea dable batirlos por su situazn, see continuará al destino [i.e., Montevideo],
quedando fuera la Esquadra." Ibid., p. 189.

Catarina Island. For over a month he had remained at Garoupas, sending out daily patrols in search of the enemy fleet, in spite of vigorous protests from Field Marshal Antônio Carlos Furtado de Mendonça who insisted that the squadron should remain closer to the main island in accordance with the royal instructions.[13] Eventually the commodore concluded that Garoupas was not as satisfactory an anchorage as he had first thought; consequently he applied to the viceroy for permission to move his ships to a station off Arvoredo. Lavradio's consent arrived on February 11, 1777, together with news that the Spanish armada had left Spain three months before.[14]

Six days later the Portuguese squadron [15] was cruising off Arvoredo when the corvette *Invencível* returned from a patrol and reported that she had seen the enemy fleet. MacDouall immediately dispatched his longboats to Desterro along with a hasty note to the field marshal that he was about to engage the enemy.[16]

By noon MacDouall's lookouts had raised seven of Casa Tilly's leading frigates, and by 3:00 P.M. the number of Spanish ships visible was so great that "it was impossible to count them." With the Portuguese squadron standing to the windward, the Spanish commander placed his warships in the van and on his starboard flank so as to screen his transports from MacDouall. As darkness fell, the wind slackened, thus preventing MacDouall from getting within firing range.

[13] Evidently no one had bothered to notify the field marshal that the viceroy had given MacDouall the option of basing himself at Garoupas instead of near Desterro, as the Crown had directed. See Antônio Carlos Furtado de Mendonça to the queen (*ca.* 1779), *RIHGB*, XXVII:1 (1864), 316–322, covering the field marshal's conversations with MacDouall and his letters to the viceroy between Dec. 17, 1776 and Feb. 17, 1777 [hereafter cited Furtado de Mendonça, Apology].

[14] Lavradio to MacDouall, Feb. 4, 1777, referred to in *idem* to *idem*, Mar. 16, 1777, and in MacDouall's reply, same date, *ABNRJ*, XXXII, 363. MacDouall immediately transmitted the news to Furtado de Mendonça, who sent it on to Böhm. On Feb. 18, the field marshal received the same information from the viceroy via an overland dispatch. Furtado de Mendonça to Böhm, Feb. 12 and 18, 1777, BNRJ, 13-4-9, nos. 65–66 (origs.).

[15] At the time the Portuguese squadron consisted of:

NAUS	FRIGATES	CORVETTES
Santo Antônio (64)	Príncipe do Brasil	Invencível
Ajuda (50)	Princeza do Brasil	Conceição
Prazeres (64)	Pilar	Sacramento
Belém (64)	Graça	S. Francisco Xavier

MacDouall to Böhm, Dec. 17, 1776, BNRJ, 13-4-5, n. 88 (orig.); *idem* to Lavradio, Mar 9, 1777, *ABNRJ*, XXXII, 359–360. Varnhagen's statement that MacDouall had "três naus, onze fragatas e outras onze embarcações" is a gross exaggeration! *Historia*, IV, 202.

[16] Furtado de Mendonça, Apologia, p. 322. The launches were to be used in the event the field marshal found it necessary to abandon the island.

The next day the Irishman tried to entice the Spanish escorts to attack him, hoping to outmaneuver them and get a chance to cut out some of the transports. His plan failed when Casa Tilly wisely refused to scatter his escorts and expose the convoy. That afternoon Mac-Douall engaged in a fruitless chase of two Spanish frigates seen hovering about Santa Catarina for over a month. They were carrying dispatches from Vértiz to Cevallos and were attempting to contact the task force, but drew off as the Portuguese squadron approached. At sundown MacDouall reversed course and returned to shadow the invasion fleet.

The nineteenth found the distance between the two opposing forces constantly widening. The Spaniards held to their southerly course, while the Portuguese squadron moved north or north-north-east as if seeking an opening in Casa Tilly's screen. Eventually Mac-Douall become discouraged, having failed to penetrate that screen or find the stragglers that Lisbon had so confidently predicted would fall into his hands. That afternoon Spanish lookouts jubilantly reported the disappearance of the Portuguese squadron, which had been last observed heading north.[17]

On the morning of February 20, when Robert MacDouall called a council of war aboard his flagship, the enemy ships were no longer visible. After reading the royal instructions and the viceroy's orders, the commodore asked his captains for their opinions as to what the squadron should do next. With but one dissenting voice[18] the officers voted to return to Rio de Janeiro to procure additional ships and new instructions. They declared that it was hopeless for them to try to prevent the enemy from proceeding with his expected landings; indeed, it would be exceedingly dangerous for the squadron to make such an attempt, now that Casa Tilly had his transports safely anchored and could devote his full attention to resisting their challenge. To fight an enemy who enjoyed such a vast superiority in the number of his warships and their firepower would be to court disaster. The captains noted that the Crown had specifically directed that the squadron ought not risk its own destruction because its loss would expose all of southern Brazil to enemy attack. Nor would it serve any useful purpose for them to sail to the Plata, as both Lisbon and Lavradio had urged, for the squadron had no landing forces of its own,

---

[17] In addition to the Spanish accounts cited in n. 1, the three preceding paragraphs are based upon MacDouall to Lavradio, Feb. 19 and Mar. 4, 1777, *ABNRJ*, XXXII, 357–359; *idem* to Martinho de Melo e Castro, Mar. 31, 1777, *ibid.*, p. 355. Cf. Lavradio to [Visconde da Vila Nova de Cerveira?] July 20, 1777, *VRL*, pp. 93–96 for a very unflattering account of MacDouall's conduct at this time.

[18] "Parecer do commandante da náu *Prazeres*, José de Melo, sobre a consulta do commandante da esquadra . . . ," Feb. 20, 1777, *ABNRJ*, XXXII, 356.

and General Böhm had not indicated any willingness to furnish them.[19]

After making another fruitless effort to chase the two Spanish frigates that had come from Montevideo, MacDouall signaled the squadron to proceed to Rio de Janeiro, leaving the Spanish armada he was supposed to defeat far astern, without ever having engaged it, without so much as firing a Parthian shot at it.

The Fall of Santa Catarina Island [20]

In the early afternoon hours of February 20 the grand armada of Spain filed into the "large, beautiful, and commodious port of Santa Catarina," or rather the Bay of Canavieiras. "The day was clear and serene. A gentle breeze blew from the East. The squadron and the convoy entered in proper formation, and in order that . . . [the Portuguese] realize that this visit was made in the name of the Catholic King, a cannonade, as is customary, accompanied the unfurling of the royal flag on all the ships." [21]

Shortly after the armada came to anchor, [22] Cevallos and his staff transferred from his flagship, the *Poderoso*, to a shallow-draft frigate. During the remainder of the day they cruised along the coast, examining the fortress at Ponta Grossa and the littoral between that point

[19] The *pareceres* of the captains are excerpted *ibid.*, pp. 355–357.

[20] The Spanish accounts cited in n. 1 continue to be useful for the invasion, but the most detailed source is the "Diario de las operaciones que executó el exercito de S.M.C. en la Isla de Santa Catalina," Lobo, III, 14–24 (hereafter cited Diario, SC). It seems almost certain from references in the Diario that map 25 in José Torre Revello, comp., "Mapas y planos referentes al virreinato del Plata," *Publicaciones del Instituto de Investigaciones Históricas*, LXXIII, was intended to accompany the diary. A much less valuable account is Manuel Fernández y Ortolan, "Relação das forças hespanholas que tomaram a ilha de Santa Catarina e Colônia em 1776–1777," first published by Francisco Adolfo de Varnhagen and reprinted by Jônatas da Costa Rego Monteiro, *A Colônia do Sacramento*, II, 183–192. Besides being sketchy, it suffers from having been written in 1812, thirty-five years after the events it describes. Among contemporary Portuguese sources, the Apology of Furtado de Mendonça is of some help in establishing chronology, but because of the author's extreme bitterness it must be used with care. More helpful is the field marshal's dispatch of Feb. 24, 1777 to Lavradio (IHGB/AUC, 1-1-29, fols. 346ʳ–348ᵛ), summarizing developments between Feb. 22 and 24. Another source, never before used to my knowledge, is Bernardo de Salazar Sarmento Eça e Alarcão (*ouvidor geral do crime*) to Lavradio, No. 30, 1777 (*ibid.*, fols. 442ᵛ–457ʳ), which is a summary of the official devassa concerning the fall of Santa Catarina (hereafter cited Sarmento, Report on devassa). Among the secondary accounts, the Spanish side is best presented in Barba, pp. 190–194, while the old work of J. F. Fernandes Pinheiro, *Ánais da província de S. Pedro*, pp. 329–334, still provides the best coverage in Portuguese.

[21] "Noticia individual," p. 44.

[22] Near Loros or Coros island. Casa Tilly stationed his six *navíos* on the edge of the convoy in case MacDouall should decide to return.

and Ponta Canavieiras to determine the best landing beach and the number of troops to send ashore.

The next day Don Pedro sent several of his aides in a *falúa* to re-check the proposed invasion area, and dispatched the *chambegüin Andaluz* to take soundings off Forts Santa Cruz and Ratones. This latter operation was meant to confuse the Portuguese about the Span-iards' intended landing place. As the *Andaluz* drew near to Fort Santa Cruz, the fort spoke briefly, putting a few balls into the war-ship but doing only minor damage. Apparently the Spaniards did not reply. At any rate, they continued their reconnaissance within firing range of the fort without further incident.

Meanwhile the defenders were endeavoring to determine what they should do in the face of the impending invasion. As soon as the armada hove into sight, the governor of Fort Ponta Grossa notified Field Marshal Antônio Carlos, who hastened to the fort for a per-sonal look. He was not reassured by what he saw. He estimated the enemy fleet at about one hundred ships, and by counting the regi-mental flags displayed on their masts, he concluded Cevallos had 12,000 troops to throw against his 2,000 to 2,500 defenders.[23] To his amazement there was no sign of MacDouall, and he realized that the enemy would be able to land without meeting any sort of naval op-position. Burdened with these disturbing thoughts, Antônio Carlos returned to his quarters. After ordering every available soldier, in-cluding hospital convalescents, to man the fortifications, he notified the viceroy, General Böhm, and Captain-General Saldanha of his plight.[24]

Two days later the governor of Ponta Grossa fortress sent a message that the Spanish were about to land. He warned that he had too few men to hold out, and that he feared his line of retreat would soon be cut off. Antônio Carlos promptly called a council of war consisting of himself, the recently arrived engineer Brigadier José Custódio de Sá e Faria, and Governor Pedro Antônio da Gama e Freitas, with whom the field marshal had constantly been at odds since they had arrived on the island.[25] The three agreed that there were no reinforcements

[23] Coeval estimates of the Portuguese garrison on Santa Catarina vary from 5,000 down to less than 2,000. The figures given in the text are based upon Sarmento, Report on devassa, probably the most objective source.

[24] Furtado de Mendonça to Böhm, Feb. 20, 1777, BNRJ, 13, 4, 9, n. 67 (orig.), which is a duplicate of the dispatch the field marshal sent Lavradio and to Captain-General Saldanha on the same date, *DI*, XVII, 272–273.

[25] Throughout his Apology, Furtado de Mendonça records his grievances against the governor, whom he considered to be an incompetent, meddlesome lackey of the viceroy. Inadvertently, he reveals that the real reason for his hostility was that when he was assigned to Santa Catarina he had assumed that he would have full charge there, but the appointment of Gama e Freitas as governor meant that he possessed only military authority.

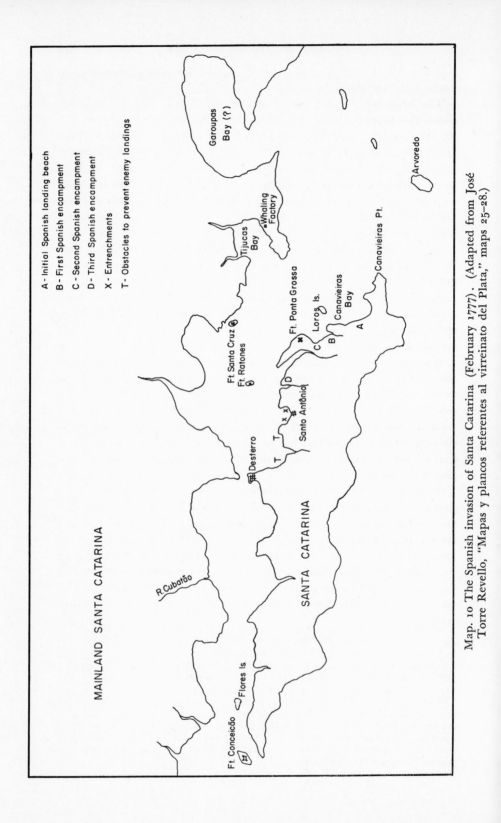

Map. 10 The Spanish invasion of Santa Catarina (February 1777). (Adapted from José Torre Revello, "Mapas y plancos referentes al virreinato del Plata," maps 25–28.)

that could be sent to the fort, but they failed to reach a decision as to what orders to give its governor.[26] The following morning word came that the Spaniards had established a beachhead at a locale called São Francisco de Paula, not far from the fortress.[27]

The initial landings had been made during the previous night (February 22). The first wave, consisting of several companies of grenadiers and Catalan volunteers, stepped ashore at 00:30 after a two-and-a-half-hour ride from their rendezvous off the island of Loros (Coros). While they deployed to occupy high ground above the beach, the launches returned to the transports and warships for reinforcements. By 8:00 A.M. six regiments and twelve field pieces were ashore. That day a new camp, Casas Viejas, was set up three-quarters of a league away from the beachhead in the direction of Ponta Grossa.

As soon as he received reports of the landings, Antônio Carlos convoked another council of war. Since the brigadier and the governor still differed on whether the fortress at Ponta Grossa should be held against an enemy attack, he sent them with another officer to examine the military situation themselves. When they returned still without reaching an agreement, the field marshal summoned all regimental officers to his headquarters. After considering the strength of the enemy already on shore, they voted in favor of abandoning the fortress before the Spaniards could invest it. Reluctantly the governor affixed his signature to their written recommendation.

That evening Field Marshal Don Victorio de Navia, author of one of the accounts of the invasion, led a patrol of 150 Catalan volunteers to reconnoiter the approaches to the citadel of Ponta Grossa. The night was clear, the moon full, but they found the going difficult. After wading up to their knees through swamps, they began the steep climb up the back of the mountain. As they advanced, they heard the barking of dogs, and correctly concluded that they were being watched. Later they heard gunfire from the fortress, which was firing upon the navío *Septentrion* and two gunboats Cevallos had sent to divert the defenders' attention. Finally the patrol returned to camp with the discouraging report that the terrain was very rugged and that it would be very difficult to capture the fortress.

The following morning, however, the Spanish found to their astonishment and relief that the fortress had already been evacuated. Its

26 In his Apology, Furtado de Mendonça makes it appear that the brigadier favored defense of the fortress, while the governor wanted it to be given up. Such an interpretation is, however, inconsistent with Gama e Freitas' later insistence that some sort of resistance be made before the island was evacuated.

27 It is interesting to note that this was precisely the beach that MacDouall had earlier suggested the Spanish could use as a landing place. See above, p. 216.

governor had made the decision himself after reading his scouting reports, but before receiving official authorization to retire. He gave up his post even though he had twenty-five to thirty-one cannon, plenty of ammunition, nearly two hundred officers and men, provisions to last twenty days, and an excellent defensive position. No wonder the Spanish chroniclers expressed gratitude to the Portuguese for having saved them "much time and labor" in order to reduce Santa Catarina's key fortress.[28]

General Cevallos immediately ordered part of his troops to occupy the citadel, and bivouacked the rest in a new camp at the foot of Ponta Grossa. Within the fortress the Spanish found the usual evidence of hasty abandonment: magazines full of munitions, and guns so imperfectly spiked that they could easily be restored to service. The Castilians also encountered a Portuguese gunnery lieutenant, José Henrique Cunha, who had become disgusted at his commander's failure to defend his position and decided to desert to the enemy. Although he may have furnished Cevallos with some useful information, it was probably not as crucial as Portuguese contemporaries and later historians believed.[29]

The same day Don Pedro sent one of his colonels to Forts Santa Cruz and Ratones to demand their surrender, promising no quarter if they offered resistance. Both governors replied that they could not comply until they had obtained permission from their superiors. They were given twenty-four hours in which to do so. To help the Portuguese make up their minds, Spanish troops were paraded conspicuously on the cliffs overlooking the forts. The next afternoon the Spaniards found both forts abandoned except for an officer and a squad of men in one, busily engaged in dumping munitions and provisions into the sea.

The following day (February 26) Cevallos occupied the village of Santo Antônio, two leagues from Desterro, and sent a delegation to the capital to demand its surrender. Back came word that the vila had already been evacuated. Don Pedro moved in quickly and issued

28 Sarmento, Report on devassa. I have stressed the situation within the fortress since I believe that its fall contributed far more to the speed with which the Spaniards were able to overrun the island than contemporary or later Portuguese writers have recognized. The anonymous author of the "Noticia individual" testifies, for example, that "El Castillo pudiera haberse defendido con decoro, porque sobre estar bien fortificado tenía buena guarnición, y aunque lo dominaban varias alturas, era obra dificultosa subir á ellas para batir, y no podía hacerse sin mucho tiempo y trabajo." Lobo, III, 45.

29 The Report on devassa incorrectly states that Cunha came from Fort Santa Cruz. Spanish contemporary sources and the Portuguese court sentence later passed against him make it clear that he commanded a battery at Ponta Grossa. As will be seen in the following section, his desertion provided one of the excuses for Portuguese abandonment of the island, but there is no indication in Spanish accounts that he provided Cevallos with any top secret information.

two proclamations to the island's inhabitants: one asserted that Spanish capture of Santa Catarina was justifiable retaliation for repeated acts of Portuguese infidelity; the other promised all civilians good treatment, and prescribed severe penalties for any Spanish soldier or sailor indulging in pillage.[30]

Two days later the last Portuguese soldier on the island surrendered. The capture of Santa Catarina had taken less than a week. It did not cost Cevallos a single casualty, nor a moment's anxiety.[31]

The Capitulation of the Santa Catarina Garrison

The decision to abandon Santa Catarina Island had been made during another stormy war council held on February 24.[32] Presided over by the field marshal, it included the brigadier, the governor, and various regimental and staff officers. After the instructions they had received from the Court and the viceroy were read aloud, the officers considered what they took to be the realities of their situation: (1) the disappearance of MacDouall's squadron; (2) the absence of the floating batteries the Court had said should be established to block the channel between Desterro and the mainland;[33] (3) the presumption that artillery lieutenant Cunha had informed Cevallos of the "secret" passes between Ponta Grossa and the island capital; (4) the fact that the enemy had already occupied their main fortress and was threatening two other forts; (5) his overwhelming numerical superiority; (6) the unlikelihood that a relief force could reach them before the Spaniards had overrun their remaining positions on the island. The council decided that these considerations provided ample ground for departing from the viceroy's injunction to give up the island only after "an exemplary defense." Although outvoted, the governor protested that at least they ought to put up a token opposition to the invaders.[34]

30 The manifesto of Cevallos, dated Feb. 20, 1777, is published, among other places, in *ABNRJ*, XXXII, 350–351. The *bando* to the troops is summarized in the Diario, Lobo, III, 18.

31 For his achievement, Cevallos was promoted from lieutenant to captain general, while 300 of his officers were upgraded one step. Fernández y Ortolan, "Relação das forças hespanholas," Rego Monteiro, *Colônia*, II, 187.

32 The following paragraph is based on Sarmento, Report on devassa. The investigator warned (fol. 450ᵛ) that the exact nature of the voting and the statements various participants had made could not be determined because "ellas [the witnesses] juram com tanta variedade sobre estes Conselhos, ou por falta de lembrança ou por confuzão de ideas. . . ."

33 The fact that such a cordon would not have prevented the Spaniards from landing at Canavieiras Bay did not impress itself upon the junta.

34 In offering an apology for his vote, the governor concluded, "últimamente senhor eu só não posso contradizer todos estes officiaes." Gama e Freitas to Lavradio,

The same day orders were passed for the troops to abandon their posts and assemble at Desterro for evacuation on the morrow.[35] It was hoped that it would be possible to keep the garrison together and march south to join General Böhm's army,[36] but that hope was considerably dimmed by the chaos that occurred during the evacuation.

Although the distance between insular and mainland Santa Catarina is only four hundred yards at the narrows, it required a day and a night (February 24 and 25) for the troops and the civilians who fled with them to negotiate that crossing. According to later testimony, there were four smacks, seven launches from the squadron, two sloops, twenty-eight whaling boats, several fishing craft, and innumerable canoes within a short distance of the capital, yet no more than eight of these craft were actually employed in the evacuation. And since their oarsmen were not to be found, the soldiers had to row themselves across the channel, loaded down as they were with packs, muskets, and personal belongings.[37]

The first objective of the retreating army was Cubatão, a small village noted for its sulfurous springs about nine or ten leagues from Desterro. There, in conformity with the viceroy's instructions, certain facilities had recently been built so that the village could serve as an emergency base in case the captaincy's garrison was forced to retire to that point.[38]

The march to Cubatão lasted three days. During that time the Portuguese army rapidly melted away. Desertions, hitherto light, now became numerous and occurred openly as desperate men forsook families and friends to take refuge in the trackless interior. Weakened by hunger—no food was served during the march—many others fell by the wayside; some lightened their load by casting away their packs

---

Feb. 24, 1777, IHGB/AUC, 1-1-29, fols. 405ᵛ-406ᵛ. When the decision to evacuate the island had been reached, the governor sent the câmara of Desterro and the provedor with their records to the reserve base at Cubatão on the mainland. *Idem* to *idem*, Feb. 23, 1777, *ibid.*, fols. 403ʳ-405ʳ. For his part the field marshal sent eight chests of his personal belongings, including silver, to São Paulo, and dispatched an aide with his son (who later became Archbishop of Braga) to Rio Grande. Report on devassa, fol. 448ʳ.

35 The message apparently did not reach the garrison of the island fort of Flores in the south channel, nor a signal station crew on Point Canavieiras, both of whom surrendered to the Spaniards on February 28. The governor of Fort Conceição, on an island just south of the main island, anticipated the order and sent his men to the mainland. He was captured along with some slaves while disposing of the munitions and putting his cannon out of action.

36 Furtado de Mendonça to Böhm, Feb. 25, 1777, BNRJ, 13, 4, 9, n. 70 (orig.), a duplicate of a dispatch sent the preceding day to Viceroy Lavradio; *idem* to Saldanha, Feb. 25, 1777, *DI*, XVII, 273.

37 The amplest account of the crossing is Sarmento, Report on devassa, fols. 452ʳ-453ʳ.

38 Sarmento declared "este sítio nem era defensável por natureza, nem o estava por arte, e podia fàcilmente ser cercado e surprehendido." *Ibid.*, fol. 447ʳ.

and weapons and tried to keep up. Only a fraction of the army reached Cubatão.[39]

On February 28 the field marshal convened still another council of war to decide whether the remainder of the garrison should try to proceed to Laguna or should capitulate to the enemy. Brigadier José Custódio, who had just returned from reconnoitering down the coast, reported that he had heard gunfire and was certain that the Spaniards were ahead of them, preparing to cut off their line of retreat. Antônio Carlos then interrogated the regimental commanders as to whether they considered their troops capable of fighting their way through to friendly forces. The colonels of the Pernambuco and Pôrto regiments[40] stoutly replied affirmatively, but the brigadier, the acknowledged expert on the geography of the region, warned that the roads were "very steep, difficult and long" and that there would be many rivers to cross before they reached Laguna. The governor lamented that he could not offer carts or beasts of burden to facilitate the march, nor boats to ford the streams "because the people did not obey him."[41] Then, on the basis of "mature reflections [so] necessary in such weighty matters," the council signed a statement declaring their belief that their situation was hopeless, and that, accordingly, they were delegating José Custôdio to treat with the enemy.[42]

The brigadier was to try to obtain free passage to Rio de Janeiro for the officers and men, but he discovered that General Cevallos had no intention of being so liberal. Don Pedro agreed to permit the officers to travel at their own expense to Rio de Janeiro, Buenos Aires, or Montevideo, as they preferred, on condition that they sign a pledge not to take up arms against Spain again during the war. However, he exempted all enlisted men from the parole, insisting that they remain as his prisoners. In addition, he demanded that all war matériel and other supplies be left behind.[43]

With these conditions, the brigadier went back to the Portuguese camp to consult his colleagues. They drew up the customary list of propositions to bargain with their adversary, but they doubtless real-

---

[39] *Ibid.*, fols. 453ʳ–454ʳ. Furtado de Mendonça wrote "Do Regim.to da Ilha tem desertado tudo, q. o m.to q. aqui poderá haver he menos de duzentas praças entrando os Off.es e creyo q. os soldados todos, e off.es Inferiores se hirão embora: o Regim.to de Pernambuco, terá hoje . . . cincoenta p.a sessenta desertores, . . . o Regim.to de Porto . . . os mesmos. . . ." To Böhm, Mar. 4, 1777, BNRJ, 13, 4, 9, n. 73 (orig.).

[40] No mention is made of what had become of the colonel of Santa Catarina's own regiment.

[41] Sarmento, Report on devassa, fol. 454ᵛ.

[42] "Termo . . . para se capitular com o inimigo," Feb. 28, 1777, Baltasar Silva Lisboa, *Annaes do Rio de Janeiro*, III, 92–95.

[43] This and the following paragraph are based on Sarmento, Report on devassa, fols. 455ʳ⁻ᵛ, and Furtado de Mendonça, Apology, pp. 329–330.

ized, as Cevallos surely did, that they were not in much of a bargaining position. The general did agree that noncommissioned officers down to standard-bearers could also return to Rio de Janeiro, and that the families and servants of both officers and noncommissioned officers could accompany them.[44]

After making a third fruitless attempt to gain additional concessions, the brigadier signed the capitulations on March 5, 1777.[45] He returned the same day to Cubatão with Spanish launches to fetch the parolees and the prisoners. The latter, apparently not appreciating the statement of their officers that they had surrendered in order to save the enlisted men from greater suffering,[46] now deserted in droves.[47] Only five or six hundred men chose to try their luck with the Spaniards,[48] and they lived to regret their decision.

Cevallos Captures Colónia but Fails to Take Rio Grande

Even before the Portuguese garrison capitulated, Don Pedro de Cevallos was planning his next move—the reconquest of Rio Grande. On February 27, the day he entered Desterro, the general outlined the

[44] Servants who were enlisted men or His Majesty's slaves were not included. See n. 45.

[45] Among other places, the capitulations are published in CB, III, 462–463, n. 1. One curious feature is Art. 8, which provided that "Los Negros de la fábricas [sic] de Aceytes de Ballenas y qualesquiera otros que huviere pertenncientes a Su Mag.ᵈ se entregaran todos de buena fé."

[46] Furtado de Mendonça, Apology, p. 329. The marshal lamely stated that prior to the signing of the capitulation, there had been ample time for the troops to desert if they were so inclined, and that he had placed no obstacle in their way. He was not troubled by the evident inconsistency of this statement with his earlier remark that the troops were too weary to go on to Laguna or Rio Grande.

[47] After experiencing great hardships, 300 survivors reached Rio Grande, and and another hundred got to São Paulo. Individuals and small groups stumbled about southern Brazil for months looking for food and refuge; some ended up in Minas Gerais, others in Rio de Janeiro. Two parties, half-crazed with hunger, made attacks upon registros in Minas Gerais and in São Paulo. Report on devassa, fols. 455ᵛ–456ᵛ; Lavradio to Melo e Castro, Apr. 3, 1777, IHGB/AUC, 1-1-29, fols. 362ᵛ–363ʳ; J. M. Figueiredo to Saldanha, Apr. 16, 1777, and Böhm to idem, May 1, 1777, DI, XVII, 269, 319; Saldanha to Böhm, June 4 and June 13, 1777, DI, XLII, 383, 393; Antônio de Noronha to Joaq[ui]m Pedro de Carn[eir]o, Aug. 29, 1777, BNRJ, 2, 2, 24, n. 97. The Mineiro captain-general wrote that the registro of Jaguari had been attacked on Aug. 1 by "35 sold.os pagos armados de Armas d'El Rey, pistolas, e cattanas do Regim.to de Pernambuco q. se pudérão escapar aos Castelhanos da Ilha de S.ta Catharina," and that they disdained the post corporal's offer to escort them to Vila Rica, saying they could make their way by themselves. The captain-general prudently ordered sergeant major Carneiro to round up the men and bring them in.

[48] Sarmento, Report on devassa, fol. 456ʳ⁻ᵛ.

next phase of his campaign in a dispatch to General Vértiz.[49] He instructed Vértiz to gather all the men he could and advance swiftly from Montevideo to the vicinity of the Lagoa dos Patos. There he was to countermarch until Cevallos himself had arrived, as he expected to do within fifteen or twenty days.[50] Don Pedro planned to force the entrance of the Lagoa with frigates and packetboats and then send in his transports. Upon a given signal Vértiz would strike from the south while Cevallos' troops hit from the north. With divine favor, prophesied Don Pedro, General Böhm's army would be crushed in the Spanish nutcracker.

The fulfillment of this plan required more than providential assistance. Successful execution depended upon precise timing, favorable weather, exceptional human efforts, and luck. The absence of any one of these factors could cause a new and possibly decisive reverse for Spanish arms.

As it turned out, the first thing that went wrong for the Spaniards was their timing. Cevallos failed to make sufficient allowance for the time necessary for Vértiz to receive his message, assemble his forces, and march 120 leagues from Montevideo to Rio Grande.[51] Moreover, Don Pedro was delayed at Santa Catarina longer than he expected. There were inventories to be made of the spoils, [52] reports and trophies to be dispatched to Madrid, prisoners to be sent to the Plata and parolees to Rio de Janeiro, [53] and security measures to be taken to prevent the island's recapture by the Portuguese.

These matters occupied Cevallos until the middle of March. He then appointed a military commandant and a civil governor to administer Santa Catarina with the assistance of a couple of thousand

49 Memoria of Don Juan José de Vértiz y Salcedo in Memorias de los virreyes del Río de la Plata, Sigfrido A. Radaelli, ed. (Buenos Aires, 1945) , pp. 91–93 (hereafter cited Vértiz, Memoria). Vértiz was evidently surprised that Cevallos planned to attack Rio Grande before proceeding to the Plata.

50 Varnhagen's statement that Cevallos intended to land at Castillos is inexact História geral do Brasil, IV, 203. As noted below in the text, Cevallos tried to stop at Castillos after failing to enter the Lagoa dos Patos, his initial objective.

51 Vértiz (Memoria, p. 92) stated that Cevallos' dispatch of February 27 did not reach him until a month later because the messenger ship encountered adverse weather.

52 "Noticia de la artillería de bronce y fierro que se ha allado en la isla de Santo Cathalina y fuertes de su comprehension," n. d., Lobo, III, 19–22.

53 The prisoners left in warships for the Plata on Mar. 8; the following day Cevallos sent three vessels to Spain with an aide-de-camp in each to convey the news of his victory; on the fourteenth four ships left for Rio de Janeiro with the parolees. Also aboard were all of the Portuguese priests on Santa Catarina who were replaced by "una nueva fundación de los Religiosos Diegos de los que han venido en la expedición." The only exception was made in favor of the curate of Santo Antônio, who for unexplained reasons (was he a quisling?) was permitted to remain. Diario, SC, p. 23.

troops, the rest he sent aboard the waiting task force. On March 20 Cevallos boarded the *Poderoso* accompanied by his staff and by Brigadier José Custódio, who decided that the climate of Montevideo was more to his liking than that of Rio de Janeiro. Owing to the usual delays interposed by the navy, the fleet did not sail until March 28.[54]

Two days at sea, the weather intervened decisively, for "a furious *pampero*" struck the convoy and continued to lash it unmercifully for more than a week.[55] Although Casa Tilly wished to turn back, Cevallos insisted that they go ahead. Nevertheless it became impossible to approach the Lagoa dos Patos, and an attempt to make the more southerly port of Castillos also proved unsuccessful. With the armada badly scattered, with many of its ships handicapped by shattered masts and ribboned rigging, and with their crews straining at the pumps to keep them afloat, the order was given to proceed to the Plata. On April 18 barely half of the eighty-three vessels that had begun the voyage at Santa Catarina limped into Maldonado, their passengers exhausted and afflicted by scurvy and a severe rash. That unseasonably early pampero probably saved Rio Grande, just as a "Protestant wind" had come to England's aid in 1588.

From Maldonado Cevallos dispatched a messenger to General Vértiz explaining his misfortune and advising him to return to Fort Santa Teresa and await further orders.[56] Then he proceeded to Montevideo, where he stepped ashore two days later.

> He was conducted to the Mother Church with all the ceremonial which is customary with the Viceroys of the Indies. The artillery of the citadel and the ships, the clarions and trumpets, the church bells, and the . . . repeated vivas truly indicated how much these people rejoiced at the arrival of their new Viceroy and former General. Everyone crowded around to see him, and it became necessary to order the soldiers to surround him [to protect him from the crush], a move which gave offense to no one. . . . Finally the Te Deum was sung, and His Excellency retired to his lodgings, giving new orders that very night for . . . the continuation of the war. . . . As His Excellency is the declared enemy of inaction and indolence, he resolved not to lose time in this plaza.[57]

So records an admiring contemporary. Actually Cevallos realized that he had no time to lose if he were to complete his campaign

54 *Ibid.*, p. 24. The "Noticia individual" gives the date of departure as Mar. 30.
55 The voyage is described in "Noticia individual," pp. 48–49, and in Fernández y Ortolan, "Relação," p. 187.
56 Cevallos to Vértiz, Apr. 16, 1777, cited in Vértiz, *Memoria*, p. 94. See also Ravignani, "El Virreinato," p. 96, n. 118.
57 "Noticia individual," p. 49. From this point on the "Diario de las providencias dadas para el sitio de la Colonia, su ataque y rendición," Lobo, III, 24–28, becomes useful.

within the space of a single season. With one eye on the weather gauge and the other fixed upon the horizon looking for the rest of his expedition, Don Pedro decided to postpone the attack on Rio Grande and to concentrate first on the capture of Colônia. He calculated that there would still be time to march against Rio Grande after Colônia was again in his hands.

Cevallos' decision was an indication of both his resourcefulness and his awareness of the desperate situation in which the defenders of Colônia found themselves. Their plight was due in part to the forthright action of Juan José de Vértiz who, as soon as he learned that a large Spanish expeditionary force was coming to the Plata, gave instructions on his own responsibility to tighten the land and sea blockade around the Portuguese outpost so as to starve its inhabitants into submission.[58]

Contemporary Portuguese sources testify graphically to the success of Vértiz' measures.[59] The last shipload of fresh food had arrived at Colônia in December 1776. In spite of good weather during the ensuing months, the only vessel to get through the Spanish blockade was a smack carrying wood; two others, loaded with provisions, fell victims of the guardacostas. The coming of cooler weather in March made it impossible to stretch the praça's meager larder by fishing and by gathering edible wild berries and herbs outside the walls, and the pangs of hunger were beginning to be felt within the citadel. To relieve the acute shortage of firewood, peach orchards behind Colônia were cut down, and the island of San Gabriel was denuded of its shrubs. By late April the garrison was on half rations.[60] A dog following a Spanish messenger into the fort was quickly smothered and

[58] Vértiz, *Memoria*, p. 90. He wrote that he had taken these steps "no obstante hallarme sin órdenes de la Corte."

[59] The last days of Portuguese Colônia are described in [Rocha to Lavradio], Colônia, June 8, 1777, IHGB, *Lata* 69, MS 1294 (an unsigned original not in Rocha's hand but certainly authored by him) ; *idem* to *idem*, Buenos Aires, Mar. 20 and [?], 1778, *RIHGB*, XXXIX:2 (1876) , 283–318; *idem* to the queen, Nov. 5, 1781, *Revista de philologia e de história*, II, fasc. II (Rio de Janeiro, 1933) , 213–225; Dr. P. Pedro Pereira Fernandes de Mesquita, "Relação da conquista de Colônia . . . ," Buenos Aires, 1778, *RIHGB*, XXXI:1 (1868) , 350–361. [The published text comprises the first part of the manuscript (BNRJ, I-1, 1, 9) ; the second (and so far as I know unpublished) part consists of a detailed description of Buenos Aires during the padre's stay there.] A document of considerable value is the petition of Colonel Domingos Correa de Mesquita to Lavradio, ca. 1778, printed in Rego Monteiro, *Colônia*, II, 165–174, from a manuscript now missing from its file in the BNRJ (I-31, 26, 1, n. 6) ! A major source hitherto overlooked is Desembargador Nicolao Joaquim de Miranda Silva e Alarcão to Lavradio, Dec. 1, 1777, IHGB/AUC 1-1-29, fols. 457ᵛ–465ᵛ, which is a summary of the devassa findings (hereafter cited Colônia devassa report) .

[60] So states Colonel Mesquita (p. 167) , though the Colônia devassa report attempts to minimize the food shortage by pointing to the testimony of the quartermaster and his scribe that the scarcity of provisions was compensated by "mais do seu equivalente em farinha"—but not in calories.

eaten half raw by famished sentries. By the end of the following month, a survivor recalled, "there were no dogs or cats left; their owners had eaten them." [61]

Thanks to intercepted dispatches from Governor Rocha intended for Viceroy Lavradio,[62] Cevallos could plan his attack against Colônia to coincide with the virtual exhaustion of its food supplies. Before making his next move he sent out officers to round up militiamen in order to guard estâncias exposed to possible Portuguese raids from Rio Grande and to block off all avenues of approach to Colônia from the north. Then he sent the larger warships back to Santa Catarina to protect the island and to seek out and destroy the Portuguese squadron. On May 20, a month to the day after the general's return to Montevideo, the first two troop laden convoys left that port for Colônia.[63]

Two days later 6,000 to 7,000 Spanish troops began debarking at the Arroyo de los Molinos, less than a league away from the Portuguese base. The Castilians immediately started unloading their ships, and were more troubled by a severe rainstorm than by the Portuguese who made no move to challenge the aggressors.[64] General Cevallos personally reconnoitered his objective and found that Colônia's fortifications had changed very little since he had last seen them. Pausing to dispatch some contingents to protect a group of ranches to the north where Colonel Rafael Pinto Bandeira was reported to be operating with a large patrol, Don Pedro ordered the rest of his troops to dig approach trenches and to assemble his formidable siege batteries.[65]

Until May 30 neither side tipped its hand. That night a Spanish patrol numbering about a hundred men made a sortie against the left flank of the citadel. Their movements were intended to mask construction of a new series of trenches and the placement of some cannon in the *chácaras* behind the praça, as well as to test the alertness of the defenders. Portuguese guards detected the patrol's approach, and abandoned a field piece to race back into the citadel with the alarm.

[61] Mesquita to Lavradio, *ca.* 1778, p. 169; again the Colônia devassa report differs, contending that if some soldiers ate dogs and cats, it was only because they were depraved, not just hungry!

[62] Padre Fernandes de Mesquita, "Relação," p. 351; Rocha to Lavradio [?], 1778, p. 301.

[63] Diario, Colônia, pp. 24–25.

[64] Rocha contended that he was obliged by his instructions not to fire upon the Spanish until they commited the first aggression. He asserted that he was merely following the viceroy's instructions of Oct. 30, 1776, but in fact he was leaning upon a rather strained interpretation of Pombal's instructions of 1775 and 1776.

[65] For the caliber and number of cannon in Cevallos' siege train see "Noticia individual," p. 52.

For a few moments the air was filled with cannon and musket fire from the fort. When it ceased the patrol withdrew, having suffered no casualties. Meantime the new guns had been positioned.[66]

The sight of the enemy in retreat was heartening to the defenders, but Governor Rocha was not elated. He knew better than to assume that a full-scale assault could be repulsed so easily. The troubled governor convened a council of war and announced his intention to ask Cevallos for terms in order to save civilians and soldiers from needless slaughter. His declaration was greeted with stunned silence. Finally the regimental commander, Colonel Domingos Correa de Mesquita, spoke up. He protested that the morale of his troops was high and that they were ready to defend Colônia "to the last drop of [our] blood." His officers backed up the colonel, but the governor still insisted that their situation was hopeless, and declared that he would take full responsibility for the surrender.[67]

Francisco José da Rocha's decision stemmed neither from panic nor from personal cowardliness, contrary to the opinions of contemporaries and later historians. It is true that the Spaniards had not yet fired their big guns on the praça, but they did not have to. It was on the verge of starvation. On May 22 a survey of provisions remaining in government warehouses and in private homes turned up forty days' supply of manioc flour and salt, twenty-odd *arrobas* of rice, a pipe of sweet oil, less than two of vinegar, a little brandy, some fish oil, and four undernourished cows—not much to sustain 1,700 souls.[68] The governor could hardly have exaggerated very much when he later claimed that the base was down to three days' provisions when he capitulated. Even the official investigator of the loss of the outpost admitted that there was food left for only six days.[69]

Besides the shortage of provisions, the governor realized that there was scant hope of help arriving from other Portuguese settlements. From obliging Spaniards he had learned of the fall of Santa Catarina and of the manner in which its garrison had surrendered. He also knew that the squadron had returned to Rio de Janeiro, and that the

[66] Portuguese accounts, particularly the Colônia devassa report, attach much more significance to this minor action than do the Spanish.

[67] Colonel Mesquita to Lavradio, *ca.* 1778, p. 168; cf., however, Colônia devassa report, fol. 462ʳ.

[68] This is a rough estimate of Colônia's population based on: (1) statement of the Diario, Colônia, that 700 troops were sent as prisoners to Buenos Aires; (2) the number of officers, noncommissioned officers, and dependents allowed to go to Rio de Janeiro given in the "Noticia individual" as 443; and (3) the list of "Famílias que ficaram na Praça da Colônia, quando esta se rendeu ao[s] Espanhóes na Guerra de 1777," n.d. but contemporary, ANRJ, Col. 67, Liv. IV, fols. 24ʳ-27ʳ, which enumerates 540 civilians, slaves, and priests.

[69] [Rocha to Lavradio], June 8, 1777; *idem* to the queen 1781 (both cited in n. 59 above); Colônia devassa report, fol. 459ʳ.

magnitude of the Spanish war fleet made it unlikely that MacDouall would be able to bring relief to Colônia.[70]

Governor Rocha had these considerations in mind when, on June 1, he sent a messenger to General Cevallos offering to surrender on the basis of twenty-two conditions.[71] Don Pedro saw through Rocha's bluff, and declined to bargain. After detaining the Portuguese emissary long enough to finish his siege preparations, Don Pedro sent him back with a demand for an unconditional surrender within forty-eight hours.[72] When Rocha appealed for more liberal terms, Don Pedro summarily rejected his request.[73]

On the fourth of June 1777 Spanish forces entered Colônia do Sacramento for the fourth time in ninety-seven years. They found the Portuguese garrison drawn up in formal parade, the troops with knapsacks on their backs, their muskets stacked before them, and their officers ready to present their swords to the victors. As the prisoners marched out the rear of the citadel they passed through two rows of triumphant Spanish soldiers to board several transports waiting to take them to Buenos Aires and new hardships.[74]

A better fate was again offered the Portuguese officers. Cevallos promised to let them return to Rio de Janeiro if they pledged not to take up arms against Spain again during the war. When they showed some reluctance in signing, Governor Rocha assured them that the practice was an honorable one, and took pen in hand and affixed his own signature on the relevant documents. Three weeks later the officers sailed, but without the governor, who elected to remain with the prisoners until the war was over, a decision he must have regretted later.[75]

<hr/>

70 Rocha to Lavradio, 1778, cited in n. 59, p. 301.

71 The author of the "Noticia individual" sarcastically comments: "propusieron en 1.° de Junio una capitulación estendida en veintidos artículos arreglados al método de que podría usar el más famoso General de la Europa, despúes de defender por un año vigorosamente la plaza mas fuerte de ella," p. 52.

72 Cevallos to Rocha, June 2, 1777, Lobo, III, 53.

73 Cevallos to Rocha, June 3, 1777, loc. cit.

74 Padre Fernandes de Mesquita wrote that the prisoners from Santa Catarina were sent to Mendoza, while those from Colônia went to Córdova. "Relação," p. 360. The author of the "Noticia individual," however, stated that the Colônia soldiers went to Tucumán (p. 54). Editor Rodolfo Garcia took exception to Varnhagen's statement (História, IV, 204 and n. 108) that the Colônia troops were sent to Mendoza, pointing out that they had gone there in 1762, not in 1777. From Cevallos' memoria, however, it appears that in 1777 the Colônia prisoners went to both places. Radaelli, ed., Memorias de los virreyes. p. 6.

75 Col. Mesquita made it appear that Rocha reached the decision to remain at the last minute; actually the governor wrote the viceroy of his intention to do so in his dispatch of June 8. He gave as his reasons "não seria louvador apresentar-me n'essa capital, deixando ficar aqui toda a tropa prisioneira, sem que ficasse com ella algum official que lhe servisse de despeito e apoio," and that he wanted to encourage their hopes of eventual repatriation. Rocha to Lavradio, Mar. 20, 1778,

Don Pedro de Cevallos entered Colônia on June 5, and had the pleasure of hearing a second Te Deum within less than two months honoring another of his bloodless victories. In accordance with his instructions, the general then ordered the citadel destroyed, an assignment to which his soldiers turned "with much pleasure." Before they were finished, the walls had been blown up by mines, the buildings torn down, and the harbor blocked by sunken ships. The stone, artillery, and munitions were then carried off to Buenos Aires and Montevideo.[76] Within a month and a half all that remained of Portugal's century-old outpost were three small churches.[77]

The destruction of the praça was convincing evidence to the Portuguese officers and civilians who witnessed its demolition of Spain's determination to put an end to the exasperating Colônia problem. As soon as the officers departed for Rio de Janeiro (July 25), the civilians were notified that they were being taken to Buenos Aires. In vain they protested that General Cevallos had already agreed to permit them to return to Portuguese soil. With only the possessions they could carry, they were transported to the new viceregal capital of the Plata, where they discovered that their time of troubles was not yet over.[78]

Cevallos returned to Montevideo on August 4 to lay plans for the recovery of Rio Grande. Early September found him at Fort Santa Teresa ready to plunge into Portuguese territory. It was then that a messenger from General Böhm brought him a royal cédula announc-

---

cited in n. 59. Nonetheless, his decision was considered an act of cowardliness by Col. Mesquita and by Desembargador Silva e Alarcão, who contended that Rocha remained behind only to escape punishment. As will be seen in Appendix II, Rocha returned to Rio de Janeiro after the war and took his punishment.

76 Gálvez to Cevallos, Dec. 10, 1777, *CB*, III, 475, referring to Cevallos' dispatch of Sept. 8, 1777; Fernández y Ortolan, "Relação," 295–296; Padre Fernandes de Mesquita, "Relação," 354; and "Noticia individual," pp. 54–55, which also contains a list of the Portuguese artillery and munitions.

77 A great deal of ink has been split over the morality of the destruction of Colônia. Even Spanish-speaking writers like Francisco Bauzá and Henrique Araña speak of the "enorme error" committed by Cevallos. See Bauzá's *Historia de la dominación espanhola en el Uruguay*, II (Montevideo, 1895), 242–243, and Araña, pp. 20–21; cf. Araña, p. 74, for Rego Monteiro's comment on this point. Considering Spain's frustrating experience with respect to Colônia, this was really the only logical way for her to put an end to the Colônia problem. Whether or not the Spanish Jesuits were the first to suggest the demolition of Colônia—a charge often made, based apparently on a remark of Padre Mesquita in his "Relação"—has never been proved, but the idea was certainly common currency among Spanish leaders since the mid-1760s. See Barba, pp. 195–197, n. 2.

78 Padre Mesquita charged that Spanish sailors stole much property from the helpless Portuguese civilians en route to Buenos Aires, and that when they arrived there Spanish customs insisted on collecting the regular duty of twenty pesos for each slave brought in, in spite of the civilians' insistence that they had no desire to sell their chattels.

ing that an armistice had been signed in Europe.[79] Doubtless the news made Don Pedro unhappy, for it caught him still short of his final goal, the expulsion of the Portuguese from Rio Grande. Good soldier that he was, however, Cevallos handed over command of a standby force to General Vértiz and returned to Montevideo with the rest of his army. After arranging to ship the main part of his expeditionary force back to the Peninsula, Don Pedro crossed the broad Platine estuary and quietly entered Buenos Aires on September 15, 1777. There he devoted his remaining months in America to the establishment of the new viceregal administration.[80] The following June he returned in failing health to Spain, where he died on December 26, 1778. Almost a year later a royal cédula bestowed the title of *marquesa de la Colonia* upon Doña Antonia de Cevallos Cortés y Calderón, in honor of her brother's most important conquest.[81]

---

[79] The "Noticia individual" covers the final phase of the Cevallos campaign in greatest detail (pp. 56–59). In accordance with the usual procedure, the original Spanish order ending hostilities was sent via Portuguese channels, i.e., the viceroy and General Böhm, while the Portuguese order went to Cevallos, who sent it to Böhm to be forwarded to Lavradio. There is evidence that Cevallos was aware of the armistice before leaving Montevideo for Santa Teresa. See Araña, pp. 44–54.

[80] For this phase of Cevallos' activities, see Barba, Chap. XIII.

[81] Cédula of Dec. 5, 1779, printed in Luis Enrique Azarola Gil, *Contribución a la historia de la Colonia del Sacramento*, pp. 230–231.

X

The Trials of Viceroy Lavradio
During the Crisis of 1777

I do not know what the Devil has got into those men, making them think
first of what they should forget, the preservation of their lives [instead of]
the conservation of their honor and that of the State.

Lavradio to Böhm, August 2, 1777

IT REMAINS to consider how the Marquis of Lavradio and his
superiors in Lisbon reacted to the series of humiliating Portuguese
capitulations just described. At no other time during his administration did Lavradio enjoy the freedom of decision that he possessed
during the crisis of 1777. While his superiors had been very explicit as
to the means for repelling the invader, they were so confident that the
Spaniards would be defeated that they did not suggest what might be
done in the event that they had miscalculated. Consequently Dom
Luís was left to improvise strategy for the defense of those parts of
southern Brazil the enemy had not yet attacked and to adopt measures for the recapture of territories that he had seized.

The Viceroy's Reactions to the Loss of Santa
Catarina and Its Garrison

As the hot, sticky month of February gave way to the somewhat cooler
temperatures of March, the viceroy waited expectantly for news of the
Spanish armada. Since February 4, when he learned that Casa Tilly
had left Cádiz,[1] he had had no report on the armada's position, but

---

[1] Strangely enough, Lisbon did not officially notify Lavradio of Cevallos' departure. Apparently the viceroy obtained his information from a merchant vessel
that left Lisbon shortly after news of the armada's sailing was received there.
Antônio Carlos Furtado de Mendonça to Böhm, Feb. 12 and 18, 1777, BNRJ, 13,
4, 9, nos. 65–66 (origs.). The French ambassador to Lisbon reported that the news
of the departure of the Spanish fleet caused no particular concern at Court since
everyone was preoccupied with the serious illness of the king. With evident relish,
he added that the Portuguese would perceive their danger when Cevallos landed
in America. Blosset to Vergennes, Dec. 31, 1776, QE, VIII, 296. Almost casually,

realized that it should already have made an appearance off the coast of Brazil. Finally, on March 6 a messenger brought a dispatch from Field Marshal Antônio Carlos, dated February 20, telling of the arrival of one hundred Spanish ships and of the disappearance of the Portuguese squadron. The same day another horseman brought news from Ilha Grande, the large island between Rio de Janeiro and Santos, that eight unidentified ships had been sighted headed for the capital. While Lavradio pondered whether this meant that Cevallos had split his task force and was sending a division against Rio de Janeiro, coast watchers signaled that six unidentified ships were approaching Guanabara Bay from the south.

At once the dreaded cry "the enemy in sight" was given. As regulars, militiamen, and homeguardsmen hurried through the streets and up the hillsides to their posts, many an oldtimer must have wondered whether Rio was about to suffer her fourth enemy invasion of the century.[2] Would the Cariocas, the Bahians, and the Mineiros stand by their guns and fight off the enemy, or would they panic as had some of their ancestors, and the city again be forced to pay tribute to get rid of unwanted guests?

Apprehensively the defenders watched as two ships passed unchallenged between Forts Santa Cruz and Laje on their way up the bay. The reason why the batteries had failed to speak became apparent as the ships drew nearer, for they turned out to be Portuguese, not Spanish. By the time they had drawn abreast of Villegaignon Island it was evident that Robert MacDouall had returned.

As he watched the ships approach their anchorage off Snakes' Island, the viceroy stared at them in disbelief. Thinking of Antônio Carlos' report of the enemy fleet before Santa Catarina, Lavradio wondered what possible motives could have prompted the commodore to return to the capital at such a critical time. When MacDouall reported and showed the viceroy the written opinions of his captains that it was futile to oppose Casa Tilly with their meager forces, Lavradio fumed. He admonished the commodore that the votes of his colleagues by no means absolved him of his responsibility, and that his cowardly conduct had probably cost Portugal the island. He added that if he had the authority to do so, he would immediately dismiss

---

Secretary Melo e Castro, who had not written Lavradio since Oct. 9, 1776, observed: "Como ao tempo em que esta carta chegar às mãos de V.Ex.a já a dita expedisão terá dado sinal de si. . . ." Melo e Castro to Lavradio, Mar. 28, 1777, BNRJ, I-2, 4, 7, n. 71.

[2] In 1710 a French pirate, Duclerc, successfully attacked the city, but was later shot; partly in retaliation a French privateer, Duguay-Trouin, sacked and levied a heavy tribute upon Rio in 1711. In 1757 a French squadron under command of the Count of Lally forcibly entered the port on its way to the Far East, causing panic and scandal when the commander was lodged in the city while his squadron underwent repairs.

him from his command.[3] MacDouall defended himself both orally and in a vitriolic exchange of letters with the marquis.[4] Ultimately both officers submitted to the Court lengthy briefs defending their views.[5]

Meantime, since the viceroy assumed that after putting up a good fight Antônio Carlos had been obliged to retreat to the mainland, he decided to send the squadron to Laguna or to São Francisco do Sul with 800 to 900 "select" troops to reinforce the field marshal. But the commodore insisted that he could not sail until his ships had been provisioned and had secured new rigging to replace that which had been lost during a storm encountered on the voyage back to Rio de Janeiro. Moreover, he pointed out that two of his ships were still at sea and that two others, the *Ajuda* and the *Graça,* were completely unseaworthy. With evident irritation the viceroy postponed the relief expedition until the missing ships should arrive, and ordered the squadron's needs supplied.[6]

Since he could not immediately send relief to Santa Catarina himself, Lavradio turned to his colleague Martim Lopes Lobo de Saldanha, captain-general of São Paulo, and asked him to rush as many men as he could to the field marshal. He realized that Saldanha's first inclination would be to strengthen the defenses of Santos, but Dom Luís assured him that the Spaniards posed a much greater threat to the border captaincies than to his own port. He asked Saldanha to relay promptly to General Böhm and to him any news he received from Santa Catarina.[7]

Three days after MacDouall's unexpected return to Rio, the viceroy made a cautiously optimistic report to the Court on the military situation. As in subsequent dispatches, he leveled severe criticism at the commodore for shirking his duty, and warned that he would not be surprised if the island fell to the enemy, but only after Antônio Carlos had put up "an exemplary defense" and had retired safely to the mainland. Lavradio hoped to render the enemy's hold on the island precarious by having the squadron cut Cevallos' supply lines to

[3] Lavradio to Manoel da Cunha Menezes, Mar. 7, 1777, *ABNRJ*, XXXII, 347-348, and *idem* to Pombal, Mar. 10, 1777, IHGB/AUC, 1-1-29, fols. 335ᵛ-341ᵛ.

[4] See the exchanges between MacDouall and Lavradio, Mar. 9-16, 1777, *ABNRJ*, XXXII, 359-363.

[5] Lavradio to Pombal, Mar. 10, 1777, cited in n. 3; MacDouall to Melo e Castro, Mar. 31, 1777, *ABNRJ*, XXXII, 355.

[6] "O Dez.r Prov.r da Faz.a R.l mandará dar p.a a Esquadra Naval o Poliame, Massame, Mantimentos, e tudo o mais q. pedirem os Comandantes p.a Conserto . . . e sobrescelentes . . . *de forma q. não possão faltar à execução das ordens com pretexto de q.l.q.r. falta.*" *Portaria* of Mar. 8, 1777, CMCM, cod. 19, fol. 166ʳ (italics added). A *portaria* of Mar. 11 authorized payment of 35,342,370 réis "p.a despezas da Esquadra Naval." *ibid.,* fol. 167ʳ.

[7] Dispatches of Mar. 7 and 9, 1777, *DI*, XVII, 190-196; cf. Saldanha's replies of Mar. 16 and [18], *DI*, XLIII, 195-200.

the Plata, and by assembling a force on the mainland to retake Santa Catarina. He predicted that if General Böhm had attacked Vértiz in the south, as he had been repeatedly enjoined to do, Don Pedro would be unsuccessful in any invasion of Rio Grande. But Lavradio could not resist observing that "if I could be closer to them [i.e., his generals] I would make them do their duty, but since they are so distant from me, each does as his caprice dictates." He ended his remarks on a confident note: if Cevallos did not receive additional reinforcements from Europe, the Portuguese cause would ultimately triumph, for "everyone, from the youngest boy to the oldest man, is prepared to strain every nerve to defend the Fatherland and the credit of the Nation to the last instant of his life." [8]

The ink was scarcely dry on these lines when the viceroy discovered the bitter truth—that the field marshal had abandoned Santa Catarina Island without having offered the enemy the slightest resistance.[9] In reporting the island's fall to Lisbon, Dom Luís professed himself stunned and heartbroken, for he insisted that Antônio Carlos had had sufficient men and supplies to make a determined defense. But Lavradio continued to hope that the field marshal would redeem himself by leading his army to Rio Grande.[10]

As soon as the viceroy learned of the fall of the island, he addressed a series of dispatches to Captains-General Noronha and Saldanha and to General Böhm regarding the defense of Rio Grande.[11] He urged Noronha to send 4,000 recruits to the southern province via São Paulo,[12] and asked the Paulista governor to expedite their passage by

8 Lavradio to Pombal, Mar. 10, 1777, cited in n. 3.

9 A shipmaster brought the initial report on Mar. 13; the following day Mendonça Furtado's dispatch of Feb. 25, stating his reasons for the evacuation, reached the viceroy.

10 Lavradio to Pombal and idem to Melo e Castro, Mar. 19, 1777, IHGB/AUC, 1-1-29, fols. 341ᵛ–346ʳ, 358ᵛ–360ᵛ.

11 In addition Lavradio wrote Manoel da Cunha Menezes, telling him of the fall of Santa Catarina, and asking for the return of the frigate Nazareth and the dispatch of any other vessels that were serviceable for the squadron. Once again Lavradio asked for the military subsidy that Bahia owed Rio de Janeiro.

12 Noronha responded by stating he would send the men as soon as he could round them up. He added: "P.a q. os habitantes desta cap.nia não dezertem p.a os çertoens della mando marchar o d[it]o corpo com o pretexto de q. tem o q. os Castelhanos fazendo na de S. Paulo um dezembarque nos vênhão atacar por q. deste modo será facilm.e conduzido até a Cid.e de S. Paulo." Noronha to Lavradio, Mar. 20, 1777, BNRJ, 2, 2, 24, n. 53. By mid-May he had 4,085 men, only 757 of them armed, en route or about to leave. The majority were "Mulatos, Mestiços, Cabras, e Negros"; the captain-general held back the whites on the pretext that Lavradio might need them later in Rio de Janeiro, but actually because he feared a black uprising if they left. Idem to idem, May 13, 1777, ibid., n. 68. For good reason Noronha said nothing about the quality of the men he was sending. Commenting on the arrival of one detachment, Saldanha wrote: "Todos estes homens vêm inteiramente nús, sem mais que humas seroulas e camiza, com muito poucas armas particulares, e estas desconcertadas. Todos os mais com humas chamadas lanças, que lhe não sei bem dar o nome." To Lavradio, Apr. 23, 1777,

furnishing them with provisions and transportation,[13] and told him to keep General Böhm informed on their progress. He warned the general that it would be some time before the Mineiros could reach him, probably not until after Cevallos had struck his initial blows. However, he minimized the menace posed by the Spanish army, asserting that it had already been weakened by hunger and pestilence. He predicted that Don Pedro would be unable to field more than 5,000 men for an invasion of Rio Grande.[14] The viceroy again recommended that Böhm occupy the pass at Santa Teresa and dispatch Pinto Bandeira to raid Vértiz' supply lines to deprive Cevallos of possible support from the south.[15]

While he was in the midst of preparing these dispatches, a message came to the viceroy from São Sebastião Island reporting that thirty sail had been sighted and were making course for Rio de Janeiro.[16] Once again the alarm was given, and again it proved unnecessary. Instead of "thirty," only three ships appeared before Fort Santa Cruz, and each flew both Spanish and white pennants.[17] Aboard were the parolees from Santa Catarina.[18]

DI, XLII, 245; see also his further comments, *ibid.*, pp. 239, 247, 251–252, 260, 274, and 276.

Neither Böhm nor José Marcelino was prepared to receive the men, and had no use for reinforcements "sem armas, sem vestidos, e sem disciplina." Böhm to Saldanha, June 12, 1777, *DI*, XVII, 324–325; J. M. Figueiredo to *idem*, Apr. 16, May 8, July 13, 1777, ibid., pp. 297, 302, and 308. Learning from the distressed Saldanha that the Mineiros were proving a great burden on the resources and that Böhm did not want them, Lavradio finally authorized the Paulista governor to send the rest home, after approximately half the contingent had gone on to Rio Grande. The story is summarized in Saldanha to Melo e Castro, Aug. 2, 1777, *DI*, XXVIII, 342–344.

13 "V. Ex.a empregará para facilitar a passagem destas Tropas, todas as bestas, gados, e mais cavalgaduras, que tiver essa Capitania, e para que os donos não fújão com ellas, V. Ex.a lhes declarará, que todas as que morrerem, ou se destruírem, lhe serão pagas pelo seu justo valor. . . ." Lavradio to Saldanha, Mar. 13, 1777, *DI*, XVII, 201.

14 The viceroy's mathematics are open to question. He knew from Court estimates and from the dispatches of Antônio Carlos that Cevallos had at least 10,000 men, and he assumed that Don Pedro would leave 3,000 at Santa Catarina. What happened to the other 2,000, he did not say!

15 Lavradio to Böhm, Mar. 13 and 24, 1777, BNRJ, 13-4-3, nos. 28–29 (origs.); *BCRG*, pp. 127–132.

16 The viceroy referred to this report almost casually in his dispatches to the Court of Mar. 19 (see n. 10 above), but curiously never elaborated further on the matter.

17 Lavradio described their approach to the harbor with considerable indignation: "aproveitando-se do vento, que lhe era favorável procuraram entrar sem pedir licença nem fazerem caso de alli haverem fortalezas; a de Sancta Cruz lhe atirou e as fez dar fundo. Lançaram a sua bandeira branca, e não continuaram a vir para dentro." Lavradio to Melo e Castro, Apr. 3, 1777, IHGB/AUC, 1-1-29, fol. 361ʳ. The previous day MacDouall's two missing ships, the *Princeza do Brasil* and the *Belém*, finally made port. They, too, may have been observed by the inhabitants of São Sebastião.

18 Portaria of Apr. 8, 1777, CMCM, cod. 19, fol. 173ʳ, authorizing delivery of

The field marshal sent Pedro Antônio da Gama e Freitas to inform the viceroy of their capitulation and to sound out his mood.[19] But the marquis refused to see any of the Santa Catarina officers, and ordered them confined to the capital's forts until an official investigation of their conduct had been made and reviewed by the king. That investigation began two and a half weeks later, when the last of the parolees arrived and the viceroy assigned a desembargador from the Relação to record the officers' testimony.[20]

A few days earlier the viceroy informed Lisbon what had happened. Enclosing the minutes of the several councils of war, the notarized decision asking Cevallos for terms, and the act of capitulation itself, Dom Luís declared that he was unable to understand how responsible officers could have forgotten all their training and their instructions and have thought only of "saving their lives [while] treading underfoot their honor and that of the Fatherland. . . ."[21] Their conduct was all the more incomprehensible when relief was under way from Rio de Janeiro, São Paulo, and Rio Grande. He failed to note, however, that when the capitulation was signed not a single man of the relief forces was en route to Santa Catarina, and that the defenders had no knowledge that such aid was coming.[22]

First Steps Toward a Portuguese Counteroffensive

Despite the loss of Santa Catarina Island and the ignominious capitulation of its garrison, the viceroy was confident that Portuguese forces

---

provisions "p.a bordo do Navio Castelhano q. está fora da barra e traz os Off.es do Reg.o de S.ta Cathar.a com as mais famílias."

[19] When MacDouall entered port after failing to attack the Casa Tilly armada, he sent Captain Arthur Phillip ashore for the same purpose.

[20] Lavradio to Melo e Castro, Apr. 3, 1777 (cited in n. 17 above), fols. 360ᵛ–364ʳ. Three days after the devassa began, the viceroy suspended it until the arrival of Brigadier José Custódio. Only months later did he realize that the brigadier was not coming, and on August 23 the investigation was resumed. It was completed by November 30. Bernardo de Salazar Sarmento Eça e Alarcão to Lavradio, Nov. 30, 1777, IHGB/AUC, 1-1-29, fols. 443ʳ, 457ᵛ.

[21] Lavradio to Melo e Castro, Apr. 3, 1777, cited in n. 20.

[22] None had left Rio de Janeiro since the squadron was unable to sail until April 1, nearly a month after the capitulation. As for Paulista reinforcements, Captain-General Saldanha reported that by April 20 he had assembled 835 recruits, but added that "Para todo este corpo . . . careço de armamento, se a V. Ex.a parecer deve hir armado [sic!], sem que mando sem elle aquelles soldados que possão tomar as armas que nos regimentos se achão dos mortos e dezertados." Saldanha to Lavradio, Apr. 23, 1777, DI, XLII, 239. The viceroy contended that General Böhm had dispatched Colonel Pinto Bandeira under forced march to Laguna with "mil e duzentos homens"; in fact, only sixteen men reached that port, arriving on April 15, forty days after the capitulation. Alcides Cruz, A Vida de Rafael Pinto Bandeira (Pôrto Alegre, 1906), p. 77.

could recover the island from the Spaniards. In formulating plans to do so, he counted especially upon the assistance of Martim Lopes Lobo de Saldanha, captain-general of São Paulo, since his captaincy was centrally located with respect to Rio de Janeiro, Santa Catarina, and Rio Grande.[23] Throughout 1777 Lavradio sent him money, munitions, and other supplies to strengthen his own defenses and to forward to General Böhm, since Spanish warships menaced the sea route between Rio de Janeiro and Rio Grande. In a rare move for the colonial era, the marquis urged Saldanha to put aside all questions of jurisdictional "etiquette," and to issue whatever orders were necessary for the protection of mainland Santa Catarina.[24] He also suggested that the captain-general send scouts to the coast opposite the Spanish-held island to gather intelligence and to establish contact with his own agents there.[25]

The viceroy realized that the proximity of large Spanish forces would be a source of major concern to Saldanha, and emphasized that the best defense of São Paulo lay in the preservation of Rio Grande. He conceded that it was possible that the Spaniards might try to occupy the port of Santos, but insisted that even if they succeeded in doing so, their advance from the coast to the plateau could easily be thwarted by a few strategically placed guards to deny them access to key passes over the Serra do Mar.[26] He thanked Saldanha for having already sent several militia companies to the town of Lajes on the plateau in southern Santa Catarina, and asked him to raise an additional 2,000 to 3,000 men to serve as a reserve for General Böhm. Sensing the need to revitalize the martial ardor of the Paulistas, the viceroy contrived the following tale which he recommended Saldanha read to influential persons in his captaincy:

[23] "A capitania de que V. Ex.a hé General hé certo ser hoje aquella, que está mais bem situada para soccorrer a todos os nossos estabelecimentos do Sul. . . ." Lavradio to Saldanha, Apr. 9/11, 1777, DI, XVII, 212; cf. Saldanha to Lavradio, Mar. 29, 1777, DI, XLII, 213.

[24] Lavradio to Saldanha, Apr. 9/11 and 28, 1777, DI, XVII, 211–224, 242; idem to câmara of São Francisco do Sul, May 2, 1777, CMCM, cod. 25, fol. 183ʳ, ordering it to honor instructions from Saldanha.

[25] One of the men upon whom Lavradio depended for information was José Rebello, a rancher and militia captain who lived on a sítio in Garoupas Bay. Apparently he and his son attempted to extort money for transporting the Santa Catarina troops ashore in their boat on Feb. 25, 1777. When the refugees reached São Paulo they had their revenge, however, and convinced Saldanha that Rebello was a quisling who had showed the enemy where the "mines" were located and had forced the Portuguese to render allegiance to the Spanish on pain of killing them. Incensed, the captain-general sent a fifty-man patrol (!) to seize Rebello, his son, and his slaves. Saldanha to Lavradio, May 5, 1777, DI, XLII, 256–257; idem to Melo e Castro, May 12, 1777, DI, XXVIII, 337–339; idem to Böhm, June 4, 1777, and to José Marcelino de Figueiredo, June 5, 1777, DI, XLII, 279–280, 284. This proved to be Saldanha's only positive contribution to the recovery of Santa Catarina.

[26] Lavradio to Saldanha, Mar. 20 and Apr. 9/11, 1777, DI, XVII, 204–205; 215–216.

It appears to me very fitting that Your Excellency make known to all the honorable Paulistas . . . that the Castilians say their most ardent desires are to avenge themselves against the Paulistas. . . . They are of the opinion that the Paulistas of today no longer possess the same valor and resolution of their ancestors; that they enjoy living more agreeably, and no longer expose themselves to the hardships and discomforts that their grandparents experienced. . . . Although [the Spaniards] promise to treat them with charity, they really intend to kill with the greatest cruelty all who fall into their hands.[27]

The viceroy also discoursed on another subject that had occasioned sharp disagreement between himself and Luís Antônio de Sousa, Saldanha's predecessor—the merits of preserving the remote frontier outpost of Iguatemí.[28] Though Saldanha regarded the retention of that fort as a useless drain on his limited reserves of men, money, and matériel,[29] Lavradio contended that it ought to be maintained, since it represented a threat to the Spaniards in Paraguay.[30] Saldanha, who was far more subservient to the viceroy than Sousa had ever been, yielded to Lavradio's advice but could not prevent the Spaniards from capturing and destroying the fort at the end of the war.[31]

Meanwhile, on April 1, MacDouall's squadron finally left Rio de Janeiro for its only successful war patrol. Lavradio ordered the commodore, whose force consisted of three naus and three frigates,[32] to prevent supplies from reaching Santa Catarina Island and to protect the ports of southern Brazil from attack. Soon after reaching the vicinity of Santa Catarina, MacDouall's lookouts sighted a Spanish saetía escorting several transports. In the chase which followed the transports got away, but the escort, the eight-gun Santa Anna, was brought to bay.[33] Her crew told their captors that a large supply convoy protected by two ships of the line and a frigate was due to arrive at Santa Catarina from Montevideo. The commodore decided to prepare a reception for them.

27 Lavradio to Saldanha, Mar. 26, 1777, ibid., p. 209.

28 See pp. 463–469, below.

29 Saldanha to Lavradio, Mar. 29, 1777, DI, XLII, 215–216.

30 Lavradio to Saldanha, Apr. 9/11, 1777, DI, XVII, 217–218; Saldanha to Lavradio, Apr. 20, 1777, DI, XLII, 241–242.

31 The presídio was overrun by "3,000" Spaniards on October 27, 1777, allegedly after the governor of Paraguay had already received news that the war was officially over. Saldanha to Martinho de Melo e Castro, Jan. 6, 1778, DI, XXVIII, 351–354; idem to Lavradio, Jan. 5, 1778, DI, XLIII, 123–126.

32 The ships were naus Santa Antônio, Belém, and Prazeres; frigates Príncipe do Brasil, Princeza do Brasil, and Pilar. Frigate Nazareth was still at Bahia, while frigate Graça and nau Ajuda were undergoing refitting at Rio de Janeiro.

33 From the sources cited in the following note it is clear that she was the same saetía that Casa Tilly had left behind at Trindade Is. to direct stragglers to Santa Catarina. See above, p. 226.

Five days later a single large warship appeared on the horizon just before dusk. MacDouall immediately ordered a general chase, led by the nau *Prazeres* and the frigates *Princeza do Brasil* and *Pilar,* the fastest ships in the squadron. As darkness fell, the pursuers and the pursued disappeared into the night; nor could MacDouall find his ships or the unknown vessel the next day. But that evening he heard gunfire, and conned his remaining ships toward its source. Early the following morning (April 21) he came upon a Spanish warship and the *Prazeres,* whose captain, José de Melo, had doggedly remained with his opponent after she had outdistanced his sister ships. Maneuvering the *Santo Antônio* ahead of the Spaniard, the commodore engaged her in a brisk duel lasting an hour and a quarter. Finally, after seeing the rest of the squadron closing in on him, the Spaniard hauled down his flag.[34]

The prisoner proved to the the *San Agustin,* a well-built seventygun ship of the line manned by 550 men. She was on her maiden voyage, having left Spain in December, 1776, to take a supply convoy to Montevideo. There she was assigned to escort another convoy to Santa Catarina. MacDouall claimed, and for once Lavradio agreed with him, that she was a better built craft than any ship in the Portuguese navy. Her capture turned out to be the one bright spot in an otherwise disastrous year for Lusitanian fortunes.

The capture of the second prize induced the commodore to cut short his cruise and return to Rio de Janeiro. Both his flagship and the *San Agustin* had suffered superficial damage, but a more serious handicap was the problem of guarding several hundred prisoners in the event of further engagements with the enemy.[35] After a round trip of twenty-six days, the squadron reentered Guanabara Bay.[36]

---

[34] During the action the *Santo Antônio* suffered fourteen wounded, while the Spanish had four dead and twenty-four wounded, some of whom died subsequently. MacDouall to Lavradio, April 26, 1777, cited in n. 36 below.

[35] Lavradio first considered sending "mais de 800 prizioneiros" from the two captured ships to Bahia, and to have them kept in the "villas do sertão." Lavradio to Cunha Menezes, May 5, 1777, cited in n. 36 below. Instead, however, he quartered them on the island of Enxadas in Guanabara Bay and set them to work on the fortifications of São João and Villegaignon. Portarias of April 30, June 11, and July 23, 1777, CMCM, cod. 19, fols. 179ʳ, 188ᵛ, and 199ᵛ. When the Spanish commander of the *San Agustin* wrote a petition asking better treatment for his men, the viceroy tartly replied that the prisoners "são tratados com a maior humanid.e e muito diferentem.e do q. o são os Portuguezes q. p.r desgraça teverão a infelic[idad]e de ficarem Prizioneiros entre os Castelhanos, e como VS se não acha constituído p.a poder requererme a respeito delles, se absterá q. lhe do o fazer, e continuando a practicar o mesmo, pode estar certo que lhe não darei mais outra resposta." To Sr. D. Jozé Fechain, Nov. 5, 1777, CMCM, cod. 25, fol. 218ʳ.

[36] The cruise is described in MacDonall [sic] to Lavradio, Apr. 26, 1777, *ABNRJ* XXXII, 353–354, which differs in detail and in emphasis from Lavradio to Melo e Castro, June 2, 1777, IHGB/AUC, 1-1-29, fols. 411ᵛ–418ᵛ; *idem* to Böhm, June 4, 1777, BNRJ, 13, 4, 3, n. 30 (orig.) [*BCRG,* pp. 132–138]; and *idem* to [Manoel da Cunha Menezes], May 5, 1777, *ABNRJ,* XXXII, 366–367.

The viceroy was jubilant about the capture of such a fine ship as the *San Agustín,* but while lavish in his praise of Captain José de Melo, he had only criticism for the commodore. Lavradio insisted that MacDouall should have remained at Santa Catarina to destroy the Spanish fleet instead of finding lame excuses to return to the capital.[37]

Smarting under the viceroy's ingratitude, MacDouall wrote to his patron, Secretary Melo e Castro, and again asked to be relieved of his command or to be dismissed from the royal service. He preferred "slavery in Barbary to the indignities I have suffered in this confused town of Rio de Janeiro," and lamented having to serve "under the direction of one who has little naval experience." He protested that he could not challenge Casa Tilly openly without risking "not only the loss of this small squadron, but of all Brazil." If only he had two additional ships of the line, he boasted grandly, he would be able to settle accounts with the Spanish squadron "and consequently take all the east coast of [South] America."[38]

In spite of his grievances, MacDouall was still in command when his squadron left (May 31) on its next patrol. For that occasion the viceroy provided his piqued subordinate with the largest force ever assembled under his command: five naus, including the new *"São Agostinho,"* and four frigates, with a total complement of 3,600 men. As before, the commodore's instructions were to prevent supplies from reaching Santa Catarina and to destroy enemy shipping within its port.

The squadron's mission was part of a general effort by which the viceroy hoped to liberate Santa Catarina. He also wrote to loyalists in the occupied territory to kidnap or suborn enemy guards and to burn the Spaniards' warehouses. By such harassment he hoped to undermine the enemy's morale so that the Spaniards would quickly succumb to a Portuguese counterinvasion.[39]

Bad News from the Court

The day the squadron sailed the frigate *São João Baptista* entered port bearing news that Dom José I was dead and had been succeeded

---

[37] See n. 36 above.

[38] MacDonall [sic] to Melo e Castro, May 6, 1777, *ABNRJ,* XXXII, 353. In a PS in English, he wrote "As a man of honor I have ever served his Majesty, has [sic] and ever shall fight [text says fright] like an English officer, but can suffer no insults any longer. I beg your Excl. will consider my case[. T]he Real Service does not go on as it should do and I can not mend it; as my friend, pity, doing my duty in spite of envey and supporting myself again[st] intrig[ues]."

[39] See sources in n. 36, and Lavradio to Saldanha, June 20, 1777, *DI,* XVII, 359.

by his daughter Maria I. The new sovereign proclaimed the usual period of mourning for her late father, six months rigorous and six months light.[40] Lavradio immediately closed all government offices for three days [41] and ordered the forts and warships in Guanabara Bay to discharge salvos in honor of the memory of their former ruler.[42]

As he attended funeral services for the departed sovereign,[43] the viceroy must have pondered the implications of a terse statement in one of the dispatches he had just received. Wrote Colonial Secretary Martinho de Melo e Castro, "The Marquis of Pombal, having obtained permission from the Queen Our Lady to resign from all his posts, left for his estate of Pombal, where he is at present." [44] The announcement was remarkably brief, but its meaning was very clear. Before the royal cadaver of Dom José was cold, his chief minister had been dismissed and banished from Court. Thus had come to an end the public career of the man who had ruled Portugal and her empire for a generation, the one who bore the real responsibility for Portugal's present involvement in an unfruitful war with Spain.

One would very much like to know how Dom Luís reacted to the news of the fall of his old patron. Only recently he had written Pombal, "I hope that Your Excellency, who has always been my patron, and whom I have served, notwithstanding my repeated protests of the lack of my talents, will now stand by me and aid me with what I need to win that glory for the State and Nation which is my only interest." [45] Yet in reporting the retirement of his chief to a subordinate, the viceroy did not betray the slightest emotion or suggestion of his true feelings.[46] Still he must have been uneasy, wondering how the new ministry [47] would evaluate his responsibility for the humili-

[40] Martinho de Melo e Castro to Lavradio, Feb. 25 and Mar. 28, 1777, BNRJ, I-2, 4, 7, nos. 73 and 86.

[41] Lavradio to various department heads, May 30, 1777, CMCM, cod. 25, fols. 187ᵛ-188ʳ. The treasurer of ordinary expenses (despezas miudas) was authorized to expend 661,666 réis for mourning clothes for government officials. Portaria of May 30, 1777, ibid., cod. 19, fol. 186ʳ.

[42] Fort São João expended thirty arrobas of powder "no Funeral de S.M."; Villegaignon, twenty; Santa Cruz, thirteen; and the small warships and hulks in the harbor unspecified amounts. Portarias of June 5, July 23, and Sept. 17, 1777. CMCM, cod. 19, fols. 186ʳ, 187ᵛ, 199ᵛ, and 211ᵛ.

[43] Details on the funeral observances in Rio are lacking, but in Salvador the captain-general reported: "Na Cathedral dessa Metrópole se eirgiu o mausoléo para as exéquias funeraes officiadas no dia 28 do passado mez, com a pompa e magnificência devida é tão relevante assumpto, pelo q.l determinei também, q. fosse o luto por tempo de hum anno, seis mezes rigoroso e seis alliviado." Manoel da Cunha Menezes to Melo e Castro, Aug. 1, 1777, ABNRJ, XXXII, 381.

[44] Dispatch of Mar. 28, 1777, cited in n. 40 above.

[45] Dispatch of Mar. 19, 1777, cited n. 10 above.

[46] E.g., Lavradio to Böhm, June 4, 1777, cited in n. 36 above.

[47] The Visconde da Villanova da Cerveira (Marquis of Ponte de Lima) became the new Secretary of Negócios do Reino, while the Marquis of Angeja succeeded

ating loss of Santa Catarina and for the probable fall of Colônia do Sacramento as well; for although Lavradio did not learn of the latter's capitulation until August 1, he certainly expected its surrender. Eagerly as he looked forward to his retirement, Lavradio did not want to be sent home in chains, as was the fate of the first viceroy of Brazil, the Marquis of Montalvo—all the more reason for achieving the recovery of Santa Catarina before a peace treaty was signed. Unfortunately Lavradio's hopes of accomplishing that objective were considerably dimmed by a singular naval "battle" fought by MacDouall's squadron.

The Naval "Action" of June 12, 1777

MacDouall's new misadventure occurred on his next patrol. While the squadron was near Laguna, the commodore sent Captain José de Melo in the *Prazeres* to land an agent near the port to obtain information about the disposition of Spanish naval units in the area. After completing his mission Melo was instructed to rendezvous with the rest of the squadron a few miles east of Laguna. When the *Prazeres* failed to appear on schedule, the commodore sent the *Ajuda,* whose captain was Dom Francisco Teles, to hunt for her.

A short time later, Teles sighted a strange vessel ahead. Because of the distance and the fact that it was already dusk, he failed to recognize her as the *Prazeres*. The captain signaled to the still visible squadron that he had sighted an unfamiliar ship. As he approached the *Ajuda,* José de Melo was also puzzled, for instead of a single vessel, he had expected to meet the entire squadron. Owing to the poor light, he failed to see either the recognition pennant flown by the *Ajuda* or her identification lanterns.

As night fell, the captain of the *Prazeres* ordered a lantern hung from his top gallants to recall his first lieutenant from the beach. Since this signal was unfamiliar to Francisco Teles, his suspicions

Pombal as president of the Real Erário. Of Cerveira, Jacome Ratton wrote: "era homem de grande erudição em sciências theológicas, muito timorato, incapaz de fazer mal com conhecimento de cauza, extrememente devoto . . . mas pouco, ou nada instruído em matérias políticas, econômicas, e de hum carácter tão irresoluto que não era capaz por si só de deliberar cousa alguma. . . ." *Recordacoens,* pp. 330–333. His opinion of Angeja was no higher: "Não me consta, que durante a administração do Marquez d'Angeja houvesse melhoramento algum na arrecadação das rendas Reaes, antes foi voz pública, que depois do seu falecimento, o Erário se achava bem desfalcado nas somas, que deixara o seu antecessor." *Ibid.,* p. 329. Surviving the fall of Pombal were Ayres de Sá e Melo, Minister of Foreign Affairs since 1775, and Melo e Castro, who now really came into his own as colonial minister. As soon as he learned of the ministerial changes, Lavradio began preparing a long summary of his administration for the benefit of his new masters. Parts of it, under the date June 20, 1777, are quoted in *VRL, passim.*

1. Execution of José Maria de Tavora,
Lisbon, January 1759

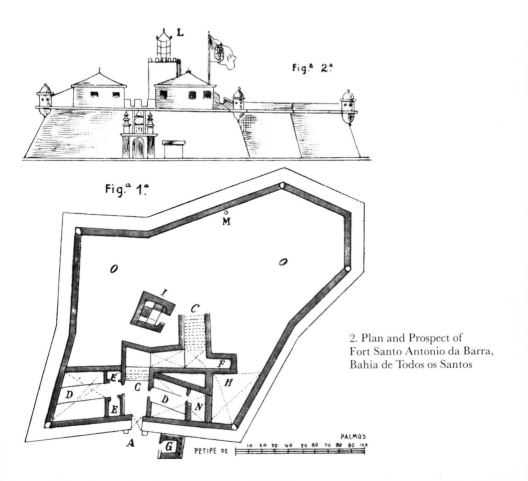

Fig.ª 2.ª

Fig.ª 1.ª

2. Plan and Prospect of
Fort Santo Antonio da Barra,
Bahia de Todos os Santos

PALMOS
10 20 30 40 50 60 70 80 90 100
PETIPE DE

3. Palace Square,
Rio de Janeiro,
1808

4. Procession of the Host
Passing the Carmelite Church,
from the Palace Square
Toward Rua Direita

5. Downtown Rio de Janeiro
in the Time of the Viceroys

6. Media of Transport
in Rio de Janeiro During the
Era of the Viceroys

7. Prospect of a Portion
of the City of Salvador,
ca. 1802

S.ᵗᵃ Catarina 15 Janⁱ 1778

Honrado Marquez do Lavradio do Meu Conselho, e do de
Guerra, Vice Rey, e Capitão General de Mar, e Terra do Estado do Brazil. Eu A Raynha vos invio muito saudar como
aquelle que prezo: Attendendo ao que participastes pela
vossa Carta de tres de Out.ᵇ do anno proximo passado da
innocencia com que se achava o Sargento Mór, que fora
do Regimento de Infanteria da Ilha de Santa Catherina
Pedro da Costa Marim, a quem se dera baixa, e se achava
prezo nessa Cidade: Fui servida despachallo no Posto de The-
nente Coronel de Infanteria, para com o d.ᵒ Posto lograr o
Soldo, que a elle compete em qualquer parte, que lhe parecer:
E Hey por bem o mandeis logo soltar, e lhe participeis o dito
Despacho, mandandolhe pagar os seus Soldos de Sargento
Mór desde o dia em que se lhe deo baixa athé a data da
Patente, que se lhe deverá passar pelo Conselho Ultrama-
rino. O que vos participo, para que assim o façaes executar. Escripta no Palacio de N. Sr.ᵃ da Ajuda em 15
de Janⁱ de 1778 // Raynha //

8. Copy of an Order
from the Queen to Viceroy Lavradio,
1778

Dom Luiz de Almeida Portugal Soares Alarcão Eça Mello Silva e Mascarenhas, Marquez do Lavradio, do
Conselho d'El Rey, Meo Senhor Fidelissimo, Marechal de Campo dos seos Exercitos, Vice-Rey, e Capitão General de Mar, e
Terra do Estado do Brazil &.ª Faço saber por que esta minha Carta Patente virem, que sendo conveniente ao serviço d'El Rey
Meo Senhor promover os postos vagos do Regimento de Infantaria da Ilha de S. Catharina, na forma do Novo Regulamento,
em Officiaes benemeritos, e tendo consideração aos merecimentos, e mais partes de Jose Rodrigues Pereira, e a achar-se servindo no
posto de Tenente no mesmo Regimento, e esperar delle continuará o Real serviço, na mesma forma, que o tem feito até o presente: Hey por bem nomear, e prover, como por esta o faço, ao dito Jose Rodrigues Pereira, em virtude da Ordem d'El Rey
Meo Senhor de tres de Setembro de mil sete centos sesenta e este, no posto de Capitão do Regimento de Infantaria da Ilha de
S. Catharina, que vagou por promoção de Simão Rodrigues, que o era, para o Governo da Fortaleza de S. Jose da Ponta grossa
da barra da mesma Ilha, com o qual posto haverá o Soldo, que lhe tocar, pago na forma das Reaes Ordens, de que se lhe formará assento nas partes, a que tocar, e será obrigado a requerer ao sobredito Senhor Patente de Confirmação pelo seu Conselho Ultramarino, e gozará de todas as honras, privilegios, liberdades, izençoes, e franquezas, que em razão delle lhe pertencerem. E o que
ordeno aos Officiaes, e Soldados seos subordinados, lhe obedeção, cumprão, e guardem suas Ordens, por escrito, e de palavra,
como devem, e são obrigados no que tocar ao Real serviço. E por firmeza de tudo lhe mandei passar a presente por mim
assignada, sellada com o Sinete de minhas Armas, que se cumprirá, como nella se conthem, e se regulará nesta Secretaria do Estado, e mais partes, a que tocar, e se passou por duas vias. Dada nesta Cidade de S. Sebastião, Rio de Janeiro. Jose Pereira Leão a fez aos seis de Junho de mil sete centos setenta e tres. O Secretario do Estado Francisco de
Almeida e Figueiredo a fez escrever.

Marquez do Lavradio

Patente porque V.ª Ex.ª há por bem nomear, e prover, a Jose Rodrigues Pereira no posto de Capitão do Regimento
de Infantaria da Ilha de S. Catharina, que vagou por promoção de Simão Rodrigues, que o era, para o Governo
da Fortaleza de S. Jose da Ponta grossa da barra da mesma Ilha, na forma, que acima se declara.

Para V.ª Ex.ª ver.

9. Patent Signed by
the Marquis of Lavradio,
1773

10. Uniforms of an Enlisted Man (left)
and an Officer (right) in
First Line Regiment, Bahia, *ca.* 1802.
The enlisted man is wearing blue breeches
and a blue coat with black epaulets
trimmed in gold and a hat piped
in yellow with a touch of white thistle
trimmed in red; the officer is wearing
white breeches, a blue coat with cream facings
and gold-worked epaulets, a scarlet sash,
and a hat piped in orange
with a head of grain;
both are wearing white stockings
and half boots.

11. Uniforms of an Enlisted Man (left)
and an Officer (right) in the
Henrique Dias Militia Regiment, Bahia,
ca. 1802. Both men are wearing
half boots, white stockings and breeches,
white coats faced and lined in scarlet
with white lace cuffs. The enlisted man
also wears a yellow cross belt,
and both have plain gold epaulets
and hats trimmed with orange piping
and a flowered device.

concerning the mystery vessel increased. When the two vessels drew within hailing distance, each captain asked the other to identify himself. The captain of the *Ajuda* thereupon resorted to a ruse that was to have fatal consequences. Answering in Spanish, he said that he was the *Santa Teresa* out of Montevideo. Not to be outdone, José de Melo, also speaking Spanish, said that he was from the Marquis of Casa Tilly's squadron, and that he had just encountered the Portuguese fleet cruising off the southern end of Santa Catarina Island.

That was enough for Francisco Teles, who ordered his gunners to open fire. José de Melo promptly returned a broadside of his own, catching the *Ajuda* as she was turning about, a maneuver that revealed three lanterns burning on her stern instead of the usual one. This unfamiliar sign was sufficient to convince José de Melo that he, too, was fighting the enemy!

Matters soon took a serious turn. Perceiving that his helmsman was bearing away from the *Prazeres,* Captain Teles grasped the wheel himself, being determined to bring his adversary to quarter. Just after he had taken the helm, a ball from the *Prazeres* shattered his leg and killed a sailor standing next to him. As Teles was carried below to surgery, he issued orders to stay with the enemy. After his leg had been amputated, he reappeared on deck and, while publicly confessing his sins, continued to conn his ship until death overtook him.

Meanwhile the commodore hastened to the scene, guided by the flashes and the sound of the guns, and boldly steered between the two unknown combatants. Although the *Santo Antônio* displayed her recognition lights, they went undetected by the duelists. Thinking himself attacked by another enemy vessel, José de Melo blazed away at the flagship, which promptly returned the fire. Suddenly Melo discerned the outlines of the flagship from the flashes of her cannon and ordered his crew to cease fire. Calling across the water, the captain of the *Prazeres* identified himself and told MacDouall that the enemy was the ship to the windward bearing three stern lights. As the rest of the squadron closed in on the unfortunate *Ajuda,* fire broke out on the deck of the *Santo Antônio,* setting off ammunition and wounding or burning forty seamen, some of them so severely that they later died. With the coming of dawn, the "action" was finally broken off.[48]

Having provisioned the squadron for three months, the viceroy was

48 The most extensive account of the melee is Lavradio to [Vila Nova da Cerveira], Aug. 25 [1777], *VRL*, pp. 114–118. See also *idem* to Melo e Castro, June 30, 1777, IHGB/AUC, 1-1-29, fols. 421ʳ–424ᵛ, and *idem* to Saldanha, Aug. 3/5, 1777, *DI*, XVII, 260–270. MacDouall's own report is unfortunately lacking. A version in which nearly every fact is given incorrectly, to the point of antedating the affair by six months, has been republished by Lucas Boiteux from a pamphlet entitled "A inadvertência," written by Portuguese Contr' Almirante Celestino Soares. See *Notas para a história catharinense* (Florianópolis [1912]), pp. 261–265.

understandably surprised to see it slipping through the dark blue waters of Guanabara Bay after having spent scarcely a month at sea. When he learned the reason for MacDouall's unscheduled return, Lavradio threw up his hands in utter disgust. He protested that his heart was unable to withstand "such extraordinary blows" as the blunders committed by Robert MacDouall and his officers who were, he was convinced, deliberately chosen for "the punishment of my sins." [49] There would soon be further disappointments.

Arrival of the Colônia Officers

On August 1 the first of the officers from Colônia reached the capital.[50] Lavradio was really not surprised to see them, but he was shocked to hear that Governor Rocha, one of his most trusted subordinates, had not defended his post before surrendering it to the Spaniards. He insisted (wrongly) that the governor had provisions sufficient to last until September or October.[51] But even if the viceroy's contention had been correct, he failed to indicate how the outcome of the Spanish siege might have been different, for since the arrival of the Cevallos expedition in America Lavradio had taken no steps to relieve the Platine outpost.

In reporting the loss of Colônia to Lisbon, Dom Luís found a new opportunity to dwell upon one of his persisting grievances, the Court's refusal to permit him to visit the borderlands to direct their defense himself. Without specifically mentioning the Crown's latest rejection of his request for license to do so,[52] the marquis pointedly observed that his rival, Don Pedro de Cevallos, had been allowed to conduct his campaign personally and had triumphed despite the obstacles raised by the Marquis of Casa Tilly and Juan José de Vértiz. Wearily, Lavradio declared that he was tired of issuing positive orders to spineless subordinates and of furnishing them with all the supplies

---

49 Lavradio to [Vila Nova da Cerveira], Aug. 25 [1777], cited in n. 48.

50 The first two of four Spanish ships bringing the returnees arrived on this day, the others having become separated in a storm. Though the Colônia officers were apparently not imprisoned like their Santa Catarina brothers, Colonel Mesquita complained that "chegando a esta Cid.e elles se vírão privados dos seus soldos, e de todo o subsídio; e cúbertos de hú oprobrio universal; até se lhe inibio a honra de aparecerem na salla [do Vice-rei]. Elles não se atrevião mesmo a andar na rua os primr.os dias, nem sahírão ao menos em q.to não tiverão a certeza q. o público de toda a ordem, não obstante, estas demonstraçoens, estava persuadido de sua innocência, e até se compadecia dos seus infortúnios." Mesquita to Lavradio, ca. 1778, Jônatas da Costa Rego Monteiro, A Colônia do Sacramento, II, 171. The Colônia devassa was opened during the month of August, 1777, and was completed by early December.

51 Lavradio to Melo e Castro, Aug. 4, 1777, IHGB/AUC, 1-1-29, fols. 425ʳ-428ᵛ; idem to Saldanha, Aug. 3/5, 1777, DI, XVII, 262–263.

52 Melo e Castro to Lavradio, Mar. 28, 1777, BNRJ, I-2, 4, 7, n. 71.

they requested, only to see his instructions ignored and the matérial go unused.[53] He could not understand "what the Devil has got into these men, making them think first of what they should forget, the preservation of their lives, [instead of] the conservation of their honor and that of the State." God grant that the generals in Rio Grande conduct themselves more honorably.[54]

Cevallos' easy conquest of Colônia convinced the viceroy that Don Pedro would soon make a second attempt to recapture Rio Grande. He predicted that the Spanish would launch simultaneous land attacks upon the Rio Pardo salient and the vila (Rio Grande), while invading the Lagoa dos Patos from the sea.[55] He estimated that General Böhm had sufficient troops to meet these attacks, but he ordered Captain-General Saldanha to keep a standby force at Lajes. Taking advantage of a report that the Spanish squadron had left Santa Catarina for the Plata, Lavradio sent a number of smacks to Rio Grande to replenish Böhm's dwindling stocks of food, munitions, and clothing.[56] In addition, he instructed Saldanha to send to the southern captaincy all the cattle and provisions he could spare.[57]

Captain-General Saldanha was also involved in a scheme the viceroy devised for the reconquest of Santa Catarina Island. He judged the time ripe for such an effort because of reports that the Spanish garrison was experiencing serious shortages of provisions and was beginning to desert in considerable numbers. Early in August the marquis unfolded his "almost infallible" plan to Saldanha, whom he asked to take charge of the island's invasion.[58] He directed the captain-general to assemble as quietly as possible as many men as he could, and to march them to concealed positions on the mainland opposite the island. While the Paulistas stood poised, MacDouall's squadron would cruise off the island making threatening gestures so as to induce the enemy to try to cover all possible invasion points. Since the Spaniards reportedly had fewer than 3,000 men on Santa Catarina, the viceroy contended that there would be many weak points in their defenses. These Saldanha's forces could invest one by

53 Lavradio to Melo e Castro, Aug. 4, 1777, cited in n. 51 above.

54 Lavradio to Böhm, Aug. 2, 1777, BNRJ, 13, 4, 3, n. 35 (orig.); BCRG, pp. 138–142.

55 Lavradio to Saldanha, Aug. 3/5, 1777, cited in n. 51 above.

56 The first four smacks to bring supplies from the capital since the invasion of Santa Catarina arrived July 1, 1777, "without having met any Spanish ship." Four more vessels reached Rio Grande early in September. Böhm to Saldanha, July 16, and Sept. 1, 1777, DI, XVII, 328–329, 332.

57 Thus reversing the usual pattern of livestock movements. Why Lavradio believed Rio Grande short on cattle, he did not say. Lavradio to Saldanha, Aug. 3/5 1777, ibid., p. 265.

58 The viceroy prefaced his remarks by saying that he would like to direct the operation himself, but since the Court denied him that privilege and since Saldanha possessed the unusual talents necessary for such an undertaking, he was asking the captain-general to serve in his stead.

one until the enemy's remaining defenses crumbled and the Portuguese again became masters of the island.[59]

Whether such an invasion stood any real chance of success, particularly under Saldanha's questionable leadership,[60] may be seriously doubted. In any case, the viceroy was obliged to call off the proposed operation almost immediately. A few days after outlining his plan to Saldanha, Dom Luís received dispatches from the Court announcing the signing of a truce with Spain, and directing him to notify all authorities in Brazil to suspend hostilities.[61] Lavradio complied at once,[62] but assured the colonial secretary that in the event that the negotiations broke down, he was prepared to drive the Spaniards from Santa Catarina Island.[63] Significantly, he did not make the same promise with respect to Colônia do Sacramento.

During the ensuing months the viceroy expressed doubts whether a peace treaty would actually be signed. With no knowledge concerning the critical situation that England faced in her mainland colonies, Lavradio was persuaded that Great Britain would surely come to Portugal's aid before letting her ally become bound by an agreement that was almost certain to be adverse to British interests.[64] Possibly Dom Luís hoped that the war would be resumed, at least until he could clear the stain upon his record by regaining Santa Catarina Island, although the critical condition of his branch of the exchequer suggests that he must have welcomed an end to heavy military and naval expenditures.[65] In January 1778, when the viceroy received copies of the Treaty of San Ildefonso [66] he forwarded them to his col-

---

[59] Lavradio to Saldanha, Aug. 3/5, 1777, DI, XVII, 266–270.

[60] The editor of Saldanha's correspondence in the Documentos interessantes series acidly observed: "Martim Lopes não era homem para emprezas desta ordem." In reply to the viceroy's instructions, Saldanha indicated that he had no money to equip the 3,000 to 4,000 men Lavradio had estimated would be necessary for the invasion, and gave no indication that he was really interested in conducting it. Saldanha to Lavradio, Aug. 12, 1777, DI, XLIII, 93.

[61] Carta régia, June 5, 1777; Melo e Castro to Lavradio, June 16, 1777, BNRJ, I-2, 4, 7, nos. 74–75.

[62] Lavradio to Böhm, Aug. 10, 1777, enclosing the Spanish royal cédula and a personal letter addressed to Don Pedro de Cevallos, BNRJ, 13, 4, 3, nos. 36 (orig.) and 40 (signed copy); idem to MacDouall, Aug. 11, 1777, CMCM, cod. 25, fol. 82^r; circular to the mestres de campo of the captaincy of Rio de Janeiro, Aug. 11, 1777, ibid., cod. 25. fol. 198^r; idem to Melo e Castro, Aug. 11, 1777, IHGB/AUC, 1-1-29, fols. 428^v–429^v, indicating that Lavradio had written to the captains-general of São Paulo, Bahia, Goiás, Minas Gerais, and Pernambuco. For the text of his message to Saldanha (Aug. 11, 1777), see DI, XVII, 270–271.

[63] Lavradio to Melo e Castro, Aug. 15, 1777, IHGB/AUC, 1-1-29, fols. 429^v–431^v.

[64] Lavradio to Böhm, Nov. 4, 1777, BNRJ, 13, 4, 3, n. 42 (orig.); BCRG, pp. 144–148.

[65] See Chap. XII.

[66] Carta régia, Oct. 11, 1777, BNRJ, I-2, 4, 7, n. 79, enclosing the treaty's text and ordering its implementation. Both reached the viceroy on January 21, 1778. Lavradio to Böhm, Jan. 23, 1778, BNRJ. 13, 4, 3, n. 44 (orig.); BCRG, pp. 153–155.

leagues without comment except to instruct Captain-General Saldanha to keep the treaty's provisions to himself.[67]

The New Rapprochement Between Portugal and Spain [68]

The Treaty of San Ildefonso was the product of a new accord between Lisbon and Madrid. Such an accommodation became possible because of the retirement from Court of the two long-time protagonists, Grimaldi and Pombal. The Genoese was the first to withdraw from the scene, having found his position in the cabinet increasingly uncomfortable since Algiers.[69] On February 19 1777, Grimaldi was succeeded by Don José Moñino, better known as the Count of Floridablanca, who had gained fame because of the prominent role he played in bringing about the suppression of the Jesuit Order when he served as Spanish ambassador to Rome. While Grimaldi was preparing to replace his successor by taking up the latter's post at the Papal Court, his archrival, Pombal, packed his bags, and on March 5 retired under duress to his estate.

When Floridablanca learned of the death of Dom José I, he decided that the moment was propitious to resume direct negotiations with Lisbon concerning their undeclared war in America. The new Spanish foreign minister, who undoubtedly anticipated Pombal's dismissal, hoped that by initiating discussions while Spain enjoyed an advantageous position, his government would earn the gratitude of the Portuguese Court and, even more important, be able to work out

---

[67] *Idem* to Saldanha, Jan. 28, 1778, *DI*, XVII, 337–339. The pertinent passage reads: "A notícia da Paz pode e deve V. Ex.a fazella publicar; porém a Cópia do Tratado, que a V. Ex.a remetto, deve V. Ex.a conservalla em si, em quanto eu não acho conveniente divulgalla." From the text which follows (*ibid.*, pp. 339–362) , it is evident that the captain-general was not advised of the seven secret articles of the treaty. It is doubtful whether the viceroy was either.

[68] Considering its importance, remarkably little has been published concerning the Treaty of San Ildefonso and the subsequent rapprochement between the Iberian powers. The pertinent volumes of the Santarem series of Portuguese diplomatic documents entirely omit the topic. Except as otherwise noted, this section is based upon Caetano Beirão, *D. Maria I* (1777–1792) , pp. 199–211, and Appendix; and Conde de Floridablanca, Memorial to Charles III, Oct. 10, 1788, with a codicil addressed to Charles IV, dated Nov. 6, 1789, published in extenso in Antonio Ferrer del Río, ed., *Obras originales del conde de Floridablanca* (Madrid, 1899) , pp. 307–350, in excerpt in *CTLA*, VII (1865) , xvii–xxii (where it is erroneously dated Nov. 6, 1781) , and in a not entirely reliable translation in William Coxe, *Memoirs of the Kings of Spain of the House of Bourbon . . . 1700 to 1788*, V (London, 1815) , Appendix 1.

[69] Coxe gives a remarkably cogent account (V, 5–13) of the reasons for Grimaldi's unhappiness in the ministry and contends that Floridablanca was his hand-picked successor.

a more advantageous settlement through direct negotiations than would likely be the case if the so-called mediatory powers (Great Britain and France) became involved in the resolution of the Iberian conflict. It is not unlikely that Floridablanca also wished to end that conflict before the deteriorating situation in the British North American colonies should make it appear desirable for Spain to go to war with Great Britain.[70]

On March 3, two days before the Santa Catarina garrison capitulated at Cubatão, Portuguese ambassador Dom Francisco Innocênio de Sousa Coutinho reported to his government that Charles III "sincerely desires the conservation of Peace" between the two Iberian governments.[71] Both the queen mother of Portugal, Dona Mariana Vitória, sister of Charles III, and her daughter, Maria I, responded to this overture by writing personal letters to the Spanish monarch indicating their desire to restore good relations with their kinsman.

Maria I advised her uncle that she had changed ministers, and that he would find the requisite sincerity and good faith in dealing with her new government. When Charles III expressed some doubts about a Portuguese cabinet which still included Martinho de Melo e Castro, whom the Spanish regarded as an Anglophile, his sister gave assurances of Melo e Castro's fidelity and denied that Britain had influenced recent Portuguese foreign policy.[72]

In May Floridablanca and ambassador Sousa Coutinho began serious discussions, and by early June they had agreed upon a truce. Then came the first reports of Santa Catarina Island's fall.[73] Floridablanca immediately demanded the cession of Santa Catarina and Rio

[70] In his memoir Floridablanca intimated as much: "*Parece que hubiésemos adivinado que la guerra era inminente con la Inglaterra. . . .*" (sic). Ferrer del Río, *Obras de Floridablanca*, p. 308. Since late 1775 Madrid had watched the situation in the English colonies by means of agents sent from New Orleans and Havana to rebel and loyalist areas. They were to determine (1) the course of the war; (2) the number of combatants on each side; and (3) their attitude toward the Spanish monarchy. Madrid was hopeful of expelling the British from the Gulf of Mexico, particularly from the Belize dyewood coast and from Florida, which England had held since 1763. Kathryn Abbey, "Efforts of Spain to Maintain Sources of Information in the British Colonies before 1779," *Mississippi Valley Historical Review*, XV (June, 1928), 56–68.

[71] Beirão, p. 199, n. 21.

[72] Maria I to Charles III, Mar. 24, 1777; Mariana Vitória to *idem*, Apr. 12 and May 3, 1777, *ibid.*, pp. 425, 200–201. Subsequently Charles III invited his sister to pay a formal visit to Spain, and late in October 1777 she did so. On the role of Mariana Vitória in the Luso-Spanish negotiations, see *ibid.*, pp. 200–201, 204.

[73] As so frequently happened, the news reached Madrid before it did Lisbon, catching the Portuguese ambassador off guard, and prompted an indignant rebuke from the colonial secretary to the viceroy. Melo e Castro to Lavradio, June 22, 1777, BNRJ, I-2, 4, 7, n. 77; published in *CB*, III, 466–467. Lavradio apologized for delaying his report, stating that he wanted to wait until he had all the facts to avoid sending an erroneous account. Lavradio to Melo e Castro, Aug. 25, 1777, IHGB/AUC, 1-1-29, fols. 431ᵛ–433ᵛ.

Grande to Spain. Sousa Coutinho, though greatly embarrassed by the field marshal's precipitate abandonment of the island,[74] replied that his government would never accede to such terms. The two statesmen continued to make counterbids while awaiting later news from America.[75] Finally, on October 1, 1777, they signed the Treaty of San Ildefonso.[76]

An examination of the terms of that treaty reveals why Viceroy Lavradio preferred to keep them from becoming public knowledge. Portugal agreed to cede to Spain Colônia do Sacramento and certain offshore islands, thus once again surrendering her claim to the north shore of the Plata as Brazil's southern boundary. The limits between Spanish and Portuguese territory in South America were defined as beginning at the Arroio Chuí, thence following the western shore of Lagoa Mirim, bending westward beyond that lagoon to skirt just east of the sources of the Rio Ibicuí, then running due north, bisecting the Uruguay River at its Pepiri-Guaçu tributary.[77] The remainder of the boundary was essentially the same as the one agreed upon in the ill-fated Treaty of 1750. The line of 1778 thus left Portugal in complete control of the Lagoa dos Patos—the chief bone of contention since 1763—but without sovereignty over the Seven Missions territory, the quid pro quo of the Treaty of Madrid. Surprisingly enough, Spain returned Santa Catarina Island to Portugal,[78] though under

[74] "Nunca esperei que fizessem huma tão indigna defença, como esta, que me traz envergonhado, e me faz passar por dores, que só as do Inferno podem ser mayores." Sousa Coutinho to the Court, n. d., quoted in Beirão, p. 205.

[75] Just after advising Lavradio of the truce, Melo e Mastro wrote him that the pressing negotiations with Madrid necessitated frequent communications from Brazil as to the military situation. He ordered him to send all the news "de expressos de Mar dirigidos a este Porto, e de terra dirigidos ao da Bahia de todos os Santos, ou ainda ao de Pernambuco," from whence the information was to be forwarded by the governors of both captaincies to the Court. Dispatch of June 17, 1777, BNRJ, I-2, 4, 7, n. 76.

[76] The Portuguese and Spanish texts of the twenty-five public and seven secret articles are given in CTLA, III (1862), 130–167. Portugal ratified the agreement on Oct. 10, and Spain followed the next day. For other published texts of the treaty see José Carlos Macedo Soares, Fronteiras do Brasil: o regime colonial, p. 190.

[77] An interesting feature of the boundary was the buffer zones established by Arts. 5 and 6. The first consisted of Lagoas Mirim and Mangueira, and the second an undefined area along the frontier from Lagoa Mirim to the Uruguay-Pepiri-Guaçú intersection. Both parties pledged themselves not to build fortifications or establish settlements within these areas. These provisions are reminiscent of the "Neutral Land" area set up unilaterally by Great Britain between her settlements and those of Spain in Georgia during the years 1750 to 1763.

[78] According to Floridablanca (Memorial to Charles III, p. 308), Don Pedro de Cevallos himself recommended that the island be given back to Portugal. He argued that (1) it would cost Spain a great deal of expense to defend it; (2) its exposed position made it an obvious objective in any future (Luso-Spanish?) war; and (3) though the Portuguese conducted whaling operations around the island, Spaniards could do better by fishing between the Platine estuary and the Straits of Magellan.

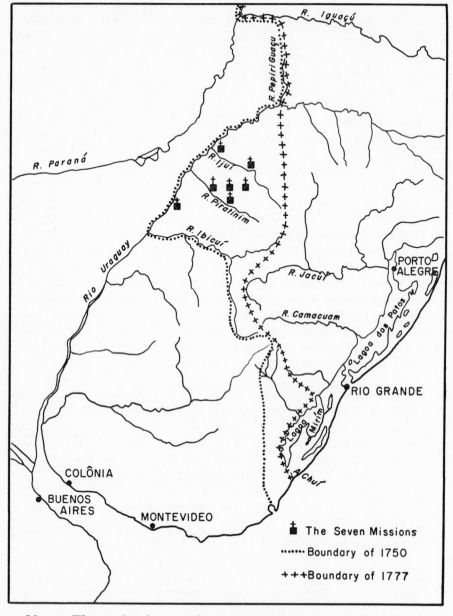

Map 11 The treaties of 1750 and 1777. (Adapted from J. C. Macedo Soares, *Fronteiras do Brasil Colonial*, map 7.)

humiliating conditions. Portugal promised to bar all foreign ships from the island and adjacent mainland except when they entered port under stress of weather.[79] Yet by a secret article *Spanish* war-

---

[79] An exception was made in the event Portugal should be at war. The passage reads: "E Sua Magestade Fidelíssima . . . promette que em tempo algum, seja de

ships and commercial vessels were promised "the greatest hospitality, and all the assistance that can be given to ships of the flag of a good ally and friend" should they elect to stop there.[80]

Other secret articles provided Portugal's new "friend" with additional forms of compensation for her apparent generosity. Among the most notable was the cession to Spain of the West African islands of Anno Bom and Fernando Pó, two vestiges of the heroic age of Portuguese discoverers, and an agreement to permit Spanish ships to call at the Portuguese islands of Príncipe and São Tomé.[81] These provisions made it possible for Spain for the first time to have direct access to the African slave markets, and meant that she would no longer be at the mercy of foreign middlemen for the chattels needed for her colonial economy.[82]

The remaining articles of the Treaty of San Ildefonso provided for the retirement of military and naval forces by both sides, exchanges of prisoners, restitution of property, evacuation of all territories transferred by the treaty, and establishment of joint commissions to survey the new boundary.[83] By another secret article several additional treaties were promised, but the only one that materialized was the "treaty of friendship and guarantee" signed at Pardo on March 11, 1778.[84]

The Question of Responsibility

The Treaty of San Ildefonso brought an end to fifteen years of intermittent fighting between Spain and Portugal, and resulted in a permanent division of the Debatable Lands between the two powers.[85]

---

paz ou de guerra, em que a corôa de Portugal não tenha parte . . . não consentirá que alguma esquadra ou embarcação de guerra ou de commércio estrangeiras entrem no dito porto de Santa Catarina, ou nos da sua costa immediata . . . *especialmente sendo embarcações de potência que se ache em guerra com a corôa de Hespanha,* ou que alguma esquadra ou embarcação de guerra ou de commércio estrangeiras entrem added. This provision was obviously directed against England.

[80] Secret Art. 6.

[81] Secret Arts. 3–5. Portuguese ships continued to have the right to call at the two ceded islands.

[82] From his Memorial, it is obvious that Floridablanca placed great importance upon these gains for the slave trade

[83] The five joint commissions did not begin their labors until 1784, and their work was still unfinished when it was terminated by a new Iberian conflict in 1801.

[84] Printed in *CTLA,* III, 168–191.

[85] The two negotiators of the treaty expressed extreme satisfaction with their handiwork. The main theme of the first part of Floridablanca's memorial (see n. 68 above) is a defense of the treaty, which he considered one of the high points of his ministry. Sousa Coutinho wrote his government that "Estou bem certo, que se não podia fazer mais útil, nem mais decorozo, e assim o julgará quem conhecer a América, e a sua situação. . . . Para compensarmos a perda a Colônia temos em primeiro lugar as férteis Campanhas do Rio Grande, e a regulação de hum País

Though Portugal lost Colônia, she retained Santa Catarına and coastal Rio Grande, while Spain continued in possession of the Seven Missions territory and the Banda Oriental. Thus each nation failed to achieve its maximum objective, that of hegemony over all of the disputed area.[86]

The question of responsibility for the Portuguese surrenders at Santa Catarina and Colônia was bitterly debated among contemporaries and became the subject of a series of judicial proceedings following the war. The rather curious findings of the magistrates and the courts-martial are discussed in Appendix II. While most Portuguese and Brazilian historians have ignored the question of culpability, the few who have considered it *en passant* have done little more than underscore the partisan assertions of one or another of the chief participants whose views they have found congenial.[87]

In his reports concerning the capitulations, the viceroy was careful to emphasize that he had done everything within his powers to put Santa Catarina and Colônia in an adequate posture of defense. He submitted lists of war matériel dispatched to both bases during his administration to prove his contention that he had furnished their commanding officers with far more equipment than had any of his predecessors. Nor could he resist the temptation to comment that if he had been allowed to take the field, the war would have had a happier ending for Portugal.

Dom Luís insisted that in spite of the Spaniards' superiority in ships, firepower, and manpower there was no persuasive reason why the Santa Catarina garrison could not have held out until relief arrived. He believed that its failure to do so was attributable partly to MacDouall's unwarranted flight, which undermined the defenders' morale, and partly to the fact that Field Marshal Antônio Carlos Furtado de Mendonça had succumbed to the evil counsel of Brigadier José Custódio, a man whom the viceroy claimed never to have trusted because of his proclivity for sowing seeds of discord wherever he went.[88]

---

imenso, reconhecido nosso, e como tal independente de questoens." Dispatch of Oct. 1, 1777, quoted in Beirão, p. 207. For an example of the conflicting views of historians, cf. *ibid.*, pp. 207–209, with Francisco Adolfo de Varnhagen, *História do Brasil*, IV, 268–269. See also Macedo Soares, pp. 167–168.

86 The Portuguese subsequently conquered and held the Seven Missions lands after a brief campaign in 1801. Jônatas da Costa Rego Monteiro, "A campanha de 1801, tomada dos 7 povos missioneiros," III Congresso de História Nacional, *Anais*, VI (Rio de Janeiro, 1938), 517–604.

87 E.g., Balthasar da Silva Lisboa, *Annaes do Rio de Janeiro*, III, 100, 106; Varnhagen, *História*, IV, 202; Boiteux, *Notas*, p. 261.

88 He neglected to remember, however, that he had once written: "Como esta tropa vae também o Brigadeiro João [*sic* for José] Custódio de Sá e Faria, oficial de muita honra e inteligência e que [h]á vinte anos serve América empregado em

The viceroy also maintained that Governor Rocha should have made a stout defense of Colônia before surrendering the praça. He admitted that the governor was short on food when Cevallos appeared before him, but insisted that there were enough provisions to last for several months. He claimed that the governor had misinterpreted his instructions, and should have challenged Cevallos when the Spaniards first landed near the citadel instead of remaining entirely on the defensive. But the errors of Rocha and Furtado de Mendonça were merely errors of judgment, the viceroy stressed, and neither was guilty of treasonable conduct; hence both merited royal clemency.[89]

Governor Rocha and the field marshal naturally took different views of the reasons for the loss of their commands.[90] Antônio Carlos evidently concluded that the best way to defend himself was to throw all the blame on his adversaries, Governor Gama e Freitas, Commodore MacDouall, and especially the viceroy. The marshal declared that the viceroy's instructions regarding the defense of Santa Catarina Island were extremely vague, and that Dom Luís had turned a deaf ear to his repeated requests for additional men and equipment to defend the island, but open-handedly gave his *criado*, Governor Rocha, everything that he wanted. He was contemptuous of the viceroy's appointment of Governor Gama e Freitas, whom he characterized as an inexperienced, youthful, wealthy dandy, and charged him with repeatedly countermanding his own orders. He protested that he had never possessed as many troops as the viceroy imagined, and that the latter greatly misled the Court as to the state of Santa Catarina's defenses. Antônio Carlos was particularly critical of the viceroy's departure from the Crown's instructions in permitting the commodore to station his ships north of the island, instead of in the channel, and of Lavradio's failure to provide floating batteries to defend that channel, even though the Spaniards had not tried (or needed) to penetrate it with their ships during the invasion, a point the marshal conveniently ignored. Finally, he charged that the viceroy deliberately rigged the investigation of the loss of Santa Catarina and the sur-

muitos e distinctos serviços, tendo dado de todas as suas incumbências uma tão excelente conta, que sempre mereceu dos Senhores Governadores a maior atenção." To Manoel da Cunha Menezes, Oct. 23, 1776, *VRL*, pp. 322–323.

89 Lavradio to Martim Lopes Lobo de Saldanha, Apr. 24, 1777, *DI*, XVII (1895), 229–230; *idem* to Vila Nova da Cerveira [?], June 20, [1777], *VRL*, pp. 104–113; *idem* to Martinho de Melo e Castro, June 4, Aug. 4, 15, and 25, and Dec. 12, 1777, IHGB/AUC, fols. 418ᵛ–420ᵛ; 425ʳ–428ᵛ; 429ᵛ–431ᵛ; 442ʳ–443ʳ.

90 According to Lavradio's successor, ex-Governor Rocha spoke in the same critical vein of the marquis as did the field marshal, whose views are summarized below Luís de Vasconcelos e Sousa to Melo e Castro, June 4, 1779, BNRJ, 4, 4, 1, n. 26. No corroboration of this statement has been found. Rocha did not express criticism of his former patron either in his letters to Lavradio written in Buenos Aires or in his later petition to the queen. See Appendix II.

render of its garrison so that witnesses could only answer questions designed to incriminate him while exonerating Lavradio and Gama e Freitas.[91]

How is one to reconcile these conflicting points of view? Certainly not by accepting either version at its face value as some historians have done,[92] for both the viceroy and the field marshal were obviously slanting their accounts to protect themselves. Still there are elements of truth in each version.

Whether Robert MacDouall played the decisive role in the loss of Santa Catarina that the viceroy and the field marshal imagined is questionable. While one may doubt that he was of flag officer caliber,[93] it is difficult to see how he could have inflicted much damage on an enemy with three times as many warships as he possessed, especially when he was under strict instructions to avoid the loss of his own force.[94] Nevertheless, it cannot be denied that the squadron's disappearance gave the army officers on the island an excuse to justify its evacuation.

The conduct of Brigadier José Custódio de Sá e Faria, the man whom the viceroy called "the principal author" of the Santa Catarina disgrace, is both enigmatic and intriguing. The brigadier was one of a number of army engineers, a group that included José Antônio Caldas and Francisco João Roscîo, who served many years in various parts of eighteenth-century Brazil as cartographers, advisers to governors on military construction, and sometimes as administrators. Like Caldas and Roscîo, the brigadier seems to have been a capable, intelligent officer of better than average cultural attainments for a person of his rank. He was also a man who clearly aroused strong feelings one way or another, as Francisco José da Rocha noted.

Since the brigadier's own account of his behavior during and after the Spanish invasion has not come down to us, we can only speculate on his motives at the time. He apparently regarded the Portuguese

91 Antônio Carlos Furtado de Mendonça to the queen [ca. 1779], *RIHGB*, XXVII:1, 292–332; the same views are expressed in the "Auto de perguntas feitas ao Illmo. e exmo. marechal de campo Antônio Carlos Furtado de Mendonça," May 15, 1778, BNRJ, I-31, 26, 1, n. 9, and in a bulky, 229-paragraph undated defense prepared by his attorney. *Ibid.*, n. 2.

92 E.g., Boiteux bases his account of the fall of Santa Catarina almost exclusively on the Furtado de Mendonça apology, and is severely critical of the "fatuous marquis" for failing to relieve the island (p. 261). Cf. *VRL*, pp. 119–121, where the author adheres to the Lavradio "line" with respect to the guilt and cowardly conduct of MacDouall.

93 This conclusion is based not only on his conduct in Brazil, but also on the fact that when he resumed service in the British navy, ca. 1780, he was given a very insignificant command. See Appendix II.

94 For a criticism of French naval strategy in the eighteenth century that applies equally to that of Pombaline Portugal, see Alfred Thayer Mahan, *The Influence of Sea Power upon History, 1600–1783* (Boston, 1928), pp. 289–290.

situation on the island and subsequently on the mainland as hopeless, and therefore recommended the evacuation of the island and the later capitulation of its garrison to avoid futile bloodshed. As a realist, he must have appreciated both the fact that the defenders were greatly outnumbered by the Spaniards and that the ill-paid and harshly treated Portuguese soldiers would desert at the first opportunity, as they actually did as soon as they were on the mainland. The fact that José Custódio remained with the Spaniards rather than accompany his fellow officers to Rio de Janeiro damned him in the eyes of contemporaries, but it does not necessarily follow that he was a traitor, as most coeval and later writers have presumed. He probably suspected that he and his colleagues were doomed to years of imprisonment before they could clear themselves—as was indeed the case—and regarded active service in Spanish America as preferable to wasting away in a Portuguese dungeon.[95]

Considering the irresolution displayed by the field marshal and his fellow officers, it is not surprising that the Portuguese garrison of Santa Catarina melted away as soon as it reached the mainland, for the soldiers had little reason to have confidence in the ability of their officers. Antônio Carlos was patently a very weak person who was unable to appreciate the problems of the viceroy or of any other Crown officer save himself. It is clear from his Apology that his chief grievance against Governor Gama e Freitas, certainly a timid person at best, was that when he was assigned to Santa Catarina the marshal had assumed he would have full powers there, and later discovered that he would have to share certain authority with the governor.[96] As for the marshal's conduct during and after the Spanish invasion, the less said the better, for by his indecisiveness and his mismanagement of the withdrawal from the island he proved himself thoroughly undeserving of his high rank.

Whether or not the fall of Santa Catarina and the capitulation of its garrison could have been averted are matters that may be open to debate, but there should be no doubt why Portugal lost Colônia do Sacramento for the fourth time in 1777. Fundamentally she forfeited the outpost by her failure to establish support bases in the Plata and to close the gap between Rio Grande and the entrepôt in the century following its initial establishment. The sieges of 1681, 1705, 1735–1737, and especially that of 1762 demonstrated the citadel's vulnerability to attack, while the persisting Spanish blockade beginning in

95 José Custódio remained in Spanish service until the end of his life. He died in Buenos Aires in 1792.

96 Santa Catarina was not the only station where senior military and civil officials (the latter also army officers) clashed. Similar friction existed in Rio Grande between General Böhm and Governor José Marcelino de Figueiredo, and in Colônia between Colonel Mesquita and Governor Rocha.

1763 was a clear indication that Madrid was determined to exclude Portugal permanently from the Plata.

While Portugal had too much at stake in Colônia for the Marquis of Pombal to admit publicly that Portugal could no longer hope to maintain the outpost, there are indications that the minister reached such a conclusion by the early seventies. The military threat that Spain posed to the Portuguese position in other parts of the Debatable Lands necessitated a decision on the allocation of Portugal's limited land and sea forces. That decision was obviously made in favor of Rio Grande, where several thousand European and colonial troops were stationed under the best European officers Pombal could obtain, and of Santa Catarina, where a relatively large part of the small Portuguese navy was assigned. No comparable military or naval forces were sent to Colônia. Indeed, on two occasions the praça's only regiment was ordered back to Rio de Janeiro to prevent the troops from falling into enemy hands. The fact that the order was twice reversed was doubtless due to Pombal's hope that the outpost could somehow still be saved. But when the British aid that Pombal confidently expected was not forthcoming, there was no alternative but to allow the entrepôt to be overrun once more. Colônia's last governor, Francisco José da Rocha, was thus left in the unenviable position of being the scapegoat for the failure of Pombal's diplomacy.[97]

During the early seventies Viceroy Lavradio recognized the precarious situation at Colônia, but he could do little about it. He was bound by instructions from Pombal and Colonial Secretary Martinho de Melo e Castro to distribute the warships, troops, and war matériel to the areas the Crown designated as having the highest defense priorities, namely Santa Catarina, Rio Grande, and (temporarily) Bahia. That Dom Luís actually hoarded in Rio de Janeiro guns and equipment that he should have sent to his dependencies, as one historian has charged,[98] is an assertion that would be difficult to prove. The point is irrelevant since the question of a shortage of guns or powder had no bearing on the decisions to surrender the Santa Catarina and Colônia garrisons. Nor can it be proved that the viceroy failed to provide his southern bastions with all the manpower he was authorized to send them. In particular, the decision to maintain a fixed garrison of six regiments in Rio de Janeiro, for which Dom Luís has sometimes been criticized, was the Crown's, not his.

This is not to say that Lavradio was blameless in his conduct dur-

---

[97] Cf. Luís Enrique Azarola Gil, *Contribución a la historia de Colonia del Sacramento*, pp. 131–132, who arrived at the same conclusion, but erroneously bases his exoneration of Rocha on Pombal's dispatch to Lavradio of May 9, 1775, which he published in excerpt (pp. 229–230), failing to realize that the Crown's first order for the withdrawal of the outpost's regiment was later countermanded.

[98] Rego Monteiro, *Colônia*, I, 428.

ing the war. As his subordinates charged, his instructions were often quite ambiguous, and were replete with unfounded assumptions and unattainable objectives parroted from the Court's overly optimistic dispatches. No doubt the viceroy and his aides merit censure for failing to provide *in advance* for the relief of Santa Catarina. The Paulistas, the troops in Rio Grande, and the Mineiros should have been prepared to go to the aid of their brothers as soon as the Spaniards launched their invasion, if not before. But such advance planning was rare in Lavradio's time. There is, of course, no assurance that Lavradio's improvised plan to recover Santa Catarina would have succeeded had the war continued and had the Court been willing to permit Dom Luís to direct the operation himself. The fact that the Court refused to allow the viceroy to assume a fighting command enabled him to assert without fear of contradiction that the Portuguese defeats would not have occurred had his request been granted, but there is nothing in Lavradio's directives to subordinates to suggest that he possessed soldierly qualities of command comparable to those displayed by his rival, Don Pedro de Cevallos.

The enforcement of a long-standing policy of prohibiting Brazil's titular administrator from leaving the seat of his government without the Crown's consent was only one of the ways that the Marquis of Lavradio found the exercise of his military authority handicapped.[99] When fellow administrators failed to comply fully with the Court's directives to furnish him with troops, supplies, and funds for the war effort, the viceroy's only recourse was to complain bitterly to those officials and to a not always sympathetic Crown. His relations with Commodore MacDouall illustrate another sort of restraint: the viceroy could not remove ranking officers in whom he lacked confidence without first obtaining royal approval. Considering the extent of his resources the nature of his instructions, the talents of his subordinates, and the checks upon his authority, it seems reasonable to conclude that the marquis performed his military duties conscientiously and did all that he could to avert the defeats that inevitably stained his record.

Among the accusations leveled against the Marquis of Pombal after his dismissal were that he had offered the head of Viceroy Lavradio to Spain in a desperate effort to obtain peace, and that he had secretly ordered the surrender of Santa Catarina Island to the Spaniards.[100]

---

[99] As noted in Chap. II, that policy dated back to 1612. It was reaffirmed shortly before Lavradio came to Rio de Janeiro, when the Crown turned down the request of the Conde da Cunha to visit Rio Grande. Francisco Xavier de Mendonça Furtado to Conde da Cunha, Mar. 18, 1767, *RIHGB*, XXXV:1, 219.

[100] João Lúcio de Azevedo, *O Marquês de Pombal e a sua época*, p. 364. Pombal issued a lengthy denial of these charges. See Chap. VII, n. 47.

Both charges were false, but it cannot be denied that Pombal was the person most clearly responsible for the drubbing that Portugal received in 1777. Whatever his merits as economic innovator and civil administrator, Pombal possessed little ability as a military strategist or diplomatist. His voluminous military instructions to the viceroy and his colleagues were conceived in unrealistic, impractical terms and were founded on false premises. Most notable among the last was his belief that since the Spanish had been defeated in Algiers by the Moors and in Rio Grande by General Böhm, the massive Cevallos armada would inevitably experience a similar fate.

Considering Portugal's inability to match Spain in manpower, naval strength, or economic resources, Pombal's borderlands diplomacy was decidedly reckless. He obviously counted heavily on Great Britain to come to Portugal's rescue with troops and ships, as she had done so often during the eighteenth century. Yet he failed to realize that in 1776 Britain was in no position to pull Portugal's chestnuts out of the fire, for she had troubles enough of her own, both in North America and in Europe, where she knew that France and Spain were waiting for an opportunity to avenge their defeat in the Seven Years' War. And so Pombal's duplicity with regard to the order suspending hostilities in Brazil backfired, and Spain responded by dispatching the second Cevallos expedition to America, with humiliating consequences for Portugal. When measured against the promises contained in the Treaty of Madrid, the results of twenty-seven years of his diplomacy concerning the Debatable Lands were distinctly barren.

It does not follow, however, that the road to peace was as easy as writers like Carnaxide and Gil Munilla have assumed.[101] It is true that Spain wished to find a permanent solution to the borderlands problem so that she could concentrate on her primary adversary, Great Britain. But Madrid wanted peace only on her own terms—Portugal's cession of Colônia and all her claims to the Plata. Portugal under Pombal was not disposed to make such concessions until she was compelled to do so.

The loss of Colônia do Sacramento in 1777 did not end Portugal's hope of acquiring all of the Debatable Lands. In 1801 a successful Portuguese campaign added the Seven Missions Lands to coastal Rio Grande, and a few years later Portuguese troops poured into the Banda Oriental ostensibly in the defense of legitimacy during the first phase of the Spanish colonial movement for independence. But al-

---

101 António de Sousa Pedroso Carnaxide (Visconde de Carnaxide), *O Brasil na administração pombalina*, p. 199; Octavio Gil Munilla, *El Río de la Plata en la política internacional, passim,* where the desire of the government of Charles III for a rapprochement with Portugal forms one of the author's principal theses.

though Portugal annexed the Banda Oriental in 1821, that achievement did not endure. Four years later the Orientales revolted against newly independent Brazil, and with Argentine help conducted a three-year war for their liberation. Ultimately Great Britain, ironically the former guarantor of Portuguese rights in the Plata, intervened for the sake of peace and profits, and forced Argentina and Brazil to relinquish their claims to the Banda, which became the buffer republic of Uruguay. For another generation the independent Spanish- and Portuguese-speaking nations of the Plata continued the rivalry they inherited from their respective mother countries. Only after the disastrous Paraguayan War (1864–1870) did Brazilian interest in the Plata abate, thus bringing to an end two centuries of attempts to realize the dream of the original sponsor of Colônia, Prince Pedro of Portugal, to unite all the continent from the Amazon to the Plata under one flag. That had turned out to be a persisting but an illusive vision.

In the long run, therefore, the undeclared war of the 1770s and the partition of 1777 proved to be decisive, but fighting that war was terribly expensive. The particular problems Viceroy Lavradio experienced in seeking the means to defray his expenses will be examined in Chapter XII, but it is first necessary to consider the fiscal reorganization of Brazil in Lavradio's time.

PART THREE

The Viceroy's Economic Problems

XI

The Reorganization of the Royal Fisc

Being indispensably necessary a complete and particular notion of all the annual revenues collected by each branch of My Royal Treasury, and of the expenses to which the same revenues are applied in order that the respective entries can be made in My Royal Treasury with the distinction and clarity that I have decreed, it is my pleasure to order the following Measures. . . .

King to Viceroy Cunha, January 18, 1764

NEXT TO the long borderlands conflict, the viceroy's most persisting problems concerned fiscal matters. Although Lavradio's predecessors had borne nominal responsibility for their branch of the royal exchequer, its actual managers were the treasury superintendents (provedores da fazenda), and the governors-general and other executive officers in the colony were expressly forbidden to meddle in the internal operations of the treasury.[1] One consequence of a series of sweeping fiscal reforms the Crown introduced in the 1760s was the downgrading of the office of the provedor. Another was the corresponding increase in the fiscal duties of the executive officers whose responsibilities ceased to be merely nominal and at times became extremely burdensome.

Structural Reorganization

Both the structural changes and the procedural innovations of the 1760s came as an aftermath of the great Lisbon earthquake of November 1, 1755.[2] Before that catastrophe no central agency existed in

[1] For example, in 1731 the Overseas Council reminded the captain-general of Pernambuco that "tendo entendido que não tendes jurisdição para vos meterdes nas materias da administração e remessa da Fazenda Real, sem expecial ordem minha para o poderdes fazer por pertencer esta só ao Provedor da Fazenda na forma do Regimento e Ordens Reaes. . . ." *Consulta* of June 2, 1731, *ABNRJ*, XXVIII (1906), 279–280; see also *carta régia* of Jan. 18, 1711 and *consulta* of July 9, 1731, *ibid.*, 262–263, and 280. The general responsibilities of the early governors-general to inform themselves with respect to the status of royal revenues and the quality of treasury personnel are outlined in 2RGG, par. 9.

[2] For an introduction to the literature concerning the earthquake, tidal wave, and conflagration and of the international reaction to the calamity, see T. D. Kendrick, *The Lisbon Earthquake* (London, 1956).

Portugal with over-all responsibility for the collection and payment of Crown moneys. Throughout the kingdom and the empire each customs officer, tax receiver, paymaster, and treasurer was individually responsible for the receipt and disbursement of the funds he handled, subject only to checks by boards of audit in the colonies and by the parent *Casa dos Contos* in Lisbon.[3] Owing to the resultant confusion and peculation the king lost a substantial portion of his revenues, and whenever fiscal crises arose, particularly during wartime and depressions, the Crown was obliged to cover deficits by devising new taxes, by calling upon its subjects to tax themselves through so-called voluntary contributions *(donativos)*, and by allowing many of its obligations to remain unpaid.[4]

After the great fire that followed the earth tremor had destroyed the Casa dos Contos and most of its records, the Pombal government conducted an intensive investigation of the Casa's operations in order to reconstruct the actual state of royal finances. These inquiries clearly demonstrated the inadequacy of the antiquated fiscal system, and led Pombal to make a fresh start. He pensioned off the personnel of the Casa dos Contos, abolished the bureau itself, and set up a new organization and a new system of accounting.

The reorganized exchequer, the Royal Treasury (styled *Erário Régio or Real Erário*), was staffed by bookkeepers and accountants familiar with advanced mercantile practices, especially the double-entry system not used by the Portuguese government before. The Royal Treasury was headed by an inspector-general, a post Pombal himself filled until his dismissal in 1777; beneath him served a treasurer-general, four comptrollers-general, and their staffs. Two of the comptrollers-general shared responsibility for Brazilian accounts.[5] Each of the four was required to prepare twice yearly balances (one dated January 1; the other, July 1–10) and, without communicating

3 The authoritative study of the Casa is Virgínia Rau, *A Casa dos Contos* (Coimbra, 1951).

4 Secondary accounts of the fiiscal system of Portugal prior to 1761 are incomplete and often confusing. Besides the excellent discussion by Miss Rau, see Caio Prado, Júnior, *Formação do Brasil contemporâneo*, pp. 318–328, and Eulália Maria Lahmeyer Lobo, *Administração colonial luso-espanhola nas Américas*, pp. 215–223, 382–394.

5 The jurisdictions of the four comptrollers-general were: (1) the Court and the province of Estremadura; (2) the remainder of Portugal plus the Algarve, the Azores, and Madeira; (3) West Africa, the State of Maranhão and the comarcas of the Relação of Bahia; and (4) the comarcas of the Relação of Rio de Janeiro, East Africa, and the Portuguese Far East. According to Ratton, it was so difficult to find persons in Portugal who were familiar with advanced mercantile procedures that the first comptrollers-general were prominent merchants who, because of their allegedly low salaries, continued to engage in business through factors. No one then seemed concerned about possible "conflict of interest." Jacome Ratton, *Recordacoens*, p. 289.

the results to his colleagues, report them to the treasurer-general. The latter then met with the inspector-general and a secretary to verify the figures. The inspector-general then reported the results to the king. In theory, therefore, only five persons in the kingdom were privy to the actual state of the finances of the realm. But more than mere secrecy was intended by these reforms. Their principal aims were to increase the efficiency of collecting the king's revenues, to reduce opportunities for peculation and fraud, and to prevent unauthorized expenditures.[6]

The creation of a new fiscal organization at home was followed by structural changes overseas. Thus during the 1760s and 1770s treasury boards (juntas da fazenda) were formed in each captaincy-general of Brazil.[7] While their composition varied somewhat from one unit to another, each was headed by a president (the senior executive officer) and five or six deputies. The latter included the senior magistrate of the unit,[8] the provedor da fazenda, the treasury procurator (*procurador da fazenda*), the treasurer-general (*tesoureiro geral*), and the chief auditor (*contador geral*) who served as the board's secretary. In the past when the provedor had complete charge of his branch of the treasury, each was responsible to the provedor mór da fazenda in Bahia but under the new system each junta was completely independent of the others and all were directly subordinate to the appropriate comptroller-general and to the inspector-general in Lisbon.[9]

According to a carta régia of the mid-seventies, the juntas were to meet two afternoons a week to transact their business.[10] Lavradio's

6 *Carta de lei*, Dec. 22, 1761, *CLP*, I, 816–830. See also Ratton, pp. 284–292.

7 There was an unauthorized treasury board in Minas Gerais as early as 1726, but it was ordered suppressed. Carta régia of Feb. 2, 1726, *RAPM*, XVI:1 (1911), 341–342. The juntas da fazenda began to function in Rio de Janeiro in 1767; in Bahia in 1769; in Minas Gerais in 1771–1772 (Teixeira Coelho, "Instrução," p. 301); in São Paulo by 1775 (*carta régia*, July 7, 1774, *DI*, XLIII, 10–13); and in Maranhão by 1780 (Raymundo Jozé de Souza Gayozo, *Compendio historico-político dos princípios da lavoura do Maranhão* [Paris, 1818], pp. 126–127); between 1765 and 1770 a board was established in Pernambuco ("Catálogo dos documentos mandados copiar pelo Senhor D. Pedro II," *RIHGB*, LXVII, 138–141). Characteristically the same term was later employed for a quite different organization. An alvará of Jan. 7, 1797 ordered "huma Junta da Fazenda á bordo de cada Real Esquadra." José da Silva Lisboa, "Synopse da legislação principal do João VI . . . ," *Memoria dos beneficios políticos do governo de . . . d. João VI* (2d. ed., Rio de Janeiro, 1940), Pt. II, p. 114.

8 I.e., in Bahia and Rio de Janeiro, the chancellor of the Relação; in São Paulo and Minas Gerais, the ouvidor; and in Maranhão the juiz de fóra. Except in Maranhão the procurator was always a deputy.

9 Alvará of Mar. 3, 1770, *CLP*, II, 451–456; cf. *carta régia* of Dec. 22, 1733 quoted in provedor mór (Bahia) to provedor (Santos), Mar. 26, 1734, *DH*, I (1928), 241–243, which illustrates the extent to which the provedores were formerly under the control of the superintendent at Bahia.

10 Carta régia, July 7, 1774, *DI*, XLIII (1903), 11. No substitutes were permitted to sit in place of members obliged to be absent from board meetings. Lavradio to Luís Antônio de Sousa, June 12, 1771, *CMCM*, cod. 15, fol. 67ʳ.

board in Rio de Janeiro probably assembled more frequently, considering the voluminous paperwork it handled. Whether the boards kept minutes of their meetings is uncertain—they do not seem to have been required to do so and none has turned up. In theory each member possessed an equal voice in the deliberations,[11] but in practice the juntas appear to have been dominated by their presidents.[12] The presidents alone were the recipients of dispatches from the highest authorities in Lisbon and could divulge or conceal information they deemed confidential. Furthermore, the presidents bore primary responsibility for the defense of their unit, and they alone were empowered to make secret expenditures from a special purse. For these reasons they cast the deciding vote even when the rest of the board assumed a contrary position.[13]

Departments of the Exchequer in Rio de Janeiro

Within each captaincy-general the treasury board exercised collective responsibility for all departments of the royal fisc, the *fazenda real* as it was generally called. Thus in Rio de Janeiro the Lavradio board supervised the following departments: (1) the office of the treasurer-general, (2) the bureau of audit (*contadoria*), (3) the provedoria, (4) the customs house (*alfândega*), and (5) the royal mint (*casa de moeda*). During wartime it also directed the work of several ad hoc agencies, notably the *junta das fragatas* that was responsible for naval procurement, the office of the military paymaster (*tesoureiro das tropas*), and the temporary junta da fazenda in Rio Grande de São Pedro. It also worked closely with the intendency-general of gold and the board of inspection (mesa da inspeção) in Rio de Janeiro. Both were headed by the same official who was the only Crown officer in the capital not subject to discipline by the viceroy.[14] Besides corre-

11 "Todos terão assento igual e votto nos Negocios q. ali se tractarem." Carta régia, July 7, 1774, *DI*, XLIII, 11.

12 For a criticism of the undemocratic character of the viceregal junta at a later time, see Luiz Beltraão de Gouveia de Almeida (chancellor of the Relação of Rio) to Dom Rodrigo de Souza Coutinho, May 14, 1799, *RIHGB*, LXV:1 (1902), 282.

13 [João Carlos Correa Lemos], "Methodo q. se pratica na Junta da Fazenda Real do Rio de Janeiro," ca. 1774, *DI*, XXXIII (1901), 19–24, at p. 20. In describing the operations of the juntas in this chapter I have relied particularly upon this report, the carta régia cited in note 10, and Sebastião Franc[isc]o Bettamio, "Plano para a administrasão da Faz.a R.al no Ryo gran de [sic] do Sul," Nov. 14, 1774, BNRJ, 13, 4, 4, n. 1.

14 The board of inspection was concerned with the promotion of sugar, tobacco, and other staples of interest to the Crown. The intendency of gold was charged with the registration of all bullion shipments and with the prevention of smuggling. The activities of both offices will be described in later chapters.

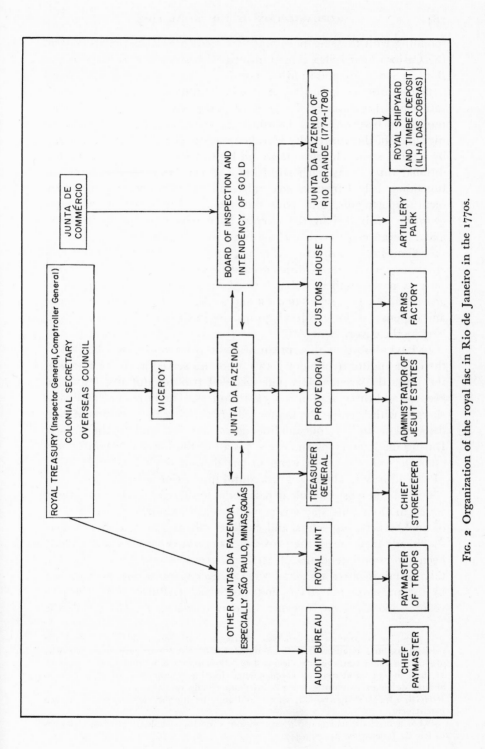

FIG. 2 Organization of the royal fisc in Rio de Janeiro in the 1770s.

ROYAL TREASURY (Inspector General, Comptroller General)
COLONIAL SECRETARY
OVERSEAS COUNCIL

JUNTA DE COMMÉRCIO

VICEROY

JUNTA DA FAZENDA

BOARD OF INSPECTION AND INTENDENCY OF GOLD

OTHER JUNTAS DA FAZENDA, ESPECIALLY SÃO PAULO, MINAS, GOIÁS

AUDIT BUREAU

ROYAL MINT

TREASURER GENERAL

PROVEDORIA

CUSTOMS HOUSE

JUNTA DA FAZENDA OF RIO GRANDE (1774-1780)

CHIEF PAYMASTER

PAYMASTER OF TROOPS

CHIEF STOREKEEPER

ADMINISTRATOR OF JESUIT ESTATES

ARMS FACTORY

ARTILLERY PARK

ROYAL SHIPYARD AND TIMBER DEPOSIT (ILHA DAS COBRAS)

sponding with these agencies and with the Royal Treasury in Lisbon, the Carioca board also communicated with sister juntas, particularly those in São Paulo and in Minas Gerais.

Before proceeding further, it may be helpful to describe the organization and functions of the major departments of the exchequer administered by the Carioca board.[15] The chief custodian of the operating funds of the viceroyalty was the treasurer-general who was assisted by a small staff. The revenues were kept in chests secured by the traditional three locks, each requiring a special key kept by a different functionary. The treasurer-general received funds from other government departments, and paid out moneys authorized by warrants (portarias) initialed by the viceroy. Such payments included salaries and allowances of civil, ecclesiastical, military and naval personnel, miscellaneous departmental expenses for goods and services, and purchases of certain commodities needed by or subsidized by the Crown, such as naval timbers, cabinet woods, and dyestuffs. The treasurer-general also kept a separate chest and a special register for the income and expenses of former Jesuit properties in the captaincy-general still held by the government.[16]

In Lavradio's time the bureau of audit (contadoria) was headed by the chief auditor (contador geral) who also served as the secretary of the junta da fazenda. His staff included two accountants, ten bookkeepers, and three apprentices (praticantes). The bureau of audit was charged with keeping the master ledgers showing the accounts of each department and all outstanding debts owed by and to the Crown. During the later 1760s and early '70s all of the bureau's records dated after December 31, 1761 were converted from single to double entry. More will be said about this procedural innovation later.

One of the most difficult departments to describe is the provedoria, which in Dom Luís' day was administered by a provedor and a corps of bookkeepers, inspectors, and clerks numbering altogether nineteen. As already mentioned, the provedores of each captaincy had formerly been the superintendents of all departments of the treasury within their administrative unit and were subject to occasional surveillance by the provedor mór da fazenda in Salvador. But in time the provedores, like the captains-general, came to operate largely outside the

15 A major source for an analysis of the organization and functions of the colonial fisc in Lavradio's time is an untitled, undated report written ca. 1770 by Manoel da Costa Cardozo for Viceroy Lavradio's use. It is located in CMCM, cod. 21, fols. 25^r–33^r, and may be supplemented by the "Mappa geral do rendimento annual de todos os empregos e officios desta cidade do Rio de Janeiro," (1781), RIHGB, LI:2 (1888), 159–181, which indicates the number of employees in each department.

16 For a brief discussion of the disposition of ex-Jesuit holdings in the captaincy of Rio de Janeiro see pp. 345–347.

control of their nominal chiefs. They also accumulated a wide variety of tasks. For example, besides over-all supervision of the operations of the various departments of the exchequer, the provedor of Rio de Janeiro was responsible for the registration of newly arrived slaves, the recruitment of crews for royal warships, and the inspection of ships being built for the Crown.

As the Marquis of Lavradio reported when he was stationed in Bahia, these tasks were too numerous and varied for any one man to perform effectively, and he was not alone in voicing such criticism.[17] A reorganization of the office was long overdue and it came with the establishment of the juntas da fazenda, for those boards collectively assumed the responsibility formerly exercised by the provedores.[18] Where they continued to exist, the provedores became primarily supply officers, but the office was abolished in Bahia in 1770,[19] where part of its functions were assigned to the newly established post of marine intendant or port admiral; the office was gradually phased out in other captaincies-general as well.[20]

Curiously enough, during Viceroy Lavradio's time the chief paymaster (tesoureiro das despezas miudas) of Rio de Janeiro continued to be a subordinate of the provedor. This officer served both as a receiver and a disburser. As receiver he collected duties on imported slaves, assessments on public officeholders' salaries, and fees on such legal documents as petitions of merit (provisões de mercês) and bond instruments (cartas de seguro). Upon written instruction from the treasurer-general, he also paid out moneys for salaries, allowances, and government purchases of goods and services.

Another subordinate of the provedor was the superintendent of warehouses (almoxarife dos armazens) whose staff appears to have been limited to a single clerk and two weighmasters (fieis). Like their

17 Oeiras to Lavradio, Aug. 26, 1769, BNRJ, I-2, 4, 6, n. 11, referring to criticisms of the office by Dom Luís and by the Conde de Azambuja.

18 Thus the Conde de Oeiras directed that "Como pelo estabelecimento da Junta da Fazenda Real dessa capitania, ficou cessando toda e qualquer jurisdição q. o Provedor la Fazenda Real podia ter no pagamento das dividas da Fazenda Real. . . ." Oeiras to Azambuja, Apr. 6, 1769, BNRJ, 10, 4, 8, n. 4.

19 Alvará of Mar. 3, 1770, CLP, II, 451–456.

20 The office was not suppressed throughout Brazil at one time, as both Rodolfo Garcia (Ensaio sôbre a história política e adminstrativa, p. 117) and Senhora Lobo (Administração luso-espanhola, p. 382) imply. It was eliminated in Minas Gerais in 1775 (Teixeira Coelho, "Instrução," p. 301), and in Rio de Janeiro in 1798, when the post of intendente da marinha was established there (Antonio Duarte Nunes, "Almanac historico da cidade de S. Sebastião do Rio de Janeiro . . . anno de 1799," RIHGB, XXI [1851], 113); the provedor's office was abolished in Rio Grande de São Pedro about 1800 (2RGG, par. 9n.), but still existed in Mato Grosso as late as 1786 (Gazeta de Lisboa, No. XXV [Sept.], 1786). It should be noted that other types of provedores, such as the provedor of the mint, continued to exist in the colony.

superiors, the warehouse superintendents accumulated a large number of tasks. Those in Rio de Janeiro were charged with the management of all royal storehouses, the marine arsenal, the artillery park (*trem da artelharia*), an arms factory, and a deposit for hardwoods. In addition, the almoxarife was responsible for equipping and provisioning the garrisons and fortresses around the capital and supplied foodstuffs to several nearby Indian villages under the Crown's protection. Because it was impossible for a single official to discharge all of these tasks efficiently, the Conde de Azambuja assigned some of these installations to separate administrators, but Lavradio's treasurer-general contended that the almoxarife dos armazens still had too many things to do.

Two other departments of the exchequer remain to be considered. One was the royal mint (casa de moeda) whose clerks, inspectors, assayers, die cutters, engravers, refiners, and stampers comprised the largest staff (thirty-nine) of all the departments under the junta da fazenda. The Carioca mint was one of two still in operation in Brazil.[21] Like its sister in Bahia, it produced two classes of metallic money, one called provincial, the other termed national money. The former was designed for internal circulation, the latter to cover remittances to the kingdom. Gold, silver, and copper coins of various denominations were minted for both purposes, and those stamped in Rio de Janeiro served the needs of government and commerce in the captaincies-general of Rio de Janeiro, São Paulo, Minas Gerais, and probably Mato Grosso and Goiás as well.[22] Lastly, there was one of

[21] The history of coinage in colonial Brazil reflects the tugging and pulling of rival economic interests. In 1694 the first Brazilian mint was opened at Bahia, allegedly upon the recommendation of Padre António Vieira. Five years later it was removed to Rio de Janeiro at the behest of its governor. Next, the entire installation was shifted for two years (1702–1703) to Pernambuco, only to be returned to Rio de Janeiro. A second mint was established at Bahia in 1715 and thereafter continued to operate until at least the end of the colonial period. A third mint was opened in Minas Gerais in 1725 but was closed in 1732, partly because of complaints by Cariocas. S[everino] Sombra, *História monetária do Brasil colonial*, pp. 106–107, 111 f.; see also Charles R. Boxer, *The Golden Age of Brazil*, pp. 29, 56–57, 59, and 196–197. In 1803 the Prince Regent of Portugal ordered both coastal mints closed; the one in Rio de Janeiro was to be transferred to Minas Gerais, that in Bahia to Goiás, but the order was later countermanded. Alvarás of May 13, 1803 and Sept. 1, 1808, Sombra, pp. 270–273.

[22] See Appendix III for indications of the kinds and amounts of coin struck by the Rio mint during the Lavradio years. The Bahian mint evidently serviced the captaincies-general of Bahia and Pernambuco, but not the northernmost captaincies, where hard cash was so short that government bills and even salaries were paid in sugar, cacao, cloves, and balls of cotton. Provedor of Pará to king, Aug. 6, 1712, and desembargador Francisco da Gama Pinto to king, July 28, 1723, Sombra, *Hist. monetaria*, pp. 141, 150–151. Although one might expect that colonial merchants in a bullion-producing colony would have less reason to complain about the shortage of hard money than in nonmineral-yielding colonies such as those of Great Britain, such was not the case. In 1790 Salvadorean merchants

the busiest of all fiscal departments, the alfândega or customs house, whose thirty employees were responsible for collecting a variety of import duties and for the prevention of contraband. Both topics will be considered later.

The Double-Entry System

Besides tightening the apparatus for the administration of the Crown's finances, the Pombal regime also introduced a sweeping innovation in record keeping by abandoning the single- in favor of the double-entry method of bookkeeping. In announcing that the new system would be put into effect throughout the kingdom and the empire, the government declared that the "new method" was "presently followed by nearly all the genteel nations (nações polidas) of Europe." [23] In fact, however, Portugal was the first to attempt to convert all government accounts to the more advanced system of record keeping.

The so-called "Italian manner" or "mercantile method" involves the dual entry of each transaction, once on the debit (left) side and once on the credit (right) side of the ledger page. The method was devised about 1300 in the major commercial centers of the Italian peninsula at a time when the operations of Italian merchant traders were becoming increasingly complex. Following the publication of Luca Pacioli's seminal treatise Summa de Arithmetica (Venice, 1494), the technique was gradually disseminated along the trade routes extending from the peninsula to leading mercantile centers beyond the Alps. It was employed by some branches of the English Treasury after 1688, but throughout the eighteenth century the Royal Exchequer of Great Britain continued to rely upon so-called charge accounts involving transactions between unequals, rather than between equals as the double-entry system requires. In France the system was introduced in some departments in 1716 and again in 1723, but both times was abandoned because of alleged "bureaucratic intransigence" and was not tried again until after the beginning of the Revolution. A few years earlier, in 1785, the Spanish government made some efforts to

petitioned the Crown to alleviate the shortage of provincial money in Bahia caused by the drainage of specie to other captaincies-general and to the Mina Coast, though the shipment of gold to the African stations was strictly forbidden. Dom Fernando José de Portugal to Martinho de Melo e Castro, Mar. 30, 1790, Sombra, pp. 250–251. For a discussion of the scarcity of hard money and of the consequent reliance upon commodity currency in the English colonies, see the sources cited and the discussion in W. T. Baxter's fine essay "Accounting in Colonial America," in A. C. Littleton and B. S. Yamey, eds., Studies in the History of Accounting (Homewood, Ill., 1956), pp. 272–287.

23 Carta de lei, Dec. 22, 1761, Tit. xii, CLP, I, 821.

establish double-entry accounting in its empire but soon abandoned them.[24]

The destruction of the Casa dos Contos and the bulk of its records provided the Pombal government with a unique opportunity to modernize the Crown's accounting procedures. But the success of such modernization depended upon a reservoir of persons familiar with the intricacies of double-entry methods, and while some elements of that method had been used by some Portuguese merchants since the seventeenth century,[25] the system was not widely understood in the Portuguese world. To remedy the scarcity of nationals familiar with what was commonly called "the Italian method" and with foreign systems of weights, measures, and currencies, Pombal established a commercial institute, the *Aula do Comércio*, in Lisbon in 1759.[26] But by Lavradio's time few if any of its graduates had reached Brazil, where the need for adequately trained accountants was evident to anyone familiar with the management of government accounts.

The Need for Accounting Reforms in the Colony

According to one student of the history of accounting, double entry offers several advantages over previous methods of record-keeping:

24 For the preceding material I have relied chiefly upon Raymond de Roover, "Aux origines d'une technique intellectuelle: la formation e l'expansion de la contabilité à partie double," *Annales d'histoire économique et social*, IX, No. 44 (Mar., 1937), 171–193, and No. 45 (May, 1937), 270–298; *idem*, "The Development of Accounting Prior to Luca Pacioli According to the Account-books of Medieval Merchants," in Littleton and Yamey, *Studies*, pp. 114–174; Frederic C. Lane, *Andrea Barbarigo Merchant 1418–1449* (Baltimore, 1944), pp. 153–158; J. E. Binney, *British Public Finance and Administration, 1774–1792* (Oxford, 1958), pp. 244–245, 256; George T. Matthews, *The Royal General Farms in Eighteenth Century France* (New York, 1958), pp. 73, 218, n. 69; and H. I. Priestley, *José de Gálvez, Visitador-General of New Spain, 1765–1771* (Berkeley, 1916), p. 82. See also two articles by B. S. Yamey, "The Functional Development of Double-Entry Bookkeeping," *The Accountant*, CIII (Nov. 2, 1940), and "Scientific Bookkeeping and the Rise of Capitalism," *The Economic History Review*, Ser. 2, Nos. 2 and 3 (1949), 99–113. The author's contention that the system was not widely used throughout the continent and did not significantly contribute to the rise of capitalism would be more persuasive had he used the papers of merchants of the time rather than depending upon coeval bookkeeping manuals.

25 See Frédéric Mauro's excellent article, "Pour une histoire de la comptabilité au Portugal: 'Le livre de Raison' de Coelho Guerreiro," *Caravelle*, I (Toulouse, 1963), 85–110. There is convincing evidence that the Jesuits in Portugal had kept accounts by means of double entry since the second half of the seventeenth century. See Luiz de Bivar Guerra, "A Administração e contabilidade dos colégios da Companhia de Jesus, nos séculos XVII e XVIII," Centro de Estudos Económicos. *Revista*, núm. 13 (Lisbon, 1953), 167–193, which is based on analysis of an "almost perfect collection" of records of the colleges of Bragança, Évora, and Elvas.

26 Statutes of Apr. 19, 1759, *CCLE*, IV, 198–205. For the shortage of persons familiar with advanced accounting procedures in Portugal, see Ratton, *Recordacoens*, p. 287; see also pp. 252 f. for his discussion of the Aula do Comércio.

"First, the records are more comprehensive and orderly; second, the duality of entries provided a convenient check on the accuracy or completeness of the ledger; third, the ledger . . . contains the materials for developing . . . statements of profit-and-loss and of capital, assets and liabilities.[27] A memorandum of about 1770 describes the recently superseded accounting practices in the captaincy-general of Rio de Janeiro and provides conclusive evidence that more simplified procedures were long overdue.[28] In the past the disbursing division (the *casa do almoxarifado da fazenda real*) of the provedoria kept only two journals (*livros de assentamentos*) to record payments of salaries and allowances, one for ecclesiastical, the other for secular personnel paid by the Crown. Payments were made at irregular rather than at stated intervals such as quarters or semesters, and were not issued automatically. On the contrary, the parish priest or government clerk, the *filho da folha,* to use the accounting parlance of the time, was required to petition the senior executive officer (for example, the viceroy) requesting sums due him. That petition initiated an elaborate, time-consuming procedure, the principal steps of which were: (1) the viceroy ordered (in writing) the provedor to confirm the obligation; (2) the provedor directed his clerk to vouch for the claim; (3) the clerk then made a search of the records, and to judge from the examples included in the memorandum that was no easy task, for the ledger sheets were arranged in triple columns crowded with a bewildering variety of entries, figures, and signatures; (4) following receipt of the clerk's report authenticating the claim, the provedor sent written confirmation of the obligation to the viceroy; (5) the latter then authorized the provedor to pay the claim; (6) the provedor next issued a pay order to his clerk. But since the pay office was open only two afternoons a week, it is scarcely surprising that "weeks, months [even] years" could pass between the dates of the original petition and the actual payment.

There was also another journal in the provedoria in which extraordinary expenditures were recorded. They, too, were authorized by the senior executive officer after a similarly involved procedure had been observed. However, since payments were recorded at random in a register called *verbas extravagantes,* it was possible for the same bill to be submitted and paid several times over.

The handling of personnel and supply records of royal warships

[27] B. S. Yamey, in Littleton and Yamey, *Studies,* p. 7.

[28] The following analysis is based primarily on "Methodo que se praticava na provedoria da fazenda do Rio de Janeiro e suas repartiçoens respectivamente à arrecadação da real fazenda com algumas notas . . . ," *ca.* 1770, CMCM, cod. 22, fols. 49ʳ–129ʳ (orig.) . This report, whose author seems to have been Manoel da Costa Cardozo, Lavradio's treasurer-general, was intended to illustrate the essential differences between the old and new fiscal procedures.

provided other opportunities for fraud. If a vessel was detained long past her original sailing date, it was likely that most of her crew would be discharged, but their names would appear on the rolls as long as the ship remained in port. The same was true of a sailor who came on board one day and left the next. In either case an overage in wages and allowances would be paid to the captain who naturally pocketed the excess. Furthermore, the only copy of the ship's manifest showing the amounts and types of cargo sent aboard from royal warehouses was delivered to the captain who was never required to make an accounting for the goods he received.

Faulty procedures in the storehouses themselves caused confusion and invited peculation. Normally the storekeeper did not forward to the provedor receipts showing the kinds and amounts of goods received until long after their arrival, thereby delaying payment for bills presented. Furthermore, since no record was kept of the unit price of goods at the time of their delivery and since the treasury customarily paid according to prevailing market prices, it was possible that a seller, when he was finally able to collect, would receive considerably more (or less) than his goods had been worth at the time of their deposit.[29] Because stock inventories were not carefully maintained, the storehouses were often oversupplied with some items and lacked others entirely. Nor were accurate records preserved to indicate what materials had been sent from the storehouses to the capital's forts or to the southern outposts. And since the captains of vessels transporting supplies to the southern bases were not required to check the goods stowed in their holds, it is easy to understand why materials requested by officials at such bases failed to arrive either because they had never been loaded or had been purloined en route.

Two final examples of faulty procedures are given here. One procedure involved suits brought by the treasury procurators against certain types of royal debtors, particularly those associated with tax contracts. Such litigation often dragged on for decades before a final settlement was reached. In the meantime the value of the debtor's encumbered estate usually dwindled to the point that neither he nor his heirs could satisfy their obligations. The other faulty procedure concerned the administration of properties seized for debts or for

[29] The author of the above-cited memorandum was obviously scandalized by the likelihood that a seller might receive more for his goods than they were originally worth, but failed to make allowances for the seller's inconvenience while awaiting payment. In Great Britain it was standard practice during this period for the prices of naval stores the government purchased to be above prevailing market rates because of uncertainties as to the date of payment and the fact that bills were sold at discount, the rate varying in accordance with the expected interval before payment. Sir William Beveridge, *Prices and Wages in England from the Twelfth to the Nineteenth Century*, I. *Price Tables: Mercantile Era* (London-New York, 1939), 623–625, 522–525.

crimes attributed to their owners. At the time of confiscation a detailed inventory of the entire estate was always ordered. Frequently, however, it was not completed until years later, when the property had already lost much of its value because of neglect and looting. By that time the initial royal custodian had often removed, disappeared, or died without having made a proper account of his stewardship. In both instances the Crown lost dearly.

The Nature of the Accounting Reforms

The new accounting procedures established in Brazil by a carta régia of 1764 were designed to correct such haphazard procedures. They were also intended to provide high colonial and Peninsular authorities with a clear picture of the status of royal finances in each unit of the empire, as well as to assure improved collection of royal revenues and more prompt payment of the king's obligations.[30] To achieve these ends the Crown ordered the establishment of a new set of records in each captaincy-general and subordinate captaincy patterned after the new types of books kept by the Royal Treasury in Lisbon. Each junta da fazenda was required to keep a master ledger to record all income and expenditures within its administrative unit. That ledger was divided into two sections, one for debts and credits accumulated before December 31, 1761, the other for annual income and expenditures after that date. A fresh ledger was to be opened at the beginning of each calendar year, and when it was closed the board was charged with drawing up a statement of the year's total income and expenditures to be reported to the appropriate comptroller-general and the inspector-general in Lisbon.[31]

The treasurer-general of each unit kept three additional annual ledgers to record the three major divisions (folhas) of royal expendi-

---

[30] Carta régia to Conde da Cunha, Jan. 18, 1764, ANRJ, Col. 60, Liv. XXXVIII, fols. 120ᵛ–121ʳ (*1.a via*); "Reprezentasão dos ministros que regem a real fazenda officiaes e livros que hé necessario criamse, e mais providencias todas de utilidade e boa arrecadassão della nesta cidade da Bahia," Aug. 16, 1766, CMCM, cod. 21, fols. 42ʳ–45ʳ.

[31] For an example of the less rigorous procedures previously followed in the recording of income and expenses, see carta régia to provedor of Santos, Mar. 22, 1736, *DH*, I (1928), 291–292. The discussion which follows is based primarily on [Lavradio?], "Methodo que com o tribunal da real fazenda tenho mandado praticar de novo nesta cidade do Rio de Janeiro para se evitarem os prejuizos, confuzoens, e dezordens, que havia na provedoria da fazenda real, e suas repartiçoens." n. d. (*ca.* mid-December 1770), CMCM, cod. 22, fols. 1ʳ–48ᵛ. This document complements the one cited in note 28 above, and the text is organized by articles situated on the right-hand side of each page, leaving the left-hand column for accompanying notes, the evident purpose being to emphasize the way double-entry accounts were arranged.

tures. In one were entered payments of ecclesiastical allowances (*cóngruas*) ; in a second were listed the unit's ordinary expenses, the salaries and other operating costs of each department. The third ledger was reserved for military expenditures. All accounts and all appointments were to run from January 1 to December 31 and were to be paid quarterly, thus eliminating the elaborate procedures previously outlined.

Each department of the exchequer was likewise required to maintain a separate set of books to prevent errors of commission and omission. For example, the chief storekeeper (almoxarife) was enjoined to have the following books: (1) a general ledger; (2) a ledger for each commodity, such as wood or farinha, regularly purchased; (3) a ledger showing current accounts with each installation the storehouse supplied; (4) a day journal to record goods received and disbursed; and (5) a journal for miscellaneous expenses (*despezas pelo miudo*). The data entered in these two journals were transferred later to the general ledger.

All ledgers were to be arranged in accordance with standard double-entry procedures. Each page of the general ledger, for example, was divided into two vertical columns, one for receipts and the other for expenditures. On the left-hand or debit side under a column labeled *o deve* were recorded the quantity of goods received, the name of the seller, the unit price, and the total amount of the purchase. Below this information were affixed three signatures, those of the almoxarife, his scribe, and the seller, attesting that the bill had been settled.[32] On the right-hand or credit side of the same page in a column headed *ha de haver* were entered the quantity of goods delivered to an agency of the government, the name of the authorized receiver, the unit price, and the total value of the delivery. This entry was verified by the signatures of the receiver, the almoxarife, and his scribe.[33]

Previously, at the end of their terms all officials who handled money were obliged to present themselves and their records before

[32] A typical entry follows:

150 Feixes de Lenha   De Pedro da Silva, cento cincoenta feixes de lenha a trinta reis; importao, quatro mil e quinhentos reis, q. logo recebo. . .

4$500

/ss/ Araujo   Pedro da S[ilv]a   Burrish

CMCM, cod. 22, fol. 11ᵛ.

[33] A typical entry follows:

300 Feixes de Lenha   A Antonio Dias Marquez, Quartel Me. do Regimento de Infantaria de Moura p.a fornecimento do mesmo regimento desde o 1.º até dez do corrente a trinta reis importao nove mil reis

9$000

/ss/ Araujo   Antonio Dias Marques   Burrish

ibid., fol. 12ʳ.

their superiors in Bahia or in Lisbon for quittance.[34] This wasteful and inefficient practice was abolished in 1760, when the Crown declared that in the future such officers should settle their accounts with the local exchequer, which would make periodic reports on the status of such accounts to the colonial secretary and the Overseas Council.[35] In Rio de Janeiro, for example, the almoxarife was required to report each Saturday with his general ledger to a room in the viceregal palace set aside for the deliberations of the junta da fazenda. There the board members went over the previous week's purchases and verified that they had been made at the lowest prices offered in the market. When satisfied with the storekeeper's report, they signed a statement that his ledger was in order. Other officials underwent similar scrutiny at intervals varying from once a month to once a quarter.[36]

New procedures were introduced to correct the casual handling of the outfitting of royal warships. As soon as such vessels entered port, the senior executive officer automatically named an ad hoc junta da fragata consisting of the ship's captain, the provedor, and an intendant,[37] which met one afternoon a week to go over the ship's accounts.[38] A separate set (jogo) of books was opened for each ship upon her arrival; in them were entered every expenditure and every item of cargo placed aboard. When the ship was ready to depart, one register was delivered to the junta da fazenda, the other remained with the captain. Duplicate rosters of the crew were also compiled, one becoming a part of the treasury board's files, the other being retained by the captain for presentation to his superiors upon his return to Lisbon. These measures were obviously intended to prevent the kinds of frauds practiced by warship captains in the past.

Other innovations were designed to reduce the leakage from sequestered properties and to provide better information concerning litigation in which the exchequer was plaintiff. With respect to confiscated estates, a separate chest, called o depozito de sequestros, was guarded in the office of the treasurer-general and the value of all gold

34 For some indications that such quittance was not always observed, see cartas régias of Dec. 13, 1685 and Apr. 20, 1688, ABNRJ, XXVIII (1906), 273-274.

35 Carta régia, Aug. 16, 1760, ANRJ, Col. 60, Liv. XXXVI, fols. 186ᵛ-187ʳ.

36 Thus, for example, the customs' receiver of Santos was required to deliver his accounts within the first ten days of each month. Carta régia, July 7, 1774 (cited in note 10 above), p. 12.

37 Presumably this was the intendant of gold, but the reference (see note 31) is not clear.

38 According to the "Methodo que se praticava na provedoria" (note 28 above, fol. 51ᵛ.), an order calling for such juntas had not been put into effect "por entrar em duvida quem havia prezedir" at such meetings. The viceroy resolved this problem of etiquette by simply directing the three dignitaries to sit at a round table! "Methodo que . . . tenho mandado praticar de novo nesta cidade." (see note 31) fol. 4ʳ.

and silver objects it contained was verified in writing by an official appraiser (*contraste*). A ledger was also kept to record deposits and withdrawals for each account. In the chambers of the junta da fazenda there was a special book in which were entered details concerning all court cases in which the treasury was an interested party, and twice a month the procurator informed the board on the current status of such suits.

Some conclusions on the effectiveness of the new procedures will be presented later. In theory the juntas da fazenda bore collective responsibility for their implementation, but the task of supervising the conversion of each captaincy-general's records to the new system fell mainly to the board's secretaries, the chief auditors, while the resolution of disputes between rival functionaries became one more duty of the senior executives.

The Filling of Public Offices

Another of the treasury boards' responsibilities was the making of appointments to vacant and nonproprietary public offices.[39] During the early colonial period such positions were filled in the private captaincies by the donataries in accordance with their charters (*doações*). In royal captaincies the governors-general were empowered to name temporary or deputy officeholders (*serventuários*) to fill vacancies or to replace persons unable to serve because of demonstrable incompetence, physical or mental disability; however, permanent appointments could only be made by the Crown, which granted title to offices in return for conspicuous service and for money payments.[40] By longstanding rule governors-general were forbidden to create new salaried positions or to name members of their personal entourage to vacan-

---

[39] No systematic study comparable to J. H. Parry's "The Sale of Public Office in the Spanish Indies under the Habsburgs," (*Ibero-Americana*, No. 37 [Berkeley, 1953]), which is more concerned with royal policy than with the incidence of venality, has ever been made for the Portuguese empire. In the section which follows my principal guides with respect to policy have been the comments of D. Fernando José de Portugal (2RGG, Chap. 7 [*DH*, VI, 323–332]), and Teixeira Coelho ("Instrução," pp. 417–423). Valuable light on the circumstances of proprietary ownership of offices in Brazil is shed by two genealogical sources: Fr. Antônio de S. Maria Jaboatão, "Catálogo geneológico [da Bahia]," ed., Afonso Costa, *RIHGB*, CXCI (Abril-Junho, 1946), 1–279; and António José Victoriano Borges da Fonseca, "Nobiliarchia Pernambucana," *ABNRJ*, XLVII–XLVIII (1935).

[40] The granting of proprietary rights to office in recompense for exceptional services appears to have been especially common during and following the ousting of the Dutch from Brazil. Thus, Antonio de Ataide de Albuquerque was conceded the office of Juiz de Órfãos of the vila of Serinhaem (Pernambuco) in 1636 "em renumeração dos bons serviços, que fez na guerra dos Hollandeses." Borges da Fonseca, *ABNRJ*, XLVII, 32.

cies.[41] The administrative heads were cautioned to guard against unsanctioned absenteeism or the naming by proprietors of unauthorized substitutes.[42] Until late in the seventeenth century office-holders do not seem to have been subject to special assessments other than half annates,[43] but in 1692 a use tax, called the *novos direitos* was established, enabling the Crown to collect about 10 percent of the annual yield of all fee-paying positions.[44]

As in contemporary Western Europe and in other parts of colonial America, private ownership of public offices became widespread in colonial Brazil, where virtually all posts except those of governors and senior magistrates could be obtained from the Crown by concession or by purchase.[45] As elsewhere, offices were sought because of their income potential and because of the prestige associated with their possession. Ranging in yearly income from a mere 10,000 réis to the handsome sum of 250,000 réis during the eighteenth century, they included largely honorific jobs like those of castellans (*alcaides*) and a wide variety of fee-earning positions such as those exercised by notaries and other clerks, porters, inspectors, and bailiffs. Minor judgeships like that of the *juizes de órfãos* who were responsible for the care of orphans and the posts of town council secretary (*escrivão da câmara*) were usually held by proprietors; so, too were certain major salaried positions, including two key fiscal offices in every captaincy, the almoxarife and the provedor.[46] Sometimes the Crown rewarded particularly able salaried officials by granting them their posts for one or more lives.[47] Other common recipients included professional soldiers, colonial merchants, a surprising number of *senhores de engenho,* and widows of all sorts of supposedly meritorious Peninsular- and

---

[41] Alvará of Dec. 3, 1621 (repeating an order of 1602), *Boletim do Conselho Ultramarino. Legislação antiga,* I (Lisbon, 1867), 217–218; 2RGG, par. 40; king to Dom Lourenço de Almeida, Sept. 6, 1716, *ABNRJ,* XXVIII (1906), 374.

[42] See several orders on this point dating from 1662 to 1668 in *ibid.,* 354.

[43] During the second half of the seventeenth century half annates were collected on notarial offices at the rate of 10 percent of their estimated annual yield. See *carta patente* of Gaspar Maciel Villasbôas, n.d. (*ca.* 1668), *DH,* XIII (1929), 35–36. Annates do not appear to have been collected in the eighteenth century.

[44] Provisão of Feb. 16, 1692, *ABNRJ,* XXVIII, 293. The order fails to stipulate the rate of the impost which I have estimated on the basis of the "Lista dos officios de justiça e fazenda da capitania de Minas Geraes . . . calculo dos seus rendimentos feito no anno de 1777," in Teixeira Coelho, "Instrução," pp. 424–431.

[45] I do not discount the possibility that senior executive and major judicial posts may occasionally have been hawked, but I have found no evidence that they were.

[46] In the 1730s even the provedor mór da fazenda was a proprietary official. See note 54 below.

[47] Such was the good fortune of Lisbon-born Pedro Cadena Vilsante who came to Brazil in the late sixteenth or early seventeenth century and served in the office of the provedor mór da fazenda of Bahia "e o fez com tão bôa ordem e cuidado que se lhe fez mercê da propriedade delle por duas vidas." Borgas da Fonseca, *ABNRJ,* XLVII, 190.

colonial-born husbands.[48] I have found no instance where the position of alderman (*vereador*) was granted for life by the Crown, a not uncommon practice in the larger cities of Spanish America; but it is interesting to note that the câmara of Recife held a proprietary interest in four offices in Pernambuco.[49] During the early eighteenth century a priest in the same captaincy owned a clerkship in the ouvidoria of Olinda said to be worth 70,000 réis a year.[50] And, surprisingly enough, the office of the provedor of Pernambuco was owned in the late seventeenth century by Simão Álvares de la Penha Deusdará, one of the very few identifiable colonial-born desembargadores of a High Court in Brazil.[51] The desembargador (and presumably the padre also) had inherited his proprietorship from his father. It was not uncommon during the seventeenth and eighteenth centuries for offices to pass from father to son to grandson (or to sons-in-law, for offices were frequently given as dowries by presumably grateful fathers-in-law) and thereby remain in the possession of one family for a century or longer.[52] Although the Crown sternly frowned against pluralism,[53] there are numerous instances of officeholders deriving income simultaneously from several posts in their possession.[54]

With the elaboration of the bureaucracy during the eighteenth century, the opportunity to acquire more than one office greatly in-

[48] For an instance of a widow seeking proprietary rights to the office of *meirinho do mar* of Rio de Janeiro, see consulta of Oct. 30, 1694, Castro e Almeida, *Inventário*, VI, 221 (nums. 1,951–53). The Pernambuco list of *ca.* 1718 (see note 49) reveals that a substantial number of proprietary offices were owned by women and exercised by male deputies.

[49] See the untitled list of public offices, their holders, and their yield in the captaincy-general for *ca.* 1718, *ABNRJ*, XXVIII, 467–473.

[50] *Ibid.*, 470.

[51] Jaboatão, "Catálogo geneológico," 143–144.

[52] Thus Bento Banderia de Melo, first escrivão da fazenda real of Paraíba after its restoration (1655) was conceded proprietary rights to the combined office of escrivão da fazenda real, alfândega e almoxarifado, a position inherited by his son, Hypólito Bandeira de Melo, and later by his grandson, Bento Bandeira de Melo, who died in 1769. Borges da Fonseca, *ABNRJ*, XLVII, 191–192. Numerous other examples of familial continuity in offices may be found in the genealogies.

[53] "Por convir ao bem publico, que nenhuma pessôa tenha dous officaes nem de serventia; nem de propriedade. . . ." Carta régia, Aug. 6, 1681, *DH*, XXXII (1936), 371–373.

[54] A classic example is that of José Pires de Carvalho e Albuquerque. The second son (with a name identical to that of his elder brother and their father) of the famous Bahian poet, José Pires (b. 1756) held the offices of *alcaide-mor* of Maragogipe, *intendente das marinhas, procurador da fazenda, provedor da alfândega* and *secretário geral do estado*. The last of these positions was an office obtained by his father in 1741 and was held by him until his death in 1774, when it passed to the elder son who yielded it to the younger in 1778. Jaboatão, "Catálogo genealógico," 174–175. For further examples see *ibid* and Borges da Fonseca, *passim.* It is interesting to note that in the 1730s Luiz Lopes Pegado Serpe was *provedor mór proprietário da fazenda real, juiz privativo* of the treasury, and also auditor general of the garrison of Salvador. *DH*, I (1928), 241 f.

creased. That elaboration occurred as a consequence of the physical expansion of the colony, the growth of its population, its greatly enhanced economic importance, and the Crown's desire to subject the colonials to more effective regulation. There are indications, however, that the number of salable offices substantially exceeded the number of potential purchasers. A list of offices in the captaincy-general of Pernambuco prepared about 1718 reveals that only fifty-five of ninety-one positions for which information is available were held by proprietors.[55] And in 1723 the Crown authorized colonial governors (with the concurrence of their ouvidores) to award all vacant and newly created positions that had not attracted proprietors to fit persons (pessôas idoneas) who agreed to contribute an initial gift (donativo) as well as a third of their yearly earnings to the Crown.[56] Three years later this policy was modified in two respects: positions valued at less than 200,000 réis per annum were declared exempt from the payment of the so-called terças partes; holders of posts worth more than that amount were required to make installment payments each semester rather than at the end of the year as originally stipulated, an innovation designed to lessen opportunities for tax evasion.[57] However, such functionaries remained temporary appointees (serventuários) rather than true proprietors and had no assurance of tenure. Indeed, a decree of 1741 declared that serventias would be awarded to whoever offered the largest gift to the Crown, provided that such assignments did not lead to the removal of competent persons for less capable ones.[58] All appointments by colonial authorities remained provisional until confirmed by the Overseas Council.[59]

Because of the difficulty of finding purchasers for judicial and fiscal posts, a carta régia of 1761 declared that the treasury board of Rio de Janeiro would be responsible for leasing such offices within its jurisdiction.[60] That jurisdiction included Minas Gerais and São Paulo

[55] See above, n. 49.

[56] Carta régia, Dec. 23, 1723, ABNRJ, XXVIII, 356–357.

[57] Teixeira Coelho, "Instrução," p. 420, Chap. 16. The terças partes assessment was subsequently construed to apply to the initial 200,000 réis of an office's yield as well as to income in excess of that amount.

[58] Carta régia, Feb. 25, 1741, ABNRJ, XXVIII, 357. According to Viceroy Portugal, "Não ha regra certa que prescreva o donativo, bem entendido que o Governador se deve regular pelo que tiver pago o Serventuario anterior, não havendo pessoa que o offereça maior." 2RGG, DH, VI, 326.

[59] Consulta of Oct. 4, 1745, ABNRJ, XXVIII, 335.

[60] Antonio de Azevedo Coutinho to Sebastião José de Carvalho, June 1, 1759, Castro e Almeida, Inventário, I, 343; carta régia, Oct. 24, 1761, ANRJ, Col. 60, Liv. XXXVII, fols. 64ᵛ–65ᵛ. The order was addressed to a board generally called the conselho da fazenda, a predecessor of the juntas da fazenda, which included the senior executive officer, senior magistrate, the treasury procurator and the Crown procurator (an officer of the Relações in Bahia and Rio de Janeiro), but not a professional accountant as did its successor.

until their juntas were established.[61] The boards were instructed to give notice each December of the availability of vacant offices by means of edicts posted throughout the captaincy-general. After the tenders had been examined, successful bidders were appointed for three-year terms beginning January 1 and ending December 31. The juntas were warned to guard against the common abuses of pluralism, nonresidence, and the employment of unauthorized substitutes.[62] Though the boards collectively approved triennial leases, the senior executive officers had the right to fill vacancies for periods of less than one year.[63]

Chief Expenditures of the Viceroyalty

A major responsibility assigned to the juntas da fazenda was the regulation of the captaincy-general's expenditures. In practice all payments were authorized by their president, the senior executive officer, who initialed warrants (portarias) addressed to the treasurer-general. Upon their receipt that officer instructed the appropriate disburser to pay out the approved sums. The principal categories of expenditure of the Lavradio board were the following: [64]

I. The Ecclesiastical Register:
   Livings and stipends

[61] I.e., respectively until 1769 and 1775. Teixeira Coelho, "Instrução," p. 418; junta da fazenda (Rio de Janeiro) to provedor of São Paulo, Nov. 4, 1767, DH, II (1928), 350–351; see also Luis António de Sousa (captain-general of São Paulo) to Oeiras, Mar. 16, 1768, RIHGB/TE, VI (1957), 69, who argued that it would be advantageous to the Royal Treasury if public offices in São Paulo were leased by a local board rather than by the one in Rio de Janeiro.

[62] Overseas Council to Lavradio, Mar. 20, 1771, BNRJ, 10, 4, 8 (unfoliated); Oeiras to junta da fazenda (Rio de Janeiro), Apr. 4, 1769, ANRJ, Col. 67, Liv. III, fols. 34[r-v]. Earlier the Conde de Azambuja had criticized illegal arrangements between proprietors and deputies whose evident purpose seems to have been tax-dodging. Azambuja to Francisco Xavier de Mendonça Furtado, Aug. 28, 1767, Castro e Almeida, Inventário, II, 179. Proprietors were obliged to take possession of their posts within one year or suffer their loss. Lavradio to Manoel Joze de Oliveira (treasury procurator), Jan. 15, 1776, CMCM, cod. 25, fols. 75[r-v].

[63] Such vacancies were filled according to the formula "em quanto estiver vago, e não for rematado pelo Tribunal da Junta da Fazenda. . . ." Portarias of May 6 and June 26, 1776 and Feb. 28, 1777, CMCM, cod. 19, fols. 47[r-v], 64[r], and 163[v]. It is interesting to note that despite the one-member-one-vote principle that was supposed to prevail within the junta, the Crown ordered that when decisions on such leases were made, "No cazo porem de votarem os Ministros de que a mesma Junta se compoem q. huma parte, e vos [i.e., the president] por outra valerá sempre o vosso voto, posto q. singular, contra a pluralidade de votos, dandome nestas cazos conta especial das razoens q. tiverdes para vos a partarez dos referidos votos." Carta régia, Oct. 24, 1761, cited in note 60 above.

[64] Adapted from "Importancia das addições que formão em suma o total de despesa das referidas thesourarias [da capitania-geral do Rio de Janeiro]," ca. 1781, RIHGB, XLVII:1, 42–43.

II. The Civil Register:
    Salaries
    Perquisites (*propinas* and *emolumentos*)
    Housing allowances
    Travel allowances
    Other expenses
III. The Military Register:
    Salaries of the general staff (officers and secretariat)
    Pay of infantry, cavalry, and artillery forces (regulars and active militia) stationed within the captaincy-general
    Clothing allowances
    Quartering expenses
    Provisions and other supplies
    Expenses of the military hospital (the ex-Jesuit college in Rio de Janeiro)
IV. The Extraordinary Register:
    Special funds distributed at the discretion of the viceroy
    Expenses of the royal storehouses
    Expenses of the provedoria
    Expenses of the intendency-general of gold
    Expenses of the customs house
    Expenses of the mint
    Expenses of the Relação
    Expenses of the arms factory
    Expenses of the marine arsenal
    Expenses of the powder house
    Expenses of the fortifications and fortresses
    Maintenance of royal warships stationed in the captaincy-general and of others while in port
    Pay and allowances of naval personnel
    Subsidy for São Paulo
    Miscellaneous obligations

The above listing is based upon a report of 1781 that gives the average yearly income and expenditures of the treasury board of Rio de Janeiro for the years 1768–1778. It is evident that most of the items included in the Extraordinary Register could properly be grouped under either the Civil or the Military Register. The fact that they were not suggests that fiscal authorities had not yet made any clear separation between continuing and nonrecurring expenses.

The relative importance of these expenditures will be discussed in the following chapter. One item in the Extraordinary Register requires explanation at this point—the annual subsidy paid by the board in Rio de Janeiro to its counterpart in São Paulo. The fact that wealthier parts of the Spanish empire, like the viceroyalty of New Spain, were expected to support less flourishing districts, such as Florida, Venezuela, or the Philippines, is well known.[65] The fact that the same practice also prevailed in Brazil is not. The origins of the Santos subsidy, an annual consignment of 4,000 cruzados (1,600,000 réis), trace back to the early eighteenth century. When the Crown created the joint captaincy-general of São Paulo and Minas Gerais (1709), it asked the governor of Rio de Janeiro whether he agreed with the new captain-general of São Paulo that the praça of Santos should be united with the joint captaincy-general. Since no royal administrator could ever concede that a rival authority should govern disputed territory, the Carioca official naturally demurred, and in 1711 Lisbon announced that Santos would henceforth be a part of the captaincy-general of Rio de Janeiro. That announcement inevitably brought forth a protest from the captain-general of São Paulo who argued with considerable logic that Santos was much closer to São Paulo than to Rio de Janeiro and was the highland city's natural outlet to the sea, but his protest was ignored. However, when São Paulo and Minas Gerais became separate governments in 1720, the Court transferred jurisdiction over the port from Rio de Janeiro to São Paulo. A major fortress was then being built at Santos, and since the resources of the remnant captaincy-general of São Paulo were deemed insufficient to bear the burden of its completion, the Crown, in 1722, assigned a portion of the customs' revenues collected in Rio de Janeiro to São Paulo for that purpose. That action was intended to be temporary, but like so many temporary fiscal measures, the subsidy became a permanent charge upon the Carioca exchequer. With payments often in arrears, the Santos subsidy continued to be a source of dispute between authorities in the two captaincies-general throughout the eighteenth century.[66]

65 For the problems stemming from subsidy payments in these areas, see John J. Te Paske, *The Governorship of Spanish Florida 1700–1763* (Durham, 1964) [*s.v.* index under "situado"]; Eduardo Arcila Farías. *Comercio entre Venezuela y México en los siglos XVI y XVII* (Mexico, 1950), Chap. 7; and John L. Phelan, *The Hispanization of the Philippines . . .* 1565–1700 (Madison, 1959) [*s.v.* index under "deficit"].

66 For details concerning the Santos subsidy, see the exchanges between the Crown and authorities in São Paulo and Rio de Janeiro between 1710 and 1720 in *DI*, LXVII (1929), 74–76, 78–79, 86A, 90, 94–96; also, Overseas Council to governors of Rio de Janeiro, May 6, 1722 and May 8, 1746, ANRJ, Col. 60, Liv. XX, fol. 17ʳ and Liv. XXI, fols. 2ᵛ–3ʳ. In 1783 the junta da fazenda of São Paulo calculated that unpaid payments due from the Carioca exchequer dating from the administrations of Gomes Freire de Andrada and the Conde da Cunha amounted to 25,500,073 réis. Junta of São Paulo to junta of Rio de Janeiro, Oct. 31, 1783, *RIHGB/TE*, VIII (1958), 85. The topic was ignored by Francisco Martins dos Santos in his superficial factual miscellany *Historia dos Santos, 1532–1936* (2 v., São Paulo, 1937).

Sources of Royal Income

The collection and management of all royal income within each captaincy-general was another important responsibility of the treasury boards. The Crown's revenues were derived from a variety of taxes, imposts, and tolls which may be conveniently grouped under the following heads: (a) major taxes on agricultural, mineral, and pastoral products; (b) duties on internal and external commerce; (c) excises; and (d) miscellaneous.[67]

The principal taxes levied on the products of agriculture, mining, and ranching consisted of the tithes (*dízimos*), the fifths (*quintos*), seigniorage, brassage and other charges collected on minted bullion, and a tax on cattle hides called the *quinto do couro*. By the bull *Super specula* (1551) collection of the tithes in Brazil was assigned to the king of Portugal in his role as Grand Master of the Order of Christ which bore theoretical responsibility for the maintenance of the colonial Church. Such tithes were classified as real, mixed, and personal, but the Crown gained from only the first two categories. Real tithes consisted of one-tenth of the estimated value of all agricultural products, while mixed tithes were levied upon livestock, fowl, wax, cheese, and honey as well as on the profits earned by sugar mills, brandy distilleries, and bread ovens. Personal tithes, generally one-tenth of the earnings from an office, trade, or business, were paid directly to the clergy at Easter. Theoretically all tithe revenues were to be used for the support of the Church, but in practice the Crown employed them for general expenses as well.[68]

During the century 1550–1650 when sugar was king in Brazil the tithes were by far the Crown's leading source of revenue from the colony. Following the mineral discoveries late in the seventeenth century, the royal fifths, generally 20 percent of mined or washed gold, became an even more lucrative source of income. Very little gold was

---

[67] Though none is complete, the following references contain useful discussions of royal income in Brazil: Teixeira Coelho, "Instrução," Chaps. XII, XIV–XX; José de Souza Azevedo Pizarro e Araujo, *Memórias históricas do Rio de Janeiro*, II, 238–248; Myriam Ellis, *O monopólio do sal no estado do Brasil (1631–1801)* (São Paulo, 1955), pp. 61–63; Augusto Olympio Viveiros de Castro, "Historia tributaria do Brasil," *RIHGB*, LXXVIII:1 (1916), 21–23; Garcia, *Ensaio sobre a hist. admin.*, Chap. XII; and Boxer, *The Golden Age, passim*.

[68] See Boxer, *The Golden Age*, p. 348, for a contemporary statement concerning the allocation of tithe income in Minas Gerais. Standard sources on the colonial tithes are Oscar de Oliveira, *Os dízimos eclesiásticos do Brasil nos períodos colónia e do império* (Juiz de Fóra, 1940), especially pp. 17, 19, 52, 54–58, 60–63; and Manoel Cardozo, "Tithes in Colonial Minas Gerais," *Catholic Historical Review*, XXXVIII (July 1952), 175–182.

found in the captaincy-general of Rio de Janeiro, but its junta da fazenda was charged with the gathering of the fifths from the interior captaincies and their remission to the Royal Treasury.[69] Seigniorage, generally 5 percent of the appraised value of minted bullion, was collected at the mint in Rio de Janeiro and was used to defray the expenses of royal warships stopping there, the cost of hardwoods shipped to the royal arsenal in Lisbon, and the salaries and victuals of Peninsular troops stationed in the colonial capital.[70] Beginning in the 1690s the quinto do couro, presumably rated at 20 percent was levied on hides exported from Colônia do Sacramento; subsequently it was extended to hide shipments from Rio Grande de São Pedro. In both cases the revenues appear to have been used for government salaries.[71]

The Crown also collected several kinds of taxes on seaborne commerce between various parts of its Atlantic empire as well as on goods transported overland from one point to another within Brazil. The most onerous was an ad valorem levy of 26 percent collected in Peninsular ports on goods shipped to the colonies.[72] Until the turn of the eighteenth century no import duties were collected in Brazil, but between 1699 and 1715 a tax called the *dízima da alfândega* was established by the principal maritime câmaras at the behest of the Crown. As its name implies, this was a 10 percent ad valorem duty levied on imported merchandise, and its revenues were earmarked for the support of local military garrisons.[73] In 1719 a so-called coast guard tax was established by the câmara of Rio de Janeiro for the maintenance of a guard ship off the Brazilian littoral,[74] and another tax bearing the same name was created in 1756 to pay the expenses of the frigate stationed off the Mina (Lower Guiana) Coast of Africa to defend Portuguese shipping against Dutch privateers.[75]

[69] On the various methods used in assessment of the tithes in Minas Gerais and the controversies stemming therefrom, see Teixeira Coelho, "Instrução," Chap. XII, and Boxer, *The Golden Age* (*s.v.* index under "Fifths"). The role of the viceroy in the gathering and remission of the fifths is described in the following chapter, see pp. 323 f.

[70] Costa Cardozo to Lavradio, *ca.* 1770 (cited in note 15 above), f. 27ʳ.

[71] Pizarro, *Memorias*, II, 247.

[72] Consulta of July 24, 1715, Virginia Rau and Maria Fernanda Gomes da Silva, eds., *Os manuscritos do arquivo da casa de Cadaval respeitantes ao Brasil*, II (Coimbra, 1958), 151.

[73] The dízima was established in Rio de Janeiro by 1699 (Pizarro, *Memorias*, II, 247), in Bahia before and in Pernambuco by 1715 (*ABNRJ*, XXVIII, 286). According to Ellis (*Sal*, p. 62) revenues collected in Rio de Janeiro from this source were assigned to meet the expenses of fortifications in Santos, Colônia, and in Guanabara Bay.

[74] For the rather complicated schedule of this impost, see Pizarro, *Memorias*, II, 246–247.

[75] José Antonio Freire de Andrada to Diogo de Mendonça, Jan. 30, 1756, *ABNRJ*, LXX, 35.

The flourishing African slave trade was too inviting a source of revenue to be neglected, and during the eighteenth century it was repeatedly tapped at various points. Thus in 1699 the Crown responded to pleas by the Bishop of São Tomé for funds to support his church by creating a tax of 1,000 réis on each slave passing through that island.[76] Two decades later, when the Portuguese were endeavoring to assure their supply of West African slaves for Brazilian mines by establishing the Ajuda factory at Whydah on the Mina Coast, another impost of 1,000 réis per slave was levied for the protection of Portuguese shipping and the prevention of smugglers along the Coast.[77] Far heavier was another impost introduced in 1714–1715 applicable to slaves imported from the African stations and reexported from Pernambuco, Bahia, and Rio de Janeiro to Minas Gerais and to Negroes born in Brazil "who by the perversity of their character are unsuitable for work in the sugar mills and fields" and could therefore be sold to work in the mines. This levy, amounting to 4,500 réis per head, seems to have been initially intended to reassure distressed sugar interests who feared that their supplies of fresh slaves would be entirely diverted to the mines, but it soon became an important source of royal income.[78]

Slaves sent to Minas Gerais were also assessed a portion of the interior customs duties called *entradas*. The entradas, established according to a schedule worked out between 1710 and 1714, were levied on all merchandise, livestock, and chattels entering Minas from adjacent captaincies-general and were expected to defray a large part of the cost of royal government in Minas. Each slave was taxed 3,000 réis, each head of cattle 1,500 réis, and each horse and mule 3,000 réis. Merchandise was divided into two classes, so-called "wet" goods (*fazendas de molhados*) and "dry" stores (*fazendas secas*). The former were assessed at the rate of 750 réis per mule-load (*carga*), generally sixty to ninety pounds, while the latter paid 1,125 réis per carga, so that a premium was placed on the importation of goods of high value rather than those of small worth. For this reason the entrada system drew strong criticism from Secretary Melo e Castro in the 1780s.[79] Cariocas may well have registered complaints themselves, for although the bulk of the imports to Minas passed through Rio de Ja-

---

76 Carta régia, Jan. 10, 1699, *ibid.*, XXVIII, 296–297.

77 *Ibid.*, 297. For the tribulations of the factory and its directors, see the excellent (but inadequately documented) study by A. F. C. Ryder, "The Re-establishment of Portuguese Factories on the Costa da Mina to the Mid Eighteenth Century," *Journal of the Historical Society of Nigeria*, I (Dec. 1958), 157–183.

78 Provisão of Mar. 27, 1714, cited in provisão of Aug. 17, 1715, *ABNRJ*, XXVIII, 295–296.

79 "Instrucção para o Visconde de Barbacena," Jan. 29, 1788, *RIHGB*, VI (1844), 41–44, pars. 81–89.

neiro, that captaincy did not share in the allocation of entrada revenues which were distributed among the captaincies-general of São Paulo, Mato Grosso, Goiás, and Minas Gerais.[80]

The entradas were collected by interior customs stations (registros) situated at strategic river crossings and in mountain passes. A number of these ports guarded the principal approaches from the littoral to Minas Gerais, others were located along cattle trails extending from Piauí, interior Bahia, and Rio Grande de São Pedro to the mining zones. At such points transit tolls (passagens), variable in amount from one station to another, were levied on livestock, carts, and travelers passing from one zone to the next. In Rio Grande, for example, each cart paid 4,800 réis and each person 120 réis before crossing the Araranguá, Mampituba, and Tramandi rivers, while in São Paulo persons crossing the Paraná en route to Minas paid 640 réis for themselves and 40 réis for each horse. Two registros on the Paraíba and Paraibuna rivers, whose tolls went to the Rio de Janeiro exchequer, were the most important in that captaincy because they were located along the heavily traveled road between the capital and Minas Gerais.[81]

The third category of royal revenues consisted of a series of excises (subsídios) levied on locally produced and imported products which for the most part can be classified as luxuries. The origins of these taxes lie in the seventeenth century when colonial câmaras repeatedly responded to appeals from their impoverished Crown for assistance in raising funds to defray vital expenses. Though portions of such tax revenues were in some instances used for municipal purposes, particularly the construction of public works and the care of foundlings (engeitados), they were primarily reserved for the payment of salaries to royal officials and for the support of military garrisons.

The principal excises created by the câmara of Rio de Janeiro are listed in Table 1.[82]

Finally, there were a number of miscellaneous sources of royal in-

---

[80] The foregoing discussion is based on Teixeira Coelho, "Instrução," pp. 404–406, which includes a breakdown of the distribution of the entradas to the four captaincies-general ca. 1776. See also Boxer, The Golden Age, pp. 347 ff.

[81] Ibid., pp. 348–349; Teixeira Coelho, "Instrução," Chap. XII; Francisco José Roscio, "Compêndio noticioso do continente do Rio Grande de S. Pedro, 1774–75," RIHGRGS, anno 22 (1942), 51; see also Myriam Ellis, "Contribuição ao estudo do abastecimento das zonas mineradoras do Brasil no século XVIII," Revista de historia, IX, No. 36 (1958), 436–443.

[82] Table 1 is based upon Pizarro, Memorias, II, 244–247; Ellis, Sal, p. 62; the consulta of Nov. 12, 1729 cited in n. 105 below; and Castro e Almeida, Inventário, VII, 22, 24–27. For a contemporary description of the excises authorized by the câmara of Olinda (Pernambuco) which sometimes set much higher duties than did that of Rio de Janeiro, see ABNRJ, XXVIII, 283–285.

TABLE 1
EXCISES ESTABLISHED BY THE CÂMARA OF RIO DE JANEIRO

Name and Date Established	Incidence	Application
Large excise on wines (1641)	8,000 rs. per pipe Madeira; 4,000 rs. per pipe of wine from Portugal or the Azores	For infantry pay and cost of fortifications
Little excise on wines (1656)	2,000 rs. per pipe of any imported wine	For municipal improvements
Excise on local brandies (1661)	1,120 rs. per *canada* (i.e., 3 English pints)	Initially for pay of garrisons around Rio de Janeiro; later also for troops stationed at Colônia
Excise on brandies from the Kingdom and Atlantic Islands	800 rs. per bbl. or 3,000 rs. per pipe	For Colônia garrison and for public works in Rio de Janeiro
Sweet oil excise (1689)	800 rs. per bbl.	To provide for an increase in the governor's salary and for care of foundlings
Salt gabelle (1689)	80 rs. per *alqueire* of imported salt	For same
Tobacco import excises (1697 and 1722)	40 rs. per lb. leaf sold at wholesale; 20 rs. per lb. sold at retail; 100 rs. per lb. snuff (*tobacco em po*.)	For support of garrisons in Rio de Janeiro and Colônia. The 1722 snuff tax was part of the coast guard levy

come. One of the oldest (dating from the late sixteenth century) was a 1 percent levy on all revenues and contracts pertaining to Brazil; its yield was reserved for so-called pious works in the kingdom.[83] Also included under this rubric were the previously mentioned assessments on public offices (*novos direitos, terças partes,* and *donativos*), quitrents (*foros*) on Crown property, fees on legal documents (such as *cartas de seguro, provisões,* and *mercês*), and chancellery fees (*dízima da chancellaria*).[84] A new item which first appeared in the revenue statement for Rio de Janeiro in 1757 was the *equivalente do contracto do tobacco.* In that year the Crown agreed to remove restrictions on commercial cultivation of tobacco within the captaincy and to abolish existing excises on imported tobacco (see Table 1) in ex-

[83] Alvará of Apr. 2, 1592, *ibid.,* 334–336.
[84] For a definition of the *dízima da chancellaria,* see António de Sousa Pedroso Carnaxide, *O Brasil na administração pombalina,* p. 107; cf. câmara of São Paulo [?] to king, Dec. 30, 1748, *DH,* II (1928), 105–106, for a dispute over its collection.

change for new levies which would provide equivalent revenue. The result was the establishment of new duties on imported slaves, brandy, and fish oil.[85] In 1772 the Pombal regime added still another tax called the *subsídio voluntário* to provide funds for the salaries of newly appointed so-called Royal Professors in the kingdom and the empire. In Brazil this tax was levied on butchered meat (one real per pound) and locally produced brandy (10 réis per *canada*).[86]

From time to time the Portuguese Crown, like that of Spain, asked colonials for other so-called voluntary contributions in order to meet extraordinary international or domestic obligations. Thus the signing of the Anglo-Portuguese marriage treaty of 1661 with its promise of a huge dowry, and of the Luso-Dutch peace treaty the same year guaranteeing the Dutch a heavy indemnity for surrender of their claims to Brazil led to special assessments that were still being collected in Brazil in 1830.[87] The expenses of the Luso-Spanish marriages of 1729 brought forth another call for voluntary colonial levies,[88] as did the devastation of Lisbon in 1755 and the destruction of the Ajuda Palace in the 1790s.[89] Contrary to their designation, there was nothing voluntary about the responses to these calls; colonials invariably protested against them, but eventually their câmaras yielded to pressures exerted by high royal authorities to vote the levies. In 1756 for example, José Antônio Freire de Andrada, acting governor of Rio de Janeiro, convoked a special meeting (which in effect was a *câmara aberto*, though it was not so styled) consisting of the aldermen and certain prominent citizens of Rio de Janeiro to consider means of contributing to the subsídio voluntário or *donativo gratuito* fund for the reconstruction of Lisbon. With the juiz de fóra voting to break a tie, the members agreed to an increase in the dízima da alfândega from 10 to 12.5 percent and to impose new taxes on wine, brandy, and sweet oil. Similarly, the câmara of Vila Rica (Minas Gerais) decided to fulfill its pledge by creating new taxes on livestock, wines, and brandies entering the captaincy-general and by placing a special impost on local brandy consumed in the city's taverns. But the câmara of Santos decided that its citizens could not afford any addi-

---

85 It is interesting to note that the new duties (800 réis per slave; 1,000 réis per pipe of local or imported brandy; and 3,000 réis per pipe of imported fish oil) were collected by officers of the mesa da inspeção rather than those of the customs house. Alvará of Jan. 10, 1757. For additional details concerning the abolition of restrictions upon tobacco growing in Rio de Janeiro, see p. 360, below.

86 Alvará of Nov. 10, 1772, *CLP*, II, 619–622.

87 The obligations Portugal assumed under these treaties amounted to the staggering sum of six million cruzados, of which about half seems to have been collected in Brazil. Francisco Adolfo de Varnhagen, *História geral do Brasil*, III, 208–210.

88 Boxer, *The Golden Age*, pp. 318–320.

89 See the article by Soares de Sousa cited in n. 106 below.

tional taxes and declined to contribute to the fund, thereby drawing an indignant demand from Gomes Freire de Andrada, the captain-general, to reconsider its vote.[90] Such extraordinary contributions were supposed to be limited to ten years, but they were invariably extended.

Problems of Revenue Collection

The Crown seldom undertook direct collection of its revenues, for Portugal, like most other nations in this period, relied primarily upon the old Roman system of tax-farming. Revenue contracts were auctioned for specified periods (usually three years, sometimes six, and occasionally for longer terms) to individuals or syndicates offering the highest bids and the most favorable terms.[91] Many authorities held that the contract system offered definite advantages over direct collection by the government: it saved the Crown the expense of maintaining a large, adequately paid administrative staff, and it supposedly assured the government a regular, steady income, since contractors were pledged to pay into the treasury portions of their bid at the beginning of their contract and at agreed-upon intervals.[92] But the Crown also stood to lose money (and often did) when contractors and their bondsmen (fiadores) defaulted despite the penalties they thereby incurred. Such defaults occurred for a number of reasons: overoptimistic bids; peculations by dishonest agents; unexpectedly poor harvests; wartime disasters; and especially the intransigence of taxpayers. Al-

90 *ABNRJ*, LXXI (1951), 52–55, 98–101.

91 For reasons not clear, the number of participants in these contracts was theoretically limited to two to three persons for small contracts and four for larger ones. Alvará of Sept. 12, 1706 (repeating alvará of Nov. 26, 1677), *ABNRJ*, XXVIII, 334. As Professor Boxer indicates (*The Golden Age*, p. 311), this regulation was not strictly enforced. For example, in 1765 the rights to the colonial whaling industry were rented to a Lisbon syndicate consisting of eight merchants headed by Inácio Pedro Quintela who also held the salt contract for Brazil. D. Alden, "Yankee Sperm Whalers in Brazilian Waters, and the Decline of the Portuguese Whale Fishery (1773–1801)," *The Americas*, XX (Jan. 1964), 272–273. Judicial and fiscal officers of the Crown were forbidden to participate in such contracts by a regulation which implied they had been accustomed to do so. Lei of Jan. 10, 1678, *ABNRJ*, XXVIII, 332–333.

92 Bernard E. Bobb, *The Viceregency of Antonio Maria Bucareli in New Spain, 1771–1779* (Austin, 1962), pp. 206–207; Matthews, *The Royal General Farms in Eighteenth-Century France*, pp. 4 ff.; and Robert Ashton, *The Crown and the Money Market 1603–1640* (Oxford, 1960), especially pp. 79–82, describe tax-farming by other contemporary governments. Ashton also notes another advantage that the Early Stuarts derived from the farming of the customs, namely that they repeatedly relied upon the farmers for large loans to meet government expenses. I do not know whether the Portuguese monarchs also borrowed from their leaseholders.

though the Crown regularly allowed grace periods beyond the terminal dates of contracts to permit final settlement of debts,[93] many contractors ended their lives in disgrace with large sums still due the Crown. More will be said about such debts later on.[94]

There was a tendency during the eighteenth century for the Crown to consolidate smaller tax farms into larger ones and to award them to a single contractor or syndicate. Thus from 1732 until 1801 the salt gabelle for all of Brazil was leased as a single contract, and from 1765 until 1801 the same was done with whaling rights in Brazilian waters.[95] As early as 1740 the five entradas contracts for Minas Gerais were triennially rented to a single contractor,[96] and that practice was also observed with some of the passagens' leases.[97] Regional contracts for revenues in more remote parts of the colony were less attractive to bidders than those in more densely populated districts because of increased costs of collection. Apparently for this reason the governor of Piauí proposed in 1752 that the dízimos of his captaincy-general be divided into seven branches (ramos) rather than be united in a single contract. A similar division of the tithes occurred in Goiás in 1778.[98]

When no bids were received or when tenders were considered unattractive, the Treasury itself "administered" the collection of particular taxes.[99] Although this method appeared to be more expensive because of administrative charges, the Crown was saved the expense of litigation over unfilled contracts, which often proved uncollectable in any event, and received moneys that it might otherwise have lost. One experienced colonial magistrate, Desembargador José João Teixeira Coelho, of Minas Gerais, strongly favored direct collection because

---

93 Originally contractors were given one year beyond their lease to settle their debts; later they were granted three years' grace. Provisão of Apr. 30, 1688, Castro e Almeida, *Inventário*, VI, 480, item 5,541; Overseas Council, Resolution of Dec. 23, 1738, Teixeira Coelho, "Instrução," pp. 401–402.

94 See Chap. XII, pp. 347–352.

95 Ellis, *Sal*, pp. 64–66, 94–95, and 97; Alden, "Sperm Whaling," pp. 272, 284, and 286. See also Boxer, *The Golden Age*, p. 311.

96 Ellis, "Contribuição ao estudo do abastecimento," pp. 446–447.

97 E.g., in reporting the conditions of the new tolls' contract for the registros of Viamão and Curitiba the viceroy observed that both "sempre andarao unidos." Lavradio to Oeiras, Feb. 9, 1770, BNRJ, 10, 4, 8 (unfoliated). On the other hand, the Overseas Council declared that the passagens of the Rio de São José in the captaincy of Rio de Janeiro should not be combined with the tolls' contact for the Rios Paraíba and Paraibuna, but did not indicate why. Ordem of Sept. 4, 1760, *PAN*, XXI (1923), 109.

98 Oliveira, *Os dízimos eclesiásticos*, p. 58.

99 For example, Sebastião Bettâmio ("Noticia particular do continente do Rio Grande do Sul," *RIHGB*, XXI [1858], 276) notes that the tithes of Rio Grande "tem andado administrados pela Fazenda Real, por não haver no Continente quem os quizesse arrematar em quanto durou a guerra, e ainda depois." The entradas of Minas Gerais were directly administered between 1765 and 1767 "por não serem alcançados os preços antecedentes." Melo e Castro, "Instrução para o Visconde de Barbacena" (cited in note 79 above), p. 49, par. 102.

"the money enters the general coffers more promptly and the people are not vexed by so much harassment (execuções) ." But the judge realized that his view was not shared by many officials since the perquisites (propinas) they customarily received from contractors could not be collected when the Treasury itself gathered the revenues.[100]

During the early colonial period the Crown often permitted contracts to be awarded on both sides of the Atlantic, thereby causing a great deal of confusion and unnecessary litigation when two leases for the same impost were let for identical or overlapping periods. To prevent such confusion the Overseas Council decided in 1731 that certain Brazilian revenue contracts would thereafter be let only in the colony, but it reserved the right to approve any contract involving changes in the usual terms, particularly when the bid was lower than those previously offered for the contract.[101] This order did not apply to Crown monopolies such as brazilwood, salt, diamonds, and whaling, which were always leased in the kingdom. Until at least the late 1760s the Council continued to auction a number of revenue contracts for various parts of Brazil.[102]

Prior to the establishment of the juntas da fazenda, most of the contracts let in Brazil were approved by the provedores of the various captaincies.[103] However, those pertaining to excises created by the câmaras were leased by the corporations themselves. They were expected to turn over the revenues received to the local treasury, an arrangement that became the source of a great deal of bickering between the aldermen and royal officials, particularly the governors and the provedores, who objected to the casual way such funds were managed and their tardy delivery to the treasury. In 1727 the Overseas Council transferred jurisdiction over the municipal excises of Olinda from its câmara to the provedoria of Pernambuco,[104] and wrote the captain-general of Rio de Janeiro to determine whether he believed it advisable to incorporate all or part of the Carioca excises as well. The captain-general, Luís Vaía Monteiro, replied that such action was not only desirable but urgently needed because the câmara's records

---

[100] Teixeira Coelho, "Instrução," p. 408. In 1726 the Overseas Council ruled that officeholders could collect propinas only once during the period of a contract, but that stipulation appears to have been ignored in practice. For the schedule of "Propinas que vencem o Governador [,] Ministro Provedor e officiaes da Fazenda," ca. 1734, see DH, I (1928) , 378; another list for 1739 appears on p. 391.

[101] Consultas of Nov. 17 and Dec. 7, 1731, DH, I, 195–197.

[102] "Relação dos contractos que se hão de pôr a lanços no Conselho Ultramarino nos dias, que abaixo se declaram, do presente anno de 1767, pelas dez horas da manhã, para se proceder na sua rematação na forma das ordens de S. Magestade," DH, II (1928) , 278–280.

[103] E.g., "Regimento dos provedores da fazenda das capitanias d'este estado," Apr. 22, 1653, Chaps. 4–7, ABNRJ, XXVIII, 300–301.

[104] Carta régia to provedor of Pernambuco, Aug. 23, 1727, ibid., 286.

were in great disorder and its payments were seriously delinquent. Four years later the King notified the câmara that he had decided to relieve it of the burdensome responsibility of managing such imposts, which henceforth would be assumed by the provedoria.[105] Wherever such annexation occurred,[106] it meant not only a further downgrading of the importance and prestige of the câmaras and a lessening of their ability to maintain municipal services formerly financed by such revenues, but also a loss of income for aldermen who had been accustomed to collect perquisites on such contracts. Though the câmara of Rio de Janeiro entered a plaintive protest against the new policy, it stood.[107] And, as already noted, when new fiscal exigencies arose in later years the Crown was not loath to appeal to colonial municipalities for additional funds.

The arrangements for the leasing of revenue contracts became another responsibility of the treasury boards. Until the formation of juntas da fazenda in Minas Gerais and São Paulo, the board in Rio de Janeiro auctioned certain contracts for all three captaincies-general.[108] With the exception of the tithes, whose collection in some captaincies-general began in July to coincide with the start of the sugar harvests, all leases ran triennially from January 1 of the first year until the last day of December of the third, another example of the Crown's efforts to standardize procedures.[109] All contracts were to

105 Overseas Council, consulta of Nov. 12, 1729 and carta régia of Feb. 22, 1731, Castro e Almeida, *Inventário*, VII, 11–12, 27. In its consulta the Council recommended that the king "sweeten" his notification to the câmara by stating that he had taken this action to relieve it of its burdens so that it could confine its economic activities to matters appropriate to the municipality. This is evidently what the king did in a letter addressed to the câmara on Feb. 22, 1731, *ibid.*, 28, item 6,120.

106 Not all colonial municipalities were deprived of control over local taxes. The city of Cabo Frio and the vilas of Angra dos Reis and Paratí in the comarca of Rio de Janeiro, for example, continued to rely heavily upon excises to meet their expenses. José Antônio Soares de Sousa, "A receita a despesa da comarca do Rio de Janeiro, em 1800 e 1801," *RIHGB*, CCXXXVIII (1958), 345, 358, and 360.

107 Câmara of Rio de Janeiro to king, Aug. 14, 1731, *RADF*, IV, 505–506; *idem* to *idem*, Dec. 29, 1732, Castro e Almeida, *Inventário*, VII, 27. The câmara humbly reminded the Crown that one of the purposes behind the olive oil excise was to provide funds for the care of engeitados, then a common problem in Brazilian cities, and stated that without such funds it could not continue to care for the foundlings because of the heavy expenses that it incurred in connection with four official annual festivals, the salary of its secretary, and the cost of maintaining an agent at Court.

108 Consulta of Aug. 29, 1760 to Conde de Bobadela, ANRJ, Col. 67, Liv. III, fols. 35[r-v]; printed in *DH*, II (1928), 277–278. The order, addressed to the Conde as president of the earlier treasury council of Rio de Janeiro, included taxes on slaves reshipped from various parts of Brazil to Minas, the chancellary duty, an impost on "wet" goods for support of the Santos' garrison, and several tolls' contracts.

109 Overseas Council, *ordem* of July 15, 1766, *RAPM*, XVI:1, 415; Oeiras to Lavradio, Nov. 18, 1768, CMCM, cod. 23, fols. 123[r]–126[r] (orig.).

be rented a month before they were to go into effect.[110] Thus, for example, on November 25, 1769, Viceroy Lavradio, serving in his capacity as president of the junta, wrote to the president of the board of inspection that from November 28 until December 4 the junta would receive tenders for the *dízimos reais* for the triennium beginning January 1, 1770, and requested him to inform prospective bidders by means of notices posted about the business district of the capital.[111] Following the award of new contracts, the viceroy reported their terms to the inspector-general of the Royal Treasury, the Marquis of Pombal.[112]

The reorganization of the colonial exchequer was largely complete, at least on paper, by the time the Marquis of Lavradio reached Rio de Janeiro. Many details remained to be worked out, and the new system was put to a severe test during the turbulent 1770s. The fiscal problems the viceroy encountered are considered in the following chapter.

110 Overseas Council, *ordem* of Feb. 10, 1759, cited in Teixeira Coelho, "Instrução," p. 399, par. 8.

111 Lavradio to Intendant General José Mauricio da Gama e Freitas, Nov. 25, 1769, ANRJ, Col. 70, Liv. V, fols. 4^{r-v}.

112 Examples of such letters of transmittal are Lavradio to Pombal, Feb. 9, 1770, Apr. 26, 1771, and June 4, 1772, BNRJ, 10, 4, 8 (unfoliated).

XII
Problems of Getting and Spending

The want of parsimony in time of peace imposes the necessity of contracting debt in time of war.
> Adam Smith, *The Wealth of Nations*

[I remind you that] it is the King's money, not mine.
I am readying a shipment of money for the troops, and even though it
is not much . . . , I always believe that a little is better than nothing.
> Lavradio to Francisco de Sousa Menezes,
> January 31, 1771 and October 13, 1772

IT HAS BEEN SUGGESTED in Chapter I that the experience that
the Marquis of Lavradio acquired with the fiscal reorganization of
Bahia was probably the major consideration that prompted Lisbon to
promote him to Rio de Janeiro in 1769. There Dom Luís found his
fiscal burdens much heavier, partly because the Rio exchequer was
larger and more important than that of Bahia, but especially because
it bore direct responsibility for providing the money for the military
and naval operations that Portuguese forces conducted between Guanabara Bay and the Plata during most of his term. Despite the economies the viceroy tried to introduce during his first years and despite
the allocation of extraordinary revenues to Rio de Janeiro during the
war years, Lavradio left office knowing that the viceregal branch of
the exchequer was more heavily debt-ridden than ever before.

First Impressions

Three months after assuming office the viceroy completed the customary report required of newly posted governors concerning the state of
royal finances in their administrative unit. Typically it was a gloomy
recital: current expenses substantially exceeded anticipated revenues,
and despite a need for urgent military reforms there were no funds to
undertake them; the Crown's obligations had reached the staggering

sum of more than 3,000,000 cruzados (1,200,000,000 réis).[1] Its creditors included members of the armed forces, ranchers, farmers, and government contractors. Some had not received a real since 1763. Sizeable sums were also owed to the Crown, but the viceroy could find no record of their amount nor any indication that his predecessors had made serious efforts to press for their payment.[2]

Dom Luís' report is, of course, further evidence of the severe and prolonged depression that Brazil and her mother country experienced during the 1760s and 1770s as a consequence of the colony's declining mineral yields.[3] But it was also typical of the kind of reporting made by newly arrived colonial officers who, while perhaps sincerely appalled by the tangled financial situation that confronted them, were also anxious to protect themselves against possible later charges of mismanagement.[4] More than three decades earlier, for example, Gomes Freire de Andrada, then captain-general of Rio de Janeiro, had protested that he lacked funds adequate to sustain Colônia do Sacramento, to succor the newly founded colony of Rio Grande de São Pedro, to provision every royal warship which touched at his ports, and to meet the general charges upon his branch of the treasury.[5] And more recently, the first of Rio's viceroys declared on his arrival at the capital that he found his treasury empty and the king indebted to his subjects by some 218,131,976 réis.[6] But while Lavradio and his fellow administrators repeatedly stressed the serious effects of such debts on the economy of their captaincies and appealed for additional revenues to meet current obligations and to pay off the arrears, the Crown seldom was willing to provide new sources of income except in time of war. Lisbon made it clear that it expected its agents to collect all sums due the king, to reduce nonessential expenditures as much as

---

[1] In the sources used in this chapter monetary data are given in réis (money of account), mil-réis (1,000 réis), contos (1,000,000 réis), and cruzados (each worth 400 réis).

[2] Lavradio to Pombal, Feb. 20, 1770, IHGB/AUC, 1-1-29, fol. 223ʳ. In 1771 the viceroy noted that the debt load of his exchequer stood at 4 million cruzados. *Idem* to Luís Antônio de Sousa, June 2, 1771, CMCM, cod. 15, fol. 64ʳ.

[3] For other indications of the depression see my "Manoel Luís Vieira: an Entrepreneur in Rio de Janeiro during Brazil's Eighteenth-Century Agricultural Renaissance," *HAHR*, XXXIX (Nov. 1959), 522; Myriam Ellis, "Contribuição ao estudo do abastecimento das zonas mineradoras do Brasil no século XVIII," *Revista de história*, No. 36 (São Paulo, 1958), 452; and H. E. S. Fisher, "Anglo-Portuguese Trade, 1700–1770," *The Economic History Review*, 2d ser., XVI (1963), 229–233.

[4] Cf. Antonio María Bucareli y Ursúa (viceroy of New Spain) to Julián de Arriaga, June 27, 1775, quoted in Bernard E. Bobb, *The Viceregency of Antonio María Bucareli in New Spain, 1771–1779* (Austin, 1962), p. 209; and Martim Lopes Lobo de Saldanha (captain-general of São Paulo) to Martinho de Melo e Castro, Nov. 18, 1775, *DI*, XXVIII (1898), 26.

[5] Andrada to the Crown, Nov. 16, 1737, Castro e Almeida, *Inventário*, VII, 267.

[6] Conde da Cunha to the Crown, Dec. 17, 1763, *RIHGB*, CCLIV (Jan.–Mar. 1962), 261–262.

possible, and to hold off the Crown's creditors as best they could.[7]

During his first months in office the viceroy became acquainted with several staff members who were to remain his chief fiscal advisers throughout his term. One was the auditor-general and secretary of the viceregal junta da fazenda, João Carlos Corrêa Lemos. A trained accountant, Corrêa Lemos had been sent by the Royal Treasury to Rio de Janeiro in 1767 to introduce the double-entry system there.[8] Dom Luís found him to be "very intelligent" and incorruptible, but stubborn, violent-tempered, excessively proud, and distrustful of his subordinates. Lavradio's successor, Dom Luís de Vasconcelos e Sousa, regarded the auditor-general as moody and truculent, but agreed with the Marquis that his knowledge of his profession made him indispensable.[9] The indispensable accountant continued to serve as secretary of the Carioca treasury board until at least 1799, and by that time had been joined in the colony by a son, João Carlos Corrêa Lemos Filho, who also became a bookkeeper in the Carioca treasury.[10]

While Corrêa Lemos remained for many years at the same post, Sebastião Francisco Bettâmio, another accountant dispatched to Brazil in 1767 to introduce the "new method," became a roving fiscal expert.[11] Initially he was assigned to Bahia, where he worked closely with Dom Luís de Almeida in introducing the double-entry system and in reducing the captaincy-general's indebtedness.[12] Subsequently he was ordered to São Paulo,[13] where he gave advice concerning establishment of the new fiscal procedures there. Next he was called to Rio de Janeiro to draft instructions for a wartime junta da fazenda being organized in Rio Grande de São Pedro. He himself became secretary of that board and was one of the few royal officials in the captaincy to earn plaudits from General Böhm.[14] After the conclusion of

7 Overseas Council, consulta of Apr. 19, 1738, Castro e Almeida, *Inventário*, VII, 362. See also the last section of this chapter.

8 Carta régia of Mar. 20, 1767, ANRJ, Col. 60, Liv. XL, fol. 56[r]. Like Sebastião Francisco Bettâmio, discussed below, Corrêa Lemos was accompanied by two assistants whose salaries were set at half of that their chiefs earned. One-third of Corrêa Lemos' salary of 1,200,000 réis was held in Lisbon to support his family. Francisco Xaxier de Mendonça Furtado to Conde da Cunha, Mar. 24, 1767, *ibid.*, fol. 56[v].

9 Lavradio, *Relatório*, p. 444; Vasconcelos to Conde de Rezende, Aug. 20, 1789, *RIHGB*, XXIII (1860), 233-234.

10 Duarte Antônio Nunes, "Almanac histórico da cidade de S. Sebastião do Rio de Janeiro, . . . anno de 1799," *RIHGB*, XXI (1851), 111.

11 Bettâmio was appointed by a carta régia of Oct. 19, 1767 (CMCM, cod. 23, fol. 142[r] [*1.a via*]).

12 See pp. 25-27, above.

13 Manoel da Cunha e Menezes to Pombal, Oct. 4, 1774, BNRJ, I-4, 3, 16, fols. 85[r-v].

14 Lavradio to Böhm, Aug. 14, 1776, BNRJ, 13, 4, 3, n. 8 (orig.). The viceroy observed, "Estimo que V. Exa. continua a achar a Sebastião Francisco Bettâmio com aquela honra e fidelidade, e zelo no Real Serviço que eu sempre lhe conheci."

the Luso-Spanish war, Bettâmio prepared a lengthy description of Rio Grande which remains an important historical source concerning the social and economic organization of the subcaptaincy.[15] A few years later he recrossed the Atlantic and by February 1784 was serving in the audit bureau for Portuguese West Africa at São Paulo de Luanda, Angola.[16]

The third member of the viceroy's fiscal team was Manoel da Costa Cardozo. A veteran treasury officer whose government service extended back at least to 1756,[17] Cardozo was a man of great wealth. He operated a large import business in Rio de Janeiro, and had landed property on the city's outskirts on which he raised indigo that he processed in a factory jointly owned with a partner.[18] At the beginning of his administration the Marquis named Cardozo as his treasurer general (tesoureiro geral), a post which made him a member of the junta da fazenda. As Lavradio's chief paymaster, Cardozo efficiently processed many hundreds of pay orders (portarias) rubricated by the viceroy for salaries, goods, and services. Dom Luís came to admire his treasurer general for his competence and his patriotism. In his memorial to his successor, he wrote that during the difficult war years Cardozo repeatedly dipped into his personal fortune to meet urgent treasury bills to conceal from the public the scarcity of funds in the Carioca treasury, yet he had refrained from demanding repayment even though the exchequer owed him more than 60,000 cruzados.[19]

The service records of these three officials illustrates a point about Portuguese administration in Brazil that should not be overlooked —that many colonials and Peninsulars enjoyed long tenures in various branches of the Portuguese fiscal system, just as did their counterparts in the British treasury and in that of the United States during its early national period.[20] Though their activities have seldom been noticed by historians, these functionaries, who ranged from minor clerks to department heads, made possible many of the achievements commonly attributed to their superiors. Furthermore, while the latter often saw only brief service at a particular station, their as-

15 "Notícia particular do continente do Rio Grande do Sul," (1780), *RIHGB*, XXI (1858), 239–299.

16 *Arquivos de Angola*, II, No. 14 (Nov. 1939), 566.

17 According to the examples appended to the "Methodo que se practicava na provedoria da fazenda do Rio de Janeiro" cited in Chap. XI, n. 28, Cardozo held the post of almoxarife (storekeeper) in 1756–1757.

18 On Cardozo's role in the indigo industry, see pp. 372–374.

19 Lavradio, *Relatório*, pp. 445–446. Cardozo continued to hold the same office under Viceroy Vasconcelos. Vasconcelos to Melo e Castro, July 15, 1781, *RIHGB*, LI:2 (1888), 185.

20 Cf. Stephen B. Baxter, *The Development of the Treasury 1660–1702* (Cambridge, Mass., 1957), pp. 140–141; and Leonard D. White, *The Jeffersonians. A Study in Administrative History, 1801–1829* (New York, 1951), Chap. 25.

sistants, who became experts in their fields, remained there for decades, thus providing that measure of guidance and continuity that is essential to the successful operation of any government.[21]

As was emphasized in the preceding chapter, the "new method" was intended to provide the Crown with a more complete and current estimate of the state of royal finances at home and overseas than had theretofore been possible. But upon his arrival in Rio de Janeiro, Viceroy Lavradio discovered that the auditor-general and his assistants had made little progress in updating and converting the accounts to the double-entry system because of persisting disagreements with older, now superseded, functionaries. Dom Luís tried to put an end to such time-consuming disputes, but not until 1770 was he able to send to Lisbon the final balance of income and expenditures for the last year of Gomes Freire's administration (1762–1763), a statement the Royal Treasury had been expecting for five years.[22]

The viceroy ordered each department under his supervision to adopt the new accounting procedures and to send him frequent statements concerning its progress. During his first years in office he submitted to the Royal Treasury monthly, semiannual, and annual balances of income and expenditures for his branch of the exchequer, even though only the last two were required. But he justified the preparation of monthly *balancinhos* as useful devices to keep the bookkeepers on their toes, and with evident satisfaction he observed the accountants posting their ledgers "day and night, Sundays and [even] Saints' Days." [23]

The viceroy's eagerness to keep a careful check on the state of royal finances within his jurisdiction drew the Court's commendation. However, the Marquis of Pombal declared pointedly that "the zeal with which Your Excellency is engaged in the Royal Service gives me reason to expect that in the future [the collection of old debts due the

21 For one other example of long service by a Portuguese officer below the rank of magistrate or governor, see the career of Antônio Coelho Guerreiro as described in Frédéric Mauro, "Pour une histoire de la contabilité au Portugal: 'Le livre de Raison' de Coelho Guerreiro," *Caravelle*, I (Toulouse, 1963), 86–87. The examples cited in the text refer, of course, to nonproprietary officeholders, but important clues concerning public offices purchased and exercised by certain families for several generations will be found in the genealogical sources cited in Chap. XI, n. 39.

22 Lavradio to Francisco Xavier de Furtado Mendonça, Jan. 4, 1770, BNRJ, 10, 4, 8 (unfoliated).

23 Lavradio to Pombal, Feb. 9, 1771, BNRJ, 10, 4, 8 (unnumbered). From the viceroy's covering letters in this codice and in ANRJ, Col. 69, Liv. I-*bis.*, it is evident that he continued to remit these three types of statements to Lisbon until at least July 1772. Dom Luís indicated that he would send monthly balances until the Court issued contrary instructions. It never did, but it is likely that when the volume of the junta da fazenda's business greatly increased during the war years, the audit bureau became too busy to prepare statements with that regularity. At least there is no mention of them in the viceroy's correspondence for his last years.

Crown] will proceed with more heat" than heretofore.[24] Lavradio tried to expedite such collections, but he enjoyed only limited success.

The State of Viceregal Finances Before 1775

Although the viceroy's correspondence contains copies of many covering letters that accompanied the balances he sent to the Royal Treasury, not a single specimen of those balances has been found. However, soon after Lavradio's retirement the auditor-general prepared a statement for Viceroy Vasconcelos indicating the viceregal treasury's average annual receipts and expenditures for the decade beginning in 1768 but weighted in favor of the relatively peaceful (and therefore more typical) years rather than those of armed conflict.[25] Despite certain omissions, that statement is the best indication that we currently have of the average yearly income and outgo of the Carioca branch of the royal exchequer during Lavradio's time. Table 2 shows its estimated annual income from all significant sources.

Several observations are suggested by Table 2. First, it is evident that by far the most lucrative source of the viceregal exchequer's income (about one third) consisted of revenues from the Royal Mint. That source yielded six times more than the tithes which, as mentioned in Chapter XI, had been the leading source of royal income from Brazil during the early colonial period. Second, the figures given for the second ranking revenue source, the dízima da alfândega, are nearly 25 percent below the receipts of the Customs House during the years 1758–1765, which averaged 182,588,603 réis a year.[26] That decline is another index of the lessening productivity of the mining

[24] Oeiras to Lavradio, July 6, 1770, CMCM, cod. 3, fol. 75ʳ (orig.) .

[25] "Mappa geral do rendimento e despeza, . . . de um anno da thezouraria geral do Rio de Janeiro, calculado no que foi possivel por um anno médio dos primeiros dez depois do estabelecimento da dita thezouraria . . . regulado pelo que se observou em outros annos, em q. esta capitania esteve em socego" (ca. May 1781) , *RIHGB*, LI:2 (1888) , 195–197; "Mappa do rendimento e despeza . . . da provedoria . . . da ilha de Santa-Catharina. . . ." *ibid.*, p. 198; "Mappa do rendimento e despeza . . . da provedoria . . . do Rio Grande de São Pedro" *ibid.*, 199–200. Another statement for ca. 1780, "Ramos que estabelecem a riqueza completa da thesouraria geral do Rio de Janeiro e praças sujacentes," (*RIHGB*, XLVII:1 [1884], 41) gives slightly different totals and includes a few items omitted from the 1781 *mappas*.

[26] Customs' receipts for the years 1757–1763 are given in "Resumo do rendimento da dízima da alfândega desta cidade do Rio de Janeiro," annex to Alexandre Rodrigues Viana to Oeiras, Sept. 10, 1764, *RIHGB*, LXV:1 (1902) , 127, while those for 1765 are reported in "Relação de todo o rendimento que tem havido na dízima da alfândega no anno de 1765," annex to Antônio Pinto de Miranda to [Oeiras?], Apr. 11, 1766, *ibid.*, 166. I have not found any indication of the receipts for 1764.

TABLE 2

ESTIMATED AVERAGE YEARLY INCOME OF RIO DE JANEIRO AND
ITS DEPENDENCIES, 1768–1778 [a]
(in mil-réis)

Source	Rio de Janeiro	Santa Catarina	Rio Grande
Dízimos reais	28,731	4,720	5,774
Seigniorage and other charges collected at the Royal Mint	169,529	—	—
Dízima da alfândega	136,875	—	—
Miscellaneous income of Customs House (including confiscations)	676	—	—
Coast Guard tax	9,521	—	—
Tax on slaves bound from Rio de Janeiro to Minas Gerais	16,063	—	—
Large wine impost	6,267	—	—
Small wine impost	4,412	—	—
Tax on brandies from Portugal and her Atlantic Islands	4,239	—	—
Tax on local brandy	4,511	—	—
Excise on olive oil	2,900	—	—
Salt gabelle	6,784	—	—
Rio de Janeiro's share of income from the salt contract	28,081	—	—
Shares of income from whaling contract	11,800	4,000	—
Assessments on government salaries	9,028	—	—
Duties on bail bonds (*cartas de seguro*)	45	—	—
Fees on petitions of merit	71	—	—
Dízima da chancellaria	1,136	—	—
Equivalent of tobacco tax	13,153	—	—
Quitrents [b]	2,070	—	—
Income from other royal property [b]	146	—	—
Revenue for royal powderhouse [b]	523	—	—
Portage fees on Paraíba and Paraibuna Rivers	11,750	—	—
Portage fees on São João River	175	—	—
Portage fees collected in Rio Grande	—	—	3,596
Quinto on hides	—	—	3,271
Income from water mill	—	—	307
Subtotals	468,486	8,720	12,948
Grand Total	490,154		

[a] Adapted from the 1781 estimates cited in n. 25.

[b] Items omitted in the 1781 estimates but included in a list for *ca.* 1780, also cited in n. 25.

zones and is reflective of the reduced purchasing power of their inhabitants. Third, Table 2 does not include income from the literary
and voluntary subsidies, apparently because it was sent to the Royal
Treasury and was ordinarily unavailable to the junta da fazenda of
Rio de Janeiro. Nor does this table list the extraordinary funds the

viceregal exchequer received from other administrative units during the mid-1770s (indicated in Table 7 below). Fourth, it is interesting to note that Rio de Janeiro's income from ordinary sources in Viceroy Lavradio's time was approximately ten times greater than that of neighboring São Paulo.[27] However, it was slightly less than 65 percent of that of Brazil's most lucrative captaincy-general, Minas Gerais, where royal income for the year 1778 amounted to 711,111,496 réis, compared with expenditures of only 193,880,226 réis.[28]

To the regret of the viceroy and the Crown, that favorable ratio between income and outgo was not duplicated in Rio de Janeiro. Table 3 shows the average yearly expenditures of the viceregal exchequer in Lavradio's time according to the computations of the auditor-general.

Several points will be noted in comparing Tables 2 and 3. First, neither the income nor the expenses of Colônia do Sacramento are listed, possibly because the audit bureau lacked such information or because the entrepôt had passed from Portuguese control in June 1777. As will be shown later, prior to that date the praça constituted a considerable burden for the viceregal exchequer. Second, even though the amount of receipts and expenditures of Santa Catarina and Rio Grande is not fully indicated by these tables, it is apparent that the two subcaptaincies generated far less revenue than they consumed; indeed, a substantial share of the military expenses charged to Rio de Janeiro was for the defense of the borderlands. Finally, it is evident that even during an average year the viceregal exchequer was out of balance by more than 100,000 mil-réis. After the Vértiz anabasis (December 1773), the gap between income and outgo continued to widen.

Before the intensification of the borderlands conflict, the viceroy continued his predecessor's policy of paying promptly what Lord Chief Justice Coke called "crying debts," that is, those owed "soldiers, mariners, tradesmen and such as live on labour," [29] and endeavored to curtail current expenditures as much as possible. One way of re-

27 According to the "Rellação de todo o rendimento certo, q. teve a fazenda real . . . de S. Paulo no anno de 1767," (DI, XIX [1896], 286), total income was a mere 26,820,503 réis. In 1776 the captain-general reported that São Paulo's receipts amounted to 47,090,599 réis. Martim Lopes Lobo de Saldanha to Martinho de Melo e Castro, Dec. 14, 1776, DI, XXVIII (1898), 248–256.

28 José Joaquim da Rocha [?], "Geographica historica da capitania de Minas Geraes" (ca. 1780), PAN, IX (1909), 69. Income from the literary and voluntary subsidies is not indicated, but see Table 7 below.

29 Early in the seventeenth century Coke divided the royal debts of England into "eating debts, such as were taken up at interest; . . . crying debts . . . , [and] pressing debts . . . ," by which he appears to have meant debts owed to socially prominent royal creditors. Robert Ashton, The Crown and the Money Market, 1603–1640 (Oxford, 1960), p. 34.

TABLE 3

ESTIMATED AVERAGE ANNUAL EXPENDITURES OF RIO DE JANEIRO AND ITS DEPENDENCIES, 1768–1778 [a]
(in mil-réis)

Charge	Rio de Janeiro	Santa Catarina	Rio Grande
I. Ecclesiastical Register			
Livings and stipends	28,242	478	852
II. Civil Register			
Salaries	34,004	3,603	4,071
Perquisites	5,058	—	—
Housing allowances	710	—	—
Travel allowances	1,579	—	—
Other allowances	2,071	—	—
III. Military Register			
General Staff [b]	14,986	1,533	—
Secretariat of same [b]	1,145	—	—
Infantry, artillery, and cavalry regiments [b]	141,104	25,898	50,801
Officers of the auxilliary militia [b]	8,198	—	
Auxiliary cavalry [b]	1,532	—	
Officers' pensions	2,744	—	—
Fortress commanders [b]	4,622	—	—
Instructors of military classes [b]	600	—	—
Vacancies in the ranks (praças mortas)	1,200	—	—
Clothing allowances	31,906	—	—
Quartering expenses	5,800	—	—
Repairs of arms and other equipment	681	—	—
Provisions and other supplies	6,040	3,101	9,168
Military hospital	30,000	4,229	4,800
IV. Extraordinary Expenses			
Special funds at the disposition of the viceroy	400	—	—
Royal warehouses	48,000	—	—
Provedoria	3,786	—	—
Intendency-general of gold	239	—	—
Customs House	3,513	—	—
Royal Mint	8,838	—	—
High Court (Relação)	221	—	—
Treasurer-general	454	—	—
Paymaster-general of troops	160	—	—
Royal Professors [b]	2,910	—	—
New inspectors of the mines of Macacú [b]	2,220	—	—
Expenses of warships and other Crown vessels while in port	41,620	565	4,556
Pay and allowances of the crew of a royal frigate as exemplified by that of the Princesa do Brasil	17,847	—	—
Fortifications and other works (obras)	11,576	1,083	—
Marine arsenal	1,406	—	—

TABLE 3 *(Continued)*

Charge	Rio de Janeiro	Santa Catarina	Rio Grande
Powder magazine	64	—	—
Arms factory	2,500	—	—
Santos subsidy	1,600 c	—	—
Miscellaneous obligations	2,957	1,806	11,150
Subtotals	472,533	42,296	85,398
Grand total	600,227		

a Based upon the sources cited in n. 25, and another estimate entitled "Importancia das addições que formão em summa o total da despesa das referidas thesourarias [do Rio de Janeiro]" (1780), *RIHGB*, XLVII:1, 42–43.

b Pay.

c Incorrectly given in the "Mappa geral" (n. 25) as 3,200,000 réis, the amount due in two years.

ducing the latter was to eliminate fraudulent practices by certain government contractors, including shipmasters, stonemasons, and carpenters, who assigned their slaves to government jobs for a few hours a day then transferred them to other tasks and billed the Crown for double the legitimate labor costs.[30] Another was to force down the prices of goods the king purchased. Dom Luís professed shock at the high prices of goods in the capital, alleging that they were two to four times greater than those prevailing in the kingdom.[31] He ordered subordinates to see that all government purchases were negotiated at the lowest possible prices, and brushed aside farmers' complaints that they had been obliged to sell their produce at less than market value.[32] Behind the viceroy's seemingly despotic policy[33] was his firm conviction that the annual deficit must somehow be reduced in order to quicken the economy, and that since the Crown declined to provide him with additional revenues to achieve that objective, it must be done by reducing the costs of government.[34]

In looking back upon his accomplishments, the marquis wrote that during his first years in office he had succeeded in reducing the arrears by 500,000 cruzados.[35] Whatever substance there may have been

30 Lavradio, *Relatório*, p. 463.

31 Lavradio to Luís Antônio de Sousa, June 2, 1771, CMCM, cod. 15, fol. 64ᵛ; *idem* to Pombal, Feb. 20, 1770 (cited in n. 2 above), fol. 223ᵛ; *idem* to Overseas Council, Dec. 9, 1774, BNRJ, 10, 4, 8 (unfoliated). For some indications of commodity prices, see Appendix V.

32 Lavradio to câmara of Laguna, Mar. 22, 1775, CMCM, cod. 25, fols. 11ᵛ–12ʳ.

33 The policy was, in fact, no more despotic than that followed during the American Revolution by officers of the Continental Congress and by officials of the various states to procure supplies from the farmers. See E. James Ferguson, *The Power of the Purse. A History of American Public Finance, 1776–1790* (Chapel Hill, 1961), chap. 4, appropriately entitled "Mass Expropriation."

34 The viceroy's views concerning the depressing effects of royal indebtedness on the colonial economy are discussed further on p. 344 of this chapter.

35 Lavradio, *Relatório*, p. 464.

to that claim—it has not been possible to verify it—the fact is that the viceroy had little more success than his predecessors in paying off the king's debts in the southern dependencies. From their founding those settlements had always been heavily dependent for financial aid upon Rio de Janeiro.[36] Yet for a variety of reasons, including their own remoteness and the greater opportunities enjoyed by officials stationed near the capital to appeal for money, there had never been an adequate flow of funds from the capital to the borderlands, a situation that often became acute in wartime. Shortly after the first Cevallos campaign, for example, the governor of Santa Catarina reported that the arrears in pay and allowances due his garrison amounted to thirty months, and that an additional 50,000 cruzados was owed to royal officials, ranchers, cultivators, and merchants in the subcaptaincy.[37] The governor of Rio Grande told a similar story,[38] and the governor of Colônia certainly could have done so.

In an effort to remedy this situation Viceroy Lavradio tried to obtain an accurate picture of the particular needs of each dependency. To that end he repeatedly asked his subordinate governors to submit detailed statements of their annual needs as well as periodic balances of the funds at their disposal. Dom Luís stipulated that their reports should be organized in accordance with the Crown's new accounting procedures, but the governors' staffs were unfamiliar with those innovations. Until Sebastião Bettâmio went to the Rio Grande in 1775, the viceroy had no competent bookkeeper whom he could spare to visit the dependencies to teach their personnel the double-entry system, nor would the Crown send him additional bookkeepers to relieve the shortage.[39] Therein lay the key weakness in the procedural

---

[36] E.g., Gomes Freire de Andrada to the king, Aug. 20, 1737, *RIHGRGS*, XXVIII, 90–91.

[37] Francisco de Sousa de Menezes to Conde Azambuja, Dec. 8, 1767, BNRJ, 7, 3, 47 (orig.).

[38] José Custódio de Sá e Faria to *idem*, Jan. 10, 1768, *RIHGB*, XXXI:1 (1868), 286–291.

[39] In rejecting a request made by Lavradio's predecessor for more bookkeepers, Count Oeiras insisted that competent persons could be found in the local business community. Oeiras to Lavradio, Aug. 30, 1769 and July 2, 1770, ANRJ, Col. 67, Liv. II-A, fols. 170ʳ and 189ʳ (both origs.). It is unlikely that many colonial merchants or clerks were familiar with the double-entry system for which they had little use. (Cf. the remarks of Professor W. T. Baxter concerning English colonial merchants' experience with double entry ["Accounting in Colonial America," in A. C. Littleton and B. S. Yamey, eds., *Studies in the History of Accounting*, pp. 279–280]). For a comparatively rare example of a New England merchant who did employ double-entry procedures, see Bernard Bailyn, ed., *The Apologia of Robert Keayne: The Self-Portrait of a Puritan Merchant* (New York, 1964), pp. 68–74. One curious indication of the shortage of bookkeepers in Rio de Janeiro at this time is provided by the experience of Gaspar Barboza Lima, former clerk of Jeronymo Serqueira Lima, a local businessman. Barboza Lima was imprisoned on a charge of stealing from his employer, but after his incarceration his victim could find no one to replace the thieving clerk who had been more familiar with the

aspect of Pombal's fiscal reforms, at least in Brazil: few colonial officers really understood the Royal Treasury's new method.

Despite his complaint about the inadequacies of the governors' requisitions, the marquis managed to send them regular allotments of funds from 1770 until 1774. But he stressed that those funds could be used only to cover current obligations, and warned his subordinates not to pay off old debts, including the Crown's promissory notes which had passed from servicemen to merchants. He cautioned the governors not to undertake any unauthorized expenditures and to pay the lowest possible prices for goods they purchased for the Crown since "it is the King's money, not mine" they were spending.[40]

The quarterly monetary consignments were dispatched aboard small coastal smacks or corvettes in parcels whose value seldom exceeded 10,000 mil-réis, a limitation designed to minimize possible losses due to hazards of the seas or capture by Spanish coast guards.[41] Aware of the perennial need for money, the viceroy apologized for not sending more and expressed his conviction that "a little is better than nothing." [42] Yet he bristled whenever a governor, responding to pressures from impatient merchants, farmers, and soldiers for sums due them, complained that funds were slow in arriving or were smaller than anticipated. Lavradio staunchly defended his staff, contending that they were doing the best they could under the circumstances.

The Shipment of Capital to the Kingdom

In addition to the relatively small remissions of capital from Rio de Janeiro to the borderlands, the viceroy bore final responsibility for

---

accounts than the owner. The latter, claiming that his business had come to a standstill, petitioned the viceroy to release his clerk to put his accounts back in order. Lavradio ordered the culprit freed on the posting of a bond to assure his future good behavior. Lavradio to Desembargador Francisco José Brandão, Nov. 13, 1770, ANRJ, Col. 70, Liv. V, fol. 118ʳ. The scarcity of colonials familiar with double-entry techniques was still observable in the early nineteenth century when the French merchant Louis François de Tollenare was living in the northeast. See *Notas dominicais tomadas durante uma viagem em Portugal e no Brasil em 1816, 1817 e 1818* (Salvador, 1956), pp. 121–122.

40 Lavradio to Francisco de Sousa Menezes, Oct. 13, 1772, CMCM, cod. 15, fol. 136ᵛ. The viceroy became so zealous in trying to curb unnecessary expenditures that on one occasion he condemned the use of powder to fire the customary salute to a departed sergeant major and demanded to know the name of the officer who had authorized it. To José Marcelino de Figueiredo, Oct. 12, 1773, CMCM, cod. 4, fol 16ʳ. The statements made in this and the succeeding paragraph are based on the viceroy's active correspondence with the governors of Santa Catarina, Rio Grande, and Colônia from 1770 to 1774, collected in the above-cited codices.

41 Later, when the Cevallos expedition was anticipated, Lavradio sent funds for the forces in Rio Grande overland via São Paulo and Curitiba.

42 Lavradio to Francisco de Sousa Menezes, Jan. 31, 1771, CMCM, cod. 15, fol. 44ᵛ.

the shipment of much larger quantities of coin and bullion to Portugal. Because of its maritime location, Rio de Janeiro served as a central collection point for revenues reserved by the Crown for uses in the kingdom. Some of those funds came from the captaincy of Rio de Janeiro, but far more originated in the captaincies-general of Goiás, Mato Grosso, and Minas Gerais; lesser sums also came from São Paulo. These revenues were sent by the juntas da fazenda of each administrative unit via armed convoys to the tesouraria geral of Rio de Janeiro. There the shipments were checked and compared with the manifests, and any discrepancies noted were reported to the remitting agency.[43] The sacks or leather bottles (*borrachas*) of coin and bullion were then packed in chests averaging 200,000 mil-réis each and put aboard royal warships for delivery to the Treasurer General in Lisbon. There the shipments were again checked against the manifests (which sometimes failed to accompany the cargoes), and the bullion was then sent to the Royal Mint to be made into coin.[44]

The captains-general of the interior were supposed to send the Crown's revenues to Rio de Janeiro at regular intervals to coincide with the sailings of the royal frigates to the kingdom, but the machinery did not work that smoothly in Lavradio's time.[45] After the abolition of the frota system in 1765, a single armed frigate periodically called at Rio de Janeiro to fetch the quintos and other royal revenues. While she was readying to depart from Lisbon, the colonial secretary (or sometimes Pombal himself) would send a fast dispatch vessel to the viceroy with a message stating the date of the warship's proximate arrival and the intended length of her stay.[46] Upon receipt of this information the viceroy immediately wrote to the captains-general asking them to forward the *rendas reais* as quickly as possible.[47] As the frigate was dropping anchor in Guanabara Bay, a viceregal proclamation appeared on the streets of Rio de Janeiro an-

43 For example, early in 1773 the junta da fazenda of Rio de Janeiro reported the arrival from Minas Gerais of thirteen bars of gold which the manifest declared to be worth 14,977,740 réis but which were appraised at 14,957,747 réis; similarly, nine bars sent from the same source to be converted at the Mint into provincial coin were said to be valued at 13,613,605 réis but were found to be worth 13,600,641 réis. Junta da fazenda, Rio de Janeiro, to Conde de Valadares (captain-general of Minas Gerais), Jan. 15, 1773, BNRJ, II, 36, 3, 48 (orig.).

44 This description rests upon the documentation cited in the remainder of this section, particularly the viceroy's correspondence with the captains-general and the ship manifests.

45 A carta régia of May 27, 1766 declared that all capital belonging to the Royal Treasury and all chests of diamonds should be sent quarterly to Rio de Janeiro. *RAPM*, XVI:1 (1911), 417. But a provisão of Oct. 4, 1771, stated that they should be remitted "em todos occasiões opportunas." Teixeria Coelho, "Instrução," p. 400.

46 Martinho de Melo e Castro to Lavradio, Aug. 8, 1770, Oct. 5, 1771, and July 10, 1772, CMCM, cod. 3, fols. 81ʳ, 152ʳ, and 170ʳ (all originals).

47 Lavradio to Conde Valadares (captain-general of Minas Gerais), Sept. 18 and Dec. 3, 1770, Dec. 1771, Jan. 4, Feb. 13, and Oct. 2, 1772, and Jan. 1, 1773, CMCM, cod. 15, fols. 29ʳ, 40ᵛ, 88ʳ, 91ʳ, 101ᵛ, 134ᵛ, 146ʳ. The viceroy was obliged

nouncing the ship's arrival and advising interested parties that her captain was prepared to receive whatever funds they wished to send to their correspondents in the mother country.[48]

These *bandos* invariably contained the reminder that the frigate would leave port without further delay (*sem prorogação do mais tempo*) on the scheduled date of her departure; often, however, the warships remained in port for weeks or even months after their supposedly unalterable sailing time. Sometimes such delays were occasioned by human adversities, such as the sudden illness of a viceroy or an outbreak of scurvy among the crew; [49] more commonly they occurred because the vessels were discovered to be so unseaworthy that they required extensive repairs, and Portuguese shipwrights were notoriously inaccurate in their estimates of the time needed for repairs. As a consequence, sailing dates were announced, canceled, rescheduled, and canceled yet again. Thus, for example, the *Graça* reached Rio de Janeiro on December 16, 1771, and the public was informed that she would remain in port only two weeks; in fact, she did not sail until March 30, 1772. Three years later the same vessel again drew the assignment to bring the fifths back to Portugal. She reached the capital early in June 1775, intending to remain a month, but because of extensive damage to her hull did not begin her homeward voyage until the following January. The departure of the *São João Baptista*, the next warship carrying bullion to Portugal, was set back a mere two months, but in 1780 the *Gigante* returned to Lisbon 216 days out of Rio de Janeiro after a long, unplanned stop at Bahia for complete overhaul.[50]

Because of Portugal's dire economic straits during the 1760s and 1770s and her heavy dependence on receipts from Brazil, such delays became a matter of serious concern to the Crown. The king's minis-

---

to remind the Count repeatedly to send certain revenues which he appears to have been withholding for his own uses. In one of his letters of transmittal to Pombal, Dom Luís noted that he was sending the quintos from Minas for the last quarter of 1770 and the first two of 1771, "porque o terceiro q. tao bem devia ter vindo, ainda até o prezente não tem chegado." Lavradio to Pombal, Nov. 2, 1771, BNRJ, 10, 4, 8 (unfoliated). Later examples of the viceroy's requests for the fifths from Minas are *idem* to Antônio Carlos Furtado de Mendonça, Jan. 14, 1774, CMCM, cod. 4, fol. 30ᵛ; and *idem* to Antônio de Noronha, Aug. 18, 1777, *ibid.*, cod. 26, fol. 141ʳ.

48 Bandos of Jan. 15 and 18, 1771; Mar. 24, 1774, BNRJ, 7, 3, 9, nos. 138, 139, and 146; bandos of June 10, 1775 (CMCM, cod. 2, fols. 162ᵛ–163ʳ), Jan. 19, 1776, and July 14, 1777 (CMCM, cod. 19, fols. 6ᵛ, 196ᵛ–197ʳ).

49 E.g., in 1767 the dispatch of the revenues was held up because of the viceroy's illness. Azambuja to Mendonça Furtado, Oct. 26, 1768, ANRJ, Col. 69, Liv. I, fols. 25ʳ⁻ᵛ. A decade later an outbreak of scurvy made it impossible for the *São João Baptista* to sail on the prescribed date. Portaria of May 30, 1777, CMCM, cod. 19, fol. 186ᵛ.

50 Bandos of June 10, 1775, Jan. 19, 1776, and July 14, 1777 (cited in n. 48 above); "Mappa do cabedal que leva o frag.ta . . . S. João Bapp.ta" (cited in n. 64 below); *Gazeta de Lisboa*, July 25, 1780.

ters repeatedly emphasized that the failure of the bullion to arrive at the anticipated times was causing "very grave prejudice" to the government, and to those members of the business community who dealt in international trade.[51] They might also have noted that since colonial merchants showed a clear preference for remitting their capital in frigates rather than in less secure commercial vessels, the tardy arrival of such remittances greatly hindered colonial trade as well.[52]

Although little seems to have been done to improve the seaworthiness of the vessels entrusted with the treasure argosies, the Crown did try to plan their sailing schedule to match that of production in the gold fields. Late in 1771 the colonial secretary asked the viceroy to report on the length of time it took to conduct bullion from producing districts to Rio de Janeiro and the seasons when it was normally transported.[53]

The viceroy's detailed reply, based presumably upon information supplied by informed persons in the capital, throws some light on the conditions of gold production and the problems of transportation between the coast and the interior in his day. In Minas Gerais, the principal gold-producing area, extraction occurred throughout the year where a system of dams and hydraulic machinery provided a constant flow of water; elsewhere, however, the miners dug up the gold-bearing gravelly subsoil (called *cascalho*) only during the dry season, and then proceeded to wash it during the rainy months, October to April. During May and June the ore was taken to the smelteries for processing and then sent on to Rio de Janeiro, usually arriving there by early August. Although the quality of the cascalho in Goiás was considered superior to that of Minas and required less washing, the distances separating the mining camps (*arraiais*) from the *Casas da Fundição* were such that the bars were not ready to leave the smelteries for Rio until sometime in June and ordinarily did not

---

[51] Oeiras to Azambuja, Sept. 11, 1767, *RIHGB*, XXXIII:1, 264. Pombal to Lavradio, Dec. 9, 1775, CMCM, cod. 14 (49/19) (orig.) ; Melo e Castro to *idem*, Oct. 9, 1776, BNRJ, I-31, 31, 1, n. 49; *idem* to *idem*, Mar. 28, 1777, BNRJ, I-2, 4, 7, n. 72.

[52] Beginning in 1734 all shipments of private capital to the kingdom were required to be made via the warships which escorted the frotas. Those sent from Maranhão were transported without charge, but others paid a fee of 1 percent. *Lei* of Feb. 28, 1736 (revising *lei* of Dec. 24, 1734) quoted in S[everino] Sombra, *História monetária do Brasil colonial*, p. 175; renewed by *lei* of Nov. 21, 1759, *CLP*, I, 569–570. However, an edict of June 10, 1766 (*CLP*, II, 251–252) gave senders the option of remitting their funds either on merchant ships or on the royal frigates. To prevent tax evasion, an *alvará* of April 17, 1770 tightened up procedures for the handling of shipments on merchant vessels by stipulating that they must be delivered to the Royal Mint in Lisbon, where the manifests would be checked and deductions of 1 percent for the Mint and 0.5 percent for the ship captain, the pilot, and the master would be made before the money would be released. *CLDA*, III, 463–465.

[53] Melo e Castro to Lavradio, Oct. 5, 1771, CMCM, cod. 3, fol. 152ʳ (orig.) .

reach their destination until August or early September. Arrivals from the mines of Mato Grosso and Cuiabá [54] were always uncertain because of the long, hazardous trip from the mining zones by the canoe convoys (*monções de canoas*) that proceeded by way of a series of rivers and frequent portages to São Paulo, where the bullion was transloaded to mule caravans and forwarded to Rio de Janeiro.[55] Ideally, Lavradio reported, if the bullion left the fields in Mato Grosso sometime in June, the preferred time for beginning the monções, it would get to the capital within two to three months. His advisers therefore recommended that the best time for the warships to pick up their collections at Guanabara would be during October and November; however, as the marquis pointed out, that would mean that the frigates would be obliged to sail back into the teeth of the Atlantic storms during the season when Portuguese captains always preferred to remain in port. All things considered, he concluded that probably the best time for the ships to reach Rio was around mid-April so that they could leave toward the end of May, thereby allowing adequate time for merchants in the interior to send their deposits for remission to their Peninsular correspondents.[56]

The viceroy's plan did not meet with the Court's favor because it meant that the bullion would reach Lisbon after midyear, considerably later than the Crown hoped to receive its badly wanted revenues. Anxious to obtain the treasure at the earliest possible date, the colonial secretary replied that the government hoped that future sailings could be arranged so that the warships would call at Rio de Janeiro toward the end of December or early January and begin their return voyage soon enough to arrive back in the kingdom by early March.[57] However, because of the shortage of warships, the need to use the few available to transport troops and war matériel to Brazil to meet the Spanish threat, and the persistence of delays in colonial ports, it proved impossible to adhere to such a schedule. Indeed, the Crown had no regular service between the Peninsula and Brazil until the establishment of the *correio marítima,* a packet service begun at the end of the 1790s,[58] but by then the volume of bullion

[54] I.e., the northern and southern mining districts of the captaincy-general of Mato Grosso, the former being situated near its capital, Vila Bela. See Charles R. Boxer, *The Golden Age of Brazil*, pp. 254–270.

[55] For a description of the difficult and perilous river trips, see *ibid.* pp. 255, 261–266.

[56] Lavradio to Pombal, Mar. 29, 1772, BNRJ, 10, 4, 8 (unfoliated). As the viceroy also noted, the two weeks that the Court normally allowed for the provisioning and loading of the royal frigates was insufficient time.

[57] Melo e Castro to Lavradio, July 10, 1772, CMCM, cod. 3, fol. 170ʳ (orig.).

[58] For a brief discussion, see Rodolfo Garcia, *Ensaio sôbre a história*, Chap. XVI. It will be recalled that the Spanish government had established a packet service between Spain and Havana in 1765 and between the Peninsula and Buenos Aires five years later.

available for shipment to Portugal had greatly diminished, as suggested by Table 4.

Table 4 provides some indication of the magnitude of capital shipments from Rio de Janeiro to Portugal over a forty-year period centering on the Lavradio years. Information for the remissions of 1749, when gold production in Brazil was approaching its peak, was taken

TABLE 4

SHIPMENTS OF CAPITAL FROM RIO DE JANEIRO TO PORTUGAL
IN WARSHIPS (A) AND IN COMMERCIAL VESSELS (B)
1749–1791
(in mil-réis)

Year	Royal Revenues	Private Capital	Totals
1749 (A)	1,383,140	4,656,708	6,039,848
1771 (A)			2,000,000
1772 (A)	1,000,000	1,800,000	2,800,000
1773 (A)	1,200,000	1,900,000	3,100,000
1774 (A)	427,396		⎫ 1,142,605
1774 (B)		715,209	⎭
1775 (B)		869,080	⎫
1775–1776 (A)	664,692	1,600,000	⎬ 4,288,723
1776 (B)		1,154,951	⎭
1777 (A)	297,179	1,804,285	⎫ 2,363,141
1777 (B)		261,677	⎭
1778 (A)	127,865		
1791 (A)	80,741		

from a contemporary listing published by Professor Charles R. Boxer.[59] The figures for 1771, 1772, and 1773 are those reported by French agents in Lisbon to their superiors.[60] It has not been possible to verify their accuracy, but the French possessed good intelligence sources in the Portuguese capital, and their estimates were probably reasonably

[59] *The Golden Age*, pp. 351–352. I have converted the sums given by weight of gold into mil-réis according to the formula described in note 61 below.

[60] Dispatches of the Marquis of Clermont, May 7, 1771, and M. de Montigny, June 16, 1772 and June 22, 1773, *QE*, VIII, 7, 32, and 54. The last citation contains a printing error, for it refers to the arrival of ten chests of bullion worth "50 million ½ de crusados," a sum far larger than any known shipment from the colony. I suspect that the true figure is 5.5 million cruzados. A dispatch of Oeiras to Lavradio dated July 3, 1770, acknowledges the arrival of eleven chests of diamonds aboard the nau *N. S. dos Prazeres,* and another of the same date states that the manifests and the rendas reais had been received but fails to disclose the amount of the latter. Both dispatches are in ANRJ, Col. 69, Liv. II-A, fols. 190ʳ–191ʳ (origs.). On December 20 of the same year the viceroy sent a covering letter for another bullion shipment aboard the nau *N. S. de Belém,* but details concerning the value of that shipment are lacking. Lavradio to Pombal, Dec. 20, 1770, BNRJ, 10, 4, 8 (unfoliated).

close to the truth. We are on somewhat firmer ground for the statistics given for 1774, since they are taken from *portarias* signed by the viceroy, that is, warrants directing the treasurer general to deliver to the warship captain so many bars or leather pouches of gold, indicating the valuation of each in terms of marcs, ounces, eighth ounces, and grains of gold,[61] and the particular revenue source from which they were derived.[62] The data for 1775–1776 are based primarily upon a list compiled in the Royal Mint in Lisbon upon the arrival of the long-delayed frigate *Graça* and are partially confirmed by viceregal *portarias*.[63] The information for 1777 was extracted from a manifest signed by the British-born captain of the *São João Baptista* on the day she left port.[64] Between frigate sailings colonial merchants relied upon commercial carriers to make remittances to their Peninsular correspondents. The amounts deposited with each merchant captain were registered with the board of inspection (mesa da inspeção) in Rio de Janeiro. In 1777 the board's president sent to Lisbon a summary of moneys dispatched on such carriers during the previous three years.[65] These sums have been entered in the second

---

[61] In order to reconcile these statistics with others cited in this chapter, I have converted data given by weight in gold into their equivalent value in mil-réis. The Portuguese gold marc contained eight ounces (*onças*), sixty-four eighths (*oitavas*), or 4,608 grains (*grãos*). Between 1713 and 1750 the official value placed on the standard unit of gold, the oitava, varied from 1,200 to 1,500 réis. See Teixeira Coelho, "Instrução," pp. 367–368. Though the magistrate states that "Do 1.º de Agosto de 1751, em que se estabeleceram as casas de fundição actuaes, principiou a valer a oitava a 1$200, e assim se está praticando" (p. 368, par. 29), authorities in Rio de Janeiro continued to calculate the oitava at 1,500 réis. E.g., a portaria of August 12, 1775 orders the sum of 10$250, "the equivalent of six eighths and sixty grains of gold-dust" to be delivered to the captain of the *Graça* (CMCM, cod. 2, fol. 187ʳ). This works out to slightly less than 1,500 rs./1/8, but the "Mappa dos cabedaes q. traz a Fragata N. S. da Graça. . . ." (note 63 below) indicates that the sums recorded for each chest were calculated on the basis of "96$000 rs. cada marco," or exactly 1,500 réis per oitava. I am therefore convinced that the conversions I have made are reasonably correct.

[62] Six portarias of Feb. 26, 1774, CMCM, cod. 2, fols. 12ᵛ–14ᵛ.

[63] "Mappa dos Cabedaes q. traz a Fragata N. S. da Graça . . . chegada do Ryo de Janeiro no dia de hoje 20 de Abril de 1776," *IHGB, Lata* 57, MS 1078. Portarias of July 19, Aug. 14, 1775, CMCM, cod. 2, fols. 177ʳ–178ʳ, 216ᵛ; and portaria of Dec. 16, 1775, *ibid.*, cod. 26, fol. 20ᵛ.

[64] "Mappa do cabedal que leva o Frag.ta . . . S. Joao Bapp.ta de q. he Com-[andant]e Guilherme Roberts . . . ; tanto dos Reaes Quintos de S. Mag.ᵈᵉ como do dinheiro de Partes," Oct. 31, 1777, CMCM, maço 9. Undoubtedly this frigate bore the revenues sent by the captain-general of Minas Gerais for the first semester of 1777. Antônio de Noronha to Lavradio, June 23, 1777, BNRJ, 2, 2, 24, n. 81. The accompanying report (given in terms of arrobas [2,048 marcs], marcs, ounces, eighths, and grains) shows the total yield of the Fifths, the *derrama*, the *escovilhas*, and the literary subsidy for that period was about 200,000 mil-réis.

[65] "Relaçam de dinheiro que se transportou para Lisboa e . . . Porto em Navios mercantes, manifestado, pelos Capitaens delles na Meza da Inspeccam . . . do Rio de Janeiro, depois de 5 de Março de 1774, em que sahio para . . . Lixboa . . . a Fragata . . . Nossa Senhora da Graça. . . ." [Jan. 29, 1776], and its continuation,

column of Table 4. For the year 1778 we have only the totals mentioned by Pombal's successor in a dispatch to the viceroy advising him of the safe arrival of the rendas reais.[66] It is probable that those for 1779 left port on the same frigate that took the Marquis of Lavradio home, but no record of them has been found. The last entry, that of 1791, is the amount of royal revenues that the Conde Rezende, Viceroy of Brazil, reported he was sending to Lisbon for that year.[67] For comparative purposes, Table 5 shows capital remissions to the kingdom from various parts of Brazil during the first half of the eighteenth century.

Several points will be noticed in comparing Tables 4 and 5. First, both reflect only remittances of bullion and coin which left Brazil through legal channels. The amount of gold that passed out of the colony illicitly during the eighteenth century cannot now be accurately determined. However, as will be contended in Chapter XIV, there is no reason to suspect that smuggling was more rampant during the second half of that century than during the first; on the contrary, with the establishment of more elaborate detection machinery after 1750 and with the onset of declining placer yields a decade later,[68] the chances are that the incidence of contraband in gold was lower in Lavradio's time than it had been during earlier decades. Second, even though the shipping point of the majority of the remittances recorded in Table 5 is not indicated, there can be little doubt that that point was Rio de Janeiro, the locus of one of the colony's two mints and the major terminus of the lines of trade between the gold-producing districts of the interior and the littoral.[69] Third, the striking decline in the volume of the rendas reais sent to Portugal from Rio de Janeiro in the 1770s appears to have been significantly

---

"Relação do dinheiro que se transportou para Portugal em Navios mercantes . . . depois de 31 de Janeiro 1776 . . . [até 21 de Outubro 1777]," Nov. 5, 1777, both in CMCM, maço 9.

[66] Marquez de Angeja to Lavradio, Sept. 11, 1778, ANRJ, Col. 67, Liv. III-A, fol. 63ʳ (orig.) . By another dispatch of the same date (ibid., fol. 62ʳ [orig.]) , the same minister reported the arrival of nine chests of diamonds but failed to mention their estimated value.

[67] Rezende to Martinho de Melo e Castro, Mar. 30, 1791, and annexes, RADF, III, 217–219.

[68] As noted in an earlier chapter, the best index of that decline is provided by the fifths collected at the smelteries in Minas. Averaging 108 arrobas a year for the decade 1752–1762, they fell to an average of 83.2 during the next decade and to 70.8 during the years 1772–1777. See the table in Teixeira Coelho, "Instrução," p. 371. Since deliveries of the quintos to Lisbon were one to two years behind collections in the Brazilian interior, the figures reproduced from this oft-cited table do not represent actual remittances for the given years. E.g., a portaria of August 14, 1775 directs the treasurer general to deliver eleven pouches of gold dust "belonging to the royal quinto of 1774 from the captaincy of Goiás" to the captain of the frigate Graça. CMCM, cod. 2, fol. 216ᵛ.

[69] In Table 5 note particularly the quantity of remittances specifically indicated as dispatched from Bahia and Pernambuco (1731ᶜ, 1735ᵈ, 1742ᵈ, 1746ᵈ, and 1749ᶠ) .

TABLE 5

CAPITAL REMITTANCES FROM BRAZIL TO PORTUGAL, 1714–1749 [a]
(in mil-réis)

Year	Royal Revenues	Private Funds	Unspecified	Total
1714	67,200	1,075,200	10,400,000	11,542,400
1717			960,000	960,000
1720 [b]	600,000	1,800,000		2,400,000
1721	118,896	1,144,738	9,530	1,273,164
1724			4,216,000	4,216,000
1725			19,520,000	19,520,000
1727	1,286,765	3,600,000		4,886,765
1729			3,200,000	3,200,000
1730			2,000,000	2,000,000
1731	2,640,000		4,400,000	} 7,542,938
1731 [c]	22,938		480,000	
1733	2,960,000	4,400,000		7,360,000
1734	1,011,200			1,011,200
1735 [c]	130,238	158,730		288,968
1736			600,000	600,000
1737	4,420,378	3,218,022		7,638,400
1738	1,200,000	1,200,000	580,911	2,980,911
1739			7,500,298	7,500,298
1740			391,991	391,991
1742	4,778,832	10,416,628		} 16,128,216
1742 [d]	5,869	926,877		
1743			1,222,962	1,222,962
1745	360,000	1,040,000		1,400,000
1746	322,400	2,740,000		} 3,395,962
1746 [c]	136,762	196,800		
1749 [e]	1,383,140	4,656,708	6,039,847	} 12,866,521
1749 [f]	22,748	370,665	393,413	

a Except for 1749 [e] and 1749 [f], this table is adapted from João Lúcio de Azevedo, *Épocas de Portugal económico: esboços de história* (Lisbon, 1947), Appendix, pp. 464–467, which is based upon a contemporary report (*QE*, V, 262–265). For the sake of uniformity, I have converted the sums given in cruzados into mil-réis.

b The Azevedo text indicates the year as 1710, but it should be 1720.

c Amount of gold aboard Pernambuco frota.

d Amount of gold aboard Bahia frota.

e Amount of gold aboard Rio de Janeiro frota. (Boxer, *The Golden Age*, Appendix VI, pp. 351–352).

f Amount of gold aboard Pernambuco frota (*Ibid.*, pp. 352–353).

greater than the diminution in the size of private remittances from the same port during that decade. While there can be no question that the rendas were falling off at an alarming rate at this time, the fact is that a substantial portion of Crown revenues ordinarily dispatched to Portugal via Rio de Janeiro and other Brazilian ports was consumed in the colony as a consequence of the intensification of the Luso-Spanish borderlands conflict. Fiscal aspects of that conflict are examined in the following section.

Fiscal Consequences of the War with Spain,
1774–1777

By April 1774 the Court had received Viceroy Lavradio's first warnings concerning the menacing advance of General Vértiz against Portuguese positions in Rio Grande de São Pedro. The colonial secretary approved Dom Luís' dispatch of reinforcements to the threatened captaincy and his decision to apply income derived from the "voluntary subsidy" to defray the cost of the buildup, but declined to authorize the diversion of other reserved funds to meet the emergency.[70]

At this time the colonial minister sought to allay the viceroy's fears that the Spaniards were about to undertake a major offensive against his southern dependencies. However, a few months later the Court itself became alarmed by the scope of Spanish preparations for the attack on Algiers. As seen in Chapter VI, Lisbon became convinced that that attack was but a prelude to a full-scale assault upon Brazil's southern settlements. To forestall such an assault, the Marquis of Pombal ordered the transfer of the three Peninsular regiments from Rio de Janeiro to Rio Grande; the mobilization of the militia on Santa Catarina Island, and its reinforcement by the Pernambuco regiment then stationed in Rio de Janeiro; and the removal of two colonial regiments from Bahia to Rio de Janeiro. In addition, Lisbon promised the viceroy the five-hundred-man Lagos artillery regiment, a thousand recruits from the Atlantic Islands, and the MacDouall squadron.

This further buildup of southern Brazil's defenses meant that the junta da fazenda of Rio de Janeiro would have to assume exceptionally heavy burdens for an indefinite period. To enable it to do so, the Marquis of Pombal ordered a substantial increase in the funds at the board's disposal. It was authorized to retain certain reserved revenues normally sent to the kingdom, including the "voluntary" and the "literary" subsidies, income from the former Jesuit properties in the captaincy, and the tax money that São Paulo ordinarily sent to Lisbon. The Carioca board was also promised an annual consignment of 40 contos from Angola and another of twice that magnitude from Bahia.[71] In addition, the captains-general of Bahia and Pernambuco

---

[70] Melo e Castro to Lavradio, Apr. 21, 1774, BNRJ, 6, 3, 24, fols. 244ʳ–248ᵛ. In a separate dispatch Pombal stated that the viceroy could also apply "the products of the Military Subsidy" to meet his increased expenditures. I have been unable to determine what revenue source he had in mind. Pombal to *idem,* same date, CMCM, cod. 14 (49/2).

[71] This is not the first time that one administrative unit in Brazil had been called upon to render financial assistance to another. The Santos subsidy paid

were directed to send to Rio de Janeiro the quarterly pay and allowances earned by their troops on loan to the viceroy.

While committing these additional revenues for the protection of southern Brazil, the Crown warned the viceroy that under no circumstances should he divert any of the royal fifths to satisfy his extraordinary expenses, for "they have indispensable applications in this Court." But Pombal assured Dom Luís that even without the quintos he would have ample funds to wage defensive or offensive war against the Spaniards.[72] That remained to be seen.

Beginning with the last months of 1774, it is possible to chart the principal disbursements of the viceregal junta da fazenda for the next three critical years.[73] As is evident from Figure 3, there was a small increase in nonmilitary expenditures, occasioned by a modest expansion of personnel in some departments to handle the increased volume of military equipment, supplies, and pay orders.[74] Although we lack complete statistics for nonmilitary payments, the omissions are not serious.[75] It is evident that such disbursements mounted far less drastically and fluctuated less radically than did military expenditures during this period. The principal categories of the latter were: the costs of outfitting and repairing the MacDouall squadron and other vessels belonging to or leased by the Crown; the strengthening of fortifications, particularly around Guanabara Bay; the purchase of wagons and livestock for the garrison in Rio Grande; the rental of quarters in Rio de Janeiro to house the additional troops stationed

---

by Rio de Janeiro has already been mentioned (Chap. XI). During its early days both Bahia and Pernambuco contributed to the expenses of Colônia do Sacramento (see "Relação do rendimento da fazenda real da cidade do Rio de Janeiro, no anno de 1700," Castro e Almeida, *Inventário*, VI, 261), and in 1753 the king ordered the Royal Mint of Salvador to send 20,000 cruzados a year to Pernambuco to help defray certain debts there. Carta régia of Sept. 18, 1753, cited in Sombra, *História monetária*, p. 212.

72 The foregoing is based upon Pombal to Lavradio, July 9, 1774, BNRJ, I-2, 4, 6, n. 60, pars. 17–18.

73 Statistical data in this section are based on an analysis of pay warrants (portarias) in CMCM, cods. 2, 15, 19, and 26, *passim*.

74 Considering the enormous amount of work involved in equipping and maintaining the squadron and the enlarged garrisons in Rio de Janeiro, Santa Catarina, and Rio Grande, the staff increases were surprisingly small. The Customs House employed seven additional clerks whose total salary amounted to 1,200 mil-réis (portaria of Jan. 2, 1775, CMCM, cod. 2, fols. 112^{r-v}); an office of paymaster of troops was opened in January 1776 with a staff of five who received 1,816 mil-réis a year ("Mappa geral do rendimento e despeza," cited n. 25 above, pp. 180–181); and a subordinate treasury board was established in Rio Grande in 1775 with less than half a dozen staff members.

75 The most notable are the salaries of the ouvidor (1,287 mil-réis per year), the juiz de fóra (1,070 mil-réis per year), and the viceroy (8,000 mil-réis per year in 1779). Lavradio was evidently paid by the Royal Treasury, but the two magistrates received their salary from the local junta da fazenda. I cannot explain why evidence of such payments is missing from the codices cited in n. 73 above.

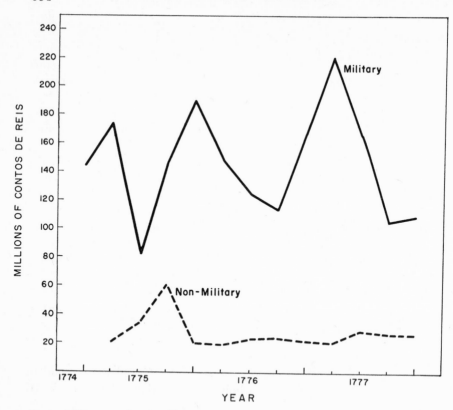

FIG. 3 Military and nonmilitary payments of the viceregal exchequer, 1774 to 1777. (Source: CMCM, cods. 2, 15, 19, and 26.)

there; the maintenance of the military hospital in the capital; the purchase of provisions for Portuguese forces in Rio de Janeiro and its dependencies and for captured Spanish prisoners; transportation charges for the shipment of troops, provisions, equipment, and consignments of money from one station to another; and the pay and allowances earned by regular and auxiliary troops and by the personnel of the MacDouall squadron. The relative importance of these disbursements is indicated by Table 6.

Table 6 brings to light several observations. One is that naval expenses, primarily for the five- to seven-ship MacDouall squadron, became exceptionally heavy. During these three years they mounted to well over 500 contos, considerably more than the land forces in Rio Grande received in pay and allowances. Little wonder that the Court ordered the squadron back to Europe as soon as peace was restored! It is also apparent why the Crown looked with disfavor upon fortification projects proposed by colonial officers, for they were also very costly. It had expressed such disfavor at the beginning of Lavradio's

TABLE 6

MILITARY PAYMENTS OF THE VICEREGAL TREASURY, 1774–1777 [a]

(in mil-réis)

Quarter	Naval Expenses [b]	Funds Sent to São Paulo [c]	Miscellaneous Purchases	Transportation	Rental for Quarters (RJ)	Military Hospital (RJ)	Fortifications		Pay and Allowances for Troops in				Allowances for Spanish Prisoners [d]
							RJ	RGSP	RJ	SC	RGSP	Colônia	
Fourth 1774	22,400	11,685	5,763	4,463	1,428	—	—	20,000	6,000	—	74,079	—	—
First 1775	42,000	—	1,473	—	—	10,600	—	—	35,000	2,707	19,369	25,800	—
Second 1775	21,800	8,000	6,200	1,679	1,759	7,800	—	2,600	33,200	—	32,222	—	—
Third 1775	50,000	6,600	5,999	—	—	4,800	—	—	19,472	7,800	50,578	—	—
Fourth 1775	61,414	—	6,448	—	2,666	11,000	—	—	51,905	14,890	32,223	8,079	—
First 1776	32,000	—	13,737	2,600	2,700	4,000	1,470	—	31,550	16,411	48,333	—	—
Second 1776	18,600	—	5,177	—	—	8,400	—	—	25,200	14,716	48,333	—	—
Third 1776	7,000	—	3,447	—	2,000	5,600	400	—	35,400	14,716	48,333	—	—
Fourth 1776	47,531	—	701	—	—	7,600	50	—	32,400	14,716	64,444	—	—
First 1777	109,338	10,000	2,858	628	—	6,600	848	—	47,600	6,500	28,200	—	800
Second 1777	56,710	8,000	17,616 [e]	—	2,700	6,800	6,984	—	38,830	—	12,000	—	5,165
Third 1777	24,000	—	26,942 [e]	1,096	—	7,500	12,876	—	28,400	—	—	—	3,596
Fourth 1777	22,807	—	8,857	1,679	2,000	6,100	6,584	—	28,400	—	4,000 [f]	—	4,479

a CMCM, cods. 2, 15, 19, 26, passim.
b Primarily incurred by the MacDouall squadron, but the junta das fragatas also disbursed funds to defray bills of other vessels belonging to the Crown.
c Includes Santos' subsidy, pay, and allowances for royal troops en route to Rio Grande via São Paulo.
d Confined on Ilha das Cobras in Guanabara Bay.

e Doubtless includes part of the costs of strengthening the fortifications of the capital.
f The figures for 1777 are evidently incomplete, for the junta da fazenda of Rio Grande reported that it had received 118,606,404 réis from the viceregal exchequer during 1777. See n. 94 below.

term when he had endorsed several proposals to modernize the defenses of Rio de Janeiro. As a result, the viceroy did not undertake any significant construction program until 1776, when he assumed the initiative and ordered the rebuilding of existing fortresses and the construction of new ones to guard against a possible Spanish attack. Then the charges for such defenses began to climb, perhaps more steeply than is apparent here, for it is likely that many of the items concealed under the rubric of miscellaneous purchases were intended for the fortresses. A third substantial and continuous military expense was the hospital, for as more and more troops entered Rio de Janeiro, the number of soldiers disabled by disease and infirmities rather than by enemy bullets grew steadily larger.

It needs to be emphasized that the statistics charted in Figure 3 and entered in Table 6 represent actual payments by the junta da fazenda, not its total expenses during the years 1774–1777. If the total expenses of the war effort were ever calculated, which is doubtful, their record remains to be discovered. Judging from the viceroy's correspondence, it appears that the board was able to meet most of its current obligations until early 1777. To be sure, there were certain exceptions. During 1776, for example, no funds were sent to São Paulo. Although payment of the subsidy was resumed the following year, the Paulista board later claimed that Rio de Janeiro still owed 25.4 contos in back payments for the subsidy and the maintenance of Paulista forces in Rio Grande during the war.[76] As Table 6 indicates, no moneys were forwarded to Colônia after the first quarter of 1775. Even before that date the viceroy advised its governor that because of the shortage of shipping and the hazards of sailing, he could not expect funds regularly and should issue the garrison ninety-day promissory notes redeemable at Rio de Janeiro.[77]

But Colônia was a lost cause and the marquis knew it. Rio de Janeira, Santa Catarina, and Rio Grande could and must be held, and the viceroy made every effort to see that their soldiers were paid regularly. When General Böhm left for Rio Grande in December 1774 he was accompanied by a year's advance pay and allowances for his troops since, the viceroy observed, soldiers were less prone to desert when paid on time.[78] The prevention of desertion seems to have

---

[76] Junta da Fazenda, São Paulo, to same, Rio de Janeiro, Oct. 31, 1783, *RIHGB/TE*, VIII (1958), 85.

[77] Lavradio to Pedro José Soares de Figueiredo Sarmento, Mar. 27, 1774, CMCM, cod. 4, fol. 41ᵛ. According to Colônia's former regimental commander, the notes were reluctantly received and heavily discounted by Colônia's merchants. Domingos Correa de Mesquita to Lavradio, *ca.* 1777 or 1778, Jônatas da Costa Rego Monteiro, *A Colônia do Sacramento*, II, 166. It will be recalled that when the outpost's regiment was returned to Rio de Janeiro briefly in 1775, it received two months' pay. That sum is recorded in Table 6.

[78] Lavradio to Böhm, Dec. 3, 1774, BNRJ, 13, 4, 2, n. 1 (orig.).

been a constant preoccupation of the marquis who never failed to
meet a payroll for those garrisons until the coming of the second
Cevallos expedition.[79]

Nevertheless, that record was achieved by allowing less pressing obligations to pile up. One such category was the quarterly allowances
due members of the clergy. Although the Crown had declared that
the clergy should be paid regularly and in full "with preference over
all other persons," since their stipends were covered by the dízimos,[80]
the fact is that the tithes were also used for other purposes, and the
clergy was often paid tardily and, according to their bishops, inadequately.[81] During the years 1775–1777 the junta da fazenda released
funds for the clergy later than for other accounts, and paid out only
about 80 percent of the authorized livings and allowances.[82] Other
accumulating debts consisted of miscellaneous bills presented by merchants, shippers, farmers, and other government creditors in the subcaptaincies. Once again, the viceroy repeated his earlier warnings to
subordinates that there was no money to pay such bills; they would
simply have to wait.[83]

As land and naval reinforcements reached Rio de Janeiro from
Portugal, the Atlantic Islands, and Bahia during the last months of
1774 and the early months of the following year, the viceregal exchequer began to feel the strain of its new burdens. Seven months after
having received the Crown's assurances that he would soon be getting
extraordinary funds from other parts of the empire, the viceroy sent
an urgent dispatch to the captain-general of Bahia advising him that
the Bahian regiments had arrived safely but in such ragged condition
that he had been obliged to provide them with complete new outfits.
As yet he had not seen "a single real" of the eighty contos that the

[79] It is difficult to tell to what extent remittances from Rio de Janeiro actually
satisfied the expenses of the outlying garrisons. In one instance where a check
is possible, it appears that current needs were adequately taken care of. In mid-
1776 the junta da fazenda of Pôrto Alegre reported that its monthly expenditures
amounted to 19,402,641 réis, of which 16,561,798 réis (or 198,741,576 réis per
annum) went to the armed forces. "Copia da conta q. em carta de 5 de Junho de
1776 remeteu a Junta da Fazenda deste continente a da cidade do Rio de Janeiro
demonstractiva das despezas necessarias cada mez . . . ," June 4, 1776, BNRJ, 13,
4, 4, n. 43. As Table 6 indicates, the Rio de Janeiro board sent over 209,440,000
réis that year to Rio Grande to pay its garrison. The subtreasury actually ended
the year with an unexpended balance of 9,669,095 réis. "Balancete da Receita e
Despeza feita neste Continente do R.o Grande . . . ," Dec. 31, 1776, BNRJ, 13,
4, 4, n. 52.

[80] Alvará of Feb. 3, 1689, CCLP, X, 186.

[81] Oscar de Oliveira, Os dízimos eclesiásticos do Brasil nos períodos da colonia
e do imperio, pp. 113, 115.

[82] According to the figures given in Table 3, the annual charges on the ecclesiastical register amounted to slightly over 29.6 contos. The portarias for the years
1775 through 1777 indicate that payments averaged about 24.6 contos.

[83] Lavradio to José Marcelino de Figueiredo, July 21, 1774, CMCM, cod. 4, fol. 55r.

Court had promised him from the Salvadorean exchequer.[84] The captain-general of Pernambuco proved equally slow about remitting funds. The viceroy sent the Court a flurry of dispatches concerning the failure of both men to assist him to the extent it had directed.[85]

Instead of expressing sympathy or reassurances that the two officers would be censured for their apparent negligence, the colonial secretary sharply reprimanded the viceroy himself. Though Melo e Castro's dispatch has already been noted in another context, it deserves to be considered a second time. The minister declared that His Majesty was pained to read all of Lavradio's

> complaints about the dearth of things you consider necessary and full of criticisms of everything that has been sent to Your Excellency . . . when He is confident that everyone in Brazil realizes that never were so many military forces nor so much war matériel, provisions [and] pecuniary aid sent to the State which Your Excellency governs . . . ; that with only the troops and resources of Rio de Janeiro the Count of Bobadela fought the Glorious Uruguayan War, triumphing simultaneously over the forces of the Indians and the Jesuit Engineers and the treacheries of the Spanish Generals . . . [who were later] expelled from Northern Rio Grande de São Pedro . . . [and everyone knows] that the Castilians of those times and now are the same Castilians.[86]

There is no indication of how the marquis reacted when he read this remarkable dispatch. Had he been so disposed, Dom Luís could have rejoined that according to Lisbon's own estimates the military threat of the mid-1770s was infinitely greater than that which confronted his predecessor two decades earlier. He could have added that at no previous time in the history of the colony had there been so many men under arms, so many dependent upon the resources of one branch of the royal exchequer as there were in 1775. But the viceroy exercised restraint and continued to try to convince the Court that he had far less funds at his disposal to fight the war than it believed.[87]

---

[84] *Idem* to Manoel da Cunha e Menezes, Apr. 10, 1775, CMCM, cod. 26, fols. 91ᵛ–92ᵛ.

[85] In the dispatch cited in n. 86, the colonial secretary referred to a group of the viceroy's letters written between Dec. 6, 1774, and May 10, 1775. These have not been found, but the substance of the viceroy's complaints about the lack of cooperation by his fellow governors is contained in Lavradio to Martim Lopes Lobo de Saldanha, Nov. 7, 1775, *DI*, XVII (1895) , 36.

[86] Martinho de Melo e Castro to Lavradio, Aug. 4, 1775, BNRJ, I-2, 4, 7, n. 14. By this date the secretary had probably received a dispatch of June 30, 1775 from Manoel da Cunha Menezes (BNRJ, I-4, 3, 16) , giving assurances that *forty* (but not eighty) contos had been sent (when he did not indicate) to Rio de Janeiro together with troops and supplies. It may be, too, that he had a similar report from the captain-general of Pernambuco who was also interested in keeping his skirts clean.

[87] Lavradio to Pombal, Oct. 31 and Nov. 19, 1776, *VRL*, pp. 336–344, 363–364.

The available evidence suggests that he had good grounds for his contention.

TABLE 7

EXTRAORDINARY FUNDS RECEIVED BY THE JUNTA DA FAZENDA OF RIO DE JANEIRO, 1774–1777 [a]
(in mil-réis)

| Source | Year | | | |
	1774	1775	1776	1777
Rio de Janeiro				
Literary subsidy	?	12,293 [b]	8,700 [c]	6,449 [d]
Voluntary subsidy	44,465 [e]	44,465 [e]	44,465 [e]	44,465 [e]
Income from ex-Jesuit properties	?	17,534 [f]	5,489 [g]	2,806 [h]
Earnings from mint	?	?	2,160 [i]	?
Minas Gerais				
Literary subsidy	5,990 [e]	5,990 [e,j]	5,990 [e]	?
Voluntary subsidy	39,950 [k]	32,313 [j]	25,672 [l]	15,683 [m]
Other		33,372 [j]	14,864 [n]	16,455 [o]
Goiás				
Literary subsidy	3,056 [e]	[j]	[p]	?
Voluntary subsidy	2,507	9,786	8,700	5,897
Other			14,957 [p]	
São Paulo				
Revenues from smelting		11,153 [q]		
Bahia				
Annual consignment		40,000 [r]		
Pernambuco				
Consignment		28,088 [s]		
Angola				
Consignment	40,000 [e]	40,000 [e]	40,000 [e]	40,000 [e]
Totals	95,968	274,994	170,997	131,755

a The "Relação dos rendimentos extraordinarios que na occazião da proxima guerra no sul auxiliaram os cofres reaes da thezouraria geral d'esta capitania" (*RIHGB*, LI:2 [1888], 203–204) was prepared by the auditor-general of Rio de Janeiro in 1781 to show the Court how little the viceregal exchequer had received by way of extraordinary income during the recent war. That report is far from complete and has been utilized here only when other sources have been lacking.

b *Portaria* of Dec. 31, 1775, CMCM, cod. 26, fols. 24 r-v.

c *Portarias* of June 30 and Dec. 31, 1776, CMCM, cod. 19, fols. 66 r and 137v.

d *Portarias* of June 30, Dec. 30 and 31, 1777, *ibid.*, fols. 192 v, 232 v–233 r.

e Estimates averaged by year by the auditor-general. See note a.

f *Portaria* of Dec. 31, 1775, CMCM, cod. 26, fol. 24 r.

g *Portaria* of June 30, 1776, CMCM, cod. 19, fol. 65v.

h *Portarias* of June 30 and Dec. 30, 1776, *ibid.*, fols. 192 v and 233 r.

i *Portaria* of Jan. 10, 1776, *ibid.*, fol. 4r.

j A *portaria* of Oct. 5, 1775 (CMCM, cod. 2, fol. 207 v) ordered delivery to the Mint of 347 marcs, 4 ounces, 7/8ths and 71 grains of gold dust pertaining to the literary and voluntary subsidies of Minas Gerais, income from confiscated properties of the former diamond contractor Felisberto Caldeira Brant, the yield of taxes on public offices and the literary subsidy of Goiás, but did not break down the amounts

Table 7 provides a more complete account than the Crown itself received of the viceregal exchequer's extraordinary income during these years. It is possible that some receipts have been overlooked, though a check of all possible sources, including a summary prepared by the auditor-general (see Table 7, note a), the correspondence of the viceroy and several of the captains-general, and other materials cited in this chapter, makes it seem unlikely that any large sums have been omitted. Assuming that ordinary revenues during this period remained at about 468,486 mil-réis a year (see Table 2), the sums listed here indicate that the total funds available to the Carioca treasury increased by 59 percent in 1775, 39 percent in 1776, but only by 28 percent in 1777. It is interesting to compare the estimated receipts for the years 1775–1777 with the record of that exchequer's actual payments.

It would appear from Table 8 that the extraordinary revenues of the viceregal treasury enabled it to defray most of its expenses during 1775 and 1776 but fell considerably short of doing so in the critical year 1777. Such a conclusion is only partially correct. In the first place, not all units that contributed extraordinary funds to Rio de Janeiro at this time did so on a regular basis. Remittances were supposed to be made toward the end of each semester, but because of problems of collection, they were often not ready at that time and were not sent until the following semester or even later. However,

---

derived from each source. Teixeira Coelho ("Instrução," p. 435) reports that in 1775 the literary subsidy of Minas produced 6,646,499 réis and the voluntary subsidy 32,312,748 réis. It is not certain that all of the income from both sources was actually remitted to Rio de Janeiro. (Here and at several other points in this table I have converted data given by weight into monetary equivalents according to the formula described in n. 61.)

k Portaria of Nov. 4, 1774, CMCM, cod. 2, fol. 82r; the figure given in Teixeira Coelho (loc. cit.) is 38,432,511 réis.

l Teixeira Coelho, loc. cit.

m Portaria of Dec. 20, 1777, CMCM, cod. 19, fols. 230 v–231 r.

n Portarias of June 28 and Nov. 23, 1776, ibid., fols. 65r–v, 128v–129r; of the total given here, 9,942,404 réis came from the sequestered property of a former ouvidor in the comarca of Rio das Velhas.

o Antônio de Noronha to Lavradio, June 23, 1777, BNRJ, 2, 2, 24, n. 81.

p Portaria of Aug. 20, 1776, CMCM, cod. 19, fol. 90v. Includes but does not separate revenues from taxes on public offices and the literary subsidy.

q Two portarias of Apr. 12, 1775, ibid., cod. 2, fols. 145 r–v.

r The report cited in note a implies that the captain-general of Bahia sent 80,000,000 réis a year to Rio de Janeiro at this time, but only one consignment of 40 contos was ever remitted. Manoel da Cunha Menezes to Martinho de Melo e Castro, June 30, 1775, BNRJ, 1–4, 3, 16. There is no evidence in this codice or in another containing the captain-general's correspondence with the Court (Library of Congress, Portuguese Collection. Register of the Correspondence of Manoel da Cunha Menezes, 1774–79, II-35-E, 1) that the Crown ever asked for or received an explanation of why no additional funds were sent from Bahia to the viceroy.

s Thezouraria Geral de Pernambuco. "Balanço geral da receita e despeza do anno de 1776," Jan. 10, 1777, IHGB/AUC, 1-1-15, fols. 105r, 106v and 107v.

most of the viceregal treasury's obligations fell due at the beginning of each quarter and (as Fig. 3 demonstrates) their magnitude fluctuated considerably from one quarter to another. The irregularity of receipts from the other captaincies therefore complicated the Carioca junta's ability to defray its obligations. Second, it needs to be emphasized again that the evidence we have concerning that board's expenditures reflects only actual payments, not total encumbrances. As will be shown later (in Fig. 4), its total obligations substantially exceeded its actual payments during these years. It is evident that as the bills mounted, the less pressing ones were simply set aside.

The growing indebtedness of the viceregal treasury during the mid-1770s is one indication that it was experiencing increasing difficulty in covering its obligations. Other evidence points to the same conclu-

TABLE 8

TOTAL INCOME AND TOTAL PAYMENTS OF THE
VICEREGAL TREASURY, 1775–1777 [a]
(in mil-réis)

	Income			Payments			
Year	Ordinary (estimated)	Extraordinary	Total	Non-military	Military	Total	Balance
1775	468,486	274,994	743,480	136,813	594,905	731,718	+11,762
1776	468,486	170,997	639,483	90,583	556,963	647,546	−8,063
1777	468,486	131,755	600,241	106,392	605,351	711,743	−111,502

a Sources: Tables 2, 6, 7, and Fig. 1.

sion. In March 1776, for example, the viceroy responded to an appeal from a regimental commander who reported that his men had not received their clothing allowance for such a long time that they had become ragged and destitute (roto e nú). The marquis expressed regret at their plight but stated that in view of the shortages of money and clothing in the capital, "there is no other remedy than to have patience and to await the coming of [new supplies from Lisbon] which I will send you as soon as I receive them." [88] The following September the treasury board in Rio de Janeiro notified its Pôrto Alegre branch to cease remitting bills to Rio de Janeiro for payment. They could no longer be settled, it said, "because the present situation does not permit more than the greatest economic prudence . . . so that the money necessary for indispensable expenses [will] not be found wanting. . . ." [89] And in January 1777 Dom Luís informed the ad-

88 Lavradio to Colonel Pedro de Moraes de Magalhães, Mar. 5, 1776, CMCM, cod. 26, fol. 73ʳ.
89 Junta da Fazenda, Rio de Janeiro, to same, Rio Grande, Sept. 4, 1776, BNRJ, 13, 4, 3, n. 10.

ministrator of one of the former Jesuit estates that the board was too hard pressed to pay for foodstuffs requisitioned from the plantation.[90]

The arrival of the second Cevallos expedition at the end of the following month spelled disaster for the viceroy in more than one way. When Santa Catarina Island fell and its garrison surrendered, the Spaniards seized the subcaptaincy's treasury. Sometime after, they apparently also intercepted a large consignment of funds intended for Portuguese forces in Rio Grande.[91] But even before these losses were known in Rio de Janeiro, Commodore MacDouall had returned and announced that he could not sail again until his ships had been rendered seaworthy, a demand that resulted in an outlay of over 100 contos. One reason the viceroy shuddered every time the squadron re-entered port that disastrous year was because each time the warships required further expensive repairs before they could put to sea again (see Table 6). Besides meeting the squadron's seemingly endless expenses, the viceregal treasury tried to provide the wherewithal to continue regular payments to the capital's garrison and to replace the captured funds it had supposedly sent to Rio Grande. Because the presence of the Casa Tilly armada made further remissions by sea hazardous, the viceroy sent pecuniary consignments for the southern captaincy overland via São Paulo and Curitiba.[92] The amounts were smaller than during previous years, a fact for which the viceroy apologized, but he assured General Böhm that the king's debts would

[90] Lavradio to M[igu]el de Albu[querqu]e de Melo (Desembargador Juiz do Confisco), Jan. 16, 1777, CMCM, cod. 25, fol. 169ʳ.

[91] I have not found any Portuguese source which gives the amount of cash in the Santa Catarina treasury at the time it fell into Spanish hands. A Spanish report indicates that there was a little over 50,000 pesos, including 10,231 belonging to the king, 30,540 to private individuals, and 10,279 to a fund for the support of orphans. "Resumen del caudel hallado en arcas . . . del Rey de Portugal, . . . de Particulares . . . y de huerfanos . . . en el campamento de Cubaton," Mar. 9, 1777, British Museum, Egerton MS, No. 374 (Bancroft Library Microfilm Collection). According to John Colbatch, in the late seventeenth century a Spanish peso was worth 750 Portuguese réis. *An Account of the Court of Portugal*, I (London, 1700), 19. I am unable to say whether the same ratio obtained in Lavradio's time. Assuming that it did, the total Spanish haul amounted to 38,287.5 mil-réis. According to the viceroy, the Castillians also seized 80,000 cruzados aboard a corvette bound for Rio Grande. Lavradio to Böhm, Dec. 8, 1777, BNRJ, 13, 4, 3, n. 43 (orig.). The assertion is suspect for several reasons: (1) there is no warrant in the files confirming that the treasurer general had issued such funds; (2) the amount was unusually large to be entrusted to a single ship; (3) it is astonishing that a cautious man like the marquis would dispatch such an argosy on the eve of the expected arrival of the Casa Tilly armada; (4) no Spanish source that I have seen mentions the capture of such treasure. It may be that the marquis conjured up a phantom capital remittance to conceal the fact that his exchequer simply could not keep up the level of its previous remissions to Rio Grande.

[92] Martim Lopes Lobo de Saldanha to Böhm, Apr. 2 and June 4, 1777, *DI*, XLII, 221 f., 281.

eventually be settled and that creditors should remain patient.[93] But it was hard for authorities in Rio Grande to remain patient when remittances from Rio de Janeiro dwindled to less than half the amount sent during the preceding year, and when they were subjected to the clamors of soldiers, sailors, government functionaries, merchants, and ranchers all demanding their due. It is not surprising to find the Pôrto Alegre junta writing an anguished dispatch to the viceroy late in 1777 reporting that the troops had not been paid since July, the militia and seamen since April, and civil officials since June. They added that large sums were also owed other creditors but that their coffers were empty and they had found is impossible to borrow money in the subcaptaincy "because in truth there isn't any." [94] That could hardly come as a surprise to the viceroy who had already resorted to desperate expedients to secure urgently needed funds for his own exchequer.

Desperate Measures

In November 1776 the marquis wrote the Court that his financial situation was becoming critical. Expenses continued to climb but because of the failure of some of the extraordinary revenues to reach him the treasury was so short of funds that he intended to try to raise a loan of 200,000 cruzados from private sources. But he warned that "In case I fail . . . it will be necessary for me to make use of the Fifths. . . ." [95] The mere suggestion that Lavradio might tap that indispensable revenue was sufficient to alarm the Court. As soon as he received the viceroy's threat, the colonial secretary acted to prevent such a calamity. He wrote Dom Luís that he did not favor his plan to raise a subscription because of the "great inconveniences which would result to the Royal Treasury" from such action, meaning that the Crown would be obliged to allocate part of its reserved funds to repay the loan. While the minister failed to suggest what alternatives the viceroy ought to pursue, he made it quite clear that one of them was not the quintos. They were sacrosanct and must always be sent to Lisbon "in tact." To make sure that the fifths were remitted in full, the Crown immediately dispatched a royal frigate to fetch them.[96]

[93] Lavradio to Böhm, Mar. 13, Aug. 2, Sept. 17, Nov. 4, and Dec. 8, 1777, BNRJ, 13, 4, 3, nos. 28, 35, 41–43 (all origs.).

[94] Junta da Fazenda, Rio Grande, to [Lavradio], Oct. 2, 1777, BNRJ, 13, 4, 4, n. 70 (orig.). A summary by the same board indicates that during 1777 its receipts totaled 187,081,302 réis, of which 118,606,404 réis originated with the treasury board in Rio de Janeiro. "Rezumo da receita do ballanço de 1777," n. d., ibid., n. 72.

[95] Lavradio to Pombal, Nov. 19, 1776, cited in n. 87 above.

[96] Melo e Castro to Lavradio, Mar. 28, 1777, BNRJ, I-2, 4, 7, n. 72.

That frigate reached Rio de Janeiro in September 1777, but by then the deed had already been done: the ever-cautious viceroy had ignored repeated statements of royal policy by dipping into the tempting coffers containing the fifths. As Dom Luís explained to the Marquis of Angeja, successor to the Marquis of Pombal, he had felt compelled to do so because of the dearth of funds in the viceregal exchequer and the lack of pecuniary assistance from the captains-general of Bahia and Goiás.[97] Without assurance that they would be paid, the viceroy continued, artisans would not work on repairs to the squadron; farmers refrained from bringing their produce to market; businessmen declined to sell their goods to the keepers of the royal warehouses; and militiamen refused to mount the capital's bastions. Consequently, he had borrowed from the fifths [98] to defray the most urgent obligations, and to lubricate the economic machinery of the captaincy which was so closely geared to the operations of the exchequer, "For as the capital available to merchants diminishes, trade falls off and His Majesty's revenues, not only from the Customs House but also from all other sources, likewise decline [and because] the farmer ceases to plant his crops . . . the Tithes are reduced." In short, said Lavradio, "When I delay making payments, entries into the coffers are held back; [but] as soon as I resume payments, [the treasury] begins to collect large receipts." [99]

The precarious condition of the viceregal exchequer prompted the viceroy to seek other ways of raising money. One measure was to ap-

[97] In several of his dispatches to the Crown and to subordinates the viceroy complained that he had not received any funds from Goiás, but that assertion is refuted by the evidence presented in Table 7. After the fall of Santa Catarina Island the viceroy did send urgent messages to the captain-general of Goiás explaining what had happened and asking that funds be sent immediately to assist his exchequer. Lavradio to Dom Antônio de Lencastre, Mar. 11 and Apr. 23, 1777, CMCM, cod. 26, fols. 135ᵛ–137ᵛ.

In Table 7 it will be noticed that the only known remittance of funds to the viceroy from Bahia was a partial shipment in 1775. Why the captain-general did not comply with the Court's original instructions to send much larger sums and why the Crown failed to reprimand him for failing to do so is something of a puzzle. But it may be conjectured that after the Court warned that the Cevallos expedition seemed headed toward Bahia, its captain-general made use of every possible real to strengthen his own defenses and no longer had a surplus to send to Lavradio. The evidence cited in n. 101 below suggests that Manoel da Cunha Menezes, like the viceroy, experienced such a shortage of funds that he was considering a public loan.

[98] Lavradio did not mention what portion of the quintos he appropriated, but it would appear that he diverted about one-third of the receipts. According to Teixeira Coelho ("Instrução," p. 371) the fifths for 1776 (the ones that would be remitted the following year) amounted to 468,179,833 réis (my conversion; see n. 61). As indicated in Table 4, remittances of the rendas reais in 1777 totaled 297,178,500 réis.

[99] Lavradio to Melo e Castro, Sept. 24, 1777, VRL, pp. 134–137. There is no indication of how Lisbon reacted to the viceroy's decision.

peal to local businessmen for a loan (unspecified as to amount) secured by his personal credit.[100] Dom Luís evidently felt that such assurance was necessary, both because he lacked authorization to pledge royal property for that purpose and because he realized that the Crown's own credit rating was worse than that of an ordinary merchant.[101] Another measure was the disposal of former Jesuit holdings in the captaincy. Their liquidation actually began before the fiscal emergency of the mid-1770s. Since Dom Luís had played a role in the formulation of royal policy on the disposition of the Black Robes' properties, it is necessary to examine some of the relevant background.

When the Society of Jesus was expelled from Brazil (1759–1760), its extensive urban and rural properties passed into the hands of the Crown. Some parcels were auctioned off in the early 1760s, but others continued to be administered by Crown officials while authorities in Brazil and the kingdom debated whether it was to the king's advantage to sell off the remaining plantations, ranches, and urban dwellings or to retain them for their income-producing qualities. Although the equipment, furnishings, livestock, and slaves on these properties were to be appraised and inventoried at the time of their confiscation, many registers were not completed until nearly a decade later; in the meantime, goods and equipment were purloined, crops were neglected, and stock herds were allowed to deteriorate.[102] Learning of such conditions, the Court directed Viceroy Lavradio to send to the Royal Treasury up-to-date inventories of the remaining ex-Jesuit properties within the captaincy of Rio de Janeiro and to dispose of them whenever the junta da fazenda received bids that equaled their appraised value.[103]

100 Lavradio to the Marquis of Angeja, Oct. 22, 1777, *ibid.*, pp. 137–138.

101 In 1779 a certain Agostinho José Barreto made the following interesting comments concerning the efforts of Crown officers in Salvador to raise a public loan: "Quanto ao empréstimo que se mandou abrir, de 3,000$000 de cruzados, não o julgo impossível, porém sim muito dificultoso de completar, visto que tal é a nossa desgraça, que tem mais crédito um mercador que o erário régio, o que na minha opinião vem de dois princípios: o primeiro, de se ter faltado muitas vêzes às repetidas promessas de pagamento das dívidas reais; o segundo de ser tão ociosa nossa legislação." Quoted without source in [Manoel] Pinto de Aguiar, *Bancos no Braisil colonial. Tentativas de organização bancária em Portugal e no Brasil até 1808.* (Salvador, [1960]) p. 27.

102 Count Azambuja to Francisco Xavier de Mendonça Furtado, Oct. 16, 1768, ANRJ, Col. 69, Liv. I, fols. 23ᵛ–24ʳ. The statements made in this and the following paragraphs are based primarily on research for a study (in progress) of economic aspects of the Jesuits' expulsion from Brazil. A brief, generally accurate account of the disposal of the Society's properties in Rio de Janeiro appears in José de Sousa Azevedo Pizarro e Araujo, *Memórias históricas do Rio de Janeiro*, V, 297–299, where, however, the author erroneously states that the plantation of Engenho Velho was still in royal hands in the 1770s. It was actually sold in 1761–1762.

103 Carta régia, Aug. 28, 1770, CMCM, cod. 3, fol. 104ʳ (orig.).

In taking note of these instructions, the viceroy offered two suggestions. He believed that it would be preferable to sell first the least desirable properties, generally those located farthest from the capital. Second, he urged that the Crown retain two of the most valuable estates, the fazendas of Engenho Novo and Santa Cruz. The former was situated near the northern outskirts of the capital, the latter occupied a large stretch of land west of the capital between the seacoast and the road to São Paulo. The Santa Cruz ranch yielded a net annual income of between nine and ten thousand cruzados (3,600 to 4,000 mil-réis), besides providing meat for the crews of passing royal frigates, charcoal for the Military Hospital and other royal facilities, and artisans (slaves) to work in the royal gun factory and other installations. He conceded that Engenho Novo had been badly administered in the past, but pointed to the growth of its annual sugar harvests from a mere three chests in 1768 to nearly fifty two years later as an indication of its value.[104] Furthermore, its lush pastures and proximity to the capital made Engenho Novo an ideal camp site for a cavalry regiment that he recommended be established in Rio de Janeiro.[105]

Some months later the viceroy passed along further reflections on the problem of the liquidation of the Jesuit properties. Noting the Crown's heavy and longstanding indebtedness in the captaincy, he suggested that bills drawn against the treasury be accepted in payment for the estates. Among the advantages that he foresaw from his proposal were: (1) that the Crown would be spared the continuing expenses incident to the administration of those properties; (2) the captaincy's debt load would be substantially reduced; and (3) as the Crown's credit improved, the captaincy's economy would be stimulated.[106]

The Crown was evidently impressed by Lavradio's proposal, for two years later it adopted it with some modifications. In March 1773 the king declared that all remaining Jesuit lands would be auctioned and that bidders would be permitted to present treasury bills dated before the end of 1761, the date regarded as marking the end of the older fiscal system, in lieu of cash for their purchases.[107] However, the Marquis of Pombal advised the viceroy that the Court had decided

104 Because charges on shipments of sugar were levied according to the number of chests (caixas) rather than by weight, the chests grew steadily larger between the sixteenth and eighteenth centuries. By the early eighteenth century they had become so large that stevedores in Lisbon complained that they were difficult to unload; accordingly, the Crown set the maximum weight for a caixa at thirty-five arrobas (1,120 lbs.). King to Luís Vahia Monteiro, Mar. 8, 1728, *RADF*, III (1896), 125–126.

105 Lavradio to Pombal, Feb. 9, 1771, ANRJ, Col. 69, Liv. I-bis., fols. 36ʳ–37ᵛ.

106 Lavradio to Pombal, July 12, 1771, BNRJ, 10, 4, 8, n. 181.

107 Carta régia, Mar. 4, 1773, cited in Pizarro, *Memorias*, V, 298.

not to keep the Santa Cruz and Engenho Novo ranches, which were also put up for sale.[108]

The viceroy yielded to the Court's wishes and nearly all the remaining Jesuit lands in the captaincy were auctioned off during the middle and later 1770s. By the end of that decade only two rural estates were left, and one of them, the fazenda of Engenho Novo, was acquired by a large syndicate in 1780. The other, the Santa Cruz ranch, was so vast and so highly appraised [109] that no satisfactory tenders were received during the rest of the colonial period.[110] The terms of the sales, which the viceroy supervised, remain to be discovered. It is evident from his memorial to his successor that they included little cash,[111] and since the viceregal exchequer could accept only old treasury paper in those transactions, the level of indebtedness it had incurred during the marquis' term was not reduced by the liquidation of the Black Robes' former properties.

The Persisting Debt Problem

In the middle of 1779 the Marquis of Lavradio left Rio de Janeiro with the knowledge that the viceregal exchequer was far more heavily burdened than it had been when he assumed office. Figure 4 indicates that treasury's yearly deficits between 1762, the date from which accounts were computed according to the "new method," and 1780.[112] It is evident that the extent of the annual deficit varied directly with the state of Luso-Spanish relations concerning the borderlands. Thus the war years 1762–1763 were followed by a continuing crisis over Rio Grande de São Pedro, climaxed by the unauthorized Portuguese offensive. The debt curve continued upward to that point; however, it fell substantially between 1768 and 1773, a period that began with the attempted Luso-Spanish rapprochement and ended in stalemate. But the march of General Vértiz in December 1773 led to a renewed buildup of Portuguese forces to defend the borderlands. The level of indebtedness again rose, sharply this time, peaking in 1777, the year

108 Pombal to Lavradio, Feb. 26, 1773, loc. cit.

109 About 1780 it was appraised at 77,227,070 réis. Luís de Vasconcelos e Sousa to Melo e Castro, July 15, 1781, RIHGB, LI:2 (1888), 193.

110 This disposition of the Santa Cruz ranch remained a source of frequent bickering among the royal officials during the remaining colonial decades. Portions of the estate still belong to the Brazilian government.

111 Lavradio, Relatório, pp. 460–462.

112 Figure 4 does not include debts owed by the subcaptaincies of Santa Catarina and Rio Grande, nor miscellaneous charges for various royal ships provisioned at Rio de Janeiro. Altogether those obligations amounted to an additional 272,646,834 réis. "Mappa da dívida passiva da fazenda real da capitania do Rio de Janeiro e provedorias suas subalternas, conforme o manifesto que se fez no principio no anno de 1780," [May 1, 1781], RIHGB, LI:2 (1888), 201–203.

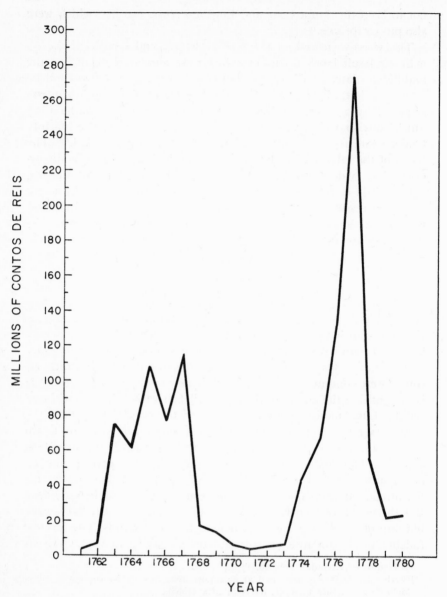

Fɪɢ. 4 Yearly indebtedness of the Rio de Janeiro exchequer, pre-1761 to 1780.
(Source: *RIHGB,* LI:2 (1888), 201–203.)

of the second Cevallos expedition but also the year when the peace
treaty of San Ildefonso was signed. The debt curve then descended to
approximately the level attained during the early 1770s.

In his report to his successor the marquis discussed at length the
debt problem and reviewed his efforts to cope with it. He concluded
that the Crown's inability to pay its bills was sapping the life blood

of the captaincy's economy and predicted that the situation would worsen rather than improve unless the Crown could be persuaded to make adequate provision for the redemption of its obligations.[113]

This was also the position taken by Viceroy Vasconcelos who in July 1781 submitted to the Court a lengthy report concerning the fiscal condition of his government.[114] In it he emphasized four major problems. First, he called attention to the continued imbalance of the viceregal exchequer whose expenses exceeded its income by over 110,000 mil-réis a year. Second, he noted that while the junta da fazenda was charged with subsidizing new agricultural crops such as indigo, cultivators quickly became discouraged when the treasury could not pay them promptly. Third, he pointed out that there were many public works in the capital remaining unfinished or still in the planning stages because of the dearth of funds. Thus the construction of the cathedral of Nossa Senhora de São Francisco, begun in 1749, had been suspended since 1753; the Customs House needed new sheds in order to protect merchandise stored there from damage by the elements; the High Court and the capital's garrison lacked their own quarters and the rental of such facilities represented a not inconsiderable sum; a much needed house of correction for vagrant women had been authorized by the Crown in 1769 but was still unbuilt a decade later; the city also needed better facilities to house its firefighting equipment. Fourth, Vasconcelos reported that while the sums due his treasury from debtors amounted to slightly over 48 contos, the exchequer itself owed more than 1,272 contos; if restricted to its ordinary income, he saw no way that those debts could be settled.

The new viceroy offered some solutions to these problems. To balance income and outgo and to enable the junta da fazenda to sustain new economic activities, he proposed that the exchequer's wartime subsidies from other administrative units be continued. Convinced of the "greatness and piety of Her Majesty" and of her desire to render justice to her subjects, he urged that the funds from the "voluntary subsidy" collected in his captaincy be retained to retire the queen's debts. And to raise additional revenues needed for the completion of essential public works, he proposed that the Crown follow the practice of other European nations and permit the establishment of a public lottery in the viceregal capital.[115]

113 Lavradio, *Relatório*, pp. 460–466.

114 Luís de Vasconcelos e Sousa to Melo e Castro, July 15, 1781, *RIHGB*, LI:2 (1888), 183–194; repr., *ibid.*, CCLVI (1962) , 200–209. Both texts seem to have been based upon a manuscript in Rio de Janeiro's National Library (BNRJ, I-3, 4, 27) , for like it, they lack six of the eleven appendices which accompanied the original. Copies of those appendices have not turned up.

115 Details concerning the proposed lottery are given in Appendix XI of the above-cited dispatch. A few years earlier, in 1769, the Marquis de Croix, Viceroy of New Spain, also proposed a lottery, which was established there two years later.

The colonial secretary found Vasconcelos' report interesting but not convincing. Ignoring its recommendations, he criticized the method by which the auditor-general had determined the viceregal treasury's active and passive debts. While the sums listed as due the Crown represented only those owed by debtors residing in the capital, the roster of debts included claims by creditors throughout the captaincy. The two sets of figures, he declared, were not congruent. Furthermore, on the basis of a report found in his secretariat, the sums actually owed to the viceregal exchequer totaled 805.4 contos, not a mere 48 contos. He added that the same source revealed that equally large sums totaling 4,020 contos were due the Crown from debtors in other parts of Brazil. If they could be collected, he concluded, the government's obligations would be greatly lessened.[116]

And there was the rub, for fully half of that enormous debt consisted of obligations dating back two decades or longer. Moreover, the colonial minister's figures represented only the amounts owed by tax farmers and did not include other kinds of debtors, notably delinquent officeholders and tax-dodging colonial merchants.[117] Nor were those debts easily recoverable, even when secured by landed property, for encumbered estates could not be sold for more than a fraction of their worth, and their seizure virtually eliminated the possibility of obtaining additional funds from bankrupt debtors or their bondsmen (*fiadores*).[118]

The particular uses of the funds the Crown acquired from this source are not apparent. See Fabian de Fonseca and Carlos de Urrutia, *Historia general de real hacienda* (1791–1793), II (6 v., Mexico, 1845–1853), 119–188.

[116] Melo e Castro to Vasconcelos, Nov. 1, 1781, BNRJ, 6, 3, 24, fols. 288ʳ–290ʳ. The report cited by the minister is reproduced here in Appendix IV. The figures given there for the amounts due from contractors in Minas Gerais between 1762 and 1780 tally with those furnished by Teixeira Coelho ("Instrução," p. 409, par. 36), suggesting that the report was based upon summaries sent to Lisbon by the various juntas da fazenda. The problem of collecting from delinquent tax farmers is further discussed by Melo e Castro in his "Instrução para o Visconde de Barbacena, . . . governador e capitão general . . . de Minas Geraes," Jan. 29, 1788, *RIHGB*, VI, (1844), 51, 57–58.

[117] According to Teixeira Coelho, by 1777 the arrears in assessments owed by officeholders in Minas Gerais had reached 344,764,089 réis. "Instrução," p. 422, par. 23; for a discussion of the practice of tax evasion by Mineiro businessmen, see *ibid.*, p. 408, par. 30.

[118] "A experiencia mostra que uma fazenda, a qual pela estimação commum, bem que phantastica, se avalia em cincoenta, cem, duzentos e mais mil cruzados, si acaso se penhora, e se põe em praça para se rematar, não apparece lançador que offereça à vista a quarta parte da sua avaliação; e de vinte fazendas que se rematam fiadas a pagamentos, apenas ha um rematante que pague passados vinte ou trinta annos." *Ibid.*, p. 407, par. 25. For a similar view with respect to the sale of debtors' property in Colonial Virginia, see Robert E. and B. Katherine Brown, *Virginia 1705–1786: Democracy or Aristocracy?* (East Lansing, 1964), pp. 111–112. Judge Teixeira added with respect to the delinquent assessments of public officeholders that "A cobrança d'esta divida é muito difficultosa, e ainda digo mais, é impossivel." "Instrução," p. 422, par. 23. Much the same was said by Viceroy Lavradio who regarded the ancient debts owed to the Crown as an illusory source of revenue. *Relatório*, p. 465.

Various remedies for dealing with the perennial problem of debt accumulation were tried or at least suggested. One aim of the "new method" was to facilitate the Crown's collection of its income. That reform, so ill-understood by many Portuguese functionaries, may have been too ambitious for the times. In any case, it failed to bring about any real improvement in the Crown's ability to manage its finances and seems to have been abandoned before the end of the century.[119] Another measure designed to improve the Crown's chances of collecting outstanding debts was a ruling by the Royal Treasury in the 1770s offering certain classes of debtors the opportunity to make installment payments proportionate to the size of their obligations and the value of their estates.[120] Judge Teixeira Coelho, long-time magistrate in Minas Gerais, made several other proposals. One already noted was that the Crown abandon the centuries-old practice of farming its taxes and collect them itself.[121] The judge also condemned the custom of allowing colonial importers grace periods in which to settle their taxes, for too often that proved to be license to evade payments altogether. In addition, he made the interesting suggestion that officeholders be required to pay their assessments at the beginning rather than at the end of each quarter of their tenure—an early advocacy of the principle of withholding! [122]

The problems of the viceregal exchequer in Lavradio's time generally mirrored those of other branches of the Royal Treasury.[123] There were never enough skilled personnel. Some were always tempted to resort to peculation, a practice facilitated by the persistence of faulty record keeping. Revenues were insufficient to defray expenditures, and the latter continued to mount in peacetime as well as in wartime. Indebtedness, which had plagued royal administrators in Brazil long before the coming of Dom Luís de Almeida, continued

119 Such is the implication of the "Plano de Fazenda" proposed on March 14, 1799 by Dom Rodrigo de Sousa Coutinho, former president of the Royal Treasury, and later an important figure during the early years of King John VI in Brazil. The Plan, in which Sousa Coutinho called for a return to the principles of 1762, is published in Pinto de Aguiar, *Bancos no Brasil colonial,* pp. 75–92; see particularly pp. 84, 88, and 92.

120 Teixeira Coelho, "Instrução," pp. 400–401, par. 12.

121 A less drastic but certainly salutory step would have been stricter enforcement of the stipulation always written into tax contracts requiring successful bidders to deposit with the Crown one-tenth to one-half of their tenders to assure payment of the remainder. E.g., *ABNRJ*, XXVIII, 300, 329–330.

122 "Instrução," pp. 408–409, 423.

123 To be sure, the viceregal exchequer also had some unique problems, such as the responsibility for the expenses of the southern captaincies. Another, which also affected other maritime treasury boards but not those in the interior, was the Crown's failure to reimburse colonial treasuries for dyestuffs, hardwoods, and other materials purchased for use in the kingdom or for resale abroad. In 1781, for example, the Carioca exchequer sent to Lisbon hardwoods for which it had paid 72,768,919 réis, and for which it never received compensation. Luís de Vasconcelos e Sousa, *Relatório,* Aug. 20, 1789, *RIHGB*, XXIII:1 (1860), 236–237.

to be "the constant companion" of those who followed him.[124] Before Lavradio's cost-conscious successor retired from his post, the passive debts of his treasury had increased from 1,272 to 2,325 contos, and that during a decade of peace.[125] Although one prominent royal official testified that the level of that indebtedness had been reduced by half during the following decade,[126] his contention is rendered suspect by a coeval statement furnished by the governor of Santa Catarina, who reported that he had been unable to find funds to pay local cultivators for foodstuffs he had purchased from them and that the arrears due his garrison had reached eighty-two months.[127] Nor did the financial situation of the seat of royal authority improve after the royal family settled in Rio de Janeiro in 1808. On the eve of Brazil's independence Dom Pedro de Alcântara, the future Emperor Pedro I, wrote his father from that city that "The debts of this Treasury go on and on. To the Bank [of Brazil is owed] approximately two thousand [contos] . . . To Yong and Finie [another] two thousand or so; to the Viscount of Rio Seco, close to a thousand; to the Arsenal do Exército, a thousand; to the Navy, eleven hundred; [and] the arrears due the Voluntarios Reaes d'El Rei [regiment] amounts to twenty-six months. . . ."[128]

Related to Viceroy Lavradio's duties as fiscal manager of Rio de Janeiro and its dependencies were his efforts to prevent the evasion of royal taxes through illicit trade and to promote the discovery and exploitation of neglected resources that might contribute significantly to the income of the king's subjects and their mother country. These subjects will be examined in the next two chapters.

[124] The phrase is borrowed from Emory G. Evans, "Planter Indebtedness and the Coming of the Revolution in Virginia," *William and Mary Quarterly*, 3d ser., XIX (1962), 517, who applies it to the problems of Virginia tobacco planters. For examples of complaints by earlier Portuguese officials concerning empty coffers and heavy debts, see Augusto Olympio Viveiros de Castro, "História tributaria do Brasil," *RIHGB*, LXXVIII:1 (1916), 36–37; see also, Antônio de Sousa Pedroso Carnaxide, *O Brasil na administração pombalina*, 99–106.

[125] Vasconcelos, *Relatório*, pp. 236–238. The Vasconcelos board made heavy outlays for the refortification of Santa Catarina Island and the restoration of its economy, the expenses of Portuguese members of the joint boundary commission set up by the Treaty of San Ildefonso, the occupation of the island of Trindade (rendezvous point of the Casa Tilly fleet in 1777), and the purchase of hardwoods and certain crops, such as indigo, subsidized by the Crown.

[126] Luiz Beltrão de Gouveia de Almeida (chancellor of the Relação, Rio de Janeiro) to Dom Rodrigo de Souza Coutinho, May 14, 1799, *RIHGB*, LXV:1 (1902), 282.

[127] João Alberto de Miranda Ribeiro, "Dados estatisticos sobre . . . Santa Catarina, 1797," BNRJ, II-35, 30, 3, n. 10.

[128] Dom Pedro de Alcântara to John VI, July 17, 1821. Portugal, Córtes Geraes, *Documentos para a historia das cortes geraes da nação portugueza*, I (Lisbon, 1833), 244; also quoted in Carnaxide, p. 105. See also Manoel Oliveira Lima, *Dom João VI no Brasil*, II (2d ed., Rio de Janeiro, 1945), 772, 785, 793, and 1168.

XIII

Problems of Economic Development

>. . . besides inspiration, every one of us may glean lessons from the history of his science that are useful, even though sometimes discouraging. We learn about both the futility and the fertility of controversies; about detours, wasted efforts, and blind alleys; about spells of arrested growth, about our dependence on chance, about how not to do things, about leeways to make up for. We learn to understand why we are as far as we actually are and also why we are not further. And we learn *what succeeds and how and why*. . . . [sic]
>
>> Joseph A. Schumpeter, *A History of Economic Analysis*
>> (London, 1954), p. 5

>The burning desire that I have of endeavoring to be useful in all respects to the service of His Majesty and the country in which I had the good fortune to be born obliges me to omit no notice of those things which contribute to the greater abundance and advantages of the State.
>
>> Lavradio to Oeiras, July 5, 1770

BECAUSE OF his heavy fiscal responsibilities and because he was in some respects a son of the Enlightenment, Dom Luís de Almeida took a keen personal interest in the economic development of the lands he governed. Conscious of the poverty of the majority of their inhabitants, the marquis encouraged increased production of some crops already long cultivated, notably sugar, and fostered new ones, particularly fibers, dyestuffs, cereals, and tobacco. Like other mercantilist-oriented imperial powers, the Portuguese government was always interested in new colonial staples that promised to eliminate the need for foreign imports and provide the mother country with a new, revenue-creating export.[1] In Lavradio's time the Crown felt a particular sense of urgency about the development of new sources of wealth in Brazil, Portugal's most important colony, because of its declining mineral yields and the steadily mounting costs of Portugal's rivalry with Spain. Consequently, the Crown encouraged the efforts of Lavradio and his contemporaries to stimulate new agricultural and ex-

[1] Cf., e.g., the efforts of the British government to promote various kinds of dyestuffs and fibers in eighteenth-century South Carolina described by C. Robert Haywood, "Mercantilism and South Carolina Agriculture, 1700–1763," *The South Carolina Historical Magazine*, LX (Jan. 1959), 15–27.

tractive industries, some of which contributed significantly to the economic revival of Brazil during the last colonial decades.

Expressions of the Viceroy's Concern for Economic Development

Of the three principal units under the Marquis of Lavradio's charge, Rio de Janeiro was not only the oldest and the most populous, but also economically the most developed. Although the captaincy boasted a few promising gold finds, its economy rested primarily on agriculture, stockraising, and trade. The captaincy's chief exports consisted of sugar, hides, and lumber products, but it also produced large quantities of manioc, beans, maize, bananas, and sugar brandy for local consumption.[2] By far the most important economic activity in Rio Grande de São Pedro (apart from rustling) was stock-raising; in Santa Catarina fishing, ranching, and subsistence farming were locally important, but that subcaptaincy produced no really significant exports and was an even greater economic liability to the Crown than Rio Grande. However, it must be remembered that the economies of both provinces were disrupted by the protracted borderlands dispute with Spain.

Despite the fact that Rio de Janeiro's dependencies had not fulfilled the expectations of their founders, Lavradio was convinced that they had promising futures if certain major problems were solved. One problem was a shortage of population. The viceroy instructed Santa Catarina's governor to interpret liberally the royal regulations permitting servicemen to marry so that they could help populate the land. He sanctioned the continuance of military exemptions for sons of the *casais* so that they could assist their parents in farming. To aid homesteaders who had lost their possessions during the first Cevallos campaign, he authorized the governor of Rio Grande to give them new lands, brood mares, and a year's rations, and arranged for the shipment of Crown-owned farm implements from Santa Catarina to the southern captaincy. However, he declined to approve petitions of settlers in Santa Catarina who wished to move to Rio Grande because he wished to stop the movement of the northern captaincy's population to the south. As already noted, Dom Luís also shipped a number of vagabonds and miscreants from Rio de Janeiro to Santa Catarina Island, where he hoped they would lead more useful lives. After the

[2] Despite their incongruities and omissions, the best sources on the products of Rio de Janeiro in Lavradio's time are the *relações parciais* of 1778/1779 prepared by the mestres de campo of the captaincy. See *RIHGB*, LXXVI:1 (1913 [1915]), 289–355.

fall of Colônia do Sacramento, he ordered assistance given to its refugee families so that they could resettle around the vila of Rio Grande.[3]

The pattern of land distribution in the southern captaincies was another impediment to their economic progress. Engrossment of land by a privileged minority who utilized only a small part of their grants yet refused to make unused portions available to persons who lacked property of their own was already an old problem in Brazil. Since the end of the seventeenth century the Crown had issued a long series of laws intended to restrict the size of land grants, and had threatened to expropriate properties whose owners failed to cultivate them.[4] Nevertheless latifundism continued to flourish, and Viceroy Lavradio considered it one of the chief reasons for the backwardness of both provinces. He repeatedly criticized the liberality of former colonial officers who had made large grants to a favored few, while many persons remained landless and the subcaptaincies continued to import food from Rio de Janeiro when they were capable of producing surpluses themselves. As he remarked to the governor of Santa Catarina, "I am certain . . . that Your Grace will reply that all those lands have already been divided, and that I know already. I also know that the distribution was poorly managed, assigning to some large amounts which they possess only for the purposes of ostentation without being able to cultivate them, while others have none, and that this was done contrary to the intentions of the king . . . which was to give to each only that portion which he could cultivate, and that if this had been done, there would not be so many persons unprovided [with lands of their own today]." [5]

He urged subordinate governors to favor married couples over single persons in the allotment of lands so that their captaincies would become more populous and therefore more productive and beneficial to His Majesty. He suggested that the governors should encourage cultivators by visiting their farms to praise their efforts and by sending other officials to do the same in districts they could not personally inspect. The viceroy cautioned against giving out lands in remote areas when partially settled zones still had parcels available, and particularly urged the establishment of ranches along the road between

---

3 Lavradio to Francisco de Sousa de Menezes (governor of Santa Catarina), June 13, 1774, CMCM, cod. 4, fol. 53^r; *idem* to José Marcelino de Figueiredo (governor of Rio Grande), Mar. 10, 1770, *ibid.*, cod. 15, fols. 12^r–13^v; *idem* to Sousa de Menezes, July 9, 1773, *ibid.*, fols. 165^r–166^v; *idem* to *idem*, Aug. 27, 1772, *ibid.*, fol. 131^r; *idem* to *idem*, Sept. 6, 1773, *ibid.*, cod. 4, fol. 7^v; *idem* to Melo e Castro, June 14, 1776, ANRJ, Col. 68, Liv. 1, fols. 3^r–4^r; *idem, Relatório*, 476–477.

4 See Charles R. Boxer, *The Golden Age of Brazil*, pp. 228–230; cf. the comments of Viceroy Dom Fernando José de Portugal, 2RGG, *DH*, VI, 368–371.

5 Lavradio to Sousa de Menezes, June 30, 1773, CMCM, cod. 15, fol. 162^r.

Santa Catarina and the upper end of the Lagoa dos Patos to provide passing travelers with provisions and mounts.[6] Despite the marquis' expressions of concern, he did not nullify existing land titles; the inequities of the allotment system persisted in the borderlands as elsewhere in the colony. Half a century later an enlightened critic denounced the "vicious distribution of lands" in Rio Grande as "absurd." [7]

For understandable reasons the captaincy whose economy was of greatest direct concern to the marquis was that of Rio de Janeiro. During his administration its northern district, the Campos de Goitacazes, famed for outlawry and sugar, became one of the two most rapidly expanding zones of sugar production in Brazil, the other being the Campinas area of São Paulo. Between 1769 and 1778 the number of sugar mills (engenhos) in the Campos nearly doubled (from 56 to 104), while the number of slaves increased from 3,192 to 4,871; production of sugar went up over 235 percent during those nine years, while that of brandy (agua ardente) doubled.[8]

The new prosperity of the Campos inevitably resulted in an increasing number of disputes over valuable sugar lands and harvests. As was his custom, the viceroy ordered several of the disputants to come to Rio de Janeiro to observe how civilized people behaved, and sent them home rather like missionaries. In his report to his successor Dom Luís spoke of a certain lawyer whom he had appointed land surveyor (juiz de sesmarias) in the Campos where he became involved

[6] Lavradio to Sousa de Menezes, June 30 and Sept. 6, 1773, CMCM, cod. 4, fols 8ʳ–9ᵛ; cod. 15, fols. 161ᵛ–163ᵛ; idem to Antônio da Veiga Cabral, Dec. 4, 1778, quoted in Francisco de Barros Moraes Araujo Teixeira Homem to Luís de Vasconcelos e Sousa, July 9, 1780, BNRJ, 9, 3, 23, n. 26; Lavradio to Böhm, Aug. 14, 1776, BNRJ, 13, 4, 3, n. 8 (orig.).

[7] Antônio José Gonçalves Chaves, "Memorias econômo-políticas" (Rio de Janeiro, 1822–1823), ed., J. B. Hafkemeyer, S.J., repr. in RIHGRGS, II (1922), 253–254; see also Paulo José da Silva Gama to Visconde de Anadia, July 25, 1803, RIHGB, XL:1 (1877), 287, concerning the problem of absentee ownership.

[8] "Relação de eng.os e engenhocas de asucar, e agoa ardente que ha no districto de Campos dos Goitacazes . . . athe o anno de 1779 incluzive," RIHGB, LXXVI:1 (1913 [1915]), 341. During the same period nine mills ceased production either because of debts, the exhaustion of firewood supplies, or the sale of their slaves; in 1778 eight new engenhos were under construction. For slightly different figures for these years, see José Honório Rodrigues, "Agricultura e economia açucareis no seculo XVIII," Brasil Açucareiro, XXVI (Sept. 1945), 314. Citing José Carneiro da Silva (Memória topographica e histórica sobre os Campos dos Goytacazes [New ed., Rio de Janeiro (?), 1907], p. 53), Dr. Rodrigues adds that 110 additional mills were built in the district between 1778 and 1783, and that by 1819 the Campos boasted 400 engenhos. Between 1775 and 1806 sugar exports from Rio de Janeiro to Portugal increased more than four-fold by volume and six-fold by value. "Tableau de la quantité de sucre et de café exportée de Rio de Janeiro pendant les années 1775, 1796 et 1806," in Louis Claude Desaulces de Freycinet, Voyage autour du monde . . . pendant les années 1817, 1818, 1819 et 1820. . . . I:1 (Paris, 1827), 235.

in so many controversies that he stimulated a minor revolt. He ordered both the official and his adversaries to Rio de Janeiro where he threw them in prison; after tempers had calmed down, he released them with the warning that he would hold each man personally responsible for any future disturbances. And if Dom Luís is to be believed, the ex-disputants became sincere preservers of law and order and he had no more trouble from the Campos on that score.[9]

To be sure, there remained the usual disagreements between landowners and renters and between indebted producers and their creditors. Several large planters who ousted squatters and delinquent tenants from their lands were supported by the viceroy.[10] A number of smaller sugar growers who also sought his protection had obtained loans from merchants in Rio de Janeiro and the city of S. Salvador dos Campos in order to build their own sugar mills. Their loans were secured by future harvests, but the merchants charged that the growers were surreptitiously selling their sugar at night so that they would have none to show their creditors. The growers denied the allegation, claiming that their crops had been smaller than anticipated because many of their sharecroppers were on militia duty for the king. The growers appealed to the viceroy requesting that a law of 1760 exempting plantations of large planters from seizure for debts be interpreted to apply to their properties too. While sympathetic with their request, Dom Luís declined to assume responsibility for such a ruling and referred the problem to Lisbon for final determination. That did not occur until 1784 when the Overseas Council concurred with a recommendation by the Treasury's counsel that the small growers be granted the same exemption as the large producers.[11]

Although sugar was by far the leading export of the captaincy of Rio de Janeiro, the viceroy was anxious to stimulate the production of other useful commodities, and responded to suggestions by subordinates and private individuals of local resources that might be profitably exploited. A case in point concerns a particular kind of hardwood which contemporaries called *tapinhoam* or *tapinhoá*.[12] Like Brazilwood, tapinhoam was found along the Atlantic coast from Pernambuco to Rio de Janeiro, but was a construction wood rather than a dyewood. Though used for many different purposes, it was particularly prized as sheathing material for the bottoms of ships be-

---

[9] Lavradio, *Relatório*, pp. 422–423.

[10] Lavradio to câmara of S. Salvador de Campos, Oct. 10, 1777 and Sept. 12, 1778, CMCM, cod. 25, fols. 203ᵛ–204ʳ, 270ᵛ–271ʳ; *idem* to Captain Vicente de Carvalho Oliveira, Feb. 20, 1776, CMCM, cod. 28, fol. 88ʳ.

[11] Alberto Lamego, *A terra Goytacá*, IV, 351–356.

[12] Perhaps the wood was the composite *Helianthus tuberosus*, known in contemporary Brazil as topinambo, topinambá, or tupinambur. *Pequeno dicionário brasileiro da língua portuguesa* (7th ed.; Rio de Janeiro, 1948).

cause of its resistance to sea organisms. However, as early as 1707 the Crown received reports that readily available stands of the trees were fast disappearing, and directed that henceforth their use be restricted to the hulls of ships. That order was renewed by the Overseas Council in 1738 when the governor of Rio de Janeiro advised that colonial merchants were still exporting tapinhoam to Holland and England and that the wood could no longer be found in the captaincies of Pernambuco or Bahia and was becoming scarce in Rio de Janeiro. The Council again reserved its use for the sheathing of vessels belonging to the Crown, and threatened violators with a heavy fine.[13]

Shortly after his arrival in Rio de Janeiro, Don Luís de Almeida was approached by an impoverished former shipbuilder then living outside the capital on a farm where he was experimenting with a method of propagating the tree from seedlings, a feat he claimed no one else had been able to achieve. The marquis inspecting his plantings, was favorably impressed, and forwarded samples to the Conde de Oeiras with the suggestion that the cultivator be suitably rewarded for his ingenuity.[14] Though his suggestion was seemingly ignored, it did elicit a dispatch from the colonial secretary inquiring where natural stands of tapinhoam were found in the captaincy, their abundance, and the method by which felled timbers were conveyed to the capital.[15] Upon receipt of the viceroy's report, a carta régia renewed the long-standing warning that such trees were reserved for the king's service and proscribed their use by private individuals.[16]

It is not likely that this warning was any more effective than earlier ones or than the blazing of the "broad arrow" on the pines of colonial New England in preventing private exploitation of coveted timbers.[17] Nevertheless considerable quantities of tapinhoam boards were thereafter regularly shipped by the royal arsenal in Rio de Janeiro to Lisbon for the construction of royal warships.[18]

While the viceroy always welcomed useful suggestions by private

[13] Carta régia, April 1, 1707, and consulta of May 6, 1738, Castro e Almeida, *Inventário*, VII, 284.

[14] Lavradio to Oeiras, July 5, 1770, IHGB/AUC 1-2-29, fols. 239ʳ–241ʳ; published in *RIHGB*, CCLV (Apr.–June, 1962), 213–214.

[15] Melo e Castro to Lavradio, Oct. 1, 1771, CMCM, cod. 3, fol. 138.

[16] Carta régia of Mar. 8, 1773 cited in Lavradio to Pombal, July 20, 1773, BNRJ, 10, 4, 8 (unnumbered). The order was modified in 1780 when individuals were permitted to purchase tapinhoam timbers unsuitable for shipbuilding from the royal arsenal in Rio de Janeiro. Melo e Castro to Vasconcelos, Dec. 4, 1780, BNRJ, I-3, 4, 26, n. 14. Earlier, Viceroy Lavradio was instructed to furnish tapinhoam boards to agents of the whaling contractor in Rio de Janeiro and those of the Companhia de Grão Pará e Maranhão for repairs of their ships. Pombal to Lavradio, Dec. 19, 1775, CMCM, cod. 14 (49/20) (orig.), and another dispatch, *idem* to *idem*, same date, ANRJ, Col. 67, Liv. III-A, fol. 16 (orig.).

[17] Cf. Joseph J. Malone, *Pine Trees and Politics. The Naval Stores and Forest Policy in Colonial New England 1691–1775* (Seattle, 1964).

[18] Thus in 1777, when the Crown ordered MacDouall's squadron to return to Lisbon, the colonial secretary suggested that the viceroy load the vessels with as

individuals, he relied particularly on the militia commanders (mestres de campo) [19] of the captaincy of Rio de Janeiro to keep him informed of agricultural conditions in the countryside where he was unable to make personal inspections. He required them to send him elaborate annual reports showing the amount of each crop produced in their district, with explanations of why harvests one year were lower than in previous years. When they attributed the incompleteness of their statistics to the unwillingness of some farmers to report the size of their harvests, Dom Luís had such individuals sent to him for a reprimand. He also ordered his field administrators to advise producers that their failure to cultivate their lands as fully as possible or to ship their crops to market promptly regardless of prevailing prices would be sufficient grounds for the expropriation of their properties; apparently, however, he never carried out that threat. Dom Luís instructed his lieutenants to send him samples and detailed accounts of useful wild plants in their districts with indications of their abundance and possible uses, and when convinced that a particular commodity could be profitably grown in the captaincy, he relied on the mestres de campo to induce farmers to try it.[20] Such was the case with tobacco.

The Viceroy's Efforts to Promote Tobacco Cultivation

Although indigenous to Brazil, tobacco did not become a significant export crop until the early seventeenth century. For a time it became Bahia's most valuable export, surpassing even sugar; during the mid-1750s as much as 200,000 arrobas of tobacco a year were shipped from the captaincy, and by the end of the century tobacco was still Bahia's second most lucrative crop. It was grown on some 1,500 plantations situated in a few favored growing areas, notably Cachoeira (locale of the best quality Brazilian tobacco), Santo Amaro, Inhambupe, and Sergipe. Of the three grades of tobacco pro-

---

much tapinhoam and *paroba* (another hardwood) as possible. To Lavradio, Dec. 21, 1777, BNRJ, I-2, 4, 7, n. 81.

[19] For a fuller discussion of the mestres de campo and their functions, see Chap. XVI.

[20] Lavradio to Miguel Antunes Ferreira, Mar. 4, 1775, CMCM, cod. 25, fols. 6ᵛ–7ʳ; *idem* to Alexandre Alvares Duarte Azevedo, May 29, 1775, *ibid.*, fol. 23ᵛ; *idem* to Miguel Antunes Ferreira, Dec. 3, 1777, *ibid.*, fol. 217ᵛ; circular to all mestres de campo, Oct. 5, 1775, *ibid.*, fol. 50ʳ; *idem* to the juizes ordinários and câmara of Rio de São Francisco, Mar. 1, 1775, *ibid.*, fol. 5ᵛ; *idem* to Alexandre Alvares Duarte e Azevedo, Feb. 27, 1777, *ibid.*, fol. 175ʳ; *idem* to Bartholomeu José Vahia, Feb. 15, 1775, *ibid.*, fol. 1ᵛ; *idem* to *idem*, Miguel Antunes Ferreira, and Ignacio de Andrade, Aug. 14, 1778, *ibid.*, fols. 264ᵛ–265ʳ; circular to all mestres de campo, Feb. 8, 1778, fols. 237ʳ⁻ᵛ; *idem* to João José de Barcelos, Jan. 25, 1779, ANRJ, Col. 70, Liv. X, fols. 86ʳ⁻ᵛ.

duced in Cachoeira,[21] the best was exported to the kingdom and sold to customers ranging from the Manchu rulers of China to French fur traders in the St. Lawrence valley; the second grade was reserved for the Brazilian market, while the third was shipped in leather-covered rolls to the African slave coast and, along with gold and brandy, constituted a prime medium of exchange for slaves.[22]

Until the middle of the eighteenth century Bahia enjoyed a monopoly on the commercial production of Brazilian tobacco; elsewhere growers could raise the plant for their own uses but not for market.[23] Brazilian markets were supplied by licensed contractors who purchased their stocks in Bahia.[24] Until 1751 the interests of the Crown and the contractors were guarded by so-called superintendents of tobacco who had offices in major colonial ports. But in that year their position was abolished and their duties were assigned to the newly created mesas da inspeção in Bahia, Rio de Janeiro, Recife, and São Luís do Maranhão. Since the Crown planned to terminate the licensing system, those boards were charged with the promotion of tobacco culture in areas where it was then retarded.[25]

The licensing system continued to apply to the captaincy of Rio de Janeiro until 1757, when restrictions on local tobacco cultivation were removed. To compensate the Crown for revenues formerly derived from the tobacco contract, new taxes were levied on slaves, sugar brandy, and fish oil.[26] Thus the government sought to promote the interests of one, or more likely two groups, namely would-be tobacco planters and slave importers, [27] at the expense of ordinary consumers.

[21] Elsewhere in Brazil only two grades were recognized, but the Cachoeira product was so highly regarded that its third quality tobacco was considered equal to the second grade produced elsewhere. "Regimento das Casas de Inspeção," [Apr. 1, 1751], Coelho e Sousa, *Systema*, IV, 92–97, Chap. III, par. 12.

[22] A scholarly history of the tobacco industry in Colonial Brazil remains to be written. Luís Amaral, *História geral da agricultura brasileira* . . . (2d ed.; São Paulo, 1958) , makes a cryptic reference (II, 114) to "Ferrário, História do fumo no Brasil" but I have been unable to locate it. The classic contemporary account (written at the beginning of the eighteenth century) of the industry in Bahia is that of Father André João Antonil, *Cultura e opulencia do Brasil por suas drogas e minas*, Pt. II; for the state of the industry there at the end of the century, see Luiz dos Santos Vilhena, *Cartas de Vilhena: notícias soteropolitanas e brasílicas*, annotated by Braz do Amaral, I, 201–205; for brief modern accounts, consult Roberto Simonsen, *História econômica do Brazil (1500/1820)* (3d ed.; São Paulo, 1957) , pp. 367–369, and the index in Boxer, *Golden Age*.

[23] *Auto* of Dec. 17, 1710, Eduardo Tourinho, ed., *Autos de correições do Rio de Janeiro*, II (Rio de Janeiro, 1930) , 19; see also n. 24 below.

[24] E.g., contract of João Serqueira Lima, approved by the king Sept. 2, 1753, *CLP*, I (Suppl.) , 258–262, especially condition X.

[25] See n. 21 above.

[26] *Alvará de lei*, Jan. 10, 1757, Coelho de Sousa, *Systema*, IV, 107–108.

[27] The interest of slave importers in having a suitable quality of locally produced tobacco available for their business is not specifically mentioned in the documenta-

While the lifting of restrictions on tobacco cultivation resulted in a rapid expansion of planting in Pernambuco, [28] that did not occur in Rio de Janeiro. Very likely the newly organized Companhia Geral do Comércio de Pernambuco e Paraíba (1759–1777) was partly responsible for the growth of production in the northern captaincy, but the *câmara* of Rio de Janeiro protested to the king that the real reason tobacco raising was not flourishing in their captaincy was because Bahian tobacco was still flooding the local market. Because of its superiority, purchasers preferred to buy the Bahian product to that locally grown; consequently farmers had become discouraged and had given up attempts to produce tobacco for sale. The only remedy that occurred to the aldermen was for the Crown to prohibit the further entry of Bahian tobacco, but the Crown had a better idea: it simply established another tax (two *tostões*) in the captaincy on imports of the Bahian product.[29]

So far as can be discovered, the viceroy did not become interested in the fate of tobacco production in Rio de Janeiro until some six years after he reached his post. Then he received a report from the local board of inspection calling attention to the fact that two recruits attached to one of the Bahian regiments stationed in the capital claimed to be familiar with the proper techniques of raising and curing tobacco. The board suggested that they be separated from service so that they could become roving consultants. Dom Luís agreed to order the release of the soldiers from their regiment and promised to write the mestres de campo to cooperate with them. He also suggested that the board draw up instructions indicating how the men should teach their skills to local farmers.[30]

Some months later these so-called experts (who may well have

---

tion that I have seen, but an anonymous late-eighteenth century manuscript notes that Rio de Janeiro was not in a good position to trade with the slave coasts because it "lacks the necessary commodity, tobacco, that leaf produced in the vicinity of Rio being greatly inferior in quality to that . . . of Cachoeira," and that consequently Carioca dealers were obliged to offer European and Asiatic goods, coin and brandies instead of tobacco for slaves. José Honório Rodrigues, *Brazil and Africa*, tr. by Richard A. Mazzarra and Sam Hileman (Berkeley-Los Angeles, 1965), p. 26 and n. 25.

[28] According to Rudolfo Garcia, by 1761 Pernambucans were producing between 20,000 and 25,000 arrobas of tobacco annually (i.e., one-tenth the yearly exports of Bahia) and were no longer dependent on Bahian tobacco for the slave trade. "A capitania de Pernambuco. O governor José César de Menezes (1774–1787)," *RIHGB*, LXXXIV (1918), 539–540.

[29] Câmara (Rio de Janeiro) to king, July 28, 1759, *RIHGB*, LXV:1 (1902), 95–96; Conselho Ultramarino, decree of Aug. 15, 1760, AHU, Livros de Registo do Conselho Ultramarino, cod. 3, fol. 112^v (Bancroft Library Microfilm Collection).

[30] Lavradio to board of inspection (in reply to its dispatch of Dec. 16, 1775), Feb. 12, 1776, CMCM, cod. 25, fols. 83^v–84^v; *idem* to Colonel Francisco António da Veiga Cabral e Câmara (commander of the Bahian regiment), May 7, 1776, *ibid.*, fol. 99^v.

been masquerading to escape the drudgery of guard duty) reported that the soil of the captaincy appeared to be unsuited to tobacco. They added, however, that promising lands did exist in the northern parts of São Paulo and offered to assist the establishment of the industry there.

Again the viceroy proved agreeable (or gullible). He authorized an appropriate travel allowance for the consultants, and wrote to officials in the towns of São Sebastião, Taubaté, São Luiz do Paraytinga, and Ubatuba asking their cooperation with the new advisers.[31] In taking such action the viceroy realized that he was exceeding his authority, since those communities were under the jurisdiction of Martim Lobo Lopes de Saldanha, captain-general of São Paulo. Accordingly, he apologized to Saldanha for issuing such instructions without first consulting him, stating that his only interest was in the economic benefits that São Paulo might derive from tobacco cultivation.[32] In equally polite terms the captain-general, who always manifested extreme deference toward the marquis, replied that His Excellency "can issue orders in this captaincy as if it were [his] own," and that he had directed the same authorities to comply fully with the viceory's orders.[33] This brief exchange is suggestive of the limits of a viceroy's actual authority in Lavradio's time.

Toward the end of his administration Dom Luís prevailed on a merchant in the capital to handle shipments to Portugal of tobacco produced in the two captaincies. It is evident, however, that he was disappointed with the lack of progress in the industry, for he urged the Court to appoint a tobacco specialist to the board of inspection to spur the industry.[34] Nevertheless, tobacco never became a flourishing crop in colonial Rio de Janeiro, and at the end of the colonial period it was still being imported from Bahia.[35]

The Fostering of Cereals: A Story of Success

More rewarding were the viceroy's efforts to foster the production of cereals in Brazil, namely wheat and rice. Though wheat was grown throughout Portugal, the mother country traditionally consumed more than she produced. For a time the Madeiras and Azores furnished the home country with wheat, but Portugal continued to import additional supplies from abroad. During the seventeenth cen-

---

[31] *Idem*, portaria of July 17, 1776, *ibid.*, cod. 19, fol. 75ʳ; *idem* to câmara of "Obatuba" and capitães mores João de Moura Negrão and Bento Lopes de Leao, Dec. 3, 12 and 16, 1776, *ibid.*, cod. 25, fols. 157ᵛ–158ʳ, 120ʳ, and 113ʳ–115ʳ.

[32] *Idem* to Saldanha, July 12, 1776, *DI*, XVII (1895), 117–119.

[33] Saldanha to Lavradio, Aug. 29, 1776, *DI*, XLII (1903), 148–150.

[34] Lavradio to Melo e Castro, May 23, 1778, IHGB/AUC, 1-2-1, fols. 5ᵛ–6ᵛ.

[35] Johan B. von Spix and Carl F. P. von Martius, *Travels in Brazil*, I (London, 1820), 187.

tury they came mostly from the Baltic and Mediterranean areas, while in the eighteenth century the Italian peninsula, France, Holland, and Great Britain sold wheat to Portugal.[36]

Before Lavradio's time wheat was grown for local consumption in São Paulo and Bahia, but was not marketed elsewhere.[37] In 1771 the marquis sent a small shipment of butter, cheese, and wheat from Rio Grande de São Pedro to Lisbon, expressing the hope that in the future Rio Grande would become the dairyland and granary of all Brazil. He observed that wheat growing was handicapped there because there were no grist mills and no one knew how to build them. He urged that milling stones and persons familiar with the erection of flour mills be sent to the captaincy from the kingdom.

The Court reacted favorably to both requests. In June 1772 the colonial secretary informed the viceroy that grinding stones would soon be shipped from Lisbon and that a search was being made for millers willing to go to the colony.[38] A few months later he acknowledged the arrival in good condition of specimens of wheat, cheese, and butter produced in Rio Grande, and announced the departure of José da Silva Lumiar (or Lumiares), a master carpenter who knew how to construct grist mills powered by wind or water.[39] Late the following year the viceroy advised Governor José Marcelino that Silva Lumiar and João Luis Bucellar, a master miller, were en route to the captaincy, and authorized payment of their salaries out of local funds.[40] Two years later, having apparently completed his mission, Silva Lumiar petitioned the viceroy for permission to return to Portugal.[41]

Within a few years wheat farming began to show some promise in Rio Grande. In 1780 Governor Sebastião Xavier da Veiga Cabral da Câmara reported that thanks to the arrival of refugees from Colônia, some 1,126 alqueires[42] of wheat had recently been sown around the vila of Rio Grande and that an additional 463 were planted in the

---

36 See Frédéric Mauro, Le Portugal et l'Atlantique au xviie siècle, 1570–1670 (Paris, 1960), pp. 295–309. The "Balança geral do commercio de Portugal com as naçoens estrangeiras no anno de 1777" (BNRJ, I-6, 4, 6) shows that Portugal imported 45,561 moios (a moio is a dry measure unit equal to 60 alqueires or 10 sacks) of wheat that year.

37 Amaral, História da agricultura, I, 69–70.

38 Martinho de Melo e Castro to Lavradio, July 10, 1772, CMCM, cod. 3, fol. 166ʳ (orig.).

39 Melo e Castro to Lavradio, Nov. 20, 1772, ibid., fol. 248ʳ (orig.).

40 Lavradio to José Marcelino de Figureiredo, Dec. 3, 1774, CMCM, cod. 4, fol. 63ʳ and portaria of same date authorizing payment of 453,112 réis comprising the earnings of both men to date. Ibid., cod. 2, fol. 100ʳ.

41 Lavradio to João Henrique Böhm, Sept. 2, 1776, CMCM, cod. 4, fol. 98.

42 According to Boxer (Golden Age, p. 356), an alqueire in the Portuguese empire was usually 1⅜ peck, but Francisco João Roscîo ("Compendio noticioso do continente do Rio Grande de São Pedro" [1781], RIHGRGS, XXIV [1948], 71) stated that the local alqueire was approximately double that of the kingdom.

parish of Pôrto Alegre.[43] By the early nineties wheat exports from Rio Grande to other parts of Brazil averaged nearly 94,000 alqueires a year,[44] and by the turn of the century the captaincy's annual harvest averaged nearly 200,000 alqueires. Over half of that amount was sent to Rio de Janeiro and points along the coast from Pernambuco in the north to Montevideo in the south. In the last colonial years wheat became Rio Grande's third-ranking export by value, behind dried meat and hides. Thus Lavradio's vision of Rio Grande as a future granary was at least partly realized in later decades.[45]

Though the captaincy of Rio de Janeiro was too tropical for wheat growing, it was the southern limit of rice cultivation in the time of the marquis. Rice was another cereal for which Portugal was dependent upon foreign sources of supply,[46] and therefore the beginnings of rice production in Brazil were welcome news to the Crown. The industry got its start in Rio de Janeiro in 1756, when a mill was built by an army engineer on the *sitio* of "Andrahy Pequeno," a Jesuit property in the valley of Engenho Velho, two leagues from the capital. The original operators failed to prosper and in 1759 sold their interests to Manoel Luís Vieira, a local businessman and brother of the talented inventor, Jerônimo Vieira de Abreu. With the aid of his brother, Manoel Luís made several technical improvements in the mill to enlarge its capacity and negotiated a partnership arrangement with a Lisbon merchant who was soon handling Vieira's rather sizeable shipments of rice to Portugal.

But Vieira soon ran into unforeseen difficulties. Early in 1762 he was imprisoned and his mill was seized because he had been accused of defrauding the heirs of a former employer. Five years later he emerged from prison and recovered his then badly run-down factory. Since he lacked funds to resume business, he persuaded some of his previous creditors to extend sufficient capital to restore the mill,

[43] Veiga Cabral da Câmara to Luís de Vasconcelos e Sousa, Dec. 22, 1780, *RIHGB*, XL:1 (1877) , 243–246.

[44] "Generos que se tem exportado do continente do Rio Grande de São Pedro em os . . . annos . . . [1790–1793]," *RIHGB*, LXV:1 (1902) , 266–267.

[45] For wheat production in Rio Grande between 1805 and 1820, see "Mapa comparativo das exportações das praças de Porto Alegre e do Rio Grande, em 16 annos consecutivos de 1805 athé 1820," in Gonçalves Chaves, "Memorias econômo-políticas" (cited in note 7 above), pp. 278–279; exports of wheat and cheese from Rio Grande to Rio de Janeiro and Bahia in 1802 and 1805 are recorded in AHU/PA-RGS, *caixa* 2, Pts. 1 and 3 (Bancroft Library Microfilm Collection) ; for cereal exports between 1816 and 1822, see "Mappa[s] da[s] exporta[ções] . . . do Rio Grande . . . no[s] anno[s] 1816 [até 1822]," in Gonçalves Chaves, pp. 292–298.

[46] During the eighteenth century Portugal imported rice chiefly from South Carolina (via England until 1730, after which it could be shipped directly to Lisbon) and from the Italian peninsula. In 1777 Portugal imported 5,088.75 quintals of rice from England and 7,271.5 from Venice and Genoa. "Balança geral do commercio de Portugal com as naçoens estrangeiras no anno de 1777," BNRJ, I-6, 4, 6, *passim*.

promising to pay both old and new obligations out of future profits. During each of the next two years Vieira's mill bought and processed as much as 100,000 arrobas of rice produced by local farmers, but before the end of 1770 the luckless entrepreneur encountered new difficulties. According to him, local merchants suddenly refused to have further dealings with him because of instructions from their overseas principals who were acting in behalf of their own British creditors. At this point Vieira turned to Viceroy Lavradio for assistance.

The viceroy listened with sympathy and interest to Vieira's story and did what he could for him. He visited the mill himself and requested the mesa da inspeção to conduct its own investigation of the plant. Convinced that it was making a valuable contribution to the economy of Rio de Janeiro, Dom Luís summoned Vieira's local creditors and urged them to continue to support him. But they refused, pleading that instructions from their Lisbon superiors gave them no alternative. The viceroy then could do no more than to forward Vieira's petition for relief and for a new loan from the Crown to the colonial minister, supported by a statement from the câmara of Rio de Janeiro and his own opinion. In his covering letter Dom Luís strongly recommended that Vieira's petition receive favorable consideration since, he said, "it is very certain that assisting this man in some form will awaken many others [here] from their lethargy to the benefit of the *pátria* and the State." [47]

Although final action on Vieira's petition was still pending when Lavradio left office,[48] the viceroy received encouragement from the Crown to promote the new industry,[49] and succeeded in finding other businessmen willing to handle the farmers' crops. The planting of the grain soon became so popular that by 1780 one writer complained that farmers had become "so preoccupied with the planting of indigo and rice . . . that . . . they do not want to plant manioc and vegetables, and for this reason farinha and beans have become very dear [here]." [50] The previous year Rio de Janeiro sent nearly 79,000 arrobas of the grain to Portugal, and by 1796 the volume of its rice exports reached 176,000 arrobas, ranking fourth by value among the captaincy's exports, after sugar, brandy, and hides.[51]

[47] To Melo e Castro, July 5, 1770, IHGB/AUC, 1-1-29, fols. 241ʳ–260ʳ.

[48] Melo e Castro to Luís de Vasconcelos e Sousa, Jan. 27, 1779, BNRJ, I-4, 4, 45 (orig.).

[49] In 1774 the colonial secretary noted "with great pleasure" the arrival of rice shipments from Rio de Janeiro, adding that "este genero tambem é importantissimo, e deve entrar em o numero dos que V. Ex. tem promovido e procurado adiantar com tanto acerto e zelo do real serviço como em bemeficio da patria em que nasce." Melo e Castro to Lavradio, Nov. 24, 1774, CMCM, cod. 13 (45/36).

[50] João Hopman to Lavradio, Rio de Janeiro, May 4, 1780, CMCM, folder marked "Diversos, 1775–1780" (orig.).

[51] "Mappa . . . das qualidades e quantidades de generos que passarão do Rio de Janeiro para o reino e ilhas desde . . . 17 de Abril até o último de Dezembro

The establishment of the rice industry in Rio de Janeiro in these decades was paralleled by similar success in Maranhão and Pará, where rice culture became even more important. Thanks to the availability of Brazilian supplies, the Crown barred the entry of rice from foreign lands in the kingdom as early as 1781.[52]

The Promotion of Fibers: A Story of Frustration

Not all economic ventures encouraged by Viceroy Lavradio turned turned out equally successfully. Despite a long series of frustrating efforts by the marquis and his contemporaries, all attempts to produce commercially acceptable fibrous materials in southern Brazil proved unavailing. Although a memorialist assured Lavradio that cotton could become a significant branch of the commerce of Rio de Janeiro if growers were assured adequate prices,[53] that captaincy did not join its northern sisters as a major cotton producer in the late colonial period.[54] Nor did sericulture prove to be a successful activity, despite Lavradio's hopes.[55]

... 1779," *RIHGB*, XLVII:1 (1884), 46–48; "Mappa dos efeitos que se transportárão desta cidade do Rio de Janeiro para os portos abaixo declarados no anno de 1796," *ibid.*, XLVI:1 (1883), 197–204.

[52] Alvará of July 24, 1781, CLP, III, 300–301. For a fuller account of the beginnings of the rice industry in colonial Brazil, see my "Manoel Luís Vieira: An Entrepreneur in Rio de Janeiro during Brazil's Eighteenth-Century Agricultural Renaissance," *HAHR*, XXXIX (Nov. 1959), 521–537.

[53] Antonio Jozé Coelho to Lavradio, Rio de Janeiro, July 9, 1771, CMCM, *maço* 31 (orig.).

[54] Although the two monopoly companies organized by the Marquis of Pombal had paved the way, Brazilian cotton exports did not become significant until the 1780s, after both companies had been dissolved. From then until the 1820s long-staple Brazilian cotton found a favored market in the Midlands of Great Britain. Edward Baines, *History of Cotton Manufacture in Great Britain* (London [1835]), pp. 304–306, 309. The relative importance of the principal producing areas from which Brazilian cotton was reexported to Great Britain in the late eighteenth century is indicated by the following table:

Source	1789	1790	1791
Pernambuco	27,010 bags [a]	28,968 bags	34,146 bags
Maranhão	9,857 " [a]	16,800 "	15,353 "
Pará	733 "	843 "	1,326 "
Bahia	519 "	1,136 "	4,035 "
Rio de Janeiro	124 "	211 "	313 "
	38,243 "	47,967 "	55,173 "

[a] "The Pernambuco bags are upon an average 140 lb. each, and the Maranham about 200 lb."

Anon., "Account of Brazil Cotton Wool exported from Lisbon," Lisbon, Nov. 12, 1792, British Museum, Add MSS 9252 (Bancroft Library Microfilm Collection); for additional details, see Amaral, *História da agric. bras.*, I, 3–64, and Stanley J. Stein, *The Brazilian Cotton Manufacture. Textile Enterprise in an Underdeveloped Area, 1850–1950* (Cambridge, Mass., 1957), Chap. 1.

[55] Lavradio to Melo e Castro, Aug. 11, 1775, BNRJ, 10, 4, 8 (unnumbered), reporting the shipment of samples of silk produced locally and requesting additional

One crop that the Crown was particularly anxious to develop in southern Brazil was hemp. In the days of sailing ships the Portuguese navy and merchant marine used large quantities of hemp for cables and hawsers, but Portugal had never succeeded in producing hemp at home [56] and was dependent upon sources of supply in the Baltic (particularly from Riga) and in Italy. Perhaps aware of the success of Great Britain in fostering hemp raising in Virginia,[57] the Crown hoped to see the industry flourish in Brazil.

Shortly after the Marquis of Lavradio become viceroy, he received notification of a contract between the Crown and one Antônio Gonçalves Pereira de Faria to establish a hemp factory in Rio Grande de São Pedro.[58] The contractor had already devoted many years in efforts to produce hemp and was destined to spend even more. In 1747 the Crown sent Gomes Freire de Andrada, then captain-general of Rio de Janeiro, a quantity of hemp seed with instructions to see that it was planted in the southern borderlands. The seed was delivered to Antônio Gonçalves, a farmer in Santa Catarina, but since it was already old it failed to mature. Subsequently, under circumstances far from clear, Antônio Gonçalves passed into the Spanish empire, returning to Rio de Janeiro from Chile in 1764 with thirty-two alqueires of hemp seed that he had managed to smuggle in via Colônia do Sacramento.

After consulting with the would-be hemp producer, Viceroy Cunha dispatched him and a nephew to Rio Grande and advised Governor José Custódio de Sá e Faria to spare neither effort nor funds in assisting Antônio Gonçalves to establish a hemp factory there since it would be of great benefit to the king.[59] After searching for a suitable location and planting what amounted to a demonstration plot, Antônion Gonçalves harvested his first hemp crop in 1766. It yielded sixty alqueires of seed, thirty-eight arrobas of combed hemp and eighty to ninety arrobas of oakum, the latter being processed by a local Scottish resident. Having demonstrated the feasibility of growing hemp in Rio Grande, Antônio Gonçalves went to Lisbon to negotiate his contract with the Crown. That instrument assured him of a twelve-year

silkworms. For reference to the efforts of an Irishman named Lourenço Belford to produce silk in the captaincy-general of Pará, see Francisco Xavier de Mendonça Furtado to [Tomé Joaquim da Costa Côrte Real?], Oct. 22, 1757, *Anais do Pará*, V (Belem, 1906), 312–313.

[56] In 1771 the Crown closed down a hemp factory at Coimbra that had been functioning since 1625 and relieved farmers in nearby districts of the necessity of planting quotas of hemp because the factory had proved more expensive to maintain than it was worth. Alvará de lei, Feb. 25, 1771, *CLP*, II, 533–534.

[57] See G. Melvin Henderson, "Hemp in Colonial Virginia," *Agricultural History*, XXXVII (Apr. 1963), 86–93.

[58] Francisco Xavier de Mendonça Furtado to Lavradio, Aug. 7, 1769, CMCM, cod. 3, fol. 46 (*1.a via*).

[59] Cunha to Sá e Faria, Oct. 6, 1764, *RIHGB*, XL:1 (1877), 235–236.

monopoly on the processing of hemp in Rio Grande and exempted his product from the payment of all royal taxes. At the end of the contract, the factory, a dozen slaves, and seed for the next harvest were to be delivered to the Crown.[60]

It was one thing to secure a contract and quite another to produce hemp. Inexplicably the contractor returned to Rio de Janeiro without any seed to begin his operations, and none seems to have remained in Rio Grande! The viceroy therefore ordered the governor of Colônia to procure a fresh supply via Buenos Aires.[61] When it arrived, the seed was planted in beds near the capital, but either the ground was foul, the season was wrong, or the seed sterile; in any case, it failed to germinate. After further delays the viceroy procured another batch of seed from the officer of a passing French ship, but before the seedlings could mature they were destroyed by a combination of heavy rains and hungry birds. A few grains were salvaged and sent by Dom Luís to Santa Catarina, where they were planted on the margins of the Rio Tubarão. Their products were delivered to Antônio Gonçalves, who in the meantime had returned to Santa Catarina; but just as he was preparing to harvest his first crop the Spaniards invaded the island and the contractor fled to Rio de Janeiro. There the viceroy assigned him a portion of the ex-Jesuit estate of Engenho Novo and directed its administrator to cooperate with him in his efforts to raise hemp. At the same time he sent seeds to one of the mestres de campo with instructions to distribute them among trustworthy farmers. Shortly after, Lavradio turned the vexatious hemp problem over to his successor.[62]

Viceroy Vasconcelos continued his predecessor's efforts to develop a hemp industry, only to encounter a new series of disappointments. At the beginning of his term the Portuguese boundary commissioner to Buenos Aires secured a fresh supply of seed from Chile which the viceroy distributed among farmers in the captaincy of Rio de Janeiro. But the new plantings failed because of inattention to their cultivation, excessive temperatures, and marauding birds.[63] After receiving new Baltic seed from Lisbon,[64] Vasconcelos decided that since Rio-

---

[60] "Condiçoens q. a V.M. offrecem Antonio Gonçalves Pereira de Faria, para estabelecer a Sementeira, e Fabrica do Linho Canhâmo," July 17, 1769, CMCM, cod. 3, fol. 47^r.

[61] Lavradio to Francisco de Souza de Menezes, Mar. 24 and Aug. 17, 1770, CMCM, cod. 15, fols. 16^r and 27^v; idem to Pedro Jozé Soares de Figueiredo Sarmento, Mar. 5, 1771, ibid., fol. 51^r.

[62] Lavradio, Relatório, p. 473; idem to João Antônio Salter de M[endon]ça (inspector of Engenho Novo), Jan. 14, 1779, ANRJ, Col. 70, Liv. X, fol. 81^v; idem to João Joze de Barcellos, Jan. 25, 1779, ibid., fols. 86^{r-v}.

[63] João Hopman reported the new failure to Lavradio with obvious relish. See note 50 above. The reason for Hopman's glee will soon be apparent from the text.

[64] The colonial secretary dispatched additional seed in 1782 and again in 1784. Melo e Castro to Vasconcelos, Oct. 24, 1784, BNRJ, I-4, 4, 1, n. 47.

grandense farmers had proven unenthusiastic about raising such a troublesome crop, a royal hemp plantation should be established in their captaincy to encourage them by example. To that end he appropriated the sizeable sum of 1,000,000 réis for the plantation's initial expenses and persuaded a priest who taught philosophy in Rio Grande to serve as its first director. A staff consisting of twenty slave couples from the fazenda of Santa Cruz, four soldiers to oversee them, a chaplain, a surgeon, an accountant, and a consultant, the redoubtable Antônio Gonçalves, then in his ninetieth year, left Rio de Janeiro for Rio Grande in August 1783.

Despite its initial promise, the royal plantation proved to be a new source of frustration to Vasconcelos and his successors. It was originally located at Rincão Cangussú, near the vila of Rio Grande. Squatters on the land were dispossessed, and although the ground was not properly ploughed, the new seed was planted. The initial harvest proved to be surprisingly good, and surplus seed was sent to Santa Catarina and Rio de Janeiro for distribution to farmers there. After this promising beginning the plantation underwent a series of relocations and alterations in management, but failed to prosper or to stimulate local cultivators to produce hemp. At the end of the colonial period a local businessman in Rio Grande noted ruefully that "today the culture of hemp is reduced to nothing." [65]

While the lethargy of Brazilian farmers was a factor inhibiting the efforts of Viceroys Lavradio and Vasconcelos to develop a colonial hemp industry, their primary opposition to the development of another kind of fibrous product came curiously from a Peninsular agent of the Crown. Known as *guaxima,* the fiber was made from the root of the *embira* bush, a hardy weed that grew extensively in the fields of Rio de Janeiro and elsewhere in the colony, for at least five varieties of the plant are recognized in Brazil.[66] Traps made of guaxima had long been used by the Indians and Negroes of the captaincy of Rio de Janeiro to capture wild life, but its commercial possibilities had been ignored until a Dutchman known as João Hopman began

[65] The most extensive accounts of unsuccessful efforts to raise hemp in Brazil are Vasconcelos to Melo e Castro, Oct. 2, 1784, *RIHGB,* CCLVI (1962), 273–280; *idem, Relatório, RIHGB,* XXIII (1860), 218–224, and Gonçalves Chaves, "Memorias econômo-políticas," pp. 270–271. The last author adds the interesting note that one reason the hemp industry did not prosper in Rio Grande was the resistance of farmers to the raising of a crop for which payments from the Crown were always uncertain, and that they deliberately boiled the seed they received before planting it so that they would not have to bother with its cultivation. The French botanist Auguste de Saint-Hilaire, who visited Rio Grande at the end of the colonial period, observed that while hemp had never flourished there, "hemp would produce very well in the humid, dark soils mixed with sand which are common in this zone." *Viagem ao Rio Grande do Sul (1820–1821),* tr. by Leonam de Azeredo Pena (Rio de Janeiro, 1935), p. 93.

[66] *Pequeno dicionário, s.v.* "embira."

to experiment with cables made of the fiber. Hopman had lived in Brazil since the 1730s and for some years had been a dealer in slaves in the capital. There he married a Portuguese lady by whom he had two daughters. Prior to the arrival of the Marquis of Lavradio, Hopman had lost his business and retired to his *chácara* in the district of Mataporcos on the outskirts of Rio de Janeiro. There he raised garden crops to supply the needs of his family and experimented with various kinds of novel plants that attracted his interest. Through his daughter, who became a servant in the viceregal household, Hopman became friendly with Dom Luís de Almeida. Because of their mutual interest in economically useful plants, the viceroy asked Hopman to experiment with various plants he hoped to promote in the viceroyalty. As a consequence, Hopman grew the first coffee produced in Rio de Janeiro, he raised mulberry trees for sericulture, and he assisted the viceroy in his efforts to produce cochineal dye.[67]

Hopman was particularly intrigued by the possibilities of manufacturing guaxima on a commercial basis. Early in 1778 he asked the viceroy to examine some cables he had made from the embira root. Intrigued, Lavradio ordered MacDouall's squadron to try them, and although they had been inexpertly made, the reports were generally favorable. Dom Luís then drafted a long dispatch to the colonial minister extolling the virtues of the new cordage that he considered superior to hemp or flax. He enclosed some samples and suggested that if they met with the Crown's approval, Hopman should be rewarded with an eight- or ten-year monopoly to manufacture it.[68] While awaiting the Court's reaction, Dom Luís ordered the mestres de campo to send him samples of embira plants found in their districts.[69]

But the Court's reaction was most unenthustiastic. Secretary Melo e Castro wrote that the Royal Cordage Factory had examined the samples and found them to be distinctly inferior to Riga hemp and of little apparent value to the navy. He curtly suggested that instead of wasting more time observing experiments with guaxima cables, the viceroy should devote his energies to the promotion of hemp.[70]

---

[67] Some references to Hopman's background are contained in Lavradio's dispatch of Jan. 12, 1778 cited in note 68. In 1782 Hopman was named a member of the mesa da inspeção, and died shortly before the end of Viceroy Vasconcelos's term. Vasconcelos, *Relatório*, pp. 223–224.

[68] Lavradio to Melo e Castro, Jan. 12, 1778, IHGB/AUC, 1-2-1, fols. 1^r–5^v; published in *RIHGB*, CCLVI, 134–138. A portaria of Jan. 3, 1778 (CMCM, cod. 19, fol. 233^v) indicates that the viceroy authorized payment of 91,440 réis to Hopman for the cables the squadron used. According to Correa de Sá, Lavradio sent four arrobas and three cables of guaxima to Lisbon, promising a future shipment of as much as 600 arrobas. *VRL*, p. 139. There is a very superficial article on guaxima by Manuel Nunes Dias, "Notícia da cultura industrial da guaxima no Brasil nos fins do seculo xviii," *Revista de Historia*, No. 24 (São Paulo, 1954), 413–418.

[69] Lavradio to Manoel Antunes Ferreira, June 16, 1778, CMCM, cod. 25, fol. 252^r.

[70] Melo e Castro to Lavradio, July 14, 1778, BNRJ, I-2, 4, 7, n. 97.

But the secretary had not heard the last word about guaxima. Despite his discouraging response, the viceroy remained convinced that Hopman's fiber had considerable merit. In March 1779 he arranged a demonstration of the comparative tensile strengths of guaxima and hemp cables at Hopman's chácara. Present were the viceroy, Hopman, João Antônio Salter de Mendonça, provedor of the Royal Treasury in Rio de Janeiro, Captain Thomas Stevens, skipper of the frigate *Princeza do Brasil*, frigate master Anastácio Rodrigues, and a scribe who carefully recorded the results of the tests whose authenticity was verified by the signatures of the witnesses. Using five samples of hemp and guaxima that had previously been examined by the inspector at the Royal Cordage Factory in Lisbon, Hopman tested pairs of cables of comparable size and thickness. In two out of four cases the local fiber proved to be superior to hemp; in a third instance it was found to be nearly as strong.[71] That confirmed Lavradio's faith in guaxima, and since the Court had not expressly prohibited its manufacture, he authorized Hopman to produce it for the local market. Soon after, Dom Luís de Vasconcelos e Sousa arrived, and Lavradio invited his replacement to witness another demonstration of guaxima cables, and before completing his report to his successor recommended the product's utility.[72]

The new viceroy continued to support Hopman's cordage project. When the Dutchman opened a plant to manufacture guaxima, the viceroy assigned a number of prisoners to work there.[73] He also recommended Hopman's appointment to the mesa da inspeção as a reward for his numerous contributions to the economy of the captaincy. Two months after approving that appointment,[74] the colonial secretary acknowledged receipt of a petition from Hopman reporting his latest improvements for weaving guaxima fibers into even stronger cords, and asked Viceroy Vasconcelos to send him some samples and an account of how they had been made.[75]

Once again samples were dispatched to the Royal Cordage Factory and for the second time its inspector, Luís António de Leiro, examined them. Senhor Leiro clearly felt that his professional reputation was at stake, for after making his tests he submitted an elaborate report to the colonial minister. In it he took pride in his nearly thirteen years' experience at the factory and reaffirmed his conviction that guaxima was worthless. Among the reasons he cited for that opinion were that the fiber was too brittle to tolerate much twisting;

71 [Experiments with guaxima], Mar. 7, 1779, CMCM, cod. 10, n.p. (orig.) .
72 Lavradio, *Relatório*, pp. 470–473.
73 In his letter to the Marquis of Lavradio cited in note 50, Hopman states that the prisoners were guarded by a detail of thirteen men, suggesting that he had a substantial working force.
74 Carta régia, June 22, 1782, BNRJ, 4, 4, 3, n. 29.
75 Melo e Castro to Vasconcelos, Aug. 2, 1782, BNRJ, I-3, 4, 28, n. 27.

that it was only half as strong as comparable hemp cables; and that in order to weave cables of equal strength it would be necessary to make them so thick that they would be cumbersome to handle. Furthermore, he doubted that such cables would last as long as hemp, and contended that they could not be reworked into oakum for caulking as was done with older hemp cables. Leiro concluded that he could conceive of no use for guaxima except as a binder twine for merchants. But he remarked that he had just tested a fiber called *tecûm* from Bahia which seemed as good as hemp, and suggested with an air of condescension that the industrious Dutchman ought to see if he could find it in Rio de Janeiro and turn his talents to its manufacture.[76]

Leiro's report rejecting guaxima was sent by the colonial minister to Viceroy Vasconcelos who passed it along to Mr. Hopman.[77] The latter became so incensed that the discovery upon which he had spent so much effort had been again rejected that he undertook new experiments designed to prove once again the fiber's merit. For a third time the viceroy sent samples to Lisbon, but he noted rather wistfully in his report to his successor that while he had found uses for the cordage in the royal arsenal in Rio de Janeiro and that it was employed in coastal shipping in Rio Grande de São Pedro, the Court remained unpersuaded of its utility. By the time Vasconcelos retired, the energetic Dutchman was no longer around to care what the Court thought, for he had passed on, and like Hopman, guaxima was soon forgotten.[78]

Indigo, Cochineal, and the Scientific Society of Rio de Janeiro

Shortly after reaching his post the Marquis of Lavradio received an inquiry from the colonial minister about an indigo manufacturing plant in the captaincy.[79] Its co-owner was the viceroy's treasurer general, Manoel da Costa Cardozo, who with an unnamed partner had built an indigo works in the 1750s called the *chárcara de anil* situated on part of the old Jesuit plantation of Engenho Velho, a few miles

[76] Luiz Antonio de Leiro e Seixas Souto Mayor to Melo e Castro, Lisbon, Aug. 7, 1784, BNRJ, I-4, 4, 1, n. 65.

[77] Melo e Castro to Vasconcelos, Aug. 14, 1784, *ibid.*, n. 29.

[78] Vasconcelos to Melo e Castro, Jan. 1, 1786, BNRJ, I-4, 4, 3, n. 36; *idem, Relatório*, Aug. 23, 1789, p. 224.

[79] I have attempted to place the Brazilian indigo industry in its global perspective in "The Growth and Decline of Indigo Production in Colonial Brazil: A Study in Comparative Economic History," *The Journal of Economic History*, XXV (Mar. 1965), 35–60, where a fuller discussion and the sources for the following paragraphs will be found.

northwest of the capital. Because of inexperience their product was not of high quality and they were unable to market it in Portugal. After failing to make a profit from their venture, the partners closed down the plant in the 1760s.

Dom Luís knew that the home government was anxious to produce the blue vegetable dyestuff in the colony since it was much in demand by European textile manufactures. He therefore persuaded Cardozo to reopen his plant, and after making certain technical improvements suggested by Jerônimo Vieira de Abreu, Cardozo produced a sample batch which the viceroy sent to Lisbon.

As he anticipated, the Court became greatly interested in the possibilities of indigo production in Rio de Janeiro. Secretary Melo e Castro wrote that if the impurities found in the samples could be eliminated, growers would find the government ready to purchase all the dyestuff they could produce. To stimulate them the secretary directed the viceregal junta da fazenda to offer cash payments for acceptable stocks in accordance with a price schedule varying with three grades of the dyestuff. The schedule would not be altered for ten years, and during that time the Crown would remain the exclusive purchaser of indigo in the colony. Because of his technical knowledge the secretary named Jerônimo Vieira de Abreu as director general of indigo cultivation and manufacture.

The viceroy acted promptly to carry out these instructions. Notices to growers of the offer to purchase indigo were soon posted about the capital. In November 1773 Lavradio instructed the new director general to determine the availability of uncultivated indigo in the vicinity of the capital and to advise cultivators to allow such plants to reach maturity so that their seeds could be harvested and distributed among growers. The following year he sent several small shipments of indigo to the kingdom, promising that more would soon follow. But he noted that because of the fiscal burdens of the local treasury board, it could not continue indefinitely to pay for the indigo it purchased, and he feared that if payments were delayed the growers would soon abandon the new crop. Delicately avoiding the obvious truth that the Crown was a notoriously poor payer, he observed that the colonists always believed that they gained more by disposing of their crops to private dealers. He suggested that they be permitted to sell indigo to the highest bidder, whether the Crown or private parties, and that when the market price was unattractively low they be allowed to dispose of their crops to the government in accordance with the already established prices. If growers were permitted that option the viceroy prophesied that Brazilian indigo would soon be moving across the Atlantic in large volume.

The colonial secretary was not as sanguine as the viceroy on the

possible effects of removal of the Crown monopoly on indigo purchases. Although the quality of recent shipments showed improvement, they were still below the Guatemalan standard; and he contended that as long as they were, Brazilian growers were deluded if
they thought that private merchants would pay them more than the
Crown. As proof, he cited the cases of certain growers in Pará and
Maranhão who some years before had tried to market their indigo
but found that no private merchant would handle it because of its
impurities. An orthodox mercantilist, the minister insisted that the
only way to assure the fledgling industry's success was to keep it
under Crown protection. Nevertheless, if the planters insisted, he
would put the matter before the king, though the viceroy could be
certain that if the Crown relinquished its control the industry would
soon "be reduced to nothing." What might happen if the local treasury board was forced to suspend payments to growers he failed to
say.

Despite misgivings as to how long the money would hold out,
Lavradio continued to promote the new culture with enthusiasm. He
urged subordinate governors to tell their farmers about the profits
they could earn from indigo. He instructed field administrators to
employ compulsion when other measures failed to persuade agricul-
turalists to raise the dyestuff, and he sought the best possible seed
from sources in Rio de Janeiro and São Paulo.

As production mounted, growers continued to seek the right to sell
their crops through private channels. In what may have been intended as a test case, Manoel da Costa Cardozo petitioned the treasury board in June 1776 for permission to sell his indigo to a woolen
mill in Oporto. In a supporting statement he recounted the tribulations he had experienced in learning how to process the dyestuff, the
encouragement he had received from the viceroy, and the stimulus
that his factory had given to indigo culture throughout the captaincy.
As he well knew, the board had no authority to grant his request, and
could only recommend its approval by the Crown. The following year
the colonial secretary granted Cardozo's petition, albeit reluctantly,
and directed the viceroy to inform growers that if they sold their best
stuff privately, they should not expect to dump the rest upon the
Crown.

As he was preparing to leave Rio de Janeiro, the Marquis of
Lavradio could look back upon his efforts to encourage the indigo industry with a sense of achievement. A few months before his departure he received a dispatch from the colonial minister advising him
that more than 7,000 pounds of indigo had recently arrived from
Brazil and that the dyestuff "has now become [such] an important
branch of our national commerce" that Portuguese mills no longer

had to rely upon foreign indigo. In his report to his successor Dom Luís summarized his efforts to aid the industry, but warned that it was essential for the Crown to allocate special funds to pay growers promptly for their crops. "It is only thus," he wrote, "that [new commodities] can be promoted in these dominions . . . , and Your Excellency knows full well that [the treasury's support] . . . far from being prejudicial to the interests of His Majesty, on the contrary, contributes additional revenues [to the Crown]. . . ."

Vasconcelos soon discovered the wisdom of Lavradio's remarks, for the industry's very success became a source of embarrassment to the local branch of the Royal Treasury.[80] In 1781 he informed the colonial minister that because of the junta da fazenda's heavy debts, it would soon be forced to suspend payments to growers if the Crown failed to make available special funds. But Melo e Castro ignored the viceroy's prediction and simply increased the price guarantees for the several grades of indigo. In 1786 Vasconcelos notified the Court that the Crown's current obligations to growers had reached 24,544,150 réis, and that the junta had suspended all further purchases. Two years later he reported that since that action greedy merchants were taking advantage of "this sad situation" to buy indigo from heavily committed growers at half the price formerly offered by the Crown. The following year, as he reviewed his administration for the benefit of his successor, Luís de Vasconcelos e Sousa was gloomy about the prospects of the indigo industry.

For a time the industry continued to flourish, and during the 1780s and 1790s Portugal advantageously reexported Brazilian indigo to continental markets when other New World supplies were curtailed by the effects of war.[81] In 1779, the year Vasconcelos succeeded Lavradio, Rio de Janeiro's indigo exports reached nearly 145,000 pounds. Seventeen years later Brazil furnished Portugal with 264,786 pounds of the dyestuff, of which over half (187,136 lbs.) came from Rio de Janeiro; most of the remainder was produced in Pará and Bahia. But 1796 appears to have been the peak year for the industry in the southern captaincy; by 1798 Rio de Janeiro's indigo exports were valued at only one-fifth of the amount estimated for 1779, and in 1800 the captaincy-general of Pará, possibly for the first time, shipped more indigo to the kingdom than did Rio de Janeiro (16,333 pounds compared to 13,156). Nevertheless, by 1812 Rio de Janeiro

[80] By the mid 1780s there were 406 indigo works between Cabo Frio and Angra dos Reis. Vasconcelos, *Relatório*, p. 189.

[81] Most notably South Carolina, where indigo production reached more than 1,100,000 pounds a year on the eve of the Revolution, and Saint Domingue, the New World's greatest producer, which averaged nearly 2,000,000 pounds a year during the third quarter of the eighteenth century. Most of the colony's 3,160 *indigoteries* were destroyed by the series of revolts that began in 1791.

was the only part of Brazil still producing indigo for overseas markets, but in 1818, the last year for which statistics are available, the captaincy's shipments amounted to a mere 6,919 pounds. Like other New World producers, the Brazilian indigo industry proved incapable of matching competition from the British-financed dyestuff industry in India.

In November 1778 the colonial secretary wrote the Marquis of Lavradio expressing his pleasure at the arrival of substantial quantities of indigo from Rio de Janeiro and commented favorably on its improved quality. "The great object now," he added, "is cochineal. . . ." [82] In contrast with indigo, cochineal is an animal dye obtained from the boiled, baked, or sun-dried bodies of female parasitical insects (*Coccus cacti*) which feed upon the prickly leaves of certain cacti, especially the cactus *Nopolea cochinellifera*, and yield various shades of red dye whose color depends on the method by which the dye is processed. The Spaniards discovered cochineal plantations (*nopaleries*) when they conquered the Aztecs, and introduced cochineal to Europe where it replaced the age-old kerms, oriental shield lice, one of the oldest of the world's dyestuffs, used since the time of Homer. Throughout the colonial era New Spain continued to enjoy a much envied natural monopoly of cochineal whose source was a highly prized state secret.[83] During the eighteenth century Spain's rivals attempted to produce cochineal in their own colonies to eliminate their dependency on Spanish sources. The year prior to the colonial minister's reference to cochineal Portugal imported some 1,360 pounds of the very expensive red dyestuff from Spain,[84] and as was the case with indigo, the Crown was interested in determining whether it could also be produced in Brazil.

Viceroy Lavradio had learned about the possibilities of producing cochineal in the colony through a discussion among members of the newly formed Scientific Society that met in his palace. This club was one of a number of similar groups of intellectuals that occasionally appeared in eighteenth-century Brazil under the aegis of viceroys or captains-general. Their membership consisted primarily of Peninsulars associated with the government, drawn together after hours by their common interests in anthropology, botany, history, medicine,

---

[82] Melo e Castro to Lavradio, Nov. 4, 1778, BNRJ, I-2, 4, 7, n. 111.

[83] William F. Leggett, *Ancient and Medieval Dyes* (Brooklyn, N.Y., 1944), pp. 69–89.

[84] "Balança geral do commercio de Portugal com as naçoens estrangeiras no anno de 1777," BNRJ, I-6, 4, 6. The same source contains a marginal comment that the year's imports of cochineal were down 5,377 pounds from the previous year, and indicates that Portugal also purchased 2,008 pounds of the dyestuff from Great Britain. Since the British colonies did not produce cochineal, this must have come by licit or clandestine means from New Spain.

physics and other subjects that could be related to their environment.[85] Superficially the Portuguese societies resembled the better known, more active, and more consequential *sociedades de amigos del país* that flourished in contemporary Spain and in parts of Spanish America,[86] and like them, they were indirectly inspired by the "arts societies" organized throughout Western Europe during the eighteenth century.[87] The Brazilian societies were of shorter duration than many of their Spanish colonial counterparts, terminating with (if not before) the expiration of the administration of their patron. Their impact on the colony was certainly far less than that of the amigos del país, partly because, in contrast with the Spanish patriotic societies, few colonials were admitted to the Portuguese groups, and also because the Crown's refusal to permit printing presses to function in the colony made it difficult for members to publish the results of their inquiries and to exchange ideas with persons of kindred interests who lived outside of Salvador and Rio de Janeiro, the two cities where such societies were formed.

All that is known about the origins of the Scientific Society is contained in a statement made in 1814 by Dr. José Henriques Ferreira, former personal physician of the Marquis of Lavradio.[88] Dr. Ferreira had proposed the formation of the academy to Dom Luís in December 1771; the viceroy readily assented, and the first meeting was held in the viceregal salon on February 18, 1772. In attendance were the viceroy as patron; the charter members, including three doctors, José Henriques Ferreira, Gonçalo José Muzzi, and Antônio Freire Ribeiro; four surgeons, Mauricio da Costa, Idelfonso José da Costa Abreu, Antônio, Mestre, and Luis Borges Salgado; and two pharmacists, the brothers Antônio Ribeiro de Paiva and Manoel Joaquim Henriques de Paiva; [89] and "a brilliant concourse" of honored but unnamed guests.

---

[85] Moreira de Azevedo, "Sociedades fundadas no Brazil desde os tempos coloniaes até o começo do actual reinado," *RIHGB*, XLVIII:2 (1885) , 265–322; Alexander Marchant, "Aspects of the Enlightenment in Brazil," Arthur P. Whitaker, ed., *Latin America and the Enlightenment* (2d ed., Ithaca, 1961) , pp. 95–118.

[86] Robert J. Shafer, *The Economic Societies in the Spanish World (1763–1821)* (Syracuse, 1958).

[87] Roger Hahn, "The Application of Science to Society: The Societies of Arts," *Studies on Voltaire and the Eighteenth Century*, XXIV/XXVII:1963, 829–836. (I am indebted to Dr. Hahn, a member of the History Department, University of California, Berkeley, for an offprint of this most interesting article.)

[88] The following discussion is based on "Sumario da historia do descobrimento da cochinilha no Brazil, e das observaçoens q. sobre ella fez no Rio de Janeiro o Dr. José Henriques Ferreira, Medico do Vice-Rei o Marquez do Lavradio," *O Patriota*, III, No. 1 (Rio de Janeiro, Jan.–Feb. 1814) , 3–14.

[89] Henriques de Paiva was the author of a small octavo volume, *Farmocopéa lisbonense* (Lisbon, 1785) , dedicated to the Marquis of Lavradio as the "fructo dos favores, com que Vossa Excellencia auxiliou os meus primeiros estudos," and of *Memorias de historia natural, de quimica, de agricultura, artes, e medicina* (Lisbon, 1790), in which the author discussed, among other topics, useful flora

The first session—the only one described in detail—was taken up with the usual dreary speeches and matters of organization. Dr. Ferreira, who was named president, made what he proudly called "an eloquent and erudite oration concerning the objects of the Academy and its utility"; Mauricio da Costa, the academy's "director of surgery," spoke on some aspects of his profession, while Antônio Ribeiro de Paiva, "director of natural history," expounded on the profit that could be derived from the study of botany. Others talked on chemistry, agriculture, and pharmacy. Finally the secretary read the organization's statutes (which have not come to light), to which the members signified their approval.

The Scientific Society appears to have met intermittently throughout Lavradio's term. From time to time other persons (not identified but probably including João Hopman) were invited to join, and the society claimed to have two corresponding members in the Swedish Royal Academy of Science. How regularly the Marquis of Lavradio participated in the Society's meetings is hard to say, for he seldom referred to it in his dispatches and (perhaps significantly) failed to mention it in his memoir to his successor.

The subject of cochineal was raised at one of the academy's first sessions. Mauricio da Costa, chief surgeon of one of the Peninsular regiments, recalled that when he had been stationed in Rio Grande de São Pedro with the joint boundary commission in the 1750s a Spanish officer who had been in Mexico pointed out to him several varieties of cacti that resembled the opuntia cactus eaten by the cochineal insects of New Spain. The surgeon lamented that his official duties had prevented him from learning more about the plant, which he had been unable to find in Rio de Janeiro. His colleagues urged him to renew his search, and several weeks later the surgeon brought to the palace some specimens of cactus that he thought resembled those he had seen in Rio Grande.

But the cactus was of no value without the insects. Evidence of what was believed to be *Coccus cacti* was first supplied by Lavradio's special agent Francisco José da Rocha. While on detached duty in Rio Grande, Rocha sent the viceroy several pieces of paper inscribed with a red ink used locally as a writing substance. After examining the paper Dr. Ferreira declared that the tint was unquestionably cochineal. Dom Luís immediately wrote for additional samples. Shortly thereafter Rocha returned to Rio de Janeiro where he had a number of discussions with Dr. Ferreira about the vermin and the cactus he had observed in the southern captaincy. Then he was sent to Santa Catarina Island to make an inspection of agricultural possi-

in Brazil. There is a copy of the first volume in the Rare Book Room of the National Library in Rio de Janeiro, but I have not seen the second.

bilities. There Rocha recognized the same sort of cactus (called tuna cactus) and insects that he had previously seen in Rio Grande. He immediately forwarded samples to the viceroy.

Rocha's discovery led to a flurry of activity. Dom Luís turned over the samples to Antônio José Castrioto, curator of the Scientific Society's new botanical garden.[90] He directed the governor of Santa Catarina to establish a large cactus plantation on the island and to dispatch new shoots from it to the capital by returning ships. The shoots were planted on another plantation, situated near Gloria Hill at the southeastern end of the city, where Antônio Ribeiro de Paiva, a member of the Society, was in charge. As cacti became available from this plantation, the viceroy sent them to his militia colonels with instructions as to the best methods of gathering the scarlet vermin and orders to see that farmers in their districts planted cactus fences around the borders of their properties. Soon the junta da fazenda was offering to purchase cochineal at prices ranging from 1,800 to 2,560 réis per pound. From time to time the viceroy sent samples of the new dyestuff to Lisbon, but he admitted that the industry had not progressed as rapidly as he had hoped, partly because the Santa Catarina plantation was lost at the time of the Spanish invasion, and also because local farmers manifested little interest in the difficult and exacting process of preparing marketable cochineal.[91]

In his memorial to Dom Luís de Vasconcelos, the marquis made the customary flattering statement that his successor's "distinguished talents" would enable him to promote cochineal more successfully than he had been able to do. Once again, Vasconcelos tried. A year after his arrival he decided to inspect the botanical garden, but on two occasions he found the gate locked and the key keeper nowhere about. When the exasperated viceroy finally gained entry he was appalled to discover the place overrun with weeds. In one corner was a withered clump of tuna cactus. The alleged reason for such negligence was provided by the botanist Joaquim José Henriques de Paiva, who petitioned to be placed in charge of the garden. He declared that no one had cared for the place since 1779, when most of the members of the Scientific Society had returned to Europe with the Marquis of Lavradio.[92] Vasconcelos responded by naming Paiva as the garden's

[90] I.e., the garden formerly attached to the Jesuit College on Castle Hill which in Lavradio's time had become the military hospital. The garden was rented to the Society for a nominal sum.

[91] The foregoing account is based upon Lavradio, *Relatório,* pp. 473–474, the Ferreira "Sumario" cited in note 88 above, and various dispatches of Lavradio which also concern the indigo industry and are cited in my "Growth and Decline of Indigo Production in Brazil." See note 79 above.

[92] Henriques de Paiva to the queen, n. d. [*ca.* 1780], BNRJ, I-3, 4, 26, n. 28. As the French cloth merchant Louis-François Tollenare noted in connection with a similar botanical garden in Pernambuco, "O jardin botânico de Olinda é ainda um

new director and assigned him a gang of galley slaves to weed the grounds properly, for he felt that they might furnish the military hospital with fresh produce and provide convalescents with a place to stroll and take fresh sea air.[93]

Though this obviously meant the primary function of the garden would no longer be experimental, the viceroy continued to promote cochineal. He assigned ten slaves from the Santa Cruz estate to plant 10,000 settings of cactus on a royal plantation, but found that local cultivators were still uninterested in producing the dyestuff.[94] He continued to purchase cochineal from Rio Grande and Santa Catarina, but advised the Court that an expert was needed to assist growers there and that his treasury lacked funds to pay for such a person or to continue to buy cochineal on the Crown's account. Toward the end of his administration Viceroy Vasconcelos remitted a sizeable shipment (nearly 10,000 pounds) of cochineal, but warned that it would be the last since the junta da fazenda had no funds to purchase any more.[95] Despite continuing interest in the establishment of the cochineal industry on a firm basis,[96] its cultivation soon ceased altogether, leaving contemporaries to debate the reasons for its abandonment.[97]

exemplo do que se encontra tão a miúde em Portugal; quero dizer: concepções sábias e bemfazejas abafadas por execuções infiéis e imprudentes." *Notas dominicais tomadas durante uma viagem em Portugal e no Brasil em 1816, 1817, e 1818* (Bahia, 1956), p. 177.

[93] Vasconcelos to Melo e Castro, Apr. 12, 1780, BNRJ, I-3, 4, 26, n. 27.

[94] "A repugnancia destes moradores a novas culturas, tantas vezes lamentada, é muito maior a respeito da coxonilha, em cuja planta vem unicamente os espinhos, sem distingam o fruto, por mais que este se lhes explique e se lhes persuada." Vasconcelos to Melo e Castro, July 15, 1781, *RIHGB*, CCLVI, 200–209; Hopman to Lavradio, May 4, 1780 (see note 50 above).

[95] Vasconcelos to Melo e Castro, Oct. 2, 1784, *ibid.*, 285–286; *idem* to *idem*, July 31, 1788 (cited in Melo e Castro to Vasconcelos, Apr. 11, 1789, BNRJ, I-4, 4, 5, n. 10).

[96] See Joaquim de Amorim Castro (juiz de fóra of Cachoeira, Bahia), "Memoria sobre a planta cactus tuna linei, vulgarmente denominada cochinilha e sobre o insecto conhecido pelo mesmo nome," [1789], Castro e Almeida, *Inventário*, III, 118–128, an essay that received a medal from the Royal Academy of Sciences in Lisbon. In 1799 Colônia-born Hipólito José da Costa Pereira (1774–1823), protégé of Dom Rodrigo de Sousa Coutinho (the future Conde de Linhares), was sent to the United States, partly to try to obtain information about the cochineal industry in Mexico and to acquire some insects from there for introduction in Brazil. Jane Herrick, "The Reluctant Revolutionist: A Study of the Political Ideas of Hipólito da Costa . . . ," *The Americas*, VII (Oct. 1950), 171, n. 3.

[97] For criticism of the Portuguese methods of producing cochineal in Rio de Janeiro, see George Staunton, *An Authentic Account of an Embassy from the King of Great Britain to the Emperor of China*, I, 186–192, and Jacinto José da Silva Quintão, "Memoria sobre a cochinilha," *O Patriota*, II, No. 4 (Rio de Janeiro, 1813), 12–14, whose unfavorable comments concerning the Scientific Society's efforts to promote cochineal provoked José Henriques Ferreira's rejoinder cited in note 88 above.

Factors that Impeded the Colony's
Economic Development

It is evident that the record of the attempts of Viceroy Lavradio and his successor to diversify the economy of the lands under their jurisdiction was a mixed one. There were some modest successes, such as indigo, rice, and wheat growing, and there were some notable disappointments, particularly cochineal, hemp, and tobacco. Both viceroys felt that their efforts to foster the economy were seriously handicapped by the lethargy of cultivators, the paucity of treasury funds, and the lack of venturesomeness on the part of the capital's business community.

The Marquis of Lavradio considered Carioca merchants less enterprising than their Bahian counterparts. He contended that most of those styled *comerciantes* (traders) were principally factors for Lisbon or Oporto merchants rather than independent operators. He singled out the firm of Francisco Araujo Pereira and Company as the only real wholesaler in Rio de Janeiro; other reputedly wealthy merchants, like Manoel da Costa Cardozo, were actually commission agents, a designation applied to ninety-eight of the 2,000 businesses registered in the capital.[98] Such agents were necessarily dependent on the instructions of their principals in Portugal who themselves were often mere intermediaries for British or other foreign interests.[99] Because of such dependent relationships, the viceroy observed, local merchants could not ship "commodities other than those which their superiors require . . . ," and since the market for the small volumes of new products he and his contemporaries were promoting was distinctly uncertain it is understandable that local merchants preferred to freight sugar, hides, and other traditional goods for which there was an established demand rather than take a chance on the newer exotic commodities whose quality was likely to be inferior to that available in the Peninsula from foreign sources. As a memorialist put it, "The merchants do not buy . . . [cotton] either because this kind of commerce is not customary, or because the quantity is always too small to

[98] "Demonstração das qualidades e quantidades de differentes ramos de mercancia mecanismo . . . que estabelecem as vantagens da sociedade do paiz," (1780) *RIHGB*, XLVII:1 (1884), 44–45.

[99] See the fine study by Allan Christelow, "Great Britain and the Trades from Cadiz and Lisbon to Spanish America and Brazil, 1759–1783," *HAHR*, XXVII (Feb. 1947), 2–29. For contemporary accounts of foreign dominance of the Portuguese economy, see Jacome Ratton, *Recordacoens*, pp. 95–96, 252, and "Etat du Portugal en 1778—réponses du consul de France a Lisbonne aux questions envoyées de Paris," Victor Magalhães Godinho, *Prix et monnaies au Portugal, 1750–1850* (Paris, 1955), pp. 336–341.

make it worth while to ship it. . . ." [100] Partly for these reasons but also because of the dearth of investment capital in the colony, the merchants of Rio de Janeiro and other parts of Brazil failed to play a dynamic role in the development of colonial trade comparable, for example, to that of the agency houses in British India at the end of the eighteenth century.[101]

As the evidence presented in the previous chapters demonstrates, the fiscal practices of the Crown itself inhibited the formation of capital in the colony. Although a leading purchaser of goods and services, the government was a notoriously poor payer, a reputation that it admittedly shared with most other European governments of the time. Nevertheless, colonial merchants and planters whose capital was tied up in unpaid government contracts were obviously deprived of funds needed for normal operations, and lacked surpluses to invest in new activities. There can be little doubt that the shortage of both royal and private financing handicapped efforts toward economic diversification in Lavradio's Brazil.[102]

But the Crown's fiscal delinquency was only one of the grievances merchants expressed to Viceroy Lavradio. They also complained about unfair competition from so-called traveling merchants (commissários volantes) who came from Europe with large amounts of goods declared as personal baggage to avoid payment of imposts on freight, and unloaded their merchandise quickly by underselling their competitors and took the next ship back to Europe.[103] Carioca merchants declared that business had been much better in the days of the frotas whose arrival coincided with the opening of fairs in the capital, where they disposed of large quantities of goods to Mineiro purchasers who were given credit until the arrival of the next frota.[104]

100 See note 53 above.
101 Amales Tripathi, *Trade and Finance in the Bengal Presidency 1793–1833* (Calcutta, 1956), Chap. 1 *et passim.* For Lavradio's observations concerning the Carioca business community, see *Relatório,* 453–454; for similar views, Manoel da Cunha Menezes (captain-general of Bahia) to Melo e Castro, Mar. 10, 1779, Castro e Almeida, *Inventário,* II, 423, and Martim Lopes Lobo de Saldanha (captain-general of São Paulo) to *idem,* Nov. 9, 1776, *DI* XXVIII (1898), 228–229.
102 Lavradio, *Relatório,* pp. 460–461.
103 The practice of merchants of accompanying shipments to their destinations dates from at least the mid-twelfth century. See Florence Elder de Roover, "Partnership Accounts in Twelfth Century Genoa," in A. C. Littleton and B. S. Yamey, eds., *Studies in the History of Accounting,* pp. 86–90. The same practice was followed by Peninsular Spanish merchants in the early days of the conquest of the Indies. See Robert S. Smith, "The Institution of the Consulado in New Spain," *HAHR,* XXIV (Feb. 1944), 62.
104 The frota system had been established in 1649 to protect Brazilian sugar fleets against Dutch assaults, and with various modifications was retained until 1765. One of the reasons given in the *alvará de lei* of Sept. 10, 1765, which abolished the frotas, was that "os interessados no commercio das ditas Capitanias [Rio de Janeiro and Bahia] constrangidos e esperarem dous, tres, ou quatro annos

But since the fleet system had been abolished (1765), the yearly volume of their trade had fallen from the 400,000- to 500,000-cruzado level to between 300,000 and 400,000. They attributed that decline not to decreasing gold yields in Minas (probably the real reason), but to the growth of manufactures in the interior.[105]

The viceroy took these representations seriously and did what he could to assist the merchants. But despite the existence of a long series of laws concerning the activities of commissários volantes,[106] he found it impossible to take effective action against them, partly because most of them came to the colony as members of ships' crews who by law were entitled to engage in limited private trade,[107] but also because they made arrangements with resident merchants to conceal the true ownership of their goods.[108] He tried to revive the capital's annual fairs, but found the merchants little interested in such a project.[109]

Lavradio was particularly concerned about the merchants' complaint that the Mineiros had become poor customers because of the growth of textile weaving in the interior. Like his master, the Marquis of Pombal, Dom Luís took a dim view of colonial manufacturing. He shared the economic views of many contemporary statesmen that the proper functions of colonies were to serve as producers of raw materials and as consumers of manufactured goods produced by the mother country, and he firmly believed that if the colonists were permitted to engage in manufacturing, the commerce (and therefore the revenues) of the kingdom would suffer.[110] Therefore he wrote to

pelos seus pagamentos, e retornos, por hum effeito necessario das ditas dilações, com prejuizos transcendentes aos seus acrédores; de sorte que não havia cabedaes, que fossem bastantes para sopportarem tão extraordinarias demoras no embolso dos ditos pagamentos." *CLP*, II, 221–222. According to Ratton, ships employed in the frotas could make only two voyages to Brazil in three years, while vessels that did not have to travel in convoy could complete two sailings in less than a year. *Recordacoens*, p. 97.

105 Lavradio, *Relatório*, pp. 456–458.

106 Notably the alvarás de lei of Dec. 6, 1755 and Mar. 7, 1760. *CLP*, I, 404–405, 726–727.

107 For a list of Peninsular and colonial products that ships' officers and men could trade in on their own account, see alvará of Dec. 11, 1756, *CCLE*, III, 538–540. Despite complaints by colonial merchants, the list was further extended in 1788. Alvará of Nov. 6, 1788, *CLDA*, IV, 112.

108 Lavradio, *Relatório*, p. 460.

109 *Ibid.*, p. 459.

110 Thus he wrote the governor of Santa Catarina, "Deve promover-se a Agricultura das Amoeiras, para se pode extrair a mayor porção de seda, q. fôr possível: *não deve consentir Fabricas de qualidade nenhũa;* todo o empenho será em q. elles cultivam todos aquelles Generos q. podem facilitarlhe um florscente commercio, ao mesmo tempo ter toda a capitania na mayor abundancia" (italics added). To Francisco de Souza de Menezes, Sept. 6, 1773, CMCM, cod. 4, fol. 9ᵛ. A quarter century later another Portuguese governor was enjoined "Vmce. observará tambem as manufacturas que mais se consomem, e informará d'isso mesmo, a fim de que se

Dom Antônio Noronha, captain-general of Minas Gerais, warning him about the harm that Mineiro "factories" were causing to the State generally and to the interior captaincy in particular. The State, he said, suffered because of the inevitable reduction of trade between Portugal, Rio de Janeiro, and Minas, but Minas itself suffered even more. He reasoned that because of the availability of locally made cloth Mineiros had less incentive to search for the gold they needed to pay for manufactures, and that as mining—the proper activity for Mineiros—diminished, so did the captaincy-general's prosperity.[111]

Dom Antônio reacted by defending Mineiro interests against the viceroy's charges. As delicately as possible he wrote Lavradio exposing the absurdity of his contentions. He denied that the decline of gold production was related to the growth of manufacturing; rather, he said, it derived from a shortage of slaves. The types of slaves engaged in weaving textiles were old and lame persons who were totally unsuited for mining or farming. He added that when he first took office he had issued instructions to subordinates to permit only the weaving of cloths of inferior quality suitable for slaves and the very poor.[112] Nevertheless, after receiving the viceroy's complaint, the captain-general took the precaution of asking his ouvidores to report the number of weaving establishments in their districts and to indicate whether they were enforcing his directive against the making of fine fabrics.[113] He also sent duplicate dispatches to Ministers Pombal and Melo e Castro defending the Mineiros against Carioca charges and declaring that the seaboard merchants were making their false allegation to cover up their failure to pay their obligations to their European creditors.[114]

animem no reino essas manfacturas, e que melhor se estabeleça *a reciprocidade entre a metropole manufactureira e a colonia agricultora.*" Dom Rodrigo de Sousa Coutinho to Fernando Delgado Freire de Castilho (governor of Paraíba), Oct. 23, 1797, *RIHGB,* VI (1865), 446 (italics added). Cf. the quite similar views of George Grenville and Pedro Rodriguez de Campomanes, prominent contemporary policy makers for the British and Spanish empires, as noted in Dora Mae Clark, *The Rise of the British Treasury* (New Haven, 1960), p. 115, n. 28, and Jaime Eyzaguirre, *Ideario y ruta de la emancipación Chilena* (Santiago, 1957), pp. 60–61 and n. 51.

111 Lavradio to Noronha, Oct. 28, 1776, the substance of which is repeated in *idem, Relatório,* p. 458, and in Noronha's reply cited in note 112.

112 Noronha to Lavradio, Nov. 19, 1776, BNRJ, 2, 2, 24, n. 31.

113 Noronha to the ouvidores of Minas Gerais, Jan. 3, 1777, *ibid.,* n. 36.

114 Noronha to Pombal and to Melo e Castro, Jan. 7, 1777, *ibid.,* n. 37. Noronha's views were shared by desembargador Teixeira Coelho who argued that without the trade of Minas, Rio de Janeiro "ha de ficar deserta e pobre" and that the prosperity of the merchant communities of Lisbon and Oporto would also be greatly lessened. "Instrução," pp. 390–391. One can almost visualize the learned judge nodding in agreement with another spokesman for the provinces who warned "Burn down your cities but leave our farms . . . ," except that he would have substituted mines for farms. See also José Eloi Ottoni, "Memoria sobre o estado atual da capitania de Minas Gerais" (1798), *ABNRJ,* XXX (1912), 305–306.

This glimpse into the economic rivalry between two admi⟩ units suggests several observations. One is that for some Crown had been anxious to eliminate cloth making in the ⟨ and had already taken some steps to prevent it.[116] But the ⟩ portant step, the famous decree of 1785, may well have been a ɑe-layed response to the Lavradio-Noronha exchange nearly a decade be-fore. That ill-understood decree was directed primarily against textile ✓ weaving in Brazil and did not, of course, bar all types of manufac-turing as is sometimes claimed.[117] It was one of the first economic re-strictions to be lifted when the Court came to Rio de Janeiro.

The Mineiro-Carioca dispute also provides another instance of the sort of economic parochialism that existed not only within eighteenth-century Brazil but also within the colonies of other nations at that time.[118] In the first years of that century, for example, the merchants and planters of Bahia secured from the Crown a preferential quota of fresh slaves entering Brazil from Africa despite the opposition of other sections of Brazil and the câmara of Luanda.[119] Forty years later the sugar interests of the littoral protested against sugar manu-facture in Minas Gerais and the Overseas Council issued an order barring establishment of additional engenhos in the interior cap-

[115] Even the sparsely settled subcaptaincy of Santa Catarina had a primitive textile industry. According to a report of 1755, there were 266 looms in Santa Catarina which annually produced 24,077 *varas* of cotton-wool and 42,181 varas of "pure cotton" cloth. "Rellação dos panos de linho e algodao que se tecerao na Ilha de Sancta Catarina e freg.as da terra firme anexas o anno de 1755 . . . ," AHC, PA/SC, *caixa* 2 (Bancroft Library Microfilm Collection). For a rather curious plan advanced at the beginning of the eighteenth century to persuade skilled Indian weavers from the Coromandel Coast to emigrate to Pará to produce textiles there, see Boxer, *Golden Age*, p. 300.

[116] According to Sebastião Ferreira Soares, *Elementos de estatistica comprehenendo a theoria da sciencia e a sua applicação á estatistica commercial do Brasil*, I (Rio de Janeiro, 1865), 67–68, a carta régia of July 3, 1766 ordered destruction of all "fabricas de tecido de algodão, linho, lá, e seda" in Brazil, but I have not seen the order. The captain-general of Pernambuco reported that by an order of Aug. 8, 1770 cloth manufacture in his captaincy-general had been forbidden. José Cezar de Menezes to Lavradio, Nov. 12, 1774, IHGB, *Lata* 439, doc. 1.

[117] Alvará of Jan. 5, 1785, *CLP*, III, 370–371; for the immediate background see Melo e Castro to [Vasconcelos], Jan. 5, 1785, *RIHGB*, X (2d ed., 1780), 213–224.

[118] Cf., e.g., the rivalry between Virginia and North Carolina over the raising of tobacco (C. Robert Haywood, "The Mind of the North Carolina Advocates of Mercantilism," *The North Carolina Historical Review*, XXXIII [Apr. 1956], 156–157), and the clashes between rival economic interests in Peru and Chile discussed in Sergio Villalobos R., *Tradición y reforma en 1810* (Santiago, 1961), excerpted in R. A. Humphreys and John Lynch, eds., *The Origins of the Latin American Revolutions, 1808–1826* (New York, 1965), pp. 136–137. The subject of intraimperial economic rivalry warrants further study.

[119] Câmara of Luanda to the king, Sept. 20, 1711, Charles R. Boxer, *Portuguese Society in the Tropics*, pp. 193–195. See also Manoel Cardozo, "The Brazilian Gold Rush," *The Americas*, III (Oct. 1946), 150–151.

taincy.[120] The protest of the câmara of Rio de Janeiro against imports of Bahian tobacco in the 1750s has already been noted. During the late 1760s and the early '70s Luís Antônio de Sousa, captain-general of São Paulo, repeatedly complained to the Crown that the growth of livestock production in Minas was harmful to his treasury since Mineiros were buying fewer animals from the southern border-lands and therefore the passagens, the tolls levied on cattle and horses that passed through his captaincy, were diminishing. He argued that the growth of ranching in Minas was harmful to the king because animals raised in the interior paid only the tithe while those that came from outside also paid the tolls; he suggested that Mineiros be enjoined to concentrate on gold mining and to refrain from diverting their slaves to "easier" forms of activity like ranching.[121] Twenty years later when another Paulista governor arranged to have slaves shipped directly from Angola to Santos so that Paulistas could sell them to Mineiros, his action drew forth a vigorous protest from the Conde de Rezende, viceroy of Brazil. Rezende acted partly because of a complaint by a Carioca slave dealer, but also because the viceregal branch of the treasury would lose 6,460 réis per slave or a total of 6,460,000 réis per thousand if the chattels entered Brazil through Santos rather than through Guanabara Bay. It was all well and good for the Paulista governor to spur the economy of his own captaincy-general, said Rezende, but not when the means he selected would be injurious to Rio de Janeiro which was, after all, the capital of the State of Brazil.[122]

The controversy between Dom Luís de Almeida and Dom Antônio de Noronha also illustrates an astute observation made by Stanley Stein, who noted that colonial executives tended to become the "vectors" of rival economic groups and to identify with and represent those that dominated the particular region they administered.[123]

[120] Noronha to Lavradio, Nov. 19, 1776 (cited in note 112 above). According to the captain-general, treasury officials had not rigorously enforced the Council's order of 1742 because of the loss in revenues restriction of the industry would entail. He estimated the annual tax yield from sugar and brandy at over thirty-one contos a year.

[121] Sousa to Oeiras, Jan. 5, 1768 and Nov. 14, 1770; idem to Melo e Castro, Oct. 20, 1772, RIHGB/TE, VI (1957), 51, 203–204, and 346; see also the exchanges between Sousa, the Conde de Valadares (captain-general of Minas), and Viceroy Lavradio, Nov. 13, 1769–Aug. 30, 1773, reproduced in Simonsen, Hist. econômica, pp. 191–194.

[122] Rezende to Melo e Castro, July 20, 1791, RADF, I, 480–481. As John Luccock wrote a few years later, "in old times . . . between some of these provinces there existed an opposition of interest, and between others open and avowed jealousies." Notes on Rio de Janeiro and the Southern Parts of Brazil . . . 1808 to 1818 (London, 1820), p. 568.

[123] The American Historical Review, LXVI (Jan. 1961), 449; cf. Hernán Ramírez Nocochea's appraisal of Ambrosio O'Higgins in Humphreys and Lynch, Origins of the Latin American Revolutions, p. 173.

However, it should be remembered that the Portuguese viceroys and captains-general of the late colonial period were also presidents of their respective juntas da fazenda, and in that capacity viewed the economic gains of a neighboring administrative unit as likely to affect adversely the income of their own branch of the Royal Treasury. Thus while Viceroy Lavradio expressed the views of Carioca merchants when he protested against the prevalence of textile weaving in Minas Gerais, he was also thinking about the resultant reduction of revenues collected at the Customs House in Rio de Janeiro.

Although the marquis supported what he considered to be the legitimate interests of local merchants, he was totally unsympathetic with their endeavors to evade the payment of taxes through illicit trade. The efforts of Dom Luís and his contemporaries to combat smugglers will be considered next.

XIV

The Contrabandist Versus the Crown

> Mere administrative watchfulness and thoroughness could never do more
> than damp their activities; it was only the triumph of free trade . . . that
> deprived them of their livelihood. . . . [U]ntil then they were able to
> match by increase of cunning and of organization the ever more elaborate
> network of the customs system—its spies, its coastguards, and its cutters, as
> well as its routine officials at the ports. . . .
>
> G. D. Ramsay, "The Smugglers' Trade:
> A Neglected Aspect of English Commercial Development,"
> Royal Historical Society, *Transactions*, Ser.
> 5, II (London, 1952), 131.

BESIDES ATTEMPTING to increase the sources of royal income by
developing new economic activities, the viceroy and his fellow administrators sought to prevent the loss of royal revenues from smuggling.
Lavradio and his colleagues were charged with preventing two basic
types of smuggling: the illicit import of slaves and merchandise, and,
the unlawful exportation of highly valued undutied commodities such
as brazilwood, gold bullion, and diamonds. Both types of smuggling
facilitated by Brazil's geography, particularly her extremely long, inadequately guarded coastline extending from the Amazon to the
Plata, with its numerous river mouths, isolated beaches, protected
coves and lagoons, and her sparsely occupied, largely unmapped or
unfortified frontiers facing the Spanish empire. As was the case with
clandestine trade in other New World empires, geography was a vital
ally of those who smuggled in Brazil.[1]

Although the origins of clandestine trade with Brazil trace back before the beginnings of the colony's formal settlement, such trade greatly
increased during the eighteenth century because of the exploitation
of gold and diamond deposits as well as the buildup of population, a
minority of whom were sufficiently affluent to be able to afford European manufactures and exotic wares from the Orient. The heavy,
often crippling duties levied on colonial imports and exports[2] and

---

[1] Cf. Carl Ubbelohde, *The Vice-Admiralty Courts and the American Revolution*
(Chapel Hill, 1960), pp. 36–37.

[2] Goods sent to Brazil paid 26 percent ad valorem on leaving Portugal and an
additional 10 percent on entering Brazil. Conselho Ultramarino, *consulta* of July
24, 1715, Virgínia Rau and Maria Fernanda Gomes da Silva, eds., *Os manuscritos do
arquivo da casa de Cadaval respeitantes ao Brasil*, II, 151 (hereafter cited Rau and
Gomes, *Manuscritos de Cadaval*).

the burden of commissions, freight, and other charges also served to encourage the smuggler to undercut the legitimate merchant. Shortly before the beginning of the Golden Age a prominent Bahian tobacco planter complained that out of a hundred rolls of tobacco he shipped to Lisbon, more than seventy-five went to pay the customs duties and freight costs. In 1756, at the apogee of the same era, the British Board of Trade calculated that on every £100 worth of English goods sent to Brazil, £68 was paid in taxes.[3] Payment of such duties might be avoided by offering suitable gratuities to ill-paid Portuguese customs officers who in their acceptance of bribes were no different than their counterparts in other imperial regimes.[4]

There were several sources of illicit trade with Brazil. One of the most important was Lisbon, the origin and terminus of most of the Brazil trade, and a city described by a French consul in the 1780s as being

> . . . full of persons exclusively occupied with contraband; individuals without industry and without fortune are registered in that class and form an army. The mansions of the nobles of the kingdom provide them with asylum, and the very guards employed at great expense to prevent fraud are the first to encourage it and to share in its profits. . . . It is possible to say without fear of exaggeration that contraband is the occupation and source of existence of a tenth of the inhabitants . . . , despite the precautions of the government to prevent that abuse. It is the same in the Colonies. Everyone there participates in deceit and is provisioned with foreign merchandise.[5]

The testimony of Consul Helfflinger is supported by that of the head of the royal customs in the kingdom who reported that large quantities of goods left the Peninsula for the colonies concealed in barrels of tar, bottles of wine, and casks of ship's biscuit.[6]

---

[3] Charles R. Boxer, *The Golden Age of Brazil*, p. 27; Violet M. Shillington and A. B. Wallis Chapman, *The Commercial Relations of England and Portugal* (London, n.d.), p. 247.

[4] Concerning dishonest customs officers elsewhere, cf. the statement by Massachusetts' Governor Francis Bernard in 1765 quoted in Lawrence Henry Gipson, *The Triumphant Empire: Thunder-Clouds Gather in the West, 1763–1766* (New York, 1961), p. 113, n. 5; see also Harry Atton and Henry Hurst Holland, *The King's Customs. An Account of Maritime Revenue & Contraband Traffic in England, Scotland, and Ireland, from . . . Earliest Times to . . . 1800*, I (London, 1908), 327–328, 362, et *passim*. For examples of the extent of the complicity of customs officers in smuggling in the Spanish empire at this time, see Herbert I. Priestley, *José de Gálvez, Visitador-General of New Spain (1765–1771)* (Berkeley, 1916), pp. 173 f., 304 f.

[5] "Notations generales sur le commerce de Portugal par [consul] Helfflinger" (1786) in Victor Magalhães Godinho, *Prix et monnaies au Portugal*, pp. 343, 347. See also Jacome Ratton, *Recordacoens*, pp. 271 ff.

[6] Ignacio de Pina Manique to Martinho de Melo e Castro, Dec. 3, 1784, *RIHGB*, X (2d ed., 1870), 225–227.

The Portuguese Atlantic Islands were another source of clandestine trade with Brazil. More important, however, were the slave entrepôts along the African coast, where Brazilian tobacco and gold were exchanged for North European manufactures furnished by English, Dutch and French vessels, and for Asiatic textiles, drugs, and spices brought by Portuguese East Indiamen.[7] When the same East Indiamen made so-called emergency stops in Brazilian ports on their outward or return voyages, their officers and men displayed great skill in evading customs officials to deal with customers ashore.[8] So, too, did foreign vessels that hovered off the Brazilian coast seeking opportunities to run in their merchandise.[9]

As already noted, there were certain types of clandestine commerce that the Crown secretly sanctioned and encouraged. One was the livestock trade between Portuguese buyers and Spanish rustlers in the Debatable Lands,[10] another was the exchange of European merchandise and Negro slaves for Spanish silver and hides. Until the 1760s that trade had been centered at Colônia do Sacramento, although it existed on a smaller scale at other points along the Luso-Spanish frontier and between the ports of Rio de Janeiro and Buenos Aires.[11] After the early 1760s the Colônia leak was largely plugged by Spanish authorities, but nearly forty years later the Portuguese Crown

---

[7] Melo e Castro, "Instrução para Marquez de Valença (captain-general of Bahia), Sept. 10, 1778, Castro e Almeida, *Inventário*, II, 443–444; *idem* to [Luís de Vasconcelos e Sousa], Jan. 5, 1785, *RIHGB*, X, 213–224, especially pars. 9–10; cf. Boxer, *Golden Age*, pp. 155–156 and 306.

[8] Boxer, *Golden Age*, p. 27.

[9] Overseas Council, Decree of Apr. 16, 1719, Livro de registro, AHU, cod. 1193 (photostatic copy in possession of Professor Engel Sluiter, University of California, Berkeley; hereafter cited OC/LR 1193); Lavradio to Felis Gonçalves Santos (capitão mor of Ilha Grande), Mar. 18, 1771, ANRJ, Col. 70, Liv. V, fol. 173ʳ; see also Louis-François de Tollenare, *Notas dominicais tomadas durante uma viagem em Portugal e no Brasil em 1816, 1817, e 1818*, pp. 353–354. The only published autobiography by a foreign smuggler who operated in Colonial Brazil that I know is the remarkably frank account by Thomas Lindley, *Narrative of a Voyage to Brazil*.

[10] See pp. 71, 81, and 101.

[11] In contrast with the general Portuguese policy of hostility toward unlicensed foreign ships calling at Brazilian ports (see pp. 403 f., below), colonial authorities were directed to be especially solicitous of the needs of Spanish vessels bound to or from the Plata and to encourage local merchants to do the same in order to establish "um negocio muito interessante" between Rio and Buenos Aires. Francisco Xavier de Mendonça Furtado to Conde da Cunha, July 23, 1766, *RIHGB*, XXXIII:1, 243–244. The celebrated English explorer James Cook, whose problems with Viceroy Azambuja will be noted later in this chapter, observed the difference in treatment of his ship and that of a Spaniard, much to his annoyance. He recorded in his journal (entry of Nov. 24, 1768) "This day a Spanish Packet . . . from Buenos Ayres put in here on her way to Spain, . . . and notwithstanding the Viceroy had all along pretended that the orders he had respecting Foreign Vessels were general yet this Vessel met with very diferent treatment from us, no Guard was put over her and her officers and crew went where ever they pleased." J. C. Beaglehole, ed., *The Journals of James Cook on His Voyages of Discovery*, I, 26.

was continuing to encourage trade between Brazil and the Spanish Platine colonies even though it was still unsanctioned by Spanish authorities.[12] Yet shortly after the turn of the nineteenth century, in another interesting example of economic parochialism the governor of Rio Grande de São Pedro argued strongly that all trade with the Spanish colonies should be prohibited since they no longer supplied silver but instead were furnishing meat, hides, wheat, tallow, and grease, thus competing with producers of the same products in his captaincy.[13]

One need not share Consul Helfflinger's conviction that all colonials partook of the fruits of smuggling to agree that all types of persons, respectable and otherwise, participated in various forms of illegal trade. As already observed, Portuguese ships' crews and their passengers frequently engaged in illicit traffic.[14] During the early days of the settlement of the mining regions some of the worst offenders were renegade friars and so-called bad clergymen.[15] In the maritime cities shopkeepers, gemsmiths, and wholesale merchants bought and sold goods illegally with the assistance of both customs officers and royal soldiers guarding suspicious ships at anchor.[16]

The fact that smuggling was widespread in other empires and in

12 See references to the colonial secretary's orders of 1798 and 1799 in 2RGG, 441–442.

13 Paulo José da Silva Gama to Visconde de Anadia, July 25, 1803, RIHGB, XL:1 (1877), 287–289.

14 That traffic included not only goods and Negro slaves but also Reinões who could not obtain passports to Brazil. In June 1771 Viceroy Lavradio refused to permit Captain José Antonio Lima leave Rio de Janeiro for Salvador, where his ship lay at anchor, on the ground that he was guilty of the "crime de commissario volante" for having introduced in the colony a number of persons without passports. Subsequently Secretary Melo e Castro ordered Captain Lima, Luís Cipriano Rabelo, captain of the Princeza Real, and a third man, Tomás Gonsalves remitted to the Limoeiro dungeon in Lisbon. Among the papers of Gonsalves was a letter of introduction signed by the viceroy's wife! Although the investigating magistrate declined to copy the letter because of the delicacy of the matter, the viceroy with evident embarrassment called the colonial minister's attention to it, stating that he had nothing to hide and that his wife was innocent of any wrongdoing. Lavradio to Melo e Castro, June 14, 1771, ANRJ, Col. 69, Liv. I-bis., fol. 46ʳ; Melo e Castro to Lavradio, Oct. 1, 1771, CMCM, cod. 3, fol. 150ʳ (orig.) ; Lavradio to Melo e Castro, Mar. 28, 1772, BNRJ, 10, 4, 8 (unfoliated) .

15 For measures directed against unauthorized friars said to be living scandalously in Minas Gerais, see ordens of May 13, 1722 and Nov. 9, 1723, RAPM, XVI:1 (1911), 461 and 396; cf. Boxer, Golden Age, pp. 54, 400, n. 60.

16 Count Cunha to Francisco Xavier de Mendonça Furtado, Nov. 8, 1766, RIHGB CCLIV (1962) 353–354. When members of one guard boat were accused of having failed to maintain proper surveillance over a suspected Portuguese smuggler at anchor in Guanabara bay, Viceroy Lavradio ordered the crew dismissed from service, shackled, and confined to hard labor for an indefinite time in the Villegaignon fortress. In view of such drastic action, it may be inferred that the soldiers had been bribed or were themselves participating in illicit traffic. Lavradio to Lt. Col. Vicente Joze de Velasco Molina, Oct. 17, 1776, (two dispatches) , CMCM, cod. 25, fols. 147ʳ⁻ᵛ.

their mother countries too [17] was of no consolation to royal authorities charged with increasing the Crown's revenues or to Peninsular or colonial merchants distressed by periodic declines in their sales and profits.[18] It is therefore not surprising that two of Viceroy Lavradio's four original instructions concerned the problems of clandestine trade and means of preventing it.[19]

The Tightening of Controls over Imperial Trade

By Lavradio's time the Crown had had a great deal of experience with smugglers in the colony and had devised a variety of countermeasures to entrap or discourage them. The apprehension of suspected smugglers was one of the prime functions of the interior customs posts (registros) that guarded approaches to the diamond-and gold-producing zones from the maritime captaincies. Those thatch-covered huts were situated in strategic spots such as river crossings and narrow mountain passes. There, besides collecting the passagens and entradas, guards checked the passports and other documents each traveler or caravan captain was required to carry. How effective these stations were in preventing contraband can only be guessed. Since their locations were known, experienced smugglers could avoid scrutiny, especially if they traveled after dark.[20] And given the grim, isolated, boring circumstances in which the guards lived, it is not unlikely that they were easily suborned.[21]

[17] Atton and Holland, The King's Customs, I, Chaps. VII–VIII; G. D. Ramsay, "The Smugglers' Trade: A Neglected Aspect of English Commercial Development," Royal Historical Society, Transactions, Ser. 5, II (London, 1952), 131–157, which concentrates primarily on the Elizabethan period; more general is Neville Williams, Contraband Cargoes. Seven Centuries of Smuggling (New York, 1961), esp. Chaps. 4–5. The literature concerning smuggling in the Spanish empire is too voluminous to need citing.

[18] See "Exposição sobre o comercio do reino oferecida a el-Rei pelo provedor e deputados dos homens de negocio de Lisboa, da irmandade do Espirito Santo," n.d. (ca. 1712–1715), Rau and Gomes, Manuscritos de Cadaval, II, 355–359; cf. Melo e Castro to [Vasconcelos], Jan. 5, 1785, cited in note 7 above.

[19] Oeiras to Lavradio, Apr. 14, 1769, IHGB, Lata 9, MS 192; idem to idem, same date, ANRJ, Col. 67, Liv. III, fol. 122ʳ. Appended to both are catalogues giving the texts of pertinent legislation.

[20] Thus Lavradio directed the câmara of Paratí (southern Rio de Janeiro) to furnish the registro in the mountains above that coastal port with fish oil so that it would not continue to be dark at night to the advantage of smugglers. Dispatch of July 10, 1771, ANRJ, Col. 70, Liv. V, fol. 209ʳ.

[21] The registros were a source of interest and sometimes annoyance to foreign travelers who ventured into the interior at the end of the colonial period. For some interesting descriptions of the facilities and their personnel, see John Mawe, Travels in the Interior of Brazil (London, 1812), pp. 113, 115, 145–146; John Luccock, Notes on Rio de Janeiro and the Southern Parts of Brazil . . . 1808 to 1818 (London, 1820), pp. 401–403, 416–421; and Gilbert Farquhar Mathison, Narrative of a Visit to Brazil, Chile, Peru, and the Sandwich Islands during the Years 1821 and 1822 (London, 1825), pp. 30–32.

If surveillance of traffic moving in the interior was spotty, the same may be said for that along the seacoast. With such an extensive littoral it was clearly impossible to maintain a thorough watch. From time to time the Crown assigned warships to patrol particular stretches where smugglers frequently appeared, but in Lavradio's day no vessels were regularly assigned to such duty.[22] A few years later, in 1785, the colonial minister outlined procedures that Viceroy Vasconcelos *ought* to follow to discourage smuggling. They included the assignment of roving beach patrols of regular and militia troops [23] and the chartering of two smacks, one to sail between Espírito Santo and Rio de Janeiro, the other to ply the southern seas between the capital and Santa Catarina. Both were to be armed and staffed by soldiers, and their captains were to stop and check all suspicious craft they encountered. Whether such vessels were actually employed is not known, but in any case they can hardly have been very effective in preventing contraband activities.[24]

Most of the machinery for the prevention of contraband was concentrated in the major ports of call such as Bahia and Rio de Janeiro. As soon as a Portuguese vessel entered port,[25] she was boarded by customs officials and escorted to an anchorage where she was guarded by two patrol boats. Port inspectors then examined passenger and cargo lists and checked passports and other documents.[26] After the captain had presented his cargo manifests and they had been found in order, the customs administrator authorized the cargo to be unloaded at the alfândega where it was examined and dutied.[27] Similar

[22] It will be recalled that MacDouall's squadron's mission was to search for Spanish invaders rather than smugglers.

[23] Such duties were already being performed by the auxiliary militia in Lavradio's time. E.g., Lavradio to Captain Francisco de Macedo Freire, Oct. 12, 1770, ANRJ, Col. 70, Liv. V, fols. 103ʳ⁻ᵛ.

[24] Melo e Castro to [Vasconcelos], Jan. 5, 1785, *RIHGB*, X, 213–224, especially pars. 29–36.

[25] Procedures for handling arrivals of unlicensed foreign ships are described in a later section of this chapter.

[26] In Rio de Janeiro newly-arrived Negro slaves were examined by the eldest alderman of the câmara who bore the title of *provedor da saude*. Lavradio to câmara (Rio de Janeiro), Jan. 31, 1771, ANRJ, Col. 70, Liv. V, fols. 155ᵛ⁻156ʳ. The basic statute regulating the passage of persons from the kingdom to Brazil was the law of March 20, 1720 (ANRJ, Col. 60, Liv. XXIV, fols. 224ʳ⁻226ʳ) which reinforced earlier decrees aimed at preventing the wholesale exodus of Peninsulars as well as the entry of foreigners to the gold fields. Subsequently passports were also required for persons seeking to leave the colony. See D. Alden, "Manoel Luís Vieira: An Entrepreneur in Rio de Janeiro . . . ," *HAHR*, XXXIX (Nov. 1959), 528–529.

[27] The dízimo da alfândega was collected on European merchandise in accordance with a book of rates (*pauta*) which Alexandre Nunes Leal (desembargador provedor da coroa e fazenda) called "antiguissima" because it failed to include a multitude of new types or units of goods received or to reflect current market values. Report to [Pombal?], Nov. 2, 1766, *RIHGB*, CCLIV (1962), 354–355; for the pauta (date of preparation unknown) see *ibid.*, pp. 355–384. British customs officers complained about the same problems. See T. S. Ashton's introduction to Elizabeth Boody Schumpeter, *English Overseas Trade Statistics 1697–1808* (Oxford, 1960), pp. 3–14.

procedures were followed before the ship was permitted to leave port.[28] Significantly, however, royal warships and private vessels chartered by the Crown were exempted from such proceedings—an open invitation for their personnel to engage in illicit traffic.[29]

At various times during the eighteenth century, particularly during the Pombaline era, the Crown tightened up the avenues of legal trade within the empire. Ostensibly this was done to prevent the smuggling of goods from one administrative unit to another, but the new restrictions also served the interests of Peninsular businessmen who wanted to reserve the lucrative Brazilian market for themselves. The Atlantic Islands, especially the Madeiras, often served as transfer points for the shipment of undutied Eurpoean merchandise to Brazil. To prevent that practice the Overseas Council repeatedly issued regulations during the first years of the century, the most stringent being a statute in 1736 that restricted trade between the islands and Brazil to natural produce of the islands, and limited the number of ships permitted to sail for Brazil each year to two from the Madeiras and three from the Azores.[30] As already noted, the slave trade between Brazil and the Portuguese colonies in Africa provided opportunities for the transshipment of illicit Asiatic goods to Brazil. In the late seventeenth century when the empire was beset by a serious depression, the Crown had encouraged legal trade between the Estado da India, the kingdom of Angola, and the State of Brazil,[31] but in 1772 direct commerce between Mozambique and Brazil was prohibited; all ships departing from the western extremity of the State of India for the kingdom were required to proceed home directly without making any interim stops.[32] The same year another measure withdrew the long-standing

---

[28] All crewmen, soldiers, and passengers preparing to leave port were warned by proclamations to go aboard twenty-four hours before their scheduled departure. Bandos of Conde de Povolide (captain-general of Bahia), Apr. 10, 1770 and Jan. 7, 1771, BNRJ, 7-3-9, nums. 136–137, and other examples in the same codex. Procedure concerning proper surveillance of Portuguese ships is described in Melo e Castro to [Vasconcelos], Jan. 5, 1785 (cited in note 7 above). It is interesting to compare Portuguese customs procedures with those of the British whose captains so often complained about Lusitanian red tape. See Elizabeth E. Hoon, *The Organization of the English Customs System 1696–1786* (New York, 1938), pp. 245–248; Lawrence A. Harper, *The English Navigation Laws* . . . (New York, 1939), Chap. VIII, especially pp. 89–91; and Atton and Holland, *The King's Customs*, I, 220–221, where the even more elaborate precautions taken with East Indiamen are described.

[29] Lavradio to Pedro José Soares Figueiredo Sarmento (governor of Colônia) and to Francisco de Sousa Menezes (governor of Santa Catarina), Oct. 22, 1771, CMCM, cod. 15, fols. 84^{r-v}.

[30] Provisões of July 24, 1709, Jan. 12, 1712, July 24, 1715, and Feb. 20, 1719; *lei* of Mar. 20, 1736, OC/LR 1193, nums. v, vii, ix, xvii, and xxi.

[31] Alvará of Feb. 3, 1672, *CCLP*, VIII, 203; and provisões of June 8, 1672, *DH*, LXVII (1945), 136–141.

[32] Alvará of Dec. 12, 1772, Coelho e Sousa, *Col. dos regimentos*, II, 131–132; Melo e Castro to Lavradio, Aug. 13, 1773, BNRJ, I-2, 4, 6, n. 32.

privilege of East Indiamen en route to the Peninsula to call at São Paulo de Luanda, Angola, on the ground that instead of legitimate "Negro goods," they left Oriental goods to be smuggled into Brazil, much to the prejudice of the Royal Exchequer and the commerce of the realm.[33] Another decree of the same year prohibited the export of undutied tobacco from Brazil to the Portuguese outpost of Macao in South China.[34] These restrictions were imposed precisely at the time when the Spanish Crown was gradually extending the principle of intraimperial free trade within its empire.[35]

The Pombal regime also acted to exclude from Brazil certain professions whose members were considered especially prone to contrabandist schemes. One group were the traveling merchants (commissários volantes) whose proscription from the colony has already been mentioned.[36] Another were the goldsmiths (ourives), many of whom were charged with conniving to defraud the Crown by concealing untaxed gold in utensils and other utilitarian objects and by counterfeiting gold coins and stamped ingots. As early as 1698 the number of goldsmiths licensed to practice their craft in the city of Rio de Janeiro had been limited to three, but that restriction was not enforced. In the first decades of the eighteenth century goldsmiths flocked to the boom towns of Minas Gerais, but royal officials finally drove them out of the captaincy in 1719. In the maritime cities of Rio de Janeiro and Salvador their shops were confined to streets known as the Rua dos Ourives, and were closely watched and frequently ransacked by suspicious officials. Nonetheless, the Crown became convinced that the only effective way to prevent collusion to evade taxes between goldsmiths, gemsmiths, and their customers was to close up all such shops. That action was taken in 1766 despite an unusually strong plea on behalf of the craftsmen by Viceroy Cunha. The royal order, which

---

[33] Alvará of June 19, 1772, *CLP*, II, 601–602; Melo e Castro to Lavradio, July 11, 1772, CMCM, cod. 3, fol. 176ʳ (orig.). Viceroy Lavradio was ordered to observe extreme vigilance with respect to East Indiamen calling at Rio de Janeiro allegedly because of stress of weather but actually to indulge in smuggling. *Idem* to *idem*, Apr. 26, 1778, BNRJ, I-2, 4, 7, n. 95.

[34] Melo e Castro to Lavradio, Jan. 18, 1773, ANRJ, Col. 67, Liv. II-A, fol. 246ʳ. As early as 1717 the Overseas Council had forbidden direct trade between Brazil and Macao. Consulta of Jan. 27, 1717, OC/LR 1193, num. 12.

[35] The only liberalizing commercial concession of the Portuguese government during the late eighteenth century was a directive encouraging trade between captaincies north and south of the Brazilian hump. Lavradio to president of mesa da inspeção, May 26, 1778, CMCM, cod. 25, fols. 247ᵛ–248ʳ. Although there was a significant growth of seagoing trade among the maritime captaincies south of the hump during the last colonial decades, there was actually little commercial intercourse between them and the former State of Maranhão, partly because of the absence of overland communications but also because of the perennial problem of sailing south from the Amazon area.

[36] See Chap. XIII, note 106.

affected 142 shops in Rio de Janeiro and 158 in Salvador, was not repealed until 1815.[37]

Smuggling Rings in Lavradio's Brazil

Like other governments then and even today, the Portuguese Crown
also relied upon paid informers for information concerning the activities of smugglers.[38] Slaves could be induced to turn in purloining
masters in the hope of gaining their freedom,[39] and freemen could
earn pecuniary rewards for reporting the misdeeds of their friends or
former comrades. Thus in 1775 the Marquis of Pombal ordered Viceroy Lavradio to publish an edict stating that while His Majesty considered contrabandists common robbers who merited severe punishment, he preferred to grant them clemency; those who revealed
known instances of smuggling were promised fifty percent of the
value of the goods discovered; even those who sang after participating
in clandestine trade were offered a full pardon and a third of the
value of the loot recovered.[40] Such terms were more generous than
those of England's celebrated Act of Indemnity for Smugglers (1736),
but it is not likely that Portuguese authorities were any more grati-
fied by the results than were the British. After all, as Neville Williams has observed, smugglers had good reason to keep silent about
their operations: "It was not so much that they had scruples about
peaching on their associates in crime—though this was hardly the best
way of ensuring they would die peacefully in their beds. Having once
come forward the self-confessed smuggler was a marked man. If he resumed his old ways and was caught in the act, his pardon for past
offenses was of no effect; he could be charged with all his crimes and
instead of a sentence to transportation would most certainly have

---

[37] Boxer, *Golden Age*, pp. 317–318, 418, n. 39. Besides the sources cited there, see
Teixeira Coelho, "Instrução," p. 293; José de Souza Azevedo Pizarro e Araujo,
Memórias históricas do Rio de Janeiro, V, 161 and 313, n. 131; and Ignacio Accioli
de Cerqueira e Silva, *Memorias historicas e políticas . . . da Bahia*, ed., Braz do
Amaral, II (Bahia, 1931), 226. For Viceroy Cunha's protest against the carta régia of
July 30, 1766, ordering the shops closed, see his dispatch of Aug. 14, 1767, *RIHGB*,
CCLIV (1962), 401–403.

[38] England's long reliance upon informers, an evidence of the weakness of a
government's policing machinery, has been analyzed by G. R. Elton, "Informing for
Profit," *Cambridge Historical Journal*, XI (1954), 149–167, and by M. W. Beresford,
"The Common Informer, the Penal Statutes and Economic Regulation," *The Economic History Review*, 2d ser., X (Dec. 1957), 221–238, the latter of whom notes
that the informer's ability to derive profit from his disclosures was not prohibited
in Britain until 1951.

[39] Lavradio to Conde de Valadares (captain-general of Minas Gerais), Jan. 18,
1771 and July 11, 1772, CMCM, cod. 15, fols. 42ʳ and 132ʳ.

[40] Pombal to Lavradio, Sept. 30, 1775, CMCM, cod. 14 (49/12) (orig.).

been sent to the gallows." [41] The Portuguese government did not exact the maximum penalty from recidivists who exhibited a distressing tendency to break their pardon and resume their former profession.[42] Nevertheless, in an age when the machinery of detection was quite rudimentary, the informer proved to be an extremely useful source of information.

In Lavradio's time informers disclosed the existence of a number of smuggling rings, or "societies" as they were called, operating in Brazil; whether they were more numerous or the scale of their activities greater than at other times during the late colonial period it is impossible to say.[43] In 1770 Secretary Melo e Castro advised Viceroy Lavradio that just after the departure of three ships from Lisbon for Rio de Janeiro a certain Vicente Vas Ferreira Sengueiro had disclosed that the pilot of one of the ships and a crew member were carrying nearly twenty thousand cruzados' worth of golden ribbons and silver and gold wire, and ordered the viceroy to make a search for it and to seize the bearers upon their arrival.[44]

Whether the culprits were found is not known, but in another instance it is possible to follow the fate of a ring of smugglers step by step from the time their activities first came to the attention of authorities in Lisbon until their apprehension in Brazil and remission to the kingdom. In the latter part of September 1775 several foreign-born goldsmiths and gem cutters, including two Frenchmen and two Hamburgers, were arrested in Lisbon. They testified that they had correspondents in Minas Gerais and in Rio de Janeiro who supplied them with illicit gold dust and diamonds. Among those whose names and addresses they furnished were a Mineiro merchant, a muleteer who traveled between Rio de Janeiro and Minas, several former gold-

41 *Contraband Cargoes*, p. 112; see also Atton and Holland, *The King's Customs*, I, 213–214.

42 For example, in 1772 the viceroy indicated that one Manoel Antônio Barata, a diamond and gold smuggler, was being sought for the third time in recent years. He had originally come to Brazil posing as a surgeon and was apprehended and sent to Lisbon, where he obtained a royal pardon. During Viceroy Azambuja's term he returned a second time to the colony as a member of a ship's crew, but his identity was revealed when the ship stopped at Rio de Janeiro and, having broken the terms of his pardon, he was again remitted to prison in Lisbon. When he obtained his release, he made his way to the diamond district of Serro Frio via Salvador, and was accused of attempting to smuggle fifty-nine oitavas of gold dust out of the captaincy-general, Lavradio to Valdares, Sept. 7, 1772, CMCM, cod. 15, fols. 133^r–v. Cf. Williams, p. 109.

43 In 1770 a carta régia declared that the traffic in illicit diamonds had reached notorious proportions and ordered colonial magistrates to submit periodic reports concerning the seizure and punishment of such smugglers. But aside from creating more paperwork, this directive seems to have been unproductive. Carta régia of Nov. 16, 1770, CMCM, cod. 3, fol. 118^r (2.a via); examples of the resulting routine reports are in BNRJ, 10, 4, 8.

44 Dispatch of Aug. 4, 1770, CMCM, cod. 3, fol. 79 (2.a via).

smiths still living in Rio de Janeiro, and a number of ex-judicial officials. On receipt of this information the Marquis of Pombal sent
urgent instructions to the viceroy aboard the galley *N. S. da Nazareth,* whose captain had orders not to permit anyone to debark or to
have contact with persons ashore in Rio de Janeiro until the viceroy
had signified permission.[45]

The ship left Lisbon September 30 and arrived in Rio during the
first week in December. On the seventh of that month Dom Luís convened the members of the Relacão in a special session. In compliance
with Pombal's very precise instructions, he then handed each magistrate written orders to proceed to the residence of one of the suspects with his scribe and a guard, to seize the accused, to search the
premises thoroughly for secret hiding places, and to gather up all
papers and put them in a box sealed with the royal arms. The box
and the investigator's written report of his mission were to be delivered to the secretary of the viceroy, the prisoner to the dungeons of
the Relacão.[46]

Within the next four days most of the suspects had been found and
locked up in the court's dungeons. However, it was discovered that
one of the principal suspects, Manoel Gonçalves Guimarães, brother
of Antônio Francisco Guimarães, both former ourives, had already
fled the capital and was living under an assumed name in the port of
Paranaguá, Santa Catarina, where he had married the daughter of the
local capitão mór. The viceroy forthwith ordered the ouvidor of the
district to seize the suspect and send him and his papers to the capital.[47] He also requested Dom Antônio Noronha, captain-general of
Minas Gerais, to arrest the Mineiro merchant implicated in the conspiracy. And, again following Pombal's instructions, he commanded
the captain in charge of the registry athwart the main highway between Rio de Janeiro and Minas not to permit anyone to proceed
along the road until three days after his courier had passed on his
way to Ouro Prêto.[48] By January 29, 1776, the viceroy was able to
turn over eight of the prisoners, including Manoel Gonçalves Guimarães, to the captain of the royal frigate *Graça* for delivery under
close guard to Lisbon.[49] Though his dispatch to the Crown has not

[45] Pombal to Lavradio, Sept. 30, 1775, CMCM, cod. 14 (49/12a) (orig.).

[46] Lavradio to members of the Relação, Dec. 7 (eight portarias) and Dec. 11,
1775 (three additional orders), CMCM, cod. 25, fols. 65ʳ–68ᵛ.

[47] Lavradio to Antônio Barbosa de Mattos, Dec. 11, 1775, *ibid.,* fols. 68ᵛ–69ʳ.

[48] Lavradio to Antônio de Noronha, Dec. 11, 1775, CMCM, cod. 26, fol. 93ʳ; *idem*
to Captain Luís Alvares de Freitas, Dec. 7, 1775, *ibid.,* cod. 25, fol. 68ʳ. It is curious
that the order closing the highway was dated four days *before* the dispatch was
addressed to Noronha!

[49] Lavradio to João Nicolão Schmerkl, Jan. 29, 1776, *ibid.,* fol. 79ᵛ; Schmerkl subsequently died while the *Graça* was at anchor in Bahia, causing a delay in the
frigate's final departure for Lisbon. The vessel reached Lisbon on April 20, 1776.
"Mappa dos cabedaes q. traz a Fragata NS de Graça . . . chegada do Ryo de
Janeiro . . . hoje 20 de Abril de 1776," IHGB, *Lata* 57, MS 1078, Pt. 2.

come to light, it was doubtless a long and full report, summarizing the procedures he had followed and the conclusions of the various investigating officers.[50]

A total of fifty-four days had elasped between the date when the viceroy first received Pombal's notification of the existence of the ring and the date when the prisoners left Rio en route to Lisbon. It has often been alleged that the colonial machinery of Portugal (like that of Spain) was slow, cumbersome, and inefficient.[51] Under normal circumstances it certainly was: proposals for improvements in administration, judicial appeals, settlements between the Crown and its creditors could take years before final action.[52] But when the Crown's vital interests were at stake, the government could and did move with remarkable dispatch.

The smugglers' ring whose apprehension has just been described was only one of a number of such groups operating between the gold and diamond fields of the Brazilian interior, the major colonial port cities, and Lisbon. Less than three weeks after Pombal had informed the viceroy about this particular "society," he ordered the breakup of another gang which dealt in diamonds, gold dust, and gold bars. Among the suspects were a ship's officer and several merchants, one of whom was known to make regular trips between Lisbon and the Mineiro intendancy of Serro Frio.[53]

The Question of Responsibility for the Apprehension of Smugglers

Three years later Dom Luís was embarrased to learn that a parcel containing 2,726 carats of diamonds had been found in the baggage

[50] The viceroy had to prod the magistrates to prepare their final reports, but it is unlikely that this significantly held up the departure of the warship. Lavradio to João Antonio Salter de Mendonça, Dec. 12 and 22, 1775; *idem* to Bernardo Salazar Sarmento Eça e Alarcao, Jan. 18, 1776, CMCM, cod. 25, fols. 69^r-70^r, 76^v-77^r.

[51] Notably by Charles R. Boxer. E.g., his *Four Centuries of Portuguese Expansion,* p. 81.

[52] A case in point: in 1767 two diamond smugglers were apprehended in Minas Gerais and were subsequently confined in either Rio de Janeiro or Lisbon. The investigating judge died before completing his report, and it was not rediscovered until eleven years later, when the Overseas Council concurred in the recommendation of the Crown attorney that while the crime was a serious one, the prisoners had already paid their penalty and should be released. The Council's recommendation was dated September 23, 1778 (*RADF,* IV [1897], 519–520), but it did not receive the royal exequateur until July 21, 1779.

[53] Pombal to Lavradio, Oct. 19, 1775, CMCM, cod. 14 (49/17) orig.; copy with enclosure naming suspects in BNRJ, I-2, 4, 7, nums. 19–20. Upon receipt of this dispatch, the viceroy ordered several magistrates in Rio, including the intendant general of gold, to apprehend the suspects. Orders of Jan. 18, 1776, CMCM, cod. 25, fols. 77^r-78^r.

of a ship's tanner, one José João, who had just arrived in Lisbon from Rio de Janeiro. The resulting investigation disclosed that José João and his brother, Manoel João, a sailor, were middlemen for a clandestine gang with branches in Rio de Janeiro and Lisbon, and that for a considerable time the two messengers had been bringing undutied merchandise to Brazil, returning to Europe with diamonds and gold.[54]

The ministry that succeeded the disgraced Marquis of Pombal in 1777 was determined to put an end to this sort of activity. In a letter rubricated by the queen the viceroy was sternly ordered to see that all colonial officials strictly observed existing laws against smugglers. In an unusual step, considering the limited scope of the viceroy's authority, the Crown directed him to appoint a trustworthy magistrate to examine whether royal officials in the Diamond District were involved in the leakage. He was directed to keep commerical traffic with the district at a bare minimum and to prohibit peddlers who entered the zone from erecting temporary dwellings that might conceal illicit exchanges.[55] In addition, the viceroy was admonished to work closely with the captain-general of Minas and with the intendant-general of gold in Rio de Janeiro to apprehend smugglers.[56]

The intendant-general in Rio appears to have received similar orders from an official who bore the impressive title of Director General of Contraband and Thefts in the Kingdom and Its Dominions and was attached to the Casa de Supplicação in Lisbon. The intendant-general was instructed to cooperate with the viceroy in the roundup of suspects and to compel his subordinates to enforce more strictly the laws against smuggling. He was also directed to examine the books of certain merchants, whose addresses were listed in an appendix, to determine whether they were involved in the newly uncovered diamond ring. There were two problems with these instructions, as the intendant-general pointed out in a prolix letter to the viceroy. First, by the time he had received the instructions news of the recently discovered diamond cache was already abroad, having been brought from Lisbon by a ship which arrived before the vessel bearing his orders. Second, he had no idea which merchants' establishments he was supposed to search, since the appendix giving their addresses had not been included! [57]

[54] Carta régia to Lavradio, Jan. 29, 1778, BNRJ, I-2, 4, 7, n. 94.

[55] It was most unusual for the Crown to authorize the viceroy to take any action within the Diamond District, for that was separately administered. The apparent reason for doing so here was that one of the principal routes of the diamond smugglers passed through Rio de Janeiro.

[56] See note 54.

[57] Manoel Pinto da Cunha e Souza to Lavradio, Apr. 13, 1778, CMCM, maço 31, n. 43 (orig.). It will be remembered that the intendant-general of gold was also president of the board of inspection and was a member of the Relação.

Whether the maritime or interior authorities should bear primary responsibility for preventing the trade in undutied gold and diamonds was a source of considerable disagreement between the viceroy and the captains-general of Minas. Shortly after Dom Luís reached Rio de Janeiro he answered a letter from the Conde de Valadares in which the latter asserted that the leakage of illicit bullion and stones was due to the laxity of the marine intendants, since contraband shipments passed ultimately through the ports of Bahia and Rio de Janeiro. Without denying their responsibility for maintaining vigilance to intercept such shipments, Dom Luís insisted that the interior intendants were especially negligent: it was their duty to name trustworthy persons to guard the registros; they were charged with locating the registries at the most strategic places; and it was their failure to alert such posts to the approach of suspected contrabandists that allowed them to slip by. In any case, said the viceroy, "our object, our obligation" should always be to work together for the good of the Royal Service. Two years later he renewed his complaint that the interior intendants were not doing as much as they could to deter smugglers.[58]

In 1778 the viceroy, in response to the previously discussed carta régia from the queen, wrote to Dom Antônio de Noronha expressing Her Majesty's concern over the persistence of smuggling. In his reply Dom Antônio stated his belief that any gold dust that passed from Minas to Rio de Janeiro did not go over the regular highway but escaped through the backlands of Bahia and entered Rio de Janeiro via Espírito Santo. While the roads and footpaths of the Bahian sertões were regularly patrolled, it was impossible to keep them under adequate surveillance because of their extent and the nature of the terrain. He admitted that effective checks on diamond smuggling should begin at the point of origin, but noted correctly that he lacked jurisdiction within the Diamond District. The captain-general concluded by insisting that the best means of curbing smuggling lay in the searching procedures that should be followed by the marine intendants.[59]

In order to protect himself against the charge that he was indifferent to a subject of vital concern to the Crown, Dom Antônio also wrote to the queen to assure her that he would cooperate fully with the viceroy to prevent smuggling. He enclosed a lengthy report prepared by two of his subordinates, the fiscal and an intendant, explaining why smuggling continued to flourish in the interior. The authors stated that smuggling in Minas had been much more common

[58] Lavradio to Valadares, Mar. 6, 1770 and Nov. 6, 1772, CMCM, cod. 15, fols. 9^r–11^r and 141^v.
[59] Noronha to Lavradio, July 22, 1778, BNRJ, 2, 2, 24, n. 145.

in the past when prices had been extraordinarily high and gold much more plentiful. They, too, expressed the view that most of the gold smuggling passed through the Bahian backlands rather than over the regular highway to Rio de Janeiro, adding that its interception depended on the vigilance of coastal authorities.

The report then turned to the theft of diamonds, which was more easily accomplished than the theft of gold. The authors noted that semiannual inspection reports the intendants had been required to prepare since 1770 had proved of slight value [60] since witnesses to the thefts were easily suborned. This was particularly true of overseers of slave gangs in the Diamond District, for since the Crown had taken over its management their salaries had diminished; as a result they had become careless in watching the slaves at work and more inclined to accept bribes to look the other way when the blacks hid precious stones. Nor had the Crown's system of licensing merchants permitted to enter the district helped, because existing regulations against suspicious persons found in the district went unenforced. The only remedies the authors could suggest to eradicate this situation were the selection of more dedicated personnel to represent the Crown in the district, the use of informers, and thoroughgoing investigations in the ports by the marine intendants. The authors noted in conclusion that although the former private contractors had failed to prevent the theft of stones, at least its incidence had been less and the industry more flourishing than it was in the late 1770s.[61]

Given the practical problems to which these various writers referred and given the universal tendency of bureaucrats to dodge responsibility whenever possible, it is understandable why such bickering went on and why the interior and coastal officials seldom worked in concert, as the Crown urged. A rare but significant example of what could be accomplished occurred during the administration of Viceroy Vasconcelos, when Mineiro and Carioca officials combined efforts to break up a notorious gang of gold smugglers in a remote part of the captaincy of Rio de Janeiro. The gang was headed by Manoel Henriques, known as Mao de Luva (Glove Hand), and a renegade Mineiro sergeant-major, Pedro Afonso Galvão de São Martinho. For some years the Mao de Luva gang had been operating several illicit gold mining camps in the mountainous backlands of the captaincy between the falls of the Macacú river and the Rio Paraibuna.[62] From time to time a few members of the gang, which included whites,

60 See note 43.

61 Noronha to the queen, July 22, 1778, with enclosure entitled "Informação sobre o extravio do ouro e diamantes," BNRJ, 2, 2, 24, n. 147.

62 The Paraibuna is the name assigned to a segment of the Paraíba river above a point which contemporaries called Tres Barras but which is known today as Tres Rios. The principal registro between Minas and Rio de Janeiro was situated at this junction.

pardos and blacks, freemen and slaves, and numbered close to fifty, had been apprehended, but the remainder continued to mine and smuggle gold with impunity. Finally, in 1785 Viceroy Vasconcelos suggested to Luís da Cunha e Menezes, captain-general of Minas, that they simultaneously send troops into the backlands to surround and capture the outlaw miners. Menezes readily agreed. The Mineiros arrived on the scene first, and after a brief skirmish they rounded up thirteen of the gang, including "Glove Hand," and seized over 680 marcs of gold dust. The attackers also destroyed three mining camps but failed to capture more than thirty members of the gang who slipped through their net.[63] Nevertheless, the breakup of the Mao de Luva gang was a significant example of what cooperation between two autonomous units of royal government could achieve. It was an example not often repeated.

The Treatment of Unlicensed Foreign Ships in Colonial Ports: The Evolution of Procedure

If royal officials could explain away their failure to catch smugglers in the sertões on the ground that they were difficult to find, they could hardly offer such an excuse to justify their inability to prevent foreign ships in their ports from engaging in prohibited trade. The captains of unchartered foreign vessels frequently sought admission to Brazilian ports on a variety of grounds, including storm-caused structural damage to hulls, masts, sails, and rigging, making their vessels unseaworthy; outbreaks of disease, particularly scurvy, among passengers and crewmen; shortages of fresh water and provisions; even loss of bearings. It was up to the senior administrative officer in each port to determine whether the captain was speaking the truth or was merely advancing pretexts in order to violate Portuguese laws against direct foreign trade with the colony.

Such laws did not exist prior to 1591. Until that date it was not unlawful for foreign persons and ships properly cleared from a Portuguese port to go to Brazilian ports in trade. Provided that they paid the established import and export duties, they could even carry Brazilian produce to foreign destinations after first calling at Lisbon for the necessary clearance.[64] That liberal policy was abandoned in 1591 in favor of one of imperial exclusivism by the new Spanish masters of

---

[63] For the voluminous documentation concerning the activities of the Mao de Luva gang and its dispersion, see BNRJ, 4, 4, 8, nums. 37–40, 68–79.

[64] The lack of any bar to direct foreign trade with Brazil during the years before 1591 is discussed in detail by Professor Engel Sluiter (University of California, Berkeley) in an unpublished paper, "The Dutch in Brazil Before 1621" read before the 1954 Congress at Recife celebrating the Tricentenário da Restauração Pernambucana.

the Portuguese empire.[65] Eleven years after assuming control of that empire Philip II issued an alvará declaring that no unlicensed foreign ships or persons would be permitted in any of Portugal's overseas possessions, excepting the Azores and the Madeiras which were considered home islands. Even chartered foreign ships were required to return from the conquests directly to Portugal without making any interim stops. Violators were threatened with dire penalties, and informers were assured of a third of the value of the illicit goods they denounced.[66]

The alvará of 1591 became the cornerstone of Portuguese imperial policy with respect to direct foreign participation in colonial trade. That policy was not significantly modified until 1808, but it was constantly challenged by foreigners seeking to trade with Brazil. Sometimes they did so *sub rosa,* that is, through residents (Portuguese- or foreign-born) in the kingdom who were allowed to engage in colonial trade; sometimes they sailed directly to the colony, occasionally lurking off the coast to signal correspondents, but more commonly sailing boldly into port, where they sought to bribe dishonest officials after justifying their presence by one or another of the already-mentioned pretexts.

With the advent of the Golden Age an increasing number of unlicensed foreign ships were attracted to Brazilian shores. In 1711, for example, the Overseas Council referred to four East Indiamen then at anchor in All Saints Bay, where they were reported as seeking to exchange European and Indian merchandise for gold and tobacco. According to the Council there were also other unauthorized ships in Rio de Janeiro and other colonial ports. It warned colonial governors against admitting foreign vessels except when truly in distress (that is, a legitimate *arribada*) or when sailing under charter in a frota; administrators who failed to observe proper precautions were threatened with a fine equal to three times their annual salary as well as the loss of their property and offices.[67] A few years later the Council noted

---

[65] It will be recalled that from 1580 until 1640 Portugal and her empire were under Spanish control.

[66] Alvará of Mar. 23, 1591, *DH*, VII (1929), 32–39. In his paper cited in note 64 above, Professor Sluiter refers to the manuscript of an earlier draft of this statute dated Feb. 9, 1591. It seems clear that the introduction of the new policy was carefully thought out before the new regulations were issued.

[67] Provisão of Feb. 8, 1711, ANRJ, Col. 60, Liv. XVIII, fols. 165^v–166^r; published in *ABNRJ*, XXVIII, 227–228. The Council subsequently added teeth to this provision when it stipulated that in the residências of retiring governors witnesses should be questioned whether those officials had admitted foreign ships and how they had treated them. It added that even though viceroys and governors-general did not undergo the general residência, a special investigation should be made after their departure for the kingdom as to how they had observed this law, stipulating that they should not be admitted to any new post until the investigation had been completed. Ordem of Sept. 7, 1715, CMCM, cod. 18, fols. 136^{r-v}. The Marquis of

reports that foreigners, particularly Frenchmen, had sought admission to Brazilian ports to effect repairs, and that their captains claimed that they lacked cash to pay for them and offered to dispose of merchandise to defray their expenses. It cautioned colonial authorities against being taken in by that old smugglers' ruse, and admonished them to exercise great vigilance whenever foreign ships were at anchor and to expedite their departure in the shortest time possible.[68]

But as the number of unlicensed ships visiting Brazilian ports continued to mount, the Overseas Council realized that the problem was more serious than it had first realized. It saw in the presence of such vessels a threat to the sources of royal income, unfavorable competition for Peninsular traders, and the opportunity for colonials to become independent of their mother country.[69] With these considerations in mind the Councillors concluded that it was imperative to go beyond the previously quite general caveats against illicit foreign trade, and proceeded to spell out precisely what precautions colonial administrators were expected to observe whenever unlicensed foreign vessels called at their ports. These regulations, embodied in an alvará of October 5, 1715, with subsequent elaborations remained in force until repealed in 1808.[70]

The machinery designed to forestall possible foreign smugglers went into operation as soon as a strange ship hove in sight of one of the forts guarding the entrance to a colonial port such as Rio de Janeiro, the illustrative example used here.[71] When her captain signaled that he wished to enter, the fort commander sent a flag message to Castle Hill reporting the ship's appearance, and dispatched a boat

---

Angeja (viceroy of Brazil) protested that this directive was a violation of the privileges of the governors-general, but in 1717 the Overseas Council reaffirmed its previous directive. Angeja to Diogo de Mendonça Corte Real, Jan. 14, 1715 [sic for 1716], Rau and Gomes, *Manuscritos de Cadaval*, II, 131; provisão of Feb. 1, 1717, *DH*, VI, 429–430. I have found no evidence that the Marquis of Lavradio and his contemporaries at Rio de Janeiro were subjected to such an inquiry; however, in 1799 the Overseas Council resolved that such testimony should still be reported to Lisbon for possible action. Resolution of Aug. 17, 1799, *loc. cit.*

[68] Provisão of Feb. 7, 1714, OC/LR 1193, num. 8.

[69] Consulta of July 24, 1715, summarized in Rau and Gomes, *Manuscritos de Cadaval*, II, 150–154, and given in full in *DH*, XCVI (1952), 175–187.

[70] CMCM, cod. 18, fols. 138ʳ–140ᵛ; published in *ABNRJ*, XXVIII, 228–230. In 1719 the Council was still unsatisfied that the new regulations were being strictly enforced and so ordered in its provisão of Feb. 16, 1719. OC/LR 1193, num. 16. The alvará of Oct. 5, 1715 was renewed by the carta régia of Feb. 25, 1734. *Anais da biblioteca e arquivo público do Pará*, VII (Pará, 1907), 241–242. For the elimination of restrictions on direct trade between Brazil and friendly nations, see the decree of June 11, 1808, *CLP*, V, 519–520.

[71] The following description is a composite based on many of the documents cited below. For a brief account of the procedures followed at the end of the century see Conde de Rezende to Luís Pinto de Sousa, Nov. 5, 1795, *RIHGB*, XXXII:1 (1869), 295–298.

to pick up an officer representing the captain. While the officer was being rowed across the bay to speak with the senior administrative officer (the governor, captain-general, or viceroy), the ship was directed to a temporary anchorage; failure to remain in the assigned space would be taken as an indication that the vessel was really a pirate and would bring the wrath of the fort's guns to bear upon her. If the administrative officer authorized the ship's entry, a harbor master from the fort went aboard and piloted her to a second anchorage. (In the case of ships plying the waters of Guanabara Bay, this was situated in front of the palace square and under the guns of the fort on Ilha das Cobras.) As the vessel approached her new anchorage, proclamations (*bandos*) were posted ashore forbidding colonials to communicate directly with the ship. To ensure that they observed that injunction and also to prevent members of the crew from slipping ashore undetected, guard boats appeared and rowed continuously around the newly arrived ship.[72]

Next a formal inquiry was made to determine why the ship had sought admission to port. This was undertaken before the captain or anyone else was allowed to come ashore, and usually before the captain's representative was permitted to return to his quarterdeck. The vessel was boarded, in response to a written directive (*portaria*) from the senior administrative officer, by a delegation of functionaries. Among them was a magistrate (in Rio de Janeiro a member of the Relação), his scribe, an interpreter, a senior officer from the local military garrison, a master shipbuilder, and in cases of reported scurvy or other maladies aboard, a physician. These officials examined the ship's papers and then proceeded to take oral testimony. The captain was first called forward, and through the interpreter the magistrate asked him a series of set questions: his name; that of his ship; her port of origin; her destination; the number of her crew and passengers; the nature of her cargo; and the circumstances that prompted his request to enter port. After he had replied, the captain was asked to step back and the same questions were put to various members of his crew. Then the delegation went ashore, but it was immediately replaced by half a dozen guards representing the alfândega, the intendant-general of gold, and various other departments; such guards remained aboard as long as the ship stayed in port. When the board of inquiry left the vessel it was usually accompanied by several crewmen who, in Lavradio's time, were taken to the audience room of the viceregal palace. There, in front of the viceroy, they were asked the

[72] Typical proclamations may be found in BNRJ 7-3-9, especially nums. 133, 143, 147, and 149. There is a good description of the so-called *rondas*, the circling guard boats, in Manoel da Cunha Menezes to Melo e Castro, July 19, 1775, BNRJ, I-4, 3, 16, n. 39.

same questions previously directed to their fellows aboard ship.

A day or two later the board of inquiry returned to the ship to deliver orally the senior administrator's decision. That decision, called the *sentença,* was based on analysis of the accumulated oral and written evidence and contained the board's conclusions as to whether the ship had really been in distress when she entered port. If not, the ship was presumed to be a smuggler; accordingly, the board formally notified the captain that he, his officers, and men would immediately be removed and imprisoned, and their ship and her cargo would be confiscated. Ultimately all would be sent to Portugal.[73] But if the ship was considered a legitimate *arribada,* that is, a vessel requiring urgent repairs, replenishment of her stores, or an opportunity for her sick to recover their health, the viceroy (or his equivalent) granted the captain's request and specified how long he would be allowed to remain in port, the number of days varying from three to as many as thirty depending upon the circumstances.[74]

After the sentença had been read aloud, it was signed by the captain and members of the board of inquiry. Then, if the captain's case seemed legitimate, he and his crew were permitted to go about their business, but they were warned to respect all the laws of Portugal, including those against smuggling, and to refrain from the use of firearms. With these injunctions the board withdrew.

If no untoward incidents occurred, the ship was able to leave port as soon as her personnel was aboard and all obligations, including port charges,[75] had been satisfied. Sometimes the date of departure approximated the day originally set in the sentença, but often the captain was forced to petition for permission to remain much longer than originally scheduled, either because of complications arising out of the problem of settling his accounts or because Portuguese ship-

[73] An exception was made in the case of Negro slaves who were sold by the treasury in Brazil after having been assessed at double the usual import duty. In the early eighteenth century confiscated goods could be sold at auction in the colony, the proceeds being remitted to the Royal Treasury. Overseas Council, resolution of Apr. 16, 1727, ANRJ, Col. 60, Liv. XXII, fols. 103^v–104^r. Later, however, the Crown ordered all seized cargoes sent to Lisbon.

[74] The allowance time reflected the estimates of members of the board. Thus, when the ship had been damaged, the master shipbuilder estimated how much time would be needed to effect necessary repairs; or when a substantial number of the crew was seriously ill, the physician guessed when they would be sufficiently recovered to put to sea again.

[75] Port charges included fees for pilotage, entrance and departure privileges, anchorage, the services of the harbor master, a "linguister," and the costs of maintaining the shipboard guards. At the end of the eighteenth century vessels entering Recife and Bahia paid initial charges amounting to 17,480 réis (£4, s18, 4d) and an additional 8,760 réis (£2, s9, 3-½d) for each day they remained in port. For unexplained reasons, these figures were considerably higher in Rio de Janeiro. Lindley, *Voyage to Brazil,* pp. 290–291. Captain Lindley considered these charges "enormous," but added "they must be paid."

wrights took longer to complete their work than had been originally estimated.[76] When the captain finally weighed anchor and headed to sea, his last responsibility was to drop the pilot at the entrance.[77] Then he set course for a distant port and bade Brazil farewell. Meantime, as his vessel was disappearing over the horizon, the senior administrative officer began drafting his report on the arribada to the Crown. When it was finished, he would attach to it the board of inquiry's report, the sentença, and all other pertinent documents.[78]

The Treatment of Unlicensed Foreign Ships: Some Case Histories

Foreigners found these procedures annoying, humiliating, and often very costly in time and money. Both contemporaries and modern historians have accused Portuguese colonial authorities of "incivility" in their treatment of foreign vessels, though in fact they were only carrying out the instructions of their government which had reason to suspect that most foreign vessels that "happened to be" in Brazilian waters were there deliberately for illicit trade. Nor should it be forgotten that other nations followed equally cautious procedures to guard against smuggling when unwanted foreign ships entered their colonial ports.[79]

But such considerations would scarcely have impressed ship's passengers like Mrs. Nathaniel Kindersley, an aristocratic English lady whose ship stopped at Salvador in the 1760s while en route to the Orient. Being of a curious nature, she sought to examine the city and its environs and was most annoyed when she was shadowed by soldiers wherever she went. However, what really aroused her ire was the fact that her request for permission to stay overnight with an English

---

[76] Secretary Francisco Xavier de Mendonça Furtado ordered Viceroy Cunha to see that the *mestre da ribeira* (the yard master) sent the poorest and slowest workmen aboard foreign vessels requiring repairs, so that their exasperated captains would think twice before putting in at a Brazilian port again! Dispatch of July 23, 1766, *RIHGB*, XXXIII:1, 244–246.

[77] Only then did the guard boat cease to accompany the ship. Beaglehole, ed., *Journals of James Cook*, I, 29.

[78] Typical of such reports are Lavradio to the king, May 24, 1769, CMCM, cod. 16 (*rascunho* apparently in the hand of the author), fols. 7^{r-v}; idem to Pombal, Mar. 30 and June 14, 1771, BNRJ, 10, 4, 8, nums. 161, 173; *idem to idem*, July 29, 1771, ANRJ, Col. 69, Liv. I-*bis*., fols. 50^{r-v}; *idem to idem*, Aug. 31, 1772 and July 27, 1773, BNRJ, 10, 4, 8 (unfoliated).

[79] For British procedures see note 28 above and Charles M. Andrews, *The Colonial Period of American History*, IV (Repr., New Haven, 1964), 246, 250–251; for a résumé of legislation concerning the treatment of arribadas in the Spanish colonies, see *Recopilación de leyes de los reynos de las Indias* (Fasc. ed., Madrid, 1791), Lib. IX, tít. 38, *passim*.

lady resident in the city was turned down by the acting captain-general on the ground that two English women under one roof was at least one too many! [80]

Mrs. Kindersley's indignation was mild compared with that of a fellow countryman, James Cook, who spent several weeks in Rio de Janeiro in 1768 while on the first of his series of historic Pacific voyages.[81] The celebrated navigator had elected to put into Guanabara Bay for water and stores, assuming that as the commander of a British warship he would be cordially received by Portuguese officials. His expectations were soon dashed, however, and he found himself involved in a hot and at times amusing verbal duel with Viceroy Azambuja.[82] The captain was affronted by the fact that guard boats circled the H. M. S. *Endeavour* as if she were bearing the plague, and protested the seemingly inhumane refusal of the viceroy to permit some of his seasick passengers to reside ashore while the ship remained in port. He disliked having to purchase his provisions through a *despachante*,[83] and was irritated to discover that his officers and men and even their commander were constantly followed when ashore. Cook stoutly denied the viceroy's contention that English sailors had to be watched to prevent them from smuggling, and complained that Azambuja had no reason to doubt the official character of his mission since he had displayed his commission. To this contention the viceroy calmly replied: "I believe you are a Gentleman of Honor and [are] incapable of deceiving me but as this is the first time I have [had] the fortune of seeing you & though the Documents be ever so sacred, . . . they are not Exempt from Contradiction[. T]his Consideration is enough for my doubt and by Consequence for my Cautions which experience in part shews me they are not without reason, because notwithstanding all care I am informed that always your People have Smugled some Goods." [84]

What was a proud lieutenant of the British Navy to do in the face of such insufferableness? He could actually do little more than fume

---

[80] Mrs. [Nathaniel Edward] Kindersley, *Letters from the Island of Teneriffe, Brazil, the Cape of Good Hope, and the East Indies* (London, 1777) , pp. 26–27.

[81] Beaglehole, ed., *Journals of James Cook*, I, cxxxviii–cxxxix, 22–29, covers Cook's stay in Rio de Janeiro (Nov. 13 to Dec. 7, 1768) .

[82] *Ibid.*, appendix I, 487–498.

[83] Anyone who has stayed long in Brazil comes to know and appreciate the services of the despachante who, among his other talents, "facilitates" the clearance of personal baggage through customs; Cook's despachante was an intermediary between the commander's storekeeper and local businessmen.

[84] Azambuja to Cook, Nov. 22, 1768, *ibid.*, I, 493. The editor in summarizing Cook's exasperating experiences in Rio de Janeiro (*ibid.*, cxxxvii–iii) displays some sympathy for the viceroy's position, but reveals his own ignorance of Azambuja's standing instructions when he terms him "ignorant," "stubborn," and "unrelenting" for his failure to behave more graciously toward the navigator.

in his journal and in his reports to the Secretary of the Admiralty.[85]
Cook paid his bills and went on his way. Though his later voyages
took him near the Brazilian coast, he carefully refrained from stopping at Brazilian ports again—precisely what Portuguese authorities
wanted.[86]

While the Marquis of Lavradio escaped any encounter with Captain Cook, he had more confrontations than he liked with Cook's
compatriots, a number of whom entered port in the early 1770s claiming to be legitimate arribadas. The record of those confrontations reveals the care with which he discharged his responsibilities toward
such intruders and how uncomfortable their lot sometimes became.

In the days of sail one could almost predict that a South Atlantic
tempest would be followed by the appearance of ships off Brazilian
ports seeking admission to recover from damage sustained during the
storm. One such vessel was the *Morse* which requested permission to
enter Rio de Janeiro on the last day of July 1770. Her captain, John
Horne, disclosed that his ship was out of Portsmouth bound for
Madras with a mixed cargo of merchandise, munitions, and passengers. After a stop at Madeira for refreshment the *Morse* ran into a
gale that broke her mainmast and ruined one of her large sails. After
Horne's statements had been verified, Lavradio drew up the sentença
giving the vessel fifteen days in which to complete necessary repairs.
But, said the viceroy, "at the end of that time he [the skipper] will
make sail immediately and [leave] this port without delay." [87] Provided, of course, that Mr. Horne had sufficient money to defray the
cost of such repairs.

Therein lay the rub, for the *Morse* evidently did not carry aboard
any cash or credit vouchers recognized in Rio de Janeiro. As a result
she was still in port nearly two months later, her captain vainly

[85] Cook to the admiralty secretary, Nov. 30, 1768, *ibid.*, 481–486. Testifying to the
effectiveness of Viceroy Azambuja's surveillance, Cook wrote: "I must not Omit
more fully to acquaint you that no one of my Boats was every permitted to pass
between Ship and the Shore without a Soldier being put in her, this practice I
was obliged to submit to [,] otherwise I could not have obtain'd the supply I
wanted. . . ." (p. 486). In a separate letter Cook expressed regret that members of
his scientific party, including Sir Joseph Banks, had been unable to make any
observations or collections in Brazil, since the viceroy would not allow them to go
ashore. Cook to the secretary of the Royal Society, Nov. 30, 1768, *ibid.*, 498–499.

[86] On his second expedition (1772–1775) Cook stopped for water and provisions
at Funchal (Madeira) and at the Cape Verdes while outbound and at the Azores
on his return. In each instance he received most of the stores that he wanted, but
the islands' governors refused to have any social intercourse with him. The only
Brazilian territory he approached on this voyage were the islands of Fernão de
Noronha which he visited in order to determine his longitude. Beaglehole, ed.,
Journals of Captain Cook, II, 21, 26–27, 668, 673–682.

[87] "Autos de exame feitos no navio Morse e preguntas feitas aos quatro inglezes
nele declarados," Aug. 1, 1770, CMCM, cod. 27, fols. 56ʳ–60ᵛ, which includes both
the shipboard and the shore inquiries and the viceroy's sentença.

pleading with the viceroy to persuade local merchants to accept drafts against the credit of the East India Company. Dom Luís supported his merchants' refusal to honor bills against the Company on the ground that they were merely complying with the terms of the alvará of 1715. Horne professed to doubt that the law had ever been previously enforced, and gratuitously suggested that "a Man cannot be too cautious how he Establishes a Precedent that may hurt his reputation by being attended with future ill consequences." Then he resorted to flattery: "I am persuaded a Nobleman enducd with the nice sentiments of Honour, so conspicuous in the Marquis of Lavaradio [sic] would hold in the utmost contempt a person who did not discharge to the best of his knowledge and ability what appeard to him to be a duty to his sovereign, as a good and faithful subject; and to his Employers an honest and trustworthy servant. . . ." [88] With that Horne requested permission to unload some copper belonging to John Company and some steel from his private stores, and proposed that their value be determined by local merchants so that he could settle his obligations and be on his way. For reasons not clear the viceroy decided by way of "a special grace" to allow the captain to do as he suggested.[89] And sometime late in October the *Morse* left for India.

A few weeks before the *Morse's* arrival another India-bound British vessel, the *True Briton,* put in at Rio de Janeiro.[90] Her captain, John Broadley, required fresh water and provisions to continue his voyage, but he was evidently apprehensive about the red tape he was likely to encounter there. Consequently, before going to pay his respects to the viceroy, Broadley hastily wrote a note to an unknown compatriot ashore:

Sir. Though I have not the Happiness of a personal acquaintance with you, yet as I know you to be the Person who conducts the Affairs for the English here, makes me take the Liberty of adressing you as I am now come in just to get refreshment for my People [. S]hould be glad to conect with no Detensions, if convenient I should be happy to see you on board tomorrow Morning[. I]f not[,] intend being on shore about 9 or 10 oclock to pay my compliments to the Viceroy, but shall expect not to be detained in the Manner my officer was yesterday, the Reason of my Writing to see [to] hear from you before I come on shore is that I would be glad

[88] Horne to Lavradio, Oct. 7, 1770, *ibid.,* fol. 63ʳ (English original) and fols. 71ʳ–72ʳ (signed copy in French). The same codex contains a number of earlier exchanges between the captain and the viceroy.

[89] Lavradio to Horne, Oct. 8, 1770, ANRJ, Col. 70, Liv. V, fols. 99ʳ⁻ᵛ. The legal justification for Lavradio's decision in this instance is not apparent from his letter, nor from any of the pertinent legislation that I have examined.

[90] "Auto de exame feito no navio inglez denominado True Britin e auto de proguntas aos tres inglezes . . . ," July 13–14, 1770, CMCM, cod. 27, fols. 126ʳ–130ᵛ, which also contains the sentença.

of your information in conducting myself here [. I]t is always my earnest desire to do everything that is proper without deragaling from the Honour of the English Nation; shall be extremely happy, either to see you or to hear from you. . . .

The more Broadley thought about it, the more anxious he became to speak with his correspondent as soon as possible. Therefore, he added a postscript: "I shall be extremely happy to see you if possible before I come on shore[. A]ny hour . . . wel make no defference[. Y]our hour shall be mine—." [91]

One would very much like to know the name of "the Person who conducts the Affairs for the English here," for despite the provisions of the Anglo-Portuguese Treaty of 1661, Great Britain did not maintain consuls in Brazilian ports at this time; nor did any other government.[92] Whether Broadley's letter actually reached its intended destination is doubtful, for the original ended up among the viceroy's personal papers, having presumably been intercepted by Portuguese guards. In any case, Broadley soon needed a friend, for two days after the viceroy had granted him permission to obtain refreshments, Dom Luís peremptorily ordered him to leave port within twenty-four hours when one of the *True Briton's* boats was seized while attempting to run forbidden merchandise ashore.[93] Somehow the captain was able to mollify the viceroy, for a week later we find him still at anchor, asking that Lavradio designate some merchants who would be willing to accept bills of credit on the East India Company, since he had

---

[91] Broadley to [?], July 13, 1770, *ibid.*, fol. 99ʳ (original in hand of the writer).

[92] About 1802 Thomas Lindley observed "Unfortunately for our commerce, no consuls, residents, or even British merchants are to be met with in the whole coast of Brazil." *Narrative of a Voyage*, p. 291. Though he was in error with respect to the absence of British residents, he was correct in his statement concerning the lack of consuls. According to article 14 of the Anglo-Portuguese treaty of 1661, four English families were permitted to reside in Brazil's principal ports (George Chalmers, *Collection of Treaties between Great Britain and Other Powers*, II [London, 1790], 286–296, at 292), but while Miss Wallis Chapman assures us that this was "a privilege which English factors afterwards declared to be of great importance" (A. B. Wallis Chapman, "The Commercial Relations of England and Portugal, 1487–1807," Royal Historical Society, *Transactions*, 3d. ser., I [1907], 167), that privilege was actually seldom exercised. There is evidence that the French government named a consul at Bahia in 1714 to assist distressed French ships entering that port, and that four years later there were four authorized English families in the same city (Rau and Gomes, *Manuscritos de Cadaval*, II, 122, 199). For some reason neither the French nor the British government continued to employ representatives at these ports. There do not seem to have been English families resident in Rio de Janeiro in Lavradio's time, although Cook refers to a certain "Capⁿ Foster an English Officer in the Portuguese Service & a Man of Honour (who hath Interested himself a good Deal in our behalf) . . . ." (Cook to the Admiralty, Nov. 30, 1768, Beaglehole, ed., *Journals of James Cook*, I, 486). It may have been Foster to whom Broadley addressed his letter, although Cook states that Foster had been imprisoned by the viceroy "for having Interested himself in our behalf." *Ibid.*, I, 486–487. No indication of his fate has appeared.

[93] Lavradio to Broadley, July 16, 1770, ANRJ, Col. 70, Liv. V, fols. 64ʳ⁻ᵛ.

found his "expenses here much more than I at first expected," and lacked sterling to defray them.[94] In view of Lavradio's already noted response to a similar proposal made a few weeks later by John Horne, it seems improbable that he approved Broadley's request. Nevertheless Broadley managed to leave port about August 1, 1770. He was fortunate to get away, considering his involvement in the case of another countryman who had just had his ship seized by the viceroy.

As the sun rose on July 19, 1770, the brig *Argyle* appeared off Fort Santa Cruz and signaled for permission to enter port.[95] She was directed to lay to, and that evening her captain, William Robertson, was rowed across the harbor to have an audience with the viceroy. According to Robertson, he had been chartered by Captain John Hasell (or Hassel), skipper of the ship *Duke of Portland*, a vessel belonging to the East India Company, to carry a cargo of iron, steel, and copper plate and bales of woolen and cotton textiles valued at £30,000 from London to the Cape Verdes. He left the Downs early in April and after a quick run reached the insular port of Santiago in the middle of May. There he was joined by the *Duke of Portland*, outbound for India. Apparently the market was poor, and since Robertson still had plenty of provisions left, he agreed to Hasell's proposal that he proceed to Jamaica to try to dispose of the rest of his cargo there. The two vessels separated early in June, the *Duke of Portland* heading for Bombay. On July 12, however, Captain Hasell showed up at Rio de Janeiro and succeeded in gaining admission to permit his passengers and crew to recover from an epidemic of scurvy and to obtain fresh water.[96] Curiously enough, the *Argyle* reached the same port a week later.[97] Was Rio de Janeiro the intended rendezvous of the two ships? The viceroy wondered.

The more Dom Luís listened to Robertson's tale concerning the adverse winds he had encountered since leaving Santiago, the more suspicious he became. He declined to allow the *Argyle* to come in, but did agree to permit her captain to visit with Captain Broadley, then about to resume his voyage to India, in order to obtain fresh provisions from the *True Briton*. For the next two days the two English skippers conferred aboard the *True Briton*, but that ship was

[94] Broadley to Lavradio, July 22, 1770, CMCM, cod. 27, fols. 100ʳ and 109ʳ (two texts, one in Portuguese by an unknown hand, one in English by Broadley).

[95] Except as noted, the following two paragraphs have been reconstructed on the basis of Lavradio to Broadley, July 29, 1770, ANRJ, Col. 70, Liv. V, fols. 96ʳ–98ᵛ.

[96] "Auto de exame feito no navio inglez denominado Duc de Portland . . . ," July 16, 1770, and sentença of July 17, 1770, CMCM, cod. 27, fols. 120ʳ–125ʳ.

[97] Whether the *Duke of Portland* was still in port at this time is unclear. Captain Hasell requested an extension of the four days originally granted him to repair his masts and to load casks (Hasell to Lavradio, n.d., *ibid.*, fols. 76ʳ⁻ᵛ [orig.]), but Lavradio's response has not been found; nor has any further reference to the ship been discovered.

seemingly in no haste to sail and dispatched few supplies to the *Argyle*. Meantime, the viceroy had turned down a written request from Robertson to enter port.[98] But after the captain persisted in his appeals, swearing that if the marquis would not allow him to sail in, he would be obliged to put into some other Brazilian harbor to supply his urgent needs, Dom Luís finally relented.

On July 23, the *Argyle* was escorted to the usual anchorage under the guns of the Ilha das Cobras, and a board of inquiry began its customary investigation. When the ship's deponents gave conflicting accounts of the vessel's intended destination after leaving the islands, Lavradio became convinced that she had deliberately sailed for Rio de Janeiro and that her captain was, in fact, a smuggler. Accordingly, on July 27 a magistrate read the viceroy's sentence to the brig's officers and men: since the *Argyle* was an apparent smuggler, she and her cargo would be immediately confiscated and her officers and men imprisoned until their punishment had been determined by the Relação.[99]

News of this drastic action must have caused consternation among other British ships then in port. The *True Briton's* captain immediately implored the viceroy to reconsider, arguing that in the past ships belonging to the East India Company had always been well treated when they found it necessary to enter American ports. The viceroy replied that if he were an English subject, he might be persuaded by the force of Broadley's arguments, but since he had the good fortune to be a Portuguese citizen and a vassal of His Most Faithful Majesty, he was obligated to enforce his master's laws, including those against the admission of foreign ships that had no legitimate reason to enter colonial ports.[100] He did, however, consent to allow the *Argyle's* crew to leave port aboard the *Morse*. When Broadley sent another note asking to see the viceroy personally about the fate of the captain and his ship. Dom Luís indicated that the matter was closed and that the *True Briton* had better get under way before he had second thoughts about the conduct of *her* captain.[101]

A few days later Will Robertson again wrote the viceroy acknowledging the latter's decision and requesting a certified copy of his written agreement with Captain Hasell "in order for my providing against him by Law When I get to London. . . ," [102] but Robertson

98 Lavradio to [Robertson], July 22, 1770 (in French, apparently in the hand of the author), *ibid.*, fols. 110ʳ⁻ᵛ.

99 "Autos de exame feito na embarcaçam igleza [sic] denominada Argile e a sentença proferida nelles," July 24–27, 1770, *ibid.*, fols. 49ʳ–52ᵛ.

100 See note 95.

101 Lavradio to "Capitão do Navio Inglez" [certainly Broadley], July 30 [?], 1770, ANRJ, Col. 70, Liv. V, fols. 95ʳ–96ʳ.

102 Will[iam] Robertson to Lavradio, Sept. 5, 1770, CMCM, cod. 27, fol. 101ʳ.

was not destined to see the Thames again for many a moon. After what must have been a long and uncomfortable winter, he and his ship's master were removed from the prison on Snakes' Island and were transported to Lisbon aboard the frigate *N. S. do Belém*.[103] There they experienced additional months of confinement in various prisons around the Portuguese capital. In May, 1772, the resident British minister, Robert Walpole, was still seeking their release and recovery of the *Argyle*.[104]

The protracted negotiations between London and Lisbon over the disposition of the *Argyle* continued for another year and a half. Finally Secretary Melo e Castro agreed to return the vessel, but insisted that Viceroy Lavradio had acted properly in seizing her.[105] Another year passed and in October 1774 the brig, by then very much the worse for her long exposure to the destructive elements of the tropics, reached Lisbon.[106] Presumably by then Will Robertson's "unhappy and unfortunate affair" was at an end.

The *Argyle* case illustrates the trouble that an unchartered foreign skipper could get into in a Brazilian port if he entered without any clear evidence of his ship's or passengers' distress and if he lacked familiarity with the Portuguese inspection procedures. It was a matter of prudence to see that one's crew carefully rehearsed their lines before exposing them to the questioning of the authorities. Nothing irritated those worthies more than a display of British arrogance, while literal compliance with the regulations pleased them immensely. For example, the Marquis of Lavradio spoke highly of Robert Preston, captain of the *Asia,* who ventured into Guanabara Bay in mid-1771 and not only saw to it that his crew refrained from offending their hosts but in conversation with the viceroy criticized the "imprudence and rashness" of Will Robertson and predicted that he would not be welcomed when he returned to England.[107]

While British and French sailors had long been accustomed to being viewed with suspicion by Portuguese port authorities, that was a new experience for Yankee mariners who first began sailing into the South Atlantic in search of sperm whales in the 1770s. One of the first to explore the grounds off Brazil was the *Leviathan*, a brig owned by

---

[103] Lavradio to Melo e Castro, Dec. 22, 1770, BNRJ, 10, 4, 8 (unfoliated).

[104] Walpole to [Weymouth?], May 26, 1772, *QE*, XVIII, 387–388.

[105] Melo e Castro to Lavradio, Nov. 8, 1773, BNRJ, I-2, 4, 6, n. 39, enclosing *idem* to [Walpole], *ca.* Nov. 1773, *ibid.,* nums. 40–41.

[106] Melo e Castro to Lavradio, Oct. 11, 1774, ANRJ, Col. 67, Liv. III-A, fol. 12ʳ (orig.), acknowledging the arrival of the *Argyle* after a voyage of 110 days. Earlier the viceroy reported that because of spoilage, it had been necessary to destroy part of the brig's cargo, and that before going to sea again, she needed extensive repairs. Lavradio to Melo e Castro, July 31, 1773, BNRJ, 10, 4, 8 (unfoliated).

[107] Lavradio to Pombal, May 10, 1771, *loc. cit.*

a Portuguese Jew, Aaron Lopez, merchant prince of Newport, Rhode Island. After exploring the neglected sperm grounds off southern Bahia in the middle of 1773, her skipper, Thomas Lothrop, headed for Rio de Janeiro to repair his leaky seams and to obtain fresh stores. Missing the harbor's entrance, Lothrop sent a boat ashore to get his bearings, but her crew was apprehended by Brazilian coast watchers. Soon after, the brig was riding at anchor off Snakes' Island and her crew was confined to the gaol on the same island.

Although Lothrop and his men denied any intent to engage in clandestine trade, the viceroy became convinced that their suspicious behavior outside Guanabara Bay resembled that of smugglers and he refused to set the captain and his men at liberty or to release their ship. But after learning that they had been fishing for sperm, a type of whale that the Portuguese had never learned to catch in deep waters, Dom Luís, ever alert to the possibility of exploiting a neglected natural resource, offered the Yankees temporary liberty and compensation if they would teach the personnel of the local whale factory their techniques for catching sperm. They did so, and during a short cruise off Santa Catarina Island late in 1773 they took six whales. The New Englanders repeated their success on two additional voyages north of the capital during the following year. But on instructions from the colonial secretary, the viceroy still refused to grant the Yankee seahunters their release. Late in 1775 Captain Lothrop and his mate succumbed to smallpox in Rio de Janeiro, and when we last glimpse the *Leviathan's* survivors a year later, two of them were writing a rather pathetic appeal to the viceroy seeking to be allowed to return home via England.[108]

Conclusion

As long as the restrictions on direct foreign trade with the Portuguese colonies persisted, the duel between the smuggler and royal officials continued, each seeking to outwit the other. Whenever the Crown devised new means for checking the activities of the illicit trader, the latter sought new ways of circumventing them. In 1795 the

[108] The preceding two paragraphs are based on sources cited in my "The Coming of Yankee Sperm Whalers to Brazilian Waters and the Decline of the Portuguese Whale Fishery (1773–1808)," *The Americas*, XX (Jan. 1964), 267–288. The *Leviathan* was not the only New England whaler to run afoul of Portuguese colonial authorities during the 1770s. In 1776 the *Rody*, another Rhode Island vessel, entered Bahia on her return from the Falkland grounds. Her captain sought to make some repairs there but lacked the cash to pay for them and was obliged to ship part of his cargo to Lisbon to acquire the necessary exchange. Manoel da Cunha Menezes to Melo e Castro, May 29 and June 27, 1776, BNRJ, I-4, 3, 6, nums. 76 and 81.

Conde de Rezende, one of Lavradio's notable successors, reported that he was continually plagued by British ships entering port on one pretext or another. Their captains always sought exemptions from compliance with the queen's regulations and displayed disrespect for authorities charged with their enforcement; the behavior of their crews was a source of constant headache to Portuguese officials. Shore parties tried to elude their shadows by suddenly separating after turning a street corner, leading their guards a merry chase. And to evade the necessity of reporting to the watch boat to pick up the required sentinel, the smuggler dispatched two boats at the same time on different courses, so that the boat officer knew not which one he should attempt to follow. To prevent unauthorized landings, the viceroy reported that he was employing seven boats to patrol the entire waterfront.[109]

But neither he nor the Crown could afford to be too sanguine about the effectiveness of such measures to deter the smuggler, for there were always officials and citizens willing to cooperate with the illicit trader whose goods were, after all, cheaper than those obtainable through legal channels. As the colonial secretary himself candidly admitted, it was impossible to prevent smuggling entirely. All that could be done was to make it as risky and expensive as possible in the hope that a majority of the contrabandists would become discouraged and abandon their profession.[110] But despite all the laws and machinery of surveillance that the Portuguese, like the British and the Spanish, adopted, the penchant to smuggle persisted.[111]

[109] See note 71 above.

[110] Melo e Castro to [Vasconcelos], Jan. 5, 1785, *RIHGB*, X, 220.

[111] During the Joanine period, for example, connivance between British merchants and Portuguese customs officers is said to have deprived the Crown of half of its import revenues. Manoel de Oliveira Lima, *Dom João VI no Brasil*, II, 773, 795.

PART FOUR

The Viceroy as Administrator

XV

Relations with Municipal, Judicial, Ecclesiastical, and Provincial Officials

> In his long viceregency of ten and a half years, the Marquis of Lavradio
> . . . dedicated himself with the greatest zeal and intelligence to all
> branches of the administration.
>
> Francisco Adolfo de Varnhagen, *Historia geral do Brasil,* IV, 251.

ALTHOUGH the military, fiscal, and economic matters considered in earlier chapters claimed much of the Marquis of Lavradio's time and energies, routine administrative tasks also required his attention, for the viceroy was charged with the supervision of all branches of government within the lands entrusted to his care.[1] This chapter will focus upon his role as director of the activities of municipal corporations (câmaras), magistrates (juizes de fóra and ouvidores), the High Court, the Church, and the commanders (mestres de campo) of militia regiments that policed the countryside. The viceroy's relations with subordinate governors and with quasi-autonomous captains-general who administered other parts of Brazil will be reserved for analysis in the following chapter.

Oddly enough, neither the regimento defining the duties of his office nor the lengthy briefing instructions Dom Luís received before coming to Rio de Janeiro specified particular guidelines for him to follow in his relations with the various branches of his government.[2] Evidently it was assumed that he would adhere to long-established policies—guarding the royal prerogative, enforcing the laws of the realm, reconciling disputes among officials and between them and the colonists, and preventing any unauthorized innovations in government, the economy, or social organization. Such, at least, appear to have been the viceroy's aims.

---

[1] With one exception; as already mentioned, the office of intendant general of gold in Rio de Janeiro was technically independent of the viceroy, although its head sometimes worked closely with him.

[2] 2RGG, *passim;* Lavradio's initial instructions are cited in Chap. V, n. 1.

The Viceroy's Relations with the Câmaras

One group whose activities the viceroy watched over were the municipal councils (câmaras) which occupied the lowest level of colonial government. Every town (vila) and city (cidade) and its hinterland (termo) was administered by such a body which included both voting and nonvoting members. The voting members, whose number varied from five to ten depending upon time and place, included one or two presiding officers (juizes ordinário; later in some cities a single juiz de fóra), several aldermen (vereadores), a procurator (procurador), a secretary (escrivão), and sometimes one or two additional officers, such as a market inspector (almotacél) and a treasurer (tesoureiro). Except for the secretary, who did not always have a right to vote in the council's deliberations but who often served for long periods, sometimes as a proprietor, these officials held office for one year and could not immediately succeed themselves. Prior to the late seventeenth century they were selected by local worthies (homens bons) through a curiously involved process of balloting designed to prevent câmaras from being dominated by members of the same family or occupational group. Nonvoting municipal functionaries included a porter (porteiro), standard-bearer (alferes), accountant (contador), and an inspector of public works (veador de obras), but in smaller communities the duties of one or more of these officials were combined.

The câmaras were concerned with a variety of municipal activities. They enacted regulations for the good government of their districts. They licensed business to operate there and collected rents on municipal properties. They fixed prices of basic commodities and levied taxes to defray their expenses and some of those of the Crown. They were supposed to provide basic public services, such as potable water and sanitation. They arranged royal and local festivals and received with appropriate ceremony their administrative superiors.[3]

As will be shown shortly, councils in the larger municipalities were relieved of some of these duties in the eighteenth century. During the turbulent seventeenth century when the Portuguese empire experi-

---

[3] No satisfactory study of municipal government in colonial Brazil exists. The best available are Edmundo Zenha, *O municipio no Brasil, 1532–1700* (São Paulo, 1948); Affonso Rui, *Historia da câmara municipal da cidade do Salvador* (Salvador, 1953); and the chapter on the same council in Charles R. Boxer, *Portuguese Society in the Tropics. The Municipal Councils of Goa, Macao, Bahia, and Luanda, 1510–1800* (Madison, 1965), which is stronger on the seventeenth century (for which the published records are much fuller) than on the eighteenth. Concerning election procedures before the 1680s, see *ibid.*, pp. 5–7.

enced serious stresses [4] and the new Braganzan dynasty (1640f.) was consolidating its position, the Crown relied upon the câmaras—in the absence of colonial assemblies—to check the activities of over-zealous colonial officials and to bear the onus of popular displeasure by devising new taxes to meet its expenses in Brazil and elsewhere.[5] The câmaras responded to their opportunities by arrogating many privileges and powers to which they had dubious right. While posing as champions of the people, they repeatedly ousted unpopular missionaries and royal officials, and sometimes even lectured royal governors on their duties.[6]

The Crown tolerated such behavior until the last years of that century, when consolidation of the monarchy and new sources of revenue derived directly and indirectly from Brazilian mines made it possible to impose effective checks on these municipal bodies. One such check involved a change in election procedures that eliminated popular balloting and gave high royal authorities the right to select new councilmen from among those nominated for municipal posts. In 1696, eight years after the new policy had been introduced at Goa in the Estado da Índia, the governor-general of Brazil and the High Court of Bahia were given joint responsibility for the naming of voting members of the câmara of Salvador.[7] It seems probable that during the next several decades royal governors in other parts of the colony, notably Pará, Maranhão, Pernambuco, and Rio de Janeiro, were also empowered to select aldermen of their leading câmaras, but the details of how and when such changes were made there remain to be discovered.

Two other measures initiated in the 1690s also affected the autonomy of the câmaras. One was an increase in the number of circuit magistrates (ouvidores) assigned to each captaincy, where their duties included general oversight of the councils' activities.[8] More direct ob-

---

[4] Notably Portugal's conflicts with the Netherlands, Spain, and Cromwellian England, and her temporary loss of colonies in West Africa and the end of Portuguese hegemony in the Far East.

[5] See pp. 304–307, above.

[6] The câmaras expelled the unpopular Jesuits from São Paulo and Santos (1640–1651), the hated Sá dynasty from Rio de Janeiro (1660), the governor of Pernambuco in 1666, and removed circuit judges (ouvidores) from Espírito Santo (1659), Itamaracá (1664), and Itanhaém (1670). For evidence of the câmaras' exercise of unauthorized prerogatives, Charles R. Boxer, *Salvador de Sá and the Struggle for Brazil and Angola,* p. 34, n. 56. In 1664 the Crown found it necessary to remind the corporations that they were still subordinate to the governors-general. Carta régia, Apr. 12, 1664, *DH,* LXIV, 357–359.

[7] Boxer, *Portuguese Society in the Tropics,* pp. 16, 74; carta régia, Nov. 22, 1696, *DH,* XXXII (1936), 411, which reversed a carta régia of Feb. 26, 1671 (*RADF,* II, 168), which had ordered royal officials to refrain from interfering in municipal elections. Cf. Rui, pp. 189–191.

[8] The usual pretext for the multiplication of ouvidores and for the introduction of juizes de fóra was the need to render justice more effective, prompt, and less

servation became possible with the appointment of the first of a new type of judge, the juiz de fóra, a university-trained, generally Peninsular-born lawyer, to preside over the more important câmaras such as those of Salvador, Olinda, and Rio de Janeiro in place of local justices of the peace (juizes ordinários).[9] In the 1720s the latter two of these councils witnessed a further reduction in their authority when the Crown transferred responsibility for the leasing of their most lucrative tax contracts from the câmaras to the royal treasurers.[10] Three decades later Brazil's four major câmaras lost control over the fixing of the prices of sugar, tobacco, and certain other commodities when that function was assigned to the newly created boards of inspection (mesas da inspeção).[11] The effect of these innovations was to lessen the significance and independence of the colony's principal municipal councils.

Although Dom Luís was in closest touch with the câmara of the city of Rio de Janeiro, he corresponded with municipal councils in other parts of the captaincy of Rio de Janeiro and in its dependencies. Much of that correspondence was purely informational in character: notifications of the existence of a state of war or peace affecting the mother country; news concerning members of the royal family; texts of new laws and decrees received from Lisbon; notices of the appointment of a new governor to one of the subcaptaincies with a reminder to the câmara of its capital to make suitable arrangements for his installation and to prepare to take the customary oath of allegiance to him.[12]

Some matters affecting the municipalities required action by the viceroy or by superior authority. An instance of the latter occurred in 1770 when the aldermen of Viamão (since 1763 the capital of Rio Grande de São Pedro) requested that their community be accorded the privileges of the city of Pôrto. That honor had thus far been conferred on only five Brazilian cities. Since the marquis had no power to grant such privileges, he merely referred the petition to the Overseas Council.[13] But he intervened personally after another council de-

---

expensive for the colonists. E.g., Overseas Council, consulta of Oct. 23, 1698, Castro e Almeida, *Inventário*, VI, 238. The general responsibilities of the ouvidores are described in the following section.

[9] The juizes de fóra were new to Brazil, but they had long existed in Portugal. See n. 36 below. On their introduction to Brazil see Sebastião da Rocha Pitta, *Historia da America Portuguesa* (Bahia, 1950), p. 303, and Zenha, *O municipio*, p. 83.

[10] See above, pp. 309–310.

[11] See Chap. I, n. 33.

[12] E.g., Lavradio, general circular of May 22, 1771, ANRJ, Col. 70, Liv. V, fol. 192ʳ; *idem* circular of May 13, 1771, *ibid.*, fol. 200ᵛ; *idem*, circular of May 29, 1777, CMCM, cod. 25, fols. 187ʳ⁻ᵛ; *idem* to câmara of Desterro (Santa Catarina), Aug. 19, 1775, *ibid.*, fol. 40ᵛ.

[13] Lavradio to Overseas Council, Oct. 9, 1770, BNRJ, 10, 4, 8, n. 119. The five cities were Rio de Janeiro, Salvador, Recife, São Luís do Maranhão and Belém.

clined to award a tax contract to a local bidder on the ground that he was not a respectable person and that his bondsmen (*fiadores*) were not men of substance. Dom Luís disapproved of their decision; the bidder and his backers might be poor but at least they were honest, and he insisted that the contract be confirmed. When the câmara refused to comply, he ordered its president to appear before him, and that seems to have ended its opposition.[14]

In remote parts of Brazil it was often difficult to recruit men to accept public offices for which the perquisites were insufficient compensation for the duties involved. That seems to have been the case in Desterro (Santa Catarina), where the câmara reported to the governor that it was unable to find men to serve in the "offices of the republic" since those eligible were enrolled in the militia and were therefore exempt from such responsibilities. The governor referred the problem to the viceroy who replied that there was no legal impediment preventing militia officers from holding public office and that they did so in Rio de Janeiro.[15]

The following year the same câmara presented a very interesting petition to the viceroy. Fr. José Antônio de Aguilar, a Dominican friar attached to the Province of Buenos Aires, had stopped at Santa Catarina while in transit to the Azores to visit relatives. Because of the shortage of priests on the island, the aldermen requested the viceroy's permission to allow the friar to remain there. Far from acceding to their request, Lavradio sternly rebuked the city fathers for even suggesting such a proposal since, he said, the king had expressly forbidden any member of the Dominican Order (one closely identified with Spain) to reside in his dominions. The câmara would henceforth "first reflect on matters which you have to present to me before doing so, so that only such as are worthy of consideration will come to my attention." [16]

For the rights conferred by these privileges, see Zenha, *O município*, pp. 98–103, and Boxer, *Portuguese Society in the Tropics*, index, s.v. "Oporto, municipal privileges of."

14 Lavradio to câmara of Santo Antônio de Sá (Rio de Janeiro), May 8 and 15, July 9 and 22, and Aug. 5, 1776, CMCM, cod. 25, fols. 99ᵛ, 102ʳ, 115ʳ, 122ᵛ–123ʳ, and 125ᵛ.

15 Lavradio to Pedro Antônio da Gama e Freitas, Nov. 28, 1775, CMCM, cod. 4, fols. 79ᵛ–80ʳ. The viceroy's recommendation appears to fly in the face of a decree of Mar. 22, 1751 by which regular and militia troops were specifically exempted from all "os empregos civís e carregos da Republica" because of various inconveniences that had arisen when they occupied both military and civil positions. *CCLE*, VI, 10.

16 Lavradio to câmara, Feb. 28, 1776, CMCM, cod. 28, fols. 87ᵛ–88ʳ. Upon another occasion when the juiz ordinário of the vila of Santa Antônio de Sá questioned one of Lavradio's orders to a townsman, the viceroy answered hotly that "as minhas determinaçoens se devem executar com a mais prompta, e cega obediencia. [S]ou . . . a dizerlhe se abstenha de entrar em semilhantes duvidas e fique advertido, de que deve ser mais comedido, uzando nas cartas respeito, com

While the viceroy encouraged communications on subjects of legitimate concern to the colony's inhabitants, he became incredibly disturbed when the citizens of Viamão expressed their uneasiness over
the military situation in Rio Grande in a petition addressed to the
acting governor of that subcaptaincy. When their petition reached
Dom Luís, he flew into a rage. Labeling the petitioners as "rebels and
disturbers of the public peace" and accusing them of being guilty of
the crime of conspiracy for daring to act in concert, he rebuked the
governor for having consorted with the citizens, thus encouraging
their abuse of familiarity, and ordered the five persons whose names
headed the petition sent to Rio de Janeiro as prisoners so that they
could receive exemplary punishment. Later the viceroy cooled off,
and on the birthday of the royal prince he pardoned the petitioners;
but at the same time he directed the acting governor to maintain all
possible vigilance to prevent a similar situation from arising again.[17]
Thus spoke the ever-cautious autocrat when confronted with the
prospect of unauthorized popular collective action.

There was little opportunity for a similar situation to develop in
viceregal Rio de Janeiro where the câmara of the 1770s appears to
have been fully subservient to the will of Dom Luís de Almeida. The
days when that corporation could defy or even depose an unfriendly
governor with relative impunity were long since past, and the prospect of another incident like the removal of the fiery Luís Vaía Monteiro in 1732 was remote forty years later.[18]

The marquis was not pleased by the performance of the câmara
when he arrived in the capital. He contended that it had become customary for well-born but impoverished men to gain council seats
which they used primarily for private gain rather than to attend to
the needs of the municipality. As a consequence, the city's property
did not yield as much as it should and many essential services had
long been neglected. To remedy this situation, he asserted that the
vereadores he selected were respectable merchants and planters who

---

que deve falar aos Senhores Vice Reys deste Estado." To Manoel José da Costa
Barreiros, Mar. 17, 1775, CMCM, cod. 25, fols. 10r-v.

[17] Lavradio to Antônio da Veyga de Andrade, May 22 and Aug. 22, 1772, ibid.,
cod. 15, fols. 122r-123v, 130v.

[18] The energetic, controversial Vaía Monteiro, governor of Rio de Janeiro 1725–
1732, has never found a biographer despite the relative abundance of documentary
materials and the significant controversies in which he became involved, notably
with the Benedictines (over ownership of the Ilha das Cobras), with the territorial magnates (over enforcement of various laws), and with the câmara of the
capital (over the control of finances and respect for the office of governor). Ultimately the câmara took advantage of his indisposition to depose him in 1732 and
he died in Rio de Janeiro the following year. For extracts from his correspondence,
see Eduardo Marques Peixoto, comp., "Luiz Vahia Monteiro, Governador da
Capitania do Rio de Janeiro . . . e a sua administração (apontamentos)," RIHGB,
Tomo especial, Pt. 3 (Rio de Janeiro, 1916), 597–660.

had the public interest at heart [19] and, he might have added, men who were amenable to his advice.

In a recent study of selected Portuguese colonial câmaras, Professor Charles R. Boxer has suggested that they were not self-perpetuating oligarchies like those which dominated some of the cabildos of Spanish America. That contention, while interesting and perhaps even plausible, is not conclusively proved.[20] An examination of the membership of the Carioca council between 1769 and 1779 does reveal that of the thirty-seven men who served as aldermen during these years, only four sat in the câmara more than one term.[21] But before we could be certain that the thirty-seven were not members of a small white elite group of planters and merchants that traditionally furnished the candidates from which the viceroys and captains-general made their selections of councilmen, we would need to know a good deal more about these men than we do. As the investigator scrutinizes the lists of the vereadores in attendance when the ouvidor conducted his annual investigation of the câmara, he wonders whether Ignacio de Foneca Lima (alderman in 1774) was related to João Antunes de Araujo Lima (1775), or to Pedro Correya Lima (1777). Was Joaquim da Silva Lisbôa (1771) a relative of Francisco Perniz Lisbôa (1772)? Or did Claudio José Pereyra da Silva (1774) belong to the same family as Manuel Rodrigues Silva (also 1774) or João Muniz Silva (1778)? In the absence of appropriate genealogical evidence, we cannot supply the answers to these questions, nor can we determine from available sources the social and economic relationships of the thirty-seven.

It is apparent from the surviving fragments of the viceroy's correspondence with the Carioca council that he took a paternal interest in its proceedings, often lecturing the câmara on measures he considered necessary or desirable. But Dom Luís was careful to allow the aldermen to save face by carrying out his recommendations in the name of the council.[22] In one instance he criticized the council for

---

19 See note 22 below. Governors-general and viceroys frequently complained about the failure of the impoverished câmaras of their capitals to repair roads, jails, fountains, and other municipal facilities, but failed to suggest where they could find money for such projects, E.g., DH, LXXXVII (1950), 31, 85, 122, 138, 148, 153, and 210.

20 Portuguese Society in the Tropics, p. 77. Professor Boxer's contention would have been news to many Salvadoreans. For an important contemporary criticism of election methods in Bahia's capital, see João Rodrigues de Brito et al., Cartas econômico-políticas sobre a agricultura e commércio da Bahia (1821) (Fasc. ed., Bahia, 1924), pp. 55–56.

21 Pedro Correyra Lima in 1769 and 1777; Antônio José Coelho (a prominent merchant) in 1771 and in 1775; Francisco de Araujo Pereyra in 1773 and in 1779; and João da Costa Pinheyro in 1773 and again in 1777. Prefeitura do Districto Federal. Publicações do Districto Federal. Autos de correições dos ouvidores do Rio de Janeiro, 1748–1820, Eduardo Tourinho, ed., I (Rio de Janeiro, 1931), [49]–63.

22 Lavradio, Relatório, pp. 448–450, 455. The annual inspections (correições) of the Carioca câmara in Lavradio's time indicate the harmony that prevailed

letting a contract for wax [23] at what he considered an exorbitant price; in another he denounced the councilmen for sharing the proceeds from the municipal butcher shop. Likewise, he condemned a council order for the removal of fruit venders (*quintandeiras*) from their accustomed places of business. When the câmara issued a building license in a military area it drew the viceroy's censure,[24] as it did when it tried to limit the number of stores licensed to sell manioc flour, corn, and beans in the city in order to protect the profits of the municipal granary.[25]

The viceroy also prodded the corporation into undertaking a modest program of improvements. Two new fountains, including the well-known *chafariz da Glória* were constructed; [26] roads were repaired and several new bridges erected; corrals and slaughtering facilities were added; the great municipal aqueduct, damaged by heavy rains, was repaired; and some of the extensive swamplands in the vicinity of the city—the source of much pestilence—were filled in.[27]

Probably the most noteworthy municipal improvement for which Dom Luís could claim credit was the establishment of a segregated quarter for the newly arrived slaves from Africa. When he came to Rio de Janeiro, one of the colony's leading slave marts, Lavradio found that it was customary for the blacks to be paraded by day throughout the city's principal streets in spite of their nakedness

---

within the corporation and in its relations with the viceroy. Typical is the standard response to the question: "Mais lhe proguntou se nesta Çidade havião Bandos e Competençias ou parçialidades de que se seguiçem pellejas, mortes, e outros damnos, e quem são os cabeças das tais parçialidades [?]," to which the alderman regularly replied: "Responderão que não havião parçialidades, Bandos que necessitaçem de opurtuno remedio, e que *tudo se achava em sossego*" (italics added). *Autos de correições*, I, [53]. That such transquility did not always prevail in viceregal Rio is suggested by the spirited defense of municipal privileges in the câmara's dispatch to the viceroy of Oct. 4, 1806. See *RADF*, II, 438–442.

23 The wax was purchased for distribution to the citizens during royal festivals.

24 Lavradio to câmara (Rio de Janeiro), July 15, 1775, CMCM, cod. 25, fol. 31ᵛ. The conflict between the governors of Rio de Janeiro and the câmaras over control of lands near the city was a never-ending one. See, for e.g., the *auto* of Dec. 17, 1710, *Autos de correições*, II, 16, and the câmara's letter to the viceroy in 1806 (cited in n. 22 above).

25 Lavradio to câmara (Rio de Janeiro), Jan. 12, 1771, ANRJ, Col. 70, Liv. V, fols. 144ᵛ–145ʳ; *idem* to Antônio Pinheiro Amado (ouvidor da comarca), Dec. 10, 1770, *ibid.*, fols. 133ʳ–134ʳ; *idem* to câmara, Jan. 21, 1771, *ibid.*, fol. 150ʳ; *idem* to *idem*, June 11, 1776, CMCM, cod. 25, fol. 112ʳ; *idem* to *idem*, Nov. 26, 1776, *ibid.*, fols. 156ᵛ–157ʳ.

26 See Noronha Santos, "Fontes e chafarizes do Rio de Janeiro," *R/SPHAN*, X. (Rio de Janeiro, 1946), 61. It should be noted that these fountains were not only for decorative purposes but were the facilities from which the townsmen, or at least their slaves, obtained water for use in their homes and shops.

27 For a discussion of the Arcos da Carioca, the great (and still standing) aqueduct completed during the long administration of Gomes Freire de Andrada, see Noronha Santos, "Aqueducto da Carioca," *R/SPHAN*, IV (Rio de Janeiro, 1940), especially p. 24.

(offensive to respectable folk) and the diseases they carried and spread; at night they were confined under the houses of the slave dealers, situated in various parts of the city. An outbreak of smallpox in 1774 was traced to a group of freshly imported slaves [28] and prompted the viceroy to decree that henceforth as soon as imported slaves had been cleared through Customs, they would be taken by boat to a district northwest of the city then called Valongo (literally long valley) and today known as Gamboa, where they would be kept in warehouses and isolated from the rest of the community. He stipulated that no more than four or five properly clothed slaves would be permitted to enter the city at a time.

Although he was probably unaware of it, Lavradio's order had precedent in the action taken by a Carioca câmara as early as 1619, when an earlier smallpox epidemic caused the council to order all suspected cases quarantined on the island of Villegaignon, which the city had acquired from the Society of Jesus for that purpose.[29] Dom Luís asserted that he had enforced his decree despite the opposition of the slave dealers, and that it had resulted in an improvement in the state of public health in the capital.[30] Actually the city continued to endure pestilences of one sort or another until the reforms of Oswaldo Cruz in the first years of the twentieth century.[31] In time conditions within the slave quarter were allowed to deteriorate, and by the Joanine period (1808–1821), when the capital experienced rapid physical expansion, the Valongo itself had become a blot on the city.[32]

According to the viceroy, the expense of these municipal improvements was partly defrayed by increased revenues brought about by more favorable terms in local tax contracts, and partly by savings gained in the better management of municipal finances. When he as-

[28] See *VRL*, p. 129, where it is stated that 5,000 persons perished in the city as a result of the pestilence. No source is given, and I have been unable to find confirmation of this statement in any of the Lavradio correspondence.

[29] Vivaldo Coarcy, *O Rio de Janeiro no século 17* (Rio de Janeiro, 1944), p. 47. For similar quarantine measures in the English mainland colonies during the seventeenth and eighteenth centuries, see Abbot Emerson Smith, *Colonists in Bondage: White Servitude and Convict Labor in America, 1607–1776* (Chapel Hill, 1947), 219.

[30] Lavradio, *Relatório*, pp. 450–451.

[31] In 1780, for example, the *Gazeta de Lisboa* reported (No. 30, July 25) that a recent outbreak of *fibres podres* (putrid fever), to which children were particularly susceptible, had just subsided in Rio de Janeiro.

[32] For two descriptions of conditions in the slave market at the end of the colonial period see *Views and Customs of the City and Neighbourhood of Rio de Janeiro . . . from Drawing taken by Lt. [Henry] Chamberlain . . . 1819 and 1820 . . .* (London, 1822), text to plate 11, and John Miller, *Memoirs of General [William] Miller in the Service of the Republic of Peru*, II (2d ed., London, 1829), 435–437.

sumed office Dom Luís found that the city treasurer, an old man who had held office for many years, had been accustomed to keep the strongbox containing the city's funds in his home, where he received and dispensed moneys haphazardly without being required to render an accounting. The chaotic state of the city's finances came to light on his death. When the chest was opened, packets of money were discovered with no indication as to their rightful owners; nor could records be found of deposits which citizens claimed to have entrusted to the treasurer for safekeeping. Not surprisingly, an audit revealed that the treasurer himself had dipped into the till for personal uses and was considerably overdrawn.

The viceroy found such carelessness unpardonable, and immediately ordered the municipal coffer conveyed to the Royal Mint. There it was opened for business on specified days of the week by the municipal treasurer who possessed one of the two keys necessary to unlock the chest and by a vereador who was given the title of inspector of deposits and the second key. To facilitate periodic audits, Lavradio insisted on the establishment of elementary bookkeeping procedures, including the maintenance of a cashbook and separate ledgers for deposits and expenditures. These reforms were embodied in a set of regulations signed by the viceroy and probably drawn up by the auditor-general, João Carlos Corrêa Lemos, for they reflected the procedures then being followed in the management of the king's revenues. As was so often the case with such salutary innovations in this era, the Lavradio regulations were forgotten soon after the marquis left Brazil. Years later in 1791, the câmara itself asked the Overseas Council for permission to restore the system of handling public funds that Dom Luís had established.[33]

The Viceroy and the Magistracy

From all indications the viceroy enjoyed unusually good rapport with the aldermen of his capital,[34] but the same was not true of his relations with the magistrates under his control, particularly the aged Jorge Botto Machado Cardozo, the juiz de fóra of Rio de Janeiro.

[33] The two preceding paragraphs are based on Lavradio, *Relatório*, pp. 449–450; [Anon.] "Methodo pello qual se estabelece novo e melhor administração para guarda, direcção a segurança do depozito geral desta cid.e," *RIHGB*, LXXVI:1 (1913 [1915]), 356–360; Lavradio to câmara (Rio de Janeiro), Apr. 25, 1777, CMCM, cod. 25, fol. 181ᵛ; Overseas Council, consulta of Nov. 14, 1791 (approved May 2, 1795), *DH*, XCV (1952), 107–109.

[34] Cf. e.g., the extremely caustic letters Viceroy Vasco Fernandes César de Menezes sent to the câmara of Salvador concerning its failure to comply with his orders. *DH*, LXXXVII (1951), 162, 178, 181, 183, 186, 201, and 205–206.

Throughout his administration the viceroy feuded with the judge whom he unflatteringly described as grossly ignorant, vain, money-grubbing, obstinate, and lethargic. He reprimanded him for failing to preside personally over city council meetings and for neglecting to perform other duties, such as the making of regular inspections of the city jail and new buildings under construction. When the judge continued to ignore Lavradio's repeated admonitions, Dom Luís summoned him to the palace, but the magistrate sulked in his home, pleading illness. The viceroy finally became exasperated and sent Machado a ukase to report promptly at 9:00 A.M. on the morrow, an ultimatum that so terrified the council president that he fled instead to the Franciscan monastery where he remained until the arrival of the marquis' replacement.[35]

The juizes de fóra were supposed to perform a variety of judicial and administrative tasks within the district where they served.[36] Despite his clashes with Judge Machado, the viceroy believed that the Crown should appoint additional magistrates of this type to supervise the activities of other câmaras in the viceroyalty; such men should be selected not only on the basis of their reputations and knowledge of jurisprudence, but also because of their patriotism, unselfishness, and tact.[37] Whether or not such criteria were given consideration, the number of juizes de fóra assigned to Brazilian municipalities was substantially increased after the arrival of the Royal Family in 1808.[38]

The juizes de fóra were local magistrates whose jurisdiction was limited to the confines of the municipality in which they resided. In terms of prestige and importance they were inferior to the circuit judges called ouvidores or, as they were sometimes styled, *ouvidores e corregedores da comarca*. The ouvidores were the first royal judges the Crown sent to Brazil during the initial phases of its colonization. In time they were outranked by the desembargadores who served in the High Courts of Bahia and Rio de Janeiro, but they were still useful royal servants in Lavradio's day. The ouvidor rode circuit over a large territory within which he exercised both judicial and administrative functions. As a judge he listened to appeals from decisions rendered by local justices, and assumed original jurisdiction over cer-

---

[35] Lavradio to Machado, Feb. 5, 1770, ANRJ, Col. 70, Liv. V, fol. 17^r; *idem* to *idem*, Dec. 9, 1770, *ibid.*, fol. 131^v; *idem* to *idem*, Oct. 2 and 3, 1776, CMCM, cod. 25, fols. 143^v–144^r, 149^r; *idem* to *idem*, Feb. 12 and 14, 1777, *ibid.*, fols. 173^{r-v}; *idem* to *idem*, July 8 and 9, 1778, *ibid.*, fols. 257^{r-v}; *idem*, *Relatório*, pp. 448–449.

[36] Among the best discussions of the functions of the juizes de fóra are Henrique da Gama Barros, *História da administração pública em Portugal nos séculos xii a xv*, 164 and 387, and Cândido Mendes de Almeida, ed., *Código filipino ou ordenações e leis do reino de Portugal*, Liv. I, tít. 65, n. 2.

[37] Lavradio, *Relatório*, p. 441.

[38] See José da Silva Lisboa, *Memoria dos beneficios políticos do governo de . . . d. João VI* (1818) (2d ed., Rio de Janeiro, 1940), Pt. 2, pp. 124–128.

tain classes of litigation. As an administrative inspector he examined the records of the câmaras of his circuit to ascertain the legality of their ordinances and to determine how well they managed their stewardship of municipal properties. He was responsible for the maintenance of roads and river crossings, and relied upon militia commanders to compel property owners to fulfill their corvée obligations. He also prepared reports for the viceroy on such matters as the conduct of particular officials, the state of timber cutting, and the quantity of harvests within his circuit. In addition, he carried out special assignments from the viceroy, seeking to verify the sources of complaints made by the colonists in their petitions to Lavradio and apprehending persons who seemed guilty of various kinds of law violations.[39]

Because of the size of their circuits and their multifarious tasks, it was difficult under the best of circumstances for the few ouvidores in each captaincy to fulfill all their duties. For that reason Lavradio recommended that three additional ouvidores be assigned to circuits under the viceroy's supervision, one for the capital district, one for the southern dependencies, and one for Espírito Santo.[40]

Apparently Manoel Carlos da Silva Gusmão, who assumed the post of ouvidor of Espírito Santo in late 1776, was no longer serving there when Dom Luís made his recommendations. Lavradio had been much annoyed when Silva Gusmão had presented his credentials to the captain-general of Bahia rather than to him. He so informed both the ouvidor and the colonial minister, pointing out that while Espírito Santo was a military dependency of Bahia, it was politically subordinate to Rio de Janeiro, and that the ouvidoria of Espírito Santo, which included the municipalities of São Salvador dos Campos and Cabo Frio in the northern part of the captaincy of Rio de Janeiro, was responsible to the Relação of Rio de Janeiro rather than to the High Court in Salvador. The ouvidor's apparent mistake illustrates the problem of overlapping jurisdictions in Colonial Brazil, and furnished Lavradio with an opportunity to renew his plea that Espírito Santo be placed entirely under the jurisdiction of the viceroy at Rio de Janeiro.[41]

[39] The above analysis is based on Diogo Pereira Ribeiro de Vasconcelos, "Breve descripção geographica, physica e política da capitania de Minas Gerais," (1806), *RAPM*, VI (1901), 799 and 826; Lavradio to Antônio Pinheiro Amado (ouvidor da comarca, Rio de Janeiro), Jan. 26, 1770, ANRJ, Col. 70, Liv. V, fol. 14^r; *idem* to *idem*, May 22, 1771, *ibid.*, fol. 190^v; *idem* to *idem*, June 8, 1771, *ibid.*, fol. 197^r; *idem* to *idem*, July 29, 1775, CMCM, cod. 25, fol. 35^r; *idem* to *idem*, Aug. 5, and 29, 1776, *ibid.*, fols. 124^v–125^v, 131^r; *idem* to *idem*, Sept. 12, 1776, *ibid.*, fols. 136^v–137^r; *idem* to *idem*, Dec. 18, 1776, *ibid.*, fol. 163^r; *idem* to *idem*, Aug. 30, 1777, *ibid.*, fol. 201^v; *idem* to *idem*, May 11 and Aug. 4, 1778, *ibid.*, fols. 245^v and 262^r.

[40] Lavradio, *Relatório*, p. 441.

[41] Lavradio, to Melo e Castro, Nov. 6, 1776, ANRJ, Col. 68, Liv. I, fols. 11^{r-v} (orig.) ; *idem* to *idem*, Dec. 19, 1776, BNRJ, 10, 4, 8 (unfoliated) ; *idem* to Manoel Carlos da S[ilv]a Gusmão, Dec. 16, 1776, CMCM, cod. 25, fols. 161^v–162^r.

Although Lavradio stressed the importance of recruiting additional qualified juizes de fóra and ouvidores to serve in Brazil, he disapproved of the type of magistrate ordinarily sent there. Most of those he had known were mere time-servers interested only in using their offices to win promotions elsewhere and in exploiting their opportunities to acquire as much wealth as possible before returning to Europe. Since their salaries were low, he contended that they deliberately encouraged litigation because of the fees they could thereby collect. And he charged that "During the nearly twelve years that I have governed in America, I have never heard of a single judge who endeavored to reconcile litigants, persuading them not to ruin themselves by continued and unjust pleas, and counselling them to abide by the solution prescribed by the laws. [Nor have] I ever found any useful project [estabelecimento] instituted by any of these magistrates." He added that on numerous occasions he had tried to mediate between contending parties, whether rich or poor. Sometimes he called them to his office to confer in person with him; on other occasions he named arbitrators to adjust disputes. His aim was to reconcile litigants so that they would cease to bring about economic ruin to each other. But the magistrates had complained that the number of law suits was becoming fewer and that their income was consequently becoming smaller. No matter, said the viceroy, the people were better off.[42]

One magistrate Lavradio undoubtedly had in mind when he was drafting his critique was Antônio Pinheiro Amado, long-time ouvidor of the district of Rio de Janeiro.[43] Relations between the viceroy and the ouvidor may never have been cordial; certainly they began to deteriorate in 1771, when Pinheiro Amado yielded to an appeal from local taverners in the capital by rescinding a câmara ordinance closing their places of business nightly between 10:00 P.M. and dawn. His countermanding order drew two sharp rebukes from the viceroy who regarded all taverns as notorious dens of iniquity and insisted that he should have been consulted before the ouvidor took such action.[44]

Like the juiz de fóra, Pinheiro Amado was a man of advanced years whose ill health prevented him from actively carrying out his duties. As a result, the viceroy repeatedly rebuked him for failing to undertake his regular inspection tours and for conducting investigations (interestingly enough called audiencias) in his own home rather

42 Lavradio, Relatório, pp. 442–443.

43 He headed the ouvidoria of Rio de Janeiro from 1766 to 1782, an unusually long tenure for such a magistrate to hold office during the eighteenth century. Autos de correições, I, 44–70.

44 Lavradio to Pinheiro Amado, Feb. 11 and 25, 1771, ANRJ, Col. 70, Liv. V, fols. 159ᵛ–160ʳ, 164ᵛ–165ʳ.

than in his official chambers. Furthermore, the ouvidor's assistants made a mockery of the law by performing their duties in street clothes rather than in the garb of their offices.[45] Of considerably more moment was his charge that the ouvidor frequently employed legal assistants to do his work for him with the result that "many times" the same attorney who served *in vice* the ouvidor in passing sentence was also employed by the defendant. While the consequences of such collusion were patently serious, Lavradio declared that it was carried on so skillfully that it was difficult to find proof of malpractice, since the advocates who signed the affidavits in the name of the ouvidor hired other lawyers to prepare their client's papers. He claimed that he had been unable to put a stop to such practices and merely called his successor's attention to their existence,[46] leaving one to wonder why he did not order the Relação to investigate such goings on.

Lavradio as a Dispenser of Justice

Considering the fact that Dom Luís, unlike some of Brazil's senior administrators, appears to have had a satisfactory working relationship with the High Court of Appeals,[47] his failure to direct it to examine the procedures of the ouvidoria is all the more inexplicable. Since he was not a desembargador, as was Viceroy Vasconcelos, the marquis did not vote in the court's deliberations. However, he did review and summarize for the Crown the findings of the desembargadores' investigations of such matters as the losses of Colônia and Santa Catarina and the apprehension of suspected contrabandists.[48] With the aid of the tribunal's chancellor, he also shifted judges from one assignment to another.[49]

Dom Luís regularly asked the judges for their written advice before issuing instructions in response to the numerous petitions received from colonials and Peninsulars. For example, when the creditors of a merchant imprisoned for an unspecified cause made claims on his encumbered estate, the viceroy asked the *ouvidor geral do crime* of the

[45] Lavradio to Pinheiro Amado, July 23 and Aug. 5, 1776, CMCM, cod. 25, fols. 123ʳ–125ʳ.

[46] Lavradio, *Relatório*, p. 441.

[47] Lavradio, *Relatório*, p. 441; cf. Luís de Vasconcelos e Sousa, *Relatório, RIHGB*, XXIII (1860), 180–181. A century before a conflict between Governor-General Roque da Costa Barreto and the High Court of Bahia resulted in the replacement of four judges. Carta régia, Mar. 22, 1680, *DH*, XXXII (1936), 333–334.

[48] See Chaps. X and XIV.

[49] E.g., portaria of Jan. 23, 1777, CMCM, cod. 19, fols. 149ᵛ–150ʳ; Lavradio to Sr. Dez.or Ouv.or Gl. do Cr[im]e Nicolão Joaqum. de Miranda S.a e Alarcão, Dec. 23, 1778, *ibid.*, cod. 25, fol. 285ʳ; *idem* to Luiz José Duarte Freire, Dez.or Chancellor da Relação, Nov. 3, 1778, *ibid.*, cod. 25, fol. 279ᵛ.

High Court for his opinion before releasing the funds.[50] When the trustee of another confiscated property requested permission to go the kingdom on private business, Lavradio approved his petition and called on one of the judges to find a suitable replacement.[51] A complaint by the Chief Provisioner (*Almotacél Mor do Reino*) of Portugal that a renter of his property in Rio de Janeiro had allowed his slaves to destroy some of the fazenda's installations but refused to undertake their repair resulted in a viceregal order to one of the desembargadores to see that such repairs were made immediately at the expense of the occupant.[52] And when a free Negro who had been convicted of murder and sentenced to ten years in the galleys and fined 100,000 réis pleaded that he had already served fourteen years but could not pay his fine because of his confinement, Dom Luís directed the ouvidor geral do crime to transfer him to the slave market so that he could be sold to the highest bidder to satisfy his fine.[53] A request by Captain-General Saldanha for an executioner to dispatch several criminals in São Paulo led the viceroy to ask a member of the court for one among the staff of its dungeons.[54]

One of the more unpleasant judicial duties of the viceroy was that of reviewing sentences of persons convicted of crimes. Where military personnel were concerned, the viceroy with the aid of the chancellor reviewed the action of the courts-martial whose sentences he could confirm, modify, or revoke; except for those recommending death (which were sent for review to the Colonial Minister [55]), his decision was final.[56] In civil cases involving large sums or important personages, the viceroy's decision could be amended or even reversed by the Desembargo do Paço in Portugal.[57]

50 Lavradio to Sr. Dezembargador Ouvidor Geral do Crime, Bernardo Sallazar Sarmento Eça e Alarcão, Feb. 29, 1776, CMCM, cod. 25, fol. 88ʳ.

51 Lavradio to João Ant.o Salter de Mendonça, Apr. 13, 1776, *ibid.*, fols. 97ᵛ–98ʳ.

52 Lavradio to Miguel José de Oliveira, May 21, 1776, *ibid.*, fols. 103ʳ–104ʳ.

53 Lavradio to Pedro Correa dos Santos, Mar. 24, 1770, ANRJ, Col. 70, Liv. V, fol. 28ᵛ.

54 Lavradio to Sallazar, Apr. 26, 1776, CMCM, cod. 25, fol. 99ʳ.

55 See the commentary of Viceroy Portugal, 2RGG, pp. 460–462.

56 Francisco Xavier de Mendonça Furtado to Lavradio, Feb. 10, 1768, CMCM, cod. 23, fol. 75ʳ (orig.) ; commonly Lavradio sent court-martial proceedings to the chancellor (or to one of the designated staff members of the Relação) with the following injunction: "Remetto a Vm.ce os dous concelhos de Guerra juntos, p.a q. vm.ce os exame, e me informe como seu parecer." Lavradio to Dez.or ouvidor geral do civel, João Antonio Salter de Mendonça, May 22, 1775, *ibid.*, cod. 25, fol. 21ʳ; the same codice contains a number of similar examples. As the number of men under arms grew during the 1770s, crimes of desertion became increasingly common. A list of 1778 enumerates twenty-seven men convicted for desertion who were sentenced for periods ranging from two to four years at hard labor. "Relação dos soldados, e tambores dos Regim.tos abaixo declarados, q. se achao cumprindo as sentenças dos Conselhos de Guerra pela culpa de dezerção . . . os quaes existem pelas Fortalezas, e Prizoens desta cidade em 10 de Novembro de 1778," BNRJ, 13, 4, 3, n. 57 (orig.) .

57 The case of one Manoel João illustrates how judicial review sometimes worked. He was accused of smuggling gold, for which the mesa da inspeção fined him

There were relatively few places in Brazil where persons sentenced for periods of confinement could be kept. Within the capital there were the city jail and the dungeons of the Relação, both located in the Corporation Hall; the various military fortresses around the city, particularly the islands of Cobras and Villegaignon; and a number of hulks anchored in the harbor. Murderers, military deserters, and persons convicted of similar crimes were often sent to such places, but there were no adequate facilities for those charged with such lesser crimes as drunkenness, brawling, child neglect, and minor thefts. Both Lavradio and his immediate successor urged the erection of a workhouse in the capital for such persons, but while the Crown approved its establishment, it failed to authorize the expenditures necessary to build it.[58]

Convicts were also exiled from their homes for varying periods. The places most frequently assigned for banishment were the fortresses of Caconada in Angola, Colônia do Sacramento, the island of Santa Catarina, and Pôrto Seguro. Between 1771 and 1779 eighty-seven persons (nearly all of them men) were sent to Angola for detention;[59] most of them were soldiers convicted of serious crimes such as desertion to the enemy, aiding and abetting deserters, bearing forbidden arms, fighting while on duty, murder, disobedience of superiors, and "gambling and knavery." Civilians, too, were dispatched to Caconada for counterfeiting, fornication, and general troublemaking. Military deserters were also sentenced to Colônia and to Santa Catarina Island. The latter and Pôrto Seguro were common destinations for civilians convicted of moral crimes such as concubinage, prostitution, sorcery, and bigamy.[60]

The circumstances that led to banishment were sometimes rather

---

50,000 réis and sentenced him to three years' exile on Santa Catarina Island; the Relação subsequently "commuted" the pecuniary penalty to two additional years of banishment, but, for reasons not given, the Desembargo do Paço granted the accused full pardon! Lavradio to Dez.r Intend.e Geral do Ouro, Manoel Pinto da Cunha e Souza, Aug. 30, 1777, CMCM, cod. 25, fols. 201ᵛ–202ʳ.

58 Carta régia, July 8, 1769, BNRJ, I-2, 4, 6, n. 9; Vasconcelos, *Relatório*, p. 183.

59 Lavradio to Captains-General D. Francisco Innocêncio de Souza Coutinho and D. Antônio de Lencastre, Feb. 25, 1771 to Feb. 26, 1779, CMCM, cods. 16 and 26, *passim*. There was one instance during Lavradio's term when a man in Angola was sentenced to hard labor on the island of Villegaignon! *Idem* to Lencastre, Sept. 26, 1776, *ibid.*, cod. 15, fol. 97ᵛ. For further discussion of the dispatch of *degredados* from Brazil to Angola, see Boxer, *Portuguese Societies in the Tropics*, pp. 197–208, and the index under "degredados."

60 Lavradio to Pedro José Soares de Figueiredo Sarmento (Governor of Colônia), Sept. 8, 1770, CMCM, cod. 15, fol. 28ᵛ; *idem* to Francisco de Souza de Menezes (governor of Santa Catarina) and to his successor, Pedro Antônio da Gama e Freitas, Mar. 1, 1774 to June 6, 1776, *ibid.*, cod. 4, *passim; idem* to José Robeiro Guimaraez e Attayde, Sept. 20, 1771, ANRJ, Col. 70, Liv. V, fols. 228ᵛ–229ʳ; *idem* to Joze X.er Machado Monteiro, Oct. 24, 1775, Jan. 5, July 20, and Sept. 16, 1776, CMCM, cod. 25, fols. 55ʳ, 72ᵛ, 122ʳ, and 137ᵛ–138ʳ.

bizarre. In one instance a distraught father of good character despaired of convincing his erring son to abandon his penchant for thievery and personally asked the viceroy to send the boy to Angola for chastisement.[61] In another a humanitarian-minded man agreed to take into his home an impoverished brother-in-law only to discover that the ingrate had impregnated his wife and a sister.[62] Then there was the case of two free *pardas* who claimed to be healers (*curandeiras*), but whose patients expired after taking remedies they had prescribed.[63] Particularly galling to the viceroy was the crime of one Francisco Jozé who appeared in Rio de Janeiro armed with a recommendation from the marquis' own wife. There he forged the viceroy's name to an order directing a squad of his personal guard to surround a citizen's home in order to extort money from the victim.[64]

The Viceroy and the Church

By no means did all criminal proceedings coming to the viceroy's attention concern delinquent seculars, for Dom Luís also dealt with trouble-making men of the cloth. Despite the fact that the Jesuits had been expelled from Portugal and her empire in 1759–1760, there were still a few Black Robes living in isolated parts of Brazil in Lavradio's time. One was Father Antônio Gomes da Silva Souto Mayor who was discovered in the captaincy-general of Goiás and upon Lavradio's order was sent to Rio de Janeiro and placed under guard in a sealed building in one of the forts until he could be transported to Portugal. The same fate befell an ex-Jesuit who had come (or possibly returned) to Brazil as a secular priest and was engaged in teaching in Rio de Janeiro when Dom Luís ordered him to Lisbon for refusing to take a special oath of loyalty to the Crown. The viceroy also directed the arrest of a former Jesuit lay brother who was found serving in one of the regiments stationed on Santa Catarina Island and whose only guilt seems to have been his former association with the Society of Jesus. Quite obviously, Lavradio and his subordinates took seriously Pombal's warnings about the alleged Jesuit conspiracy! [65]

61 Lavradio to D. Antônio de Lencastre, Nov. 9, 1772, *ibid.*, cod. 15, fol. 142ᵛ.
62 Lavradio to D. Antônio de Lencastre, Feb. 10, 1773, *ibid.*, fol. 151ʳ.
63 Lavradio to D. Antônio de Lencastre, Nov. 20, 1775, *ibid.*, fol. 78ʳ.
64 Lavradio to D. Antônio de Lencastre, Mar. 9, 1776, *ibid.*, fols. 83ᵛ–84ʳ.
65 Lavradio to Lt. Col. Luis Manoel da Silva Paes, Sept. 5, 1770, ANRJ, Col. 70, Liv. V, fol. 82ʳ; *idem* to Oeyras, Sept. 6, 1770, *ibid.*, Col. 69, Liv. I-*bis*, fols. 19ᵛ–20ʳ; *idem* to *idem*, Dec. 16, 1770, *ibid.*, fols. 29ʳ⁻ᵛ; *idem* to Melo e Castro, Dec. 9, 1771, BNRJ, 10, 4, 8 (unfoliated) ; *idem* to Francisco de Souza de Menezes, Apr. 17, 1773, CMCM, cod. 15, fol. 157ʳ. For Pombal's belief that there existed a Jesuit conspiracy against Brazil, see pp. 110–111, above.

Jesuitophobia was also involved in the arrest of two other clerics whose case reveals rather clearly the subservience of colonial ecclesiastical authorities to secular control in Lavradio's time, as well as the extreme sensitivity of secular authorities to criticism from the pulpit. The case concerned an incendiary sermon preached by the so-called rebel preacher Padre Manuel Furtado de Mendonça, vicar of the parish of S. João da Barra in the traditionally turbulent district of Campos dos Goitacazes in the northern part of the captaincy of Rio de Janeiro. The Padre's misfortunes began on September 9, 1770, when his friend P. Antônio José Pereira Carneiro, rector of the seminary of Lapa in São Salvador dos Campos, invited him to the seminary to deliver the annual sermon to celebrate St. Peter's Day. Padre Mendonça chose as his text Matthew 16: 16–18: "And Simon Peter answered and said, Thou are the Christ, the Son of the Living God. And Jesus answered . . . That thou are Peter, and upon this rock I will build my church; and the gates of hell shall not prevail against it." As he warmed up to his message, the preacher launched into an embittered denunciation of the excessive temporal regulation of the Church which, he said, was deprived of its right to curb abuses, since such authority was considered contrary to the laws of the State. He closed his sermon by asking, "Grant, Most Vigilant Pastor and Most Holy Father, your protection to change the jurisprudence, that the natural right be independent of privilege, that what is ordered in our sanctuaries be reaffirmed in our palaces, that the sinners have no other refuge than that of penitence, that the laws of the princes do not attempt to do more than enforce the laws of God and that any bishop may work properly to correct wrongs without opposition." [66]

Among those who heard the message was the ouvidor da comarca, Dr. José Ribeiro Guimarães de Atayde, who very likely was the Padre's principal target. The indignant magistrate immediately reported this "seditious sermon" to the viceroy and charged that, in effect, the sacerdote had asserted that "the State of the Church was dominated by Princes and secular Justices, contrary to its exemptions and liberties. . . ." Lavradio immediately ordered the imprisonment of Padre Mendonça, the seizure of all his papers, and the launching of an investigation into all aspects of the case to determine whether the priest customarily repeated such charges in public and whether he had contact "with any of the individuals of the pernicious Company of Jesus or associates of its brotherhood."

The viceroy's order reached the ouvidor in São Salvador while he was continuing his tour of inspection. Padre Mendonça was also in that vila, having come to town to take part in the feast of the Eleven

66 Alberto Lamego, *A Terra Goytacá*, IV, 57–58; the entire sermon is published in the appendix to this volume, pp. 435–449.

Thousand Virgins. After the festivities were over, the magistrate invited the padre, who was then preparing to return to his parish by canoe, to come to his residence to attend "the operas" in celebration of the saints' day. The unsuspecting priest accepted and remained overnight in the ouvidor's lodgings. The next morning he was suddenly confronted by the ouvidor, three scribes, the local bailiff, and two justices of the peace, accompanied by a squad of soldiers, and was placed under arrest. When he inquired the cause for his seizure, the ouvidor merely informed him that it was done by order of the viceroy. Subsequently he was confined to the common gaol along with "factious Negroes and mulattoes," though there existed other, more decent facilities where he could have been incarcerated, or so wrote his friend Padre Carneiro to the secretary of the Bishop of Rio de Janeiro. In the meantime Padre Mendonça's widowed mother was driven from her home, and a rigorous search of the premises turned up her son's papers, including a copy of the incriminating sermon.

Two months later Padre Mendonça was sent under guard by launch to Rio de Janeiro, where he was detained on Ilha das Cobras. Meantime, ouvidor Guimarães de Atayde began his formal investigation, taking the testimony of thirty witnesses and examining the accused's papers. Among them was an allegedly Jesuitical letter from Padre Carneiro to Padre Mendonça. The former soon further excited the suspicions of the magistrate by publicly condemning him as a *corregedeiro*, an offensive term the ouvidor regarded as an insult to the judicial authority he represented. Before long, Padre Carneiro was on his way to Snakes' Island to join Padre Mendonça.

As for the sermonizer, he was repeatedly interrogated by Judge José Maurício da Gama e Freitas, but failed to disclose his involvement in any conspiracy. During his initial questioning, the priest lamely defended himself by arguing that in his sermon he was referring to the heresy of certain foreign princes who relieved their subjects of obedience to the Supreme Pontiff, and that he had not meant to imply that the rulers of Portugal were guilty of that practice, nor had he intended to foment rebellion among the king's subjects. In a later interrogation Padre Mendonça attributed his persecution to the personal malice of the ouvidor because he had protested against that official's imposition of a tax on sugar mills and *engenhocas* in the Campos area, where it had never been levied before.

While the Padre's examination by secular authorities continued, Dom Frei Antônio do Desterro, Bishop of Rio de Janeiro, began his own inquiry into the St. Peter's Day proceedings. In a letter remarkable for its docility and its deference to secular authority, the Bishop wrote Secretary of State Melo e Castro that as soon as he learned about the sermon, he had ordered an ecclesiastical inquiry. He assured the secretary that most of the Church "is pure and free from such an abominable sin" as treason; nevertheless this did not compensate for the great sorrow (*magoa*) that the incident had caused His Reverence "because the repeated examples of my fidelity and also my pastoral vigilance in this [diocese] had given me reason to expect that there were no errant sheep in this small flock." It is clear that the aged bishop, who was at pains to show that he was even outdoing the viceroy in eliminating sedition from the Church, was extremely embarrassed by the St. Peter's Day sermon.[67]

After reviewing the evidence, desembargador Gama e Freitas advised the viceroy that Padre Mendonça was more culpable of idiocy than of sedition. Lavradio himself concluded that the priest was basically a good but poor man who used his small income to support his widowed mother and his aged sister. He had displayed bad judgment but had intended no wrong. Nevertheless, the always conservative Dom Luís concluded that without an express order from the king he could not release the priest; consequently the devassa and the offending padre were sent to Lisbon. There Mendonça languished in the Limoeiro dungeons for three years, finally securing his release in 1774. After returning to Brazil to resume his vicarage, the righteous priest sued the ouvidor for what amounted to defamation of character, but his suit was eventually quashed by the Overseas Council.[68]

Jesuits and presumed Jesuit agents were not the only clerics who fell afoul of the viceroy. In 1773 he dispatched three quarreling Benedictines to Lisbon for chastisement, and exiled the abbot of the Benedictine convent in Rio de Janeiro to the Order's monastery in São Paulo. Three years later he sent back to the kingdom an obstreperous vicar of the district of Sabará (Minas Gerais), and expelled from the captaincy of Rio de Janeiro a priest who refused to turn over a quantity of lime to secular authorities for use on the fortifications.[69]

Aside from such occasional disciplinary problems, relations between Church and State in the diocese of Rio de Janeiro seem to have been

67 Dom Frei Antônio do Desterro to Melo e Castro, Mar. 30, 1771, *ibid.*, pp. 82–85, n. 66. The Bishop, who was installed in the See of Rio de Janeiro in 1746, died there on December 5, 1773 and was buried in the Benedictine monastery. Lavradio to *idem*, Dec. 13, 1773, ANRJ, Col. 69, Liv. I-*bis.*, fol. 92ʳ.

68 The previous paragraphs are based especially on *idem* to José Ribeiro Guimaraens e Attayde, Oct. 8 and Nov. 17, 1770, ANRJ, Col. 70, Liv. V, fols. 105ᵛ–106ʳ, 119ᵛ–120ʳ; *idem* to Pombal, July 23, 1771, BNRJ, 10, 4, 8 (unfoliated); and Lamego, IV, 56–85, the fullest account, told from manuscript sources then in the author's private collection.

69 Pombal to Lavradio, Aug. 14, 1773, BNRJ, I-2, 4, 6, n. 37; Melo e Castro to *idem*, Oct. 14, 1773, *ibid.*, n. 38; Lavradio to Manoel Gonçalves Anjo, Jan. 29, 1776, CMCM, cod. 25, fol. 80ʳ; *idem* to Antônio Pinheiro Amado, Feb. 22, 1776, *ibid.*, fol. 86ʳ.

tranquil during Lavradio's stay.[70] The viceroy's alleged piety may have had something to do with that; certainly the recent expulsion of the Jesuits did, for that draconic measure, coupled with others such as the Pombal regime's efforts to restrict the number of candidates for the priesthood,[71] threw leaders of the colonial Church on the defensive.

We know little about the history of that Church, and most of what we have learned concerns the activities of the Jesuits who until the eve of their expulsion were politically, economically, and culturally dominant among the regular clergy serving in Brazil.[72] The secular branch was not as large, as wealthy, or as politically active as its counterpart in the Spanish colonies.[73] Though the Inquisition was founded in Portugal in 1547, it never established offices in Brazil as the Holy Office of Spain did in its empire. Nor did the Brazilian clergy gather together in impressive and lengthy councils like those which met several times in the viceroyalties of Peru and New Spain to discuss problems of religious discipline and dogma. While Portuguese bishops were included among the triumvirate of dignitaries who administered the colony in the absence of governors-general or viceroys, they never served singly as temporary or regularly appointed heads of the colony, as some prelates did during the early days of the Spanish empire; nor did they emulate their fellow bishops by pitting their prestige and power against that of the viceroys. For these and other reasons the sources of friction between the Portuguese episcopacy and senior royal officials, though never wholly absent, appear to have been markedly less common and certainly less acrimonious than was so often the case in the adjacent empire.[74]

[70] See the extremely flattering appraisal of Lavradio by D. José Joaquim Justiano Mascarenhas Castello Branco to Melo e Castro, May 31, 1779, *RIHGB*, LXIII:1 (1901), 84. Mascarenhas was one of the few Brazilian-born clergymen to occupy a diocese in Brazil during the colonial period. He was born in Rio de Janeiro in 1731 and served as bishop of Rio de Janeiro from 1773 until his death in 1805. "Prelados do Rio de Janeiro desde 1560 até 1871," *RADF*, III (1896), 288.

[71] See Chap. I, n. 74.

[72] The only truly outstanding work on the Church in colonial Brazil is Serafim Leite, S. J., *História da companhia de Jesús no Brasil* (10 vols., Rio de Janeiro, 1938–1950), which includes references to conflicts between the secular and regular branches of the clergy.

[73] E.g., compared with the thirty dioceses and ten archepiscopal provinces of colonial Spanish America, Brazil possessed six dioceses (Belém, Maranhão, Olinda, Rio de Janeiro, São Paulo, and Mariana [Minas Gerais]) and one archepiscopal province (Bahia) at the end of the eighteenth century, reflecting differences in the size of the flocks the Church served and also in its wealth. The two northern bishoprics were suffragan to the patriarchate of Lisbon, the others were subordinate to the archbishopric of Salvador.

[74] E.g., the highly charged conflicts between the episcopacy and the viceroys of New Spain which in two instances (1624 and 1642) resulted in the latters' removal from office had no parallels in colonial Brazil.

Although the sovereigns of Portugal possessed as extensive powers over the colonial church as the rulers of Spain enjoyed, they did not delegate them as fully to their viceroys. In their capacities as vice patrons the Spanish viceroys were concerned with ecclesiastical appointments, removals, and transfers; they oversaw elections by governing bodies of the Church; and they controlled the publication of Papal legislation addressed to the faithful.[75] Among these responsibilities the only one that directly concerned Portuguese viceroys was the removal of ecclesiastics from their offices for disciplinary reasons. Other aspects of patronage were administered from Lisbon by the old Board of Conscience and [Military] Orders,[76] the Overseas Council, and the secretaries of state.

Patronage matters were therefore not one of the primary duties of the Portuguese viceroys or the governors-general before them. It is significant that patronage is not among the topics discussed either in the revised regimento of the office of the governors-general or in the briefing instructions given to newly posted officers.[77] It is also noteworthy that neither Lavradio nor his successor considered it necessary to discuss the status of the Church in their terminal reports, though Spanish viceroys always devoted a section of their *memorias* to the *gobierno ecclesiástico*.[78]

From time to time Dom Luís issued administrative orders to members of the parish clergy. He asked them to carry out a variety of assignments such as the organization of supplies needed by the govern-

[75] For a convenient summary of the patronage responsibilities of the viceroys of Spanish America, see Lillian Estelle Fisher, *Viceregal Administration in the Spanish-American Colonies* (University of California. Publications in History, XV, Berkeley, 1926), Chaps. 5–6; cf. Bernard E. Bobb, *The Viceregency of Antonio Maria Bucareli in New Spain, 1771–1779* (Austin, 1962), Chaps. 2–3. Bucareli, a contemporary of Lavradio, became much more deeply involved in ecclesiastical problems than did the marquis.

[76] The Mesa da Consciência e Ordens was created in 1532 by João III to advise him on matters of religious policy. After an apostolic bull of 1551 authorized the permanent union of Portugal's three military Orders (Santiago, Aviz, and Christ) with the Crown, the board assumed responsibility for administering the lands and revenues belonging to those Orders. Since the ecclesiastical revenues of Brazil were assigned to the Order of Christ, the board became concerned with the distribution of the tithes for the support of the Church in the colony and advised the king on the disposal of benefices, ecclesiastical appointments and the like. Its responsibilities were defined in the regimentos of Aug. 12 and 23, 1608, *CCLP*, I, 228–245; see also Boxer, *Salvador de Sá*, pp. 36–37; and Marcelo Caetano, "O Govêrno e a administração central após a restauração," *Historia da expansão portuguesa no mundo*, III:1 (Lisbon, 1940), 191.

[77] See Chap. V, n. 1. The statement also applies to the Crown's instructions to the captains-general.

[78] Lavradio did not specifically mention the Church in his *Relatório*. Vasconcelos, who did, confined his remarks to a discussion of the problem of immorality among friars residing in the capital. Vasconcelos to Conde de Rezende, Aug. 20, 1789, *RIHGB*, XXIII (1860), 181–182. For references to the terminal reports of the Spanish viceroys, see Chap. XVII, notes 10 and 17.

ment, the submission of information concerning the conduct of their parishioners, including public officials, and the preparation of reports on demographic and economic characteristics of their parishes.[79] In the performance of these duties the curates worked closely with the heads of the rural constabulary.

The Role of the Mestres de Campo

Beyond the urbanized limits of the capital, the maintenance of law and order was the responsibility of captains-major (capitães-mores) who led companies of the home guard (ordenanças) in the smaller towns, and especially the mestres de campo, the colonels who commanded first-line militia regiments (auxilários) in rural districts. Professor Boxer has noted that in addition to their military duties these great landed magnates (poderosos da terra) performed a variety of administrative tasks in the backlands where salaried royal officials such as the ouvidores seldom ventured.[80] While he implies that these prototypes of Brazil's latter-day coroneis were unique to the interior captaincies, they were also important cogs in the administrative machinery of the coastal captaincies.

In the Marquis of Lavradio's time there were eight mestres de campo in the captaincy of Rio de Janeiro, each of whom was responsible for two to six parishes.[81] Four administered districts now within the state of Guanabara (Greater Rio de Janeiro) ; one supervised parishes along the northern periphery of Guanabara Bay; another those along the bay's eastern littoral; two others were responsible for the municipalities of Cabo Frio and São Salvador dos Campos. All but two received their patents before Dom Luís assumed office,[82] a reminder that the viceroys had little political patronage at their disposal.

Professor Boxer has observed that the militia commanders were usually the largest landowners in their districts,[83] and this seems to have been the case with those who served under the Marquis of Lavradio. Miguel Antunes Ferreira, who administered the parishes of N. S. do Amparo de Maricá and S. José de Itaborahy on the littoral

---

[79] E.g., Lavradio to Padres Bento José Barrozo, Alberto Caetano, and Henrique Jozé de Carvalho, May 11 and 30 and July 15, 1776, CMCM, cod. 25, fols. 100^v, 108^r, and 121^r.

[80] The Golden Age of Brazil, p. 307.

[81] By comparison, there were eighteen mestres de campo in the larger captaincy-general of Bahia. Felisbelo Freire, História territorial do Brasil, I (Rio de Janeiro, 1906) , 194–195.

[82] Their patents, dated March 18, 1767 to July 4, 1768, may be found in ANRJ, Col. 60, Liv. XL, passim.

[83] See n. 80 above.

east of the capital, owned eighty-two slaves and two engenhos, one of which produced forty chests (caixas) of sugar and ten pipes of brandy (agua ardente) a year. Ignacio de Andrade Soutomayor Rendon possessed seventy slaves and several mills which annually processed 152 caixas of sugar and up to seventy-six pipes of brandy. João José Barcelos Coutinho was by far the greatest slaveholder (210) in the Goitacazes and had a mill whose yearly capacity was rated at twenty-five "engenhos de asucar"[84] and four pipes of brandy. Another mestre de campo, Alexandre Alvarez Duarte e Azevedo, owned extensive lands along the Rio Macacú northeast of the capital. These were all men of exceptional substance, for the average planter in the captaincy possessed fewer than ten slaves and probably ground between ten and twenty chests of sugar per harvest.[85]

Within their districts these uniformed symbols of royal authority performed a wide variety of tasks, some routine in nature but others in response to specific orders from the viceroy. They recruited and drilled adult males in the community to serve as potential reinforcements for the first-line troops. They guarded the seacoast, looking for suspicious vessels hovering offshore and warning the capital when such craft were sighted. Their forces rooted out renegade slave camps (quilombos) and smugglers' nests, and rounded up gypsies (ciganos), alleged sorcerers, rebellious slaves, quarrelsome neighbors, and other miscreants. They checked the passports of nonresidents loitering in their district and searched for escaped prisoners and deserting soldiers. Except for the slaves, who were publicly whipped in the pillory of the nearest town, they remitted their prisoners under guard to the capital, where they were either incarcerated or taken before the viceroy for a stern lecture. Dom Luís charged these officers with enforcement of directives prohibiting such practices as the adulteration of manioc flour sent to market or the use of toxic fish poison in streams used by local inhabitants for drinking water. He asked them for details regarding the numerous petitions he received on such matters as land disputes and charges of misconduct by officials in their districts. He depended on them to mobilize the economic resources of their districts needed for the war effort and to persuade local cultivators to plant the new crops he was promoting.[86] In cooperation with the parish priests, the colonels prepared for the viceroy's use detailed reports (mapas) on the population structure, the number of sugar mills and slaves, and the quantity of sugar, brandy, dressed timber, dye-

84 I have been unable to determine the precise meaning of this unit of measure.
85 "Relações parciaes apresentadas ao Marquez de Lavradio," [1778/1779], RIHGB, LXXVI:1 (1913 [1915]) , 293, 300–301, 328, and 337.
86 See Chapter XIII.

stuffs, cereals, and other commodities produced in their districts.[87] In effect, these field administrators were the eyes and ears of the viceroy in the countryside and performed duties roughly analogous to those exercised by the *capitaine de la milice* in the seigneuries of New France.[88]

Because of the power these magnates wielded, there was always the temptation for them to abuse their authority, a matter of concern to the viceroy who kept as tight a reign on them as possible. As he wrote Luís de Vasconcelos, "it should not be forgotten that from time to time it is necessary to alter benevolence with severity toward these men; otherwise, they will become abusive and it is the people who have to suffer." [89] To be sure, it was much easier for him to exercise surveillance over the colonels within the relatively narrow confines of the captaincy of Rio de Janeiro than it was for the captains-general of the vast expanses of Minas Gerais, Mato Grosso, Bahia, or Grão Pará to do so. Lavradio insisted that the field commanders remain in their districts at all times except when he specifically authorized them to come to the capital, but when he did call for them, he demanded that they appear promptly.[90] Not infrequently he rebuked the *poderosos* for misinterpreting or neglecting his instructions, for seizing persons

[87] This analysis is based on the active correspondence of Lavradio with the militia officers in CMCM, cod. 25 and ANRJ, Col. 70, Liv. V, *passim.* I have not seen any of their letters to the viceroy.

[88] Also called *capitaine de la côte* and *de la paroisse.* For a discussion of their origins and functions, see Gustave Lancetot, "Les Troupes de la Nouvelle-France," *Canadian Historical Association. Annual Report* (1926), pp. 40–42, and E. R. Adair, "The French-Canadian Seigneury," *Canadian Historical Review,* XXXV (Sept. 1954), 193–195. There were, of course, significant differences between the French and Portuguese militia commanders in their socioeconomic status in the community and in the scope of their activities. In New France the capitaine de la milice was nominally subordinate to his seigneurial lord whereas in Brazil the mestre de campo was himself a *latifundista* with authority over large areas beyond his own property; the capitaine's responsibility was limited to his particular seigneury. I have the impression that the mestre de campo played a more vital role in the administration of the Brazilian countryside than did his counterparts in rural Spanish and English America. On the militia in the Spanish empire see Lyle N. McAlister, "The Reorganization of the Army of New Spain, 1763–1767," *HAHR,* XXXIII (Feb. 1953), 1–32 and Robert L. Gilmore, *Caudillism and Militarism in Venezuela 1810–1910* (Athens, Ohio, 1964), pp. 99–106. Among the few studies on the militia in the English colonies are Jack S. Radabaugh, "The Militia of Colonial Massachusetts," *Military Affairs* (Spring 1954), 1–18, and John W. Shy, "A New Look at Colonial Militia," *William and Mary Quarterly,* 3d ser., XX (Apr. 1963), 175–185.

[89] Lavradio, *Relatório,* p. 437.

[90] *Idem,* circular to all mestres de campo and capitães mores, Feb. 26, 1771, ANRJ, Col. 70, Liv. V, fols. 165ᵛ–166ʳ; one can surmise the dressing down in store for the recipient of a one-sentence dispatch such as the following: "Logo q. Vm.ce receber esta partirá p.a cid.e p.a me vir fallar." *Idem* to M[igu]el Ant[un]es Ferreira, Oct. 9, 1776, CMCM, cod. 25, fol. 143ʳ. The same codice contains numerous other directives written in the same vein.

without his sanction, for recommending appointments of men he considered to be unqualified for military positions, and for despotic behavior provoking complaints from their settlers. On balance, however, Lavradio pronounced himself well satisfied with the performance of these very useful colonial-born district administrators.[91]

Conclusion

As the foregoing indicates, the viceroy was kept busy communicating on a wide variety of topics with many different types of officials within the territories directly under his control. In doing so, he was obliged to evaluate the capabilities and culpabilities of personnel not of his own choosing. He relied on them to check each other, as well as on the constant flow of petitions from the settlers concerning the behavior of their officials. Though he clearly had no use for popular participation in government, he was responsive to legitimate complaints of misconduct by public functionaries, but like a good modern editor, he refused to take cognizance of anonymous accusations.[92] Because of differences in age, training, field experience, temperament, and social status, clashes among salaried and nonsalaried officials and between them and the viceroy were doubtless inevitable. The wonder is not that such conflicts arose, but that they were not more common, more divisive. The Pombaline style of government with its emphasis on extreme deference and literal obedience to royal authority and its discouragement of dissent may have been partly responsible for their relative absence; but so, too, was the character of the viceroy himself. For though the marquis was demanding, impatient, and sometimes haughty and peevish, he abhorred factional controversy. But if the maintenance of harmony was the tone that he constantly struck in his instructions to subordinates, the record of his relations with the governors of the subcaptaincies and his fellow captains-general reveals a quite different sonance.

91 *Idem, Relatório,* pp. 421, 436–438.

92 Typical of his reactions to such complaints is the following: "Vejo o q. Vm.ce me representa a respeito de Verissimo Alves, e a carta q. VM.ce me diz ser do mesmo sobre o qual devo dizer-lhe q. como hé carta sem nome, não merece credito, nem della deve Vm.ce fazer cazo, q. he o mesmo q. eu faço com todas as q. se me escrevião sem serem assignadas . . . ; e só no cazo de se verificarem alguas das couzas q. contem a mesma carta e constando estas por pessoas fidedignas [sic], q. as prezenciassem hé q. Vm.ce me deve dar conta para eu proceder. . . ." Lavradio to P[adr]e Vicente Ferreira Noronha, May 22, 1776, CMCM, cod. 25, fol. 104ᵛ.

XVI

Relations with Governors
and Captains-General

I therefore nominate you Viceroy and Captain General of the Land and
Sea of the State of Brazil for the term of three years and longer until
it is My pleasure to name your successor. . . . And in order that the affairs
of my service be well governed . . . I give you power and authority over
all the Generals, field masters, fortress captains . . . and over all *fidalgos*
and . . . other of my subjects regardless of quality, state, or condition. . . .

> Patent of Dom Antônio Álvaro da Cunha,
> Conde da Cunha, June 27, 1763, *PAN*, II, 3–4.

[The King] orders me to explain to Your Excellency that although the
Viceroys of Bahia bore the appellation of Viceroys of all the State of
Brazil, [they] did not bestow officers, nor govern in the other captain-
cies [-general] which have governors subject to His Majesty . . . [and] that
the same therefore holds good in [the] captaincy of Rio de Janeiro where
Your Excellency is Viceroy with respect to Bahia, Pernambuco &c.

> Francisco Xavier de Mendonça Furtado to Conde da Cunha,
> February 4, 1765, ANRJ, Col. 67, Liv. I-A, fols. 76^{r-v} (orig.) .

THE TWO QUOTATIONS that begin this chapter illustrate the
differences between the theoretical and the actual limits of the territorial authority of Brazil's eighteenth-century viceroys. In theory they
were charged with the management of the king's domains throughout
the length and breadth of the colony, but in reality they administered
only a small part of them. Within their respective spheres the viceroys
and the captains-general were the heads of separate but often inter-
related hierarchies. In critical times, such as the mid-seventies, the
Crown did grant the viceroys exceptional war powers and placed certain captains-general under their orders. However, since it failed to
equip the viceroys with coercive powers and since it continued to
issue the captains-general instructions which at times were at variance
with the viceroys' directives, the captains-general retained their traditional options of compliance. Thus the Marquis of Lavradio was always obliged to deal with his fellow senior administrators on the basis
of *primus inter pares* rather than as *supereminentia*. The captains-
general, like the viceroys, were ultimately answerable for their acts to
the Crown, but the subordinate governors of Colônia, Rio Grande de

São Pedro, and Santa Catarina were immediately responsible to the viceroy.[1] The problems Dom Luís de Almeida encountered with both types of executive officers are explored below.

The Viceroy and the Subordinate Governors

During the Marquis of Lavradio's administration six men governed subordinate units of the viceroyalty. They included two governors of Colônia, Pedro José Soares de Figueiredo Sarmento (1764–1775),[2] and Francisco José da Rocha (1775–1777); two governors of Santa Catarina, Francisco de Sousa Menezes (1765–1775) and Pedro Antônio da Gama e Freitas (1775–1777); and two governors of Rio Grande de São Pedro, José Marcelino de Figueiredo (1769–1771; 1773–1780) and Antônio da Veiga de Andrade, who filled the office on an interim basis from 1771 to 1773. All were high-ranking military officers who with one exception held or attained the rank of colonel during their administrative tenure.[3] Three (Rocha, Gama e Freitas, and Veiga de Andrade) had been aides of the viceroy. Except for Gama e Freitas, who served briefly as captain-general of Minas Gerais in 1775, none seems to have had prior administrative experience before assuming his borderlands post. The background of Francisco José da Rocha has been discussed earlier,[4] and that of José Marcelino de Figueiredo will be considered shortly. Nothing of significance is known about the previous careers or family relationships of the others.[5]

Like the viceroy, the borderlands governors conducted a wide-ranging official correspondence. Besides reporting regularly to Lavradio, they issued instructions to their own corps of subordinates and corresponded with each other. The governors of Colônia and Rio Grande also exchanged insults with their counterparts in neighboring Spanish territories. Since they faced common military and economic problems, the governors of Rio Grande and Santa Catarina often shared information with the captains-general of São Paulo. However,

---

[1] Oeiras to Lavradio, Apr. 14, 1769 (2nd instruction), par. 23, *RIHGB*, XXXI:1, 298–299.

[2] The roster of officeholders in Varnhagen erroneously lists Colonel Francisco Antônio Cardoso de Menezes as governor of Colônia from 1769 to 1775. Francisco Adolfo de Varnhagen, *História geral do Brasil*, V, 306.

[3] The exception, José Marcelino, was promoted from colonel to brigadier in 1774 as a reward for his role in turning back the Vértiz expedition.

[4] See pp. 120–124, above.

[5] It is tempting to assume that Pedro Antônio da Gama e Freitas was related to José Mauricio da Gama e Freitas, a member of the Relação of Rio de Janeiro and president of the mesa da inspeção during Lavradio's regime, but I have not found positive evidence of such a connection.

the subordinate governors did not communicate with other captains-general or with the Court; the viceroy was always the channel through which they received instructions from Lisbon.

Only in one instance did the Marquis of Lavradio recall a governor to confer with him, but he endeavored to keep in close touch with each of his lieutenants. On the average of twice a month smacks plied between Rio de Janeiro and its dependencies with dispatches from and to the viceroy. Most dispatches concerned the military, economic, and routine administrative matters discussed in previous chapters. Sometimes Dom Luís found occasion to praise the efforts of his subordinates; more often he scolded them for misinterpreting their orders, for overstepping their authority, and for becoming involved in conflicts with other officials.[6] In such instances he lectured them on what he called his "system of government." He insisted that the king's commands must always be blindly obeyed,[7] but emphasized that His Majesty's service suffered when his colonial officers behaved despotically and became embroiled in fruitless feuds. Caution, suavity, and tact were far more effective than fire or iron, for "If two stones are struck together with equal force, both will break into pieces; however, if one, even though it be the smaller, is gently rubbed against the other, dislodging by degrees the sod which clings to it, . . . neither . . . will be damaged and both can contribute to the strength of the edifice: prudence, moderation, toleration, perseverance, and time have always conquered the greatest difficulties in the world." [8]

A frequent recipient of such paternal advice was an officer who in Brazil was called José Marcelino de Figueiredo but whose true name was Manuel Jorge Gomes de Sepúlveda. Shortly after the end of the Peninsular War of 1762–1763, Captain Sepúlveda (1735–1814), a cavalry officer, became involved in a barroom scuffle with several British officers who were amusing themselves by disparaging the abilities of the Portuguese sovereign. The infuriated captain killed one of the Britons, and British authorities demanded that he be held accountable for his crime. But Sepúlveda seems to have been too socially prominent to be treated like a common criminal; besides, from the Portuguese point of view he deserved praise rather than punishment.

---

6 These generalizations are based primarily on the viceroy's correspondence with his subordinates in CMCM, cods. 4, 15, and 26, *passim*.

7 "As Reaes Ordens . . . [d'El Rei] . . . devemos todos obedecer às cegas, olhando somente para o verdadeiro espirito dellas, sem entrarmos na disputa se forão bem ó mal passadas, poiz basta serem determinadas, pella Real Rezolução do mesmo S.or em que asista aquela alta e superior comprienção, q. a Divina Providencia depozitou nos soberanos senhores, para obrarem com aserto em todos as determinações . . . e devemos executalas no seo literal sentido, sem lhe [sic] darmos interpretação algũa." Lavradio to Sousa de Menezes, Apr. 25, 1770, CMCM, cod. 15, fol. 18ᵛ.

8 Lavradio to Francisco José da Rocha, July 21, 1772, *ibid.*, fol. 118ʳ.

Nevertheless it appeared expedient to get him out of the kingdom until the incident had been forgotten. In 1765 he turned up in Rio de Janeiro bearing the pseudonym of José Marcelino de Figueiredo and orders that he be assigned to one of the Peninsular regiments stationed there. In an accompanying dispatch the colonial secretary informed the viceroy of the circumstances behind the subterfuge and stressed that the fact the captain was serving in the colony under a false cognomen must remain secret.[9] So far as can be determined, that secret was well kept, for no one ever hinted in his official correspondence that José Marcelino de Figueiredo had ever been known by any other name. Several months before the Marquis of Lavradio came to Rio de Janeiro, José Marcelino left port to assume the post formerly held by José Custódio de Sá e Faria as governor of Rio Grande.[10]

Dom Luís de Almeida was doubtless acquainted with the circumstances behind José Marcelino's presence in Brazil and very likely disapproved of his past conduct, which he would have considered unbecoming a gentleman. Thus he may have been unfavorably disposed toward the governor from the beginning of their relationship. Certainly the viceroy soon found abundant reasons to criticize his behavior, sometimes over quite trivial matters. For example, when he learned that the governor had designated a newly formed Rio-grandense militia company as the Royal Volunteers (after his own former regiment in Portugal), Dom Luís reprimanded José Marcelino for having acted without first clearing the name with him. In any case, he observed testily, the name was singularly inappropriate since the king had already disbanded that regiment for disciplinary reasons; instead, he insisted, the company would be called the Select Volunteers. When the governor sought to intervene in a dispute between an engineering officer and a curate by writing directly to the Bishop of Rio de Janeiro, he drew the viceroy's censure again for having failed to consult him first. Dom Luís also reproved José Marcelino for auctioning a ranch belonging to the king, asserting that as president of the junta da fazenda that was his responsibility. In another instance he rebuked the governor for ignoring an order from the same treasury board to dispatch certain moneys to the capital. He also accused him of failing to display proper respect in his dispatches for the viceregal office, and contended that his despotic behavior was

9 Francisco Xavier de Mendonça Furtado to Conde da Cunha, Mar. 1, 1765, Varnhagen, *História*, V, 289.

10 Auto de posse, Mar. 9, 1769, *Revista do Archivo Público do Rio Grande do Sul*, No. 7 (Sept. 1922), 15–17. For an uncritical sketch of José Marcelino's service as governor, see Florêncio de Abreu, "Govêrno de José Marcelino de Figueiredo no govêrno de São-Pedro—1769 a 1780," Congresso sulriograndense de história e geografia. *Anais*, II:3 (1937) 177–204.

a source of unrest among the troops and populace in the subcaptaincy.[11]

As for the target of these salvos, the governor calmly insisted that he had always acted in the best interests of the Royal Service and that God would judge whether he had erred.[12] But the marquis was unwilling to await the Deity's verdict. In June 1771 he hinted that because of the governor's complaints of ill health he was considering relieving him of his duties. Two months later the viceroy peremptorily informed the governor that Lieutenant Colonel Antônio da Veiga de Andrade was coming to replace him, and that as soon as he arrived José Marcelino would return to the capital where he would discover "that I am capable of showing you that I can make my subordinates obey me as they should." [13]

José Marcelino spent a year and a half in Rio de Janeiro learning that lesson.[14] Meantime the viceroy directed his replacement to conduct an investigation of his predecessor's administration. In particular, he was to inquire whether the governor had failed to execute, respect, and keep secret the viceroy's orders; whether he had mistreated civilians and military personnel and had been petulant in his relations with the câmara of Viamão; and whether he had mishandled royal property.[15]

The charges were serious enough but the proofs were evidently defective, for in June 1773 José Marcelino resumed his post.[16] But he was soon joined by a shadow, Gaspar José de Matos, another of the viceroy's aides.[17] Matos escorted a detachment of troops from Rio de

11 Lavradio to José Marcelino de Figueiredo, Apr. 20, 1770, Jan. 28, Mar. 13, and June 17, 1771, CMCM, cod. 15, fols. 20ᵛ, 44ʳ, 52ʳ, and 67ʳ⁻ᵛ. *Idem* to Antônio da Veiga de Andrade, Oct. 26, 1771, *ibid.*, fols. 89ʳ–90ᵛ.

12 José Marcelino de Figueiredo to Lavradio, July 6, 1771, CMCM, cod. 28, fol. 65ʳ (orig.).

13 Lavradio to José Marcelino, June 9 and Aug. 14, 1771, *ibid.*, cod. 15, fols. 66ʳ, 72ʳ⁻ᵛ.

14 There is no evidence to support the contention of Alcides Cruz that José Marcelino returned to Portugal in 1771 and came back to Brazil two years later. *Vida de Raphael Pinto Bandeira* (Pôrto Alegre, 1906), p. 92.

15 Lavradio to Veiga de Andrade, Aug. 27, 1771, CMCM, cod. 15, fol. 74ʳ.

16 Some historians, including Varnhagen (*Historia*, V, 289), have argued that when José Marcelino returned to Rio Grande, he began a second term, but that was clearly not the case. Lavradio indicated to the Governor's interim replacement that "Com approvação d'El Rey . . . , torno a mandar a esse Continente . . . ao Coronel Jozè Marcelino de Figueiredo, *para continuar o governlo debaixo da mesma pose* e homenagem, q. se lhe deu no anno de mil setecentos e seçenta e nova . . . ." To Veiga de Andrade, Apr. 5, 1773, *ibid.*, fol. 154ʳ (italics added). He wrote substantially the same to Governors Francisco de Souza de Menezes and Pedro Jozè Soares de Figueiredo Sarmento in dispatches of Apr. 17, 1773, *ibid.*, fols. 156ᵛ–157ᵛ.

17 Gaspar José de Matos Ferreira e Lucena, son of a field marshal, enrolled in Lavradio's Cascaes regiment on Aug. 7, 1762; he accompanied Dom Luís to Bahia with the rank of lieutenant, and there became his aide-de-camp with the rank of captain. He followed Lavradio to Rio de Janeiro where he became inspector of the

Janeiro to the subcaptaincy, but he went sent there primarily to keep an eye on the governor.[18] After receiving favorable reports from him, Lavradio expressed satisfaction that the governor had improved his relations with subordinates.[19] Two years later he even found occasion to praise the "tireless zeal" of José Marcelino, by then promoted to brigadier.[20] But the two soon had another falling out, and Dom Luís warned his successor to be on guard against José Marcelino's arbitrary, disobedient actions.[21]

The Viceroy and the Captains-General

Although a viceroy could recall a disobedient governor and recommend the naming of his successor, he could not do that with intractable captains-general. Their nomination and removal was determined entirely by the Crown, though in specific instances the viceroy was authorized to designate interim replacements. But he could not summon uncooperative captains-general before him nor personally inspect their districts, much less dispatch troops there to compel compliance with his wishes. It is true that the patents of the captains-general continued to include reminders of their subordination to the viceroys,[22] but such inferiority was purely nominal. Neither Lavradio's initial instructions nor those issued to his fellow senior administrators required them to submit to his jurisdiction in administrative,

---

viceregal guard, part of which he led to Rio Grande in 1774. Subsequently he returned to Rio de Janeiro to become supervisor of a new royal gun factory. From 1780 to 1796 he served as colonel of the regiment of dragoons in Rio Grande. In May, 1808 he became a lieutenant general, and in 1821 he retired as field marshal. Matos to the Queen, Lisbon, Dec. 15, 1796, AHU/PA-RGS, *maço* 1; "Officiaes do Estado Maior do Exercito no Brasil em 1808," *RADF*, II (1895), 479.

18 Lavradio to José Marcelino, Aug. 9, 1773, CMCM, cod. 4, fol. 14ʳ.

19 Lavradio to José Marcelino, Oct. 12, 1773 and June 13, 1774, *ibid.*, fols. 14ᵛ–16ʳ, 52ᵛ.

20 Lavradio to José Marcelino, Oct. 1, 1775, *ibid.*, fol. 75ᵛ.

21 Lavradio, *Relatório*, p. 484. Soon after the marquis left Brazil, the governor was again removed from office, this time as a consequence of a personal feud with the formidable Rafael Pinto da Bandeira, but such scrapes seem to have had no adverse affect on his later career. Before returning to the kingdom, where he officially regained the use of his original name in 1783, he married a member of the prestigious Sá e Benevides family in Rio de Janeiro. In Portugal he rose to the rank of field marshal by the end of the 1780s, and was then serving as governor of the city of Bragança and as commanding general of the province of Tras os Montes. During his last years he participated in the liberation of Portugal from the French. Abreu, "Govêrno de José Marcelino de Figueiredo," pp. 199 f.; Melo e Castro to Luís de Vasconcelos e Sousa, Nov. 28, 1783, BNRJ, 4, 4, 5, n. 15; Cruz, *Pinto Bandeira* p. 93; *Gazeta de Lisboa*, XLIII (2d suppl.), Jan. 3, 1789 and XLVI (2d suppl.) Nov. 17, 1789; José Feliciano Fernandes Pinheiro, *Anais da província de S. Pedro*, p. 140, n. 2.

22 See the comments of D. Fernando José de Portugal appended to 2RGG, par. 39.

economic, or fiscal matters.[23] The viceroy did have primary responsibility for the colony's defenses, but even when the Crown specifically directed certain captains-general to provide him with men, matériel, and funds for that purpose, Dom Luís was obliged to phrase his appeals for such assistance in the form of *requests* rather than *commands*, as he was accustomed to address subordinate governors and others within his own hierarchy. And when such requests proved unavailing, he had no recourse but to complain to the Crown.

Biographical details concerning the captains-general of Lavradio's time are meager. The first of the two who served in Pernambuco during Dom Luís' administration was Manuel da Cunha Menezes, afterwards Conde de Limiar(es) . Cunha Menezes was the son of an officer in the household of Queen Mariana of Austria and was one of several members of his family to hold high office in late-colonial Brazil.[24] He came to Pernambuco at the youthful age of twenty-seven and remained there from 1769 until 1774, when he was promoted to Bahia where he served until 1779. According to one historian, contemporaries considered him exceptionally able and honest.[25] An examination of some of his correspondence [26] indicates that he was conscientious, cautious, and jealous of his prerogatives—common traits of most of Lavradio's fellow administrators. His successor in Pernambuco was José César de Menezes (1774–1787) , no relation of Cunha Menezes but the son of Fernandes César de Menezes, viceroy of Brazil from 1720 to 1735. They came from a long line of nobles who had traditionally supplied the Crown with sons for military and administrative posts throughout the empire. Forty years old when he arrived in Olinda, José César had seen military service in the kingdom and

23 E.g., Martinho e Melo e Castro, "Instrução com q. S. Mag. manda passar á Goiás o Governador José de Almeida e Vasconcelos," Oct. 1, 1771, *RIHGB*, XXVII:2 (1864), 234–259; [*idem*], "Instrução militar para Martim Lopes Lobo de Saldanha, . . . capitão-general . . . de S. Paulo," Jan. 14, 1775, *ibid.*, IV (2d ed., 1863) , 350–362; and *idem*, "Instrução para D. Antônio de Noronha, . . . capitão general . . . de Minas Geraes," Jan. 24, 1775, *ibid.* VI (2d ed., 1865) , 215–221. For Lavradio's initial instructions, see Chap. V, n. 1.

24 The Cunha Menezes (sometimes written Cunha e Menezes or Cunha de Menezes) were the Wentworths of late-colonial Brazil. One of Manoel's brothers, Luís da Cunha e Menezes, served as captain-general of Goiás (1778–1783) and Minas Gerais (1783–1788) ; another brother, Tristão da Cunha e Menezes, also served as captain-general of Goiás (1783–1798) , while a cousin, D. João Manoel de Menezes, held the same post between 1800 and 1804. Francisco da Cunha e Menezes, captain-general of São Paulo (1782–1786) , India (1786–?) , and Bahia (1802–1805) , may have been another brother. According to Pizarro (*Memorias históricas do Rio de Janeiro*, VIII:1, p. 112) , Manoel's widow married his brother, Luís.

25 F. A. Pereira da Costa, "Governadores e capitães generaes de Pernambuco, 1654–1821," *Revista do Instituto Historico Archeologico e Geografico Pernambucano*, No. 58 (June, 1903) , 452–455.

26 Particularly a register of his correspondence with the Court between 1774 and 1779 in the Library of Congress. Portuguese Collection, II-35-E, 1.

in India. When he completed his tour of duty in Pernambuco he left behind not only a reputation as a forceful, energetic, impartial administrator, but also a natural son, Pedro César de Menezes who later became captain-general of Piauí (1803–1805).[27]

During the latter part of Lavradio's stay in Rio de Janeiro the captain-general of Minas Gerais was Dom Antônio de Noronha (1775–1780), who may have been related to that long line of men of the same name who served in India from the sixteenth to the eighteenth centuries. Judge Texeira Coelho who worked closely with Dom Antônio considered him an able, industrious, humane administrator, and stated that when he relinquished his post Minas had lost a true restorer.[28] Another accorded that sobriquet was Dom Luís Antônio de Sousa, captain-general of São Paulo (1765–1775), whose background and relations with the Marquis of Lavradio are described in the next section. Little is known about his successor, Martim Lopes Lobo de Saldanha (1775–1782), save that his family were *fidalgos* from the province of Alemtejo and claimed that their ancestors had fought along with King Sebastian at the ill-fated battle of Alcacarquibir (1578). He does not appear to have been related to Cardinal Saldanha, the *bête noire* of the Jesuits. Enough has already been said about Captain-General Saldanha in earlier chapters to indicate that he was the most deferential among the captains-general with whom Viceroy Lavradio had close relations. He was also the most mediocre in abilities and at best must be characterized as a mere time-server. Ultimately he was removed from office to face charges of despotic conduct.[29]

Nothing of significance has come to light concerning the backgrounds of others who served as captains-general in Brazil during Lavradio's tenure. It would appear that the captains-general had more administrative experience behind them than the subordinate governors, and that they came from a higher social station, one that in some cases was not far removed from that of the Marquis of Lavradio.

Since Rio de Janeiro was the port of call for warships carrying some of the captains-general to and from their stations, the viceroy had an opportunty to confer personally with several of those officials when they passed through his capital. In 1771–1772 José de Almeida Vasconcelos and Luís de Albuquerque de Melo, respectively captains-

---

[27] Rodolfo Garcia, "A capitania de Pernambuco no governo de José César de Meneses (1774–1787) ," *RIHGB*, LXXXIV (1918) , 533–560.

[28] "Instrução," p. 362.

[29] For an uncritical scissors-and-paste sketch, see Dulce de Campos, "O governo do capitão-general de São Paulo Martim Lopes Lobo de Saldanha, 1775–1782: notas e apontamentos," *Revista do Arquivo Municipal [de] São Paulo*, Ano 14, CXVII (Jan.–Mar. 1948), 3–50.

general of Goiás and Mato Grosso, stayed in the city for more than six months before leaving for the interior.[30] The next year Dom Francisco Innocêncio de Sousa Coutinho, retiring captain-general of Angola, spent more than a month with Lavradio before continuing home to assume his responsibilities as ambassador to Spain.[31] In 1775 Dom Antônio de Noronha and Martim Lopes Lobo de Saldanha held extended discussions with Dom Luís before they took up their duties.[32] But none of the captains-general came to Rio de Janeiro during their terms, for they were not permitted to leave their posts without special royal authorization.[33]

Nevertheless, the captains-general were supposed to keep the viceroy informed of their activities.[34] Some did, though none sent him periodic status reports like those subordinates once submitted to the governors-general. Lavradio's correspondence with the executive officers of units adjoining Rio de Janeiro (São Paulo, Minas Gerais, and Bahia) always ran heavy. It was less abundant with the captains-general of Pernambuco and Angola. Dom Luís seldom heard from the administrators of Mato Grosso and Goiás,[35] and had no contact with those in Pará or Maranhão. Some captains-general, such as those

[30] Lavradio to Conde de Valadares and to Antônio Carlos Furtado de Mendonça, Dec. 2, 1771, CMCM, cod. 15, fols. 87ʳ–88ʳ; Balthasar da Silva Lisboa, *Annaes do Rio de Janeiro*, VI, 357–358.

[31] Lavradio to Melo e Castro, Jan. 15, 1773, BNRJ, 10, 4, 8 (unfoliated); *idem* to Antônio de Alencastre, Feb. 19, 1773, CMCM, cod. 15, fol. 150ᵛ.

[32] Lavradio to Bartolomeu José Vahia, Apr. 4, 1775, CMCM, cod. 25, fol. 15ʳ; Lobo de Saldanha to Melo e Castro, Apr. 24, 1775, *DI*, XXVIII (1898), 1–4. Earlier Luís Antônio de Sousa stayed nearly a month with the Conde da Cunha before passing to São Paulo. Sousa to Overseas Council, Dec. 1, 1767, *DI*, XXIII (1897), 250–256. As will be noted later, Sousa was obliged to spend several months in the viceregal capital before returning to Portugal. Among other dignitaries whom Viceroy Lavradio entertained were the governor of Goa, the archbishop of Salvador, and the bishop of São Paulo. Lavradio to Furtado de Mendonça, Jan. 14 and Apr. 15, 1774, CMCM, cod. 4, fols. 30ᵛ, 46ʳ.

[33] There were at least two reasons why the Crown did not permit its senior officers to leave their posts at will. One was the traditional view that administrations always needed the guiding hands of their heads to function properly; the other was the fear of the possibly cabalistic nature of unauthorized meetings by high colonial functionaries. It will be recalled that the Crown did authorize Dom Antônio de Noronha to proceed from Ouro Prêto to Rio de Janeiro if the viceroy required his assistance to defend his capital, but that Dom Luís never exercised his option to call for him.

[34] In 1722 the Overseas Council directed the captains-general of Minas and São Paulo to "dar conta do estado do seu governo ao vice-rei . . . ainda que não haja novidade, . . . porque convem que o governo geral seja inteirado de todas as noticias." *Consulta* of Oct. 26, 1722, *RAPM*, XVI:1 (1911), 399; *DI*, XVIII (1896), 72.

[35] Much to Lavradio's chagrin. On more than one occasion he wrote "Hâ muito tempo q. não tenho tido o gosto de saber da estimavel saude de V. Ex.," a tactful reminder that the interior administrators were supposed to keep him informed of their activities. To Jozê de Almeida e Vasconcelos (captain-general of Goiás), Nov. 26 and Dec. 23, 1772, CMCM, cod. 15, fols. 144ʳ and 146ʳ.

in Bahia and Pernambuco, communicated with each other more often than they did with the viceroy. Most, though not all, wrote to the Crown more frequently than to Lavradio.

Some of these exchanges concerned personal affairs. Though such subjects were occasionally mentioned in regular dispatches (*cartas de oficio*), they were often reserved for special letters called *cartas familiar*. These were actually highly stylized documents in which the authors congratulated one another on their appointments, promotions, or impending retirements, and commiserated with each other on the common ailments that afflicted them all. The viceroy and the captains-general also shared news concerning life at Court, the achievements of members of their families, and the performance of officers stationed in their districts who were protégés of their correspondents.[36]

The bulk of Lavradio's active and passive correspondence with the captains-general pertained to military, fiscal, economic, and routine administrative matters affecting the Royal Service. Because of the viceroy's central position, the Crown sometimes used him as a channel of information to alert the captains-general to problems of common concern such as the prospect of war or peace or the expected arrival in Brazilian waters of large numbers of contrabandists. During the mid-seventies the viceroy also periodically informed the captains-general on the status of the borderlands conflict.[37]

Although Dom Luís cautiously shied away from the captains-generals' request to interpret the wishes of the Crown,[38] he was not loath to offer them paternal advice on methods to employ in governing their districts.[39] Such gratuitous advice is one indication of his desire to enlarge his sphere of influence, a common trait among bureaucrats. On more than one occasion he suggested to the colonial secretary that the viceroys ought to have more powers than they were customarily granted.[40] Presumably he meant powers over the captains-

---

[36] E.g., Luís Antônio de Sousa to Conde da Cunha, Dec. 5, 1767, *DI*, XXIII (1896), 247–248 (a farewell message) ; *idem* to Conde d'Azambuja, Dec. 4, 1767, *ibid.*, 248–249 (welcoming the new viceroy to Brazil). Lavradio sent and received similar messages. E.g., Lavradio to D. Francisco Innocêncio de Sousa Coutinho, July 7, 1771, CMCM, cod. 15, fol. 69^v; *idem* to Antônio Carlos Furtado de Mendonça (acting captain-general of Goiás), Aug. 8, 1771, *ibid.*, fol. 71^v.

[37] E.g., by a "carta circular a todos os Generaes" of May 7, 1776 (CMCM, cod. 26, fols. 109^v–110^v) he reported the Portuguese victories of March 31–April 1, 1776 in Rio Grande. A notation indicates that copies were sent to the captains-general of Angola, São Paulo, Minas Gerais, Goiás, Bahia, and Pernambuco.

[38] His customary response was "Ask the King or be guided by your own judgment." E.g., Lavradio to Luís Antônio de Sousa, Mar. 16 and Apr. 23, 1770, CMCM, cod. 15, fols. 16^r and 18^r.

[39] E.g., Lavradio to José César de Menezes, July 12, 1775, IHGB, *Lata* 186, MS 4693A, fols. 101^r–104^r; and *idem* to Manoel da Cunha Menezes, Oct. 23, 1776, *VRL*, pp. 319–331, especially pp. 325–327.

[40] Lavradio to Melo e Castro, Oct. 6, 1772 and [?], 1773, cited in *VRL*, pp. 40 and 128. Unfortunately I have not been able to locate copies of these dispatches.

general, but the marquis' own attempts to intervene in areas beyond those directly assigned to him were conspicuously unsuccessful.

One such occasion arose in 1770 after the death of a captain-general of Goiás. Failing to discover a royal directive outlining the procedure to be followed in such instances, the local authorities in Vila Boa turned for advice to their ouvidor. The magistrate suggested that they do what was done under similar circumstances in Bahia and Pernambuco, namely convoke a meeting of Vila Boa's câmara, its leading citizens (*homens bons*), and its principal royal officials to elect a temporary junta. After the junta named a triumvirate consisting of the ouvidor, a militia sergeant-major, and the câmara's eldest alderman, that body notified the viceroy of their election.

Far from approving this procedure, Dom Luís declared that it was highly irregular and insisted that he alone had the power to designate an interim head of Goiás.[41] Consequently he assigned Brigadier Antônio Carlos Furtado de Mendonça to administer Goiás until the king had appointed a new administrator, and ordered the junta to dissolve itself. The junta received the viceroy's rebuke with ill humor since its members believed that their election had been in accordance with the practice followed elsewhere, but after a token protest, they resigned.

The differences of opinion between officials in Goiás and the viceroy in this matter led to an alvará that must have disappointed both sides. In the future, the Court directed, whenever an executive officer died in office or was incapable of performing his duties, a triumvirate consisting of the senior ecclesiastical, judicial, and military authorities would automatically assume the reins of government and hold them until the king had named a successor.[42] Thus while the Crown denied colonials a voice in the selection of interim regimes, it also deprived the viceroy of the possibility of extending his influence to other administrative units. Eight years later the new procedure went into effect when the next captain-general of Goiás left his post before his successor arrived. The junta that took over on that occasion notified the viceroy of that fact, and Lavradio could do no more than acknowledge their existence.[43]

Another locale where the Marquis of Lavradio was tempted to intervene was in his former captaincy-general, Bahia. In 1774 the efforts of Captain-General Manoel da Cunha Menezes to fill out the regi-

41 In the first dispatch cited in note 43 below, the viceroy rested his claim on an unidentified order to Conde de Bobadela issued in a similar situation many years before.

42 Alvará of Dec. 12, 1770, *CLP*, II, 521–522.

43 The foregoing is based on Lavradio to Antônio José Cabral de Almeida, Damião José de Sá Pereira, and Antônio Thomaz da Costa, May 10, 1770, *RIHGB*, XXVII:2 (1864), 231–232; *idem* to câmara of Vila Boa, n. d. [1770], ANRJ, Col. 70, Liv. V, fol. 56ʳ; and *idem* to junta of Goiás, July 29, 1778, CMCM, cod. 26, fols. 148ᵛ–149ʳ.

ments he was sending to Rio de Janeiro stirred up the usual unrest, particularly in Vitória, Espírito Santo. That community's câmara petitioned Cunha Menezes to exempt its citizens from the draft, alleging that their port was too strategically important (because it gave access to Minas Gerais) and exposed to Indian attacks to have its manpower depleted. Evidently the viceroy, who always wanted full jurisdiction over Espírito Santo, heard of the petition, for he urged the captain-general to comply with the aldermen's request. Cunha Menezes, clearly piqued at the marquis' interference, wrote a testy letter to the câmara asserting that theirs was the only disloyal part of his government.[44] Nevertheless he sent the well-known engineer José Antônio Caldas to take charge of the port's defenses since, as the captain-general informed the Court with some sarcasm, the viceroy had expressed personal concern for its security.[45] A few months later the captain-general's recruiters aroused further discontent in the district of Porto Seguro, north of Espírito Santo. After its capitão mor and ouvidor complained that the draft would "ruin" their district, Dom Luís initially stayed Cunha Menezes' order for the enrollment of recruits there; then, admitting that he lacked jurisdiction in the district, he urged the ouvidor to appeal to Cunha Menezes, suggesting that if that remedy failed he should apply to the king.[46]

The viceroy also sought to exert his influence in other captaincies-general. His criticism of the use of Negro slaves in textile manufacturing in Minas and of the alleged negligence of Mineiro officials in preventing contraband trade there has already been discussed,[47] as have his efforts to encourage tobacco growing in São Paulo.[48] But Lavradio carefully refrained from issuing orders directly to the subordinates of either captain-general without consulting their chiefs.[49] It may be that he was particularly cautious in his relations with Paulista officials as a result of his encounters with their dynamic captain-general, Luís Antônio de Sousa.

44 The captain-general was not telling the truth, for apart from Pôrto Seguro (where similar unrest existed), there was also popular opposition to recruiting in Sergipe. See his dispatch cited in n. 45.

45 Cunha Menezes to Melo e Castro, Apr. 15, 1776, BNRJ, I-4, 3, 16, n. 70.

46 Petition of câmara of Vitória, [Sept. 16, 1775]; Lavradio to [Cunha Menezes], Oct. 31, 1775; Cunha Menezes to câmara, Dec. 15, 1775, Castro e Almeida, Inventário, II, 312, 318–319; idem to Melo e Castro, Apr. 16, 1776, cited in n. 45; Lavradio to capitão mor Anastácio Joaquim Moita Furtado, Oct. 10, 1775, CMCM, cod. 25, fols. 55ʳ–56ʳ; idem to ouvidor José Xavier Machado Monteiro, May 26, 1776, ibid., fols. 106ʳ⁻ᵛ.

47 See pp. 383–384 and 401.

48 See p. 362.

49 In one instance he advised a curate responsible for opening up part of a road between Rio de Janeiro and São Paulo to refer all questions concerning the section of that road within São Paulo to its captain-general and those pertaining to the part within Rio de Janeiro to himself. Lavradio to Padre Henrique Jose de Carvalho, July 15, 1776, ibid., cod. 25, fol. 121ʳ.

Lavradio Versus Luís Antônio de Sousa

Of all the captains-general who served in Brazil during Viceroy Lavradio's administration, Luís Antônio de Sousa was the most energetic, possibly the ablest, and certainly the most contentious. In the annals of São Paulo he is called the restorer because he became its first captain-general after a seventeen-year lapse during which São Paulo was governed from Rio de Janeiro. Having lost control over Minas Gerais in 1720, the Paulistas were deprived of two additional territories in 1748 when Mato Grosso and Goiás became separate administratve entities. As part of the same reorganization São Paulo was downgraded from the rank of captaincy-general to that of a mere district of Rio de Janeiro, administered by a governor at Santos who was subordinate to the captain-general of Rio de Janeiro, Gomes Freire de Andrada, Conde de Bobadela.[50] Shortly after Bobadela's death (January 1, 1763), the câmara of São Paulo petitioned the Crown to restore São Paulo to its former status, claiming that it had not been effectively administered from Rio de Janeiro. When the Conde da Cunha, first of Rio's viceroys, confirmed the need for a stronger government in São Paulo, the Crown decided to restore it as a separate captaincy-general.[51]

The first of the new line of independent administrators, forty-three-year-old Dom Luís Antônio de Sousa Botelho e Mourão, lord of the manor of Mateus (Morgado de Mateus), was a brother-in-law (and cousin) of two prominent Portuguese ambassadors,[52] and like them came from an aristocratic family that traced its lineage to a bastard of Afonso III (1248–1279), though the quality of Dom Luís' blood presumably had been corrupted by that of his great grandmother, Maria Teresa Coloen, an Irish commoner. Like his father, a cavalry officer who fought in the War of the Grand Alliance (1702–1713), Dom Luís became a soldier and commanded the second Braganza regiment

[50] Marco Antônio de Azevedo Coutinho (colonial secretary) to Dom Luiz Mascarenhas (captain-general of São Paulo), May 1, 1748, DI, XVI (1895), 166–168. The Crown's reorganization of Brazil in 1748 requires further study, particularly the reasons for the extinction of the captaincy-general of São Paulo, a subject Paulista historians prefer to pass over in silence. For further reference to the career of the Count of Bobadela, see Chap. II, n. 75.

[51] Overseas Council, consulta of Dec. 12, 1763, RIHGB/TE, V (1957), 341; Francisco Xavier de Mendonça Furtado to Conde da Cunha, Feb. 4, 1765, DI, XI (1896), 211–213; repr. in DI, XLVII (1929), 144.

[52] Dom Francisco Innocêncio de Sousa Coutinho and Dom Vicente de Sousa Coutinho, respectively ambassadors to Madrid and Versailles during the mid-1770s. As will be noted later, the former had previously been captain-general of Angola.

during the Peninsular War of 1762–1763.[53] Two years later he embarked for Brazil on his most important administrative assignment.[54]

The new captain-general soon demonstrated that he had no intention of being a mere time-server. Indeed, a review of his administration strongly suggests that he was bent on establishing a record that would commend his name to the Crown when a more important post became available[55] Certainly he seldom missed an opportunity to impress the Court with his statesmanlike qualities, gratuitously offering his opinion on such matters as the importance of retaining Portugal's "Gibraltar" (Colônia), and the profit she might derive from a rapprochement with Spain.[56] Few men in his position would have offered such unsolicited advice to their superiors, and it is inconceivable that Sousa did so without an ulterior purpose in mind.

Like other colonial administrators, including the Marquis of Lavradio, Sousa was concerned about the backwardness of the lands he governed. He offered several reasons for São Paulo's impoverishment, including the ignorance and slothfulness of the Paulistas, the rootlessness of Peninsulars who sojourned in the captaincy, the excessive dependence of both groups on slave labor, the dispersed character of the captaincy's inhabitants, and the wastefulness of an agricultural system that knew neither the plow nor the value of manure (*estrume*).[57] Though he accomplished little of direct benefit to agricul-

---

[53] "Requerimento de D. Luís Antônio de Sousa . . . por seu procurador, o filho, D. José de Sousa . . . a [Maria I]," post 1775, *RIHGB/TE*, VII (1957), 56; Américo Brasiliense Antunes de Moura, "Govêrno do Morgado de Mateus no vice-reinado do conde da Cunha. S. Paulo Restaurado," *Revista do Arquivo Municipal*, LII (São Paulo, 1938), 9–155, is the first part of what promised to be a full-length study of Sousa's administration but covers only the years 1765–1767.

[54] The chronology of Sousa's progress toward his post illustrate the leisurely pace with which Portuguese colonial administrators commonly assumed their offices. He was appointed on Dec. 14, 1764, but did not take his oath at Court until Feb. 18, 1765. He sailed from Lisbon on Mar. 27, arriving in Rio de Janeiro June 20. There, pursuant to his instructions, he consulted with the Conde da Cunha until July 16, when he sailed for Santos, arriving eight days later. But he did not ascend the plateau to be installed by the câmara of São Paulo until Apr. 7, 1766, nearly a year and a half after his appointment. Sousa to Overseas Council, Dec. 1, 1767, *DI*, XXIII (1896), 250, 255.

[55] In 1767 Sousa hastily wrote the Conde de Oeiras to assure him that although his wife had petitioned the king that he be allowed to return home upon the completion of his three-year term, he was willing to serve overseas as long as he could be useful and that his family could get along without him. One might infer that Sousa was glad to be away from a domineering spouse, but it is more charitable to assume that he hoped to remain in São Paulo long enough to establish a record that would warrant his promotion. Sousa to Oeiras, July 3, 1767, *DI*, XXIII (1896), 185–186.

[56] E.g., Sousa to Oeiras, Oct. 14, 1766 and Jan. 28, 1768, *ibid.*, 134–138, 371–373. Other examples of Sousa's views on the proper military strategy the Portuguese should observe are discussed below.

[57] Sousa to Oeiras, Dec. 23, 1766, Jan. 30 and 31, and Mar. 11, 1768, *ibid.*, 1–10, 374–383, and 392–396.

ture, Sousa sought to spur the Paulista economy by encouraging the formation of a wholesale syndicate in Santos to promote Paulista exports to the kingdom, thereby emulating the Crown's monopoly companies for the development of northern Brazil.[58] Distressed that no new towns had been established in the captaincy since 1705 and that many of its inhabitants were living beyond the pale of the law or the church, he created nineteen new parishes and founded half a dozen vilas soon after taking office.[59]

The founding of two of these communities–Lajes situated on the "road" between Curitiba and Viamão in the highlands of Santa Catarina, and Guaratuba, located in the bay of the same name on the littoral of the present state of Paraná–involved Sousa in one of several protracted boundary controversies. Though both towns were within lands claimed by the governors of Santa Catarina and therefore by the viceroys, Sousa contended that São Paulo's southern boundary properly extended to the Rio Pelotas, and thus included all of the present states of Paraná and mainland Santa Catarina.[60] In the north he lay claim to a twenty-league stretch of land bordering on Minas Gerais, and tried unsuccessfully to enlist the support of three viceroys to sustain São Paulo's position in that dispute.[61] In the southwest the captain-general encroached on lands already contested by the captains-general of Mato Grosso and the Spanish governors of Paraguay.

As in all such boundary controversies between rival colonial authorities, there was a measure of sheer aggrandizement behind Sousa's aggressive moves. But he also seems to have had other objectives in mind. One was to increase the sources of income of São Paulo, one of the colony's poorest administrative units. That was his prime reason for seeking control over Paulista settlements along the Mineiro frontier and for contesting with the viceroys the right to award the passagens contracts for Viamão and Curitiba.[62] Another may have been a wish to improve his own image, at that time the subject of derisive placards posted on church doors in his capital.[63] And by posing as the

[58] Sousa to Oeiras, Feb. 2, 1768, and appendices. *Ibid.*, 383–392.

[59] Sousa to Oeiras, Dec. 23, 1766, *ibid.*, 1–10; Aluizio de Almeida, "O maldito Iguatemí," *Revista do Arquivo Municipal*, IX (São Paulo, 1944), 111–151, at 122.

[60] Sousa to Azambuja, Dec. 19, 1767, *DI*, XXIII, 300. Lajes remained a bone of contention between administrators of São Paulo, Santa Catarina, and Rio de Janeiro until it was finally separated from São Paulo and assigned to Santa Catarina by an alvará of Sept. 9, 1820. Max Fleiuss, *História administrativa do Brasil*, 110.

[61] See Sousa's correspondence with Viceroys Cunha, Azambuja, and Lavradio, Aug. 28, 1765 to Oct. 29, 1772, *DI*, XI, 252–263. Sousa's successor, Martim Lopes Lobo de Saldanha, carried São Paulo's case for the disputed territory to the Crown. Saldanha to Melo e Castro, Apr. 28, 1778, and appendixes, *RIHGB/TE*, VII (1957), 168–174.

[62] See particularly Sousa to Oeiras, Jan. 5, 1769, and *idem* to Overseas Council, Feb. 28, 1769, *DI*, XIX (1896), 211–216, 304–309.

[63] Sousa to Oeiras, July 3, 1767, *RIHGB/TE*, V (1957), 432.

militant defender of Paulista interests, he seems to have intended to revive the Paulistas' pride in their past achievements.

This last aim was reflected in Sousa's multipronged expansionist program, initiated soon after his arrival in São Paulo. One prong led to Lajes, founded in 1766. A second was extended the following year with the building of a fortified outpost on the northern margin of the Iguatemí river, twenty leagues west of the Sete Quedas or Guairá Falls and only fourteen leagues from the Spanish town of San Isidro Labrador de Curuguatí in northeastern Paraguay (see Map 4 facing p. 61). Like other foci of Paulista interest at this time, Fort Iguatemí, to use one of its several names,[64] lay within the old Guairá mission field that an earlier generation of Paulistas had devastated in the 1620s and 1630s.[65] When the Spanish Jesuits abandoned that field and took their Indian neophytes with them, the Portuguese lost interest in the area. But that interest was revived a century later, first by the search for suitable transportation routes to link the livestock sources of the south with the gold fields of Mato Grosso and Goiás in the north, and later by attempts to delineate the Luso-Spanish boundary established by the Treaty of Madrid.[66] After the abrogation of that agreement, Lisbon became concerned lest the Spaniards, particularly the Jesuits, reoccupy the mission field and thus drive a wedge between Lusitanian Platine settlements and those farther north. To prevent such a move and to assure Portuguese control of the middle Paraná and the cattle lands to the east, the Crown instructed Sousa to erect a fortification on the Rio Iguatemí.[67]

Soon after construction of the fort started, several hundred Paulistas began to extend other prongs into the lands south of São Paulo by venturing along the eastern tributaries of the Paraná River. Although these scouting parties were termed *bandeiras,* the historian Basílio de Magalhães has correctly noted that these were not the typical private, spontaneous expeditions connoted by that term but were deliberately organized and funded by Captain-General Sousa.[68] Between 1768 and 1771 eleven such expeditions canoed through the waters of the Tibagí, a major tributary of the Paranapanema, and the Ivaí, the next sizeable southerly tributary of the Paraná; others examined the Piriquí and the Iguaçú rivers and explored the *campos de Guarapuva,*

---

[64] Initially it was called Cachoeira dos Prazeres; then it became Nossa Senhora dos Prazeres (after the patron saint of Sousa's household); and finally Nossa Senhora dos Prazeres e São Paula do Iguatemí.

[65] See pp. 63–64, above.

[66] In fact, on of the boundary commissioners, José Custódio de Sá e Faria, built a temporary stockade on the Iguatemí River in 1755.

[67] For the background to the founding of the presidio, see the article cited in n. 59.

[68] *Expansão geográfica do Brasil colonial* (3d ed., Rio de Janeiro, 1944), p. 346.

situated between the headwaters of the Tibagí, Piriquí, and Iguaçú.[69]
In the course of their searches these *bandeirantes,* the last of a long
cycle which began nearly two centuries before, discovered remains of
old Jesuit missions, including groves of bananas and oranges, and ruins
of two long-forgotten sixteenth-century Spanish settlements (Villa Rica
de la Guairá and Ciudad Real) ; but their main objective, apart from
securing this vast territory for Portugal and especially for São Paulo,
was the perennial quest for precious wealth.[70]

The construction of the advanced base on the Iguatemí and the
unveiling of the eastern sertões of the Paraná were thus already
under way when the Marquis of Lavradio first arrived in Rio de
Janeiro. Captain-General Sousa wasted little time in informing the
new viceroy about the nature of these enterprises and requesting support for them. "The two things of greatest concern to this Government," he told Lavradio, "are the Guatemy Establishment on the
frontiers of Paraguay and the expeditions that are now conquering
and securing the backlands of the Tibagí." Since both were of great
utility to the Royal Service and since he had already exhausted his
own resources, he was obliged to apply to the viceroy for money,
arms, munitions, and "all sorts of implements" to sustain them.[71]

The marquis responded cautiously to these requests, partly because
that was his nature but also because he wanted to establish in Sousa's
mind his subordination to the Viceroy of Brazil. It is probable that
the Conde de Azambuja had briefed Lavradio about the aggressive
tactics of the new Paulista administrator, and it was important to remind him of his place. Consquently, Lavradio declared that before he
acted on Sousa's request he should be more fully informed on condi-

[69] A key source, prepared by one of the promoters of these parties, is the summary by Afonso Bot[elh]o de S[ão] Payo e Souza, Curitiba, Dec. 19, 1772, *DI,* IV
(1896), 37–53.

[70] One report that may have rekindled interest in the Paraná sertões was that
by a Carmelite friar who declared that stones appearing to be diamonds had been
found in the headwaters of the Tibagí. Gomes Freire de Andrada to Sebastião
José de Carvalho e Melo, Dec. 12, 1755, Jaime Cortesão, ed., *Alexandre de Gusmão
e o tratado de Madrid (1750),* Pt. V, 48. Paulista activities along the affluents
of the Paraná during this period are richly documented. Most of the printed
sources are cited in Magalhães, *op. cit.,* pp. 340–357, but see also *RIHGB/TE,*
VI (1957), 52, 81–82, and 205–209 for Sousa's first reports to the Crown concerning
these operations; Toetônio José Juzarte, "Diário da navegação do Rio Tietê, Rio
Grande, Paraná e Rio Guatemi" (1769–1771) [Affonso de E. Taunay, *História das
bandeiras paulistas,* III (2d ed., São Paulo [ca. 1960]) 239–296] is a fascinating
account of travel by canoe from the port of Araraitaguaba (Pôrto Feliz) on the
Tietê, west of the city of São Paulo, to Iguatemí. See also below, n. 92, for
another important diary. Besides Magalhães, useful secondary sources include
Carvalho Franco, *Bandeiras a bandeirantes de São Paulo* (São Paulo, 1940), pp.
289–311, and Aluizio de Almeida's previously cited essay (see above n. 59). None
of these authors has examined the administrative controversies that these activities
engendered.

[71] Sousa to Lavradio, Feb. 13 and 14, 1770, *DI,* XIX, 431–436.

tions within São Paulo and the motives behind his expansionist pro-
grams. He promised to send what supplies he could, but warned that
his warehouses were badly depleted and that he had little money in
the treasury.[72]

Sousa understood the meaning behind the viceroy's unenthusiastic
response. He replied tartly that since he had already given Lavradio's
predecessors detailed accounts of his projects, he had considered it
unnecessary to do so again. But after briefing the marquis, he reminded him that the king had ordered their governments to work in
concert and that the Crown had directed him to turn to the viceroys
for whatever munitions and equipment he needed.[73]

The viceroy turned aside Sousa's thrust by praising him for the
skill with which he was administering the captaincy-general and by
reassuring him that he would furnish "everything that is necessary" to
assist in its preservation and material progress.[74] But the more he reflected on Sousa's expansionist activities, the less he liked them. Early
in 1771 he expressed his misgivings to the Marquis of Pombal. The
very success of such enterprises, he warned, could lead to their un-
doing, for if gold and diamonds were actually found in the Paraná
backlands they would provide new opportunities for smuggling and
would surely excite the cupidity of the Spaniards who were militarily
stronger in the interior than were the Portuguese. The Castilians
would then find pretexts to wage war over the disputed area and
might invade São Paulo "which is destitute of forces to defend itself."
It was for these reasons, he added, that the Conde de Bobadela had
opposed the opening up of those sertões, and because of the "very
delicate" nature of the operations in progress he felt it necessary to
alert His Majesty to their possible consequences.[75]

Soon after, the viceroy received additional reports from Sousa on
promising discoveries in the sertões of the Tibagí and the Ivaí.
Lavradio thanked him for the news and stated that he hoped the king
would approve Sousa's expenditures in support of the bandeiras;
however, he refused Sousa's request for additional funds and explained
his own fiscal burdens. When Sousa chose to ignore the viceroy's explanation and continued to press for pecuniary aid for his frontier
enterprises, Lavradio became annoyed and brusquely informed him
that his appeal was "entirely impractical" because of the critical condition of his own treasury. He promised to pay up the arrears owed
for the Santos subsidy and to furnish that stipend at regular intervals,
but warned that he could do no more. He considered it "a little ex-

---

[72] Lavradio to Sousa, Apr. 17, 1770, CMCM, cod. 15, fols. 17r-v.
[73] Sousa to Lavradio, June 30, 1770, DI, XXXIV, 219–222.
[74] Lavradio to Sousa, Oct. 5, 1770, CMCM, cod. 15, fol. 31v.
[75] Lavradio to Pombal, Jan. 14, 1771, ANRJ, Col. 69, Liv. I-bis., fols 32v–33r.

traordinary for us to undertake the possession of a very large country without first having the people or the means to sustain and defend it," and stated that his previously expressed approval of Sousa's ventures assumed that they had already been cleared with the Crown.[76]

But if the viceroy thought that Luís Antônio de Sousa was going to be easily deterred from pursuing his expansionist enterprises, he soon learned otherwise. Confronted by Lavradio's reluctance to provide him with assistance on the scale he had expected, the captain-general appealed to the Crown, emphasizing the limits of his own resources and alleging that the Spaniards were already making threatening gestures against the Iguatemí presídio. That brought the response desired. The Court ordered the viceroy to send Sousa "whatever quantities" of funds he needed in order to defray "necessary and indispensable expenses," but characteristically failed to indicate where the money was to come from. The Crown also instructed Lavradio to dispatch Brigadier José Custódio de Sá e Faria and two aides to São Paulo to make an inspection of Fort Iguatemí, and directed him to send Sousa a company of artillery, one or more companies of infantry, and several small pieces of artillery.[77] The captain-general thus won the first round, and the viceroy admitted as much.[78]

Although the marquis conceded that he had been temporarily out-manuevered, he still did not share the Court's enthusiasm for the efforts of Sousa to win control of the Paraná backlands. He made that clear in two long and personally revealing dispatches to the captain-general in April 1772. He began by observing that the acquisition of new territory and the conversion of untamed Indians could be of real benefit to São Paulo and to the State, but insisted that such undertakings required careful planning and reflection so as to discover the appropriate means and ends. The two primary objects of conquests, he argued, are to acquire new resources and to diminish those of the enemy. In the case of São Paulo there was no demonstrable need for additional lands since the captaincy already possessed more than its present population could develop. In his judgment the acquisition of additional lands at this time would cause the Paulistas to disperse further and to dissipate their energies and resources so that in the end they, rather than the Spaniards, would become weaker. Furthermore, said Lavradio, if such lands were to be taken away from Indians who presently occupied them, he was opposed to their acquisition.

[76] Lavradio to Sousa, Feb. 27 and June 2, 1771, CMCM, cod. 15, fols. 48ᵛ–49ᵛ, 63ᵛ–64ᵛ.

[77] Two cartas régias of Aug. 13, 1771, CMCM, cod. 3, fols. 134ʳ and 136ʳ (both *única vias*), not sent until Oct. 1. Melo e Castro to Lavradio, Oct. 1, 1771, *ibid.*, fol. 144ʳ⁻ᵛ (orig.) ; printed in *VRL*, pp. 167–169.

[78] Lavradio to Sousa, Jan. 13, 1772, CMCM, cod. 26, fols. 83ᵛ–84ʳ; *idem to idem*, Apr. 14, 1772, *ibid.*, cod. 15, fols. 107ᵛ.

Reviewing the centuries-old record of Portuguese treatment of the Indians, he candidly observed that "we suffer now the fruits of our [past] cruelty . . . from the first . . . we have scourged these People." He asked, "after taking their estates from them is it to be wondered that they [now] distrust and fear us?" Rather than by brandishing the sword, the viceroy counseled, the Portuguese should win over the Indians by examples of piety and kindness. That would take longer than outright conquest, he admitted, but it would pay invaluable dividends. He emphasized that he was not in principle opposed to new conquests, but that he favored prudent expansion consistent with existing means.

This led Lavradio to make several additional points. In response to Sousa's queries [79] he stated that he favored retention of Fort Iguatemí, but recommended that soldier-farmers should be encouraged to settle in the vicinity of the presídio to relieve it of its present dependence on external sources of food.[80] But until the frontier with Paraguay had been rendered secure, he felt that it was unwise to proceed with the conquest of the Tibagí hinterlands. He insisted that he had complied fully with the Court's latest instructions to support Sousa and that he would continue to do so as far as his means permitted. But he reminded the captain-general that his primary responsibilities were the protection of Rio de Janeiro and the defense of its southern outposts, and that he therefore had no troops to spare. Besides, a regiment of 800 Paulista volunteers would be worth more than 3,000 Peninsulars or Cariocas because the Paulistas were already familiar with the techniques of fighting in bush country. If Sousa believed that he could not recruit such a force, the viceroy added shrewdly, then it was evident that he lacked the manpower to sustain his ambitious projects. To give his remarks additional weight, he concluded by noting that he had discussed these matters with the captains-general of Goiás and Mato Grosso who were staying with him, and that both shared his views.[81]

It is likely that the viceroy sent the Court copies of these carefully considered observations. Certainly he renewed his warning that Sousa's aggressive moves were likely to serve as pretexts for Spanish movements against Rio Grande or Colônia. But the colonial secretary countered by saying that the Spaniards had no need to find pretexts in order to turn bellicose and discounted the probability that they would attack the borderlands. Still, he repeated his earlier reminder that the viceroy and the captain-general should work together to co-

---

[79] Sousa to Lavradio, Apr. 8, 1772, *RIHGB/TE,* VI (1957) , 294–295.

[80] It will be recalled that the viceroy gave the same advice to the governors of Santa Catarina and Rio Grande.

[81] Lavradio to Sousa, Apr. 14 and 30, 1772, CMCM, cod. 15, fols. 108ʳ–116ᵛ.

ordinate the defenses of southern Brazil, just as the captains-general of Pará, Goiás, and Mato Grosso were supposed to cooperate in the defense of northern and western Brazil. The minister sent similar advice to Captain-General Sousa, stressing one of his favorite maxims that in unity there is strength and that the strength of Brazil depended on the existence of a common accord among the administrators of contiguous districts. At the same time he vetoed Sousa's proposal to undertake a "diversion" against the Spaniards via Iguatemí. He observed that if the Portuguese attacked the enemy along the road between Curaguatí and Asunción, they would be obliged to travel over exceedingly difficult terrain, while their adversaries could easily retaliate by striking the Portuguese where they were most vulnerable, that is, in Rio Grande, and, he reminded Sousa, its loss would mean the loss of "the most important barrier" between Spanish positions and his own captaincy-general.[82]

But Luís Antônio de Sousa was not a man easily parted from his cherished beliefs. Despite the secretary's opposition to his "diversionary" project, he continued to argue in favor of a concentration of Portuguese forces at the interior presídio rather than in Rio Grande, a position he considered militarily inferior to Iguatemí. Among the advantages he claimed for that outpost were that it could provide (1) security for the pastures east of the Paraná between Western Rio Grande and São Paulo; (2) protection for Mato Grosso and Goiás against enemy moves from Paraguay; (3) opportunity for the development of clandestine trade with Spanish settlements there and for attacks on such towns in the event of Castilian assaults upon either Colônia or Rio Grande; and (4) pressure on the Spaniards to divide their forces between Buenos Aires and Asunción to guard against a possible Portuguese inland offensive.[83] Sousa thought that he had discovered justification for such an offensive in October 1773 when he received reports from the governor of Iguatemí that the Spaniards had erected a fort nearby and were thought to be advancing on his position. In alarm the captain-general wrote the viceroy suggesting that the enemy be attacked at once.[84]

The viceroy strongly disagreed. In a long reply ringing with sarcasm he observed that he had no doubt that the Spaniards *were* building such a fort, but neither its existence nor mere rumors con-

[82] Melo e Castro to Lavradio, Nov. 20, 1772, CMCM, cod. 3, fols. 188ʳ–195ʳ and BNRJ, 4, 4, 60 (both origs.); printed in *VRL*, pp. 171–181. *Idem* to Sousa, same date, BNRJ, I-2, 4, 6, n. 28.

[83] Sousa to Lavradio, Apr. 6, 1773, *RIHGB/TE*, VI (1957), 359–360; *idem* to *idem*, May 14, 1773, *DI*, XXXIV, 138–144; *idem* to *idem*, Sept. 9, 1773, *RIHGB/TE*, VI, 374–375; *idem* to Melo e Castro, Nov. 13, 1773, *DI*, XXXIV, 93–103; *idem* to Pombal, Nov. 15, 1773, *ibid.*, 103–104.

[84] Sousa to Lavradio, Oct. 31, 1773, cited in Lavradio's reply (see n. 85).

cerning the enemy's intentions warranted beginning a war, for only the king could sanction that. The Castilians' real intentions could best be determined if Brigadier José Custódio made the inspection that the Court had directed him to undertake more than a year before. He urged that he carry out that assignment as soon as possible.[85]

This dispatch was hardly finished before the viceroy received the first news of the departure of the expedition led by General Vértiz for Rio Grande.[86] He immediately wrote again to Captain-General Sousa and directed him to forward to Rio Grande the troops he had on loan from Rio de Janerio. He implied that he had called earlier for their transfer, and noted bitterly that had they been sent they would already be in a position to assist in the subcaptaincy's defense.[87] Though the Vértiz anabasis failed to attain its objective, Luís Antônio de Sousa reached the inevitable conclusion that the Spaniard would never have attempted his incursion had Iguatemí been properly strengthened. He was convinced, he told the Court, that the funds and manpower sent to Rio Grande could be put to better advantage at Iguatemí.[88]

By now even the Court's patience with its opinionated captain-general had become exhausted. In April 1774 the colonial secretary sent Sousa two strongly worded reprimands, both left open for the viceroy to read, seal, and forward.[89] First, the minister invoked the name of the king to prohibit the captain-general from diverting any forces intended for Rio Grande for the support of Iguatemí. Second, he dismissed as valueless a lengthy paper in which Sousa had expounded on the merits of his "expensive and impractical" diversionary project. Third, he forbade him to authorize any more expeditions to the sertões of the Ivaí and Tibagí until he had provided the Crown with "the most exact and rigorous information concerning the deportment of the discoverers toward the Indians." Fourth, he enjoined Sousa not to "promote, prepare or plan" any military undertaking unrelated to the defense of Rio Grande or Iguatemí, for "His Majesty prizes much more the loss of a single league of territory in the southern part of Portuguese America than fifty leagues of exposed sertão in its interior. . . ." Lastly, he sternly condemned both Sousa

85 Lavradio to Sousa, Dec. 12, 1773, CMCM, maço 15 (rascunho). The viceroy sent a copy of this dispatch to Lisbon. Idem to Melo e Castro, Dec. 13, 1773, cited in Chap. V, n. 81.

86 See pp. 125 f.

87 Lavradio to Sousa, Dec. 14, 1773, CMCM, maço 15 (rascunho).

88 Sousa to Melo e Castro, June 18, 1774, DI, XXXV (1901), 28–285; excerpted in RIHGB/TE, VI, 418.

89 Melo e Castro to Lavradio, Apr. 22, 1774, CMCM, cod. 13, fol. 20ʳ (orig.).

and Brigadier José Custódio for the latter's failure to conduct his urgently needed inspection of the Iguatemí praça.[90] It was clear that Lavradio had won the second round, but the final and decisive one was still to come.

Meanwhile, prodded by the exasperated minister's rebuke, Brigadier José Custódio left the city of São Paulo on his long-delayed inspection trip early in October 1774.[91] Accompanied by four officers and twenty-two artillerymen, he took the classic canoe route from the river port of Araraitaguaba (Pôrto Feliz) on the Tietê River to the interior, paddling along the Tietê until its confluence with the Paraná, down the latter to the Iguatemí, and up the Iguatemí to the praça, a distance of 301 leagues which the party covered in fifty-eight days.[92]

Two months later the brigadier summarized his findings in a devastating report to the Court.[93] He found that the praça was ample enough to accommodate 3,000 men, though its garrison numbered only a tenth as many. Except for two white infantry companies, the garrison consisted of Negroes, mulattoes, and criminals "who have little to lose." Forty-two soldier-farmers ("adventurers") were engaged in raising crops, ninety-five were guards, and the remainder were either at work on the fortifications or were suffering from various sorts of illness. Morale was exceedingly low because the soldiers were ill paid and fed and had seen 499 of their comrades carried off by pestilence during the past six years. Understandably, the survivors hoped that the king would order them to retire from such a pestiferous, forbidding place. Not only was the fort situated in an unhealthy area, but the brigadier considered it strategically vulnerable from higher ground. He saw no indication that the Spaniards were active in nearby streams; their closest settlements lacked anything suitable to warrant illicit trade with them, and because of the character of the terrain it was virtually impossible to approach Asunción from the fort. In short, the inspector's long-awaited report confirmed the viceroy's misgivings and the Court's suspicions, and, by demolishing

90 Melo e Castro to Sousa, Apr. 21, 1774 (two dispatches), BNRJ, I-2, 4, 6, nos. 52 and 53; idem to José Custódio de Sá e Faria, same date, ibid., n. 54.

91 Precisely why he tarried so long in the Paulista capital remains a puzzle. In April 1773 Sousa indicated that the brigadier was about to leave to make his inspection, but two months later he reported that the engineer still had not completed arrangements for his trip. Sousa to Lavradio, Apr. 6, 1773, RIHGB/TE, VI (1957), 360; idem to Melo e Castro, June 3, 1773, ibid., 362.

92 "Diario da viagem que fez o brigadeiro José Custódio de Sá e Faria da cidade de S. Paulo á praça de Nossa Senhora dos Prazeres do Rio Igatemy," RIHGB, XXXIX (1876), 227–277.

93 José Custódio de Sá e Faria to Melo e Castro, Iguatemí, Feb. 4, 1775, ibid., 217–227.

Sousa's major arguments in favor of the advanced base, cast serious doubt on his judgment.[94]

Nevertheless, José Custódio's report probably had no immediate bearing on Sousa's future, for by the time it reached Lisbon the Court had already decided to transfer the captain-general to Minas Gerais, thus in effect giving him a promotion.[95] But nearly a year ensued between the date when the Crown made its intention known and the arrival of Sousa's successor. During that interval the viceroy managed to abstain from becoming involved in further controversies with Sousa. His dispatches to the captain-general were limited to instructions concerning the movement of troops and supplies to the south. To ensure compliance, the viceroy always reminded Sousa that he was sending copies of such directives to Lisbon so that the Court could determine how well the captain-general was discharging his responsibilities.[96]

Sometime before Martim Lopes Lobo de Saldanha arrived in São Paulo to relieve Sousa, the viceroy learned that the Court had changed its mind concerning the reassignment of Sousa. Instead of proceeding to Minas, he was ordered home—without any promise of a new position.[97] That must have been a severe blow to the ambitious Morgado de Mateus, and understandably he wished to avoid a meeting with Dom Luís de Almeida who was indirectly responsible for blocking his advancement. When the marquis heard that Sousa was planning to sail for the kingdom by way of Bahia, thus bypassing Rio de Janeiro, he sent an urgent message to São Paulo advising the retiring captain-general that the royal frigate Graça was then in Guanabara Bay and had ample accommodations awaiting him.[98] Sousa, in fact, did sail aboard the Graça, but though the viceroy had assured him that she would leave "infallibly" on July 10, 1775, she was unable to get under way until the following January.[99] Luís Antônio

94 It may be recalled that Spanish forces overran and destroyed Fort Iguatemí in October, 1777. See Chap. X, n. 31.

95 Pombal to Lavradio, July 15, 1774, par. 10, RIHGB, XXXI:1, 303–307.

96 Lavradio to Sousa, Sept. 20 and 22 and Dec. 12, 1774, and Jan. 13, 1775, CMCM, cod. 26, fols. 84ᵛ–90ᵛ; idem to idem, Mar. 27, 1775, ibid., cod. 4, fols. 68ʳ⁻ᵛ.

97 I have been unable to locate the dispatch or dispatches in which the Crown countermanded its earlier order shifting Sousa to Minas, and therefore cannot say what, if any, explanation it offered. It was not unusual, of course, for the Court to change assignments of colonial officers before they went overseas, but in Sousa's case no alternative position at home was offered. His petition (note 53 above) describes him as being "sem posto."

98 Lavradio to Sousa, June 10, 1775, CMCM, cod. 4, fol. 71ʳ.

99 The sources are regrettably silent on whatever direct contacts existed between the two men during this period. The "Relação dos passageiros e prezos q se embarcão no Rio de Janeiro a bordo da fragata . . . N.S.ra da Graça" (ca. Jan. 31, 1776) [IHGB, Lata 71, MS 1344] shows that Sousa's party included an aide, two priests, two criados, two pretos, two mulattoes, and a Paulista.

de Sousa thus spent more than six months in Lavradio's capital, and uncomfortable months they must have been!

Conclusion

The protracted dispute between Viceroy Lavradio and Captain-General Sousa was far from unique among senior colonial officers in Brazil. For example, Professor Boxer has written with reference to the experience of an earlier viceroy,

> Like other viceroys and governors-general . . . , the Count of Sabugosa was not always on the best of terms with his senior (and largely nominal) subordinates. . . . [H]e carried on a veritable vendetta with . . . the governor of Minas Gerais. . . . The latter returned his dislike, and . . . these two fidalgos denounced each other in their respective correspondence with the Crown. . . . Beyond periodically enjoining these two governors to coöperate amicably, the Crown did nothing to resolve this feud, obstinately refusing to dismiss either of them. . . . [T]hough it did not make for administrative harmony [this] fitted in with the colonial system of checks and balances, which ensured that the misdeeds or mistakes of any one governor would speedily be reported by a disgruntled colleague.[100]

This is a generally accurate appraisal of the way the Crown managed its senior colonial administrators. Like the Spanish government, it encouraged tale-bearing correspondence from high-level officers to prevent possible collusion against its vital interests. However, the administrators did not need to be prodded to divulge the nature of conflicts with their rivals, for they were always anxious to persuade the Crown of their own devotion to duty and to protect themselves against possible charges of misconduct. Consequently, disputants like Luís Antônio de Sousa and the Marquis of Lavradio sent Lisbon copies of all key dispatches exchanged with their adversaries. As the foregoing section suggests, the Crown served as umpire, sometimes intervening to support one disputant, sometimes the other. While it is true that it seldom successfully reconciled feuding administrators—indeed, it is questionable whether it ever seriously tried [101]—its patience was definitely limited. Colonial officers always served at the Crown's pleasure, and when they sufficiently incurred its displeasure as a result of cowardly or treasonable acts, malfeasance, serious bad judgment, or

---

[100] *The Golden Age of Brazil*, p. 145.

[101] In 1728, for example, the Overseas Council advised the king that it was "not very convenient for Your Majesty's service that governors and senior officials who serve with them be on too friendly terms because it is very advantageous that they should be fearful of each other. . . ." for this was a principle of good government. Consulta of Nov. 12, 1728, *DH*, XC (1950), 174.

mere intransigence, as in Sousa's case, they were likely to suffer consequences ranging from a sharp reprimand to removal from office or even heavy fine, exile from the Court or the kingdom itself, or imprisonment.

It might seem surprising that the Marquis of Pombal, generally considered a centralist, did not place the captains-general, like the borderlands governors, fully under the viceroys' control and discipline so that the realities of the viceroys' authority corresponded to their titles. The Crown actually took a step in the direction of greater administrative centralization within Brazil during the long regime of Gomes Freire de Andrada (1733–1763) who, though only a captain-general, exercised authority over a far more extensive area than did the contemporary Salvadorean viceroys.[102] But such broad territorial jurisdiction was never conferred on the Rio viceroys,[103] for Pombal was as reluctant as his predecessors to entrust them with the authority of true vice-kings. That reluctance stemmed partly from his deep-seated distrust of the high nobility from whom the viceroys were drawn, partly from his centralizing impulses that tended always to tighten the Crown's grip on all levels of the imperial bureaucracy, not to delegate its powers to lieutenants. And such was the policy that his successors followed.[104] Pombal's aim was to keep the locus of power entirely on the Portuguese side of the Atlantic. When it was transferred temporarily to the Brazilian side (1808–1821), the days of Brazil's subordination to Portugal were numbered. But long before that shift occurred, the Marquis of Pombal had passed from the scene, as had the Marquis of Lavradio.

[102] See Chap. II, n. 75.

[103] There is no evidence to support Professor Burns' contention that Pombal "increased the power of the viceroy" as part of his efforts "to make royal power absolute." E. Bradford Burns, ed., *A Documentary History of Brazil* (New York, 1966), p. 137. Indeed, there was a further contraction of the viceroys' territorial jurisdiction at the end of the colonial period. In 1807 the Crown established the captaincy-general of Rio Grande de São Pedro and assigned its head responsibility for Rio Grande and Santa Catarina. "Alvará de regimento de que deve usar o gov.or e cap.m. gen.al da nova capitania de Saó Pedro," Oct. 16, 1807, AHU/CU/LR, cod. 169, fols. 148v–155r (Bancroft Library Microfilm Collection).

[104] In 1796 and again in 1804 the Crown contemplated revision of the standing instructions (regimentos) defining the duties of the viceroys and captains-general and asked incumbents for their recommendations. For two responses, see 2RGG, *passim*, and Dom Francisco de Assis Mascarenhas (captain-general of Goiás), "Regimento que observão os governadores, e capitaens-generaes da capitania de Goiáz . . . com hum treslado de todas as ordens regias q. o ampliaraó, ou restringiraó," July 20, 1806, AHU/CU/LR cod. 1229 (Bancroft Library Microfilm Collection). Significantly neither respondent suggested that the viceroys be equipped with greater authority.

XVII

Portrait of a Viceroy and Critique
of a Regime

> My self-love does not blind me to the point of inducing me to defend all
> my resolutions as judicious; I did what I could, and what my talents per-
> mitted . . . I never put off any tasks which appeared likely to prevent my
> falling into error. . . .
>
> . . . my system consist[ed] in keeping the people in peace and obedience,
> promoting their legitimate interests (*utilidades*), bestirring them from
> their customary idleness, and at the same time . . . [in] finding ways to
> augment the interests of His Majesty and the revenues of this Cap-
> taincy. . . .
>
> Lavradio to Vasconcelos, *Relatório*, June 19, 1779

IN THE EARLY MONTHS following the termination of the Luso-
Spanish war the Marquis of Lavradio anxiously looked for word from
the Court that he would soon be relieved and allowed to go home.
Occasionally troubled by unspecified maladies and yearning to rejoin
the family he had left behind more than a decade before, particularly
to see for the first time his new grandchildren, the weary viceroy
wrote Captain-General Saldanha in January 1778 that he fervently
hoped for news that he could return to the kingdom and enjoy the re-
laxation that he so badly needed.[1] The same week he learned of his
nomination to the Council of War, normally an indication that his
recall would soon be at hand.[2] Any anxiety that he may have felt
about his future status was dispelled by a warm personal letter from
the Marquis of Angeja, Pombal's successor, congratulating him on his
praiseworthy administration during a difficult period in Portugal's
history.[3] But not until the end of the year did the colonial secretary

---

[1] Lavradio to Saldanha, Jan. 28, 1778, *DI*, XVII (1895), 338; over seven years
before, the viceroy had expressed the hope that he would be relieved as soon
as he completed the three-year term prescribed in his patent, but he must have
known that the Court seldom felt bound by that commitment. *Idem* to Luiz Pinto
de Souza, Oct. 17, 1770, CMCM, cod. 15, fols. 35ʳ⁻ᵛ.

[2] Lavradio to Böhm, Jan. 23, 1778, BNRJ, 13-4-3, n. 44 (orig.); *BCRG*, pp. 153–
155.

[3] Angeja to Lavradio, Nov. 1777, quoted in *VRL*, pp. 141–142.

inform him—and then almost casually—that he was being replaced.[4]

During his final months in Brazil the retiring viceroy devoted his energies to various matters requiring his special attention. One was the working out of details for the relocation of the former civilian residents of Colônia, the return of Santa Catarina Island from the Spaniards, and the fulfillment of other provisions of the Treaty of San Ildefonso.[5] Dom Luís continued to display a personal interest in new lines of economic activity within the captaincy of Rio de Janeiro, such as the production of indigo and the manufacture of guaxima cordage.[6] He also supervised repairs to his palace so as to make it as comfortable as possible for his successor.[7]

Lavradio's successor, Dom Luís de Vasconcelos e Sousa, possessed impressive credentials for his assignment to the most exalted post in the Portuguese empire. The son of the Marquis of Castelomelhor and brother of the Conde da Calheta, the new Dom Luís was a member of the Council of Finance and the Casa de Suplicação. Some eight months after his appointment desembargador Vasconcelos finally reached Rio de Janeiro on March 30, 1779, having survived a harrowing encounter with a Yankee corsair that chased his frigate, the *Nazareth,* and had the effrontery to put a ball through his personal wardrobe.[8] Vasconcelos assumed his duties on April 5, following several days of amicable conferences between the incoming and outgoing viceroys. But the Marquis of Lavradio was obliged to remain in Rio de Janeiro for another two months until the *Nazareth* had received the diamond shipments from Minas and was ready to sail back to Portugal.

Lavradio was not condemned to spend his remaining months in the colony in idleness, for he used them to comply with an unexpected directive Vasconcelos had brought him from Lisbon. In that dispatch the colonial secretary called on the marquis to provide his successor with "a general instruction" concerning the government of Rio de Janeiro and its dependencies.[9] What prompted such an order at this time is hard to say, for though Spanish viceroys had long been re-

4 Melo e Castro to *idem,* Sept. 15, 1778, BNRJ, I-2, 4, 7, n. 101. The secretary's announcement came in the third paragraph of a rather general dispatch, and his tone was markedly cool by contrast with that which he expressed in a special letter he addressed to Lavradio's successor a decade later announcing his recall. *Idem* to Vasconcelos, Sept. 20, 1788, BNRJ, I-4, 4, 6, n. 35.

5 Lavradio, *Relatório,* pp. 485–486.

6 See pp. 369–374.

7 Lavradio to João Antônio Salter de Mendonça, Sept. 10, 1778, CMCM, cod. 25, fol. 270ᵛ.

8 Luís de Vasconcelos e Sousa to Melo e Castro, Apr. 23, 1779, IHGB/AUC, 1-2-1, fols. 9ʳ–11ᵛ; D. Alden, "The Marquis of Pombal and the American Revolution," *The Americas,* XVII (Apr. 1961), 376 and n. 27.

9 Melo e Castro to Lavradio, Jan. 13, 1779, BNRJ, I-2, 4, 7, n. 113.

quired to submit *memorias* or *relaciones de gobierno* to their replacements,[10] that practice had not been regularly followed in the Portuguese empire. It is true that a law of 1628 enjoined Portuguese viceroys, governors, and ambassadors to send to the Court a status report on their offices before they could claim their final year's salary,[11] and that since 1655 the viceroys of India had been required to give their successors "the advice and information you judge convenient to my royal service and to the well-being and security of that State," [12] but neither injunction had been consistently enforced. Though he was not the first Portuguese viceroy to draft a written briefing for his replacement,[13] Lavradio appears to have been the first of his rank in Brazil to do so.[14] While his successor was also directed to prepare such a report,[15] no later viceroy of Brazil seems to have done so, though at least one captain-general did.[16]

[10] A considerable number of those instructions have been collected and published. For a listing of such collections, see Sigfrido A. Radaelli, ed., *Memorias de los virreyes del Río de la Plata,* pp. x–xi. Although they did not prepare terminal reports comparable to the *relaciones,* English and French colonial governors submitted status reports to the Crown during their administrations and were occasionally called on to record their impressions after having retired from office. A noteworthy example of the latter type of report, and one for which I am indebted to my colleague Max Savelle who called it to my attention, is M. de la Galissonnière, "Memoir on the French Colonies in North America" (1750), E. B. O'Callaghan, ed., *Documents Relative to the Colonial History of the State of New York* . . . X (Albany, 1858), 220–232, but though broad in its sweep, it lacks the precise sort of information usually found in the *relaciones.*

[11] *Decreto* of Sept. 30 and carta régia of Oct. 31, 1628, *CLP,* IV, 136, 138. The wording is remarkably similar to that in the decrees of Dec. 16, 1628 and Nov. 23, 1631 by which Philip III spurred Spanish viceroys to prepare such reports under the same kind of threat (*Recopilación de leyes de los reynos de las Indias,* [Fasc. ed., Madrid, 1791], *Lib.* III, tít. 14, *ley* 32), an interesting example of the efforts of the Philippine rulers of Spain and Portugal to impose uniform administrative practices on the dual empire. One of Lavradio's immediate predecessors prepared such a terminal report for the Court (Conde da Cunha to Melo e Castro, Apr. 25, 1767, *RIHGB,* CCLIV [Jan.–Mar. 1962], 393–395), but whether the Marquis did also is not known.

[12] *Carta de guia* of Mar. 15, 1655, cited in Felippe Nery Xavier, ed., *Instrucção do Ex.mo Vice-Rei Marquez de Alorna ao seu successor o . . . Marquez de Tavora* (2d ed., Nova Goa, 1856), p. 7 n.

[13] E.g., the Alorna instruction, cited above, was prepared in 1750.

[14] "[E] se esta minha narração não satisfazer a toda a curiosidade de V. Exc., se sirvirá de desculpar-me por ser este papel original, isto é, ser eu o primeiro que dou uma conta ao meu successor. . . ." Lavradio, *Relatório,* p. 409. Subordinates sometimes drafted similar reports for their superior's use. An example is Jozé Xavier Machado Monteiro to Lavradio, May 10, 1772, CMCM, *maço* 30, enclosing the sender's "Rellação individual do q. tenho feito nesta capitania de Porto Seguro no espaço de sinco annos, q. tenho servido de ouvidor."

[15] Vasconcelos to Conde de Rezende, Aug. 20, 1789, *RIHGB,* XXIII (1860), 143–239.

[16] Antônio Manoel de Melo e Castro Mendonça (captain-general of São Paulo, 1797–1802) to Paulo Antônio José da France e Horta, Dec. 28, 1802, *DI,* XLIV (1915), 129–157.

Compared with the terminal reports of the Spanish viceroys, Lavradio's *relatório* was not long, occupying only seventy-seven printed pages.[17] Though quite differently organized,[18] it nevertheless unfolded systematically. Dom Luís began with a description of the geographic extent of the lands directly administered by the viceroy,[19] then described the military situation he found in Rio de Janeiro and its dependencies when he took up his duties. These introductory sections were followed by others, focused primarily on the captaincy of Rio de Janeiro, concerning his dispositions with respect to its defenses, the various branches of his government, the treatment of colonials, and the development of its economy. The last parts of the report related the administrative, military, and diplomatic problems that affected the subcaptaincies of Santa Catarina and Rio Grande during his regime. Interspersed within each heading were comments concerning the policies of his predecessors, his own "system," his recommendations to the Court and to his successor. *En passant* he identified key personnel who could be trusted and others who needed to be closely watched. Though the Marquis devoted particular attention to the deficit problem of the viceregal exchequer, he passed over the details of the recently concluded borderlands war, a subject doubtless still painful to him. Significantly, he said nothing about his relations with the Church or its status in the colony; [20] nor

17 That of his successor was a fifth longer. As the complexities of administration increased, so did the length of the memorias of the Spanish viceroys. That of Francisco de Toledo, viceroy of Peru 1569–1581, was only thirty pages, but those of his successors down to 1651 averaged sixty-two pages (Ricardo Beltrán y Rózpide and Ángel de Altolaguirre, eds., *Colección de las memorias o relaciones que escribieron los virreyes del Perú* [2 v., Madrid, 1921–1930]). By contrast, the memoria of Lavradio's counterpart in Peru, Manuel de Amat y Junient (1761–1776) extended for 820 pages! Vicente Rodrigues Casado and Florentino Perez Embid, eds., *Memoria de gobierno del virrey Amat* (Seville, 1947). The relaciones of Lavradio's contemporaries in the new viceroyalty of the Plata were much shorter. Pedro de Cevallos' was only nineteen pages, though Juan José de Vertíz' ran to 172 pages. Radaelli, *op. cit.,* pp. 3–197.

18 The relaciones were commonly divided into four major heads (in varying order) : general administration; ecclesiastical affairs; finances; and military affairs. See Beltrán y Rózpide and Altolaguirre, *op. cit., passim*. There is little generic resemblance between the Alorna instruction (see n. 12) and the Lavradio report, for the former is divided into three subjects—relations with the subject peoples; relations with the representatives of other European powers established on the subcontinent; and the performance of the several branches of viceregal government—and allots less than a third of the space to the last topic.

19 Here he borrowed liberally from a report prepared by the military engineer Francisco João Roscîo. Roscîo to Lavradio, Feb. 15, 1779, CMCM, *maço* 7 (orig.) . The same bundle contains a second unsigned draft of this report plus another (*idem* to *idem,* Mar. 5, 1778 [orig.]) of the same type on Santa Catarina and Rio Grande de São Pedro.

20 Vasconcelos devoted one paragraph to the Church, a discussion of the problem of immoral friars living in the capital. Vasconcelos, *Relatório,* pp. 181–182.

did he include any detailed account of conditions in other parts of the so-called State of Brazil—further reminders, if there need be, of the limits of viceregal authority in colonial Brazil.[21]

The English translator of this document has described it as "unnecessarily diffuse and periphrastic." [22] If judged by modern editorial standards, that appraisal is correct, but if measured by the accepted style and content of such reports in Lavradio's day, the relatório is more deserving of praise than of criticism. Its tone is modest rather than boastful, and its author, unlike many Spanish viceroys, refrained from exaggerating his own achievements. Nor was he guilty of maligning the character of his not always tractable nor responsible subordinates.[23] On the whole, the relatório is an orderly, reliable résumé of conditions that the newly retired viceroy had found upon assuming office, the methods he had employed to improve them, and the status of those he left to try the talents of his successor.

Shortly after affixing his signature to the relatório (June 19, 1779), the marquis sailed for Lisbon with an entourage that probably included his personal physician, José Henriques Ferreira, and two of his former aides, Camilio Maria Tonelet and Gaspar José de Matos, both of whom were at the beginning of distinguished military careers.[24] On reaching his destination (August 20, 1779), the marquis went to the royal palace of Queluz to pay his respects to the queen, then hastened to rejoin his family at the Lavradio palace situated on an eminence overlooking the Tagus in the northeast quarter of Lisbon.[25]

In contrast with the voluminous record of his activities in Brazil,

---

[21] Vasconcelos' relatório is likewise restricted in its coverage to Rio de Janeiro and its two dependencies.

[22] John Armitage, *The History of Brazil,* II, 243. The Armitage translation (II, 161–242), though readable, is unreliable for scholarly purposes since it omits important passages and contains a number of misspellings of proper names. The ANRJ, BNRJ, and IHGB all have MS copies of the relatório, but I am unaware of the location of the original, if it still exists.

[23] E.g., he limited his remarks concerning the officer primarily responsible for the ignominious surrender of the Santa Catarina garrison to the following: "Do regimento de Moura é seu Coronel Antonio Carlos Furtado de Mendonça: este official por ora está impedido, pareceme desnesessario fallar n'elle" (p. 431). Cf. Appendix II for that officer's traducement of Lavradio.

[24] The *Gazeta de Lisboa* cited in n. 25 below does not list the members of Lavradio's party, but Major Matos wrote General Böhm that these three expected to sail with the Marquis. Matos to Böhm, Aug. 20, 1778, BNRJ, 13-4-3, n. 60 (orig.). Dr. Ferreira had already received license to return to the kingdom with his family. Melo e Castro to Lavradio, May 12, 1778, ANRJ, Col. 67, Liv. III-A, fol. 57ʳ.

[25] *Gazeta de Lisboa,* Aug. 21, 1779. The palace is mentioned in *The Journal of William Beckford in Portugal and Spain 1787-1788,* Boyd Alexander, ed. (London, 1954), p. 121.

there are few hints as to how the marquis spent his remaining years.[26] It is unlikely that he underwent a residência, for such terminal investigations had fallen into desuetude, at least for high-ranking colonial officers, before Lavradio's time.[27] Certainly Dom Luís experienced no disgrace during his last years, for he became a member of the Council of War and by 1786 was named president of the *Desembargo do Paço,* the highest tribunal in the realm. The official gazette occasionally mentions his presence at various state functions such as the marriages and funerals of members of the royal family. Curiously, his name does not appear on the lists of those distinguished personages in attendance at the meetings of the Academia Real das Sciencias. The *Gazeta de Lisboa* of November 17, 1789 did report that the marquis was among those on whom the queen had recently bestowed the Grand Cross of the Order of Christ. That was destined to be the last award Dom Luís de Almeida received on this planet, for six months later (on May 2, 1790), he died of unreported causes while in his sixty-first year.[28]

According to Monsenhor Pizarro, when news of the marquis' death reached Rio de Janeiro the Cariocas sincerely mourned his passing. The cleric obviously regarded their lamentations as well deserved, for he depicted Lavradio as a pious, compassionate, affable, urbane, humane colonial officer who, despite his exalted station, was always accessible to the ordinary folk and was ever mindful of their interests. Though he was a zealous servant of the Crown, he was neither rigorous nor sanguinary; such a man, said Pizarro, knew well how to fulfill his duties to the Lord and to Caesar.[29] Later historians have concurred with the chronicler's evaluation, and have awarded the Marquis of Lavradio high marks as a colonial administrator. Robert Southey termed his views as "scientific and liberal," but added wryly that "even if they had been more steadily encouraged by the Government, the Brazilians were not ripe for them." Other nineteenth-century historians, such as Varnhagen, Fernandes Pinheiro, and

[26] His biographer and descendant, Correa de Sá, is entirely silent concerning the marquis' last years.

[27] Frequently in the eighteenth century officials were specifically exempted from the residência. E.g., Antônio José Victoriano Borges da Fonseca, "Nobiliarchia Pernambucana," *ABNRJ* XLVII (1935), 201 (*s.v.* Antônio Felippe de Bulhões da Cunha). When colonial officers were removed from their posts as a consequence of serious charges preferred against them, an investigation of their administration was naturally undertaken. E.g., *ordem* of May 5, 1732 (*RAPM,* XVI:1 [1911], 348–349) concerning the residência of D. Lourenço de Almeida, former captain-general of Minas Gerais.

[28] *Gazeta de Lisboa,* Apr. 30 and May 14, 1785; July 29, 1786; June 21, 1787; Sept. 19, 1788; Nov. 17, 1789; Apr. 9 and May 2, 1790.

[29] José de Souza Azevedo Pizarro e Araujo, *Memórias históricas do Rio de Janeiro* V, 215–218.

Rocha Pombo, praised Lavradio as "an excellent and enlightened administrator," one who was "mild tempered, prudent, obsequious, and just," and among the ablest colonial officers to serve during the reign of José I. These appraisals have been echoed by twentieth-century Brazilian historians including Max Fleiuss, Pedro Calmon, Caio Prado, Júnior, and Lourival Gomes Machado.[30]

Such flattering tributes, which rest largely on the relatório, Lavradio's only widely read exposition, are in some respects confirmed by the extensive record the marquis left behind. That record—documents written by, to, or about Lavradio—makes abundantly clear that he was, indeed, a hard working, extremely conscientious servant of the Crown. Like many another Portuguese senior administrator,[31] he devoted much time to drafting and revising—frequently in his own hand—countless, often lengthy dispatches to his superiors, peers, and subordinates. If the tone he employed when writing to his lieutenants was sometimes caustic and imperious, that which he used in his ofícios to the Crown was always studiously deferential. He labored long hours over the many papers that constantly crossed his desk—judicial proceedings; the accounts of the exchequer; dispatches from the Court, fellow administrators, and subordinates; the reports of the mestres de campo and the parish curates; and those innumerable petitions from office holders and private individuals. Many of the documents needing his approval were of a purely routine or even trivial character that in modern governments would be handled by minor functionaries. But in the Portuguese regime, as in the Spanish, no subject was too insignificant to require the attention of the administrative chief. By dispatch, signature, or rubric the viceroy passed on such matters as applications for temporary leaves of absence by military and civil personnel; the authorization of a wooden leg for a wounded veteran; the drawing of a new clothing allowance for a group of shipwrecked artillerymen; and the incarceration of a protesting father so that his daughter could be married.[32] In each instance

30 Significant estimates of Lavradio's abilities as a viceroy may be found in Robert Southey, History of Brazil, III (London, 1819), 664; Armitage, History of Brazil, II, 159; Francisco Adolfo de Varnhagen, História do Brasil, IV, 251–252; João F. Rocha Pombo, História do Brazil, VI (Rio de Janeiro, [1905]), 422; J. C. Fernandes Pinheiro, "Os últimos vice-reis do Brasil," RIHGB, XXVIII:2 (1865), 237; Max Fleiuss, História administrativa do Brasil, p. 58; Caio Prado, Júnior, Formação do Brasil contemporâneo, 308; Pedro Calmon, História do Brasil, IV (Rio de Janeiro, 1959), 1204; and Lourival Gomes Machado, "Política e administração sob os últimos vice-reis," in Sérgio Buarque de Holanda et al., Historia geral da civilização brasileira, I:2 (São Paulo, 1960), 367–371.

31 Cf. Charles R. Boxer, The Golden Age of Brazil, p. 147.

32 The manuscript codices used in this study are full of similar examples. In more than one way did the viceroy's job resemble that of the king's. See Charles R. Boxer, Four Centuries of Portuguese Expansion, p. 81, for a discussion of trivial as well as important matters requiring the king's attention.

Dom Luís sought to make his action coincide with the expressed wishes of the Crown; whenever in the slightest doubt, he referred the question, no matter how unimportant, to Lisbon for an answer.[33] Prudence and caution were the constant words of advice that he gave to his colleagues and subordinates, and they were truly the watchwords by which he lived. Only in rare instances, such as his appropriation of part of the quintos in 1777, did Dom Luís deliberately depart from his instructions. There was no place in his philosophy for *obedezco pero no cumplo,* the famous noncompliance formula employed by Spanish colonial officers. Indeed, Lavradio could easily have concurred with the statement of a noted sixteenth-century Mexican viceroy who vowed that he would not "take a step beyond royal orders unless I see the stream is leaving its bed; even though a matter weigh less than a hair, I shall not act without consulting Your Majesty." [34]

Nor would the Marquis have considered absenting himself from his seat of government without license from the king. He was fully aware of the deep-rooted conviction that Portuguese authorities shared with those of Spain—that administrative chiefs must remain constantly at their posts to oversee the work of subordinates who could not be trusted to make any sort of decision by themselves.[35] But from Lavradio's point of view adherence to that policy posed several disadvantages. One was that he was forced to remain an armchair commander because the king would not allow him to go to the borderlands to direct military operations. (There is no reason to suspect that his presence there would have altered the outcome of the fighting, for, contrary to the assertions of Pedro Calmon and others, Dom Luís did not possess the soldierly qualities of a Bobadela, much less those of a Cevallos.) Another disadvantage of his confinement was that he had no opportunity to gain personal familiarity with the lands and peoples he administered. During his eleven years of service in the colony the marquis never ventured more than a few leagues away from his palace.[36] Then, too, the fact that he was always on the job meant

[33] Thus he declined to prescribe the boundary limits of a newly established Indian village in the captaincy of Rio de Janeiro, insisting that their determination must be left to the king. Lavradio to Desembargador Manoel Francisco da S[ous]a e Veiga, Apr. 1773, BNRJ, II-34, 15, 40 (orig.). An Angeja (the Marquis of Angeja, viceroy of Brazil, 1714–1718) might assert as viceroy that he was competent to make such a decision, but never a Lavradio. Cf. Boxer, *The Golden Age,* pp. 147 and 399, n. 45.

[34] Martín Enríquez de Almansa to the king, Jan. 10, 1574, quoted in Philip Wayne Powell, "Portrait of an American Viceroy: Martín Enríquez, 1568–1583," *The Americas,* XIV (July, 1957), 7.

[35] Cf. Magali Sarfatti, *Spanish Bureaucratic-Patrimonialism in America* (Institute for International Studies: University of California, Berkeley, 1966), p. 25.

[36] In Rio de Janeiro he once climbed the top of a mountain known as o Pico, overlooking fort Santa Cruz at the entrance to Guanabara Bay, to study plans for its fortification. Late in his administration Dom Luís spoke of making a secret tour

that he never enjoyed any respite from the constant drudgery of his official tasks—there were no vacations for colonial officers in his day—and it is little wonder that there were occasions when the viceroy's patience wore thin with laggard subordinates or insufferable foreign sea captains.

The extent to which the marquis may properly be considered an enlightened administrator depends on precisely what is meant by that term. If it is defined as one who was highly cultured, free from prejudices, opposed to tradition, given to original ideas and possessed of the tenacity to see them bear fruit, then Lavradio does not qualify. If, on the other hand, it is applied to one who exhibited sincere concern for the welfare of those entrusted to his care, then Dom Luís merits the designation. Nothing is more precious than a human life, he once told a colleague, and his expressions of grief when he received reports of accidental deaths among the troops he sent south appear genuine.[37]

As is evident from Chapter XIII, the viceroy took a keen interest in the exploitation of neglected natural resources, partly because their development would bring new prosperity to Brazilians. But that was distinctly a secondary consideration in his mind, for he was thinking primarily about the benefits that the kingdom, particularly the royal exchequer, might derive from the promotion of new products. Nevertheless, Dom Luís deserves credit for having lent the prestige of his office to the efforts of the Vieiras, Hopmans, Coelhos and others who directly contributed to Brazil's agricultural renaissance. Though the degree of his active participation in the celebrated Scientific Society of Rio de Janeiro remains unclear, it appears that his dedication to the advancement of science has been exaggerated. Consistent with his willingness to encourage certain forms of economic activity that might redound to the benefit of the mother country was his opposition to colonial manufacturing, partly because of the alleged harm such activity caused Carioca importers, but especially because it competed with cloth making in the mother country. But as Armitage once said, "His ideas on commerce . . . were those of the age in which [he] . . . lived." [38] So, too, was his strong paternalistic strain, reflected in his advice to his peers and subordinates and in his orders to militia colonels to compel farmers to grow certain crops, even though the execution of such instructions was likely to arouse resentment.

Although Dom Luís professed to take "no notice of the murmurs of

---

of the captaincy of Rio de Janeiro, but there is no indication that he ever realized that ambition. Lavradio to Captain Luiz Alvares de Freitas Bello, June 23, 1778, CMCM, cod. 25, fols. 253ᵛ–254ʳ.

[37] Lavradio to Martim Lopes Lobo de Saldanha, Apr. 26, 1776, DI, XXVII (1895), 109; idem to Böhm, Jan. 26 and Feb. 13, 1775, BNRJ, 13-4-2, nos. 9 and 10; BCRG, pp. 36–41.

[38] History of Brazil, II, 159.

the people," he lent an attentive ear to their expressed grievances against their neighbors and the king's officers.[39] Many of his directives to magistrates, militia commanders, and parish priests called for verification of reports of misconduct by colonists and royal officials and for the remission of offending parties directly to him. He enjoined subordinates to carry out his instructions "with all possible suavity" so as to avoid vexing the king's subjects.[40] Their failure to do so was likely to result in a peremptory order to report to him to explain their behavior, and when such personal interviews—one of the hallmarks of his regime—failed to produce the desired results, a few nights in the Relação's dungeon were likely to do so. While the marquis was as firmly opposed as any man of his class to popular participation in the affairs of government, he did as much as he could to benefit the colonists since their well-being contributed directly to that of the mother country.

This did not mean that Lavradio had a very high estimate of the Brazilians or that he was particularly fond of them. His dispatches, like those of his peers, are full of references to the "natural slothfulness and carelessness of the Americans," [41] and he advised his successor that "The general character of Americans in these parts . . . is that of lethargy, humility, and obedience. While they are sober in their habits, they are . . . prone to vanity and hauteur. But these defects are easily overcome. They are robust and capable of all sorts of labor, and do what they are told. However, if they are not given careful instructions, they often remain in a state of inactivity until they are reduced to extreme poverty." [42]

Unflattering as these remarks are, Dom Luís' appraisal was shared by most Portuguese colonial officers of his time and by Peninsulars generally. Not long before Lavradio wrote these lines the English traveler William Dalrymple attended "a little farce" in Lisbon where "the manners of the inhabitants of Brazil were ridiculed with some humour; they represented them as a very formal and pedantic people, and brought them in with a suite of [N]egroes, monkeys, parrots &c. [T]here was a kind of low wit introduced in it, which seemed to give greater satisfaction to the audience, than any other part: an old woman frequently breaking wind in her master's face, produced infinite applause, even from the boxes." [43]

Like most of us, the marquis bore his share of prejudices. Along

---

39 Lavradio, *Relatório,* pp. 455–456.

40 E.g., Lavradio to Antônio Pinheiro Amado (ouvidor da comarca), Jan. 26, 1770, ANRJ, Col. 70, Liv. V, fol. 14ʳ.

41 E.g., Lavradio to Oeiras, July 5, 1770, IHGB/AUC, 1-2-29, fols. 239ʳ–241ʳ. and *idem* to Melo e Castro, Feb. 25, 1774, *VRL,* p. 181.

42 Lavradio, *Relatório,* p. 452.

43 *Travels through Spain and Portugal,* p. 150.

with the Marquis of Pombal and many other Lusitanians, he distrusted foreigners generally, particularly Spaniards and Britons. Though the treatment of the Indians never became one of his major responsibilities as it had been for his sixteenth-century predecessors, and although he was not inclined to romanticize about the Amerindians' primordial existence as did some of his contemporaries, the viceroy was acutely conscious of the wrongs Europeans had committed against them and was especially solicitous of their welfare.[44] But in common with most *Reinóes* of his time, Lavradio had far less esteem for African Negroes.[45] The fact that he once ordered an Indian *capitão mor* removed from his post for having degraded himself by marrying a Negress has been noted by several authors.[46] On another occasion he dismissed a *capitão mor* whom the Indians of the village of Mangaratiba (Rio de Janeiro) certified was not of their blood but was a mulatto.[47] The captain-general of Bahia reported that the marquis sent home a number of Bahian soldiers "because of physical defects, illnesses, and [the fact that they were] of the pardo breed." [48] Further confirmation of Lavradio's dislike for Negroes is provided by a Brazilian-born chronicler of Angola who observed that during the customary hand-kissing ceremonies at the viceregal palace Dom Luís would not allow colored militia officers to approach him but insisted that they make their bows from the doorway after their white colleagues had paid him their respects.[49]

The viceroy also possessed pronounced antipathies toward certain professions. He considered lawyers to be greedy parasites, apothecaries common robbers, taverners custodians of dens of iniquity, and ecclesiastics sowers of intrigue and discord.[50] Sometimes he carried his

[44] Apart from his correspondence with Captain-General Sousa regarding the activities of the Paraná bandeiras (see Chap. XVI, pp. 363 f.) , that concern was reflected in various ways, such as Dom Luis' order for a judicial inquiry to determine whether the Indians of a newly formed community had been deprived of lands and cattle that properly belonged to them (see note 33 above) , and his request that several Indian boys being educated by a priest be sent to him so that he could see the progress they had been making in their studies. Lavradio to Padre José da Silva Furtado, Sept. 5, 1775, CMCM, cod. 25, fol. 42ᵛ.

[45] Concerning racial attitudes in the Portuguese empire, see Charles R. Boxer, *Race Relations in the Portuguese Colonial Empire 1415–1825*, and José Honório Rodrigues, *Brazil and Africa*, tr. by Richard A. Mazzara and Sam Hileman (Berkeley, 1965) , pp. 57 f.

[46] Alfredo de Carvalho, *Frases e palavras—problemas históricas e etimológicos* (Recife, 1906), pp. 41–42; Boxer, *Race Relations*, p. 121; and Rodrigues, p. 58. The source, which none of these authors cite, is Lavradio to Antônio Pinheiro Amado (ouvidor da comarca), Aug. 6, 1771, ANRJ, Col. 70, Liv. V, fol. 214ʳ.

[47] Lavradio to Antônio Pinheiro Amado, Dec. 4, 1775, CMCM, cod. 25, fol. 60ʳ.

[48] Manoel da Cunha Menezes to Melo e Castro, June 30, 1775, BNRJ, I-4, 3, 16.

[49] Elias Alexandre da Silva Corrêa, *Historia de Angola* (1792) , I (Lisbon, 1937) , 84 n.

[50] Lavradio, *Relatório*, pp. 442–443; *idem* to Francisco de Souza Menezes, May 27 and Oct. 13, 1771, CMCM, cod. 15, fols. 62ᵛ–63ʳ, 137ʳ.

prejudices to absurd lengths, as when he ordered the grandson of a taverner dismissed from his militia post simply because of his grandfather's occupation.[51] The best that can be said about Lavradio's social attitudes is that he was a man of his times who was incapable of rising above them.

Measured by the standards of achievement set by that small group of truly outstanding governors of colonial America,[52] the Marquis of Lavradio cannot be ranked as a great colonial officer. His regime did not mark a major turning point in the life of the colony, nor did he leave any enduring monument to testify to his accomplishments. He was not a figure of heroic fighting qualities, nor an erudite law-giver, nor a man of gifted literary attainments. Indeed, it is questionable whether the strong-minded Marquis of Pombal would have selected a man of such qualities as Brazil's nominal administrative chief. But Dom Luís was far from being a mere time-server. Within the narrow limits of authority granted him he performed his many tasks faithfully, selflessly, tirelessly, and deliberately. It is plain that those limits were territorially and substantively much less extensive than those of the viceroys of the Spanish empire.[53] The title viceroy of Brazil was not really descriptive of the position that Lavradio occupied, nor did his office possess that mystique of eminence that for centuries had been associated with the position of viceroy in Spanish America. Like his counterparts, the marquis was burdened with endless paperwork that made his position more akin to that of a well-paid clerk than to that of a decision-making executive.[54]

51 Lavradio to Manoel da Silva Braga, May 29, 1775, *ibid.*, fol. 24ʳ.

52 Depending on the criteria applied, such a group might include Antonio de Mendoza, Francisco de Toledo, Martín Enriquez de Almansa, Luís de Velasco II, and the second Revillagigedo in the Spanish empire; Robert Hunter, William Keith, Thomas Pownall, Cadwallader Colden, and Thomas Hutchinson in the English mainland colonies; Count Frontenac, the Marqueses de Vaudreuil, and the Count de la Galissonnière in New France; Mem de Sá, Salvador Correa de Sá; Francisco Barreto de Menezes, and possibly António de Albuquerque in Brazil.

53 Cf. Lillian Estelle Fisher, *Viceregal Administration in the Spanish-American Colonies* (Berkeley, 1926), pp. 335 f.

54 The earnings of Brazil's titular senior administrators had risen steadily since the founding of royal government. Between 1549 and 1602 the salaries of the governors-general climbed from 400,000 réis per year to 1,200,000. The Conde da Cunha, the first of the Rio viceroys received 4,800,000 réis per year, and that seems to have been Lavradio's salary too. However, his wife petitioned the Queen that her husband was actually receiving less than the former Salvadorean viceroys because they were able to collect certain emoluments and perquisites not available to the viceroys at Rio de Janeiro, and asked for an adjustment. Accordingly, the Queen agreed to advance the Marquis 30,000 cruzados (12,000,000 réis) to defray his expenses and asked him to render an accounting as soon as he returned to Lisbon. The salary of Lavradio's successor was elevated to 8,000,000 réis per year and remained at that level during the term of the Conde de Rezende beginning in 1789. Martinho de Melo e Castro to Lavradio, Jan. 1, 1779, BNRJ, I-2, 4, 7, n. 112; carta régia to Luís de Vasconcelos e Sousa, Jan. 25, 1779, ANRJ, Col. 67, Liv. IV, fol. 4ʳ (orig.). See also Rocha Pombo, *Historia do Brazil*, V, 370–371.

Though he failed to realize the unattainable ambition of his master, the Marquis of Pombal, to extend Brazil's frontiers to the Uruguay and the Plata, he helped to prevent the permanent loss of territory that Portuguese forces could reasonably expect to hold. The expenses of defending the borderlands proved extremely heavy, and despite the fact that the viceroy assiduously pushed the Pombaline fiscal reforms, he was unable to arrest the steadily mounting burden of royal indebtedness in the colony. Coming to Brazil in a period of economic recession, Dom Luís was energetically responsive to suggestions for the development of alternative sources of wealth, and thereby contributed to the resuscitation of Brazilian agriculture at a critical time during the last colonial decades. Considering his lack of professional training for administrative tasks, the magnitude of the problems he faced, and the sort of guidance and support he received from his superiors, Dom Luís de Almeida discharged his manifold responsibilities as constructively, beneficially, and competently as could be expected.

The long and eventful administration of Viceroy Lavradio occurred during the third phase of Portuguese rule in Brazil. The first was the propietary era of the 1530s and 1540s when the Crown endeavored to promote the conquest, settlement, defense, and exploitation of the lands it claimed in South America by extensive delegations of its rights to private individuals. But the donatarial regime did not prove as adaptable to the extensive and already inhabited mainland as it had in the Atlantic Islands. As a consequence, the second phase of royal administration was initiated in 1549 with the establishment of a supervisory regime at Salvador headed by a governor-general. The next century and a half witnessed the taming of the littoral, the pacification and partial elimination of the indigenous population, the planting of Portuguese outposts from the remote forests of the Upper Amazon Valley to the seacoast opposite Buenos Aires in the Platine estuary, the development of an agricultural, slave-based economy, the gradual phasing out of enclaves of private government, and several reorganizations of the royal administration that progressively reduced the effective authority of the governors-general. This last trend was continued during the third phase (ca. 1690–1808) when large mineral bonanzas were uncovered and worked, agriculture underwent periods of decline and revival, and population, both black and white, substantially increased in numbers and moved inland from the already settled coastal zones. Additional territory was appropriated in the west and south, and rivalry between Spain and Portugal for hegemony in South America reached its apogee. Colonial life underwent increased regimentation through legislation and the creation of a more elaborate bureaucracy—a bureaucracy centered in captaincies-general whose heads were nominally dependent upon viceroys at Salvador and later at Rio de Janeiro, but who were mainly answerable directly to the Crown. The last phase (1808–1822) came during the Court's residence in Brazil, when many long-standing socioeconomic restrictions were eliminated, governmental institutions were upgraded and further centralized, and Brazil became a co-kingdom.

The most significant commentaries on Brazil's colonial administration have been implicitly or explicitly focused upon the second and third of these phases. Writing during the last phase, Robert Southey, the first foreigner to undertake the ambitious task of summarizing Brazil's colonial experience, concluded his three-volume *History* with a critical appraisal of the Portuguese regime. In it he condemned the governors for their exercise of despotic authority "regulated by no laws, checked by no usages, standing in no fear of public opinion, and controlled by no responsiblility . . . as absolute as so many Bashaws. . . ." He characterized the administration of justice as "scandalously remiss," and termed the persistence of the systems of tax farming and royal monopolies, especially that on trade, as "at once wasteful and oppressive." But, writing in 1819, Southey concluded that "Fair prospects, and glorious ones, are before them [that is, the Brazilians] if they escape the curse of Revolution." [55]

Brazil, of course, did not escape the contagion of revolution, and in the mid-nineteenth century two of her most influential historians, Francisco Adolfo de Varnhagen and João Francisco Lisboa, published two quite different views of the former Portuguese regime. In his impressively researched, largely narrative *General History* of the colonial period, Varnhagen, the Paulista-born historian and diplomat, found that regime more worthy of praise than of blame. He admitted that the Crown and its agents sometimes made mistakes because of inexperience, inadequate information, poor communications, and sheer bad judgment, but he insisted that such shortcomings were contrary to the meritorious intentions of the Crown. Though he conceded that colonial executive officers were sometimes unjust, arbitrary, and despotic, he pointed out that the Crown circumscribed their powers by the privileges awarded to the magistracy, the câmaras, and the heads of the Church and by the restrictions imposed on the governors' activities. On the whole, Varnhagen concluded, Colonial Brazil was no worse governed than was the mother country.[56]

[55] *History of Brazil*, III, 869–877.
[56] *Historia geral do Brasil*, III, 267–269; IV, 248–250. (Varnhagen's first edition was published in Rio de Janeiro between 1854 and 1857.)

And no better either, responded Lisboa. The Maranhense essayist, journalist, lawyer, and politician could find little good in what he regarded as the record of Portuguese misrule. In his famous *Jornal de Timon* Lisboa condemned the laws Portugal applied to Brazil as "confused, incomplete, contradictory [and] oppressive," and charged that the governors, the magistrates, and even the câmaras were united to form a "general system of oppression and tyranny" against the colonists and the Indians. Although he admitted that there were a few well-meaning colonial officers, he contended that they were powerless to offset the "pernicious influence" of the vast majority of officials whom he characterized as ignorant, corrupt, nepotistic, despotic, and vicious.[57]

Despite the fact that his polemic was directed at the particular frontier conditions prevailing in the Amazon area and was less thoroughly researched than Varnhagen's much broader and fuller narrative, Lisboa's strictures gained acceptance among leading Brazilian historians who applied them to the colonial regime as a whole. For example, J. M. Pereira da Silva, the author of an early multivolume synthesis of the founding of the Brazilian empire, followed Lisboa's interpretation with only slight modification. He agreed with Varnhagen that the Crown intended to protect the colonists against the abuses of their governors, but lamented that "unfortunately practice did not correspond to theory," partly because the Crown was too far away from its agents and communications were too slow to permit adequate checks on their conduct.

Pereira da Silva found the Crown itself at fault because of its unwise choice of colonial officers who were either "inept fidalgos" who had neither training nor talent for administration and owed their appointments to their influence at Court or were excessively proud but impoverished soldiers who lacked understanding of how to govern civilians and whose only merits were their valor and audacity. Such men, he claimed, came to Brazil with the sole aim of acquiring fortunes as quickly as possible. They did so by extortions and thefts and by imposing such terror that the settlers seldom dared to raise their voices in protest for fear of the consequences. When they did, he charged, the damage had been done before the Court was cognizant of it, and the peculating officials managed to escape punishment by destroying evidence against them and by conspiring with those who were sent to investigate wrongdoing. Although he, too, admitted that occasionally honorable, conscientious, even able officers made their appearance, he agreed with Lisboa that they were exceptions to the

[57] *Jornal de Timon,* reprinted in Lisboa, *Obras,* III (São Luis do Maranhão, 1865), 83–91, 93–97, 166–169, and 171–179.

run of ignorant, corrupt despots who governed Brazil.[58] The argely negative portrayal of Brazil's colonial administration ap- in the prolix and poorly researched multivolume history of ..l by the turn-of-the-century historian José Francisco da Rocha ... .bo whose remarks on this subject represent a paraphrase of Lisboa and Pereira da Silva.[59]

Among modern interpreters of Brazil's colonial past, two of the most knowledgeable, Caio Prado, Júnior, and Charles R. Boxer, are impressed by different features of Portugal's colonial administration and therefore reach somewhat different conclusions about its character. In his perceptive analysis of that regime [60] Prado, the able Paulista Marxist essayist, notes that with the exception of the donataries, who soon disappeared as significant elements in the administration, the institutions that Portugal introduced in Brazil were replicas of those that existed at home rather than adaptations and innovations tailored to the colony's frontier environment. Conforming to its Peninsular model, the colonial regime consisted of multiple hierarchies with ill-defined functions and limitations. Modern concepts of the separation and division of powers were alien to such a regime in which administrative entities were united only in their subordination to the Crown. He points out that such agencies, like their Peninsular counterparts, were concentrated in urban centers, though most of the population was dispersed throughout the countryside and was therefore largely beyond the effective range of royal authority. The instrumentalities of that authority were, in his view, cumbersome, inflexible, inefficient, and lacking in appropriate expertise.[61] Consequently sound fiscal management was absent; public order largely insecure; and justice expensive, extraordinarily complicated, slow, and inaccessible to the majority of the population. Prado observes that the government provided remarkably few public facilities, betokening the fact that the administration was not geared to render services but existed primarily to produce revenues for the king, his Court, and other favored parties in the realm. Thus while he discounts as exaggerated the contention of earlier writers that the colonial regime was notoriously despotic, Caio Prado, Júnior, emphasizes its exploitive character.[62]

58 Historia da fundação do imperio brazileiro, I (2d ed., Rio de Janeiro, 1877), 106–113. The first edition appeared in Rio de Janeiro between 1864 and 1868.

59 Historia do Brazil, V, 403.

60 For Prado's functional analysis see his Formação do Brasil contemporâneo, pp. 297–336, 361–362.

61 E.g., he notes that the gold intendencies of Minas Gerais were administered by jurists without benefit of technical advisors such as geologists, mineralogists, or engineers. Ibid., p. 332.

62 "Um objective fiscal, nada mais que isto, é o que anima a metrópole na colonização do Brasil. Raros são os atos da administração ou administradores que fazem exceção à regra." Ibid., p. 335.

Professor Boxer's unsurpassed knowledge of the Lusitanian empire in the Old and the New Worlds leads him to take a less harsh view of the Portuguese government.[63] He contends that the Crown took a sincere, paternal interest in the just treatment of its colonials and was usually receptive to their legitimate complaints. Without denying the Crown's exploitive purposes, he observes that "If the Crown squeezed a great deal of gold out of its vassals . . . , it also made innumerable payments and maintained an enormous pension list wherein figured widows and orphans in remote colonies as well as parasitic courtiers at Lisbon."[64] He depicts its overseas governors as haughty, race-conscious, stern, quarrelsome officers, the best of whom were enlightened, courageous, and tirelessly devoted to the Crown's interest and to their own,[65] in contrast with others who were unimaginative, indecisive, cowardly do-nothings. On the whole, Mr. Boxer leaves his readers with the impression that the imperial regime did not weigh heavily on the average colonial.

It is possible to concur with many of the criticisms of the Portuguese regime expressed by previous students, particularly if it is understood that such judgments may be equally applied to other contemporary colonial governments. All European colonies in the early modern period existed primarily for the advantages they offered their mother countries, and only those activities that were considered beneficial or at least noninjurious to the vital interests of the mother country were deemed permissible. For that reason each mother country forbade certain forms of manufacturing in its colonies and reserved especially valued resources exclusively for its own uses. Similarly, each imperial power restricted the right to engage in direct trade with its colonies to its own subjects and denied that privilege to outsiders. If England adopted a more liberal immigration policy with respect to the settlement of foreigners in her colonies than did Portugual or Spain, that was partly because her colonies lacked the prized mineral resources found in the Iberian empires and envied by their rivals.

As D. K. Fieldhouse has observed, the administrative institutions and the degree of freedom that each mother country bestowed on its colonies mirrored the institutions and privileges that existed at home.[66] The growth of parliamentary influence at the expense of royal author-

---

[63] See particularly *The Golden Age*, pp. 146, 198, 204, and 314–315.

[64] *Ibid.*, p. 204.

[65] Professor Boxer is fond of contending that the governors of colonial Brazil commonly and illicitly engaged in private trade (see *ibid.*, index, *s.v.* "Governors, engage in trade and commerce") but nowhere adduces convincing evidence to support such a charge.

[66] *The Colonial Empires: A Comparative Survey from the Eighteenth Century* (London, 1965), p. 20.

ity in eighteenth-century Great Britain was matched overseas by the rise of popular assemblies that contested the right to govern with executive officers appointed by the Crown. In eighteenth-century Portugal and Spain parliamentary bodies (*Cortes*) no longer met and centuries before had ceased to serve as restraints upon the royal will, while in the colonies municipal bodies (cabildos and câmaras), the most likely spokesmen for colonial aspirations, were politically ineffective before representatives of the Crown. By the Marquis of Lavradio's time control over the imperial bureaucracy was far more centralized in Portugal and Spain than it was in Great Britain.[67] Yet while there are indications that during the 1760s and 1770s England was considering the naming of a powerful executive to supervise its mainland colonies,[68] no comparable centralizing tendency may be discerned within the less compact Iberian empires in the late colonial period. Indeed, one important effect of the administrative reforms of the Bourbons was to lessen the stature of the viceroys of Spanish America,[69] and enough has already been said to indicate that the Braganzas before, during, and after Pombal were not inclined to make the viceroys of Brazil true vice-kings.

It is true, as Caio Prado, Júnior, has asserted, that the bureacracy of Colonial Brazil was concentrated in the cities, but in most instances it is hard to see what agencies could have been effectively relocated outside of the capitals. Certainly there was a need for additional ouvidores to dispense justice in the countryside, as well as for

[67] *Ibid.,* pp. 61–63; see also Charles M. Andrews, *The Colonial Period* (New York, 1912), pp. 140–141, 147–148.

[68] In 1760, for example, the Reverend Samuel Johnson, author of "Questions Relating to the Union and Government of the Plantations," renewed his "old plea" for "some gentleman of great dignity and worth" to be appointed by the Crown "in the nature of a Vice Roi, or Lord Lt. to reside in New York." Quoted in Carl Bridenbaugh, *Mitre and Sceptre. Transatlantic Faiths, Ideas, Personalities, and Politics 1689–1775* (New York, 1962), p. 216. In the view of Clarence E. Carter the position of the commander-in-chief of the British Army in North America was intended to serve as an imperial instrument for administrative centralization. "The Significance of the Military Office in America, 1763," *American Historical Review,* XXVIII (1923), 475–488, and "The Office of Commander in Chief: A Phase of Imperial Unity on the Eve of the Revolution," in Richard B. Morris, ed., *The Era of the American Revolution* . . . (New York, 1939), pp. 170–213; but cf. John Richard Alden, *General Gage America* . . . (Baton Rouge, 1948), pp. 83, 86, and 88.

[69] Besides the division of the viceroyalty of Peru into three vice-royalties, the largely autonomous status attained by the captains-general of Chile, and the creation of the Provincias Internas regime in the northern parts of New Spain, I am thinking of the establishment of the intendency system that lessened the military, fiscal, and judicial powers of the viceroys (John Lynch, *Spanish Colonial Administration, 1782–1810. The Intendant System in the Viceroyalty of the Rio de la Plata* [London, 1958]), and the creation of the office of regent (1776) which assumed many of the viceroys' duties with respect to judicial administration (Fisher, *Viceregal Administration,* p. 29).

more strenuous efforts to keep such magistrates in the field rather than permit them to spend most of their time in their headquarters where they, like the *corregidores* of Spanish America, found the amenities of life more attractive than those available in the backlands. Even more urgent were procedural changes in judicial processes to simplify the settlement of litigation affecting private interests. But, as suggested by the Pombaline fiscal innovations, structural and procedural reforms did not necessarily produce basic improvements. Those reforms also suggest that the Portuguese Crown continued to rely too heavily on persons trained in law and in military affairs to conduct the technical operations of administration for which they lacked the requisite special competence. But persons with the training or skills comparable to those of the French intendants, for example, were not to be found either in the Portuguese colonies or at home.

Although contemporaries sometimes expressed the opinion that the bureaucracy of Colonial Brazil needed to be reduced in size, it was not, in fact, impressively large. In Lavradio's day the total number of salaried administrative personnel in the nine captaincies-general probably did not exceed 1,500 or one per 1,036 registered inhabitants.[70] But it should be remembered as Caio Prado, Júnior, has noted, that the bureaucracy was concerned with relatively few primary tasks: the enforcement of law; the promotion of the interests of the faith; the maintenance of external defense and internal security; the collection and disbursement of revenues. And in return for its demands on the colonists for their obedience, their abstention from exercising any popular voice in the direction of the affairs of government, their enrollment in military levies, and above all their payment of taxes, the Portuguese regime provided fewer services than any other imperial government between the sixteenth and the early nineteenth centuries.[71] In its orientation the Portuguese colonial bureaucracy was service-seeking rather than service-rendering.

[70] For Brazil's population in the 1770s, see Appendix I. In Bahia and Rio de Janeiro, the two captaincies-general where there were the largest number of administrative positions, there were an estimated 500 employees in the former (a ratio of 1:574 inhabitants) in 1779 and 192 in the latter (a ratio of 1:875) in 1781. Martinho de Melo e Castro, "Instrução para o Marquez de Valença," Sept. 10, 1779, Castro e Almeida, *Inventário*, II, 437–455; "Mappa geral do rendimento annual de todos os empregos e officios de justiça e fazenda d'esta cidade do Rio de Janeiro," (1781), *RIHGB*, LI:2 (1888), 159–181. By contrast, the total number of federal employees in the United States in 1801 stood at 2,120 (a ratio of 1:2,650) and grew to nearly 7,000 (a ratio of 1:1,429) by 1821. Leonard D. White, *The Federalists. A Study in Administrative History* (New York, 1959), p. 255; U.S. Bureau of the Census, *Historical Statistics of the United States, Colonial Times to 1957* (Washington, D.C., 1960), p. 710, Table Y-241. Information on the number of state employees during these years is lacking.

[71] Cf. Prado, p. 333.

Like the colonial regimes of France and Spain, that of Portugal was paternalistic, legalistic, authoritarian, and quasi-patrimonial,[72] but it was not purposefully despotic. To be sure, some governors and some magistrates were petty capricious tyrants who were dishonest, cynical, and corrupt; others were upright officials who carried out their duties conscientiously, competently, and constructively. A few rendered conspicuous service to the Crown, but most were less interested in making a record of achievement than in marking time and keeping their records sufficiently unstained so that they could qualify for more attractive positions at home. In the absence of career-line studies, one would be hard put to estimate what percentage of colonial officers fitted into any of these categories.

Because the senior administrative officers and the magistrates were the executors of a remote arbitrary authority, it was inevitable that they became the targets of charges of wrongdoing by ill-informed, disgruntled, frustrated, and jealous Peninsulars and colonials. In some cases the charges were no doubt based upon substance, but in others they were simply reactions to situations unfavorable to the complainant, situations for which the targets of their abuse were personally blameless. Furthermore, it should be remembered that if the bureaucrats exhibited undesirable personal traits, so did the governed. If fiscal officers defrauded the king of his revenues, so did merchants, miners, and planters whenever they found the opportunity. Despotic behavior was certainly discernible within the chambers of the governors' palaces; but it could also be seen on the estates of the sugar barons of the coast, in the mining camps of the interior, and on the cattle ranches of the west and the far south. It is absurd to say that colonials were the silent victims of oppression, for the record demonstrates otherwise. That record consists not only of the formal protests the câmaras filed against their superiors and the occasional (but remarkably infrequent) outbursts of popular unrest, but also the flights of colonials to avoid the recruiter, their desertion from the armed

72 In recent years several scholars, including John Te Paske (in two unpublished papers), Magali Sarfatti (*Spanish Bureaucratic-Patrimonialism*), and Richard M. Morse ("The Heritage of Latin America," in Louis Hartz, ed., *The Founding of New Societies* . . . [New York, 1964], p. 157), have applied the Weberian model of the patrimonial state to the Spanish empire, but so far as I know no one has tried to see whether the model also fits Portuguese Brazil. In part, it does. For example, among the policies of the patrimonial ruler which Professor Morse identifies with the Spanish regime in America are: (1) "limiting the tenure of royal officials" [equally true in the Portuguese regime]; (2) "forbidding [such] officials to acquire family and economic ties in their jurisdictions" [as indicated in this chapter, such a rule was not followed in Brazil]; and (3) "using inspectors and spies to supervise all levels of administration" [parish priests, mestres de campo, juizes de fóra, ouvidores, and occasionally members of the Relações, did investigate the conduct of particular individuals, but the Portuguese never assigned special investigators comparable to the Spanish *pesquisidores* or *visitadores* to undertake general or specific examinations of large administrative units].

forces, their evasion of taxes, and their concealment of provisions to prevent them from being commandeered by an impecunious government.

But such forms of protest existed in all empires at this time, and the fact that widespread colonial opposition to Portuguese rule did not occur until the second decade of the nineteenth century may have been attributable to several factors; among them, the lack of opportunity for collective action within the colony, the low level of literacy and informed opinion, and the extent to which colonials actually participated in their own government. The rosters of public offices, the hints contained in administrative correspondence, and the genealogies of the patriarchal families of the northeast suggest that members of the Brazilian elite were closely allied with Peninsular bureaucrats by indirect as well as direct connections. By indirect connections I refer to marriages as well as less formal unions between Peninsular officials and members of the local aristocracy. Such bonds united colonial dynasties with Peninsular governors, senior magistrates, treasury and customs officials. But colonials themselves held important public offices. As indicated in Chapter XVI, colonial-born landed magnates were responsible for the maintenance of law and order in nonurban parts of the colony. A significant number of colonials became governors and magistrates in Brazil and in other parts of the empire. In Bahia the former office of provedor mór da fazenda passed repeatedly from colonial-born father to colonial-born son, and in other administrative units the office of royal treasurer remained the property of certain colonial families for generations—a situation unthinkable in the Spanish empire. Members of the colonial elite owned dozens of minor judgeships and clerkships acquired by purchase or as gifts from the king, and colonials served on the juntas da fazenda and the mesas da inspeção.[73]

The full extent of colonial participation in the government of Brazil awaits further study. It is clear that whether colonial- or Peninsular-born, many members of that bureaucracy were hard-working agents of the Crown. Few among them were outstanding performers; certainly none rivaled the contributions to the theory of colonial administration of such important treatisers as Juan Matienzo, Veitia Linaje, or Solórzano Pereira; and few could match the statesmanlike qualities of Antônio Vieira, Antônio Rodrigues da Costa,[74] or Ale-

[73] Among other sources, the statements regarding the participation of colonials in the royal regime are based upon a reading of José Victoriano Borges da Fonseca, "Nobiliarchia Pernambucana," *ABNRJ*, XLVII–XLVIII (1935) and Antônio de S. Maria Jaboatão, "Catálogo genealógico [de Bahia]," ed. Afonso Costa, *RIHGB*, CXCI (April–June 1946), 1–279.

[74] A member of the Overseas Council and the author of a remarkable memorial concerning the problems of governing Brazil. See "Consulta do Conselho Ultramarino a S. M., no anno de 1732, feita pelo conselheiro Antonio Rodrigues da

xandre de Gusmão. As a group the members of Portugal's regime in Brazil were exceedingly cautious and contentious; they were extremely jealous of their prerogatives, and they were limited in their conception of administrative problems by their immediate horizons.

English writers of the eighteenth and nineteenth centuries were accustomed to refer to Portugal's New World colony as "The Brazils." They employed the plural noun wisely, for there were many Brazils, not one. The seeds of Brazilian separatism were planted with the founding of the quasi-feudal captaincies during the sixteenth and early seventeenth centuries; they were nourished by the captaincies-general of the seventeenth and eighteenth centuries; and they produced bitter fruit in the divisive regional revolts of the nineteenth and twentieth centuries. If Portugal failed to integrate Brazil socially, culturally, economically, and administratively, the formula for such integration has continued to elude the efforts of the governments that have succeeded hers.

Costa. . . ." *RIHGB*, VII (2d ed., 1866), 498–506. For biographical details, see Boxer, *The Golden Age*, pp. 325, 367–368.

Reference Matter

Appendix I

Distribution of the Population of Brazil, 1772–1782 [1]

PLACE	TOTAL	PERCENT
Rio Negro	10,386	0.6
Pará	55,315	3.5
Maranhão	47,410	3.0
Piauí	26,410	1.7
Pernambuco	239,713	15.4
Paraíba	52,468	3.4
Rio Grande do Norte	23,812	1.5
Ceará	61,408	3.9
Bahia	288,848	18.5
Rio de Janeiro	215,678	13.8
Santa Catarina	10,000	0.6
Rio Grande de São Pedro	20,309	1.3
São Paulo	116,975	7.5
Minas Gerais	319,769	20.5
Goiás	55,514	3.5
Mato Grosso	20,966	1.3
TOTAL	1,555,200	100.0

[1] Adapted from adjusted totals given in D. Alden, "The Population of Brazil in the Late Eighteenth Century: A Preliminary Survey," *HAHR*, XLIII (May, 1963), 191. Reprinted with permission of Duke University Press.

Appendix II

The Quest for Culpability for the Capitulations of 1777

THE UNSAVORY STORY of the efforts of Portuguese authorities to affix responsibility for the losses of Santa Catarina Island and Colônia do Sacramento in 1777 has never been told with any degree of accuracy or completeness.[1] Besides revealing some aspects of judicial procedures in Portugal at this time, that story casts light upon the conception of justice in this eighteenth-century kingdom.

As already indicated in the concluding chapter of this study, there is no indication that the government of Maria I considered the Marquis of Lavradio personally responsible for the borderlands disasters. Indeed, the marquis continued to be welcome at Court and to hold important public offices until the end of his life.

Such was not the case with Dom Luís' old patron, the Marquis of Pombal, whose last years were spent in disgrace on his sixteenth-century estate of Pombal.[2] Though in ill health, he continued to turn out prolix memorials defending various aspects of his long ministry. In 1779 the Crown sent two judges, both former protégés of Pombal, to his residence to interrogate their former chief on his conduct in office. How prominently foreign policy figured in their questioning is not apparent. In any case they failed to shake the octogenarian ex-minister's defense that everything he had done—the suppression of the Pôrto revolt, the imprisonment and exile of the nobility, the trial and execution of the Távoras, the expulsion of the Jesuits, and the rest—had been approved by the late king. Fortunately for Pombal, Dom José I was not able to refute him.

Nevertheless Pombal's enemies found opportunities to humiliate him further. In 1780 a royal decree ordered a review of the Távora case and declared the original decree of January 12, 1759, framed by Pombal himself, null and void. The following April fifteen of eighteen judges found that all persons named as guilty of conspiring to murder King José I were innocent of the charges. But the crowning blow came with the publication of a decree of August 16, 1781, in which the queen de-

---

[1] Compare the account given here with Francisco Adolfo de Varnhagen, *História do Brasil* . . . , IV, 202, nn. 101–103, and 231; and Lucas Alexandre Boiteux, *Notas para a história catharinense*, p. 275.

[2] On Pombal's last years, see João Lúcio de Azevedo, *O Marquês de Pombal*, Chap. XI and John Smith (Conde de Carnota), *Memoirs of the Marquis of Pombal*, II (London, 1843), Chaps. XXV–XXVII.

clared Pombal to be "a criminal worthy of exemplary punishment." However, in deference to his ill health, his advanced age, and his request for pardon, Maria I absolved him from corporal punishment but continued his exile from Court.[3] Nine months later the once dreaded minister passed to his ultimate reward.[4]

The first of the Marquis of Lavradio's subordinates to clear himself of culpability for the Portuguese defeats was Robert MacDouall. In June 1777 the colonial secretary empowered the viceroy to remove the commodore from command if Dom Luís still found him insubordinate, and promised that additional instructions on the Irishman's fate would be sent "with the utmost brevity possible." Six months later, the Crown ordered MacDouall sent to the kingdom aboard the first available ship. He was to be accompanied by all documents bearing on his conduct, and was allowed to travel as a private citizen rather than as a prisoner.[5]

When MacDouall reached Lisbon in May 1779, he was incarcerated at the *sítio* of Nossa Senhora da Ajuda. There a court-martial composed of nine naval officers and presided over by the auditor general of the navy reviewed his conduct in Brazil. They examined twenty-nine specific charges, nearly all of them based on statements in Viceroy Lavradio's dispatches. The board found that MacDouall had spoken the truth on various occasions when he certified that his ships lacked essential provisions and were unfit for sea duty. Citing the viceroy's own dispatches, they confirmed the commodore's contention that every officer whom he had appointed had been approved by Lavradio. The officers concluded that MacDouall's admitted intemperance stemmed from his excessive zeal for the royal service rather than from any disrespect for the viceroy.

Then the board examined the Irishman's role in the events of 1776 and 1777. It cited the Court's expression of gratitude to MacDouall for his brave conduct during the naval action of February 19, 1776, in the Lagoa dos Patos as sufficient proof of the king's satisfaction with his behavior on that occasion. The board concluded that MacDouall's decision to shadow the Casa Tilly armada in February 1777 was consistent with his instructions, and declared that his failure to attack the enemy was due to a lack of wind rather than to cowardice. It praised him for his capture of the *San Agustín*, and found reasonable his statement

3 The Portuguese text of the decree is given in Smith, II, 387–388; an English translation appears on pp. 352–354.

4 The *Gazeta de Lisboa's* obituary of May 17, 1782 reads: "Veio notícia do Pombal de haver morrido alli, depois d'huma prolixa moléstia, o Marquez daquelle título, a 15 deste mez, no 83 º da sua idade." Smith (II, 365) states Pombal died on May 5, while Azevedo (p. 389) goes even further astray, placing the date as August 8.

5 Martinho de Melo e Castro to [Lavradio], June 22, 1777, J. F. Fernandes Pinheiro (Visconde de São Leopoldo), *Anais da província de S. Pedro* (Rpr., Rio de Janeiro, 1946), pp. 357–359; *idem* to *idem*, Dec. 22, 1777, *RIHGB*, XXXI:1, 348–349.

that he subsequently returned to Rio de Janeiro because his prisoners had informed him that the Spanish armada was headed in that direction, even though that assertion could not be supported by any of the known facts. Strangely enough, the court-martial board made no mention of the subsequent naval engagement between MacDouall's own ships. The board concluded that the commodore had conducted himself honorably and valorously throughout his cruise in Brazil, and, on July 30, 1779, it ordered him set free.[6]

This was not the last that the Portuguese were to see of MacDouall. After his liberation he rejoined the British navy, and on May 3, 1781, he appeared outside Guanabara Bay in the nine-gun frigate *Shark* seeking permission to enter the port for water and fresh produce. He claimed that he had recently given his supplies of both items to a British merchant vessel bound for India.

The port officer consulted with Viceroy Vasconcelos, who was suspicious of MacDouall's motives, and ordered him to anchor outside the bay beneath the guns of Fort Santa Cruz. In addition he placed the customary guard boat around the *Shark* to prevent any communication between the ship and persons ashore. Later the viceroy agreed to furnish MacDouall with his needs, but insisted on sending them to him rather than allow the British officer to enter the port even though he still retained his commission in the Portuguese navy.[7] Vasconcelos also rejected the request of William Roberts, an English captain of a Portuguese frigate, to visit MacDouall, and was greatly irked when the Englishman did so anyway.[8]

After MacDouall left Rio de Janeiro, a Spanish prisoner who had escaped from his ship testified that the Irishman's real purpose in stopping at Rio was to ascertain whether a Spanish ship had arrived there

---

[6] "Sentença proferida no conselho de guerra sobre o processo verbal do Coronel do Mar Roberto MacDoual," July 30, 1779, BNRJ, I-31, 26, 1, n. 7. Compared with the long, drawn-out civil and military tribunals' deliberations concerning MacDouall's army colleagues, the naval board's decision was reached in an incredibly short time. The fact that MacDouall was a British subject undoubtedly had a bearing on the board's action.

[7] The *Gazeta de Lisboa* of Dec. 18, 1779, announced that the queen had issued a decree confirming MacDouall's appointment as Coronel do Mar.

[8] Luís de Vasconcelos e Sousa to Martinho de Melo e Castro, May 7, 1781, which includes the report of the *patrão mór* to the viceroy on May 3; Vasconcelos to MacDouall, May 4; MacDouall to the commandant of Fort Santa Cruz, May 7; and William Roberts to Vasconcelos, May 7, BNRJ, 4, 4, 3, nums. 58–63. The *Gazeta de Lisboa* published a summary of the viceroy's report in its August 21, 1781 issue.

In his report the viceroy expressed doubts as to whether he should have informed the viceroy of Buenos Aires that the English frigate had appeared in Guanabara Bay. The colonial secretary replied that under the terms of the peace treaty signed by Spain and Portugal in 1777, the viceroy ought to notify his Spanish counterpart concerning the presence of all British warships but not commercial vessels in Brazilian waters. He also approved of Vasconcelos' treatment of MacDouall. Melo e Castro to Vasconcelos, Aug. 17, 1781, BNRJ, 4, 4, 3, n. 24.

from the Plata with bullion or whether Vasconcelos was sending a frigate to Buenos Aires to fetch the silver. Apparently the English had learned that the Spanish were using Portuguese ships to transport bullion back to the Peninsula in order to prevent its capture by British warships.[9]

Not all of the Marquis of Lavradio's former subordinates were as fortunate as Robert MacDouall in their encounters with the Portuguese judicial machinery. Francisco José da Rocha, former governor of Colônia do Sacramento, returned to Rio de Janeiro from Buenos Aires with other repatriates from the entrepôt in the early months of 1779.[10] In the capital he discovered that the judge who had conducted the investigation on the loss of his post had placed all the blame for its fall on his shoulders.[11] In June, about the time the Marquis of Lavradio left the capital, the ex-governor was sent home as a prisoner of state.[12]

In Lisbon Rocha was confined to the tower of Fort São Vicente de Belém to await trial. Apparently the Crown rejected a petition he submitted asking for his freedom, for in November 1781 he drew up a rather rambling memorial to the queen justifying his conduct in signing Colônia's capitulation.[13] His plea availed him nothing, for he was convicted of the crime of lèse-majesté and condemned to death. However, in January 1784 the queen commuted his sentence to permanent exile in Angola. Three months later the Council of War, of which it will be remembered the Marquis of Lavradio was a member, directed that the modified sentence be carried out.[14] So far as is known, Rocha spent his last days in that remote African colony, a victim of circumstances for which he was hardly responsible.[15]

---

[9] Francisco Antonio España [y Menezes] to Vasconcelos, May 7, 1781, BNRJ, 4, 4, 3, n. 64. The report was criticized in the *Gazeta de Lisboa* (Sept. 11, 1781) which contended that the Spaniard had exaggerated the size of the British fleet of which MacDouall was allegedly a member. On Spain's use of Portuguese ships during the war to transport silver to the Peninsula, see Conde de Floridablanca to Charles III, Nov. 6, 1789, *CTLA*, VII, xxv–xxvi.

[10] Viceroy Vasconcelos reported that Rocha reached Rio de Janeiro a few days after his own arrival there. Vasconcelos to Martinho de Melo e Castro, June 4 1779, BNRJ, 4, 4, 1, n. 26.

[11] A summary of the *devassa* is given in Desembargador Nicolão Joaquim de Miranda Silva e Alarcão to Lavradio, Dec. 1, 1777, IHGB/AUC, 1-1-29, fols. 457ᵛ–465.̣

[12] See n. 10 above.

[13] Rocha to [?], Nov. 5, 1781, a covering letter for his "Defeza" which follows. Alberto Lamego, "O último governador da Colônia do Sacramento: Francisco José da Rocha," *Revista de philologia e de história*, II (Rio de Janeiro, 1933), 212–225. Lamego published these documents in order to refute the contention by Pizarro that Rocha died in Angola (Pizarro e Araujo, *Memórias históricas do Rio de Janeiro*, IX, 374), but he was unaware of the documents cited in n. 14 below.

[14] Decree of Jan. 8, 1784, BNRJ, I-31, 26, 1, n. 10; *consulta* of the Council of War, Mar. 24, 1784, *ibid.*, n. 11.

[15] Another victim of circumstances was Padre Ramos Louzada, vicar of the Paulista frontier post of Iguatemí. When that presídio was attacked by a large force

Seven years thus passed between the fall of Colônia and the final sentencing of Francisco José da Rocha. But it took even longer to conclude the investigations of the loss of Santa Catarina Island and the subsequent surrender of its garrison. As noted in Chapter X, those investigations began in April 1777 when the viceroy ordered Judge Bernardo de Salazar, a member of the Relação, to begin a devassa concerning the reasons for that capitulation. A few days later Lavradio suspended the inquiry pending the return of Brigadier José Custódio de Sá e Faria. By August of that year it had become apparent that the brigadier had no intention of returning to Portuguese soil; accordingly, the devassa was reopened. By November 30 Judge Salazar had concluded his questioning of the imprisoned officers and submitted his report to the viceroy. In it he centered his criticisms on the mismanagement of the island's evacuation and on the officers' failure to maintain discipline among their troops during the march to Cubatão. But unlike the magistrate who handled the Colônia inquiry and focused his charges exclusively on that outpost's governor, Judge Salazar did not single out particular individuals for censure.[16]

Even before the results of this investigation were known in Lisbon, the colonial secretary directed Viceroy Lavradio to order the Relação of Rio de Janeiro to proceed "without loss of time" to try all persons accused of responsibility for the loss of Santa Catarina and to forward the tribunal's sentences to Lisbon for approval.[17] Two months later, however, the minister reversed himself and instructed Lavradio's replacement, then still in Portugal, to send the prisoners back to Lisbon under close guard. He stressed that they should not be dispatched on the same frigate that was to bring the Marquis of Lavradio home. The prisoners actually left Rio de Janeiro two weeks before the marquis' departure.[18]

As soon as the Santa Catarina officers reached Lisbon they were recommitted to prison, and the Casa de Suplicação, one of Portugal's senior tribunals, was directed to pass final sentence on the prisoners.[19] While their case was being considered, Field Marshal Antônio Carlos Furtado de Mendonça filed a petition denying the court's jurisdiction,

---

of Spanish troops from Paraguay, late in 1777, its garrison deposed the commandant and elected the padre in his place. For having subsequently signed the act of capitulation the padre was confined in the dungeon of the fortress of Santos for twenty years. *Revista do Instituto Histórico e Geográfico de São Paulo*, VI (1900), 248n.

[16] The devassa is summarized in Bernardo de Salazar Sarmento Eça [e Alarcão] to Lavradio, Nov. 30, 1777, IHGB/AUC, 1-1-29, fols. 442ᵛ-457ʳ.

[17] Melo e Castro to Lavradio, Dec. 22, 1777, *RIHGB*, XXXI:1, 348-349.

[18] Melo e Castro to Vasconcelos, Jan. 31, 1779, BNRJ, 6, 3, 24, fols. 275ᵛ-276ᵛ; Vasconcelos to Melo e Castro, June 4, 1779, BNRJ, 4, 4, 1, n. 26.

[19] Carta régia, Mar. 20, 1780, *CLP* (Suppl.), 482-483; there is a copy in BNRJ, I-31, 26, 1, n. 15.

claiming that he was entitled to trial by a military court.[20] The Casa ultimately concluded that since none of the senior officers was guilty of treason, it lacked cognizance in their case.[21]

But that decision did not apply to one junior officer who had been implicated in the loss of Santa Catarina Island, Lieutenant José Henriques Cunha, an officer in the artillery regiment of Rio de Janeiro. It may be recalled that when the commander of the Ponta Grossa fortress evacuated his post, one of his battery officers, Lieutenant Cunha, joined the Spanish forces instead of retiring with the rest of his colleagues.[22] Subsequently the senior Portuguese officers agreed that evacuation of the island was imperative because of the certainty that the artillery officer had revealed to the Spaniards all of the island's secret passes and the weak points in its defenses.[23] Even though that supposition remained unsubstantiated—indeed, contemporary Spanish sources contain no indication that Cunha supplied the enemy with confidential information—the Casa de Suplicação accepted the presumptive evidence and convicted the lieutenant of being a "rebel and traitor to his king and fatherland."

The tribunal's sentence is a reminder that however much the Enlightenment had penetrated the Iberian Peninsula, the teachings of Beccaria had not.[24] It ordered the culprit bound by a rope and dragged behind a horse through the principal streets of Lisbon to the waterfront square of Ribeira Nova. There his head was to be severed from his body, and the latter burned and the ashes cast into the sea. His head was to be conveyed to Santa Catarina Island and exposed on a high gate at Fort Ponta Grossa "until the weather consumes it" to remind others of the fate awaiting traitors. In addition, the lieutenant's estates were declared confiscated, and his memory was condemned to infamy.

Only one essential element was missing when the court passed this barbarous sentence: the subject, for José Henriques Cunha was tried in absentia! [25]

Meanwhile a special court-martial board, called a council of war, had reached a decision concerning the conduct of the other Santa Cata-

20 "Por excepção declinatória, e via melhor de dir.to diz o . . . Marechal de Campo Antônio Carlos Furtado de Mendonça o seg.te. . . ." n.d. [1781?], BNRJ, I-31, 26, 1, n. 1.

21 *Acordãos* of Nov. 8 and Dec. 14, 1781, *ibid.,* n. 16. The court's decisions were based on a rather puzzling interpretation of Liv. I, tít. 74 and Liv. V, tít. 6, par. 2 of the Código Filipino. The first title concerns the duties of *alcaides móres,* or commanders of *praças* and castles, and the second specifies when such officers became guilty of the crime of *lèse-majesté.*

22 See Chap. IX, p. 234.

23 Antônio Carlos Furtado de Mendonça to the Queen [1779], *RIHGB,* XXVII:1, 324.

24 Cf. the punishment meted out to the Tupac Amaru conspirators in Peru a few months earlier.

25 Sentence of Mar. 5, 1782, BNRJ, I-31, 26, 1, n. 13.

rina officers,[26] and a remarkable decision it was. First, the board absolved three senior officers of the Santa Catarina regiment and the commanders of Forts Conceição and Ponta Grossa [27] of all responsibility for the loss of the island, holding that they had kept their posts until ordered to evacuate them. For "evident proofs of constancy and valor" in the island's defense, it recommended that each be indemnified for salaries accumulated since his imprisonment.

Next the board took up the case of the field marshal. It stated that the evidence proved he had diligently prepared the island's defenses in accordance with instructions from the viceroy and the Court. It found that his order for the evacuation of the island was justified because of MacDouall's retirement, the likelihood that the Spanish would soon cut off his retreat, and the nature of the viceroy's instructions.[28] Similarly, it found no fault with the garrison's subsequent capitulation, holding that it was inevitable because of the difficulties of the road to Laguna, the lack of supplies to sustain the march,[29] and the certainty that the Spaniards were already masters of the southern end of Santa Catarina. Consequently the council declared Antônio Carlos Furtado de Mendonça innocent of all charges.

Not wishing to show discrimination, the board also declared ex-governor Pedro Antônio da Gama e Freitas guiltless. After all, it said, he was a mere subordinate of the field marshal and possessed no independent military authority of his own. Moreover, the governor had conducted himself honorably on all occasions before, during, and after the coming of Cevallos.

Nor did the council think that Brigadier José Custódio de Sá e Faria merited punishment. With considerable logic it declared that he could not be held responsible for any of the major deficiencies in the island's defenses, since he had arrived at Santa Catarina only a short time before the Spaniards. It also asserted that he bore no blame for his opinions in the several councils of war, since he had honestly expressed his convictions. It insisted that the fact that the brigadier did not go back to Rio de Janeiro after the capitulation could not be construed as evidence of his guilt, and alleged that General Cevallos had refused to let him return.

[26] The council, appointed by a decree of April 16, 1782, consisted of eleven officers ranging from lieutenant generals down to sergeants major. *Ibid.*, n. 4. Apparently this was an *ad hoc* tribunal not the Council of War sitting as the Conselho de Justiça. See carta régia of Aug. 20, 1777, *CLP*, III, 154.

[27] Simão Rodrigues, former commander of Fort Ponta Grossa, had already died in prison.

[28] The council failed to note, however, that Lavradio authorized abandonment of the island only after a vigorous defense had been conducted.

[29] The board failed to point out that the reason for the shortage of supplies was that neither the field marshal nor the governor had made arrangements to have them conveyed to the mainland.

Finally the board considered the cases of six lesser regimental officers. It found that they had all performed their duties faithfully, and had even argued with their superiors at the Cubatão meetings in favor of continued resistance to the Spaniards. Their courageous attitude earned the council's recommendation that they be promoted.[30]

One is left to speculate on how the Court reacted to this masterful "whitewash." Final action on the council's report was not forthcoming until the queen announced her decision two and a half years later. At that time she dismissed from her service both the field marshal and the ex-governor.[31] Five of the six officers whom the military board had recommended for promotions were retired at their existing ranks, but without salary compensation for their years of imprisonment. Three others were also retired but allowed to collect their accumulated pay. Another trio who had died in prison were declared innocent, and their families were authorized the pay they had earned until their demise. On the fate of Brigadier José Custódio, there was only silence.

The queen ordered that the sentence of the military board should not be made public, and directed that all records pertaining to the loss of Santa Catarina should be lodged in the offices of the secretary of war, where they should be guarded with the greatest secrecy and circumspection "to the end that this matter remain in perpetual oblivion." [32] And for good reason!

30 Sentence of July 1, 1783, Balthazar Silva Lisboa, *Annaes do Rio de Janeiro*, III, 106–114; there is a copy in BNRJ, I-31, 26, 1, n. 12.

31 The text calls him Pedro José da Gama instead of Pedro Antônio da Gama e Freitas.

32 Carta régia of Jan. 14, 1786, *CLP*, II (Suppl.), 570–571; the copy in BNRJ, I-31, 26, 1, n. 8, gives the date as Jan. 11, 1786.

Appendix III

Money Struck at the Mint in Rio de Janeiro, 1768–1779 [a]
(in mil-réis)

A. Value of Coin of the Realm (in Gold)

YEAR	DENOMINATION		
	6,400 rs.	3,200 rs.	1,600 rs.
1768	2,712,909	—	—
1769	2,452,186	—	—
1770	2,333,728	—	—
1771	2,582,586	—	—
1772	2,416,922	5,005	—
1773	2,583,744	—	2,771
1774	2,322,880	—	—
1775	2,161,760	—	—
1776	2,494,170	—	—
1777	2,218,042	—	—
1778	2,419,936	—	—
1779	2,613,402	—	—

B. Value of Provincial Coin

YEAR	GOLD DENOMINATION			SILVER DENOMINATION		
	4,000 rs.	2,000 rs.	1,000 rs.	600 rs.	3,000 rs.	150 rs.
1768	—	—	—	—	—	—
1769	97,488	—	—	—	—	—
1770	—	—	—	8,032	—	—
1771	31,956	6,798	1,444	7,440	7,708	520
1772	—	—	—	—	—	—
1773	68,272	9,442	—	—	—	—
1774	139,252	11,746	6,000	11,663	—	—
1775	225,452	—	—	—	—	—
1776	99,060	—	—	—	—	—
1777	198,268	—	—	—	—	—
1778	10,964	—	—	—	—	—
1779	—	—	—	—	—	—

[a] "Mappa de toda a qualidade de moedas que girão n'esta capitania, cunhadas na real Caza da Moeda no Rio de Janeiro do anno de 1768 até 1796," *RIHGB*, XLV:1 (1883), 191–193. The table does not reveal the total volume of coin in circulation in Rio de Janeiro and its neighboring captaincies-general during these years, for they also received occasional shipments of provincial coin struck at the royal mint in Lisbon. For example, an alvará of March 20, 1774 directed the Royal Treasury to remit "moedas provincias" worth 4,089,980 réis to Rio de Janeiro. S[everino] Sombra, *História monetária do Brasil colonial* (Rio de Janeiro, 1938), p. 231. The following year the treasurer general at Rio de Janeiro forwarded to the junta da fazenda of São Paulo a shipment of copper coin valued at 16,000,000 réis received from Lisbon. *Portaria* of May 22, 1775, CMCM, cod. 2, fol. 158r.

Appendix IV

Account of What Is Owed to the Royal Treasury in the Different Captaincies of Brazil from the Yield of Contracts Rented and Administered [ca. 1781][a]
(in réis)

CAPTAINCY OF RIO DE JANEIRO
Amount which is owed until the end of 1761 471,263,214
Amount which is owed from 1762 until 1767
   inclusively 28,927,509
Amount which is owed from 1768 until the present 305,243,076
   Total 805,433,799

CAPTAINCY OF MINAS GERAIS
Amount which is owed until the end of 1761 946,186,601
Amount which is owed from 1762 until 1771
   inclusively 623,583,631
Amount which is owed from 1772 until the present 588,562,545
   Total .... 2,158,332,777 [b]

CAPTAINCY OF S. PAULO AND SANTOS
Amount which is owed until the end of 1761 87,068,002
Amount which is owed from 1762 until 1774
   inclusively 30,236,739
Amount which is owed from 1775 until the present 24,090,806
   Total 141,395,547

CAPTAINCY OF GOIÁS
Amount which is owed until the end of 1761 113,278,018
Amount which is owed from 1762 until 1772
   inclusively 44,416,710
Amount which is owed from 1773 until the present 121,241,301
   Total 278,936,029

CAPTAINCY OF BAHIA
Amount which is owed until the end of 1761 176,371,258
Amount which is owed from 1762 until 1768
   inclusively 34,440,490
Amount which is owed from 1769 until 1777 12,348,200
   Total 223,159,948

CAPTAINCY OF PERNAMBUCO
Amount which is owed until the end of 1761 264,863,662
Amount which is owed from 1762 until 1777 28,617,095
   Total 293,480,757

[CAPTAINCY OF] PARAÍBA
Amount which is owed until the end of 1761 15,186,401
Amount which is owed from 1762 until 1777 17,041,451
   Total 32,227,852

[Captaincy of] Rio Grande do Norte

Amount which is owed until the end of 1761	21,166
Amount which is owed from 1762 until 1777	9,153,987
Total	9,175,153

[Captaincy of] Ceará

Amount which is owed until the end of 1761	13,658,642
Amount which is owed from 1762 until 1776	46,960,138
Total	60,618,780

[Captaincy of] Pará

Amount which is owed from 1776 and 1777	10,562,669

[Captaincy of] Angola

Amount which is owed until 1761	145,475
Amount which is owed from 1762 until 1772	3,326,362
Amount which is owed from 1773 until 1777	4,084,696
Total	7,556,533
Total	4,020,879,844

a Undated appendix to Martinho de Melo e Castro to Luís de Vasconcelos e Sousa, Nov. 1, 1781, BNRJ, 6, 3, 24, fols. 289^r–290^r. It will be noted that the report omits the captaincies-general of Maranhão and Mato Grosso, but does include the captaincy-general of Angola.

b The subtotal is incorrectly given as 258,332,777.

Appendix V

Commodity Prices in Southern Brazil, 1740–1777
(in réis)

SAVE FOR ANTONIL's oft-quoted listing of the cost of commodities in the gold fields of Minas Gerais at the opening of the eighteenth century,[a] our knowledge of the prices of goods and services in eighteenth-century Brazil, their movement over time or their variation from one part of the colony to another, is abysmal. Royal officials seldom particularized about such matters in their reports to the Crown, and the records of purchases by institutional users, such as the Holy Houses of Mercy (*Casas de Misericórdia*) and the various religious Orders, especially the Jesuits, remain to be found and analyzed. Some helpful clues are provided by scattered references in the manuscripts used for this study and in the printed inventories of Jesuit properties made within a few years of the Society's expulsion from Brazil. Except when otherwise noted, the prices given below are those prevailing within the captaincy of Rio de Janeiro in the indicated years.

I. Physical Installations:
A battery of boiling vats and furnaces for
processing sugar (1775) 620,000
A brandy distillery (1775) 300,000
A pottery shop (1775) 500,000
A sugar refinery (1775) 1,600,000
A sugar mill with attached stock pen (1775) .... 600,000 [b]
Average yearly rental of a house (*moradia de
casa*) in the city of Rio de Janeiro (1740) .... 83,433 [c]

II. Livestock:
A cow ready for slaughter (1759) .... 5,000 [d]
A milk cow (1759) .... 4,500 [d]
A heifer (1759) .... 1,000 [d]
A cow with calf (1775) .... 4,500 [b]

---

[a] E.g., Charles R. Boxer, *The Golden Age of Brazil*, pp. 330–332.

[b] "Autto de inventario e avaleação da r.al fazenda do Engenho Novo e todas suas pertenças. . . ." Oct. 14, 1775, *RADF*, III (1896), 517–524; IV (1897), 14–18, 121–126, 162–167.

[c] "Relação de todas as casas, foros e chãos que ha nesta cidade [do Rio de Janeiro] pertencentes aos padres da Companhia nas ruas que abaixo se declara" (1740), *ibid.*, II, 367–370. The list gives 91 properties whose rentals varied from 19,200 to 200,000 réis.

[d] "Auto de sequestro feito na fazenda de Sam Cristovão e terras a ella pertencentes," Nov. 9, 1759, *ibid.*, I, 140–142; 273–278; 316–321

A female calf (1759) .... 2,500 [d]
A horse of prime quality (unspecified as to type)
  suitable for the viceregal guard (1776) .... 16,000 [e]
A gray horse of prime quality (1759) .... 10,000 [d]
A gray horse in poor condition (*destrocado*)
  (1759) .... 2,000 [d]
A sorrel horse of good quality (1759) .... 5,000 [d]
A yoke of oxen (1759) .... 16,000 [d]
A ram (1759) .... 640 [d]

III. Provisions:
  One arroba of jerked beef (1770) .... 800 [f]
  One dozen dark cinnamon (1765) .... 4,000 [g]
  One alqueire of manioc flour (1766, 1770) .... 300 to 340 [h]
  One measure of sweet oil (1767) .... 960 [i]
  One alqueire of salt (São Paulo, 1768) .... 880 [j]
  Table allowance for one day's food for captured
    Spanish naval officers (1777) .... 400 [k]

IV. Clothing:
  Cost of outfitting a Negro slave for one year (São
  Paulo, 1768) :
    A pair of flax breeches 560
    A baize cloak 1,320
    A baize waistcoat 1,600
      Total .... 3,480 [j]
  A pair of shoes suitable for soldiers (1770) .... 750 to 850 [l]

V. Labor:
  Value of an unskilled Negro slave without
  observable physical defects (1775) :
    A child under 8 years of age 14,138
    A young slave (8 to 14 years of age) 34,700
    A prime slave (15 to 25 years of age) 47,666
    A mature slave (26 to 45 years of age) 44,160
    An old slave (46 to 65 years of age) 25,555
  Value of a skilled slave:
    A carpenter aged 60 56,000
    A coppersmith aged 44 55,000
    A mason between 48 and 54 years of age .... 45,000 to 64,000
    A shoemaker aged 27 76,000
    A steward (*feitor*) aged 40 70,000

e *Portaria* of July 20, 1776, CMCM, cod. 19, fol. 77[v].
f CMCM, cod. 22, fol. 11[v].
g *Ibid.*, fol. 85[r].
h *Ibid.*, fols. 89[r] and 11[v].
i *Ibid.*, fol. 87[r].
j Luis António de Sousa to Oeiras, Jan. 31, 1768, *DI*, XXIII (1896), 382.
k CMCM, cod. 19, fol. 185[r].
l Lavradio to Francisco José Brandão, June 30, 1770, ANRJ, Col. 70, Liv. V, fol. 58[v].

A steward aged 50 ....   45,000 [m]

Cost of a day's labor performed by an unskilled
    Negro slave (1777) ....   60 [n]

Cost of a day's labor performed by an unskilled
    free Indian (1777) ....   25 [n]

[m] Average prices computed from appraisals given in the Engenho Novo inventory (see note b above) which identifies 168 slaves by name, age, and particular skill. The value of a mature slave seems excessively high when compared with the price of a prime slave. It is possible that some of the mature slaves possessed skills not indicated in the inventory.

[n] CMCM, cod. 19, fols. 151^v and 155^r.

Bibliography

THERE IS an abundance of source material in manuscript and print for the two major themes of this study, the development of Brazil's colonial administration and Luso-Spanish Platine rivalry. The continuing interest in military and diplomatic history in Brazil, Argentina, and Uruguay and the persistence of boundary questions between those nations after Independence have stimulated the publication of documents on the colonial antecedents of such problems. It is safe to say, however, that what has appeared in print is only a fraction of what is available in manuscript. A really thorough examination of the rivalry between Portugal and Spain in America during the colonial period would require research in the archives of Spain, Portugal, France, Great Britain, Argentina, and Brazil.

Several important commentaries and collections of Portuguese laws pertaining to colonial Brazil were published during the eighteenth and nineteenth centuries, but they are very scarce today. Moreover, none is complete, and, none suggests the extent to which administrative practice departed from the rules laid down in the statutes. The only way that problem can be effectively attacked is to examine the administrative correspondence on colonial Brazil. For some offices in certain areas, such as São Paulo, a significant body of such material has been published, but for the most part it remains in manuscript. The archives of Brazil contain vast quantities of official correspondence for the second half of the colonial period. One finds in such depositories originals or copies of dispatches between the Crown and its overseas representatives; correspondence among colonial officers from the lowest (municipal and rural) to the highest levels; reports on military and economic conditions; statistics on population and commerce; fortification designs; maps; charts; texts of laws, proclamations, licenses, land grants, and the like. What one does not usually encounter in Brazilian depositories are the originals of letters from colonial officers to the Crown, the recommendations of Peninsular councils and tribunals to the king, or communications between members of the Portuguese cabinet. For such materials one must go to Portugal.

Manuscript Materials

The resources of four archives in Brazil were tapped for this study.[1] Each contains a certain amount of material duplicated in the others, such as additional originals or copies of royal dispatches, but each also possesses many documents not available elsewhere.

THE ARQUIVO NACIONAL

The Arquivo Nacional, Brazil's largest documentary repository, possesses extensive holdings from the mid-seventeenth to the end of the nineteenth century. For a catalog of its historical manuscripts, see "Catálogo dos livros da secção histórica do Arquivo Nacional," *PAN*, XIII (1913) and XVI (1916). Some of the individual collections, such as numbers 60, 67, 68, and 69, have been calendared in the archives' *Publicações*. While such lists are helpful in searching for particular documents, they would have been more useful had they been organized by codexes instead of simply by date. The most important codexes for this study were:

Collection	Livros
60	1, 4, 7, 18, 19, 20, 22, 24, 34, 36, 37, 38, 39, 40, 41, 45
67	1, 1A, 2, 2A, 3, 3A, 4
69	1, 1 *bis*
70	1-10
73	5, 6
94	7
157	8

THE BIBLIOTECA NACIONAL

Like the Arquivo Nacional, the Biblioteca possesses a very large manuscript collection for the second half of the colonial period. The *fichário* or card file in the Manuscripts Section is difficult to use because of the relatively few subject headings, the not always logical classification of manuscripts, and the lack of sufficient cross references. In recent years the Biblioteca has resumed publication in its *Anais* of calendars of documents concerning the history of particular states, such as Maranhão, Pernambuco, Bahia, São Paulo, and Paraná. The

---

[1] In addition, I have made selective use of documents in British and Portuguese archives available on microfilm in the Bancroft Library of the University of California. For a guide to its holdings, see Mary Ann Fisher, "Preliminary Guide to the Microfilm Collection of the Bancroft Library" (University of California, Berkeley, 1955). I also consulted a microfilm of a register of the correspondence of Manoel da Cunha Menezes, captain-general of Bahia, 1774–1779, in the Library of Congress.

Manuscripts Section also has several typewritten shelf lists of portions of its holdings. Such lists indicate both old and new call numbers, and, while tedious to use, the serious investigator must consult them to obtain an idea of the extent of the Section's holdings. Just as helpful as any catalog is a sympathetic functionary who often can turn up unsuspected riches. In this connection I wish to record my gratitude to Hélio de Albuquerque who called my attention to many valuable items.

The principal codexes and folders (*pastas*) that I consulted in the Manuscripts Section were:

2, 2, 24	Livro segundo das cartas de Antônio de Noronha (captain-general of Minas Gerais), 1776–1779.
4, 4, 1 to 4, 4, 11	Correspondência activa e passiva de Luís de Vasconcelos e Sousa (1780–1790). Eleven codexes, each containing a table of contents, of correspondence between Lavradio's successor and Peninsular authorities.
6, 3, 24	Cartas régias, 1765–1807. A nineteenth-century copybook containing several important dispatches from the Court to Lavradio.
10, 4, 8	Cartas de Seu Magestade Fidelisima (*sic*), e provisoens do Conselho Vltramarino, expedidas ao illustrissimo e excelentisimo senôr d. Luiz de Almeyda . . . Marquez do Lavradio . . . Anno de MDCC (*sic*).
	Judging from the way this codex is bound, the state of its preservation, the quality of its paper, and the hand of the copyist, I suspect that this was once a part of the personal collection of Viceroy Lavradio, for it is markedly similar to the codexes owned today by Sr. Marcos Carneiro de Mendonça (see below). When I found the codex it was uncataloged and without pagination. It is a register of about 450 pieces of active correspondence of the viceroy with various Peninsular authorities during the years 1769–1779.
13, 4, 1 to 13, 4, 9	Correspondência de General João Henrique de Böhm. Nine codexes containing the general's passive correspondence from the viceroy and various authorities in Santa Catarina, Rio de Janeiro, and Rio Grande. Nearly all are originals. Codex 13, 4, 5 contains original dispatches of Robert MacDouall not cataloged under his name in the *fichário*.
I-2, 4, 6 to I-2, 4, 7	Collecção das ordens mais necessárias e curiozas . . . do Rio de Janeiro, 1597–1779. Correspondence from the Crown to senior administrators of the captaincy-general of Rio de Janeiro. About half of the seven codexes pertain to the years 1750–1777, and the last two are indispensable for the Lavradio administration.

I-28, 26, 2   Letter book of João Henrique de Böhm, 1775–1777. Rough drafts of the general's letters to the viceroy.

I-31, 26, 1   Untitled *pasta* containing sixteen contemporary copies of the official investigations and sentences of the officers implicated in the Portuguese defeats of 1777.

I-31, 26, 11   *Pasta* containing dispatches (mostly originals) of Pombal and Martinho de Melo e Castro to Lavradio, Jan. 15, 1776 to July 31, 1776

I-31, 31, 1   A continuation of the same correspondence, mainly for August through October 1776.

MANUSCRIPT COLLECTION OF SR. MARCOS CARNEIRO DE MENDONÇA

Among the most important manuscripts consulted for this study are those now owned by Sr. Mendonça, for they comprise the majority of Viceroy Lavradio's own papers. The collection was offered for sale by the viceroy's descendants to the Instituto Histórico e Geográfico Brasileiro in 1925, but it evidently lacked the funds to purchase them.[2] In the 1940s the descendants of the viceroy in Portugal became hard-pressed financially and gave the majority of their historical manuscripts to a wealthy Portuguese sportsman as collateral for a loan. When the family was unable to repay its debt, its creditor invited the Brazilian Foreign Office (the Itamaratí) to make an offer for the papers. Four years elapsed and the Itamaratí had still not concluded the negotiations when Sr. Mendonça, a Brazilian industrialist with a deep interest in the career of the Marquis of Pombal, learned of the collection while on a visit to Lisbon. After four days of discussions, the papers were his for approximately $300![3] Meanwhile, the Lavradio family sold the remainder of its collection, a relatively small part of the original corpus, to Sr. Angelo Pereira of Lisbon, who still owns these papers.[4]

The fact that colonial officers commonly retained official documents in their personal possession after leaving their posts is well known, but we have little information as to the extent and variety of papers they took with them. The Mendonça Collection indicates the wide array of materials that one such official, the Marquis of Lavradio, took home with him. Except for miscellaneous materials labled "Geral" or "Maço," all documents are preserved in bound codexes. The Collection is organized as follows:

Cod. 1   Livro de cartas correntes dos rendimentos reaes da capitania da Bahia . . . principiado no anno de 1769. Extra

[2] Agenor de Roure, second secretary of the Instituto Histórico, called attention to the offer in his report for 1925. *RIHGB*, XCVII (1925), 479. The catalogue is published on pp. 495–505.
[3] Conversations with Sr. Mendonça in 1957.
[4] I am obliged to Professora Virgínia Rau for this information.

large; 57 folios of double-entry accounts for Bahia covering the years 1766–1769.

Cod. 2   Cartas e portarias do illmo. e excelentisimo senhor D. Luiz de Almeyda, Soares, Portugal, Esa, Alarcàm, Sylva, Mascarenhas, Marquez do Lavradio . . . Capitam general de màr, e terra do Brazil, expedidas aos ministros da relaçam dele. Anno de MDCC[LXXIV]. 217 folios. *Portarias* to treasury officials and viceregal proclamations, Feb. 9, 1774, to Sept. 1, 1775.

Cod. 3   [untitled] 261 folios. Dispatches from the Court to Lavradio, Aug. 19, 1768, to Nov. 20, 1772.

Cod. 4   Livro do registro das cartas doz generaes das differentes cap. nias deste eztado, expedidas pella secret. a do mesmo &a. 105 folios. Continuation of cod. 15; correspondence of Lavradio with subordinate governors, Aug. 9, 1773, to Jan. 17, 1777.

"Geral 5"   Notícias estatísticas da capitania do Rio de Janeiro . . . 1778–1779. Loose bundle of accounts by the militia colonels of the economic condition of each district in the captaincy of Rio de Janeiro. Published in *RIHGB*, LXXVI:1, 289–355.

"Geral 6"   [untitled] Loose bundle of letters from J. H. de Böhm to Lavradio, Dec. 23, 1774, to Nov. 29, 1775.

"Geral 7"   [untitled] Loose bundle of reports by the army engineer Francisco João Roscîo to Lavradio, written 1778–1779. Copied almost verbatim by the viceroy in the first part of his relatório.

"Geral 8"   Relação das amostras de madeiras, que tem hido para a corte. Report of shipments of local timbers to the royal naval arsenal in Lisbon.

"Geral 9"   Dinheiro q. tem hido p.a Lx.a desde o anno de 1776 thé o de '77. Three extremely valuable documents. The first two are records of private capital sent on merchant vessels to Lisbon and Pôrto between April 1774 and November 1777. The third is the manifest of funds deposited aboard a royal frigate in 1777 for transmission to Portugal.

"Geral 10"   Experiência do linho guaxima. Report of tests made on a local fiber thought to be as useful as hemp.

"Geral 11"   Ofícios, requisições, memórias e instruções do Brigadeiro Jacques Funk.

"Geral 12"   [untitled] 23 dispatches from Martinho de Melo e Castro to Lavradio, 1770–1777.

"Geral 13"   [untitled] 45 dispatches from Martinho de Melo e Castro to Lavradio, 1773–1774.

"Geral 14"   [untitled] 23 dispatches from Pombal to Lavradio, 1774–1775.

Cod. 15   Cartas particulares expedidas pela Secretaria de Estado a . . . Excelentissimo Snr. Luís de Almeyda . . . Marquez do Lavradio, Governador e Capitam General da Capitania da Bahia. Ano de MDCCLXIX. 169 folios. In spite of the title, this contains active correspondence of Lavradio with various captains-general and subordinate governors from Nov. 13, 1769, to Aug. 7, 1773, and precedes cod. 4 in this series.

Cod. 16   [untitled] 94 folios. Correspondence of Lavradio as captain-general of Bahia to the Court and to local officials.

Cod. 17   Patentes dos postos providos pelo . . . Marquez do Lavradio, Ano de MDCC[LXXII]. 233 folios. Miscellaneous appointments made between November 1772 and November 1774.

Cod. 18   [untitled] 175 folios. Contains originals of Pombal's four initial instructions to the Marquis of Lavradio upon his appointment as viceroy.

Cod. 19   [untitled] 247 folios. A continuation of cod. 2 containing warrants and proclamations issued by Viceroy Lavradio between January 1776 and March 1778.

Cod. 20   [untitled] 241 folios. A continuation of cod. 17 covering appointments made between November 1774 and September 1776.

Cod. 21   Cartas e papéis pertencentes ao governo do ilmo. e exmo snr. Marquez do Lavradio na capitania da B.a. 431 folios. Miscellaneous correspondence, 1766–1769.

Cod. 22   [untitled] 146 folios. Manual explaining the defects of the "old" method of bookkeeping and the advantages of the "new" one, with examples of both procedures as they were employed in the exchequer of Rio de Janeiro. Prepared ca. December, 1770.

Cod. 23   [untitled] 201 folios. Dispatches of Lavradio to the Court, 1767–1769.

Cod. 24   Patentes dos postos providos p.lo D. Luís de Almeyda . . . governador e capitam generàl da capitania da B.a MDCCLXVII. 364 folios. Miscellaneous appointments made between April 1768 and November 1772. Precedes cod. 17 in the series.

Cod. 25   [untitled] 286 folios. 326 letters written by Viceroy Lavradio to the chancellor of the Relação of Rio de Janeiro, other magistrates, municipal councils in Rio de Janeiro, Santa Catarina, and Rio Grande de São Pedro, and the militia colonels of Rio de Janeiro between February 1775 and late 1778.

Cod. 26 [untitled] 155 folios. Folios 4 to 26 contain *portarias* and proclamations that fill a gap between codexes 2 and 19. The remainder contains miscellaneous letters from the viceroy to various captains-general and governors, in part duplicating material contained in cods. 4 and 15.

Cod. 27 [untitled] 130 folios. Correspondence and investigative reports concerning foreign ships which entered Rio de Janeiro (mainly during 1770) on various pretexts.

Cod. 28 [untitled] 135 folios. Original dispatches of Francisco José da Rocha to Lavradio from Rio Grande de São Pedro between November 1771 and early 1773.

Cod. 29 [untitled] 133 folios. Original dispatches of Francisco José da Rocha to the viceroy from Colônia between January 1775 and December 1775.

"Maço 30" [untitled] Miscellaneous papers including reports of cultivators of indigo in the captaincy of Rio de Janeiro and a report on the manufacture of butter and a method of adding color to it.

"Maço 31" [untitled] Miscellaneous papers including reports from Lavradio to the Crown concerning the military situation in Rio Grande during 1773–1775.

INSTITUTO HISTÓRICO E GEOGRÁFICO BRASILEIRO

The extensive manuscript holdings of the Instituto are divided into two sections, each with a separate card catalog. Loose documents are filed in metal boxes called *latas*. They include single or small groups of dispatches from the Crown to various colonial authorities, miscellaneous fiscal reports, inventories of confiscated Jesuit properties, bills of lading, and the like. The *Catálogo dos manuscriptos do Instituto Histórico e Geográfico Brasileiro existentes em 31 de Dezembro de 1883* (Rio de Janeiro, 1884) describes much of this collection, but unfortunately some of the materials listed there can no longer be located in the Instituto.

The section called the Arquivo Ultramarino consists of bound volumes of transcripts made in Portugal by scholarly missions during the nineteenth century. Included are the correspondence of the captains-general of Brazil to the Crown during the second half of the eighteenth century. Unfortunately there is no index to the individual codexes, which average between 250 and 300 folios, so that it is a slow task to work through them. Among the many latas and codexes that I examined, two of the latter (AUC 1-1-29 and 1-2-1) were particularly helpful. The first contains some of Lavradio's dispatches to Lisbon written during the early seventies and a large portion prepared during the late seventies. Neither group is available in other Brazilian archives. The second includes dispatches from Luís de Vasconcelos e Sousa to the Crown.

UNPUBLISHED DISSERTATIONS

Canales, José, "Rio Grande do Sul in Luso-Spanish Platine Rivalry, 1626–1737," University of California, Berkeley, 1959.

Rodríguez, Mario, "Colônia do Sacramento: Focus of Spanish-Portuguese Rivalry in the Plata, 1640–1683," University of California, Berkeley, 1952.

PRINTED MATERIALS

BIBLIOGRAPHICAL AIDES AND REFERENCES

The standard bibliographical sources were of slight help for this specialized study. Well-known works such as Augusto Victorino Alves do Sacramento Blake, *Diccionário bibliográphico brasileiro* (7 vols., Rio de Janeiro, 1937), and Innocêncio Francisco da Silva, *Diccionário bibliográphico portuguez . . .* (22 vols., Lisbon, 1858–1923) proved unfruitful since their compilers include only persons who left published works, and colonial administrators were rarely literary figures. The celebrated *Bibliographia Navalis; or, Impartial Memoirs of the Lives and Characters of Officers of the Navy of Great Britain . . . 1660 to . . . [1793]* by John Charnock (6 vols., London, 17— to 1798), which contains sketches of officers who reached flag rank in the royal navy, was of no assistance since none of the British naval officers mentioned in this study appear to have attained that distinction. The most helpful auxiliaries were:

"Arquivo do Marquez do Lavradio. Lista completa do archivo do vice rey do Brazil Marquez do Lavradio . . . ," *Revista do Instituto Histórico e Geográfico Brasileiro,* XCVII (1925), 495–505. Catalogue of the complete Lavradio archives, of which the largest portion is today in the possession of Sr. Marcos Carneiro de Mendonça in Rio de Janeiro.

Borba de Moraes, Rubens, and William Berrien, eds., *Manual bibliográfico de estudos brasileiros* (Rio de Janeiro, 1949). The sections on history in this cooperative bibliography are uneven and incomplete, but it continues to be a useful starting place for almost any topic pertaining to the colonial period.

Cardiff, Guillermo Furlong, ed., "Cartografía jesuítica del Río de la Plata," Facultad de Filosofía y Letras. *Publicaciones de Investigaciones Históricas,* LXXI (Buenos Aires, 1936). The most important published collection of seventeenth- and eighteenth-century maps on the Platine area. Part I discusses the sources of the plates which comprise Part II.

Ferreira, Vieira, "Legislação portugueza relativo ao Brasil," *Revista do Instituto Histórico e Geográfico Brasileiro*, CV (1929), 201–229. A listing of Portuguese laws still in force in Brazil in 1823, when the Constituent Assembly voted to continue their enforcement until a new code had been drafted. Unfortunately the sources where the texts may be found are not given.

Macedo Soares, José Carlos de, *Fronteiras do Brasil: o regime colonial* (Rio de Janeiro, 1939). Gives texts of various treaties affecting Brazil together with maps and source collections where the treaties are published.

Pereira e Sousa, José Caetano, *Esbôço de um diccionário jurídico, teorético e prático, remissivo as leis compiladas e extravagantes.* 3 vols. in 1 (Lisbon, 1825–1827). A unique, very rare, and exceedingly valuable aid to the student of Portuguese administrative history. The compiler, a lawyer, spent many years searching for legislation applying to particular offices and practices in the Portuguese government. The work was finished after his death by his son. The copy that I used in the Sala dos Livros Raros of the National Library in Rio de Janeiro lacks pagination and is badly worm-eaten and water-damaged. There is another copy at Coimbra.

Rio de Janeiro, Arquivo Nacional, *Publicações do Arquivo Nacional,* I-- (Rio de Janeiro, 1886--). Includes a useful series of calendars of documents kept in the archives. The emphasis of the first sixteen volumes is on the eighteenth century; thereafter it shifts to the Independence and Early National periods.

Torre Revello, José, ed., "Mapas y planos referentes al virreinato del Plata," Facultad de Filosofía y Letras. *Publicaciones de Investigaciones Históricas,* LXXIII (Buenos Aires, 1938). Another valuable collection of maps for the Platine area, dating in the main from the second half of the eighteenth century.

PUBLISHED DOCUMENTS

Included here are some of the numerous printed collections of Portuguese legislation, standard Brazilian documentary sets, and series of documents pertaining to Luso-Spanish Platine rivalry. The compilations of statutes contain considerable duplication and none are truly complete. All possess tables of contents but lack badly needed detailed indices. Many of the secondary works listed under Later Books possess valuable documentary appendices.

Andrade e Silva, José Justino de, ed., *Collecção chronológica da legislação portuguesa.* 10 vols. (Lisbon, 1854–1859). Part of an ambitious, never-finished project designed to publish all Portuguese legislation between 1603 and 1826, this collection is actually limited to the seventeenth century. Includes *regimentos, alvarás,* and decrees arranged in a strictly chronological fashion. Fundamental.

Archives diplomatiques, Commission des, *Recueil des instructions données aux ambassadeurs et ministres de France* . . . . 26 vols. in 27 (Paris, 1884–1934). Vol. III includes instructions to French representatives at Lisbon during the time of Pombal.

Argentine Republic, Archivo General de la Nación, *Documentos referentes a la guerra de la independencia.* Ser. II. *Campaña del Brasil: antecedentes coloniales.* 3 vols. (Buenos Aires, 1931–1941). The most important published collection of documents on Luso-Spanish Platine rivalry and a model of how things like this should be done. Each volume contains an excellent, if pro-Spanish, introduction, a detailed table of contents, and an index. The documents, taken from archives in Spain and Argentina and occasionally from printed Brazilian collections, include correspondence between Spanish authorities in the Plata and the Peninsula, dispatches between Lisbon and Rio de Janeiro, and exchanges between local Spanish and Portuguese authorities. Volume I (1535–1749) was edited by Carlos Correa Luna, Vols. II (1750–1762) and III (1762–1778) by Ismael Buchich Escobar.

Boletim do Conselho Ultramarino. Legislação antiga. 2 vols. (Lisbon, 1867). A culling from other published collections. Volumes I (1446–1754) and II (1755–1834) emphasize legislation applicable to the colonies.

Brazil, Biblioteca Nacional, *Anais (Annaes) da Biblioteca Nacional,* I-- (Rio de Janeiro, 1876--). Because of its consistent high quality, the *Anais* must be rated as Brazil's best historical publication. In it have appeared scholarly articles, catalogues, and calendars of documents in the National Library and in Portuguese archives, and important collections of administrative and diplomatic correspondence.

———, *Documentos históricos.* I-- (Rio de Janeiro, 1928--). The first two volumes were published under the auspices of the Arquivo Nacional; the rest by the Biblioteca Nacional. Includes administrative correspondence and various kinds of legal documents dating from the mid-sixteenth to the early nineteenth centuries. The series is strongest from the mid-seventeenth to the mid-eighteenth century and is comparatively thin on the late eighteenth century.

Calvo, Carlos, ed., *Colección completa de los tratados, convenciones, capitulaciones, armisticios y otros actos diplomáticos de todos los estados de la América latina.* 11 vols. (Paris, 1862–1869). Includes texts of important treaties and other diplomatic instruments bearing on the Debatable Lands.

Castro e Almeida, Eduardo de, comp., *Inventário dos documentos rela-*

tivos ao Brasil existentes no Arquivo de Marinha e Ultramar de Lisboa. 8 vols. (Rio de Janeiro, 1913–1936). Also published in *Anais da Biblioteca Nacional*, XXXI, XXXII, XXXIV, XXXVI, XXXVII, XXXIX, XLVI, and L. A partial calendar of papers transferred from the old depository to the Arquivo Histórico Colonial which numbered more than 200,000 loose documents and 300,000 codexes. Of 337 boxes *(caixas)* on Bahia, 84 are catalogued and excerpted in Vols. I-V (1613–1807), while 44 of the 219 concerning Rio de Janeiro are covered in Vols. VI-VIII (1617–1755). The seventeenth century is poorly represented for Bahia, but appears more prominently in the Rio volumes. After the series was suspended upon the death of the compiler, 1,343 additional items pertaining to Rio de Janeiro (1752–1757) were published in the *Anais*, Vol. LXXI (1951).

Coelho e Sousa, José Roberto Monteiro de Campos, ed., *Systema, ou collecção dos regimentos reaes: contém os regimentos pertencentes á fazenda real, justiças, e militares . . .* 6 vols. (Lisbon, 1783–1791). This poorly organized but essential series extends from the late sixteenth to the late eighteenth centuries. Volumes IV and VI are especially useful, for they contain the *regimentos* of the Relações of Bahia and Rio de Janeiro as well as those of the Conselho Ultramarino and the Mesas da Inspeção.

Collecção chronológica de leis extravagantes, posteriores á nova compilação das ordenações do reino publicadas em 1603 . . . até . . . 1761. 6 vols. (Coimbra, 1819). The first four volumes contain alvarás and leis, the last two decretos and cartas régias. Three of the six volumes emphasize the years 1750–1761. Volume 6 contains a chronological index for the entire series.

Collecção das leys, decretos, e alvarás que comprehende o . . . reinado de . . . D. Joze o I. . . . 5 vols. (Lisbon, 1771–[1800?]). Sometimes called the *Coleção Galhardo* after the name of the royal printer who published this collection of offprints of legislation pertaining to the years 1750–1800. Now largely superseded by Delgado da Silva *(s.v.)*.

"Correspondência passiva do Tte.-Gal. João Henrique de Böhm," *Boletim do centro rio-grandense de estudos históricos.* Ano I, No. 1, Rio Grande, October, 1939, pp. 10–160. Contains Viceroy Lavradio's dispatches to Böhm from December 1774 to April 1778, of which the originals are in BNRJ 13, 4, 2 and 13, 4, 3. These are obviously printed from another source, presumably a *livro de registro* in Rio Grande do Sul. One of the most important portions of the viceroy's correspondence now in print.

Cortesão, Jaime, ed., *Alexandre de Gusmão e o tratado de Madrid. (1750).* 9 vols. (Rio de Janeiro, 1950–1963). A fundamental source for an evaluation of Gusmão as a statesman and for the antecedents of the treaty of 1750.

Delgado da Silva, António, ed., *Collecção da legislação portuguesa de*

1750 a [1820]. 6 vols. plus 3 supplements (Lisbon, 1830–1847). Standard collection for the period. Of great value for administrative and economic legislation pertaining to Brazil.

Legg, L. G. Wickham, ed., *British Diplomatic Instructions, 1689–1789.* VII, *France,* Pt. IV, *1745–1789.* Royal Historical Society, Camden. 3d ser., XLIX (London, 1934). A source overlooked by Brazilian and Portuguese historians. Contains the well-edited instructions of the Secretary of State for Foreign Affairs to his ambassadors in France. Provides insights into British policy vis-à-vis Portugal. Unfortunately the instructions sent to British representatives at Lisbon have not been published.

Mendes de Almeida, Cândido, ed., *Código philippino ou ordenações e leis do reino de Portugal recompiladas por mandado d'el-rey d. Philippe I.* 14th ed. (Rio de Janeiro, 1870). The authoritative and last edition of the Philippine code of 1603. The scholarly annotations of the editor make this one of the greatest pieces of erudition produced by a scholar in nineteenth-century Brazil.

Prefeitura do Districto Federal, Publicações do Archivo do Districto Federal, *Autos de correição dos ouvidores do Rio de Janeiro,* Eduardo Tourinho, ed. 3 vols. (Rio de Janeiro, 1929–1931). Reports of the annual visitations of the ouvidores to the câmara of Rio de Janeiro from 1640 to 1800.

Radaelli, Sigfrido A., ed., *Memorias de los virreyes del Río de la Plata* (Buenos Aires, 1945). Includes terminal reports of Cevallos, Vértiz, and their successors.

Rau, Virgínia, and Maria Fernanda Gomes da Silva, eds., *Os manuscritos do arquivo da casa de Cadaval respeitantes ao Brasil.* 2 vols. (Coimbra, 1956–1958). From the Restoration (1640) to the early eighteenth century the Dukes of Cadaval were senior advisers to the kings on administrative policy. This is a calendar of some of the papers that remain in the Cadaval family's possession and pertain to Brazilian affairs during the later seventeenth and early eighteenth centuries (to 1724). The editors have been generous in their summaries, and have done an excellent job of indicating the importance of a collection which is no longer open to scholars.

Recopilación de leyes de los reynos de las Indias, . . . Fasc. ed., 1791. 3 vols. (Madrid, 1943).

Rio de Janeiro, Arquivo Municipal, *Archivo do Districto Federal: revista de documentos para a história de cidade do Rio de Janeiro,* A. J. Melo Moraes Filho, ed. 4 vols. (Rio de Janeiro, 1894–1897). The *Revista* published a great variety of documents pertaining to the administrative, economic, and social history of colonial Rio de Janeiro.

Rio de Janeiro, Instituto Histórico e Geográfico Brasileiro, *Revista do*

Instituto Histórico e Geográfico Brasileiro. I-- (Rio de Janeiro, 1839--). A major documentary source for the colonial period.

——, *Tomos especiais.* 15 vols. (Rio de Janeiro, 1956–1959). A calendar of documents in the Arquivo Histórico Ultramarino bearing on São Paulo, 1619–1781, similar in conception to the Castro e Almeida series (see above). Though poorly edited, these volumes are extremely important and demonstrate the need for comparable series for Pernambuco and Minas Gerais.

São Paulo, Arquivo do Estado de São Paulo, *Publicação official de documentos interesantes para a história e costumes de São Paulo,* I-- (São Paulo, 1895--). One of the most important documentary series for the student of colonial administrative history, for it includes the correspondence—chiefly seventeenth- and eighteenth-century—of the governors of São Paulo with all levels of colonial authorities and with the Crown.

Sousa, Manoel de Barros (Visconde de Santarém), and L. A. Rebello da Silva, eds., *Quadro elementar das relações políticas e diplomáticas de Portugal com as diversas potências do mundo.* . . . 18 vols. (Lisbon and Paris, 1842–1860). The most important collection of texts and excerpts of diplomatic documents bearing on Portugal from the sixteenth to the late eighteenth centuries. Volumes II and VIII concern Portugal's relations with France and Spain down to early 1777; Vol. XVIII concerns Portugal's relations with Great Britain to 1815 but material for the years 1777–1780 is not included. The first eight volumes were prepared by Santarém from materials in Portuguese, Spanish, and French archives; the remaining volumes are largely an editing of his notes.

COEVAL OR NEAR CONTEMPORANEOUS WORKS

[Anon.] "Almanaques da cidade do Rio de Janeiro para os anos de 1792 e 1794," *Anais da Biblioteca Nacional,* LIX (1937), 189–[355]. A valuable source for who was who in Rio de Janeiro at the end of the eighteenth century. The editor, Rodolfo Garcia, suggests António Duarte Nunes as the author.

Beaglehole, J. C., ed., *The Journals of Captain James Cook on His Voyages of Discovery.* 3 vols. plus atlas to date. Hakluyt Society. Extra ser. (Cambridge, 1955–1967). As near as possible to a definitive edition of Cook's voyages. Volume I includes documents concerning Cook's stop at Rio de Janeiro in 1768.

Bulkeley, John, and John Cummins, *A Voyage to the South Seas in His Majesty's Ship the Wagner in the Years 1740–1741,* with an introduction by Arthur D. Howden Smith (London, 1927). The *Wagner,* one of Anson's ships, was wrecked on the coast of south Chile. Part of her crew subsequently made their way by long boat to the

Brazilian coast, stopping at Rio Grande de São Pedro, Rio de Janeiro, and Salvador. Bulkeley, a warrant gunner, did the writing,
and has some very uncomplimentary things to say about Portuguese
officials and Brazilian society.

Byron, John, *A Voyage round the World in His Majesty's Ship the
"Delphin," commanded by the Honorable Commodore Byron.* . . .
2d ed. (London, 1767). "Foul-weather Jack" Byron, grandfather of
the poet, spent several weeks in Rio de Janeiro in late 1764, and has
some interesting things to say about the character of the city and
the weakness of its defenses.

Caldas, Jozé António, *Notícia geral de toda esta capitania da Bahia
desde o seu descobrimento até o prezente anno de 1759.* Facs. ed.
(Bahia, 1949). An encyclopedia of useful knowledge concerning the
administration, church, economy, defenses, and revenues of Bahia
in the 1750s.

Dalrymple, William, *Travels Through Spain and Portugal* (London,
1777). A mediocre travel account by an English major in the Irish
brigade stationed at Gibraltar who made a five-month trip on horse-
back through Spain and Portugal. Appended is an important ten-
page account of the Algiers debacle taken from eyewitnesses.

Forges, Evariste Désiré de (Vicomte de Parny), *Oeuvres d'Evariste
Parny.* 5 vols. (Paris, 1808). A French poet bound for the Orient
whose ship was driven by bad weather to seek refuge in Rio de Janeiro in 1773. Volume I includes Parny's letter of September 1773
to his brother telling of life in Rio de Janeiro and of his meeting
with Viceroy Lavradio, for whom he failed to provide a descriptive
sketch.

Gazeta de Lisboa, 1778–1820. For the late eighteenth century this is
an invaluable source which contains a wide array of information
concerning court life, important governmental appointments, ship
arrivals and departures, and the weekly state of the money market
in Lisbon.

[Grimaldi, Marqués de], *Respuesta a la memoria que presentó en 16
de enero de 1776 el Exmo Señor Don Francisco Inocencio de Souza
Coutiño, embaxador de S. M. F.* . . . *Apéndice de documentos.* . . .
(Madrid, 1776). Essentially a white paper defending the diplomatic
position of Spain in the dispute with Portugal concerning Rio
Grande de São Pedro. Republished in Calvo, *Colección . . . de los
tratados,* III.

Lindley, Thomas, *Narrative of a Voyage to Brazil: Terminating in the
Seizure of a British Vessel and the Imprisonment of the Author and
the Ship's Crew . . . with General Sketches of the Country . . .
and a Description of the City and Provinces of St. Salvadore and
Porto Seguro.* . . . (London, 1805). The author, an English contrabandist, was imprisoned in Salvador in 1801–1802. He was a keen

observer and provides valuable insights into the economic and social life of Bahia at the beginning of the nineteenth century.

Nunes, António Duarte, "Almanac histórico da cidade de S. Sebastião do Rio de Janeiro . . . anno de 1799," *Revista do Instituto Histórico e Geográfico Brasileiro*, XXI (1858), 1–176. Comparable in value to the first item in this section.

Ratton, Jacome, *Recordacoens de . . . sobre occorrências do seu tempo em Portugal . . . 1747 . . . [até] 1810* (London, 1813). Ratton was a French-born, Portuguese-naturalized cloth merchant who spent most of his life in Portugal and for many years was an official of the Junta do Commércio. He knew and describes many of the important people of his time in Portugal and was a strong admirer of Pombal. His discussions of economic conditions during the Pombaline years are particularly valuable.

Staunton, George, *An Authentic Account of an Embassy from the King of Great Britain to the Emperor of China*. . . . 2d ed., 3 vols. (London, 1798). Staunton, secretary of the first British embassy to China, spent several weeks in Rio de Janeiro in 1792. His extensive account (I, 160–215) describes the economy and society of the city and environs.

Teixeira Coelho, José João, "Instrucção para o governo da capitania de Minas Geraes" (1780), *Revista do Instituto Histórico e Geográfico Brasileiro*, XV (1852), 257–476. Desembargador Teixeira Coelho, who served on the Relação of Pôrto at the time this instruction was completed, spent eleven years in Minas Gerais and on the basis of his experience prepared this handbook for future captains-general, describing the laws in force, the powers and restrictions on the authority of the captains-general, and the status of the Mineiro economy. A very important and unique work for the study of colonial administration.

Tollenare, L[ouis-] F[rançois] de, *Notas dominicais tomadas durante uma viagem em Portugal e no Brasil em 1816, 1817 e 1818* (Bahia, 1956). Tollenare was a French cotton buyer who lived and traveled throughout the Northeast but he was most familiar with Pernambuco. He was a remarkably keen but cautious and honest observer, and filled his notebooks with his observations concerning government, the church, social structure, recreation, and the economy.

Vilhena, Luiz dos Santos, *Cartas de Vilhena: noticias soteropolitanas e brasilicas*, annotated by Braz do Amaral. 3 vols. (Bahia, 1921–1922). Vilhena was a professor of Greek who lived in Salvador from 1787 to *ca.* 1804. His essays are encyclopedic in coverage and while they emphasize economic, political and social conditions in Bahia, are informative for other parts of Brazil as well. Their value is enhanced by numerous maps, plates, and tables.

White, John, *Journal of a Voyage to New South Wales* (London, 1790).

The author, a British surgeon on a convict ship bound for Australia, spent several weeks in Rio de Janeiro in 1787, and proved himself a first-rate observer of the daily life of the city's inhabitants.

LATER BOOKS

Armitage, John, *The History of Brazil, from the . . . arrival of the Braganza family in 1808 to . . . 1831.* 2 vols. (London, 1836). Intended as a continuation of Southey's History (*s.v.*), the narrative is mainly political and the interpretation is unflattering to the Portuguese regime.

Araña, Henrique, *Expedición de Don Pedro de Cevallos al Rio Grande y Río de la Plata* (Rio Grande, 1937). Useful primarily for the initial publication of certain documents concerning the second Cevallos expedition.

Azarola Gil, Luis Enrique, *Contribución a la historia de Colonia del Sacramento: la epopeya de Manuel Lobo seguida de una crónica de los sucesos desde 1680 hasta 1828 y de una recopilación de documentos* (Madrid, 1931). A pioneer work based on multiarchival investigations. Like all works on Colônia, it is thin on the years 1763–1777. Especially valuable for its documentary appendices.

Azevedo, João, Lúcio, *O Marquêz de Pombal e a sua época.* 2d ed. (Lisbon, 1922). The earliest of the modern critical studies of Pombal. Azevedo saw Pombal as a well-meaning but arbitrary, autocratic enlightened despot.

Balbi, Adrien, *Essai statistique sur le royaume de Portugal et d'Algarve.* . . . 2 vols. (Paris, 1822). A comprehensive analysis of various aspects of the Portuguese government during the late eighteenth and early nineteenth centuries. The author, a professor of geography, physics, and mathematics, consulted manuscript as well as printed sources.

Ballesteros y Beretta, Antonio, *Historia de España y su influencia en el mundo.* 9 vols. (Barcelona, 1929).

Barba, Enrique M., *Don Pedro de Cevallos, governador de Buenos Aires y virrey del Río de la Plata* (Buenos Aires, 1937). A doctoral dissertation done at the University of Madrid and based on multiarchival Spanish sources. Though the author failed to consult relevant Portuguese materials, this remains the most extensive study of the career of Don Pedro, particularly as it related to the Platine area.

Beirão, Caetano, *Dona Maria I* (*1777–1792*). 4th ed. (Lisbon, 1944). Standard work on the dreary years after the fall of Pombal. Mainly a study of court life.

Bermejo de la Rica, Antonio, *La Colonia del Sacramento* (Toledo, 1920). An important diplomatic study which includes many documents bearing on Colônia found in the Archivo General de las Indias (Seville).

Boiteux, Lucas Alexandre, *Notas para a historia catherinense* (Floria-nopolis, 1912). Admiral Boiteux has an undeservedly high reputation in Brazil as an historian. This book is marred by many errors and is chiefly worthy of note as one of the few surveys of Santa Catarina.

Boxer, Charles R. *Four Centuries of Portuguese Expansion, 1415–1825: A Succinct Survey* (Johannesburg, 1961).

————. *Portuguese Society in the Tropics. The Municipal Councils of Goa, Macao, Bahia, and Luanda, 1510–1800* (Madison, 1965).

————. *Race Relations in the Portuguese Colonial Empire, 1415–1825* (Oxford, 1963).

————. *Salvador de Sá and the Struggle for Brazil and Angola, 1602–1686* (London, 1952).

————. *The Golden Age of Brazil 1695–1750. Growing Pains of a Colonial Society* (Berkeley, 1962).

Five basic studies by the foremost contemporary historian of the Portuguese empire. Few can rival his superb knowledge of printed sources, his ability to make deft use of selected manuscript materials, or his felicitous style.

Caetano, Marcelo, *De Conselho Ultramarino ao Conselho do Império* (Lisbon [?], 1943). A brief and disappointing work from the pen of an able historian who devotes a single superficial chapter to the years 1643–1833. Demonstrates the need for an adequate study of the Overseas Council.

Carnaxide, Visconde de (António de Sousa Pedroso Carnaxide), *O Brasil na administração pombalina (economia e política externa)* (Rio de Janeiro, 1940). The title notwithstanding, this is a study of what the author, a Catholic apologist for João V, regards as the misguided policies of Pombal. It is based upon archival materials in Portugal and Brazil, but the research is far from exhaustive.

Carnota, John Smith Athelstane, Conde de, *Memoirs of the Marquis of Pombal; with Extracts from His Writings, and from Despatches in the State Paper Office.* 2 vols. (London, 1843). Smith was an English-born secretary of the Duke of Saldanha, a nephew of Pombal. His biography is exceedingly partial to Pombal and is chiefly valuable for its documentary excerpts.

[Corrêa de Sá], D. José d'Almeida, *Vice-reinado do d. Luiz d'Almeida Portugal, 2° marquez de Lavradio 3° vice-rei do Brasil* (São Paulo, 1942). The only biography of Viceroy Lavradio, this was written by one of his admiring descendants who used a portion of the family papers. The text is little more than a stringing together of documentary quotes with very haphazard citations. Two-thirds of the volume consists of documentary appendices, which include many items that I was unable to find in Brazilian archives.

Cruz, Alcides, *Vida de Raphael Pinto Bandeira* (Pôrto Alegre, 1906). As the only biography of this colorful frontier captain, the book is indispensable, but a more detailed and dispassionate modern study is much needed.

Fernandes Pinheiro, José Feliciano (Visconde de São Leopoldo), *Anais da província de S. Pedro* (Rio de Janeiro, 1946). A reprinting of the 1819 edition, the work of an eminent Brazilian statesman and governor of Rio Grande during the early national period. Based firmly upon local archival sources, it is the best of the older histories of Rio Grande and contains a clearly written, though anti-Spanish text.

Fleiuss, Max, *História administrativa do Brasil*. 2d ed. (São Paulo, 1925). A well-known work by a former president of the Instituto Histórico e Geográfico Brasileiro. Only sixty pages pertain to the colonial period, and they are encyclopedic rather than analytical and include a number of serious errors.

Gama Barros, Henrique da, *História da administração pública em Portugal nos séculos XII a XV*. 2d ed., Torquato de Sousa Soares, ed. 11 vols. (Lisbon, 1945–1954). A distinguished work in the Herculano tradition. Fundamental for an understanding of the evolution of Portuguese administrative institutions.

Garcia, Rodolfo, *Ensaio sôbre a história política e administrativa do Brasil (1500–1810)* (Rio de Janeiro, 1956). Lectures given in 1930 by one of Brazil's most eminent historians covering various colonial institutions, primarily for the first half of the colonial period. Though superficial, the essays are well worth reading.

Gil Munilla, Octavio, *El Río de la Plata en la política internacional. Génesis del virreinato* (Sevilla, 1949). A dissertation based mainly on Spanish archival materials. Although Portuguese printed works are listed in the bibliography, the author clearly did not consult them. The result is a pro-Spanish, anti-British, anti-Portuguese study of the international role of the Plata, *ca.* 1760 to *ca.* 1780. The book includes important documentary appendices.

Lamego, Alberto, *A terra goytacá à luz de documentos inéditos*. 2d ed., 7 vols. (Niterói, 1951). A solidly based local history of the northern part of the captaincy of Rio de Janeiro which reprints important documents from Portuguese archives.

Lobo, Eulália Maria Lahmeyer, *Administração colonial luso-espanhola nas Américas* (Rio de Janeiro, 1952). An ambitious attempt to write a comparative history of Portuguese and Spanish colonial administration which fails to come off because of too much indigestion and the absence of sufficient analysis.

Lobo, Miguel, *Historia general de las antiguas colonias hispano-americanas*. 3 vols. (Madrid, 1875). In spite of its title, this is primarily concerned with the Platine area. The third volume includes the texts of many important documents bearing on the second Cevallos expedition.

Luz Soriano, Simão, José, História do reinado de el-rei d. José e da *administração do Marquês de Pombal.* . . . 2 vols. (Lisbon, 1867) . A chronicle of Pombal's triumphs in Europe by one of his most ardent defenders. Includes texts of many of Pombal's memorials concerning Luso-Spanish Platine rivalry.

Mauro, Frédéric, *Le Portugal et l'Atlantique au xvii*e *siècle, 1570–1670* (Paris, 1960). An impressive, broadly conceived, thoroughly researched study of Portugal's Atlantic empire during the indicated years with special emphasis on Brazil.

Oliveira, Oscar de, *Os dízimos eclesiásticos do Brasil nos períodos da colonia e do imperio* (Juiz de Fora, 1940) . The basic study stressing legal rather than fiscal aspects of the subject.

Pereira da Silva, João Manuel. *Historia da fundação do imperio brasileiro.* 7 vols. (Rio de Janerio, 1864–1868) ; 2d ed., 3 vols. (Rio de Janeiro, 1877) . The first volume of this dated but still useful study concerns the institutional background to the establishment of the Brazilian empire as viewed from an anti-Portuguese, mildly anticlerical perspective.

Pizarro e Araujo, José de Sousa de Azevedo, *Memorias históricas da provincia do Rio de Janeiro.* 10 vols. (Rio de Janeiro, 1820–1822) ; 2d ed., 9 vols. (Rio de Janeiro, 1945–1948). A mine of badly organized information derived from local archival sources. Particular emphasis is given to ecclesiastical affairs. The first six volumes focus on Rio de Janeiro and its dependencies, the last three on the remainder of Brazil.

Porto [Afonso] Aurélio, *História das missões orientais do Uruguai.* 2d ed., 2 vols (Pôrto Alegre, 1954) . The foremost study of the Jesuit missions in Rio Grande before the expulsion of the Society.

Prado, Júnior, Caio, *Formação do Brasil contemporâneo: colônia.* 2d ed. (São Paulo, 1945) ; tr. by Suzette Macedo as *The Colonial Background of Modern Brazil.* (Berkeley and Los Angeles, 1967) . A brilliant series of essays on the colonial roots of modern Brazil by one of Brazil's leading Marxist historians. The essay on colonial administration is the best brief analysis in print.

Rau, Virgínia, *A Casa dos Contos* (Coimbra, 1951) . The basic study of the "old" Portuguese fiscal system and the bureau of audit.

Rego Monteiro, Jônatas da Costa, *A Colônia do Sacramento, 1680–1777.* 2 vols. (Pôrto Alegre, 1937) . Based solidly on published and manuscript sources, this is the most detailed study of the Colônia problem from the military and diplomatic aspects, but it, too, is thin on Colônia's last phase. The second volume consists of documents.

———, *Dominação espanhola no Rio Grande do Sul, 1763–1777* (Rio de Janeiro, 1937) . The only monograph on the Spanish occupation, it is founded on multiarchival sources in Brazil. Though abundantly documented and generally sound in analysis, the work is weak on the Portuguese reaction to the mounting of the second Cevallos expedition.

Rodrigues, José Honório, *O continente do Rio Grande* (Rio de Janeiro, 1954). A brief introductory essay sketching some of the salient lines of colonial development in Rio Grande and based largely upon articles and monographs by Riograndense historians.

Trípoli, César, *História do direito brasileiro (ensaio)*. 3 vols. (São Paulo, 1936). Volume 1 *(Epoca Colonial)* emphasizes colonial courts and legal procedures but omits a great deal.

Varnhagen, Francisco Adolfo de (Visconde de Porto Seguro), *História geral do Brasil antes da sua separação e independência de Portugal*. 5 vols., 5th ed. (São Paulo, 1956). First published over a century ago, this remains the greatest history of colonial Brazil. Varnhagen was especially strong on the sixteenth and seventeenth centuries, where he did most of his original research. The later centuries are comparatively less well founded or synthesized. The utility of the later editions has been enhanced by the abundant bibliographical annotations provided by editors Capistrano de Abreu and Rodolfo Garcia.

Zenha, Edmundo, *O município no Brasil, 1532–1700* (São Paulo, 1948). Based exclusively upon printed materials, this is a useful study of the influence of the colonial câmaras during their period of greatest importance.

ARTICLES

Abreu, Florêncio, "Govêrno de José Marcelino de Figueiredo no govêrno de São-Pedro—1769 a 1780," *Anais do segundo congresso de história e geografia sul rio-grandense*. II (Pôrto Alegre, 1937), 177–207. Based on the Böhm correspondence and exchanges between the governors of Rio Grande and Viceroy Lavradio, this is an attempt to rehabilitate José Marcelino by emphasizing his positive contributions.

Alden, Dauril, "Manoel Luís Vieira: An Entrepreneur in Rio de Janeiro During Brazil's Eighteenth-Century Agricultural Renaissance," *Hispanic American Historical Review*, XXXIX, November, 1959, 521–537.

———, "The Growth and Decline of Indigo Production in Colonial Brazil: A Study in Comparative Economic History," *Journal of Economic History*, XXV, March, 1965, 35–60.

———, "The Marquis of Pombal and the American Revolution," *The Americas*, XVII, April, 1961, 369–382.

———, "The Population of Brazil in the late Eighteenth Century: A Preliminary Survey," *Hispanic American Historical Review*, XLIII, May, 1963, 173–205.

———, "Yankee Sperm Whalers in Brazilian Waters, and the Decline of the Portuguese Whale Fisher (1773–1801)," *The Americas,* XX, January, 1964, 267–288.

Azevedo, J[oão] Lúcio de, "Política de Pombal relativo ao Brasil," *Novas epanáforas. Estudos de história e literatura* (Lisbon, 1932), pp. 7–62. A by-product of the author's interest in Pombal, this is a sketchy study of the minister's impact upon Brazil emphasizing his diplomatic and military policies, his attack on the Jesuits, and his economic aims.

Caetano, Marcelo, "O govêrno e a administração central após a restauração," *História da expansão portuguesa no mundo,* III:1 (Lisbon, 1940), 189–198. An excellent brief account.

———, "As reformas pombalinas e post-pombalinas respeitantes ao ultramar. O novo espírito em que são concebidas," *Ibid.,* III:1, 251–260. Global in approach.

Carvalho Mourão, João M., "Orgãos administrativos e judiciários da colônia no período decorrido de 1500 a 1763," *Anais do IV congresso de história nacional,* IX (Rio de Janeiro, 1954), 403–460. Encyclopedic in coverage, but poorly digested. Provides useful detailed data on the functions of many colonial offices.

Christelow, Allan, "Great Britain and the Trades from Cadiz and Lisbon to Spanish America and Brazil, 1759–1783," *Hispanic American Historical Review,* XXVII, 1947, 2–29. A first-rate study of the changes in British commercial policy vis-à-vis Spanish and Portuguese America during these years.

Fernandes Pinheiro, J. C., "Os últimos vice-reis do Brasil," *Revista do Instituto Histórico e Geográfico Brasileiro,* XXVIII:2, 1865, 225–273. A study of the viceroys of Rio de Janeiro from 1763 to 1790 based upon MSS in the Instituto Histórico. Primarily useful for the inclusion of extensive excerpts from the sources.

Garcia, Rodolfo, "A capitania de Pernambuco no governo de José César de Menezes (1774–1787)," *Ibid.,* LXXIV, 1919, 533–560. A thin sketch of one of Lavradio's contemporaries.

Moura, Américo Brasiliense Antunes de, "Govêrno do Morgado de Mateus no vice-reinado do conde da Cunha. S. Paulo restaurado," *Revista do Arquivo Municipal.* LII (São Paulo, 1938), 9–155. A promising beginning of an uncompleted study of the administration of Luís António de Sousa.

Ravignani, Emilio, "El virreinato del Río de la Plata (1776–1810)," in Ricardo Levene, ed., *Historia de la nación Argentina,* IV:1, 2d ed. (Buenos Aires, 1940), 33–234. A well-founded, clearly organized study by one of Argentina's best historians who used both Spanish and Portuguese materials.

INDEX

Accounting procedures: reform of, 25, 291f.; need for reform of, 288f.; weaknesses of reform of, 316, 322-323. *See also* Royal Treasury

Albuquerque, José Pires de Carvalho e, pluralism of, 296 n. 54

Alfândega. See Customs House

Algiers crisis, effects of on Portuguese strategy, 154-155, 160-168

Almoxarife (Customs superintendent), 295

Almoxarife dos armazens (superintendent of warehouses), 285-286

Altamirano, Father Lope Luis (Jesuit delegate to Luso-Spanish boundary commission), 91

Amado, Antônio Pinheiro (*ouvidor* of Rio de Janeiro), 433-434

Andonaegui, Don José (governor of Buenos Aires), 92

Andrada, Gomes Freire de, Conde de Bobadela (captain-general of Rio de Janeiro, Minas Gerais, and São Paulo): 45, 54, 307, 313, 459; recommends consolidation of southern Brazil under aegis of Rio de Janeiro, 72 n. 41; opposes colonization of Rio Grande de São Pedro under private auspices, 77; Portuguese commissioner for execution of Treaty of Madrid, 90-93; authority of greater than viceroys, 472

Andrada, José Antônio Freire de, 306

Andrade, Antônio da Veiga (interim governor of Rio Grande de São Pedro), 122, 448, 451

Angeja, Marquis of, 257 n. 47, 473

Aranda, Count of, Pedro Pablo Abarca y Bolea (ambassador to France), 166, 167, 172, 196

Araujo, Francisco Gil Garcia de, accused of "atrocious crimes," 19

Arriaga, Julián de (minister of war in Spain), 101, 166 n. 85

Arroio Chuí, 61, 265

Atlantic Islands, of Portugal: reinforcements sent to Brazil from, 139; source of illicit trade, 390. *See also* Homesteaders (*casais*)

Aula do Comércio (commercial institute), 288

Ayres de Sá. *See* Melo, Ayres de Sá e

Azambuja, Count of, Dom Antônio Rolim de Moura Tavares (second viceroy of Rio de Janeiro), 6 n. 12, 27, 54, 286, 409

Bahia de Todos os Santos, captaincy of, 31

Bahia de Todos os Santos, captaincy-general, 40; economy of, 14-15, 359-360; military forces of, 20-22; thought to be Cevallos' objective, 204, 211; defensive preparations at to thwart Cevallos, 205-207; Lisbon concludes Cevallos will not attack, 213. *See also* Menezes, Manoel da Cunha *and* Salvador, City of

Banda Oriental, 59, 199, 210, 275

Bandeira, Rafael Pinto (*Riograndense* rancher and war hero), 123, 242, 452 n. 21; biobibliographical note, 130 n. 68; accused of defrauding the king, 122-123; victories of against Spanish detachments, 130-131; lauded by Böhm, 149; surprise attack of, on San Martín, 168; captures Fort Santa Tecla, 183; rewards of, 192-193; ordered to raid Banda Oriental, 210

Bandeirantes, 63-64

Bandeiras, last cycle of, 462-464

Bettâmio, Sebastião Francisco (accountant), 25-26, 156, 322; biographical sketch, 314-315

Blasco, Miguel Ángelo (Milanese engineer), 137 n. 94

Board of Conscience and [Military] Orders, 442

Board of Inspection (*mesa da inspeção*), 282, 360, 424; established in major Brazilian ports, 12; functions of, 12 n. 33, 45 n. 78, 306 n. 85, 329

Bobadela, Conde de. *See* Andrada, Gomes Freire de

Böhm, João Henrique de (Austrian general), 52, 215 n. 90, 222 n. 121, 336; sent to Brazil, 112; assigned to Rio Grande de São Pedro, 134, 137, 145-146; pessimistic reports of, 148-149; relations of, with Lavradio, 52, 145-146, 149-150, 153, 210-211; ordered to hasten expulsion of Spaniards, 154; inspection tour of, 156; character of, 157; expels Spaniards from Lagoa dos Patos, 182-187; commended by Pombal for victories, 192; instructions of concerning defenses against Cevallos, 203-204, 206, 210; death, 157 n. 50, 187 n. 35

Botanical gardens, 379-380

Boundary controversies among colonial executives, significance of, 461-462

Brazil, administration of: beginnings of royal government in, 30f.; stages of reorganization of, 34-35, 39, 72, 459, 485-486; character of, 446, 471-472, 479, 491; appraisals of, 399, 486-494

Brazil, agricultural renaissance of, 356-380 passim, 481

Brazil, early history of, 10-11

Brazilians: Lavradio's low estimate of, 482; character of, 491; extent of participation by, in colonial regime, 493

Broadley, John (captain of the True Briton), 411-414

Bucareli y Ursúa, Francisco de (governor of Buenos Aires), 107

Cachoeira (Bahia), center of tobacco production, 359-360

Caldas, José Antônio (military engineer), 270, 458

Câmara, Sebastião da Veiga Cabral e (future governor of Rio Grande de São Pedro), 132-133, 156 n. 46

Câmaras: membership of, 296, 422; and voluntary contributions, 306-307; of Olinda and Rio de Janeiro lose control over excises, 309-310; duties of, 422-423; reduction in powers and privileges of, 423; Lavradio's relations with, 424-428; contention not oligarchies unproven, 427

Campos de Goitacazes, 356-357, 444

Canavieiras, bay of, 230

Canoe convoys (monções de canoas), 327

Capitação (head tax), 12

Capitães mores (governors): duties of, 31-32; restrictions on, 32-33; terms of, 33; qualifications of, 34. See also Governors, subordinate

Capital, remission of, to Portugal, 323-332 passim

Captaincies-general: origins of, 39-40; an "intimate association and close defensive alliance," 43

Captaincy system, 11, 31

Captains-general, office of: duties of, 18, 31-32; character of occupants, 34, 454; relationship of, to viceroys, 42, 208, 447; relations of, with Viceroy Lavradio, 452f.

Cardozo, Jorge Botto Machado (juiz de fóra of Rio de Janeiro), 430-431

Cardozo, Manoel da Costa (entrepreneur and treasurer-general of Rio de Janeiro): biographical sketch, 315; probable author of report on fiscal system, 289 n. 28; and indigo production in Rio de Janeiro, 372-374

Carvajal y Lencastre, José de (president of the Council of the Indies), 86-88, 94

Carvalho, Paulo de (brother of Pombal and inquisitor-general of Portugal), 27

Carvalho e Melo, Sebastião José de. See Pombal, Marquis of

Casa dos Contos (Bureau of Audit), 280, 288

Casa Tilly, Marquis of (Spanish admiral), 201, 225, 226, 229

Casais (homesteaders), 70 n. 31, 73, 77, 354

Casas da fundição. See Smelteries

Castillos Grandes, meeting of boundary commissioners at, 91

Castro, Martinho de Melo e. See Melo e Castro, Martinho

Cerveira, Visconde da Villanova da, Marquis of Ponte de Lima, 257 n. 47

Cevallos, Don Pedro de (two-time victor over the Portuguese and first viceroy of the Plata), 195, 342, 347-348; biographical sketch, 200; and the Guaraní War, 92-93; first campaign against the Portuguese, 94-101 passim; urges attack on Portugal, 196, 197, 198; analyzes plan for attack on Brazil, 197; second campaign against the Portuguese, objectives, 198-199; secret appointment as viceroy, 200, 213; preparations of, 201; departure of, from Cádiz, 224; debate of concerning attack on Santa Catarina Island, 225, 227; and the fall of Santa Catarina Island, 230f.; failure to retake Lagoa dos Patos, 238-240; reception of at Montevideo, 240; and second capture of Colônia, 241-245 *passim;* impact of on Portuguese vice-regal exchequer, 342-348; death of, 246

Charles III (King of Spain, 1759-1788), 94, 165 n. 83, 196-197, 264

Choiseul, Duc de (Foreign Minister of France), criticism of Pombal by, 109 n. 116

Clergy in Brazil: criticism of recruiting practices of, 21, 53 n. 107, 476; discipline of, 437-440; character of, 441; as administrative agents, 442-443; absense of mention of, in Lavradio's terminal report, 476

Cloth-making in Brazil, 383-385

Cochineal, 376-380

Coelho, José João Teixeira (royal judge), opposes tax-farming, 308-309

Coimbra, Manoel Soares (grenadier commander), 184

Colônia do Sacramento: 60, 138, 211, 336; founding of, 66-68; historiography concerning, 68 n. 24; first captured by Spaniards, 69; first reestablished by Portuguese, 69; sailing time between, and Buenos Aires, Montevideo, Santa Catarina, and Rio de Janeiro, 69-70; population of, 71, 243; contraband trade at, 94 n. 49, 96 n. 64, 102, 138, 211, 390; captured for third time by Cevallos (1762), 96; returned to Portuguese control for third time, 101; blockade of, 84, 101, 114-115, 117-119, 241, 243; as a listening post, 119; Spanish plan for attack on (1771), 126; "not a praça [but] a prison," 158; deliberate sacrifice of, ordered by Pombal, 16of.; garrison of returned from Rio de Janeiro, 167-168; second order for withdrawal of garrison of, not received, 220; vulnerability of, 220-221; capture of and destruction of, by Cevallos (1777), 241-245; inability of Portugal to maintain, 271-272; resettlement of refugees from, 355. *See also* Rocha, Francisco José da

Colonial Secretary, office of, 9

Communications: problems of, 34, 191 n. 55, 264 n. 73, 327; sailing time between Rio de Janeiro, Colônia, and intermediate points, 69-70; between Rio de Janeiro and Lisbon, 144

Companhia do Grão Pará e Maranhão, 12

Comptrollers-general, of Royal Treasury (Lisbon), jurisdictions of, 280 n. 5

Conselho da Índia, 10 n. 24

Conselho Ultramarino. See Overseas Council

Contadoria (bureau of audit, Rio de Janeiro), composition and functions of, 284

Convoy system (*frotas*), 12, 324, 382-383

Cook, James: problems of, at Rio de Janeiro, 390 n. 11, 409-410

Correio marítima (packet service), 327

Corridas (livestock round-ups), 81, 122-123

Cotton exports from Brazil, 366

Coutinho, Francisco Innocêncio de Sousa (Portuguese ambassador to Madrid), 166, 213, 455; and Grimaldi, 172, 173; delivers tampered note to Grimaldi, 189; warns of impending attack on Northern Brazil, 204; negotiates with Floridablanca after Spanish victories, 264-265

Crime and punishment, 435-436, 444

Cubatão (coastal village, Santa Catarina), 236, 238

Cunha, José Henrique (Portuguese gunnery lieutenant), 234, 235, 503

Custódio, José. *See* Sá e Faria, José Custódio

Customs House (*alfândega*) 287, 317, 389, 393. *See also* Dízimo da alfândega

Degredados (exiles), 70 n. 32, 135 n. 84, 436-437

Depression in Brazil, 313, 317-318

Desembargadores (senior magistrates), installation of, 20 n. 65

Desertion. *See* Military service

Desterro (capital of Santa Catarina), 61, 72, 73 n. 42, 236

Deusdará, Simão Álvares de la Penha, colonial-born member of Relação of Bahia, 296

Diamond District, 12, 13, 400, 401, 402

Dízima da alfândega (import duty), 302, 318, 393 n. 27

Dízimo. See Tithes

Donataries, 31, 43

Donativos (voluntary contributions), 280, 297, 306-307

Double-entry system, origins of, 287. *See also* Accounting procedures

Economic parochialism, manifestations of, 383-387, 391

El Ferrol expedition, 136, 141

Entradas (interior customs duties), 303

Epidemics, 429

Erário Régio. *See* Royal Treasury

Estado do Brasil, 35, 43

Estado do Maranhão, 35, 40

Falta de braços, myth of, 209
Faria, Antônio Gonçalves Pereira de, efforts of to produce hemp, 367-369
Fazenda real. See Royal Treasury
Ferreira, José Henriques (physician of Viceroy Lavradio), 377-378, 380 n. 97, 477
Fifths, royal *(quinto)*, 12, 301, 324; collection of, 302, 326-327; not to be diverted, 333, 343; Lavradio threatens to use, 343; and does, 344
Figueiredo, José Marcelino de, pseud. for Manuel Jorge Gomes de Sepúlveda (governor of Rio Grande de São Pedro), 121, 142 n. 114; biographical sketch, 449-450, 452 n. 21; acrimonious relations of, with Lavradio, 450-452
Floridablanca, Count of, José Moñino (foreign minister of Spain), 263-265
Foreign consuls, presence of, in Brazilian ports, 412
Foreign ships, unlicensed: procedures concerning in colonial ports, 403-408
France, relations of with Portugal and Spain: hopes for alliance to include Portugal, 109f.; Aranda directed to request Louis XVI to mediate Luso-Spanish dispute, 166; Grimaldi considers mediation unnecessary, 167; Grimaldi reconsiders, 172; declines to propose mediatory congress, 190; hope of ministers of to localize Luso-Spanish conflict, 193; aid sought by Spain for possible attack on Portugal, 197
Freitas, Pedro Antônio da Gama e (governor of Santa Catarina), 140, 231, 235, 252
Frotas. See Convoy system
Funk, Jacques (Swedish military engineer); 52, 54, 112; biographical sketch, 112 n. 129; promoted to field marshal and assigned to Rio Grande de São Pedro, 140; authorized to return to Rio de Janeiro, 210 n. 68
Furtado, Francisco Xavier de Mendonça (Colonial Secretary), 10, 19, 90 n. 37

Gálvez, José de (minister of the Indies), 195, 196, 198, 226 n. 6
Garoupas Bay (Porto Belo?), 61, 75, 228
Gastón, Miguel, squadron of, 202 n. 29
Goiás, captaincy-general of, 40, 339, 455, 457
Gold, 12; production of, in Minas Gerais, 326-327

Goldsmiths *(ourives)*, harassment of, 395-396
Gómez, Don Antonio (commander of Seven Missions), 127-131 *passim*
Governor, ideal qualities of, 3
Governor-general, office of: authority of and restraints upon early occupants, 31-34; average tenure of occupants during sixteenth, seventeenth, and eighteenth centuries, 33; occupants' attitudes toward, 34; general character of occupants of, 34; diminution of authority of after Dutch war, 35-40. *See also* Viceroy of Brazil, office of
Governors, subordinate: duties of, 448-449; relations of with Viceroy Lavradio, 448-452. See also *Capitães mores*
Grão Pará, captaincy-general of, 40, 455
Great Britain: refuses to aid Portugal against Spain after Seven Years' War, 103, 109; dominant position of, 108-109; relations of with Portugal, 109-111; aid sought from by Pombal, 171; lack of assurances from necessitates suspension of hostilities, 172-173; ambassador of to Spain tampers with Portuguese note, 189; declines to propose mediatory congress, 190; Grimaldi convinced is unable to assist Portugal, 191; Pombal continues to hope for aid from, 192; Portuguese dependency on, 262; and possible war with Spain, 264. *See also* Pombal, Marquis of
Grimaldi, Marquis of (foreign minister of Spain): negotiations with Portugal after Squillace revolts, 108f.; overture to resume negotiations concerning borderlands, 166; suspends hostilities against Portuguese in Plata, 167; uneasiness of, 171-172; rejects Portuguese note, 173; Pombal's view of, 190; is convinced Great Britain unable to aid Portugal, 191-192; favors attack on Brazil rather than Portugal, 196; retirement of, 263
Guairá missions: founded and abandoned, 63; remains discovered, 463
Guaraní War, 92-93, 200
Guaxima (fiber), 369-372
Gusmão, Alexandre de (royal counsellor and diplomat): biographical sketch, 87 n. 19; hostility of toward Pombal, 9; architect of Treaty of Madríd, 87-90; critique of Colônia discovered by Francisco José da Rocha, 158

Hardcastle, George: 177, 181, 185; role obscure during MacDouall's attack in

Lagoa dos Patos, 178 n. 5; leads naval force into Lagoa dos Patos, 150-151; role during successful attack on Spaniards in Lagoa dos Patos, 185-186; in charge of naval defenses of entrance to Guanabara Bay, 222-223

Hasell (Hassel), John (captain of *Duke of Portland*), 413, 414

Hemp-growing, problems of, 367-369

Henrique Dias battalion, 21, 162

Homesteaders. See *Casais*

Hopman, João (Dutch-born farmer), 369-372, 378

Horne, John (captain of the *Morse*), 410-411

Iguatemí (Portuguese frontier post): establishment of alarms viceroy of Perú, 126; Lavradio favors retention of, 254, 466; Luís Antônio de Sousa and the role of, 462-470 *passim;* overrun by Spaniards, 501-502 n. 15

Indians: Guaraní oppose Portuguese occupation of Seven Missions lands, 91-93; of Rio Grande de São Pedro, Portuguese efforts to woo, 93, 137; Spain demands return of after Seven Years' War, 102; Lavradio's concern about treatment of, 121, 124 n. 42; Portuguese policy toward, Lavradio's criticism of, 465-466; Lavradio's attitude toward, 483

Indigo, production of, 372-376

Innocent XI (Pope), bull *Romani Pontificis*, 67

Intendants: marine (Bahia), 25; interior (Minas Gerais), 12, 401

Intendant-general of gold (Rio de Janeiro), 12, 45 n. 77, 282, 400-401, 421

Jesuitophobia, 437-440. *See also* Pombal, Marquis of

Jesuits, 9; opposition to, draws Portugal and Spain closer together, 106-108, 112, 115

—Portuguese, 35; alleged conspiracy of with Great Britain, 111; Lavradio warned against, 116; former properties of, 284, 332, 345-347; accounting methods of, 288 n. 25

—Spanish: Guairá missions, founded by, 63-64; Paraná missions, founded by, 64; Uruguay-Tape missions, founded by, 63-64; Seven Missions, founded by, 66; opposition of to Treaty of Madrid, 89; expulsion of, from Spain and the Indies, 107-108

José I (king of Portugal, 1750-1777): selects Lavradio as tutor, 6; surprise selection of Pombal by, 8; death of, 194, 256-257, 263

Juíz de fóra (municipal judge), 424, 431

Junta(s) da fazenda: established at Bahia, 25; in the other captaincies-general, 281; in Rio Grande de São Pedro, subordinate status of, 155, 282; functions of, 282, 294, 297, 302, 310-311, 324, 332, 345

Junta das fragatas, 282

Kesselberg, Fredrick (Danish sea captain), 178, 179

Kindersley, Mrs. Nathaniel, experience of in Salvador, 408-409

Lajes (Paraná), founding of, 74, 461, 462

Land: assignment of, criticism of, 123; engrossment of, 355; disputes over, 356-357

Lavradio, Marquis of (Dom Luís de Almeida Portugal Soares Alarcão Eça Melo Pereira Aguilar Fiel de Lugo Mascarenhas Silva Mendonça e Lencastre): ancestry and birth, 4; early career, 4-5; captain-general of Bahia, 6, 13-27; promotion to Rio de Janeiro as viceroy, 27-28; reports on conditions at new post, 51-56; initial instructions as viceroy, 116; protests failure of Crown to provide assistance, 133-134; full war powers given to, 141; promoted to lieutenant-general, 141; yearns for field command, 143, 250, 260, 480; assumes responsibility for untimely victories, 174-175; reports victories, 188-189; preparations of to defeat Cevallos, 206f.; optimism of despite arrival of Cevallos, 249-250; stunned by loss of Santa Catarina Island and capitulation of its garrison, 250, 252; calls for 4,000 Mineiro recruits, 250-251; plans counteroffensive, 252f.; refuses to see Santa Catarina parolees, 252; responsibility of, for defeats, 272-273; hopes for retirement, 473; replaced, 474; terminal report (*relatório*) of, 474-477; final years, 477-478

—character of, 446, 449, 479-485; paternalism of, 153, 427, 481; humanitarianism of, 465-466; prejudices of, 482-484

—relations of: with Pombal, 6-7, 135, 141, 257; with Böhm, 52, 154-155; with MacDouall, 248-249, 256, 260; with the Church, 437-443; with sub-

Lavradio, Marquis of (*continued*)
ordinate governors, 448-452; with co-
equal captains-general, 208, 452-471.
See also Böhm, João Henrique de *and*
MacDouall, Robert
—jurisdictional conflicts of, 432, 457-
458; cf. 253
—as an administrator: efforts to encourage economic development, 26,
354-387 *passim;* praise of, 27-28, 135,
141, 473; concern of regarding treatment of Indians, 121, 124 n. 42; rebuke of by colonial secretary, 170, 338;
activities of as president of treasury
board of Rio de Janeiro, 312-349
passim; justification of for appropriat-
ing part of fifths, 344; obtains loan
secured by personal credit, 345; recommends disposal of Jesuit properties,
346; concern of regarding poverty in
colony, 353; view of colonial manufactures, 383; role of concerning suspected foreign smugglers, 410-416;
view of magistrates sent to Brazil,
433; judicial duties of, 434-435; "system of government," 449, 473, 481-
482; later appraisals of, 478-485
Lemos, João Carlos Corrêa (accountant),
314, 430
Lippe, Count of, William of Schaum-
burg-Lippe Bükelburg (reorganizer of
Portuguese army), 5-6
Lisbon: effects of earthquake in, 9, 279,
306; illicit trade in, 389
Livestock: left by Spanish Jesuits in
Rio Grande de São Pedro, 64; and
motivation for occupation of southern
borderlands, 69f.; wild cattle and
horses in Rio Grande, 78; value of,
509-510. See also *Corridas*
Lobo, Dom Manoel (founder of Colônia
do Sacramento), 68
Lopez, Aaron (merchant prince of Newport), 416
Lothrop, Thomas (captain of the *Leviathan*), 416

MacDouall, Robert: biographical note,
139 n. 99; arrival at Rio de Janeiro
from Portugal, 146; Lavradio's instructions to, 147; reluctance of to attack
Spanish warships, 147-148; criticism
of, by Lavradio, 148, 155, 181, 182 n.
20, 248-249, 256, 260, 268; criticism of,
by Böhm, 153; plans of, to assist
Böhm, 169; naval engagement of, in
Lagoa dos Patos, 176-182 *passim;*
praise of and promotion by Pombal,

182; interview with Lavradio, 212-
213; instructions of concerning defense
of Santa Catarina Island, 214, 218-
219; criticism of, 216; departure for
Santa Catarina, 218; fails to engage
Spanish fleet, 228-230; returns to Rio
de Janeiro, 248-249; successful patrol
of, 254-256; appeal of to Secretary
Melo e Castro, 256; misadventure of,
258-260; responsibility of, for Portuguese defeats, 270; returns to Lisbon,
499; cleared of all charges, 499-500;
subsequent return to Rio de Janeiro,
500-501. *See also* Naval squadron, Portuguese
Maldonado, port of, 61, 71, 240
Manufactures: alleged growth of, in
Minas Gerais, 383-384; restrictions imposed on, 385
Mao de Luva gang, 402-403
Maranhão, captaincy-general of, 40
Maria I (queen of Portugal, 1777–1816),
257, 264, 499, 505
Mato Grosso, captaincy-general of, 40,
327, 339, 455
Matos, Gaspar José de (viceregal aide),
132 n. 75, 451-452 n. 17; 477
Melo, Ayres de Sá (ambassador to Spain
and later secretary of foreign affairs),
107, 172 n. 120
Melo e Castro, Martinho de (minister
to Great Britain and later colonial
secretary), 264, 303; succeeds Mendonça Furtado as colonial secretary
(1770–1792), 10; reports Britain's unwillingness to aid Portugal, 109-110;
instructions of, to Viceroy Lavradio
concerning defense of borderlands,
137f.; rebukes Lavradio, 170; is confident Cevallos would be defeated,
202-203; criticizes Viceroy Vasconcelos'
report on Crown's indebtedness, 350
Mendonça, Antônio Carlos Furtado de,
6; interim captain-general of Goiás,
457; transferred to Santa Catarina Island, 138; confers with Lavradio, 147;
flattery of, by Lavradio, 170 n. 107;
instructions of regarding defense of
Santa Catarina, 211-212, 215; protests
removal of squadron, 228; and fall of
Santa Catarina Island, 231f.; and capitulation of forces, 235-238; instrument of Sá e Faria?, 268; apology of,
269-270; responsibility of, for Portuguese defeats, 271; trial of, 502, 504
Menezes, Francisco Barreto (governor-
general, 1657–1663), 36-37
Menezes, Francisco de Sousa de (governor of Santa Catarina), 140

Menezes, José César de (captain-general of Pernambuco) , 139, 453-454

Menezes, Luís da Cunha e (captain-general of Minas Gerais) , 403

Menezes, Manoel da Cunha (captain-general of Pernambuco and of Bahia): 139; biographical sketch, 453; instructions of, concerning expected Spanish attack, 205-206; relations of, with Lavradio, 218, 457-458

Mercantile method. *See* Double-entry system

Mesa de inspeção. See Board of Inspection

Mesa do Desembargo do Paço, 33 n. 19, 478

Mestres de campo: duties of, 359, 444-445; prototypes of *coroneis,* 443-446; Lavradio's reliance on, 444-445; Lavradio's policy toward, 445-446

Military engineers. *See* Blasco, Miguel Ángelo; Caldas, José Antônio; Funk, Jacques; Roscîo, Francisco João; *and* Sá e Faria, José Custódio

Military service: unpopularity of, 21, 162 n. 67, 458; desertion from, 52-53 n. 103, 70, 81, 119, 236, 238 n. 47, 336-337, 435 n. 56, 436

Militia: Henrique Dias battalion, 21, 162; reactivation of (1766) , 111; Lavradio's attitude toward, 207; police activities of, 443-446

Minas Gerais, captaincy-general of, 12, 40, 395; revenues produced by, 339; trade of with Rio de Janeiro, 383; alleged manufacturing in, 383-384; livestock raising in, 386; problem of smuggling in, 395, 397, 398, 399 n. 52, 401-403. *See also* Diamond District; Fifths, royal

Mint(s): staff and functions, 286, 430; conflicts over location of, 286 n. 21; of Salvador, 15; master of, accused of embezzlement, 22-23; of Rio de Janeiro, money struck at, 118 n. 9, 506; revenues from, 317, 318; expenses of, 320

Money, scarcity of, 118, 286 n. 22

Monteiro, Luís Vaía (governor of Rio de Janeiro) , 309-310, 426

Montevideo, port of, 60; founding of, 71; abortive Portuguese attack on, 78; "does not deserve the name of port," 227; reception of Cevallos at, 240

Mourão, Luís Antônio de Sousa Botelho e. *See* Sousa, Luís Antônio de

Naval squadron, Portuguese: promised Lavradio, 138; elements of begin to

arrive in Rio de Janeiro, 146; status of, in mid-1775, 153 n. 38; in late 1776, 217 n. 94; in February, 1777, 288; assigned to guard Santa Catarina Island, 154; melee of, 258-260; expenses of maintaining, 334; ordered back to Europe, 334, 358 n. 18. *See also* MacDouall, Robert

Navia, Don Victorio de, 198, 233

Negro slaves: and defense of Bahia, 205; uprising of, feared in Minas Gerais, 209; and defense of Santa Catarina Island, 215; aged and lame as weavers, 384; use of as informers, 396; Lavradio's dislike for, 483; value of, by age and skill, 510. *See also* Slave trade, Negro

Noronha, Dom Antônio de (captain-general of Minas Gerais) : character of, 454; and troop reinforcements, 208-210; as defender of Mineiro interests, 384; and difficulties of combatting smuggling, 401; discussions of with Lavradio, 455

Novos direitos (assessments on public offices) , 305

Óbidos, Conde de, Dom Vasco de Mascarenhas (second viceroy of Brazil), 37-38

O'Reilly, Alejandro, 165, 198

Osório, Tomás Luís (commander of Fort Santa Teresa) , 97 n. 69

Ouvidores (circuit magistrates) , 423, 431-432. *See also* Amado, Antônio Pinheiro

Ouvidoria (tribunal) , 35

Overseas Council (*Conselho Ultramarino*) , 75; downgrading of, by Pombal, 10; functions of, 297, 442; orders certain revenue contracts leased in Brazil 309; and prevention of clandestine trade, 404, 405

Pacioli, Luca (author of *Summa de Arithmetica*) , 287

Pais, José da Silva: recommends Desterro as capital of Santa Catarina, 73 n. 42; supports plan for private colonization of Rio Grande de São Pedro, 77; and the founding of Rio Grande, 78-79; favors retention of Rio Grande over Colônia, 81-82

Paiva, Manoel Joaquim Henriques de (pharmacist and member of Scientific Society) , 377, 379

Paranaguá, port of, 59, 398

Passagens (transit tolls) , 304

Paulistas as warriors, 150, 160, 204; "scourges of the Jesuit and the Castilians," 140; praised by Lavradio, 144; Böhm's estimate of, 169; Lavradio's attempt to stimulate ardor of, 253-254

Pedro II (prince and later king of Portugal, 1667–1706), and founding of Colônia do Sacramento, 67

Peninsulars, restlessness of, 460

Pernambuco, captaincy-general of, 39-40, 339. See also Menezes, José César de

Pombal, Marquis of, Sebastião José de Carvalho e Melo (dominant minister of Portugal, 1750–1777), 6, 398; early years of, 7-8, 111; appointed secretary of state for foreign affairs and war, 8-9; policies of, 9, 110, 113, 472; opposes Treaty of Madrid, 90; demands Spain evacuate Lagoa dos Patos, 102; jesuitophobia of, 108, 110-111, 116, 190; and negotiations with Grimaldi toward settlement of borderlands dispute, 108f.; appeals of for aid from Great Britain, 136, 160-161, 171, 206; plan of to sacrifice Colônia, 160-162; determines to profit from Spain's defeat at Algiers, 166f.; reasons for ordering suspension of hostilities in Brazil, 172; finally sends order, 174; mind of, 182 n. 21; spurns, then accepts offer of French mediation, 189; underestimates seriousness of Cevallos expedition, 202; misinterprets reasons for British mobilization, 206; instructions of, for defense of Santa Catarina Island, 214; fiscal reforms of, 288f., 322-323, 351; as inspector-general of Royal Treasury, 311; fall of, 257, 263; responsibility of, for Portuguese defeats, 273-274; investigation of regime of, 498-499; death of, 187 n. 35, 499 n. 4

Pombaline epoch, 11

Population: of Brazil in Pombal's time, 10, 497; of Salvador, 15 n. 48; of Rio de Janeiro, 46; of Colônia do Sacramento, 71; of Santa Catarina, 73; of Rio Grande de São Pedro, 80

Portarias (warrants), 298, 329

Propinas (perquisites), 299, 309

Provedor (mór) da fazenda, offices of, 24, 295, 296; reorganization of, 279, 285; staff of, 281, 284; functions of, 284-285, 309; gradual elimination of, 285 n. 20

Provedoria, 284, 299

Public lottery, proposed by Viceroy Vasconcelos, 349

Public offices: Lavradio recommends standards for fillment of, 24; the filling of, 294f.; Brazilians in, 296; assessments on, 305

Quinto. See Fifths, royal
Quinto do couro, 301

Ratton, Jacome, 7

Real Erário. See Royal Treasury

Regimento (standing instructions), 32, 38 n. 45

Registros (interior customs stations), 156, 304, 392, 398, 401

Relação (high court of appeals): functions of, 11 n. 29, 18-19, 398-399, 406-407, 434-435; terms of judges of, 33 n. 19

—of Bahia: early history of, 11, 15; Lavradio's criticism of, 19-20; sentence of challenged by colonial secretary, 19

—of Rio de Janeiro, 11, 48, 299, 434; Lavradio's comments on, 51-52

Rendimentos préteritos, defined, 25

Residências (terminal investigations), 19 n. 58, 478

Responsibility for Portuguese defeats, 268-274, 498-505

Rezende, Conde de (Viceroy of Brazil), 386, 417

Rice, cultivation of: in Rio de Janeiro, 365; in Maranhão and Pará, 366

Ricla, Conde de (minister of war in Spain), 166 n. 85, 196

Rio de Janeiro, captaincy of: governors of unwilling to remain subordinate to governors-general, 35-39 passim; general description, 45-46; population of (ca. 1780), 46; economy of, 354-381 passim

Rio de Janeiro, captaincy-general of, 40, 44-46

Rio de Janeiro, city of: succeeds Salvador as titular capital of Brazil, 43; rise in importance of, 44; a major administrative center, 45; description of, 46-51; jubilation in concerning Portuguese victories, 188; French attacks on, 248 n. 2; alarms in, 248, 251; merchant community of, character of, 381; improvements in during Lavradio's regime, 428-430

—fortifications of: need for repair of, 54; claimed incapable of withstanding a British attack, 109; respected by Cevallos, 197 n. 6; improvements in, by Lavradio, 221-223; expense of, 334-336

Rio Grande de São Pedro, captaincy of: 59, 218, 221, 251, 319, 342; geography of, 60-63; historiography concerning, 74 n. 51; Portuguese settlement of, 74-82; population of (1780), 80; economy of, 80-81, 354-369 *passim;* first Cevallos campaign in, 97-98; Spain's determination not to evacuate, 99f.; refusal of Pombal to surrender Portuguese claims to, 102f.; first Portuguese campaign against Spaniards in, 104f.; persisting stalemate in, 116-175 *passim;* unsuccessful Portuguese naval attack in, 176-182; Portuguese victories in, 182-187; reaction to, in Rio de Janeiro, 187-188; reaction to, diplomatic, 189-194; reaction of Spain to, 195-202 *passim,* 224f.; plans for new Portuguese offensive based in, 210-211; Cevallos' planned second invasion of, 239-240, 245; fiscal burden of, 319. *See also* Guaraní War; Jesuits, Spanish; Treaty of Madrid; Treaty of San Ildefonso

Rio Grande de São Pedro, vila of: captured by Cevallos (1763), 97-98; reoccupied by Portuguese forces (1776), 186-187

Rio Pardo, Portuguese fort of, 101, 129

Robertson, William (captain of the *Argyle*), 413-415

Rocha, Francisco José da (viceregal aide and governor of Colônia): biographical sketch, 120; mission to Rio Grande de São Pedro, 120-124; named governor of Colônia, 140; leaves Rio de Janeiro for Colônia, 146f.; questions wisdom of retaining Colônia, 157-160; decision of to surrender, 243-244; elects to remain with imprisoned troops, 244; criticism of, by Lavradio, 269; and cochineal, 378-379; conviction of, 501

Roscîo, Francisco João (military engineer), 54, 270, 476 n. 19; sent to borderlands to assist in defense of, 133; named inspector of fortifications of Rio de Janeiro, 222; Lavradio's high regard for, 222 n. 122; geographical report of, 476 n. 19

Royal Extraction. *See* Diamond District

Royal Treasury: status of branch of at Salvador, 22, 26; embezzlement at, 22-24; embezzlement elsewhere in the colony, 24 n. 87; status of branch of at Rio de Janeiro on Lavradio's arrival, 312; chief expenditures of, 298-300, 333-336, 342; sources of income of, 301f., 317-319, 339-340; debts owed to, 316-317, 350, 507-508; debts owed by, 321-322, 342-343, 347-352

Sá e Benavides, Salvador Corrêa de (governor and captain-general of southern captaincies), 37, 66

Sá e Faria, José Custódio (military engineer), 54, 231, 450, 502; biographical sketch, 104; efforts of to expel Spaniards from Lagoa dos Patos, 105-106; promoted for achievement in Rio Grande de São Pedro, 114 n. 141; criticism of, by F. J. da Rocha, 123-124; sent to São Paulo to inspect Fort Iguatemí, 465; reprimanded by colonial secretary, 468; inspection trip of, 469-470; assigned to Salvador, 205; transferred from Salvador to Santa Catarina, 214-215 activity of during Spanish invasion, 231-235 *passim;* role of in capitulation of Portuguese forces, 237-238; accompanies Cevallos to Plata, 240; alleged evil counsel of, 268; enigmatic character of, 270-271; found not guilty, 504-505; death of, 271 n. 95

Saldanha, Martim Lopes Lobo de (captain-general of São Paulo), 6, 139; biographical sketch, 454; urged by Lavradio to rush troops to Santa Catarina, 249; asked by Lavradio to organize counteroffensive, 253, 261-262; relations of, with Lavradio, 362; discussions of, with Lavradio, 455

Salvador, city of, 14-16

Santa Catarina, captaincy of, 59, 140; geography of, 60-63; historiography of, 71-72 n. 37; settlement of, 71-74; economy of, 74, 354-355; fiscal burden of, 319. *See also* Santa Catarina Island

Santa Catarina Island, 146, 176, 181; as a way station, 72; defenses of ordered strengthened, 138; MacDouall's instructions concerning defense of, 147, 154, 214, 216-217, 218-219; land reinforcements sent to, 162; predicted to be Cevallos' objective, 213; Spanish plans for conquest of, 197-199; preparations by Portuguese for defense of, 213-214, 216-219; final Spanish decision to attack, 225-227; MacDouall and defense of, 227-230; fall of, 230-235; Lavradio's efforts to recover, 252f.; reasons for its return to Portugal, 265-266. *See also* Mendonça, Antônio Carlos Furtado de *and* Treaty of San Ildefonso

Santa Tecla: cattle station at, 91; Vértiz erects fort at, 129; capture of, 149, 183

Santa Teresa, fort: 199, 206; captured by Cevallos (1763) , 97; Böhm ordered to recover, 210; Cevallos returns to in preparation for second invasion of Rio Grande, 245

São José do Norte, *Riograndense* town of, 105, 106

São Miguel, fort, 79, 206; captured by Cevallos (1763) , 97; Böhm directed to anchor defenses at, 137; Böhm fails to capture, 187 n. 38; Cevallos fears Böhm may have seized, 199

São Paulo, captaincy-general of, 40, 386; dismemberment of, and restoration of, 459. *See also* Paulistas as warriors; Sousa, Luís Antônio de; *and* Saldanha, Martin Lopes Lobo de

—subsidy of, 299-300, 336

Scientific Society, of Rio de Janeiro, 376-379

Sericulture, 366

Seven Missions: founded by Spanish Jesuits, 66; mines suspected to exist in, 75; conquered by Portuguese, 268 n. 86, 274. *See also* Guaraní War; Treaty of Madrid; Treaty of Pardo; *and* Treaty of San Ildefonso

Seven Years' War, and the Debatable Lands, 96f.

Silva Pais, José da. *See* Pais, José da Silva

Slave trade, Negro: volume of, to Rio de Janeiro and Salvador, 14; Rio de Janeiro as a center of, 44; to Colônia prohibited by Lavradio, 119; taxes on, 303, 306, 318; tobacco and, 360; quotas of, 385; as an avenue for smuggling, 390; fresh arrivals confined to segregated quarters in Rio de Janeiro, 428-429. *See also* Negro slaves

Smelteries (*casas de fundição*) , 12, 326

Smuggling. *See* Trade, illicit

Sousa (Botelho e Mourão), Luís Antônio (captain-general of São Paulo) , 6, 139, 254; ancestry and biography, 459-460; Lavradio ordered to assist, 125; ambitions of, 460f.; achievements of, 461f.; complains of livestock raising in Minas Gerais, 386; relations of, with Lavradio, 463-471; reprimanded by colonial secretary, 468; scheduled promotion, 470; recall of, 470

Sousa, Luís Pinto de (Portuguese plenipotentiary to London) , 171, 206

Sousa, Tomé (first governor-general of Brazil) , 31

Squillace revolts, in Spain, 106-107

Subsídio voluntário. See Taxes, tolls, and excises

Subsídios (excises) . *See* Taxes, tolls, and excises

Sugar: importance of in Brazil in seventeenth century, 10; relative significance of in Pernambuco, Bahia, and Rio de Janeiro, 44 n. 70; size of chests of, 346 n. 104; expansion of growing of, in Campinas and the Campos de Goitacazes, 356; planters of exempted from seizure for debts, 357; complaint against production of in Minas Gerais, by Luís Antônio de Sousa, 385-386

Tapinhoam (hardwood) , 357-358

Tax-farming, 307-311

Taxes, tolls, and excises, 301f.; *terças partes*, 297, 305; *subsídios*, 304-307; *subsídio voluntário*, 306; excises, jurisdiction transferred from municipalities to provedoria, 309-310. *See also* **Tax-farming**

Terças partes (assessments on public offices) . *See* Taxes, tolls, and excises

Tesoureiro das despezas miudas (chief paymaster) , functions of, 285

Tiro de cañón (Spanish formula defining limits of Colônia) , 84

Tithes (*dízimos*) , 311; classification of, 301; average yield from, in captaincy-general of Rio de Janeiro, 318; funds used for nonecclesiastical purposes, 337

Tobacco, 10; tax on, 305, 318; cultivation of, in Bahia, 359-360; in Pernambuco, 361; Lavradio's efforts to promote raising of, in Rio de Janeiro, 361-362; in São Paulo, 362

Tonelet, Camilio Maria (viceregal aide) , 149 n. 29, 477

Trade, illicit: at Bahia, 19; between Rio de Janeiro and Buenos Aires, 67, 390 n. 11; part of motivation for founding of Colônia do Sacramento, 67; at Colônia, 67, 86, 94 n. 49, 96 n. 64; Laguna as a center of, 72; in Rio Grande de São Pedro, 123; Fort Iguatemí planned as center of, 467; volume of unlikely to have been greater during second half of eighteenth century than first, 330; forms of, 388; sources of, outside of Brazil, 389-390; evidence of, 391 n. 16, 397-399; difficulties in preventing, 392-417 *passim;* use of informers to detect, 396-397; sale of slaves introduced via, 407 n.

78; persistence of, 416-417. *See also* Foreign ships, unlicensed

Trade, legitimate: between Portugal and Bahia, 14; Rio de Janeiro, 381; annual fairs at Rio de Janeiro, 382-383; restrictions on, 394-395. *See also* Convoy system; Slave trade, Negro; Traveling merchants

Traveling merchants (*comissários volantes*), 382, 395

Treasury. *See* Royal Treasury

Treasurer-general, office of, 284

Treaty of 1661, 412

Treaty of 1750. *See* Treaty of Madrid

Treaty of Fontainebleau, 99, 100

"Treaty of the Frontier," 100, 120

Treaty of Limits. *See* Treaty of Madrid

Treaty of Madrid, 86-95 *passim*

Treaty of Pardo (1761), 85

Treaty of Paris (1763), 99

Treaty of San Ildefonso, 262, 263, 265-267, 474

Treaty of Tordesillas (1494), 83-84

Treaty of Utrecht (1713-1715), 85

Trindade, island of, 225, 254 n. 33

Valadares, Conde de (captain-general of Minas Gerais), 401

Valdelirios, Marquis of, Gaspar de Munibe Garavito de León y Tellos (Spanish diplomat and boundary commissioner), 90 n. 38, 101

Vasconcelos, António Pedro de, opponent of Treaty of Madrid, 90

Vasconcelos e Sousa, Luís de (successor to Lavradio as viceroy), 379-380, 500; biographical sketch, 474; fiscal report of, 349; and promotion of new products, 368-380 *passim;* and capture of a smuggling gang, 402-403

Vértiz y Salcedo, Juan José (Governor of Buenos Aires and later viceroy): biographical sketch, 117 n. 4; expedi-

tion of, against Portuguese positions in Rio Grande, 125-132; warns that Portuguese forces in Rio Grande are too strong for him to expel, 166; denies knowledge of Cevallos expedition, 223; ordered by Cevallos to menace Rio Grande, 239; tightens blockade of Colônia, 241; fiscal consequences of expedition of, to vice-regal exchequer, 319, 347

Viceroy of Brazil, office of: conflicting opinions concerning extent of authority of, 29-30; permanent establishment of, 40; jurisdictional limits of, 42-43, 362, 447-472 *passim;* limited patronage of, 443; Lavradio recommends greater authority for, 456; salary of, 484 n. 54; title not apposite, 484. *See also* Governor-general, office of

—duties of, 43, 454-455, 479-481; military, 143-144; toward captains-general, 208, 452f.; fiscal, 281-282, 298; economic development, 353f.; prevention of illicit trade, 405-408; with respect to local administration, 421-434, 443-446; judicial, 434-437 *passim;* toward the Church, 437-440; as a channel of information, 449, 456

Vidal de Negreiros, André, 36, 38 n. 45

Vieira, Manoel Luís (rice merchant), 364-365

Vieira de Abreu, Jerônimo (inventor), 364, 373

Walpole, Robert (British minister to Portugal), 415; quoted on Pombal, 190 n. 49; warning by, concerning El Ferrol expedition, 135-136

Whaling, 14 n. 44, 416

Wheat farming, 362-364

Zabala, Don Francisco Bruno de, 131-132